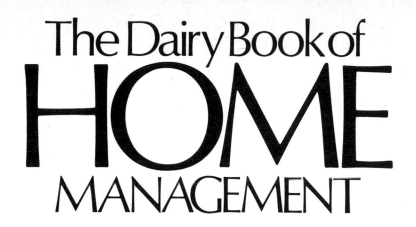

The Dairy Book of HOME MANAGEMENT

Published by Macdonald Educational Ltd
on behalf of the Dairy Industry

New edition first published 1980

© Milk Marketing Board 1980
ISBN 0 356 07296 7
Made and printed by
Purnell & Sons Ltd, Paulton

General Editor: Neil Tennant

Contributors
Food and Cookery: Carol Clarke
Home Maintenance: Pauline Swaine,
    Percy Blandford
Home Improvement: Brenda Greysmith
Gardening: David Carr
Home Crafts: Lindsay Vernon, Sue Biro,
    Violet Stevenson
Pet Care: Tina Hearne
Beauty and Health: Veronica Kruger, Brian Ward
Law and Finance: Andrew Martin
Family Occasions: Sheila Fullarton

Managing Editor: Chester Fisher

CONTENTS

METRIC WEIGHTS AND MEASURES

The United Kingdom is in the process of changing over from the old Imperial system of weights and measures to the metric system used by most other countries.

The metric system is simpler than the Imperial because it is based on tens. There are four basic units — kilogram, metre, litre, °C — and other units simply derived from these.

The KILOGRAM (kg) is the unit for weighing. One kilogram is a little over two pounds. The GRAM (g) is one thousandth of a kilogram; the metric TONNE (t) is a thousand kilograms, which is just less than an Imperial ton.

The METRE (m) is the unit of length. One metre is a few inches over a yard. The MILLIMETRE (mm) is one thousandth of a metre, or ten millimetres is a centimetre. The KILOMETRE (km) is a thousand metres, which is about five-eighths of a mile.

The LITRE (l) is the liquid measure. One litre is a little less than two pints. The MILLILITRE (ml) is one thousandth of a litre.

The DEGREE CELSIUS (°C) or degree centigrade is the unit of temperature. 0°C is the freezing point of water; each increase of 1°C is equivalent to an increase of 1 4/5 °F; and 100°C is the boiling point of water.

Weights and measures in the 'Food and Cookery' chapter are given in both metric and Imperial units. These conversions are only approximate but the proportions are accurate within one set of units. So for best results use either Imperial or metric units but do not mix them.

The tables given here conform to the British Standards conversions.

WEIGHT

1 lb	=	0.4559 kg
1 kg	=	2.205 lb

½ oz	=	14 g
1 oz	=	28 g
2 oz	=	57 g
3 oz	=	85 g
4 oz	=	113 g
8 oz	=	227 g
1 lb	=	454 g
2 lb	=	907 g
3 lb	=	1.36 kg
4 lb	=	1.81 kg
7 lb	=	3.17 kg
1 st	=	6.35 kg
2 st	=	12.69 kg
4 st	=	25.38 kg
1 cwt	=	50.76 kg
1 ton	=	1015.26 kg

10 g	=	0.4 oz
25 g	=	0.9 oz
50 g	=	1.8 oz
100 g	=	3.5 oz
200 g	=	7.1 oz
500 g	=	1 lb 2 oz
1 kg	=	2 lb 3 oz
2 kg	=	4 lb 7 oz
3 kg	=	6 lb 10 oz
4 kg	=	8 lb 13 oz
5 kg	=	11 lb
10 kg	=	22 lb
100 kg	=	221 lb
1 t	=	2205 lb

LIQUID

1 pint	=	0.568 litre
1 litre	=	1.760 pints

1 fl oz	=	28 ml
2 fl oz	=	57 ml
3 fl oz	=	85 ml
4 fl oz	=	114 ml
5 fl oz	=	142 ml
10 fl oz	=	284 ml
1 pint	=	568 ml
2 pint	=	1.137 l
3 pint	=	1.705 l
4 pint	=	2.273 l
6 pint	=	3.408 l
1 gal	=	4.546 l

50 ml	=	2 fl oz
100 ml	=	4 fl oz
200 ml	=	7 fl oz
300 ml	=	11 fl oz
400 ml	=	14 fl oz
500 ml	=	18 fl oz
1 l	=	1 pint 15 fl oz
2 l	=	3 pints 10 fl oz
5 l	=	8 pints 16 fl oz
10 l	=	17 pints 12 fl oz

LENGTH

1 in	=	25.4 mm
1 m	=	39.37 in

1 in	=	25 mm	=	2.5 cm
2 in	=	51 mm	=	5.1 cm
3 in	=	76 mm	=	7.6 cm
6 in	=	152 mm	=	15.2 cm
1 ft	=	305 mm	=	30.5 cm
2 ft	=	610 mm	=	61.0 cm
1 yd	=	914 mm	=	91.4 cm
2 yd	=	1.838 m		
10 yd	=	9.144 m		
440 yd	=	402 m		
1 mile	=	1609 m	=	1.609 km

10 mm	=	1 cm	=	0.4 in
20 mm	=	2 cm	=	0.8 in
30 mm	=	3 cm	=	1.2 in
50 mm	=	5 cm	=	2.0 in
100 mm	=	10 cm	=	3.9 in
200 mm	=	20 cm	=	7.9 in
300 mm	=	30 cm	=	11.8 in
500 mm	=	50 cm	=	1 ft 7.7 in
1 m	=	1 yd 0 ft 3 in		
2 m	=	2 yd 0 ft 7 in		
3 m	=	3 yd 0 ft 10 in		
5 m	=	5 yd 1 ft 5 in		
10 m	=	10 yd 2 ft 10 in		
1 km	=	1094 yd		

TEMPERATURE

To convert °F to °C:
Subtract 32, multiply by 5 and divide by 9.
To convert °C to °F:
Multiply by 9, divide by 5 and add 32.

0°F	=	−17°C
20°F	=	−7°C
32°F	=	0°C
40°F	=	5°C
50°F	=	10°C
60°F	=	16°C
70°F	=	21°C
80°F	=	27°C
90°F	=	32°C
98°F	=	37°C
100°F	=	38°C
150°F	=	66°C
200°F	=	93°C
212°F	=	100°C

0°C	=	32°F
10°C	=	50°F
20°C	=	68°F
30°C	=	86°F
40°C	=	104°F
50°C	=	122°F
100°C	=	212°F

FOOD AND COOKERY

FOOD AND COOKERY

EATING FOR HEALTH

CATERING FOR YOUR FAMILY'S NEEDS

Food fuels and maintains the body: to keep healthy, we need a balance of different kinds of food. The wheel of health (below) gives a good guide to a healthy diet.

Protein Builds new tissue. This is why growing children need proportionately more protein in their diet than adults. Good sources of protein are meat, poultry, fish, cheese, nuts and pulses.

Carbohydrates An energy source, found in quantity in starch and sugars.

Fats Fats provide twice the energy of any other food — and in addition they are also used for cooking.

Minerals Most balanced diets contain enough minerals, but sometimes they need to be augmented. Iron and calcium are most important, with smaller quantities of iodine, sodium and potassium, all found naturally in food or water.

Vitamins Vitamin A is present in oily fish, liver, butter and orange/red vegetables, such as carrots.

Vitamin B has several groups: they help the body use oxygen and form new blood cells. Yeast, wheat germ and liver are good sources of B vitamins.

Vitamin C is ascorbic acid, which helps form connective tissue. It is found in fresh fruit and raw vegetables.

Vitamin D is needed for the growth of healthy bones. Oily fish — and sunlight — are potent sources.

Vitamin E has many wondrous properties ascribed to it but these have yet to be proved. It occurs widely in many foods.

Vitamin K helps blood to clot. A deficiency is rare.

As your family grows, their dietary needs will change, but the most important factor is that good eating habits are introduced right from the start.

THE BABY

Breast feeding is best for the baby and the mother. Breast milk provides the baby with the right blend of protein, fat and carbohydrate, and the feeding helps establish a close bond in these early days.

Sometimes it is difficult to get the milk established, but try to persevere.

As a substitute, there are modified versions of cows' milk which can be made up for bottle feeds. Make sure all the equipment is properly sterilized, and don't be tempted to make the mix too concentrated: follow the advice of your health visitor and the instructions on the pack of powdered milk.

Make sure you visit the health centre regularly to

The Wheel of Health shows the foods you need for a balanced diet. Use protein foods for body growth; fresh fruit and fresh vegetables for vitamins; and carbohydrates and fats for energy.

check your baby's progress. If extra vitamins or minerals need to be given, they'll be prescribed.

Only a few years ago it was common practice to introduce solid food to a baby's diet at a very early age. Often this meant that cereals were added to a baby's bottle feed from as early as several weeks old.

However, nowadays it is realized that solids are unnecessary for a baby before the age of four months and that usually babies do, in fact, have enough nutrients to last, naturally, from birth to six months. Make sure your baby eats some form of puréed cereal between four and six months, then gradually introduce puréed fruits, vegetables and other foods. Orange juice or rose-hip syrup is a good source of vitamin C.

By the time the infant is one year old, he or she will be able to eat quite a range of foods in various forms. Your baby will also enjoy sucking and biting on rusks and biscuits with all six or so teeth. Don't over-salt the food or add too much sugar: the baby's organs are still developing and will not be able to cope with an excess.

Introduce solid foods gradually, but never try to force anything unpopular. There are whole generations for whom the mention of spinach produces only a grimace and a shudder.

THE PRE-SCHOOL CHILD
Between the ages of one and five your child is growing rapidly. The eating habits you establish will be crucial for the rest of his life.

Bones and teeth are developing, which means that a regular supply of calcium is needed. Provide it in the form of milk, cheese and yogurt. Encourage your child to end a meal with an apple, a carrot, or cheese — recently found to be a weapon against dental decay.

THE YEARS AT SCHOOL
Start the day with a good breakfast: supply protein and energy foods for your children — and the adults in the family.

There is no need to provide bacon and egg, with toast and lashings of butter. Muesli, bran, fresh fruit, raisins, yogurt or milk provide an excellent start to the day. School meals are carefully balanced, nutritionally, and provide valuable nourishment to school children.

Towards adolescence there is a huge spurt in growth, with a need for added nutrients. At this time, encourage your children to cook, boys as much as girls. It will be a good start to adult life and will teach them the importance of goodness and flavour in a pleasant way.

ADULTS
With an understanding of the importance of good food habits, there shouldn't be any problems. But there are special circumstances in which diet plays a major part.

PREGNANCY AND LACTATION
When pregnant, you eat for two — but not in the folklore sense of eating twice as much. You must, though, keep healthy for your baby, as well as yourself. Make sure your intake of protein, calcium, iron and vitamins is adequate.

During pregnancy and after, in breast feeding (lactation), make sure your diet includes milk, cheese and yogurt; meat and poultry; fish and eggs; fresh vegetables and fruit; and wholemeal bread and cereals. If you need extra vitamins or iron supplements, you will be able to get them from your health centre.

SLIMMERS
If any member of the family is overweight it is important that they be helped back to their correct weight. A balanced diet is still necessary but as we normally eat many foods to excess, we can safely cut down without damaging our health. Try not to rule out foods with a high nutritional value, such as milk, cheese, meat, fish, eggs, fruit and vegetables, although the amount you eat of each may need to be reduced. Cut down on sugary foods such as cakes, sweets and biscuits, which contribute very little to the diet. Fatty foods and fried foods are also high in calories, as is alcohol, and consumption of these should be watched, and strictly limited.

INVALIDS
Illness in the family may require special diets. Proper feeding often plays a very important part in the way that an invalid recovers from illness or an operation. The sick person may have no appetite and so the food must be presented particularly attractively. Small portions should be given with plenty of variety in the food presented. Colourful edible garnishes can play a significant part in invalid cookery.

DIABETICS
The treatment of all diabetics, even those who require insulin, will necessitate some degree of dietary restriction. The diabetic's in-

FOOD AND COOKERY

take of carbohydrate foods must be controlled. Once the basic principles of the carbohydrate exchange system are understood, the diabetic's meals can easily fit in with those prepared for the rest of the family.

GRANDPARENTS

Older people are less active and use less energy, but a balanced food intake is important — vital, even.

If you have elderly relatives living with you or in easy reach, you can make sure they eat what they need. The problem arises for people who live on their own. They may find food for one proportionately much more expensive than catering for a family; they may not have good appetites and perhaps don't feel like making the effort to cook. The worrying result is that many old people make do with a cup of tea or an easy, convenient filler which supplies none of their nutritional needs.

There is no easy solution, but if you are a senior citizen or if you have elderly neighbours, try to start a kind of shared shopping. Six eggs, a packet of butter and a block of cheese can easily be divided among three people, and there will be no waste.

If you have older relatives living with you, tempt their appetites by providing a little of everything, as long as there is no contra-indication from the family doctor. Make sure that calcium and vitamin D are offered — in the form of milk, cheese, tuna, pilchards and sardines, for instance. They help prevent brittle bones. A deficiency could lead to disablement in an elderly person.

MEAT

CHOOSING MEAT

Throughout Great Britain you will find the widest possible variety of cuts and joints of meat. This is the result of a partnership. The farmer rears the kind of stock the butcher demands, and this in turn is dictated by his customers' preferences. There are regional variations in cutting carcases of meat, and the names of cuts and joints are different throughout the country. The ones listed here are those most commonly used. Thanks to sophisticated methods of cold storage, home-killed and imported meat of good quality is available all year.

Always buy from a reliable butcher who selects meat with care and stores it under the right conditions. Make the most of his knowledge and skills: never be afraid to ask his advice about 'best buys'. If you want an unusual cut or something which needs special preparation, order it at least a few days in advance.

Before you buy meat, work out how much you want to spend, what time you have for preparation and cooking — and, of course, how many people you are going to feed. As a general rule, allow 100–150 g (4–6 oz) of boneless meat per person and 175–350 g (6–12 oz) of meat on the bone. Cheaper and tougher cuts of meat are as nutritious as the more expensive ones. They just need careful cooking to make them tender.

For more information on nutrition and health, see pp. 270–275. See also Beauty and Health, pp. 313–315.

BEEF

Comes from steers or uncalved heifers. It is still the most popular meat in Great Britain, for its versatility as well as its flavour and food value. British beef is most plentiful in autumn, but imported beef is available throughout the year. All beef should be hung by the butcher or wholesaler for about ten days to tenderize before it is sold.

What to look for Only freshly cut meat is a bright colour. Exposure to the air turns it brown, but if the meat is fresh, this does not affect its eating quality at all. The colour of the fat will range from white to pale yellow: the food the animal ate determines this.

Lean meat is muscle and the texture varies according to the age of the animal and the cut of beef. Muscles used frequently — those in the neck and legs, for instance — will be more coarsely grained and show visible connective tissue (gristle). This meat needs long, slow cooking to make it tender. Cuts with little gristle, such as rump or fillet, are used for roasting and grilling. Cheap cuts are often used to make mince. It is better to buy the meat in a piece and mince it at home.

Brisket An economical buy, sold on the bone or boned and rolled; excellent for braising and pot-roasting. You will often find it salted for pressed or corned beef.

Chuck and blade After the outer fat has been removed, this cut is usually boned and sold as chuck or blade bone

A good display of fresh meat.

FOOD AND COOKERY

steak. It needs long, slow cooking and is best braised, stewed or used in pies.

Flank (thick flank or top rump) A lean joint, cut from the hindquarters. Whole, it may be slow-roasted, pot-roasted or braised; in slices, braised or fried.

Flank (thin) An inexpensive cut which contains gristle. It becomes tender after slow cooking. It is often sold pre-salted or as mince.

Neck and clod A cheap cut, usually sold as stewing steak or mince.

Rib (fore) The traditional cut for roast beef. Usually sold on the bone but you may buy it boned and rolled.

Rib (thin and thick) Some-times known as middle rib, this joint is ideal for slow or pot-roasting and braising. You will often find it boned and rolled.

Rib (wing) Excellent for roasting. Often sold boned and sliced as steaks.

Shin (foreleg) and leg (hind-leg) A lean cut with a good flavour and a high propor-tion of gristle. It needs long, slow cooking, so use it for stews, casseroles and stock.

Silverside A lean, boned joint. Roast it fresh, or buy it salted and boil it with car-rots. Dumplings are a tradi-tional accompaniment.

Sirloin This is an expensive but delicious and tender cut of beef. You can buy it on the bone or boned and rolled for roasting. It is often cut into slices for grilling. The fillet is sometimes used in dishes like Beef Wellington.

Steaks The most tender cuts of beef are often sold sliced, as steaks. Fillet, sirloin and rump are the best. When you eat a Tournedos steak in a restaurant, it comes from the fillet, as does a *filet mignon* and a Chateaubriand. An entrecôte comes from the top part of the sirloin. Other popular steaks are T-bone, Aitch-bone and Porterhouse.

Topside Excellent for long, slow cooking, because it can be tough, this is a lean, bone-less joint.

VEAL
The best British veal comes from 3- to 4-month-old calves which have been reared on a

BEEF

rib (thin and thick)

chuck and blade

rib (fore)

neck and clod

rib (wing)

shin

flank (thick)

brisket (rolled)

special diet of milk and fatty foods. This helps to keep their flesh very pale in colour. This meat is very expensive though and 'bobby calves' (less than three weeks old) and imported veal are the types more often seen in the shops. Holland is the chief exporter of veal to this country.

Veal is a very lean meat and can be very bland. It is much improved by being generously larded before it is roasted (to keep the meat moist) and by being cooked with other, more flavourful ingredients. Stuffings and rich sauces are commonly served with veal and your seasoning can be on the generous side. Although it is an expensive meat, the leanness means that there is little or no waste.

What to look for Veal should be moist, soft, fine-grained and covered with a very thin layer of creamy white fat. Don't buy flabby wet meat, dry brown meat or mottled, bluish meat. The colour of veal will vary from off-white to pale salmon pink; the flavour is always delicate.

Breast An economical cut sold boned and rolled for roasting, or diced for pies and stews.

Escalope A slice taken from the haunch, cut transversely across the grain of the meat. It is usually beaten until thin, then coated with egg and breadcrumbs, and fried.

Fillet The most expensive cut from the top of the leg. It has no wastage. It may be bought whole, for roasting, or in slices, as *médaillons*.

Knuckle A cheaper cut from the lower part of the leg. Braise or stew it. The shin is often cut into pieces 5–8 cm (2–3 in) long. Rich in marrow, they are cooked with tomatoes, herbs and wine to make the classic Italian dish *Osso Buco*.

Leg A large and expensive joint: use it for roasting.

Loin A large joint from the back. It can be sold on the bone or boned and rolled, but is often cut into chops.

Neck (best end) Most often sold boned, stuffed and rolled for roasting; but often bought on the bone in a piece or as cutlets.

Neck (middle) A cheaper cut, used for braising, stewing and in pies.

Scrag An inexpensive, boney cut, used for stews.

Shoulder Known as 'oyster' when boned, this is the most economical roasting joint.

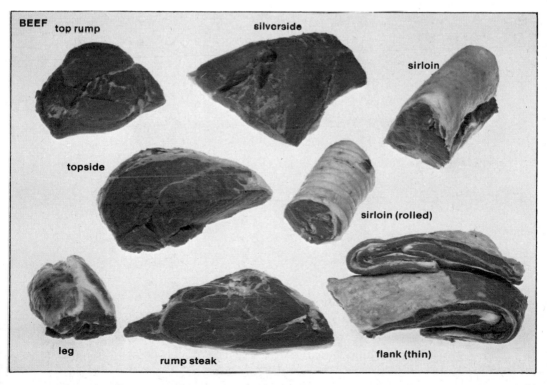

BEEF top rump · silverside · sirloin · topside · sirloin (rolled) · leg · rump steak · flank (thin)

FOOD AND COOKERY

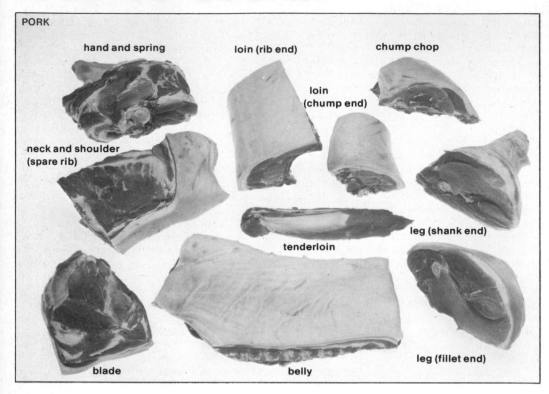

PORK

hand and spring   loin (rib end)   chump chop

loin (chump end)

neck and shoulder (spare rib)

leg (shank end)

tenderloin

blade   belly   leg (fillet end)

PORK

Pork is a rich, succulent meat. It doesn't keep well, which is why, in the past, it used to be eaten fresh only in the winter months. However, thanks to good refrigeration, British pork is now available throughout the year. Almost every part of the pig is used, whether as prime roast or sausages.

What to look for Fresh prime pork should be firm, a delicate pink and finely grained. The fat should be firm and white, the bones pinkish-blue, and the skin or rind smooth and free from hairs. It is the skin that forms crackling on a roasted joint.

Pork retains more flavour if cooked on the bone, but frequently it is boned and rolled ready for stuffing. It must always be well cooked.

Belly This is sometimes known as streaky. It is ideal for an economical stuffed and rolled roast and the thin end can also be grilled. It tends to be rather fatty. Spare ribs, used in Chinese cooking, come from this cut.

Tenderloin (fillet) This runs under the backbone. It is very lean but not so well flavoured, and can be roasted, grilled or fried.

Hand and spring Together these form a large roasting joint, but they can also be sold separately. Hand is the lower part of the shoulder and spring the knuckle end, often used for casseroles.

Leg A large, expensive roast-ing joint which can be cut into two: fillet end (top of leg) and shank end. The fillet is sometimes cut into steaks, and the trotters are usually salted and boiled or used to make brawn.

Loin This comes from the middle back of the animal and is a choice cut for roasting on the bone, or boned, stuffed and rolled. Loin chops come from the rib end of the loin; chump chops from the leg end. Both are good for grilling or frying.

Neck and shoulder (spare rib and blade bone) A large roasting joint which is economical and particularly good when boned, stuffed and rolled. When divided into blade and spare rib, can be roasted, braised or grilled.

LAMB

Most lamb is slaughtered at about six months; mutton comes from sheep at least 18 months old. British lamb is available between March and November and is most plentiful between August and November. New Zealand lamb is at its best between December and June.

What to look for Young lamb is firm, fine-grained, and pale pink to pink-brown, while meat from older animals is slightly darker. The fat should be creamy-white and crisp. Joints should be plump with a good proportion of lean meat and a moderate layer of fat. There is usually little gristle.

All cuts, except the neck, can be roasted and the individual chops from them may be grilled or fried. Some forequarter cuts are casseroled, stewed or made into pies.

Breast A most economical cut, often boned and rolled for roasting or braising.

Leg An expensive cut from the animal's hindquarters, this is sold on the bone or boned, stuffed and rolled for roasting. It is often divided into two joints: the *fillet* (thick end), often sliced for grilling and frying; and the *shank* (thin, knuckle end).

Loin This is usually divided into *loin end* and *chump end* and cut into chops for grilling, frying and braising. Chump chops are oval, with a small central bone. They are meatier and more expensive than loin chops, which have a T-shaped bone. *Noisettes* are taken from the loin, boned, trimmed of fat, and shaped into rounds.

Neck (best end) From the loin end of the neck, this is the most economical and versatile cut. It can be roasted on the bone (use two equal-sized pieces to make a *crown roast* or *guard of honour*); boned and rolled; or split into cutlets for grilling and frying.

Neck (middle and scrag) These cuts contain a great deal of bone and fat and are traditionally used for making broth, and in both Lancashire hot pot and Irish stew.

Saddle A joint for special occasions — the whole loin cut from both sides of the animal. Order it in advance from your butcher and roast in a moderate oven.

Shoulder Cut from the forequarters, this is an inexpensive roasting joint, especially when boned to form a cavity and stuffed with a substantial stuffing mixture. Though fatty, it is tender and succulent roasted on or off the bone. It may be divided into the blade and knuckle to make two small roasting joints.

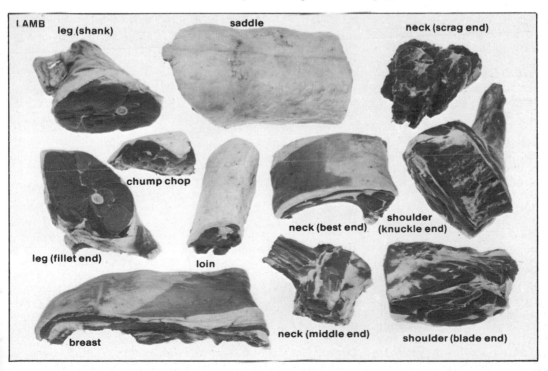

LAMB
leg (shank) · saddle · neck (scrag end) · chump chop · neck (best end) · shoulder (knuckle end) · leg (fillet end) · loin · breast · neck (middle end) · shoulder (blade end)

FOOD AND COOKERY

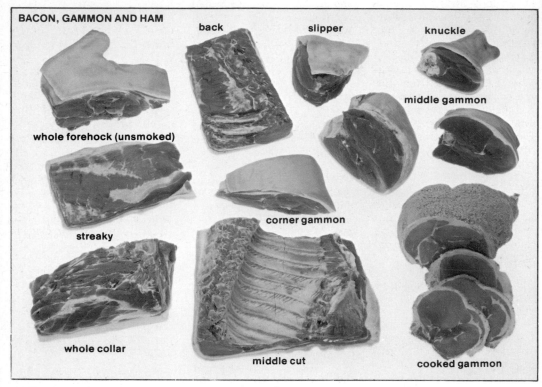

BACON, GAMMON AND HAM

back

slipper

knuckle

middle gammon

whole forehock (unsmoked)

streaky

corner gammon

whole collar

middle cut

cooked gammon

BACON, GAMMON AND HAM

For centuries, pork has been 'cured' with salt to preserve it. As bacon, gammon and ham, it is still very popular in Britain. Grilled or fried, served roasted, braised or boiled, cuts of bacon combine good flavour and food value with cheapness. There is little waste and the cooking water after boiling makes excellent stock.

What to look for Just under half the bacon we eat comes from home-bred pigs; much is imported from Ireland, Denmark and other countries. Most bacon is cured 'Wiltshire' style. The pig, other than the head, feet, bones and offal, is lightly cured in a salt brine as two 'sides' for about two weeks.

When taken out of the brine, the bacon is 'green', with a delicate flavour and pink flesh. Later it may be smoked to preserve it even longer. Smoked bacon has a stronger, saltier flavour.

Bacon is most often sold in rashers. Gammon is the leg of the bacon, cured with the rest of the side; ham is also leg, cured to the local recipe.

Back Most often cut in rashers but sometimes sold as a joint, boned and rolled for baking or boiling. Look for lean, *long back* rashers for grilling; *middle* or *through-cut,* sold as rashers or in the piece, and *prime back,* for frying or grilling in rashers or braising or boiling in the piece. Bacon chops come from this cut and can be fried, grilled or braised.

Collar An inexpensive cut from the neck. Soak before cooking and serve it hot or cold as a joint.

Forehock The whole foreleg, and one of the cheaper bacon joints. Often cut into the *butt* and *foreslipper,* both excellent for boiling, and *small hock,* a tough cut which should be casseroled, boned.

Gammon An expensive cut, usually sold in four joints: *corner, middle, hock* and *slipper.* The large rounded rashers usually come from middle gammon; all joints can be boiled or baked.

Streaky Sold in rashers, this is the cured equivalent of belly pork. Fry or grill it; use it to cover (bard) poultry and game when roasting.

Ham The hindleg of the pig, cut when it is still fresh pork. There are many different cures: look for York ham, a mild-flavoured, very delicate meat, or the rarer Bradenham and Suffolk cures. Every country has different ways of treating ham: Virginia ham comes from pigs fed on peanuts and peaches; Kentucky from hogs fed on wild acorns and clover. From Europe come hams which are often eaten raw as the first course in a meal.

OFFAL
Offal are the parts left after the slaughtered animal has been dressed: the liver and kidneys are most popular but all are highly nutritious.

Calf's liver The most expensive liver, with a mild flavour.

Lamb's liver The most popular liver, excellent for grilling or frying.

Pig's liver Stronger in flavour than lamb's liver but softer in texture, ideal for pâtés and casseroles.

Ox liver May be soaked in milk or salted water to reduce the strength of its flavour; ideal for casseroles.

Calf's kidney The most tender kidney, but often difficult to obtain.

Lamb's kidney Good for grilling and frying; must be light brown and firm.

Pig's kidney Suitable for grilling or frying, also often used in casseroles.

Ox kidney Tougher, so requires long, slow cooking for stews, steak and kidney pies and puddings.

Ox and lamb's tongue Readily available and may be bought fresh or salted. Both should be soaked in salted water before cooking in fresh water with a *bouquet garni*. The skin and bone must be removed before being pressed in jellied stock. Lamb's tongue may be served hot with parsley sauce.

Lambs' and pigs' hearts Best stuffed and then slowly casseroled or braised.

Ox heart Much larger than lamb's or pig's and often added, chopped, to stews.

Brains Calves' and lambs' brains are simple to prepare. After soaking for about two hours in cold, lightly salted water, simmer gently for about 20 minutes and then press them as they cool. They can then be sliced, coated in flour and fried in butter.

Sweetbreads The two parts of the thymus gland, one in the throat and one in the chest cavity. Calves' and lambs' sweetbreads have the best flavour, while that of the ox is tough and strong in flavour. They require careful preparation but are delicious served with a cream sauce.

Tripe The lining of an ox's stomach. Tripe from the first stomach is referred to as the 'blanket' and that from the second stomach is called the 'honeycomb'. It can be stewed in milk or sliced and deep fried. As tripe has already been par-boiled, the butcher will advise on the length of cooking time.

Calves' feet and pigs' trotters Ideal for making stock. They may also be boned, stuffed and roasted, or boiled for adding to brawn.

Oxtail Excellent braised. It should be skinned and jointed by the butcher, and be lean and deep red in colour.

Ox cheek Used for stews and brawn; very economical.

Head Sold whole or in halves, salted or fresh and mainly used for brawn. Calf's head may be boiled and served whole with a cream sauce; sheep's head is used for soups and stews.

Marrow bones The fore and hind legs of beef cattle. The marrow inside them should be pale pink, and adds a delicious flavour to home-made stocks and soups.

Sausages A combination of lean meat, fat, cereal and seasoning. Many butchers have their own recipe, but the percentage of lean meat the sausage must contain is stated by law.

Black pudding This is sausage-shaped, made from pig's blood and pork fat and stuffed into pig's intestines before boiling. It is served sliced and grilled or fried.

STORING MEAT
Without a refrigerator Fresh meat must be kept as cool as possible, preferably in a meat safe which allows circulation of air. Always use meat that was bought minced and cooked meats on the day of purchase.

In a refrigerator Keep raw and cooked meat separate and loosely wrapped in foil or film at 2°–6°C (35°–43°F).

In the freezer Meat will keep for varying lengths of time.
   Before freezing, trim the meat and remove excess fat. Trimming helps ensure neat

FOOD AND COOKERY

Appropriate maximum storage times for meat in the home.

	Days in meat safe	Days in refrigerator	Months in freezer −17°C (0°F)
Uncooked meat			
Beef	2	3-5	12
Pork	2	2-4	6
Lamb	2	3-5	9
Bacon rashers	4	7	1
Bacon vacuum-packed rashers	5	10	3
Mince	same day	1	3
Offal	same day	1-2	3
Sausages	1	3	3
Cooked meats			
Casseroles with bacon	1	2	3
Casseroles without bacon	1	3	6
Ham	same day	2-3	2
Meat pies	1	1	3
Sliced meat with gravy	1-2	2-3	3
Sliced meat without gravy	1-2	2-4	2
Pâté	1	2	1
Stock	same day	4	6

Reproduced by kind permission of 'British Meat'

packing, and fat can become rancid. If you are freezing chops, rashers or slices of meat, put sheets of grease-proof paper between each portion. Pack the meat in thick-gauge polythene bags or in foil. Exclude as much air as possible to prevent de-hydration and 'freezer burn'.

If you have bought meat in bulk, make sure you freeze minced meat and offal first, then small cuts followed by large joints. Everything should be clearly labelled. The date on which the meat was frozen must be shown so that you will know by when it must be eaten, and nothing be wasted. Don't overload the freezer; the storage tempera-ture must be −17° (0°F). Adding extra food will raise the temperature in the freezer and the contents will start to thaw.

Thawing meat Joints are best thawed in the refrigerator for one or two days before cook-ing but, if cooked from frozen, place a meat thermo-meter in the thickest part half way through cooking to ensure that the centre of the joint is thoroughly cooked. Do not allow the thermo-meter to touch the bone. Boned and rolled joints should always be thawed be-fore cooking.

TENDERIZING MEAT

Sometimes steaks and veal escalopes are beaten to crush tough fibres; mincing meat has the same effect. Tough cuts, used for stews and braises, are often marinated for a few hours in an aro-matic mixture with herbs, spices and an acid, such as wine or cider. As the meat soaks, the acidity in the mari-nade helps tenderize it.

A stew cooked in wine tastes even better, reheated thoroughly, the day after it is cooked. If you have a pre-pared meat dish and want to freeze it, follow the freezer manufacturer's instructions.

COOKING MEAT

OVEN ROASTING
Only tender joints are suitable for oven roasting. Beef may be served under-done, but make sure veal, lamb and pork are cooked thoroughly. There is no agreement about the best heat; the temperatures given here are for slow roasting, an increasingly popular method.

Pre-set the oven to 100°C (350°F) Gas Mark 4. Put the weighed joint on a grid in-side a roasting tray. If it is very lean, rub it with lard, dripping or good cooking oil. With pork, make sure the rind is scored (the butcher will do this) and brush the cut surface with oil and salt so that you will get crisp crackl-ing. If you want very accu-rate timing, use a meat thermometer. Insert it into the joint before cooking.

Beef 20–25 minutes per 450 g (1 lb) plus 20–25 minutes. Using a meat thermometer, register 60°C (140°F) for rare beef: 70°C (160°F), medium; 80°C (180°F), well done.
Veal 35 minutes per 450 g (1 lb) plus 35 minutes. With a meat thermometer, register 80°C (180°F).
Lamb 25-30 minutes per 450 g (1 lb) plus 25-30 minutes. Using a meat thermometer, register 80°C (180°F).
Pork As for veal.
Bacon and gammon See the times given for boiling in your recipe. Simmer for half the stated time, drain, then roast in the oven for the rest of the cooking time, at 220°C (425°F) Gas Mark 7, basting frequently. The tempera-ture, with a thermometer, should be 70°C (160°F).
Spit roasting To spit roast in the oven, follow the times given above. Under direct heat, allow 15 minutes per 450 g (1 lb) plus 15 minutes.

PRESSURE COOKING
Reduces the cooking time by up to 75 per cent. Follow manufacturer's instructions.

MICROWAVE COOKING
Not suited to cuts requiring long slow cooking. Follow manufacturer's instructions.

GRILLING/FRYING
Times vary: a beef steak may take 7–10 minutes; a thin veal escalope 4; a pork chop 15–20 minutes.

Grilling Pre-heat the grill. Brush the meat with butter or oil and add seasoning.
Frying Shallow-fry meat in butter, dripping, lard or oil. Cook at a high temperature to start with then lower the heat until the meat is cooked through.

STEWING
This is a slow method of cooking for tougher cuts of meat. The meat is accom-panied by vegetables, herbs and seasoning, and sim-mered in stock, water, wine or another liquid.

To prepare the meat, cube it, toss in seasoned flour and fry quickly to seal in the juices. Remove the meat and fry vegetables in the pan until golden. Stir in a little flour to absorb the fat then replace meat, pour on sufficient liquid to just cover and sea-son. Simmer on the stove or in the oven at 160°C (325°F) Gas Mark 3, for 1½-3 hours.

BRAISING
Braising is a slow method of cooking for less tender cuts of meat such as brisket, spare rib chops and offal. To pre-pare the meat, roll in sea-soned flour and fry quickly in hot fat using a heavy-based pan or casserole. Remove the meat and lightly fry vege-tables in its juices. Return the meat to the pan, barely cover the bed of vegetables with liquid, season, and cook slowly on a very low heat on top of the cooker, or in the oven for 2–3 hours at 160°C (325°F) Gas Mark 3. When the dish is cooked, reduce the liquid by boiling and pour over the meat. Slow cookers are also good for braising.

POT ROASTING
Small, tougher cuts of meat such as brisket and topside are suitable for pot-roasting. The oven-proof pan or cas-serole must have a tightly-fit-ting lid and a thick base, and be large enough to hold the joint comfortably without it touching the sides.

Fry the meat in a little fat until brown. Remove and cover the base of the pan with a bed of chopped root vegetables. Replace the meat and cook on the top of the cooker turning the meat fre-quently for 45–50 minutes.

BOILING
Salted meat and tongues are customarily boiled, but whole unsalted joints may also be cooked in this way.

Soak salted meat in cold water overnight. Drain, pour over fresh water, season, add a *bouquet garni*, a chopped onion and root vegetables. Bring to the boil, simmer slowly in a pan with a tightly-fitting lid. Allow about 20–25 minutes per 450 g (1 lb) plus 20–25 minutes.

REHEATING
When meat is to be reheated, it is important to bring it to the boil and then simmer for 20 minutes.

FOOD AND COOKERY

CARVING MEAT

This is simple if you have a good carving knife, a two-pronged fork and a steel for sharpening the knife. The same principles apply for roast or boiled cuts.

The meat will keep hot for about ten minutes once it has been removed from the oven or from the boiling liquor. Put it to rest in a warm place to allow the meat to 'set' — it makes carving much easier. Adjust your timing to allow for the accompanying vegetables to be cooked, but not overdone, and to allow time for a sauce to be made or gravy thickened. Meanwhile keep meat hot without over-cooking it.

Carve the meat on a flat surface, one on which it will not slip about. A spiked carving dish is ideal as it also catches the juices. First, loosen the meat from around any exposed bones (see diagrams alongside). Hold the joint in place firmly with the carving fork and use the knife to slice steadily across the grain of the meat. Generally, beef is carved fairly thinly, and lamb in thick slices. But how you carve is up to you. Whether you serve thick or thin slices is purely a matter of personal preference. Follow the diagrams for meat on the bone.

ACCOMPANIMENTS

There are many traditional accompaniments to roast and grilled meats. Their flavours enhance the meat.

Roast beef
Horseradish sauce, mustard, Yorkshire pudding.
Fried steaks

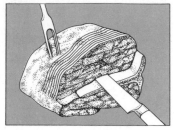

Sirloin of beef Slice downwards towards the bone on one side, then loosen the beef from the bone. Turn the joint over and repeat the action on the other side.

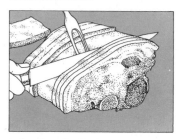

Loin of pork Remove the chine bone. Remove the crackling if wished, before you carve towards the bone. Cut into slices.

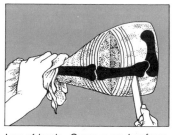

Leg of lamb Carve a wedge from the centre of the leg. Continue carving on both sides of the wedge, with the knife at an angle. Turn over and slice along the leg.

French or English mustard; fried onion rings.
Grilled steaks
Maître d'hôtel (parsley and lemon) butter, mustard, watercress.
Roast veal
Breadcrumb and parsley stuffing, bacon rolls.
Roast lamb, lamb chops
Mint sauce, red currant jelly.

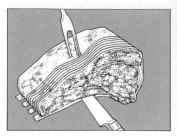

Forerib of beef Remove the back-bone (chine bone). Loosen the meat from the rib bones. Carve the beef downwards towards and between the rib bones.

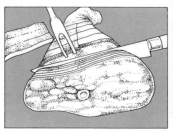

Leg of pork Remove some of the crackling. Slice down to the bone, then over the top of the bone. Turn over and slice towards the thin end.

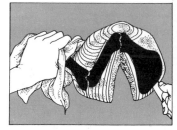

Shoulder of lamb Cut a wedge down between the upper arm bone and blade bone. Carve downwards first, then horizontally across the shank bone.

Serve mutton with onion sauce and apricot and walnut stuffing.
Roast pork, pork chops
Apple sauce; sage and onion stuffing; orange and water-cress salad.
When roasting lamb or pork, nick the skin in four or five places and insert pieces of garlic or sprigs of rosemary.

POULTRY

CHOOSING POULTRY

Fresh or frozen, poultry of excellent quality is available all the year round from butchers and supermarkets.

Poultry is defined as a bird bred for the table: chicken, boiling fowl, duck, goose and turkey come into this category. So does guinea fowl, which used to be a game bird.

As with meat, decide in advance what you want in terms of your budget and the number of portions you will serve. Don't think of chicken only in terms of roasting: you will often find an old, tough bird which will make an excellent casserole, cooked with vegetables and herbs. Many butchers sell packs of giblets — necks and internal, edible parts of chicken from which you can make broth or stock. Chicken livers, fresh or frozen, can be used, fried and served on toast or made into a pâté.

When you buy frozen poultry, make sure it is completely thawed before you cook it; there is a risk of salmonella poisoning from partly-thawed poultry. Once thawed, take out the giblets. Rinse the inside of the bird by holding it under a running tap and letting the water run through. Dry the bird carefully, inside and out, with kitchen paper.

Turkey tends to be dry and generous barding of the breast with streaky bacon will help keep the flesh moist. Duck is boney and even a large one will not feed more than four. Goose is flavourful but fatty and, like duck, will not go as far as chicken. To get extra value from your bird, use the bones for stock and the tasty fat for cooking.

COOKING AND SERVING

CHICKEN

Chicken joints Sold as individual portions. Casserole with vegetables, herbs and spices, in stock or wine. Alternatively, grill plain or season and coat with egg and breadcrumbs and shallow fry.

Poussins Young chickens, about six to eight weeks old. They weigh from 450–900 g (1–2 lb), and serve one or two people. Season, brush with melted butter, and grill, turning frequently.

Broilers Twelve-week-old chickens; they weigh from 1.1–1.4 kg (2½–3 lb), and will feed three to four people. Roast at 190°C (375°F) Gas Mark 5, allowing 20 minutes per 450 g (1 lb) plus 20 minutes.

A game bird, in all the beauty of its plumage, and a selection of poultry. *Left to right, back row:* capon, wild duck, domestic duck. *Centre:* Guinea fowl, turkey, boiling fowl. *Front row:* single and double poussins, roasting chicken.

Large roasters 1.8–2.3 kg (4–5 lb) birds, they should serve six people. Roast at 160/170°C (325°F) Gas Mark 3 for 25 minutes per 450 g (1 lb), plus 25 minutes. Baste regularly with the bird's juices as it cooks.

Capons 10–12 weeks old, these birds serve eight to ten people. Their weight is usually 2.7–3.6 kg (6–8 lb). For cooking times, see 'Large roasters'.

Boiling fowls Usually poultry 18 months or older. Cook with wine, cider or stock, vegetables, herbs and spices. Boil, steam or casserole for about two hours until tender.

FOOD AND COOKERY

DUCK

Duckling A bird up to six weeks old, weighs 1.6–1.8 kg (3½–4 lb) and will serve two people.

Duck 1.8–2.7 kg (4–6 lb), serves three to four. Roast at 160°C (325°F) Gas Mark 3, allowing 25 minutes per 450 g (1 lb) plus 25 minutes.

Duck is a fatty bird so do not brush with butter before cooking and do not baste. Instead, prick the skin with a fork to allow the fat to run out during cooking.

GOOSE

Most geese weigh about 2.7–5.5 kg (6–12 lb) and will feed from six to twelve people. Roast as for duck.

GUINEA FOWL

Guinea fowl weigh from 550 g–1.7 kg (1¼–3¼ lb) according to their age. Roast the younger birds, coated with butter or barded with streaky bacon. Use older, tougher guinea fowl in casseroles.

TURKEY

Look for a 4.5–6.3 kg (10–14 lb) bird for 12 servings. Roast as for chicken, basting frequently.

ROASTING

Buy a plump, young bird. Look for a pliable breast bone. When you buy a fresh duck or goose, choose one with yellow feet and bill.

Poultry, with or without a stuffing, is often trussed. This is not necessary for most small birds and roasting chickens, but it helps keep a turkey in shape as it cooks.

Stuffing After the bird has been cleaned, put a savoury stuffing in the neck end. It is unwise to stuff the body cavity but put in a peeled apple, onion or orange with a little butter to give the bird extra flavour and to add moisture. Traditional accompaniments to poultry are: roast potatoes, Brussels sprouts, chipolata sausages and gravy from the bird's juices.

Stuff the neck end of a chicken with parsley and thyme, mixed with fresh breadcrumbs, and add a sage-and-onion stuffing to duck or goose. For turkey use a chestnut stuffing. Use a bread sauce with chicken or turkey; a sweet-sharp apple sauce with duck. Serve cranberry sauce and grilled bacon rolls with guinea fowl and turkey.

Trussing After the bird has been prepared, pull the loose neck skin over the opening and fold the wings back over the skin. Push a skewer through the body, just behind the thighs. Secure the wings with string looped around the skewer and, turning the bird over, tie the thighs together.

Roasting poultry Put the bird on a grid in a roasting tin. Put it into the pre-heated oven, covered with butter or 'barded' with rashers of streaky bacon so that it does not dry out during cooking. Turn it from time to time to make sure it is evenly cooked on all sides. Spoon out the juices from the pan to baste. Add a little cider halfway through cooking, to add flavour to duck and goose. You may cover the bird with a sheet of aluminium foil as it cooks, but take off to allow browning and crisping for the final 15–30 minutes. To test for 'doneness', push a skewer into the thigh. If the juices run clear, the bird is cooked. Let the bird stand for a while, keeping hot, to make carving easier.

ROASTING TIMES FOR TURKEY			
Weight		Cooking time in hours	
kg	lb	160°C (325°F) Gas Mark 3	230°C (450°F) Gas Mark 8
2.7–3.6	6–8	1½–3½	2¼–2½
3.6–4.5	8–10	3½–3¾	2½–2¾
4.5–6.3	10–14	3¾–4¼	2¾–3
6.3–8.1	14–18	4¼–4¾	3–3½
8.1–9.0	18–20	4¾–5½	3½–3¾
9.0–10.8	20–24	5¼–6	3¾–4¼

CARVING AND JOINTING

Carving chicken First remove the stuffing. Insert the blade of the carving knife between the leg and the body and cut through. Sever the thigh from the drumstick. Repeat with the other leg. Carve off the wings, taking some of the breast meat too. Carve the breast in long downward slices and divide between the portions.

With a small chicken, fewer portions will be possible. Cut off the legs but leave them whole. Carve off the wings with the breast attached. Hold the knife close to the carcass to avoid leaving breast meat on the bone.

Portioning chicken For 4 portions, cut along the breastbone and open out the bird. Either cut along the backbone or cut it out completely. Cut each chicken half diagonally between leg and wing. For 6 portions, cut off the legs and wings and then cut off each side of the breast.

Carving turkey First cut the drumsticks away from the body. Leave the thighs attached to the breast. Cut away both wings. Carve the white meat from the breast in long slices, carving down from the breastbone. Carve the dark meat from the drumsticks and from the thighs, holding the drumsticks upright. Make up portions of dark and white meat mixed.

If the turkey has been stuffed, spoon out the stuffing before starting to carve and then add a little to each portion when you are dividing the meat.

Carving duck or goose Remove the stuffing if applicable. Cut away the legs and, with a goose, divide into two. Then cut away the wings. Cut down along the breastbone. On each side of the breast make cuts through the meat parallel to the first cut. Loosen the meat from the carcass by cutting upwards, holding the knife close to the body of the bird.

Portioning duck Duck can often be too small or boney to carve. In this case portion it as you would a chicken.

STUFFINGS

Use stuffings to give a more attractive shape to poultry. They give extra flavour and help stretch out the portions.

Only stuff the neck end, never the body cavity, as there is a chance that it may not cook through thoroughly.

Always remove stuffing from bird after carving and allow to become cold separately.

Duck and goose may be stuffed from either end.

For a simple stuffing, combine fresh white breadcrumbs, one beaten egg, seasoning, butter and fresh herbs. Use sage, parsley or tarragon. Moisten with a little water, and add finely peeled lemon rind.

To make a sausagemeat stuffing, combine sausagemeat with a lightly fried, finely chopped onion, breadcrumbs and a beaten egg. Season to taste and, if liked, add chopped, boiled chestnuts, or a large cooking apple, sliced into small pieces.

Never freeze a bird ready-stuffed: it will deteriorate rapidly.

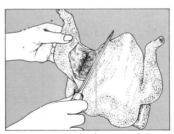

Jointing a chicken Clean the bird and pull each leg away from the body. Using a sharp knife, slice through between the thigh and the carcass. Sever the wings and slice off each breast.

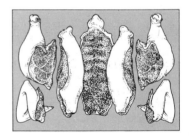

Chicken joints Use the legs and breasts of young chickens for grilling. Serve hot, with a devilled sauce, or cold for a picnic or barbecue. Casserole joints of a boiling fowl or use to make soup.

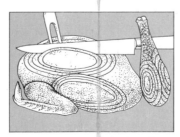

Carving a turkey Use a sharp carving knife to cut away the drumsticks. Slice off the wings. Carve the white meat from the turkey breast and the dark meat from drumsticks and thighs.

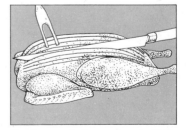

Carving a duck or goose First spoon out the stuffing if you are using one. Then sever the legs and the wings from the body. Slice downwards on either side of the breastbone.

FOOD AND COOKERY

GAME

If game is to be tender it must be young. Age is easily determined when the game is fully feathered or furred which is one good reason for buying it this way. Generally speaking, look for plumpness, pale coloured feet and soft, downy plumage in birds, and soft pliable ears in rabbits and hares. Venison is sold in joints so you will have to rely on your butcher.

Game birds must be hanged to increase their flavour and promote tenderness. This is not easy for everyone and, if you order your game well in advance, a butcher will do it for you. Rabbits do not need hanging but hares do, and the preparation of both — skinning, paunching, catching the blood — is messy and more easily dealt with by a butcher. If a bird has not been drawn this must be done, except with quail.

Grouse Roast at 200°C (400°F) Gas Mark 6 for about 40 minutes. Bard well and stuff or put butter in the body cavity. Serves one to two.
Partridge Cook as grouse. Older birds should be braised or casseroled.
Pheasant Roast at 220°C (425°F) Gas Mark 7 at 20 minutes per 450 g (1 lb).
Pigeon Roast for 15-20 minutes at 220°C (425°F) Gas Mark 7. Young birds may be jointed and grilled, older birds casseroled.
Quail Sold oven ready but undrawn. One bird serves one person. Roast at 200°C (400°F) Gas Mark 6 for 15 minutes. Can also be grilled.
Wild duck Three varieties are common in the UK, teal, mallard and widgeon. They will normally serve one to two people. Bard and roast at 220°C (425°F) Gas Mark 7 for 20-30 minutes.

Hare Bard and roast at 180°C (350°F) Gas Mark 4 for about 2 hours. Braise or casserole older animals having first marinated them in red wine.
Rabbit Roast as for hare, grill joints and casserole or braise older animals. Marinate in herbed and spiced oil and wine before cooking.
Venison Roast, braise or grill the loin and haunch, first marinating as for hare. Roast at 190°C (375°F) Gas Mark 5 for 35 minutes per 450 g (1 lb), keeping the joint moist. Braise for 2½–3 hours.

TABLE OF POULTRY AND GAME IN SEASON

● Months when of best quality
o Available all time

	Seasons											
	J	F	M	A	M	J	J	A	S	O	N	D
Poultry												
Chicken	o	o	o	o	o	o	o	o	o	o	o	o
Duck	o	o	o	o	o	o	o	●	●	●	●	●
Goose	●	●	o	o	o	o	o	o	o	●	●	●
Guinea fowl	o	●	●	●	o	o	o	o	o	o	o	o
Turkey	o	o	o	o	o	o	o	o	o	o	o	o
Game												
Grouse								●	●	●	o	o
Partridge	o								o	●	●	o
Pheasant	o									o	●	●
Pigeon	o	o	o	o	o	o	o	●	●	●	o	o
Quail	o	o	o	o	o	o	o	o	o	o	o	o
Wild duck	●	●						●	●	●	●	●
Furred Game												
Hare	●	●	●					o	o	●	●	●
Rabbit	o	o	o	o	o	o	o	o	o	o	o	o
Venison	●					●	●	●	●	●	●	●

FISH

CHOOSING FISH

White and oily fish are both rich in protein, and oily fish contain vitamin D which helps develop good teeth and strong bones. It is often prescribed to pregnant women and young children in the form of cod liver oil.

Although we are surrounded by waters which are extensively fished, it is difficult to buy fresh fish in many parts of the country. However, fish commercially frozen is very good: because it is frozen soon after being caught this does not affect its flavour drastically. Keep it in its pack and store in the freezing compartment of your refrigerator for the recommended length of time. Once thawed, do not refreeze.

If you are lucky enough to have a good fishmonger, use his skills. It is not difficult to gut and fillet fish yourself, but the fishmonger has the sharp filleting knives and the expertise to do it quickly and professionally. Fresh fish doesn't keep well: if possible, cook and eat it the day you buy it. In any case put the fish in your refrigerator, covered for safe storage.

Cured fish, from the expensive delicate salmon to the breakfast kipper, has been enjoyed in Great Britain for

In the fish basket **1** skate. On the slab, from left to right **2** rainbow trout **3** haddock **4** brill **5** smoked mackerel **6** herring **7** cod **8** Dover sole **9** mackerel **10** whitebait **11** plaice **12** sea trout **13** red mullet **14** sardines

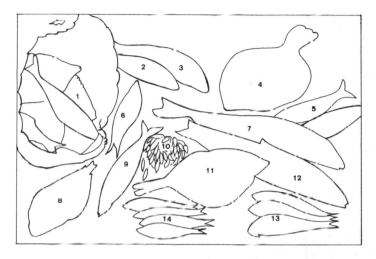

23

FOOD AND COOKERY

centuries. Look for it in a good delicatessen as well as on the fishmonger's slab. It is also available frozen.

WHAT TO LOOK FOR
White and Oily fish When you buy fresh fish, look for brightness. The eyes should be prominent, the gills red, the scales sparkling. The body should be firm and there must be a fresh smell.

Cured fish Look for plumpness. Smoked fish which is curling around the edges and looks dry has probably been kept for too long.

WHITE FISH
Bass A round fish with delicate flesh. Bake or poach a large fish; grill or fry smaller ones.

Bream Sea bream is a round fish, with coarse scales. It has sweet, tender flesh. Bake larger fish with a stuffing; grill or fry smaller fish.

Brill A firm, white, flat fish which looks like a turbot and has a similar but less succulent taste. Bake, grill or poach.

Cod Cod is round, with close, white flesh and a mild flavour. It is usually bought in steaks or as fillets. Grill, bake or fry.

Coley A fish which is always sold filleted. When raw, the flesh is greyish, but becomes white after cooking. Because cod has become expensive, coley is often used instead. You can fry, grill or bake it.

Dab and Flounder Part of the plaice family, with soft,

white, sweet flesh. Grill, fry or bake.

Dogfish Also called flake, huss and rig, this is a firm-fleshed member of the shark family. It used to be known, incorrectly, as 'rock salmon'. Use it in casseroles, soups and fish stocks.

Haddock Part of the cod family. Buy it whole, or in cuts or fillets. It has firm, fine-textured white flesh. Bake, grill or fry.

Hake A member of the cod family. Cook as for cod and enhance its taste with a well-flavoured sauce.

Halibut A large, flat fish, most often sold in cutlets. Bake whole, with a stuffing; fry, grill or poach. Mock halibut is smaller.

Plaice One of the most popular fish in this country. It has a greyish upper side with bright orange spots and a white underside. Plaice has soft, sweet flesh. Use it whole, fried or grilled, or filleted. You may use plaice in recipes which call for the more expensive sole.

Rockfish Also known as catfish. Look for firm, pinkish-coloured flesh; use for fish stews and soups.

Skate A flat fish with large 'wings' — the part we eat. The sweet flesh comes away from the bones easily; grill or fry in butter.

Sole Dover sole is often thought to be the best of all white fish. Its flavour is delicate but not insipid; its flesh firm but creamy. Grilled,

fried on the bone, or filleted, sole is often served with a sauce. Dover sole is oval, its upper side is brownish, with irregular black markings; its underside is white. Ask your fishmonger to skin it. Lemon and witch soles are cheaper. Their flavour is not quite as good but they are excellent value: fry, grill or poach them. Serve with a sauce.

Turbot A large flat fish, with a creamy flavour; cook as for halibut, preferably whole.

Whiting A round fish, part of the cod family. Whiting is bony, but has soft, flaky flesh and a delicate flavour. Bake, fry or poach it.

OILY FISH
Carp A freshwater fish which can taste muddy. To prevent this, soak for about three hours beforehand in salted water. Especially good stuffed and baked.

Conger eel A saltwater fish with a greyish black skin. It has a distinctive flavour and is ideal for stews, soups and fish kebabs.

Herring A small, oily fish with creamy-coloured flesh. Bought whole, it is often brushed with melted butter, seasoned, sprinkled with oatmeal and grilled or fried.

Mackerel A cheap, tasty saltwater fish. It is round, with a silvery underside and a blue and green striped upperside. It is usually grilled, but you can stuff and bake it. Cut its slightly oily flavour with a gooseberry or apple sauce.

Mullet (grey) This is a large estuary fish with firm flesh.

Small grey mullet are best grilled and served with savoury butter, and larger ones stuffed and baked.

Mullet (red) A uniquely flavoured red-skinned saltwater fish, best grilled or baked and served with butter, lemon and seasoning.

Perch Requires careful cleaning. Remove hard scales by plunging into boiling water. Best grilled and served with melted butter.

Pike A freshwater fish of great size and very coarse flesh. Prepare by soaking, and then boil, or bake with a stuffing. Pike is traditionally used in *quenelles*.

Pilchard Large sardine, often sold in cans. Pilchards make very economical fish dishes.

Salmon A migratory fish sold as steaks or whole. Excellent poached and garnished with cucumber, sprigs of parsley and lemon wedges, and delicious served cold with mayonnaise.

Sardine Sardines are young pilchards which are usually bought canned in oil or tomato sauce, but may also be bought fresh. If canned, serve cold or grilled on toast.

Smelt or sparling Small strong-tasting fish, which is best rolled in breadcrumbs and deep fried.

Sprat Small fish similar to herrings, but silver-skinned. Young sprats, known as brislings, are canned in oil or tomato sauce. If you buy them fresh, flour, deep fry and sprinkle with lemon juice and black pepper.

Trout (rainbow) This is the most common. It has creamy flesh and is best grilled and served with maître d'hôtel butter, or fried and served with almonds.

Trout (river or brown) Distinguished from rainbow trout by its darker skin.

Trout (sea or salmon) A pink-fleshed fish, salmon-like in flavour. Cook in the same way.

Whitebait Very small herring or sprat, about 4 cm (1½ in) in length and silver-skinned. Especially good coated in flour and deep fried until crisp, served with lemon juice, salt and pepper.

CURED FISH

Fish used to be cured at home, in salt, vinegar or by smoking, as a method of preservation when fresh food was not available.

You may still pickle fish: keep it in the refrigerator and use within a few days. A hot smoker adds flavour but does not preserve the food: cold smoking preserves the fish. It is possible to build a cold smoker at home, but you need specialist advice.

Anchovy Small, silvery fish, often used in savouries, pizzas and salads, anchovies are most often bought cured and canned in oil.

Smoked cod's roe You will find it in delicatessens and fishmonger's shops. Use it to make *taramasalata*, a Greek hors d'oeuvre.

Smoked haddock Arbroath smokies are small haddock, smoked to a dark golden brown. Spread them with butter, grill or cook in the oven, and eat hot with buttered toast.

Finnan haddock are smoked and pale yellow. To make Kedgeree, for a hearty breakfast or light supper, cook gently in milk and butter. Drain and add boiled, long grain rice and chopped hard-boiled eggs. Add a little more butter, mix well, and season to taste. Serve on a large platter.

Bismarck herring Fillets pickled in spiced vinegar with sliced onion.

Bloater A herring cured in brine, then lightly smoked. Grill or fry.

Buckling A herring which has been smoked and lightly cooked. Eat with brown bread and butter.

Kipper The most popular smoked herring. It can be bought boned, fresh or frozen. Spread with butter and grill.

Rollmop A brined herring fillet, sprinkled with sliced onion, then rolled up and secured with a cocktail stick. Put in a pickling jar, cover with spiced vinegar, sometimes sweetened, with a bayleaf; keep in a cool place and eat after 5 days.

Smoked mackerel Sold ready to eat. To make a pâté, skin, and pound with soured cream. Season with salt, freshly ground black pepper and lemon juice to taste.

Smoked salmon and trout The best of smoked fish, always sold ready to eat. Buy them plump and juicy. When serving, add thinly sliced brown bread, butter, freshly ground black pepper, and wedges of lemon. Horseradish sauce goes well with smoked trout.

25

FOOD AND COOKERY

PREPARING FISH

Scaling and cleaning Put a few layers of kitchen paper on your work surface or chopping block. Using a blunt knife, scrape away the scales from tail to head. Rinse thoroughly under running water.

Cleaning a round fish Take a sharp knife and split the fish along the belly. Scrape out the entrails (inner parts). Cut off the head, just below the gills. Cut away the fins. If you want to fillet and skin the fish, leave the tail. Rinse again with cold water.

Cleaning a flat fish With the point of your knife, make an incision just behind the head on the upper (dark) side. Scrape out entrails and rinse.

Filleting A round fish will give you two fillets; a flat fish, four. Hold the fish by its tail and, using a sharp knife, cut along the backbone. With *round fish,* turn skin down and lift off the backbone gently, running the knife along behind it as you raise it. Pick off any smaller bones that have not come free. With *flat fish,* cut round behind the head and free the two upper fillets from the backbone, using the knife. Turn the fish over and repeat the process.

Skinning First sprinkle salt on your fingers so you can get a firm grip on the fish's tail. *To skin round fish* Make an incision just below the head, then loosen the skin. Pull it towards the tail, easing it up by running the blade of a knife underneath it. Pull the skin off gently, using the knife when you need it. *To*

skin flat fish Again, sprinkle salt on your fingers so you can grasp the tail firmly. Make a slit and pull off the skin towards the head. Turn the fish over, and skin the other side.

COOKING

Fish should be cooked at a relatively low temperature to prevent the flesh from becoming tough. The fish is cooked when the flesh parts easily from the bones.

Baking Bake in the centre of a pre-heated oven at 180°C (350°F) Gas Mark 4 allowing 25–30 minutes for whole fish and 10–20 minutes for fillets and steaks. A small amount of liquid and butter may be added: baste frequently. The fish can be stuffed and covered in foil, in which case it will take about 8 minutes per 450 g (1 lb) for large fish plus 10 minutes. Steaks take about 20 minutes.

Poaching Totally immerse the fish in seasoned fish stock. Bring just to the boil, and then reduce to a bare simmer for 8–10 minutes. This is an ideal method of cooking white fish because the liquid can be used to make a sauce.

Deep frying Coat the fish in egg, flour and breadcrumbs or batter and immerse in hot oil: 160–170°C (312–325°F). Test to see whether the oil is hot enough first by dropping a small piece of bread into it. The bread should turn a light golden colour and rise to the surface within 30 seconds when the oil is ready.

Shallow frying The oil or butter should come half-way

up the fish. Cook the fish for approximately 10 minutes, depending on its thickness. This is an excellent method for small whole fish and steaks or fillets.

Grilling Score whole, round fish with shallow diagonal cuts to allow the heat to penetrate the flesh. Brush white fish with melted butter. Baste and turn the fish as it cooks. Once the grill has become hot, allow 10–15 minutes for steaks, cutlets and whole fish, and 4–5 minutes for fillets.

Steaming Put fillets in the top half of a steamer or double saucepan, season and cook for 10–15 minutes over boiling water. As steaming is the purest way of cooking fish, it is a popular method of preparing white fish for invalids and young children.

ACCOMPANIMENTS

Most fish has a delicate flavour: serve it with a sauce which has a contrasting taste.

There are many variations on white sauce including cheese, mustard and parsley. They add zest and flavour.

Make a fresh tomato sauce or one from fish stock, thickened with flour and butter, and enriched with white wine and cream.

Oily fish, like mackerel, are the better for a sharp, piquant sauce. To make gooseberry sauce, simply simmer gooseberries (topped and tailed) with sugar, adjusted to taste.

For grilled or fried fish, serve savoury butters, a home-made mayonnaise, horseradish or tartare sauce.

SHELLFISH

All shellfish should be bought fresh and clean. Molluscs — mussels and oysters among them — are bought live. Look for tightly closed shells which open as they are cooked.

Prawns, crabs and lobsters are crustaceans. They are usually sold boiled before you buy them.

Clams Serve raw — or you can cook them like mussels. Clam chowder is a classic American dish. They are also good in a tomato sauce with spaghetti.

Cockles A symbol of London life, like a trip to Southend or a visit to the music hall. You will usually buy them shelled and cooked. Serve them with vinegar and brown bread and butter.

Crab Usually bought precooked — boiled by the fishmonger. He will usually

This picture shows a selection of the shellfish widely available in the British Isles.
1 lobster **2** small and large crabs **3** clams **4** king prawns **5** two varieties of live oyster **6** scallops **7** winkles **8** whelks **9** shrimps **10** mussels **11** shelled cockles

FOOD AND COOKERY

'dress' it for you — removing the white meat from the claws and the brown meat from the shell. If you have a live crab, put it in a pan of cold water, bring it up to the boil and cook for 15–20 minutes. Add a sliced onion, bayleaf and seasoning.

Serve crab with a salad and mayonnaise or as a savoury souffle. When preparing remove inedible parts (dead men's fingers).

Lobster As with crab, it is far easier to buy a lobster which has been boiled. Cooking the lobster isn't a job for the squeamish as it must be cooked alive. Tie the tail in the curled position to the body and then plunge head-first into boiling water. Boil for 15-20 minutes according to the size. Ensure that all inedible parts (dead men's fingers) are removed.

Mussels Molluscs with blue-black shells, always sold live. Scrub them thoroughly first, discarding any which are part-open. Remove any barnacles and cut away the seaweed-like beard.

Rinse thoroughly, then cook, often in wine, sliced onion and herbs. If any mussels are still closed after cooking, throw them away.

Oysters An expensive food now, mostly eaten in restaurants, oysters used to be a cheap and common dish until, in the middle of the nineteenth century, oyster beds dried out or became polluted. After that, good oysters became exclusively the province of those who could afford them.

British oysters, from Whit-stable, Cornwall and other areas, are still regarded as the best in the world. Prepare them as you would mussels: scrub well. Open and serve raw on the half-shells, with slices of brown bread, butter, lemon wedges and a sprinkling of cayenne pepper.

Prawns and shrimps Usually sold cooked, they are available all the year round fresh in their shells, shelled or canned. Live, they are brownish in colour. Put them into a pan of boiling water for about 5 minutes (15–20 for Dublin Bay prawns–scampi). To shell, hold between your finger and thumb and pull off the tail

shell first; then twist off the head. Peel away the rest of the shell. Prawns and shrimps make delicious hors d'oeuvres.

Scallops Most often bought, opened, on the half-shell, fresh or frozen. Look for a bright orange roe surrounded by plump, creamy-white flesh. Clean them carefully, cutting away any beard or intestinal threads. Ease them from the half-shells, slice the white parts, and poach in dry white wine for about ten minutes. Add the orange coral after five minutes. Take them out and keep warm; use the cooking liquid as the base for a white sauce.

The white parts are also good sautéed in butter — rich but very delicious.

Whelks and winkles Traditional London treats. They are almost always sold from market stalls, cooked and cold, on little dishes with seasoning in the form of rough malt vinegar, salt and pepper. You need a pin to prise the winkles out of their shells. If you are lucky, you may be served sliced brown bread, to mop up the juices.

Crab Having twisted off legs and claws, pull the body from its shell. Remove the intestines (above) and halve the body to reach the rest of the meat.

Mussels After you have scrubbed the mussel clean and scraped the shell, use a sharp knife to cut away the beard (above). Rinse well before cooking.

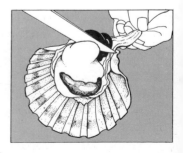

Scallops Using a sharp knife, scrape off the 'beard' (above). Gently ease the scallop from its shell with the same knife; cook according to your recipe.

WHITE FISH — Fish in Season — Months of Year

Legend:
- ● Months when of best quality
- ○ Available all time

Fish in Season	J	F	M	A	M	J	J	A	S	O	N	D
Bass					●	●	●	●				
Bream, sea						●	●	●	●	●	●	●
Cod	●	●	●		○	○		●	●	●	●	●
Coley, saithe	○	○	○			○	○	○	○	○	○	○
Dogfish (huss, rig, flake)	●	●	●	●	●	○	○	○	●	●	●	●
Flounder	●	●			○	○	○	○	●	●	●	●
Haddock	●	●	○		○	○	○	○	○	○	●	●
Hake	●	●	●					●	●	●	●	●
Halibut	●	●	●	●					●	●	●	●
Mock Halibut	●	●	○	○	○	○	○	○	○			
Plaice	●	●	●		○	○	○	○	○	○	○	○
Skate	●	●	●							●	●	●
Dover Sole	●	●	○	○	●	●	●	●	●	●	●	●
Lemon Sole	●	●	○	○	●	●	●	●	●	●	●	●
Turbot	○	○	○	●	●	●	●	●	○	○	○	○
Whiting	●	●	○	○	○	○	○	○	○	●	●	●

OILY FISH — Fish in Season — Months of Year

Legend:
- ● Months when of best quality
- ○ Available all time

Fish in Season	J	F	M	A	M	J	J	A	S	O	N	D
Carp	●	●	●			●	●	●	●	●	●	●
Conger eel	○	○	○	○							○	○
Herring	●	●				●	●	●	●	●	●	●
Mackerel	●	●	●	○		○	○	●	●	●	●	●
Mullet, grey	●	●				●	●	●	●	●	●	●
Mullet, red					●	●	●	●	●	●	●	●
Perch	●	●	●			●	●	●	●	●	●	●
Pike	●	●	●			●	●	●	●	●	●	●
Pilchard	●	●	●	○	○	○	○	○	○	○	○	●
Salmon						●	●	●	●	●		
Sardine			●	●	●	●	●	●				
Smelt or Sparling	●	●	●									
Sprat	●	●	●							○	○	○
Trout, rainbow	○	○	○	○	○	○	○	○	○	○	○	○
Trout, river or brown			●	●	●	●	●	●				
Trout, sea or salmon			●	●	●	●	●					
Whitebait		●	●	●	●	●	●					

SHELLFISH — Fish in Season — Months of Year

Legend:
- ● Months when of best quality
- ○ Available all time

Fish in Season	J	F	M	A	M	J	J	A	S	O	N	D
Clams	○	○	○	○	○	○	○	○	●	●	●	○
Cockles	●	●	●	●	○	○	○	○	●	●	●	●
Crab	○	○	○		●	●	●	●	●	○	○	○
Lobster	○	○	○	●	●	●	●	●	○	○	○	○
Mussels	●	●	●						●	●	●	●
Oysters	●	●	●						●	●	●	●
Prawns & Shrimps	○	○	○	○	○	○	○	○	○	○	○	○
Scallops	●	●	●						●	●	●	●
Whelks	●	●	○	○	○	●	●			●	●	●
Winkles	●	●	●	●	●	●	●		○	●	●	●

FOOD AND COOKERY

VEGETABLES

CHOOSING VEGETABLES

Above all, look for freshness. Green vegetables should be fresh and crisp; roots and tubers firm; bulbs — such as onions — dry and free from mildew.

Always buy vegetables in the quantities you need: don't be tempted to buy more than you can use. As a general rule, avoid small vegetables, which may be tasteless, or overgrown ones, which can be coarse. However, always keep a look out for seasonal bargains.

Artichokes (globe) Cut off the stalk and the tougher outside leaves. Rinse well under running water, making sure no grit remains between the leaves, then drain.

The artichoke has an inedible 'choke' above the heart, or fond, the most succulent part of the vegetable. You can scoop it out with a teaspoon when it is raw or when it is cooked.

Cook the artichoke in boiling salted water, for about 35–40 minutes. You can tell when it is done: the leaves pull out easily. Drain upside down in a colander.

Serve hot with melted but-

ter or Hollandaise sauce; cold with mayonnaise or vinaigrette dressing.

Artichokes (Jerusalem) Scrub and peel, plunge quickly into cold water and lemon juice to prevent discoloration, then boil in salted water with additional lemon juice for 15–20 minutes or steam for 20–25 minutes and drain. Alternatively, remove skin after cooking, and serve with melted butter or Hollandaise sauce.

Asparagus Cut off the woody ends and scrape along each stalk, wash, and tie into bundles of about six, with all the heads together. Trim the stalk ends of the bundle to an even length. Boil upright for 10–15 minutes, taking care not to overcook in case the heads become mushy. To eat, hold by the stem and dip in melted butter, or serve cold with mayonnaise.

Aubergines Cut off the stem and leaves around it, and slice it thinly. Sprinkle salt over the cut surface, and leave for about 30 minutes before rinsing with cold water. Serve fried in slices; whole, use it stuffed and baked. Use aubergine in *Moussaka* and *Ratatouille.*

Avocados Usually eaten as a starter or in salads; buy ripe. Cut in half lengthways, remove the stone and brush with lemon juice to prevent browning. Serve with a vinaigrette dressing or fill the halves with prawns and a light cocktail sauce.

Beans (broad) When young and tender cook in the pod, but large ones should be podded, boiled in salted water for 15–20 minutes and drained, then tossed in melted butter with parsley or served with a parsley sauce.

Beans (French) Slender, stringless beans, prepared by trimming the ends and cooking whole in boiling salted water for about 5–10 minutes, or steaming until soft.

Beans (runner) Larger and coarser than French beans. Trim the ends, slice thinly and cook in the same way.

Bean sprouts (Mung beans) Rinse under cold water and strain well; fry in oil for 1–2 minutes. Serve with salads, cold meats or traditional Chinese dishes.
Growing bean sprouts at home Soak 175 g (6 oz) beans overnight in a warm place and transfer the sprouting

1 potatoes 2 cauliflower 3 lettuce
4 parsley 5 fennel 6 broccoli
7 celery 8 cabbage 9 celeriac
10 parsnips 11 courgettes
12 turnips 13 swede 14 chicory
15 kohlrabi 16 avocados
17 aubergines 18 spinach 19 leeks
20 sweet corn 21 globe artichokes
22 sweet peppers 23 runner beans
24 shallots 25 Brussels sprouts
26 cucumber 27 tomatoes
28 watercress 29 radishes
30 French beans 31 carrots
32 okra 33 mushrooms 34 onions

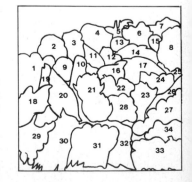

beans to a tray covered with blotting paper or an absorbent kitchen towel. Keep in a dark, warm place for about six days, watering every day, to produce white shoots.

Beetroot Cut off the stalks 2.5 cm (1 in) above the root and wash, handling with care, to prevent the beetroot from 'bleeding'. Add a little vinegar to the cooking water and boil for about 45 minutes or bake at 160–170°C (325°F) Gas Mark 3 for 1–2 hours, moistened with butter and loosely covered with foil. Peel off the skin when ready, but do not prod to test tenderness. Serve with vinegar or melted butter, hot or cold.

Broccoli The white variety is best broken into florets or cooked in boiling water whole, like cauliflower. The purple variety and the green (Calabrese) have a delicate flavour and are best steamed for about 10–15 minutes, then drained and buttered.

Brussels sprouts Remove outer leaves, wash and cut a small cross in the stalk end of larger sprouts to ensure thorough cooking. Boil in salted water for about 10 minutes, drain, and toss in butter, seasoned with pepper.

Serve Brussels sprouts with chestnuts: use equal quantities of both. Slit the sides of the chestnuts and boil for about 2 minutes to soften the skins. Remove from the heat, peel and put on to simmer for about 40 minutes. After 30 minutes cooking, put on the sprouts in a separate pan. Drain both, mix in a serving dish and serve with butter, salt and freshly ground pepper.

Cabbage Remove outer leaves, cut in half and remove the hard centre. Wash thoroughly, slice and cook in a small quantity of boiling, salted water for 5–10 minutes. Drain and serve at once with a knob of butter. Red cabbages can be pickled and are excellent served as an accompaniment to cold meats. Use white cabbages to make coleslaw.

Carrots Scrape or peel thinly, cut off the ends, and slice, dice or cut into strips. Simmer for about 10 minutes. New carrots can be cooked whole and drained then served with melted butter and chopped parsley. They are an excellent addition to stews and casseroles, or grated raw in winter salads with onions and cabbage.

Cauliflowers Remove outside leaves and make a cut across the stalk. Wash, and cook in boiling salted water with the stem down, or steam for 10–15 minutes, according to size. Alternatively, divide into individual florets and cook for 5–10 minutes before serving with butter and salt and pepper or a cheese sauce. Raw florets are excellent served with savoury dips.

Celeriac Known as the 'turnip-rooted celery', it has a strong celery flavour. Peel, slice and cook in boiling, salted water for 20–30 minutes. Drain well and serve with melted butter or a sauce. Alternatively steam, fry, make into a cream soup, or grate raw into salads.

Celery Separate the stalks, scrub thoroughly in cold water, and drain. Excellent served raw with cheese or cooked in boiling salted water for 15–20 minutes. Alternatively braise and serve with a gravy-like sauce.

Chicory Cut off the stem and outer leaves and remove the core before wiping. Generally eaten raw as part of a salad, but can be cooked by plunging into boiling salted

Artichoke After cutting away the stem and tough outer leaves, spoon out the hairy 'choke' to leave the sweet 'fond'.

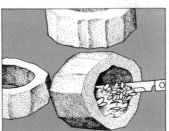

Marrow Peel the whole marrow, then cut into thick slices. Using the point of a sharp-bladed knife, scrape away the seeds.

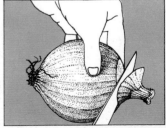

Onion First trim off each end, using a sharp-bladed vegetable knife. Then peel away the skin and rinse onion in cold water.

water, with lemon juice, for 15–20 minutes, or braised in butter and water. Serve with a sauce, or seasoned with herbs.

Corn Avoid overripe golden yellow kernels which have lost their sweetness. Remove silky threads and outside leaves and cook in boiling water (unsalted to prevent toughening) for 5 minutes or more, according to size. The corn is ready when a kernel can be easily removed from the core. Alternatively cut away the corn from the cob after cooking. Drain and serve with a liberal amount of butter and salt and pepper, fry in butter, or serve cold with salad vegetables.

Courgettes Trim the ends, wash and slice, but do not peel. Sauté in melted butter in a covered pan for 5–10 minutes or steam or boil until tender. They can be stuffed and baked or used as an ingredient in Ratatouille, itself an excellent accompaniment to roast beef and lamb cutlets.

Cucumbers Usually eaten raw and sliced with or without peel. Add cucumber to a salad, a chutney or a cold soup. Cucumbers can also be steamed for 5-10 minutes, or sautéed in butter. They can be rather indigestible.

Endive Curly-leaved, lettuce-shaped salad vegetable with a distinct flavour. Trim the stalk and remove outer leaves before washing. Serve cold as a salad.

Fennel Trim both ends, and cook whole in boiling salted water for 30–40 minutes. Cut into slices and serve with melted butter. Alternatively sauté slices in butter for about ten minutes or serve raw with a cheese salad.

Kale There are two varieties available: curly kale, which has tight, curly leaves, and Borecole, with large, flat leaves. Both are prepared and cooked like cabbage or used raw in a winter salad.

Kohlrabi A large stem with green leaves which resembles a turnip in taste. It should be eaten when young and tender. Prepare by removing the leaves and peeling thickly. Leave whole, if small, or chop and cook in boiling water for about 30 minutes, until soft. Alternatively steam and serve with a sauce, or coat cooked slices in batter and fry.

Leeks Remove outer leaves, cut off root end and top, and split down the centre or slice. Wash thoroughly to remove dirt and grit between the layers and cook in boiling

salted water for about 15 minutes, until soft. Drain and serve with a cheese sauce. Leeks are also excellent in flans and soups, or stuffed and baked in the oven.

Lettuce Available in many varieties, it can be cabbage-shaped, with soft or crisp leaves, or long with crisp leaves and a sweet taste. Long-leaved Cos is mainly available throughout the summer months and the round soft-leaved variety is sold all the year round.

Remove the outer leaves, separate remaining ones and wash well in cold salted water before drying thoroughly in a clean towel or draining in a colander. Serve as a salad or make into a cream soup.

Marrow Wash the skin and cut in half to scoop out seeds. Stuff with minced beef and breadcrumbs and bake for about 20 minutes at 180°C (350°F) Gas Mark 4. Alternatively peel large marrows, cut the flesh into cubes or rings and cook in boiling salted water until soft. Serve with a well-flavoured tomato or cheese sauce.

Mushrooms Cultivated mushrooms include button, flat and open varieties which require only peeling or wiping before use. Sauté in butter for 3–5

Place the onion on a chopping block to slice. Cut downwards, turning the onion with the blade facing the centre.

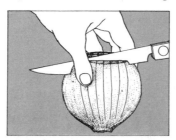
Hold the onion firmly and slide across the grain. If you want onion slices, cut right through to the base.

To chop an onion, turn it on its side and slice into large or small chunks. Have a bowl ready to contain the pieces.

FOOD AND COOKERY

minutes and use in a large selection of savoury dishes including casseroles, pizzas and quiches. May also be used raw in salads.

Mustard and cress Trim the stalks with scissors, removing the roots, and wash in a colander. Drain well and use to make appetizing salads and garnish sandwiches.
Growing mustard and cress at home Sprinkle cress seeds over a sheet of damp blotting paper or absorbent kitchen paper. Keep damp. Two or three days later sprinkle mustard seeds over the paper and about five days later it should be ready.

Okra Often known as 'lady's fingers' this is a green pod vegetable much used in Indian, Caribbean and Greek cooking. Trim the ends and leave whole or slice, according to the recipe. It is usually sautéed for 5–10 minutes.

Onions They can be boiled, fried, braised, baked or steamed and are extremely useful in most savoury dishes. Cut off the ends and remove outer skin. To dice, cut in half and lay cut side downwards on the board. Then slice across and lengthwise. English varieties have a stronger flavour than the larger, mild Spanish onions.

Parsnip Trim the ends, peel thinly and wash. Parboil for 5 minutes and drain. Roast in the pan with the joint of meat, at 200°C (400°F) Gas Mark 6 for 40 minutes. Alternatively cook in boiling salted water for 30–40 minutes, until soft, or sauté for about 10 minutes until golden brown.

Peas Cook fresh peas when they are still young and tender in lightly salted water for 10–15 minutes. Drain and serve with a knob of butter and a sprig of fresh mint. (When they are extra sweet they can be cooked and eaten in the pod.) The season for fresh peas lasts only six weeks, but they are also frozen, canned or dried.

Peppers Young peppers are green and turn red when fully ripened. Trim off the stalk end, cut in half and remove seeds before slicing. Use raw in salads; add to casseroles and other savoury dishes. Alternatively, remove the core and seeds with the tip of a sharp-bladed knife and stuff, halved or whole, with a savoury rice mixture and bake in the oven.

Potatoes There are many varieties of this versatile staple vegetable. Some are 'floury': use for mashing or baking in their jackets; others have a closer, more waxy flesh: use them for roasting and chipping.

Among the many good, all-purpose main crop potatoes are King Edward, Maris Piper, Pentland Crown and Kerr's Pink. Desirée and Majestic are excellent for roasting and chipping, and cold in salads.
Boiled Scrape new potatoes and simmer in salted water for 15–20 minutes. Drain and serve with butter, fresh mint or parsley. Alternatively, make a potato salad, using a vinaigrette or mayonnaise dressing. Boil older potatoes in their skins, or peel as thinly as possible. Simmer, whole, for 20–30 minutes until soft but unbroken.
Casseroled Arrange thinly sliced old or new potatoes in a lightly greased pie or flan dish, season with salt and pepper and spread each layer with butter. Bake at 190°C (375°F) Gas Mark 5 for 1¼ hours or until tender. Serve in the dish.
Chips Cut potatoes into slices and then into sticks, soak in salted water for about 30 minutes to remove excess

Duchesse After the potatoes have been creamed, spoon into a piping bag fitted with a nozzle. Pipe into rosettes.

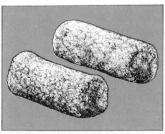

Croquettes Creamed potatoes, rolled into sausage shapes, dipped into beaten egg, coated with breadcrumbs and deep-fried.

Matchstick chips Slice the potatoes and soak in salted water. With a sharp knife cut into matchstick widths before frying.

starch, and drain. Heat oil or lard to 190°C (375°F) in a large pan or deep-fat fryer, testing the temperature by dropping in a potato stick, which should rise to the surface immediately the fat is ready. If you use a deep fryer, quarter fill the basket with a batch of potatoes, fry for about three minutes and drain on kitchen paper. Continue until they have all been partly cooked. Finally fry all the chips rapidly for a further three minutes, drain on kitchen paper and serve immediately.

Creamed Mash and, over gentle heat, beat in a knob of butter, salt and pepper and a little milk. Beat well until light and fluffy.

Crisps Very thinly sliced potatoes, cut in rounds. Soak in cold water, drain and deep fry rapidly for about 3 minutes. Salt and serve.

Croquettes Roll mashed potato into small sausage shapes and coat with egg and breadcrumbs. Fry in deep fat until crispy and golden brown. Fried onion, chopped nuts or grated cheese can be added to the mixture to give extra flavour.

Duchesse Cream potatoes with an egg yolk, and pipe into rosettes on a greased baking tray. Bake at 200°C (400°F) Gas Mark 6 for about 25 minutes until golden.

Fried or sautéed Boil until

Jacket Top the potatoes with butter and season generously. Add cheese and a finely chopped fresh herb.

almost cooked, slice and fry slowly in melted butter until golden brown.

Jacket Scrub large, even sized potatoes and prick all over with a fork. Bake at 190°C (375°F) Gas Mark 5 for 1–1½ hours, depending on size, until tender. Cut in half lengthways or cut a diagonal cross in the top, and serve with cheese, butter, salt and pepper and chopped chives.

Mashed Boil potatoes, drain, and using a potato masher or fork, beat until smooth with a little added butter over a low heat, then season.

Matchstick chips Prepare and cook as for chips but cut the sticks into julienne strips (fine matchstick sizes) and reduce the cooking time to only three minutes in total.

Roast Peel and quarter potatoes and parboil for 5–10 minutes, then drain. Transfer to a meat roasting tin in a hot oven 220°C (425°F) Gas Mark 7 for about 45 minutes or until crisp and golden brown. Roast around a joint of meat or a chicken or turkey if there is room.

Pumpkin Skin, cut in half, remove seeds and fibrous centre and cut into cubes. Cook in boiling water for about 15 minutes until tender and serve with other vegetables. Pumpkin can also be made into pumpkin pie; a delicious cinnamon flavoured sweet which is traditionally served in America at Thanksgiving.

Radishes Cut off the leaves and roots and wash well. May be eaten raw; often cut into waterlily shapes and used as a garnish. Alternatively cook in boiling salted water for 5–10 minutes, according to size, until tender. Drain well and serve with melted butter.

Salsify Often referred to as 'oyster plant', this is a delicate-flavoured root vegetable. It should be scrubbed and scraped quickly, cut into 2.5–5 cm (1–2 in) lengths and cooked in boiling salted water with added lemon juice for 20–30 minutes. Drain and serve with melted butter and chopped herbs or with a sauce, such as Hollandaise.

Sea Kale Similar to thin celery stalks in appearance, it can be eaten raw with cheese and salad or cooked and served with melted butter or a sauce. Trim the ends, wash and tie in bundles like asparagus. Boil or steam for about 20 minutes until tender, but still crisp.

Shallots A small, mild-flavoured onion. Prepare and cook in the same way as onions. Frequently pickled, added to a casserole or served with baby carrots in a cream sauce.

Spinach Remove any bruised leaves and rinse thoroughly to get rid of clinging grit. Trim away the base of the stalks and centre ribs. Put the wet leaves in a pan and cook over gentle heat for about 10 minutes. You should not need to add extra water. Drain well, and serve with a knob of butter, salt, freshly ground nutmeg and pepper.

Swede A round root vegetable with a purplish-coloured outer skin and orange-yellow sweet flavoured flesh. Scrub and peel thickly, dice or slice and boil or steam for about 20 minutes. An excellent addition to stews and home-made soups, swedes can also be roasted around the joint in the oven at 200°C (400°F) Gas Mark 6 for about 1 hour, according to size.

FOOD AND COOKERY

Sweet potatoes Not related to the potato, this is an elongated or round tuber which can be white, red or purple; it has a sweet taste. Use it like a potato; scrub, peel and boil, fry, bake or roast.

Tomatoes Although the tomato is a fruit, it is used as a vegetable. There are many varieties, from the large bright red Spanish to the smaller English tomato with its unique flavour and aroma. The skin is loosened by plunging into boiling water for 2–3 seconds, then into cold water. Tomatoes can be eaten raw in salads, fried, grilled, baked or steamed, and used in sauces with pasta and in savoury dishes.

Turnips Early turnips with green and white skins are available from April until July, and can be eaten raw, peeled and thinly sliced. Maincrop turnips with coarse flesh and thicker skins need to be boiled for 20–30 minutes according to size. Alternatively steam for 30–40 minutes. Add to a stew or serve with equal quantities of mashed potato, carrot or parsnip and plenty of butter.

Watercress Select fresh green leaves. Wash and serve raw with salads, use as a garnish to savoury dishes, or make into a soup.

VEGETABLE GARNISHES
Cucumber Before slicing, score the skin of the cucumber lengthways with a fork to give a decorative effect. If liked, make the slices into twists or butterflies and use for garnishing pâtés and plates of sandwiches.

Gherkins Fan shapes are made by slicing lengthways and opening out.

Radishes Make 'roses' by slicing lengthways through the radish and putting into iced water to open up.

Tomatoes Using the point of a sharp-bladed vegetable knife, make incisions around the middle, then carefully separate the two halves.

SALADS
Salads are marvellous. Everyone knows about their nutritional value but, using a few basic dressings (see p. 59), you can provide everything from a refreshing, palate-cleansing finish to a dinner, to a meal which is satisfying, varied and complete in itself.

Spring
Buy early-crop, thin-skinned new potatoes. Scrub and boil for 10–12 minutes in salted water, with sprigs of fresh mint. Drain thoroughly, slice, then toss, still hot, in a vinaigrette dressing. Chill in the refrigerator, and add chopped mint or chives just before serving. If you have no fresh herbs, finely chopped onions or spring onions also make a delicious potato salad.

Cold asparagus can be served with a vinaigrette dressing or mayonnaise.

Summer
Enjoy salad vegetables at their best. You will find a variety of lettuces: Cos and Webb's have the best flavours and firmest textures. Look for curly endives and fresh, dark green watercress. Handle green salad vege-

tables very carefully because they can discolour quickly. Tear off outer leaves. Throw away bruised ones, but reserve tough leaves for cooking with sweet, young green peas and small onions. Lettuce can be used to make a cold summer soup, light and creamy.

Wash the lettuce well under running water, then drain or dry on a kitchen towel. Place in a polythene bag in the refrigerator. Make a vinaigrette dressing in your salad bowl and add the salad greens just before serving. Toss lightly to coat the leaves with the dressing.

Autumn
As summer blends into autumn, you'll find small, sweet tomatoes which have ripened late. Scald, skin, and peel. Place in a salad bowl which has been wiped around with a halved clove of garlic. Add orange slices, watercress and a vinaigrette dressing. Test for seasoning: you may want to add a little sugar and lemon juice. Chill before serving. Tomatoes and chopped spring onions also make a good salad with a vinaigrette dressing flavoured with mint.

Winter
You will find imported lettuces in the shops — but if they are tired and wilting, don't buy them. Instead make use of the wide range of root vegetables. Shred a small white cabbage and add sliced apples. Stir in some mayonnaise, and add halved walnuts. Celeriac, thinly sliced, blends well with mayonnaise; grated carrot and turnip with a vinaigrette dressing.

Vegetables in Season	J	F	M	A	M	J	J	A	S	O	N	D
Artichoke, globe	○	○	○	○	○	●	●	●	●	○	○	○
Artichoke, Jerusalem	●	●	●							●	●	●
Asparagus	○	○	○	○	●	●	○	○	○	○	○	○
Aubergine	○	○	○	○	○	○	○	○	○	○	○	○
Avocado	○	○	○	○	○	○	○	○	○	○	○	○
Beans, broad				●	●	●	●	●	●			
Beans, French	○	○	○	○	○	●	●	●	●	○	○	○
Beans, runner							●	●	●			
Beetroot	●	●	●	●	●	●	●	●	●	●	●	●
Broccoli	●	●	●	●	●	●		●	●	●	●	●
Brussels sprouts	●	●	●					●	●	●	●	●
Cabbage	●	●	●	●	●	●	●	●	●	●	●	●
Carrots	●	●	●	●	●	●	●	●	●	●	●	●
Cauliflower	●	●	●	●	●	●	●	●	●	●	●	●
Celeriac	●	●	●							●	●	●
Celery	●	●				●	●	●	●	●	●	●
Chicory	○	○	○	○	○				○	○	○	○
Corn							●	●	●			
Courgette	○	○	○	○	○	●	●	●	●	○	○	○
Cucumber	○	○	○	●	●	●	●	●	●	●	○	○
Endive	○	○	○	○	○	●	●	●	●	○	○	○
Fennel	○	○	○	○	○	○	○	○	○	○	○	○
Kale	●	●	●	●	●						●	●
Kohlrabi	○	○	○	○			○	○	○	○	○	○
Leeks	●	●	●	●	●				●	●	●	●
Lettuce	●	●	●	●			●	●	●	●	●	●
Marrow							●	●	●	●		
Mushroom	●	●	●	●	●	●	●	●	●	●	●	●
Mustard and cress	●	●	●	●	●	●	●	●	●	●	●	●
Okra	○	○	○	○	○	○						○
Onions	●	●	●	○	○	○	○	○	●	●	●	●
Parsnip	●	●	●	●					●	●	●	●
Pea					●	●	●	●	●			
Pepper	○	○	○	○	○	○	○	○	○	○	○	○
Potato	●	●	●	●	●	●	●	●	●	●	●	●
Pumpkin								●	●	●	●	●
Radish	○	○	○	●	●	●	●	●	●	●	○	○
Salsify	○	○	○	○	○					○	○	○
Sea kale	●	●	●					●	●	●	●	●
Shallot	●	●	●						●	●	●	●
Spinach	○	○		●	●	●	●	●				○
Swede	●	●	●	●	●				●	●	●	●
Sweet potato	○	○	○							○	○	○
Tomato	○	○	○	○	○	●	●	●	●	●	○	○
Turnip	●	●	●	●	●	●	●	●	●	●	●	●
Watercress	●	●	●	●	●			●	●	●	●	●

FOOD AND COOKERY

FRUIT

CHOOSING FRUIT

Fruit provides roughage and citrus fruits are an important source of vitamin C.

Buy fresh, firm fruit and eat within a few days. Store in a cool, dry place. All fruit is seasonal but there are good supplies of imported fruit when nothing home-produced is available. Seasonal gluts can produce bargains.

In the shops, fruit should be marked with its country of origin and class. The most usual are Class 1: first-class fruit, with no defects; and Class 2: good fruit with a few small blemishes. The gradings follow regulations laid down by the EEC.

Apples There is a wide variety of apples, both home-produced and imported. For eating apples, try Cox's Orange Pippin, with a pale green skin flecked with orange-red streaks. It has crisp, juicy flesh and is excellent for storing. Crispin is a recently introduced variety; bright green, large and crisp. Golden Delicious apples have pale green skins, which turn yellow on keeping, and a bland flavour. Russets are crisp and nutty, under their golden-brown, flecked skins.

Worcesters have thick red skins, flecked with green, and their white flesh is sweet and juicy.

Cooking apples are larger than eaters, and they have a sharp, sour flavour. Look for Bramley's Seedling, with a deep green skin and soft, fine-flavoured flesh. Grenadier is another good cooker, with firm flesh. Other varieties include Early Victory, Lord Derby and Newton Wonder.

To cook apples, wash, peel and chop, then cook over a gentle heat with a little water, and sugar to taste. Add seasoning: one or two cloves, ground cinnamon or lemon peel. To bake apples, wash and core. Fill the cavity with dried fruit, brown sugar or honey and bake in the oven on a tray until soft.

Crab apples are tiny, sharp-flavoured fruit which grow wild and are used mainly in preserves.

Apricots Eat fruit raw when just ripe or halve and remove stone, simmer in a little water with sugar, and use as a pie filling or in desserts. Dried apricots must be soaked overnight in water for cooking. Give them, raw, to children as a healthier alternative to teeth-damaging sweets.

Bananas Avoid overripe bananas; slightly underripe fruit can be kept for longer or used for cooking. Use in fruit salads and sweets: slice just before serving and dip in lemon juice to prevent any discoloration.

Bilberries (Whinberries or Whortleberries) Dark blue berries, grown wild or commercially, not unlike black currants in flavour. Cook with sugar and use to make superb pies and cheesecakes.

Blackberries Blackish-purple raspberry-shaped fruit which grow wild or are cultivated. They are used to make jellies and wines, in apple pies and as the toppings to cheesecakes.

Blackcurrants These fairly large black berries have a slightly sour flavour and are ideal for making jams and jellies, pie fillings, drinks and sauces for desserts.

Cape gooseberries Used in preserves or for decoration: peel back the dry 'petals' and dip into fondant.

Cherries Common types are White and Black Heart cherries. They are excellent eaten

A rich harvest of fresh fruit, both home-grown and imported. When locally produced fruit is at its best, eat it raw or add to salads and desserts.
1 Bramley apples   2 Yellow honeydew melon 3 Green honeydew melon   4 White grapes
5 Bananas   6 Two melons — Ogen and Watermelon
7 Pineapple   8 Grapefruit
9 Czar plums   10 Granny Smith apples   11 Red currants, with stalks removed   12 Two pears,

Comice and William   13 Black grapes   14 Clementines
15 Tydeman's apples
16 Pomegranates 17 Kiwi fruit (Chinese gooseberries) 18 Paw paws (Papayas)   19 Oranges
20 Mandarin oranges
21 Mangoes 22 Nectarines
23 Limes   24 Rhubarb   25 Figs
26 Persimmons   27 Dates
28 Cranberries   29 Lemons
30 Blackberries   31 Strawberries
32 Raspberries 33 Black currants
34 Gooseberries

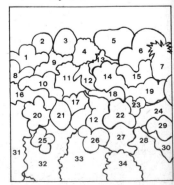

raw in fruit salads. Use the sourer Morello cherries for pies, preserves and home-made wines.

Clementine This cross between a tangerine and an orange is popular at Christmas time. It has seeds and a thin, yellowish-orange rind.

Cranberries Small dark red berries with a sour taste. They are normally stewed and made into a jelly or sauce and traditionally served with turkey at Christmas.

Dates Often dried, packed in boxes or pressed into a solid block for culinary purposes. They are delicious in cakes and biscuits.

Figs These are green or purple with a large number of small seeds embedded in red flesh. Also available dried. Serve fresh figs raw or stewed as a dessert; dried, in biscuits and puddings.

Gooseberries Many varieties are available. They can be eaten raw or cooked, in tarts, fools and puddings. Prepare by topping and tailing with a pair of scissors.

Grapefruit A thick-skinned yellow juicy fruit eaten for breakfast or as an appetizer to a meal. Cut in half, loosen flesh with a sharp knife, remove pips, and serve grilled, sprinkled with sugar, or divide into segments and mix with orange segments and mint leaves. Useful for adding to home-made lemonade and marmalade.

Grapes Black and white grapes are eaten raw or used in fruit salads. In many countries they are made into wine or dried to form raisins. If not seedless, cut in half, and take out the pips with a knife. A good idea is to make frosted grapes to serve with coffee after a dinner party. Wash and dry the grapes, hold by the stalk and dip into lightly beaten egg white then dust with caster sugar.

Kiwi fruit (also known as Chinese gooseberries) Rare, egg-shaped fruit with furry brown skin and green seeded flesh. Eat as a dessert fruit or use for preserves.

Kumquat An oval orange fruit shaped like a plum. It comes from Japan among other places and is used mainly for decoration or in marmalade.

Lemons These vary in thickness and size and are used in flavouring sweet dishes and cakes, for marmalade, lemonade and garnishing food and drinks.

Limes This citrus fruit has a green skin and a sour taste. It is used mainly for fruit drinks and marmalade.

Loganberries Dark red in colour and similar in shape to raspberries. They can be eaten raw or poached in a sugar syrup and used in puddings or preserves and wines.

Loquats Scarce, plum-shaped, yellow fruit with creamy, slightly sour flesh.

Lychees Small stone fruit with hard red-brown skin and white flesh. They have a slightly acidic flavour, and are often sold canned.

Mandarin oranges A fruit with thin, bright orange skin. Most popular at Christmas time. The segments are available canned and can be used in a wide selection of pudding recipes.

Mangoes These vary in size and colour (green, yellow or red), have a hard skin, a large centre stone and soft flesh with a spicy taste. Serve as a

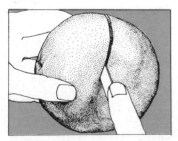

Preparing grapefruit **1** Slice the fruit in half with a sharp-bladed knife.

2 Carefully loosen the flesh from the skin with a curved grapefruit knife.

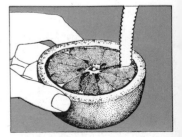

3 Using the same knife, separate the individual segments of grapefruit.

dessert fruit or make into chutney.

Melons Slice, remove seeds and serve as a starter or for a dessert. Cut into segments, shape into balls, or fill the hollowed-out melon half with fruit salad. The melon is ripe when it is slightly soft to the touch at each end.

Charentais melons are small, round and sweetly scented. They have orange flesh and pale yellow, wrinkled skins. Honeydew melons are oval, with tough yellow skins and pale green flesh. Ogen melons are round, with yellow skins and pale yellow, juicy flesh. Cantaloup melons have dark green skin and yellowish flesh. Watermelons are largest of all, with dark green to purple skin and bright red, watery flesh.

Nectarines They resemble peaches but have a smooth skin. Eat them raw or use in recipes which would normally call for peaches.

Oranges Of the many varieties available, the sweet dessert Jaffa, eaten alone or in fruit salads and puddings, and the bitter Seville, used in marmalade, are the best known. Blood oranges have a sweet red juicy flesh and navel oranges are distinguished by a raised growth at one end.

Ortanique This orange-yellow thin-skinned fruit is a cross between a tangerine and an orange and used for both desserts and marmalade.

Passion fruit Plum-shaped with crinkly hard skin, and seedy flesh which is sweet and juicy. Excellent for combining with other fruit in fruit salads and desserts.

Pawpaws Smaller than a melon but similar in texture, this oval-shaped fruit has a smooth yellowish-orange skin when ripe. Its flesh is pinkish-orange with black seeds down the middle. Serve in the same way as a melon.

Peaches Eaten raw or used in fruit salads, in pies and other sweets. The most common kind is 'cling-stone', with a stone which is difficult to separate from the flesh. To remove the skin, plunge into boiling water for a few seconds, cool and peel with a knife. Home-grown peaches are available throughout the summer.

Pears Dessert and cooking pears are available. The most popular types are Conference, William's and Comice. When pears are ripe

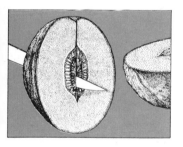

Preparing a melon **1** Slice lengthwise with a sharp knife, then cut again into quarters.

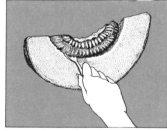

2 Slice the melon quarters into segments. Scoop out the seeds from each piece.

3 Gently separate the flesh from the skin. Chill before serving with sugar or a pinch of ground ginger.

Preparing a pineapple **1** Slice off the top and stem, then cut into slices.

2 Use a grapefruit knife with a serrated blade to cut away the skin.

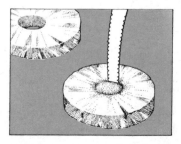

3 Remove the woody, indigestible centre from each slice of pineapple.

FOOD AND COOKERY

eat them raw or remove core and use in sweets and preserves. An excellent dessert is pears poached in cider, served with cream or chocolate sauce.

Persimmons Similar in shape to large tomatoes with soft flesh and an acidic flavour. Use the pulp for jams and fruit puddings.

Pineapples Large fruit with rough brownish-orange skin, stiff green leaves and juicy yellow flesh. Often bought canned and used for a variety of sweet dishes. Prepare a fresh pineapple as illustrated, or hollow out the flesh and fill with fruit salad for an attractive party sweet.

Plums There is a large range available. Among the most popular dessert and cooking plums are Czar, Greengage, Pershore and Victoria. Eat raw, or use in pies, puddings and preserves. Damsons are small purple plums with a good, sharp flavour: usually served cooked.

Pomegranates Round, with reddish-orange skin and bright red flesh embedded with seeds. Cut in half and eat by sucking the flesh from the seeds.

Quinces A yellowish green fruit with a shape somewhere between an apple and a pear. It has a hard flesh and is difficult to peel. It can't be eaten raw, but is delicious made into preserves and highlights the flavour of apples. Available late September-October.

Raspberries Red juicy berries often sold with their inner hulls removed. They are excellent served with cream in meringue nests, puréed and made into fools and ice cream, or used for jams.

Redcurrants Bright red berries, ideal for using in fruit salads and for making jellies. Remove fruit from the stalk by running a fork down the length of it.

Rhubarb It can be available 'forced' in winter, when it has pink stalks, or from March to June in its main crop with thicker, greener stalks and a sourer taste. Remove the leaves (which are highly poisonous), wash and drain well before stewing or poaching with sugar for puddings, pies and crumbles.

Satsumas Seedless fruit, similar to tangerines and easy to peel. They are available throughout the winter.

Strawberries The popularity of this fruit is reflected in the increasing demand for 'pick-your-own' strawberry fields during the summer months. The flesh is red and juicy and has tiny pips on the surface. Hull and serve with fresh cream, scones or ice cream or make into jam.

Tangerines A small orange-like fruit which is easy to peel. Delicious despite its many pips.

Ugli This is a cross between a grapefruit and a tangerine. It has greenish-yellow skin and sweet flesh.

Whitecurrants These are quite rare, but when you can get hold of them, serve them for dessert with sugar.

NUTS

Almonds Available shelled or unshelled. They are covered in a thin brown skin, which can be removed by blanching in boiling water for about 2 minutes. They usually have a slightly bitter flavour.

Brazil nuts Often associated with Christmas, these long, hard brown nuts are sold both shelled and unshelled.

Chestnuts Available fresh in a tough outer skin. Remove by making a slit at both ends. Boil for about 10 minutes or place in an oven before peeling skin off. Also obtained in cans or dried, they give an unusual nutty flavour to stuffings and puddings.

Coconuts Coconuts have a fibrous brown outer shell and are traditionally associated with the fairground. They contain milk which can be drained out by making a hole at one end. When it is empty crack the coconut open to reveal its white flesh. This can be sold separately, ground and dried and is suitable for making chocolate-coated sweets and puddings. It is also used in curries.

Filberts A variety of hazel nut, completely covered with a husk.

Hazel or cob nut Shell these, using nut crackers or a heavy weight, and remove skins if necessary by blanching in boiling water for about 2 minutes. Ideal for making muesli, and using in sweet dishes.

Walnuts Available in shells or shelled for use in cakes and puddings.

Fruit in Season	J	F	M	A	M	J	J	A	S	O	N	D
Home-produced fruits												
Apples	●	●	●	●	●	●	●	●	●	●	●	●
Crab apples									●	●		
Apricots	●	●		●	●	●	●					●
Cherries						●	●	●				
Pears	●	●	○	○	○	○	○	○	●	●	●	●
Plums								●	●			
Quinces										●	●	
Home-produced soft fruits												
Bilberries							●		●			
Blackberries								●	●	●	●	
Blackcurrants							●	●				
Blueberries							●	●				
Gooseberries					●	●	●	●				
Loganberries							●	●				
Raspberries							●	●				
Redcurrants							●	●				
Rhubarb			●	●								
Strawberries						●	●					
White currants								●				
Imported citrus fruits												
Clementine	●	●									●	●
Grapefruit	●	●	●	●	●	●	●	●	●	●	●	●
Lemon	●	●	●	●	●	●	●	●	●	●	●	●
Lime	●	●	●	●	●	●	●	●	●	●	●	●
Mandarin	●	●	●								●	●
Orange	●	●	●	●	●	●	●	●	●	●	●	●
Ortanique	●	●	●							●	●	●
Satsuma	●	●	●							●	●	●
Tangerine	●	●	●								●	●
Ugli	●	●	●								●	●
Imported fruits												
Bananas	●	●	●	●	●	●	●	●	●	●	●	●
Cape gooseberries	●	●	●	●	●	●	●	●	●	●	●	●
Chinese gooseberries	●	●						●	●	●	●	●
Coconuts	○	○	○	○	○	○	○	○	○	○	○	○
Cranberries	●	●										
Dates	●	●	●								●	●
Figs								●	●	●		
Grapes	●	●	●	●	●	●	●	●	●	●	●	●
Lychees	●	●										●
Mangoes	●	●	●	●	●		●	●	●			
Melons	○	○	○	○						○	○	○
Nectarines								●	●	●		
Water melon						●	●	●	●			
Pawpaws						○	○	○	○	○	○	○
Peaches							●	●	●			
Persimmon	●									●	●	●
Pineapple	●	●	●		●	●	●		●	●	●	●
Pomegranates	●								●	●	●	●
Nuts												
Chestnuts										●	●	●
Hazel or cob nuts	○	○	○	○	○	○	○	○	○	●	●	●
Walnuts	○	○	○	○	○	○	○	○	○	●	●	○
Almonds	○	○	○	○	○	○	○	○	○	○	○	○
Brazil nuts	○	○	○	○	○	○	○	○	○	○	○	○

FOOD AND COOKERY

MILK AND CREAM

Milk should be stored in a cool place, preferably in the refrigerator, as it is highly perishable. It is packaged in sterile bottles or cartons and so will keep best in its own container. Cover jugs, even in the refrigerator, to prevent milk from absorbing flavours from other foods. Wash milk jugs well before refilling, and never mix new milk with old as this is how bacteria are transferred.

GRADES OF MILK

Pasteurised milk (silver cap) Pasteurising is a process which destroys harmful micro-organisms. The milk is subjected to mild heat, 71°C (161°F) for 15 seconds, then rapidly cooled to not more than 10°C (50°F). It will keep perfectly well for two–three days in a refrigerator.

Homogenised milk (red cap) Milk which has been heated and forced through a small aperture to break down the fat globules into small particles which remain evenly suspended throughout the milk, preventing the formation of a 'cream line' at the top of the bottle. The milk is then pasteurised. Keeps two–three days in a refrigerator.

Ultra Heat Treated or 'Long Life' milk (pink cap) Milk which has been homogenised and heated for an extended time at a lower tem-

Rich, fresh cream turns the simplest dessert into a treat. For a special fruit salad, add a little liquer, such as Grand Marnier or Cointreau, to the fruit. Chill and serve with fresh cream.

Piping cream **1** Chill cream and bowl for at least 30 minutes. Whip, quickly at first, then slowly, until it stands in peaks.

2 Fit a forcing bag with a nozzle. Place it over a cylinder for easy filling: a cheese grater is ideal for this purpose.

3 Spoon in the whipped cream until the forcing bag is full. Lift the bag out carefully, twisting the top around to close it.

perature, and then subjected to an ultra-high temperature treatment of not less than 132°C (270°F) for one second. Keeps for several months unopened, without refrigeration: see the date code on the carton. Once opened, keep as for pasteurised milk.

Sterilised milk (blue cap) Milk which has been homogenised, bottled and vacuum-sealed, then heat treated to not less than 100°C (212°F) for 20-30 minutes before cooling. Once opened, refrigerate; unopened it will keep for a minimum of seven days but several weeks is usual.

Channel Islands and South Devon milk (gold cap) Milk from cows of Jersey or Guernsey and South Devon breeds, with a minimum butterfat content of four per cent. It may be pasteurised or untreated. Keeps two–three days in a refrigerator.

Untreated milk (green cap) Raw milk from attested herds which has not undergone any form of heat treatment; bottled under licence at a farm.

FRESH CREAM
Because of its rich smoothness and versatility, fresh cream is much used in cooking. It can be used to thicken soups, enrich sauces, and cover puddings

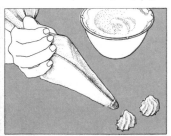

4 Hold the forcing bag firmly and pipe the cream on to a cake or dessert, or on a baking sheet for freezing.

as well as being the main ingredient in such desserts as syllabubs and ice creams. It can be used as a pouring cream or whipped and is one of the simplest ways of turning an ordinary pudding into a treat.

Buy fresh cream in small quantities and store in a refrigerator. Once opened, cover with cling film or foil to prevent tainting by other foods. Use within a few days of purchase.

Double cream This has a butterfat content of not less than 48 per cent. It is a rich, pouring cream; use it to serve with a fruit-based pudding. Whipped, it can be frozen for up to one month.

Whipping cream It has a minimum butterfat content of 35 per cent. It is thinner than double cream but whips well and is cheaper. Use it to pipe onto cakes and for desserts. It can also be bought ready-whipped and sold in tubs, ideal for decorating cakes.

Single cream It has a butterfat content of not less than 18 per cent. Pour it over fruit salad or into coffee; add to sauces or the cooking liquids of casseroles. Single cream cannot be whipped.

Half-cream This has a butterfat content of not less than 12 per cent. It cannot be whipped. Serve with coffee.

Clotted cream It has a minimum fat content of 55 per cent, and is produced by heating cream to 82°C (180°F). After cooling, the crust is removed and the cream is packaged.

Fresh clotted cream can be kept in the refrigerator for several days: serve it with scones and strawberry jam.

Soured cream Commercially soured to give a clean piquant flavour.

LONG-LIFE CREAMS
Sterilised cream With a minimum butterfat content of not less than 23 per cent, this cream is homogenised, then heat treated in bottles. It will keep, unopened, for up to two years in an ordinary food storage cupboard; refrigeration is not necessary.

Ultra Heat Treated cream After homogenisation it is subjected to heat treatment at 132°C (270°F) for one second. The cream is rapidly cooled and packed in aseptic, foil-lined containers. The date stamp on the container will tell you how long you can keep it.

Extended life cream This has a minimum fat content of 48 per cent and is heat-treated and vacuum-sealed in a bottle. It will keep for two–three weeks in a refrigerator, unopened.

Frozen cream There are many brands of commercially frozen dairy creams: keep according to the manufacturer's instructions.

HOW TO WHIP CREAM
The optimum fat content for whipping is 35–40 per cent. In order to get the best results, ensure that the bowl, whisk and the cream are very cold: put them in the refrigerator for about 30 minutes. Whip quickly at first until a matt finish is obtained and then reduce the speed until the cream stands in peaks.

Over-whipping will give the cream a poor, buttery texture and will make it difficult to pipe. It also spoils the creamy taste.

FOOD AND COOKERY

BUTTER

Butter, with its unmistakable taste, is another versatile dairy product. Salted or unsalted it can be used in a variety of dishes or simply spread on toast.

TYPES OF BUTTER

Lactic butter This is made from ripened cream which has been soured by the addition of a culture. Its flavour is full and slightly acidic. Most European butters are 'lactic'; packed in silver wrapping.

Sweet cream butter This popular butter comes from pasteurised cream. It has a bright colour and a mild, creamy flavour. It is excellent for pastry-making. Most British, Irish and New Zealand butters are 'sweet cream', packed in gold foil wrapping.

STORING BUTTER

Refrigerating Keep butter in its wrapper in the refrigerator until you want to use it. Keep salted butter for a maximum of one month; unsalted butter for up to three weeks.

Freezing Butter is best eaten fresh, but it may be frozen for up to three months. Overwrap the original wrap with freezer film or foil, and label.

Savoury butters
To garnish grilled meat, fish or baked potatoes, make a savoury butter. Cream the butter with the back of a fork and add chopped, fresh herbs. The addition of parsley and lemon juice makes Maître d'hôtel butter: serve it with a steak. Chive butter is especially good with baked potatoes. You can also beat in crushed garlic, anchovies or mustard.

Sweet butters
Use them to accompany Christmas puddings, mince pies or steamed puddings.
Brandy or rum butter Cream 85 g (3 oz) butter with 85 g (3 oz) caster sugar. Beat in 2–3 tablespoons of brandy or rum, adding a few drops at a time. For extra flavour, add a pinch of cinnamon to rum butter and use moist, brown sugar instead of caster. To make *almond butter,* cream the butter with the sugar and add 15 g (½ oz) ground almonds with 1–2 drops almond essence. Put in a dish, and leave to harden in the refrigerator until ready to use.

YOGURT

Usually made from skimmed milk, the food values of yogurt are increasingly appreciated and many people make it at home.

Use it, in its natural flavour, to make a health-giving breakfast, with a tablespoon of bran or muesli, with brown sugar and fruit. When you make a curry, add sliced cucumber or onion to yogurt for a deliciously cooling accompaniment.

Commercial yogurt All yogurt sold in this country contains a live culture unless labelling indicates that it is heat treated. *Low-fat yogurt* has the same fat content as skimmed milk, and *whole-milk yogurt,* the same fat percentage as whole milk. *Whole-fruit yogurt* contains fruit in a sugar syrup, whereas with *fruit-flavoured yogurt,* the taste comes from fruit syrup.

Storing yogurt Keep cool, otherwise the dormant bacteria become active and produce more acid which impairs the flavour of the yogurt and also causes it to separate.

Keep all yogurt in the refrigerator for four-five days. Heat treated yogurt keeps longer: look for the date stamp on the cap.

You can freeze fruit yogurt for up to three months because it has a high sugar content. Thaw in the refrigerator for 24 hours, or for one hour at room temperature.

Making yogurt at home For a simple and economical recipe, see p. 8 of The Dairy Book of Home Cookery.

Butterballs Cut chilled butter into small squares. Scoop out portions and place between two butter pats. Lightly rotate the top pat to form balls.

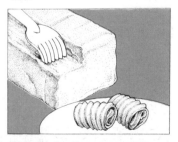

Buttercurls Use a special curling tool and run it along the block of cold butter in a straight line. Chill in the refrigerator in a bowl of water before using.

CHEESE

Cheese is made from the milk of a cow, goat or sheep. Milk is ripened by the addition of a 'starter' culture of lactic acid bacteria which turns milk sugar (lactose) into lactic acid. The milk sours as it ripens, separating into the solid curds and the liquid whey. The curds form the basis of the cheese we eat, helped by added rennet.

Because of differences between the cheese-making processes of various countries, there is a huge variety of cheeses available from all over the world.

Buying and storing cheese
Buy cheese fresh if you can, and in the quantity you will use over four or five days. Wrap loosely in cling film or aluminium foil and store in a cool larder or in the refrigerator.

About an hour before serving, take out of the refrigerator, unwrap it and allow the cheese to 'breathe' so that its full flavour is brought out.

You may buy cheese, prepacked, with storage times printed on the package. As with cheese cut fresh, make sure it isn't dry, cracked, sweaty or oily. Always buy from a good grocer or a reliable supermarket where fast turnover ensures freshness.

The cheeses listed here represent the range of home-produced and imported cheeses most available throughout Great Britain. With unfamiliar cheeses, buy small portions to see if you like their taste.

HOME-PRODUCED CHEESE (LIGHTLY PRESSED)

Caerphilly Originating from

1 Farmhouse Caerphilly
2 Gouda 3 Edam 4 Roquefort
5 Emmenthal 6 Gruyère
7 Red Cheshire 8 Red Leicester
9 Blue Cheshire 10 Fourme
d'Ambert 11 Bleu de Bresse
12 Camembert 13 Mozzarella
14 Port Salut 15 Coulommiers
on straw 16 Bel Paese 17 Blue
Stilton 18 Gorgonzola 19 Sage
Derby 20 Creamery Brie
21 Farmhouse Brie de Meaux
22 Livarot 23 Neufchâtel
24 Reblochon 25 Petit Pont
l'Evêque 26 Goat milk cheese,
log-shaped 27 Double
Gloucester with chives
28 Farmhouse Sage Lancashire
29 Cendré 30 Mi-chèvre
31 Fresh, salted goat milk cheese
32 Goat milk cheese sold in a
pyramid shape 33 Crottin, a
harder, cured goat milk cheese
34 Soft, lightly pressed goat milk
cheese 35 Fresh, lightly salted
goat milk cheese, covered in red

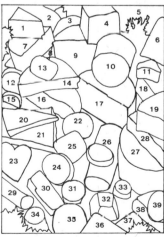

wax for protection 36 Gjetost, a
typical brown whey cheese
37 Garlic and herb cheese
38 Poivre d'Auvergne, a Fondu or
processed cheese 39 Boursin,
coated with black pepper

FOOD AND COOKERY

Wales, this is a creamy white cheese with a semi-smooth texture and a mild flavour. Ideal for a cheeseboard, for filling celery and making savoury spreads.

Lancashire A white, crumbly cheese with a tangy flavour. Famous for cooking in sauces and toasting.

White Wensleydale Originally made by the monks at Jervaulx Abbey, this mild, creamy-coloured cheese with its unique taste goes well with apple pie.

HOME-PRODUCED CHEESE (HARD-PRESSED)

Cheddar Easily the most popular cheese available in the UK, with a firm, crumbly texture and a taste which becomes more mellow as the cheese ages. It is ideal for cooking, serving with biscuits, or toasted on bread. Look for *Farmhouse Cheddar,* a matured cheese with a rich flavour. Ireland, New Zealand and Canada also manufacture Cheddar cheese.

Cheshire Both red and white have a crumbly texture and a mild, slightly salty flavour. Excellent served with cake, fruit and biscuits. *Blue Cheshire* is also available.

Farmhouse Cheshire is normally made from the milk of a single herd of cows. This tasty cheese is of high quality, due to its slow maturing period of at least six months.

Derby A pale cheese with a smooth texture and a mild flavour which matures with age. *Sage Derby* has chopped sage leaves added which gives the cheese extra flavour and an attractive, marbled appearance.

Dunlop A traditional mellow Scottish cheese, produced mainly in the islands of Arran and Islay.

Double Gloucester A bright orange-yellow buttery cheese, with a smooth and close texture and mild flavour. Eat with salad or fruit at the end of a meal.

Leicester A buttery soft cheese with a rich orange appearance, and fairly mild taste. An excellent cooking and eating cheese.

BLUE VEINED CHEESES

The blue veins in these cheeses are produced by the growth of penicillium moulds. Stainless steel needles are used to produce air holes in the cheese to allow the moulds to grow. Some blue veined cheeses are still ripened in cool caves where the mould grows naturally.

Blue Stilton The 'King of Cheeses' has a characteristic rich flavour and creamy, blue-veined body, formed by allowing the penetration of a penicillium mould. Traditionally accompanied by port.

Blue Wensleydale When blue mould is introduced into white Wensleydale it gives it a distinctive rich flavour. The cheese takes longer to mature than white Wensleydale.

Stuart A Scottish blue-vein cheese from the mould *penicillium roquefort.* It is a rich and creamy cheese with a delicious nutty flavour.

MORE UNUSUAL CHEESES

Applewood Cheddar cheese smoked over applewood.

Caboc A rich, creamy Scottish cheese, pale in colour, with the surface rolled in toasted oatmeal. Ideal for spreading on biscuits.

Cotswold A cheese based on double Gloucester and flavoured with chives.

Crowdie This is a skimmed milk soft curd cheese with a sharp tangy flavour. Its manufacture follows the methods once used on Scottish farms.

Garlic A full-fat soft cheese with chopped fresh leaves of wild garlic herb. It is coated with flaked oats and nuts.

Ilchester A Cheddar-based cheese, flavoured with beer and garlic. It has a soft texture and a good flavour.

Red Windsor A red-streaked, crumbly-textured, Cheddar-based cheese with a flavour similar to mild Cheddar. Ideal for eating with biscuits or in salads.

Walton A soft cheese, based on Cheddar and mixed with Stilton and walnuts.

Fresh cheeses Cottage, cream and curd cheeses are soft, mild and slightly acidic. A 'starter' culture is added to pasteurised milk or cream to produce soft acid or cream cheese. This method is based on the traditional home-made cheese recipe.

PROCESSED CHEESES

Made by breaking down other cheeses, e.g. Cheddar and Cheshire, and adding emulsifying salts. The cheese is bought pre-packed and may be flavoured with celery, ham, prawn or a similar ingredient. Its texture is smooth.

IMPORTED CHEESES

Brie A French cheese made from cows' milk. It has a soft pale yellow appearance and an edible crust.

Camembert A famous French cheese from Normandy with a creamy, pale yellow appearance and a soft crust. Like Brie, it is made from cows' milk, but has a much stronger taste.

Danish Blue Made from homogenised milk with a high cream content. A blue-veined cheese with a salty flavour and soft, slightly crumbly texture.

Edam A Dutch cheese made from partly skimmed milk, encased in a red wax rind. It has a slightly rubbery texture and mild flavour.

Emmenthal A full-flavoured cheese with a slightly sweet, nutty taste. Like Gruyère, it is hard-pressed but has larger holes. It melts easily: use it with an equal weight of Cheddar in a cheese sauce.

Gorgonzola An Italian cheese with a mottled green appearance and a coarse brown rind. It has a firm texture and a sharp taste.

Gouda A soft Dutch cheese with a high butterfat content. Golden in appearance and creamy in taste.

Gruyère A hard, pale yellow cheese with small holes and a brown, wrinkled rind, made in France and Switzerland. Excellent for cooking, and delicious for fondues.

Mozzarella A soft Italian curd cheese with a slightly sour taste. It is ideal for use in pizzas and lasagna.

Parmesan A hard Italian cheese, its strong fragrance and flavour make it ideal for cooking, and it adds a finishing touch when finely grated and sprinkled over soups and pasta dishes.

Roquefort A crumbly, salty blue French cheese, made from ewes' milk. A mould develops naturally in the cheese to give the characteristic green veins.

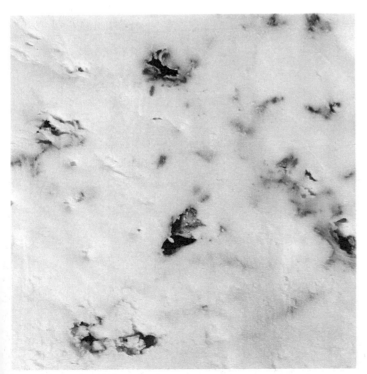

A close-up of a blue veined cheese. The veins are thriving colonies of the mould, penicillium roquefortii.

Once cheese like this was left to ripen in damp, dark caves and the mould invaded naturally. Now, because of commercial pressures, almost every cheese is inoculated with spores of mould before being left to ripen.

No blue veined cheese is alike. The variety of 'white' cheese influences the flavour and texture, even though the mould growth is the same. Roquefort, with its pungent taste and crumbly texture, is as different from soft, salty Danish blue as that cheese is from Stilton or blue Cheshire. One thing they have in common is the way they ripen from the centre outwards, as the veins spread.

Serve with water biscuits or wholemeal bread, butter and slices of crisp celery, a bunch of watercress or a green salad. Add home-made pickles or chutney and fresh fruit.

FOOD AND COOKERY

EGGS

The colour of the egg you buy does not affect its food value — although a speckled brown egg, fresh from a farm, boiled and served in an egg cup with home-baked, toasted bread and creamy butter is the image of an ideal breakfast for many people.

Commercially produced eggs are generally sold in date-stamped cartons. Sizes one–two (70–65 g; 3–2½ oz) are *large;* three–four (60–55 g; 2½–2 oz) are *standard;* sizes five-six (50-45 g; 2-1¾ oz) are *small;* size seven is under 45 g (1½ oz).

There is no need to refrigerate eggs but if you do, take them out one hour before using. This prevents cracking and makes whisking easier.

Separating eggs Have two small basins ready. Crack the shell sharply on one, let the white pour into one bowl and tip the yolk into the other.

Whisking Use eggs brought to room temperature. Beat vigorously using a whisk, fork or electric whisk to incorporate a large volume of air. Do not leave to stand; use straight away.

Folding in egg whites Using a metal spoon, gently cover the beaten egg whites with the thicker mixture, without beating, to avoid loss of air.

Boiling eggs Place eggs in cold water and then bring to the boil. Time eggs from the point of boiling and simmer thereafter as shown below.

Type	Size	Minutes
Soft-	5–6	2½
boiled	3–4	2¾
	1–2	3
Medium-	5–6	3½
boiled	3–4	4
	1–2	4½
Hard-	1–2	10
boiled	3+	9

Frying eggs Use about 50 g (2 oz) butter or lard for four eggs. Heat the fat until it starts to bubble, then lower the temperature as you drop in the broken eggs, one at a time. Fry for about two minutes (or to taste). Remove with a slice.

Scrambling eggs For four eggs, allow 25 g (1 oz) butter. Beat the eggs, and season with a little salt and pepper. Melt the butter in a heavy-based pan over a low heat, then mix in the eggs, stirring with a wooden spoon, until they are thick and creamy.

Poaching eggs There are two methods of poaching eggs: the easier is to use a poaching pan. You need a little skill and practice to poach eggs directly into water.

Using a wide, shallow pan, add water, bring to the boil, then reduce to a very gentle simmer. Break eggs into a saucer and slip them into the water, one at a time. Let them simmer.

Making omelettes An omelette is one of the most versatile and creative dishes you can make with eggs. You can choose any kind of filling, savoury or sweet.

In a Spanish omelette, add a prepared blend of lightly fried onions, peppers, diced cooked potato, bacon — or whatever else you have to hand.

For a basic omelette, allow two eggs for each person, 5 ml (1 teaspoon) water, and about 15 g (½ oz) butter.

Break the eggs and beat lightly with the water. Season to taste. Heat the butter in a heavy-based omelette or small frying pan until it sizzles, then pour in the eggs. Tilt the pan so that the mixture cooks evenly. When the omelette is almost set, add a filling, then fold.

SIZES OF EGGS

one　　two　　three　　four　　five　　six　　seven

STORE CUPBOARD FOODS

RICE

Originally associated in this country with traditional rice pudding, the economical versatility of rice is being recognized and it is now used in many exciting and popular dishes.

Long grain rice originates from many countries, but look for *patna* and *basmatti* rice from India, and long grain rice from the USA. Use in savoury dishes. During cooking the long grains become fluffy and separate.

If you buy it pre-packed, it may be described as 'easy cook', 'separate grain', 'pre-fluffed', 'specially processed' or 'non-stick', which indicates that the rice has been subjected to steam treatment before milling to increase retention of food value.

'Pre-cooked', 'instant', 'quick-cook' and 'express', are names found on packaging, which indicate that the rice has been pre-cooked and dehydrated, and so requires soaking before cooking according to the manufacturer's instructions.

Short or round-grain rice Many brands sold here come from China and Australia. Use for rice puddings and other sweet rice dishes. The grains tend to become sticky on cooking.

Brown rice has increased in popularity, because its unmilled state results in the increased retention of vitamins and minerals. Used in savoury dishes, it has a distinct, nutty flavour.

Wild rice Used in savoury dishes. This is not a true rice but the seed of a wild grass from the USA and Canada.

Cooking rice Remember that raw rice will treble in weight after cooking. For perfect, fluffy rice, simmer in a covered pan for about 15 minutes, with about twice its own volume of water.

Allow 50 g (2 oz) dry rice per person, and about 40 minutes cooking time if you're using brown rice. Alternatively cook in a covered dish, with the correct proportion of water, at 180°C (350°F) Gas Mark 4, for about 40 minutes. If necessary, keep hot in a sieve over water.

For fried rice, use well-drained boiled rice which is slightly undercooked. Rice can be flavoured with stock cubes, dried soup mixes, tomato juice or herbs during the cooking process. If too much rice has been cooked, use to make a tasty rice salad with chopped tomatoes, peppers and celery. Rice will freeze successfully for up to six months in a sealed container.

For a rice pudding use 50 g (2 oz) short grain rice with 575/600 ml (1 pint) milk and 25 g (1 oz) sugar and bake at 150°C (300°F) Gas Mark 2 for 2-2½ hours.

Five different varieties of rice. From the left: **1** long-grain (patna) **2** medium grain (Carolina) **3** Italian (Arborio) **4** brown rice **5** round, short-grain rice.

FOOD AND COOKERY

PASTA

Pasta is dough: hard (durum) wheat and water, commercially processed is the most familiar, but it is possible to make at home. There are hundreds of different shapes: spaghetti and macaroni are most familiar, but look for noodles — tagliatelle or fettuccine; pasta shaped in shells and bows, and flat sheets (lasagne). Quite often, spinach is added for colour: look for 'verdi' on the packet.

Pasta is often served with a tomato, beef or cheese sauce before the main course of a meal but it can be the main dish, served with butter, freshly ground black pepper and lashings of grated Parmesan cheese.

Cooking pasta Allow 75-125 g (3-4 oz) pasta per person, and cook in a large quantity of boiling salted water for 8-15 minutes, depending on the size and thickness of the pasta, or according to packet instructions. Usually allow 575-600 ml (1 pint) water and 1 level teaspoon of salt for every 50 g (2 oz) pasta, and take care not to overcook or it will become sticky. Cook spaghetti in whole strands by holding it at one end and letting it slowly sink into the boiling water. Drain, rinse well with hot water, re-heat with a little butter over a low heat and serve.

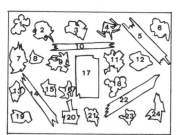

Pasta comes in a variety of shapes.
1 *Tortellini* tiny 'little hats' filled with meat or cheese. Cook and serve with a sauce **2** wholemeal *tagliatelle* **3** *grosso rigata*, usually cooked and then stuffed **4** *pennini* **5** *zitoni* **6** *tagliatelle verdi*, coloured with spinach **7** egg-enriched *tagliatelle* **8** *anellini*, tiny soup shapes **9** *tortiglioni*, spirals **10** *capellini* **11** *farfalle*, shaped like bows or butterflies **12** freshly made *tagliatelle* **13** *ravioli*, small cushions of pasta filled with meat or cheese **14** *spaghettini* **15** *stelline*, star-shaped pasta for soups **16** *conchigliette*, small shell shapes **17** *lasagne verdi*, used in baked dishes with layers of meat in a tomato sauce and topped with a white sauce and cheese **18** *conchiglie*, large shell shapes, cooked and served with a rich tomato or meat sauce **19** *granigna rigata* **20** *cannelloni*, cook, then fill with a meat or cheese stuffing and serve with a sauce **21** *ruote* **22** *spaghetti* **23** *nocchette*, another pasta for soup **24** *penne*

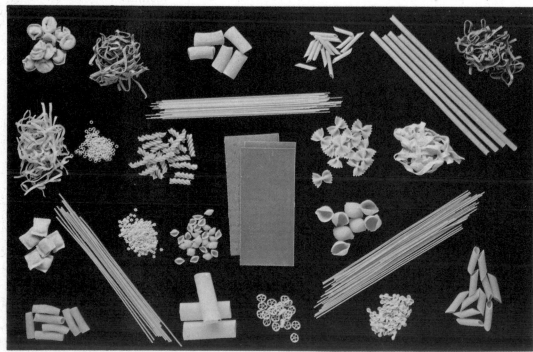

PULSES

Dried beans, peas, split peas and lentils. These should be soaked overnight in cold water or for 2-3 hours in boiling water. Allow 25-50 g (1-2 oz) per person; drain and cook in fresh boiling salted water. Lentils do not need soaking.

Butter beans and dried peas Usually used in soups and stews or served with butter.

Haricot beans Soaked and cooked with bacon, treacle and spices and served with a tomato sauce, are *baked beans.*

Kidney beans. Soak overnight, cook and serve with minced beef, chilli powder and spices to make *Chilli con Carne.*

Cooking times for pulses

Lentils   30-40 minutes
Split peas   30–45 minutes
Peas   1½–2 hours
Haricot and
Kidney beans   1–1½ hours
Soya beans   2–3 hours
Butter beans   1–1½ hours

OTHER DRIED FOODS

Textured vegetable protein (TVP) Processed soya bean is used mainly for extending fresh meat.

Pearl barley Polished grain, used to thicken soups or included in meat dishes.

Oatmeal Dried and husked grain ground to different grades of fineness, and used traditionally in porridge, biscuits and parkin.

Rolled oats Crushed, partly cooked grain, used to make quick porridge, breakfast muesli and biscuits.

Semolina, sago and tapioca All used for milk puddings, but obtained from different sources. Semolina is hard wheat which has been coarsely milled. Sago is pith from the trunk of the sago palm. Tapioca is the root of the cassava plant from the West Indies.

DRIED FRUIT

Apricots With their sweet-sharp flavour, apricots are great favourites in sweet and savoury dishes. Reconstitute in water overnight, then use with walnuts and breadcrumbs to make a stuffing for lamb; purée for a soufflé or make into jam.

Currants Small, hard fruit dried from tiny grapes. Use them in cakes and buns.

Dates A fruit known and enjoyed for at least 2,000 years, used in salads, stuffings, cakes and puddings.

Prunes Dried plums, rich in vitamin A. For a good flavour, soak overnight in weak tea or water and red wine. Use with apple to make a stuffing for goose; or cook, purée and whip with cream.

Raisins Dried Muscat grapes, rich and subtly flavoured, raisins are perhaps the most versatile of dried fruits. Use in puddings, cakes, with rice for a savoury stuffing, or for a breakfast muesli.

Sultanas Soft, sweet and seedless, use sultanas, plumped up in hot water, in cakes and puddings.

Other dry stores include breakfast cereals, flours (cornflour, rice flour and wheat flour), sugars, syrups, essences, flavourings and condiments.

Left to right:
1 butter beans **2** soya beans
3 red and brown lentils **4** two varieties of split peas **5** whole dried peas **6** haricot beans

FOOD AND COOKERY

HERBS AND SPICES

HERBS

Herbs have been used as much for their healing powers as their flavours at least since 2500 BC, when the earliest detailed information was recorded in China.

Growing herbs Make a herb bed in your garden, or grow herbs in pots on your windowsill. Grow those that you will use most frequently in the kitchen.

Drying herbs Pick herbs, rinse in clear water, tie in bunches with string, and hang upside down to dry — outside, in the sunshine; in an airing cupboard; in your kitchen or in an oven at a very low temperature.

You can keep the green colour of parsley and mint if you first blanch them for a few seconds in boiling water.

Once dry, crumble the leaves and pack into small jars. Cover, label with the date, and store in a cool, dark, dry place.

Buying dried herbs Always buy dried herbs in small quantities. Label with the date of purchase and keep for no longer than six months.

TYPES OF HERBS

Basil A pungent herb, used with tomatoes, especially in pasta sauces and salads.
Bay This slightly sweet leaf is used in a *bouquet garni*, to flavour casseroles and soups, and to garnish pâtés.
Chervil This has a delicate, slightly spicy fragrance. Use it in omelettes, soups, sauces, savoury butters and potato salads.
Dill Both stalks and seeds have an aromatic flavour, a little like caraway, but milder. Use it in dishes which contain cucumber and fish.
Fennel The leaves and bulb have an aniseed flavour. Use with fish, lamb or in sauces.

Marjoram A small-leaved herb, used mainly for flavouring meats, savoury stuffings and tomato dishes.
Mint A fast-spreading garden herb with many varieties. A traditional accompaniment to roast lamb, use also to garnish vegetables, fruit salads and cold drinks.
Oregano Related to marjoram but stronger and hotter. Used in Italian dishes.
Parsley A very popular, mild-flavoured herb, used for garnishing. It is included in a *bouquet garni*, for flavouring sauces, soups, and a wide variety of meat and vegetable dishes.
Rosemary A highly aromatic herb, used to give added flavour to roast lamb, poultry and potatoes.

1 garlic **2** bay leaves **3** parsley
4 bouquet garni **5** chives **6** mint
7 thyme **8** fennel **9** rosemary
10 basil **11** chervil **12** dill
13 tarragon **14** savory **15** sage
16 horseradish **17** oregano and marjoram

Sage A strong-flavoured herb, used in a stuffing with onion for rich meat and poultry; gives its unique flavour to Sage Derby cheese.

Savory There are both summer and winter varieties of this slightly peppery herb. Use it with eggs, fish, salads and green beans.

Tarragon Two varieties are widely available, French and Russian: French has the better flavour. Use tarragon to flavour vinegar; in chicken dishes and with eggs.

Thyme A strongly flavoured herb, with a sweet aroma. An essential part of a *bouquet garni*, add it to meats and stuffings.

SPICES

Spices come from tropical plants. They are the edible, aromatic parts dried: the fruit, berries, bark, roots or buds of the plants.

Allspice Small berries, with a flavour of cloves, nutmeg and cinnamon. Use ground, in cakes, meat casseroles and milk puddings.

Cardamom A seed with a tough shell: crack it to release the eucalyptus-like flavour, and use in curries.

Caraway The seeds of this herb are used in bread, cakes and East European dishes.

Cayenne Pepper from ground chillis. It is very hot, so use with care.

Chilli A fruit grown in warm and tropical countries. As spices, the pods may be bought green or red.

Cinnamon The inner bark of a tree grown in India and Sri Lanka. Use it in puddings, mulled wine and meat casseroles, whole or powdered.

Cloves Dried buds from a tropical tree, cloves, whole or ground, are used with apples, hams, and milk puddings.

Coriander A plant whose origins are in southern Europe and the Middle East. Use its spicy seeds in curries and stuffings.

Cumin A small herb, whose aromatic seeds are used in curries, and with rice, beans and pickles.

Fenugreek Seeds used in curry mixtures.

Garam masala A mixture of ground spices, used to flavour Indian food just before serving. It most often contains cardamom, cinnamon, coriander, cumin, cloves, ginger and pepper.

Ginger A warming spice with a sharp, tangy taste. Buy it fresh, dried, powdered or crystallized.

Mace The outer covering of nutmeg, mace is sold powdered or as 'blade mace'. Use in sauces and stews.

1 tamarind **2, 3, 4** mustard powder, black mustard, white mustard **5, 6** whole and ground cloves **7, 8** ground and dried red chillis **9** pickled green chillis **10** cumin **11** fenugreek **12** cayenne **13** powdered saffron **14, 15** whole and ground ginger **16** vanilla pods **17** ground fennel **18** sesame seeds **19** allspice berries **20, 21, 22** whole white and black peppercorns; ground white pepper **23, 24** whole and ground cardamom **25** coriander berries **26, 27** blade and ground mace **28** paprika **29** poppy seeds **30** ground coriander **31, 32** ground and whole nutmeg **33** ground cinnamon **34** turmeric **35** garam masala

FOOD AND COOKERY

Mustard Yellow (white) and black mustard are in greatest demand. The ground seeds are used in a variety of different combinations, often with added spices and wine vinegar, to give zest to beef, ham and cheese.

Nutmeg The seed of a tropical tree, covered with a scarlet network of mace, nutmeg has a pleasant, crisp flavour. Grate and add to milk puddings, custards and cakes.

Paprika From a sweet red pepper, buy it ground to add a sweet pungency to a goulash, or to garnish a sauce.

Pepper The most widely used of all spices, both black and white pepper come from a tropical climbing vine. Black peppercorns are the berries, dried in the sun. White peppercorns have been husked of their outer skin.

Poppy seed Tiny seeds; sprinkle on bread, pies, mashed potatoes or noodles.

Saffron The most expensive spice used in cookery, saffron comes from the stigma of a crocus. Gold in colour, with a subtle, slightly bitter taste, use it to flavour fish soups, rice and some rubbed-in cakes and buns.

Sesame An important food plant; use the nutty seeds to flavour cakes and biscuits.

Tamarind The pods of the tamarind tree are pulped to make a delicate, slightly sour ingredient for curries.

Turmeric Always sold ground, turmeric comes from a plant related to ginger. It is bright yellow, with a warm, pungent flavour. Use it with rice and in curries.

Vanilla The plant is a variety of orchid. Its pods are dried, giving a sweetly scented flavour to milk puddings and cakes.

STOCK

This is an all-important cooking liquid which is used as the basis for soups, casseroles and sauces. It should be well flavoured but be complementary to the ingredients of the finished dish. Vegetables with strong flavours, such as parsnips, should be used sparingly.

Fresh bones and those left over from joints can be used, together with vegetable trimmings. Add extra vegetables, herbs and possibly wine or another liquid for extra flavour and cover with water. Bring to the boil and then simmer. Brown stock or game stock takes about 3 hours; fish and vegetable stock only 30 minutes. Do not cook fish stock for longer or it acquires a nasty sticky taste from the bones. Be careful with fish bones that are strongly flavoured.

Strain cooked stock, leave to cool and skim. Use immediately or store, covered, in the refrigerator for 2-3 days. Reboil before use.

Brown stock Makes 1.8 litres (3 pt).

225 g (8 oz) marrow bones
450-675 g (1-1½ lb) shin of
    beef (roughly chopped)
20 g (¾ oz) dripping or oil
1 leek (cleaned)
1 onion (peeled and chopped)
100-125 g (4 oz) carrots
Bouquet garni
Salt and pepper

Cover the bones with water and simmer for about 10 minutes. Meanwhile, preheat the oven to 220°C (425°F) Gas Mark 7. Drain the bones, then put into a roasting pan with the beef and dripping (or oil).

Brown for about 30 minutes, turning from time to time. Put the roasted bones and beef in a heavy-based pan; cover with cold water and add the prepared vegetables and seasoning. Bring to the boil. Skim scum from the surface and cover, then simmer for about 3 hours, adding additional water if required. Strain, cool, and remove the fat. Add extra seasoning to taste.

White stock Use veal bones and add vegetables, herbs, seasoning and water. Bring to the boil, then simmer, remove scum and strain.

Fish stock Makes 575–600 ml (1 pt).

450 g (1 lb) fish bones and
    trimmings (head and skin)
1 onion (peeled and chopped)
Salt and pepper
Bouquet garni

Wash the fish trimmings and bring to the boil with 575–600 ml (1 pt) of water. Remove scum and add chopped onion, seasoning and bouquet garni. Cover the pan and simmer for about 30 minutes on a low heat. Strain and use immediately.

Game stock Use a carcass and cleaned giblets and cook as for white stock, simmering for 2-3 hours. Strain and remove the fat before use. Ideal for making use of chicken and turkey carcasses.

Vegetable stock Made by using a variety of chopped vegetables: cabbage, lettuce outer leaves, and clean peelings from carrots and parsnips with added seasoning. Simmer and strain through a sieve lined with a piece of muslin before use.

SOUPS

There are many varieties of soup, both thick and thin, ranging from consommés and broths to iced soups, bisques (fish soups) and fruit soups. All soups are simple and enjoyable to make at home. You can make good use of chicken carcasses and un-cooked bones and, if there is a glut of tomatoes in your garden, fresh soup is just one excellent way of making use of them.

Consommé Clarified brown stock enriched with lean beef, or chicken stock enrich-ed with chicken. A first course soup, completely clear and with a robust flavour.

Broth A thin soup made from fresh bones and vegetables cooked in water very slowly and for a long time. The meat and vegetables are served in the soup. Similar soups can be made using stock as a basis. These soups make hearty meals with the simple accompaniment of fresh bread.

Puréed soup Made from fresh vegetables cooked in stock and then puréed, or from fruit poached in water and then puréed. No further thickening is generally required.

Cream soup Rich and thick, made from puréed vege-tables (or fish or poultry), enriched with cream and but-ter. Egg yolks can also be used. A béchamel sauce often forms the basis of the soup and the main ingredients are cooked in this before being puréed.

Minestrone A meal in itself. First make a brown or chicken stock, allowing 1.1 litres (2 pt) for four servings. Pour a little oil into a heavy-based pan and add chopped onion, carrots, celery and leeks. Cook gently for a few minutes and add chopped bacon, a crushed garlic clove and tomato purée or canned tomatoes. Pour on the strained stock, add two bay leaves and basil, oregano or marjoram. Add dried haricot beans which have been soaked, and simmer gently for about one hour. Test for seasoning. At this stage you can add extra vegetables in season and some pasta shapes. A little red wine can also go in. Cook until the pasta is tender, another 15-20 minutes, and serve in warm bowls, topped with grated parmesan cheese.

Soups, thick and thin, are easy and very satisfying to make at home. With a good stock, some vegetables and meaty bones you can make a meal in a bowl and serve simply with fresh bread.

FOOD AND COOKERY

SAUCES

Sauces enrich cooked foods in different ways. They may use some of the cooking liquor, with added thickening, to enhance the taste. They may act as a contrast: a sharp apple sauce cuts across the richness of pork; cheese sauce boosts the mild flavour of a cauliflower. Or you may use a cold sauce — vinaigrette with a salad, red currant or mint with lamb.

ROUX-BASED SAUCES
A roux is a blend of equal quantities of fat (most often butter) and flour, cooked over a gentle heat before a liquid and seasoning are added. You can make a thin, pouring sauce or a thick sauce for coating and binding foods.

White sauces: use milk or a white stock for the liquid. For brown sauces, use a brown stock. For a white sauce, cook the fat and flour together for about two–three minutes; for a brown sauce, until it colours.

Basic white sauce Melt 15 g (½ oz) butter in a saucepan over a low heat. Blend in 15 g (½ oz) flour. Cook for 2–3 minutes, then add 275–300 ml (½ pint) milk or white stock, slowly at first, then more rapidly as the sauce begins to thicken. If the sauce goes lumpy, strain it through a sieve into a clean pan, using a wooden spoon.

Flavour with grated cheese, herbs such as parsley, mustard — whatever the recipe recommends. For a full range of white sauces, see pp. 129-132 in *The Dairy Book of Home Cookery*. See p. 133 for brown sauces.

BLENDED SAUCES
You can thicken cooking liquid with cornflour or a blend of uncooked butter and flour (known as *beurre manié*). For the former, blend about 15 g (½ oz) cornflour with a little milk or cooking liquid, then stir it into the cooking liquor until smooth and slightly thickened. For *beurre manié*, blend together equal quantities (about 15 g (½ oz)) each butter and flour, then add in small dollops to the cooking liquid, stirring all the time until it is blended.

GRAVY
Made from the juices of a

It is essential that a white roux-based sauce should be brought to the boil and then simmered.

TABLE OF ROUX-BASED SAUCE CONSISTENCIES

Type of sauce	Fat	Flour	Milk or other liquid	Use
Thin sauce	15 g ($\frac{1}{2}$ oz)	15 g ($\frac{1}{2}$ oz)	275–300 ml ($\frac{1}{2}$ pt)	Base for soups
Pouring sauce	20 g ($\frac{3}{4}$ oz)	20 g ($\frac{3}{4}$ oz)	275–300 ml ($\frac{1}{2}$ pt)	For fish, meat, vegetable and sweet dishes
Coating sauce	25 g (1 oz)	25 g (1 oz)	275–300 ml ($\frac{1}{2}$ pt)	Coating foods
Panada (very thick sauce)	50 g (2 oz)	50 g (2 oz)	275–300 ml ($\frac{1}{2}$ pt)	To bind foods, base for soufflés

roasting joint or bird. For *thin gravy*, pour away and discard the fat from the roasting tin and add stock from the vegetables cooking on the stove to the juices. Season to taste. For *thick gravy*, pour off most of the fat (while retaining the juices), then add flour to the tin. Stir over a gentle heat until it browns, then add water or a stock cube. Taste, and season if necessary. Bring to the boil and simmer for a few minutes.

EGG-BASED SAUCES
Hollandaise is the most famous; serve warm with fish, poultry and vegetables.

Hollandaise sauce For 4–6 servings, you need 225 g (8 oz) butter, beaten yolks of 4 eggs, the juice of $\frac{1}{2}$ lemon, salt and pepper. Heat water in a large saucepan until it reaches simmering point; meanwhile melt the butter in another pan. Put a large bowl over the simmering water and whisk the egg yolks, adding a little water. As soon as they begin to thicken, remove from the heat and whisk in the melted butter, slowly at

first, until the sauce becomes smooth and glossy. Add the lemon juice and season to taste.

This sauce isn't difficult to make: just make sure you cook it over gentle heat. If it begins to curdle, strain into a clean pan and beat in another egg yolk. For variations, see p. 129 of *The Dairy Book of Home Cookery*.

COLD SAUCES
Basic Mayonnaise Recipe
2 egg yolks (size 1 or 2)
2·5 ml ($\frac{1}{2}$ level teaspoon) each of dry mustard, salt and caster sugar
2·5 ml ($\frac{1}{2}$ teaspoon) Worcestershire sauce (optional)
Pepper
275–300 ml ($\frac{1}{2}$ pt) salad oil
30 ml (2 tablespoons) vinegar or lemon juice
15 ml (1 tablespoon) hot water
Put yolks, mustard, salt and sugar, Worcestershire sauce (if used) and pepper into bowl. Beat until smooth. Add half the oil, a drop at a time, and continue beating until mayonnaise is very thick. Stir in 15 ml (1 tablespoon) vinegar or lemon juice. Beat in rest of oil gradually, about

10 ml (2 teaspoons) at a time. When all the oil has been added, stir in last 15 ml (1 tablespoon) of vinegar and the hot water. (The water helps to prevent separation.) Adjust seasoning to taste. Transfer to covered container. Will keep refrigerated for up to 2 weeks. For variations, see p. 126 and p. 131, *The Dairy Book of Home Cookery*.

Vinaigrette (salad) dressing To dress a salad for about four people, beat together 90 ml (6 tablespoons) of good olive or cooking oil with 30 ml (2 tablespoons) of wine or cider vinegar, or the juice of 1 lemon. Add a little dried mustard, sugar, salt and pepper.

Fruit-based sauces Simmer red currants, cranberries or apple slices with a little water, then add sugar to taste. See pp. 130–134 for other sauces, in *The Dairy Book of Home Cookery*.

For custards, chocolate and jam sauces, see pp. 136–139 of *The Dairy Book of Home Cookery*.

FOOD AND COOKERY

BATTERS, BISCUITS AND SCONES

MAKING BATTERS

Traditionally batters are associated with Shrove Tuesday and pancake tossing, or with Yorkshire pudding served as a starter or as an accompaniment to roast beef. This mixture of milk, eggs and flour can be made into a large number of other exciting dishes: fruit pancakes, fritters and crêpes suzettes.

Proving the pan To avoid the problem of pancakes sticking to the pan a non-stick pan may be used, but better 'prove' a small heavy-based shallow frying or pancake pan as follows. Heat the pan with 2 tablespoons of oil until a faint haze appears. Remove from the heat, add a tablespoon of salt to the oil and rub with kitchen paper until the surface is sealed and shiny. Remove surplus salt and repeat if necessary. The pan is then ready for use.

Pour a little oil and butter in the pan, heat until a faint haze appears then pour off the excess into a small dish placed next to the hob. Return the pan to the heat to ensure it is very hot before the batter is poured in.

Basic Pancake Batter

100 g (4 oz) flour
Large pinch of salt
1 egg
275 ml (½ pt) milk
1 tablespoon melted butter

Sift flour and salt into bowl. Beat to smooth creamy batter with egg, half the milk and melted butter. Stir in remaining milk and use as required. There is no need to let the batter stand before using,

although it may be left, covered, in the refrigerator.

Pour in 2-3 tablespoons of basic pancake batter mixture, tilting the pan to cover it evenly. It should take about 1 minute to brown one side, before tossing or flicking over with a palette knife. If the pancake is becoming brown too rapidly, turn the heat down. Serve immediately, sprinkled with lemon juice and sugar.

Pancakes may be kept warm if layered with sheets of greaseproof paper and then placed on a plate over a pan of boiling water or wrapped in aluminium foil and kept warm in a preheated warm oven. Makes eight-ten small pancakes.

For more pancake ideas, refer to *The Dairy Book of Home Cookery*, pp. 141-143.

Basic Coating Batter
For coating fish, meat, vegetables.

100 g (4 oz) plain flour
¼ level teaspoon salt
1 egg
15 ml (1 tablespoon) melted butter
150 ml (¼ pt) milk

Sift flour and salt into bowl. Beat to smooth creamy batter with unbeaten egg, butter and milk. Use as required.

Sweet Fritter Batter
Use to coat fruit such as apple rings, banana slices, and pineapple chunks.

50 g (2 oz) plain flour
Pinch of salt
5 ml (1 level teaspoon) sifted icing sugar
60 ml (4 tablespoons) lukewarm water
10 ml (2 teaspoons) melted butter
White of 1 egg

Sift flour and salt into bowl

and add sugar. Gradually mix to a thick smooth batter with water and butter. Whisk egg white until stiff and fold into batter mixture.

Yorkshire Pudding
Make up the pancake batter as described. Preheat the oven to 220°C (425°F) Gas Mark 7 and put 2–3 tablespoons hot dripping or oil into a baking tin or individual patty tins. Heat until a faint haze appears and pour in the batter. Bake just above the centre of the oven for 30-35 minutes.

Toad-in-the-Hole
Preheat the oven to 200°C (400°F) Gas Mark 6. Place 450 g (1 lb) pork sausages in a greased baking tin and bake for 10 minutes turning once. Remove from the oven and pour over made-up pancake batter and bake as for Yorkshire pudding.

MAKING BISCUITS

Biscuits can be made up with a number of variations from one basic mixture. They are at their best when freshly baked, but can be kept in an airtight tin for a week.

Biscuits made from syrup or honey should be left on the baking tray when taken out of the oven to harden before being placed on a wire cooling rack.

Basic Biscuit Recipe

225 g (8 oz) self-raising flour
Pinch salt
150 g (6 oz) butter
100 g (4 oz) caster or sifted icing sugar
1 beaten egg

Sift the flour and salt into a mixing bowl. Rub in the butter finely until the mixture resembles fine breadcrumbs, then add the sugar. Mix to a very stiff dough with the beaten egg.

Turn out on to a lightly floured board and knead gently until smooth. Put into a polythene bag or wrap in aluminium foil and leave to chill for about 30 minutes.

Roll out thinly and cut into about 30 rounds with a 5 cm (2 in) plain or fluted biscuit cutter. Put the biscuits on to greased baking sheets and prick well with a fork.

Bake in an oven preheated to 180°C (350°F) Gas Mark 4, for 20-30 minutes. Leave on trays for a few minutes before transferring to wire cooling racks. When cold, store in an airtight tin.

Biscuit variations To the basic biscuit recipe try adding one of the following:

40 g (1½ oz) chopped walnuts and 2.5 ml (½ teaspoon) vanilla essence.

50 g (2 oz) chopped almonds and 2.5 ml (½ teaspoon) almond essence.

1 level teaspoon finely grated lemon or orange rind.

50 g (2 oz) currants.

50 g (2 oz) chopped glacé cherries.

7.5 ml (1½ level teaspoons) mixed spice or cinnamon.

50 g (2 oz) desiccated coconut and 2.5 ml (½ teaspoon) vanilla essence.

50 g (2 oz) grated plain chocolate or small chocolate drops.

For a variety of other biscuit recipes see *The Dairy Book of Home Cookery* pp. 220-224.

BISCUIT CRUST

An uncooked crust which makes an ideal base for cheesecake and other creamy dessert fillings.

150 g (6 oz) biscuits, for preference, digestive or ginger
75 g (3 oz) butter
Sugar (optional)

Crush biscuits with a rolling pin, or use a liquidizer. Melt the butter over a low heat and add the sugar, if used.

Stir until evenly combined and use to line a flan ring or pie dish, using the back of a spoon to smooth the mixture. Chill in the refrigerator for two hours before filling.

MAKING SCONES

Make scones for afternoon teas, spread with butter, jam and cream. It is important to get the consistency of the dough right. Insufficient liquid may result in heavy, badly risen scones; using too little, you find them spreading and shapeless. Avoid using too much baking powder because this results in an acid taste. The first rolling out will produce the best results, but the trimmings can be kneaded together and re-rolled to cut out as many scones as possible. Bake in a hot oven or on a griddle.

Basic Scones

225 g (8 oz) self-raising flour
2.5 ml (½ level teaspoon) salt
50 g (2 oz) butter
25 g (1 oz) caster sugar
150 ml (¼ pt) milk
For fruit scones, add 25-50 g (1-2 oz) sultanas and/or currants
For cheese scones, add 5 ml (1 level teaspoon) dry mustard, pinch Cayenne pepper and 50 g (2 oz) grated Cheddar cheese and omit sugar.

Sift flour and salt into bowl.

Rub in butter finely, add sugar and/or any additional ingredients; add milk all at once. Mix to a soft, but not sticky, dough with a knife. Turn out on to a lightly floured board and knead quickly until smooth. Roll out to about 1 cm (½ in) thickness. Cut into 16-18 rounds: savoury scones are usually cut with a plain biscuit cutter and sweet scones with a fluted cutter. Transfer to buttered baking tray. Brush tops with milk, and add a sprinkling of grated cheese to cheese scones. Bake at top of oven at 230°C (450°F) Gas Mark 8 for 7-10 minutes or until golden and well risen. Cool on a wire rack and serve while fresh.

Dropped Scones

225 g (8 oz) self-raising flour
2.5 ml (½ level teaspoon) salt
15 ml (1 level tablespoon) caster sugar
1 egg
275 ml (½ pt) milk
25-50 g (1-2 oz) melted butter

Sift flour and salt into bowl. Add sugar and mix to a smooth creamy batter with the whole egg and half the milk, then stir in rest of milk. Brush large heavy frying pan or griddle with melted butter and heat. Drop small rounds of scone mixture in batches from a tablespoon into the pan. Cook until bubbles show on surface. Turn over carefully with a slice or palette knife and cook for further 2 minutes. Keep in a folded tea towel, to stay warm and moist.

Potato scones Boil 225 g (8 oz) floury potatoes and sieve while hot. Add sifted flour to make a stiff dough, a pinch of salt and a little butter. Roll out and cook on a griddle or in a greased pan.

FOOD AND COOKERY

PUDDINGS AND DESSERTS

Puddings and desserts should be chosen carefully to complement the main course and, preferably, be prepared well in advance of serving.

If you use the oven, think about fuel costs. If you have the main course cooking on a top or centre shelf, put an egg custard or rice pudding in the bottom of the oven. Puddings served with custard are typically associated with British kitchens but, to the French gourmet, ice creams, mousses, soufflés and gâteaux are traditionally served after the cheese board.

Basic Steamed Pudding
150 g (6 oz) self-raising flour
Pinch of salt
75 g (3 oz) butter
75 g (3 oz) caster sugar
1 beaten egg
75–90 ml (5–6 tablespoons) milk

Sift flour and salt into bowl. Rub in butter finely. Add sugar. Mix to fairly soft consistency with egg and milk. Stir briskly until well combined. Transfer to a prepared pudding basin and *steam* for 1½–2 hours.

Alternatively *bake* pudding at 190°C (375°F) Gas Mark 5, for 15 minutes and reduce temperature to 160°C (325°F) Gas Mark 3 and bake for a further 35-40 minutes. Serves 4.

Preparing a pudding basin
Lightly butter a ¾–1 litre (1½–2 pt) pudding basin and line the base with a small round of greaseproof paper. Fill the basin ⅔ of the way up with mixture and make a cover with a piece of buttered,

greaseproof paper. Cover with a sheet of pleated aluminium foil and secure with string, making a handle to make lifting out easier.

Traditionally, steamed suet puddings are spooned directly into a cloth and knotted at the top. *Steam* in a large saucepan, on a trivet or in a steamer or pressure cooker, keeping the water halfway up the basin side and maintained at a very gentle simmer.

For a further selection of steamed pudding recipes see *The Dairy Book of Home Cookery*, page 150.

JELLIES, MOULDS AND MOUSSES

Light, delicate desserts, set by gelatine, these desserts can be prepared and chilled well in advance of serving.

Using gelatine In order for the dessert to set properly, the gelatine must be completely dissolved. Sprinkle 1 envelope or 3 rounded teaspoons powdered gelatine into warm water and stir briskly. Stand the container in a pan of warm water over low heat and stir until the gelatine is dissolved, when the solution turns clear. If you are making a milk jelly, never add gelatine to very hot milk or it will curdle, nor to icy cold milk mixtures, as they would then set in small rubbery globules.

This amount will set 575–600 ml (1 pint). Add the dissolved gelatine while it is cool, but not set, to a little liquid brought to room temperature. Mix thoroughly and then add the dissolved gelatine solution to the other liquid ingredients. It should stir in easily.

Basic Milk Jelly
20 ml (4 level teaspoons) powdered gelatine
45 ml (3 tablespoons) hot water
50 g (2 oz) caster sugar
575 ml (1 pt) milk

Put gelatine and hot water in a basin. Stir over pan of boiling water until gelatine is dissolved; meanwhile put sugar and milk into saucepan. Stand over very low heat until sugar dissolves. Take off heat when gelatine and milk are both lukewarm, combine by pouring milk gently on to the gelatine, stirring well. Pour into a ¾ litre (1½pt) mould, first rinsed with cold water. Leave to set in the refrigerator and turn out on to a serving plate. Serves 4.

Basic Cream Mould
45 ml (3 tablespoons) water
15 g (½ oz) granulated sugar
15 ml (3 level teaspoons) powdered gelatine
275 ml (½ pt) fresh double cream
275 ml (½ pt) sweetened cold custard
5 ml (1 teaspoon) vanilla essence

Put water, sugar and gelatine in a basin. Stir over a pan of boiling water until gelatine and sugar are dissolved. Leave until cool. Whip cream until lightly stiff. Remove any skin from custard, beat until completely smooth, then whisk in cooled gelatine solution and vanilla essence. Fold in whipped cream, then leave in refrigerator until mixture just begins to thicken and set, stirring occasionally. Transfer to ¾ litre (1½ pt) mould, first rinsed with cold water. Chill until firm and set. Turn out on to plate and serve with fruit. Serves 4–5.

Basic Cold Soufflé

15 ml (3 level teaspoons)
  powdered gelatine
45 ml (3 tablespoons)
  hot water
2 eggs (size 1 or 2), separated
50 g (2 oz) caster sugar
Grated rind and juice of
  1 lemon
150 ml (¼ pt) fresh
  double cream
For decoration: 40 g (1½ oz)
  finely chopped, shelled
  walnut halves or blanched
  and toasted almonds; 60 ml
  (4 tablespoons) fresh
  double cream, whipped;
  angelica stems or
  crystallized violet petals

Tie 10 cm (4 in) strip of doubled greaseproof paper round
a 575/600 ml (1 pt) soufflé
dish, making sure paper
stands 4–5 cm (1½–2 in) above
edge of dish. Brush inside of
strip with salad oil.

Put gelatine and hot water

in a basin. Stir until dissolved, over a pan of boiling
water. Whisk egg yolks and
sugar together in a bowl over
a pan of hot water until very
thick and pale. Remove bowl
from hot water and continue
whisking until mixture is
cool. Gently whisk in
dissolved gelatine, lemon
zest and juice. Keep in a cool
place until just beginning to
thicken and set. Meanwhile
whisk cream until fairly
stiff, and beat egg whites to a
stiff snow.

Gently fold lemon mix-
ture into cream, and fold in
beaten whites. Pour into prepared soufflé dish (mixture
should reach almost to top of
paper). Chill until firm and
set. Just before serving, ease
paper away from mixture
with a knife dipped in hot
water and discard. Gently

Pies, syllabubs, meringues, ice
cream, cream moulds and
mousses are all popular desserts.
Decoration can make a simple
sweet look splendid.

press chopped nuts against
sides of the soufflé. Decorate with whipped cream and
angelica or crystallized violets. Serves 4.

Basic Mousse

450 g (1 lb) fruit
  (raspberries or
  strawberries)
3 eggs (size 2)
2 egg yolks
100 g (4 oz) caster
  sugar
15 ml (1 tablespoon)
  powdered gelatine
  (20 ml [4 teaspoons] for
  a firmer set)
45 ml (3 tablespoons) water
275 ml (½ pt) double cream,
  whipped
Grated chocolate

Reserve a few fruit for decoration and put the remainder in a pan over gentle heat and simmer for 5 minutes, until soft.

Rub fruit through a sieve into a bowl. Whisk all the eggs and sugar over a pan of hot but not boiling water until thick and creamy and the mixture leaves a trail over the surface. Remove from the heat, place the bowl in a bowl of iced water and whisk until thick and cool. Dissolve the gelatine and water over a pan of boiling water, stir quickly into fruit and whisk in egg mixture. Fold the whipped cream into fruit mixture when beginning to set. Spoon into serving dish and decorate with grated chocolate and reserved fruit. Serves 4.

For a further selection of cold desserts see *The Dairy Book of Home Cookery*, pp. 157-170.

SYLLABUBS
Syllabubs are creamy, smooth and rich. They are made with eggs, cream and sugar, and subtly flavoured with sherry, marsala, sweet wine, brandy or liqueur. The most popular is probably lemon syllabub. The lemon offsets the richness and makes the syllabub an excellent dessert for a special meal. It is, of course, prepared in advance, which is always useful when you are entertaining. Let the sugar absorb the flavour of the liquor before mixing.

Basic Syllabub
150 ml (¼ pt) white wine
30 ml (2 tablespoons)
   lemon juice
10 ml (2 level teaspoons)
   finely grated lemon rind
75 g (3 oz) caster sugar
275 ml (½ pt) fresh double
   cream

Put wine, lemon juice, zest and sugar into a bowl. Leave for minimum of 3 hours. Add the cream and whip until the mixture stands in soft peaks, then transfer to 6 sundae glasses and place in refrigerator until ready to serve. Serves 6.

EGG CUSTARDS
Custards can be divided into *pouring sauces,* used to accompany puddings, pies and stewed fruit, and *baked* or *steamed* — puddings in themselves.

The greatest difficulty in making egg custards is to prevent the egg from curdling; do not over-cook at too high a temperature or add the egg too quickly to hot liquid. For a pouring sauce use a basin standing over a pan of simmering water or a double saucepan. Five ml (1 teaspoon) blended cornflour will help to prevent a pouring custard from curdling. Stand the dish or dishes for a set custard which is to be cooked in an oven, such as crème caramel, in a *bain marie*: a heatproof dish placed inside a roasting tin which has been half-filled with cold water.

Basic Custard Sauce
2 eggs (size 3)
10 ml (2 level teaspoons)
   caster sugar
275 ml (½ pt) milk
2·5 ml (¼ teaspoon) vanilla
   essence (optional)

Beat eggs with sugar and 45 ml (3 tablespoons) milk. Heat rest of milk to lukewarm, and beat into eggs. Pour into top half of double saucepan over gentle heat and cook, stirring frequently, without boiling, until it thickens.

Pour into jug and stir in vanilla essence. Serve hot or cold. Serves 4–6.

Basic Baked Egg Custard
3 eggs (size 1 or 2) or
   yolks of 4 eggs (size 3)
575 ml (1 pt) milk
25 g (1 oz) caster sugar
Grated nutmeg

Beat eggs with milk and strain into a ¾ litre (1½ pt) buttered heatproof dish; stir in sugar. Sprinkle surface lightly with nutmeg and stand the dish in a roasting tin half filled with water. Bake in the centre of the oven at 160°C (325°F), Gas Mark 3 for up to an hour. Serves 4.

For a further selection of egg custard recipes, see *The Dairy Book of Home Cookery,* p. 149 — Coffee, Chocolate, Orange and Lemon Custard p. 139 and Crème Caramel p. 163.

TRIFLES
Trifles are layers and layers of delicious ingredients. It is like having several desserts in one: sponge soaked with liqueur, fruit, home-made custard and lashings of whipped cream. And a trifle need not stop there. Fruit, nuts, crushed caramel, chocolate, glacé and crystallized fruit can all be used as decorations.

Sugared trifle sponges are nicest for the base. Soak these with a liqueur or other alcohol to complement the fruit you will be using. Sherry, Cointreau, Marsala or brandy can all be used. If you do not want to use alcohol, fruit juice can be used instead. Top with your chosen fruit (fresh or cooked) and a thick pouring custard.

Spread generously with whipped cream and decorate as you wish.

Basic Trifle

1 stale sponge cake
or 6 trifle sponges
Strawberry or raspberry jam
(optional)
425 g (15 oz) fresh or cooked
fruit, canned sliced
peaches or pear halves
30 ml (2 tablespoons) sherry
575 ml (1 pt) thick custard
275 ml (½ pt) fresh double
cream
Toasted almonds

Cut sponge cake(s) into slices and arrange in a large glass trifle dish or spread the fingers over the base. If desired, spread with strawberry or other red jam. If using canned fruit, drain (reserving the juice) and reserve some fruit for decoration. When you use fresh fruit, reserve a few berries or slices. Sprinkle sherry and drained fruit juice on sponge then add most of the fruit, spread on top of the sponge. Spoon on warm thick custard and leave until cold. Whip cream and spoon or pipe over the custard. Decorate with reserved fruit and almonds. Chill before serving. Serves 4.

MERINGUES

Meringues, made from egg whites, provide the topping for many appetizing desserts. Meringue shells can make delicious sweets, filled with raspberries or oranges and fresh cream. Take care to make sure the whisk and bowl are clean and free from any traces of egg yolk. Use eggs at room temperature and use a balloon whisk or an electric mixer.

Basic Meringue
2 egg whites
100 g (4 oz) caster sugar
Pre-heat the oven to 110°C

(225°F) Gas Mark ¼. Put egg whites into a clean dry bowl and whisk until stiff and in peaks. Add half the caster sugar a little at a time and continue beating until meringue is smooth and close textured and stands in firm peaks. Fold in rest of sugar, and pipe or spoon rounds of this mixture on to a baking tray covered with rice paper or non-stick greaseproof paper. Bake in the oven until dry and crisp but not brown.

Halfway through the cooking the meringues can be taken out and the base pressed in lightly to make space for a filling. Turn over shells and return to oven. Remove and cool on wire rack.

Alternatively the meringues can be piped into 2 circles and, when cooked, sandwiched together with fresh cream, fruit or chestnut purée. For more meringue recipes, see *The Dairy Book of Home Cookery*, pp. 226–227.

ICE CREAM AND SORBETS

Ice cream and sorbets are delicious and easy to make at home. Ice cream is basically a custard enriched with fresh double cream and a sorbet is a water ice, a sugar syrup flavoured with fruit juice or purée. The right sugar content is important for the consistency of the ice cream or sorbet, and you must freeze it quickly.

Dairy Ice Cream

275 ml (½ pt) fresh single
cream
75 g (3 oz) caster sugar
2 eggs (size 1 or 2)
5 ml (1 teaspoon) vanilla
essence
275 ml (½ pt) double cream

Turn refrigerator to the coldest setting or the freezer dial to 'quick-freeze' about 1 hour

before proceeding. Heat single cream. Cream together sugar and eggs and add cream. Cook over hot water until thick. Stir in vanilla essence. Strain mixture into ice-cube tray or loaf tin. Freeze for 45 minutes or until it has frozen about 1 cm (½ in) around the edges of the tray. Pour mixture into bowl and beat thoroughly. Add double cream, lightly whipped. Return to tray or tin and refreeze for 2 hours or until firm. Transfer to the refrigerator for 30 minutes before serving.

For further ice cream recipes, see *The Dairy Book of Home Cookery*, pp. 171–174.

Basic Sorbet

275 ml (½ pt) water
100 g (4 oz) caster sugar
225 g (½ lb) fresh or frozen
fruit (blackcurrants or
similar)
2 egg whites

Heat sugar and water gently, until sugar has dissolved. Bring to the boil then simmer for 10 minutes until you have a concentrated sugar syrup. Set aside to cool.

Prepare fruit and cook over low heat, with 30–45 ml (2–3 tablespoons) of water, for 10 minutes. Rub through a sieve into a bowl to form a purée. Make up to 575 ml (1 pt) with sugar syrup and, when cool, place in a freezer container in the freezer compartment until firm.

Whisk egg whites until stiff. Put the frozen purée in a bowl and break up with a fork, before folding in the whisked egg whites. Return to the container and freeze until firm. To avoid separation of the egg whites the mixture may have to be rewhisked at intervals throughout the freezing process. Serves 4–6.

FOOD AND COOKERY

MAKING PASTRY

The art of making pastry has been surrounded by much mystique but it is simply the skill of combining fat, flour and water in the correct proportions according to your recipe; handling lightly but firmly in a cool environment; and baking in a hot oven. To obtain good light, crisp results, make sure ingredients, working surface and utensils are cold: if possible, keep them in the refrigerator before using. Cold hands also help.

After you have prepared the pastry, let it rest for about 20 minutes in a cool place before baking. The amount of water added is important as hard or tough pastry is caused by too much water as well as over-handling; and soft, crumbly pastry which is difficult to roll out, is due to insufficient water.

Basic Shortcrust Pastry
For pies, flans, tarts and pasties. The basic proportions are always half fat to flour.

200 g (8 oz) plain flour
2·5 ml (½ level teaspoon) salt
100 g (4 oz) butter or
  margarine
Cold water to mix —
  allow 5 ml (1 teaspoon) per
  25 g (1 oz) flour

Sift flour and salt into bowl. Add fat and cut into flour with a knife. Rub with fingertips until it resembles breadcrumbs. Sprinkle water over and mix to stiff paste with a blunt knife. Draw together with your fingertips, turn out on to lightly floured board and roll out as required. Bake according to recipe.

If not used immediately, transfer to polythene bag or wrap in aluminium foil and place in refrigerator.

Rich Shortcrust Pastry
For excellent sweet pastry, for mince pies and fruit tarts.

200 g (8 oz) plain flour
Pinch of salt
125 g (5 oz) butter
1 egg yolk
7·5 ml (1½ level teaspoons)
  caster sugar
20-25 ml (4-5 teaspoons)
  water

Make in the same way as basic shortcrust pastry, adding sugar and egg yolk with the water. Chill and roll out.

Rolling out and baking pastry
First lightly flour a pastry board. Use a rolling pin with short light movements, turning the pastry. Roll to a thickness of about 0.5 cm (¼ in). Use the dish as a guide to size and use the rolling pin to lift the pastry into the dish. If

making a pie, reserve some pastry for the lid. Press firmly into position excluding all air pockets and avoid stretching, which could cause the pastry to shrink back from the edges during cooking. Prick the bottom with a fork and fill. When making a pie, roll out the covering and seal the edges with water. Make a slit in the centre to let out the steam during baking. Bake at 200°C (400°F) Gas Mark 6.

Baking blind This is the term applied to baking a pastry flan case before adding the filling. Line a flan ring placed on a baking sheet. Place a sheet of greaseproof paper or aluminium foil on the base and sides of the flan ring, and press down the pastry. Add dried beans to weigh down the pastry as it cooks. Bake for 15 minutes at 200°C (400°F) Gas Mark 6 and remove paper before baking for a further 5–10 minutes until evenly browned.

Finishing and decorating Leftover strips of pastry can be used to make pastry leaves or tassels on a pie: brush with an egg wash, using beaten egg yolk mixed with a little water. Brush sweet pies with milk. Make a slit in the

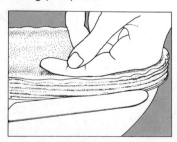
Use your fingers and a knife to seal the edges of a pie and then to knock up and flute.

When baking blind, cover the pastry with greaseproof paper and weigh down with dried beans.

Leftover pastry can be used to make decorations for the top, in leaf-shapes for example.

centre to let out the steam and finish the edges of pies by crimping with the thumb or with the back of a fork. For open flans make a lattice effect, by interweaving long pieces of pastry. For cheese pastry see *The Dairy Book of Home Cookery*, p. 212.

Suet Crust
For boiled and steamed puddings.

200 g (8 oz) self-raising
  flour
2·5 ml (½ level teaspoon) salt
5 ml (1 level teaspoon) baking
  powder
100 g (4 oz) shredded
  beef suet
125 ml (¼ pt) cold water
  to mix

Sift flour, salt and baking powder into bowl. Add suet and mix to a soft paste with water. Turn out on to floured board. Knead until smooth and roll out to about 0.5 cm (¼ in) thickness. Use the pastry as required.

Lining and covering a pudding basin From the rolled-out pastry, cut out a quarter of it to use as a lid. Fold the rest around a greased 1.2 litre (2 pt) pudding basin, moulding to fit. Roll the remaining pastry for the cover. Put in the filling, cover, and brush the edges with water; seal. Cover with a pleated piece of greaseproof paper to allow for expansion during cook-

ing. Place cloth over and tie string around the rim of the basin or use aluminium foil as a lid.

Hot-Water Crust Pastry
For raised pies.

300 g (12 oz) plain flour
2·5 ml (½ level teaspoon) salt
1 egg yolk (size 3)
60 ml (4 tablespoons) milk
60 ml (4 tablespoons) water
25 g (1 oz) butter
75 g (3 oz) lard

Sift flour and salt into bowl; make a well in the centre. Beat yolk with 15 ml (1 tablespoon) milk and pour into well. Pour rest of milk and water into saucepan. Add butter and lard. Heat slowly until butter and lard melt, stirring all the time. Bring to a brisk boil. Pour into the bowl and mix with a wooden spoon until ingredients are well blended.

Turn out on to floured board and knead quickly until smooth. Put into bowl or basin standing over pan of hot water. Cover with clean tea-towel and leave to rest for 30 minutes.

Roll out warm pastry to 0.5 cm (¼ in) thickness and use as required.

Raised Pie Using hot-water crust pastry cut two-thirds of it off to use to mould around the base of a jam jar or alternatively to line a loose-

bottomed cake tin or pie mould. Keep the rest of the pastry in a warm place, wrapped in greaseproof paper. With a 900 g (2 lb) jam jar, mould the warm dough two-thirds of the way up the jar and remove when cool. Fill with meat, often diced pork and veal, well seasoned, and cover the pie with the remaining pastry. Seal by moistening the edges and, with scissors, cut the border and make a slit in the centre of the lid. Decorate with pastry leaves, brush with beaten egg and surround with a protective layer of paper tied with string, to prevent collapsing. Bake at 220°C (425°F) Gas Mark 7 for 20 minutes. Reduce to 150°C (300°F) Gas Mark 2 and bake for a further 1½ hours, testing with a skewer when cooked. Pour stock in through the centre hole and leave to set before serving.

Choux Pastry
An easy pastry to make for superb chocolate éclairs and delicious profiteroles.

75 g (2½ oz) plain flour
Pinch of salt
150 ml (¼ pt) water
50 g (2 oz) butter
2 eggs (size 3), well beaten

Sift flour and salt. Put water and butter into a saucepan and heat slowly until butter melts, then bring to a brisk

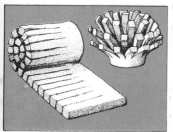
Make a tassel by cutting evenly along a strip of pastry, rolling it up and opening out the top.

To line a pudding basin, roll the pastry (see above), fold in four and lower into the basin.

To add liquid to a pie, leave a hole in the middle and pour in stock through a funnel.

FOOD AND COOKERY

boil. Lower heat and add all the flour. Stir briskly until ingredients form a soft mix and leave the sides of the pan clean. Remove from heat, cool slightly and add eggs gradually, beating hard until mixture is smooth, shiny and firm enough to stand in soft peaks when lifted with a spoon. Use immediately, or leave in saucepan covered with the lid to prevent drying out. For a variety of recipes using choux pastry, see *The Dairy Book of Home Cookery,* pp. 169 and 242.

Flaky Pastry

150 g (6 oz) butter
200 g (8 oz) plain flour
1·25 ml (¼ level teaspoon) salt
125 ml (¼ pt) chilled water
5 ml (1 teaspoon) lemon juice

Divide butter into four equal portions and chill three of them. Sift flour and salt into bowl. Rub in unchilled portion of butter. Mix to soft paste with water and lemon juice. Turn on to floured board and knead thoroughly. Put into polythene bag or wrap in aluminium foil. Chill.

Roll out to 0.5 cm (¼ in) thick rectangle, measuring about 45 cm x 15 cm (18 in x 6 in). Using tip of knife, spread one chilled portion of butter (in small flakes) over the top third and middle third of rectangle to within 2.5 cm (1 in) of edges. Dust lightly with sieved flour.

Fold in three, envelope style, by bringing bottom third over middle third and folding top third over. Seal open edges by pressing firmly together. Put into polythene bag or wrap in aluminium foil and chill for 15 minutes. Remove from bag or unwrap. With folded edges to left and right, roll out again into 45 cm x 15 cm (18 in x 6 in) rectangle. Cover with third portion of butter as before. Fold, seal and chill. Repeat again, adding last portion of butter, and chill. Roll out again. Fold and seal, return to polythene bag or wrap in aluminium foil. Chill.

Roll out to 0.5 cm (¼ in) thickness and shape according to your recipe. Rest for 20–30 minutes in a cool place before baking in a pre-heated oven at 220°C (425°F) Gas Mark 7 for 15–20 minutes.

Rough Puff Pastry

200 g (8 oz) plain flour
1·25 ml (¼ level teaspoon) salt
150 g (6 oz) butter
125 ml (¼ pt) chilled water
5 ml (1 teaspoon) lemon juice

Sift flour and salt into bowl. Cut butter into tiny dice and mix together water and lemon juice. Add butter to flour, using a knife, to mix to a fairly soft, crumbly paste with water and lemon juice.

Draw together with fingertips, turn out on to floured board and shape into block. Roll out to 0.5 cm (¼ in) thick rectangle, measuring about 45 cm x 15 cm (18 in x 6 in). Fold in three, envelope style, by bringing bottom third over middle third and folding top third over. Seal open edges by pressing firmly together. Give pastry a quarter turn so that folded edges are to right and left. Roll out, fold and turn three more times before baking.

If possible, put folded pastry into polythene bag (or wrap in aluminium foil) and chill about 15 minutes between rollings. Use according to the recipe you are following.

Puff Pastry

225 g (8 oz) butter
225 g (8 oz) plain flour
1·25 ml (¼ level teaspoon) salt
5 ml (1 teaspoon) lemon juice
Chilled water to mix

Put butter into clean cloth, squeeze well to remove surplus moisture and to make it soft and pliable. Shape into 12.5 cm (5 in) square block. Sift flour and salt into bowl. Mix to soft paste (about same consistency as butter) with lemon juice and water. Turn out on to floured board and knead well. Roll out to rectangle measuring 30 cm x 15 cm (12 in x 6 in).

Stand butter on lower half of the pastry rectangle. Bring top half over so that butter is completely enclosed. Press open edges firmly together and put into polythene bag or wrap in aluminium foil. Chill.

Remove from wrapping. With fold on right, roll to a 45 cm x 15 cm (18 in x 6 in) rectangle, and fold in three as for flaky pastry. Seal edges, wrap and chill. Repeat, until pastry has been rolled, folded and chilled seven times. Return to polythene bag or wrap in aluminium foil. Chill at least 30 minutes before rolling out to 0.5 cm (¼ in) thickness and shaping according to your recipe. After shaping, let the pastry rest 30 minutes in a cool place before baking in a pre-heated oven.

To make a variety of exciting dishes using these pastries see *The Dairy Book of Home Cookery,* pp. 34–35 (vol-au-vents);p. 200 (cheese and onion pasties); p. 238 (cream horns); p. 242 (cream slices).

MAKING BREAD

There is nothing quite like the aroma and flavour of home-made bread — and if it is made in bulk, loaves and rolls can last several weeks in the freezer. In fact loaves will keep for months.

Flour For the best results use 'strong' flour (with high gluten content) to obtain a large volume and open texture. Dense, coarse textured brown bread with a nutty taste can be produced from wholemeal flour (containing 100 per cent wheat) or wheatmeal flour (80–90 per cent wheat, including germ and some bran).

Yeast Buy fresh yeast which is creamy in colour, firm to touch and easy to break. Keeps up to 5 days in a cool place.

It is essential that all equipment is warm, as yeast is killed by extreme heat or cold during fermenting. However, yeast can be stored, deep frozen, successfully. Dried yeast is more convenient because it can be stored for a much longer time (up to six months) and so is ideal in times of emergency.

Remember that dried yeast is more concentrated: 25 g (1 oz) fresh yeast equals 15 g (½ oz) dried yeast.

Salt Important to improve flavour and strengthen the gluten in the flour, but too much will destroy the yeast, resulting in heavy, uneven bread.

Liquid Water alone, or a mixture of water and milk, can be used to produce the correct consistency.

Fat Used to soften and en-

rich doughs for making buns, tea bread and savarins.

Sugar Important for the bread to rise, as it is a source of food for the yeast although too much will kill the yeast.

Kneading and rising Kneading is essential for the strengthening and development of the gluten, to enable the bread to rise. Push the dough over towards you, pushing down and away with the knuckles and giving the dough a quarter turn before repeating the procedure. Alternatively, use the dough hook on the mixer, until the dough becomes firm and elastic. Cover with a lightly greased polythene bag and allow about 1 hour in a warm place (airing cupboard or over a pan of hot water). Alternatively, leave to rise in the refrigerator overnight and, before shaping, return the dough to room temperature. Short-time bread requires no rising stage.

Knocking back and proving Re-knead to knock out the air

1 Cottage 2 Cholla 3 French
4 Bloomer 5 Farmhouse
6 Sesame 7 Light rye
8 Wheatmeal 9 Scoffa
10–13 Small Rolls 14 Pot
15 Milk 16 Dark rye
17 Granary 18 Wholemeal
19 Currant loaf 20 Date loaf

FOOD AND COOKERY

bubbles, and to produce a well-risen and even-textured loaf. *Knock back*, throwing the dough on to a board, pounding it with your fists, and throwing it down again on the breadboard. Repeat the process three times. Shape as shown below, put into tins, cover with greased polythene and leave to rise at room temperature until double in size (*proving*).

Baking Remove polythene and bake in a hot oven at 200–230°C (400–450°F) Gas Mark 6—8, according to the recipe. Loaves will take 30–35 minutes and rolls 15–20 minutes. It helps to improve the texture of the loaf if a bowl of hot water is placed at the bottom of the oven to create steam. On removal the bread should be golden brown.

Short-time Bread Recipe
25 g (1 oz) fresh yeast
25 mg ascorbic acid
450 ml (¾ pt) warm water
675 g (1½ lb) strong flour
15 ml (1 tablespoon) salt
5 ml (1 teaspoon) caster sugar
15 g (½ oz) butter

Dissolve yeast and ascorbic acid in water. Sift dry ingredients into a bowl. Rub in butter. Add liquid and bind mixture. Knead, wrap in polythene and leave to rise. Knock back and shape into tin. Wrap and leave in a warm place until double.

FAULTS IN BREAD-MAKING

Coarse, open texture Too much liquid; over-proving; oven too cool.

Texture uneven, with large holes Incorrect knocking back; insufficient mixing; over-proving.

Heavy, close texture Insufficient kneading or proving; yeast killed.

Crumbly and stales quickly Over-proving; oven at too low temperature; flour too soft; too much yeast.

Yeasty flavour Too much or stale yeast; over-proving.

Pale crust Cool oven; insufficient sugar.

Dark crust Hot oven; too much sugar.

Thick crust Oven too cool.

Loaf rises over tin Too much dough in tin; over-proving.

Cracks in crust Too much liquid; under-proving; oven too hot.

Flat top Poor shaping of dough; dough too wet; insufficient salt.

Dough collapses when put into oven Over-proving.

For a variety of recipes, see *The Dairy Book of Home Cookery* pp. 248–255.

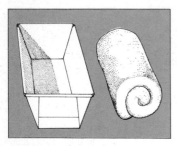

Shaping Roll up like a Swiss roll or fold in three and put in tin with fold at the bottom.

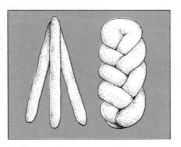

Plait Roll out three strips of dough with a slight bulge in the centre of each and plait loosely.

Coburg Roll dough into a ball and flatten slightly. Cut a cross into the top before proving.

Cottage Two balls, one half the size of the other. Put small ball on top and indent with a spoon.

Crown Divide dough into six balls and arrange with sides touching in a cake tin.

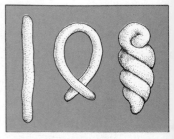

Twist Pull one end of a strip of dough over the other. Twist the loop on itself and tuck in ends.

MAKING CAKES

There are various basic ways of making cakes. Rubbing in is the simplest, with or without eggs; creaming is the method used for rich cakes; the whisking method produces fat-free sponges and the melting method moist cakes such as gingerbread.

Baking cakes is easy and satisfying but faults can occur sometimes, for the following reasons.

Badly shaped cake Tin unevenly lined; careless filling; wrong consistency.

Sunken cake Excess raising agent; oven too slow; underbaking; opening the oven door and letting in cold air.

Close, heavy texture Oven too slow; underbaking; mixture too wet; insufficient raising agent.

Coarse, open texture Excess raising agent; uneven mixing in of flour.

Peak top or cracked top Tin too small; oven too hot; tin placed too high in the oven.

Dry cake Insufficient liquid; excess raising agent.

Speckled, hard sugary crust Excess sugar; oven too slow; sugar too coarse.

Uneven rising Tilted and unevenly placed in oven or oven may need adjusting.

Preparing the Cake Tin Grease lightly with melted fat or oil and line with greaseproof paper or foil. For a rich fruit cake, which requires long cooking, use double greaseproof paper and surround the outside of the tin with a double sheet of greaseproof paper to prevent overcooking. Small paper cases can be used on a baking sheet for buns. See *The Dairy Book of Home Cookery*, p. 229.

Fats Butter or margarine are best for cake-making; they give a good flavour and longer keeping time to the cake.

Flour If self-raising flour is used there is no need to add any additional raising agent. For rich fruit cakes and whisked sponges, plain flour should be used, with a quantity of raising agent accord-

A selection of cakes to make at home and serve for both family and party teas. Rich fruit cakes and cream-filled sponges, moist flapjacks, buttery scones topped with jam and cream, and home-made biscuits with nuts and fruit are all equally tempting and delicious to eat.

FOOD AND COOKERY

ing to the recipe. Sieve together before use.

Raising Agents Use cream of tartar and bicarbonate of soda in a 2 to 1 ratio to make baking powder. More often, buy it ready made. Yeast and eggs are other raising agents.

Eggs Eggs act as a raising agent and also help to bind the ingredients together in plain cakes.

Sugar Caster sugar is ideal for sponges although it is more expensive than granulated sugar. Brown or Demerara sugar makes good gingerbread and parkin and additionally gives a rich, dark appearance.

Fruit Wash dried fruit and glacé cherries and dry thoroughly. Coat fruit in some of the weighed flour, to prevent sinking during cooking. Chop large pieces of candied peel, dates and nuts.

Baking Times vary and so do temperatures; see individual recipes.

Cooling Leave to settle for a few minutes before moving a knife around the cake tin. Once the cake is ready, carefully turn it upside down on to a rack to allow it to cool before filling or icing.

Storing Most cakes are best eaten fresh, but gingerbread and rich fruit cakes improve on keeping, and should be stored, wrapped in aluminium foil, and placed in air-tight tins. Never store both cakes and biscuits in the same tin, otherwise the biscuits will go soft. Refrigerate all cream cakes.

RUBBED-IN CAKES
Use no more than half the ratio of fat to flour.
225 g (8 oz) plain flour
10 ml (2 teaspoons) baking powder
a pinch of salt
50-75 g (2-3 oz) fat
50-75 g (2-3 oz) sugar
50-100 g (2-4 oz) flavouring (nuts, fruit etc)
150 ml (¼ pt) milk

Sift the dry ingredients (flour, salt, baking powder and spices) first; then rub in the fat. Add sugar and any dried fruit, according to the recipe. Make a well in the mixture.

Beat the eggs thoroughly and mix into the well of the cake mixture, with any liquid flavouring. Bake small cakes in a hot oven, large cakes in a slow oven.

See pp. 237 and 239 of *The Dairy Book of Home Cookery*.

CREAMED CAKES
Creamed cakes are made from equal quantities of fat and flour. It is important that the butter is at room temperature before you start.
100 g (4 oz) softened butter
100 g (4 oz) sugar
2 (size 3) eggs
100 g (4 oz) self-raising flour
pinch of salt
Beat the butter and sugar together vigorously. Add the eggs one at a time and finally the dry ingredients sifted together. Bake at 180°C (350°F) Gas Mark 4 for about 25-30 minutes.

RICH FRUIT CAKES
These are made by the creaming method, with the addition of dried and glacé fruit and chopped peel. The quantities are from 100–650 g (¼–1½ lb) fruit and peel to each 225 g (8 oz) flour. Bake very slowly at 140°C (275°F)

Gas Mark 1 for 2½–3 hours. Make at least 2–3 weeks in advance to allow to mature. Store by wrapping in layers of greaseproof paper or foil.

For almond paste, butter cream frosting, glacé and royal icing, see *The Dairy Book of Home Cookery*, p. 245. For a variety of other rich cake recipes, see *The Dairy Book of Home Cookery*, pp. 232–4.

WHISKED CAKES
Being fat free and, therefore, particularly light these sponges should be baked as soon as they are mixed.
75 g (3 oz) plain flour
a pinch of salt
3 size-2 eggs
75 g (3 oz) caster sugar
Sift the flour and salt on to greaseproof paper. Whisk the eggs and sugar together over hot water until thick and creamy. Fold in the flour. Bake at 190°C (375°F) Gas Mark 5 until just firm and lightly coloured, about 15 minutes.

MELTED CAKES
Moist and sticky cakes are made by this method.
450 g (1 lb) plain flour
45 ml (3 tablespoons) baking powder
a pinch of salt
150 g (6 oz) sugar
150 g (6 oz) fat
150-300 g (6-12 oz) sweet flavouring (golden syrup, honey, marmalade etc)
275 ml (½ pt) milk
The sugar, fat and sweet flavourings are melted and then mixed into the sieved dry ingredients, with the milk. A beaten egg can also be added. Bake at 180°C (350°F) Gas Mark 4 until well risen (1½ hours). Allow to cool for 15 minutes before turning out of tin.

PRESERVING

Preserving has been used since people first learned to cook. Today it is a way of keeping flavours at their best, but in earlier centuries it was a method of survival.

All food is subject to decay from micro-organisms, bacteria, yeasts and moulds. Some are harmless; others, not. The object of preserving food is to inhibit all decay. Sugar, salt, vinegar and alcohol are agents of preservation. Heat treatment can preserve fruit, a traditional method of preserving being drying, and freezing is a new one. Canning is greatly used commercially.

You do not have to be a self-sufficiency enthusiast to enjoy making preserves at home: in fact, more and more people are turning to it. If you have a glut of fruit in your garden, make it into jams, jellies and chutneys, to last through the winter and beyond. Even if you don't have a garden, you can buy red cabbage to make a crisp pickle, which will have a far better flavour than any you can buy in shops. If you visit a pick-it-yourself strawberry farm, pick some extra berries for jam.

One of the greatest pleasures in making preserves is to give them as presents. Add a few drops of liqueur to bottled fruits; present crystalized fruit in pretty, ornamented, gift-wrapped boxes. Home-made gifts are always really appreciated.

Equipment needed A good-quality preserving pan is a worthwhile investment if you intend to make preserves from year to year. Never use a copper pan for pickles or chutneys: the copper reacts with the vinegar and spoils the flavour. If you do not own a preserving pan, use a wide, heavy-based pan made from stainless steel or aluminium. Don't leave fruit to stand in an aluminium pan: the acid may pit the surface of the metal.

You may re-use jars that have been carefully sterilized. Buy commercially produced waxed paper and cellophane seals to cover them. You can use screw-top lids with chutneys and pickles, provided they have plastic linings.

When you make jellies, you can buy a jelly bag, but it is quite easy to strain the juice through some six layers of butter muslin, first scalded; or even use a clean, scalded tea towel.

Choosing fruit and vegetables Choose slightly under-ripe, acid fruit for jams and jellies; even-sized fruit for bottling; crisp, young vegetables for making chutneys and pickles.

PROCESSING TIMES FOR BOTTLING FRUIT

All times are shown in minutes

Fruit	Hot water bath	Pressure cooker	Oven	
berries and currants, apple slices	2	1	Up to 2 kg (4 lb)	40
			2½ to 5 kg (5 to 10 lb)	60
gooseberries, rhubarb, stone fruits (whole), citrus fruits	10	1	Up to 2 kg (4 lb)	50
			2½ to 5 kg (5 to 10 lb)	70
solid-pack apples, purée halved stone fruits, pineapple, strawberries	20	4	Up to 2 kg (4 lb)	60
			2½ to 5 kg (5 to 10 lb)	80
whole tomatoes, figs, pears	40	5	Up to 2 kg (4 lb)	70
			2½ to 5 kg (5 to 10 lb)	90
solid-pack tomatoes	50	15	Up to 2 kg (4 lb)	80
			2½ to 5 kg (5 to 10 lb)	100

FOOD AND COOKERY

JAMS

The best fruit for jam-making contains a high level of pectin, a substance under the skin which, when the fruit is cooked with sugar, helps it to set. Apples, apricots, black and red currants, plums and damsons and sharp gooseberries are ideal. Among fruits low in pectin are strawberries, grapes, pears, rhubarb and cherries. To make a successful set with these, add a fruit rich in pectin: blackberry and apple jam, for example, or strawberry with red currants. Alternatively, add lemon juice, apple, red currant or gooseberry juice, or a commercial pectin. Follow your recipe.

There is a test to find out if there is enough pectin: pour a little cooked juice into a glass containing methylated spirits and swill it around to see if a large clot forms from the juice, in which case, there is sufficient pectin for a firm set.

Sugar Use granulated or the more expensive preserving sugar. Warm in a low oven for about 20 minutes before adding to the cooked fruit for a fast set.

Making jam While you make the jam, put your storage jars into a very low oven to warm.

Prepare the fruit; cut away any bruised parts, rinse, stone or hull. Measure out an equal quantity of sugar to fruit but, if the fruit is sour, you can increase the amount to taste. For low pectin fruit, use also commercially bottled pectin, following the manufacturer's instructions for quantities. Simmer the fruit (and pectin) in a pan, stirring, until it becomes soft and pulpy. Stir in the warmed sugar and bring to the boil, stirring all the time, until the sugar dissolves. Keep at a fast boil until the jam sets, after about 15–20 minutes.

Checking the setting point The easiest method is to use a cold saucer test. Put a saucer in the refrigerator. After the jam has been boiling for about 10 minutes, spoon a little on to the saucer. Push it with your finger. If it wrinkles, it is set. Alternatively, spoon out a little of the jam, and allow it to cool for a few seconds. Drop the jam from the edge of the spoon. If the drops form into flakes which break away clearly and sharply, the jam is ready. You can also use a sugar thermometer: it should register 110°C (230°F).

Skimming, potting and covering If there is any scum on the surface of the jam, skim it off with a metal spoon.

Take the warm jars out of the oven, and pour in the jam, using a small jug or a funnel. Cover immediately. Label, including the date the jam was made, and store in a cool, dark, dry place.

For a variety of recipes for home-made jam, see *The Dairy Book of Home Cookery,* pp. 256–259.

JELLIES

Jellies are made from the juice of cooked fruit, strained through a jelly bag, then brought to the boil and cooked with sugar to a set. Because only the juice is used, the yield is much smaller than that of jams. This explains, in part, why wild and damaged fruit is often used. Traditionally, jellies made from wild fruits complement different meats and game.

MARMALADES

Marmalades are made from citrus fruit. Use Seville oranges for a fine, bitter flavour; or use a mix of sweet oranges, grapefruit, lemon or lime.

COMMON FAULTS IN PRESERVE MAKING

Poor set is usually due to insufficient boiling after the sugar has been added; insufficient acid; overripe fruit or excess sugar in relation to pectin and acid.

Poor colour may be caused by over-boiling after adding the sugar, overripe fruit or insufficient acid.

Sugar crystals are usually due to over-boiling but excess acid could also be the cause.

Air bubbles appear if the jam is left to cool for too long before pouring it into the jars.

Mould on the surface is usually because of insufficient sugar or low sugar concentration. The remedy is to remove the mould, reboil and use for cooking.

Fermentation is caused for the same reasons as mould or because of warm storage.

Cloudy jelly appears if the bag has been squeezed when the juice is pressed through.

Layer of syrup is because of too much acid. For a variety of recipes for home-made jams and marmalades see *The Dairy Book of Home Cookery* pp. 256–259.

PICKLES

Pickles are made from vegetables or fruit, preserved in vinegar.

To make a spiced vinegar For 1 litre (1½ pints) malt, cider or wine vinegar, add a cinnamon stick, and level tablespoons (15 ml) of whole cloves, black peppercorns, allspice berries and blade mace. If you like the flavour, add a dried chilli or peeled garlic clove. Drop the spices into the vinegar, cover and leave for about two months; or bring the vinegar to the boil, add the spices and leave for two hours. To make a sweet, spiced vinegar for fruit, add 900 g (2 lb) sugar to the vinegar, dissolve, and add mace, ginger, cloves, a cinnamon stick, allspice and a slice of lemon peel.

When you pickle vegetables, pack in cooking salt overnight; then rinse and dry. Cover with vinegar.

Poach fruit in the sweetened vinegar before packing in jars and sealing.

CHUTNEYS

These are a mixture of fruit (such as apples and tomatoes), sugar and spiced vinegar; cooked to the consistency of jam. They are at their best after three months.

BOTTLING FRUIT

Bottling sterilizes fruit to prevent contamination from micro-organisms. It is an excellent method of preserving fruit — in a sugar syrup for best results — to retain its flavour.

Before the advent of freezers, bottling was one of the most usual methods of preservation: it is now popular again. You may flavour bottled fruit with brandy, a liqueur, or a reduced, sweetened wine. Add lemon or orange zest, and spices.

Preparing fruit for bottling Make a syrup, using about 225 g (8 oz) sugar dissolved in 575/600 ml (1 pint) water. As an alternative, flavour with honey or golden syrup, dissolved in the water.

Prepare the fruit, peeling, halving and stoning as necessary. Have ready well-rinsed bottling jars: those most often on sale are Kilner or Le Parfait. Fill the jars with fruit, pour over hot syrup, remove air bubbles and seal the lids, according to the manufacturers' instructions.

Process in a hot water bath by placing the jars on a trivet, making sure they do not touch each other, in a deep, wide pan. Cover with warm water up to the lids of the jars and heat the water up to 88°C (190°F) over 30 minutes, or for the time recommended.

Alternatively, use a pressure cooker, using water 2.5 cm (1 in) up the jars, and bring to 2½ kg (5 lb) pressure for the recommended time; or process in the oven.

BOTTLING VEGETABLES

There is a rare but potentially fatal spore in vegetables which causes botulism poisoning. This spore is killed in acid — which is why bottled fruit is safe — but can thrive in the low-acid environment of bottled vegetables, even when heat-processed. As a result, *bottling vegetables is not recommended*.

When you bottle tomatoes, make sure you add a teaspoon of lemon juice because most varieties available are less acidic than they once were.

OTHER METHODS OF PRESERVING

Drying This is the oldest method of food preservation. Use it if you have access to gentle heat, with free circulation of air: in an airing cupboard or Aga stove. You may dry fruit in an oven, but it is expensive in fuel.

Apple and pear rings, plums and mushrooms dry well. Dip in salt water and spread out on a cake rack or sew on a string, with space between.

Salting There are many ways of salting meat, fish and vegetables. Check your recipe and remember that salting at home does not ensure long-term preservation, although it adds flavour when the food is cooked.

Storing Apples, pears and root vegetables can be stored over winter. Keep them in a cool, dry, dark place.

Smoking To preserve meat or fish by smoking requires presalting, drying in a cool place, with a regulated temperature, and then smoking in a cold smoker. This is not practicable to attempt at home, unless you have ideal conditions and a fair amount of experience.

The flavour of smoked food can be achieved at home though, using a hot smoker. There are several different makes on the market and the process is not difficult. The smoking kits come complete with instructions and recipes and everything that you will need apart from methylated spirits. The kits are very compact too.

Many different foods can be hot smoked. Remember, you are not preserving the food, simply cooking it and adding flavour. Fish, meat sausages, bacon, ham, poultry, cheese and some vegetables can be hot smoked.

FOOD AND COOKERY

FREEZING

Freezing is the most recent, simplest, and one of the best methods of preserving food. The kind of freezer you buy will be determined by the size of your family and the space at your disposal. In addition, most refrigerators have a freezing compartment which will keep frozen food for one to three months, according to the star markings shown.

Packaging Food must be good quality and carefully wrapped as cold air inside a freezer dries out food. Heavy duty polythene, aluminium foil or purpose-made cardboard containers with lids are ideal. If you are packaging food in a polythene bag, suck out any air with a straw or squeeze the pack before securing. Label with freezing and 'use-by' dates, type of food and weight. Pack carefully: bad packaging will cause cross-flavouring and 'freezer burn'.

Freeze food quickly by setting the 'fast freeze' switch a few hours beforehand to avoid the food having a poor appearance and poor texture on thawing. Once food has been frozen on the coldest shelves, it can be transferred to storage compartments and the dial reset. Make an inventory of all foods in stock.

Thawing Food taken from the freezer should be thawed slowly in a refrigerator or a cool place. Foods containing a high proportion of liquid must be heated slowly. Thawed foods should never be re-frozen.

In a power failure, do not open the door; the food will keep cold up to 24 hours.

MEAT
Preparation Remove excess fat. Wrap in aluminium foil, then overwrap in thick polythene bags. Interleave chops, steaks and hamburgers with greaseproof or waxed paper.

Storage life See chart given on p. 16.

Thawing times For steaks, chops and stewing steak, five to six hours in the refrigerator; two to four hours at room temperature. For a joint under 1.5 kg (3 lb 4 oz), six to seven hours per 450 g (1 lb) in the refrigerator; two to three hours at room temperature. For a joint over 1.5 kg (3 lb 4 oz), six to seven hours per 450 g (1 lb) in the refrigerator; two to four hours at room temperature.

POULTRY AND GAME
Preparation Remove the giblets from poultry and game birds. Wrap in foil, then in heavy-duty polythene.

Storage life Chicken, one year; game birds, six to eight months; turkey, six months; duck and goose, four to six months.

Thawing times For a whole bird, eight hours per 450 g (1 lb) in the refrigerator. For joints, two to three hours per 450 g (1 lb). Thaw completely before cooking.

FISH AND SHELLFISH
Preparation Clean and fillet. Small fish can be frozen whole. Use greaseproof or waxed paper between individual portions. Pack in thick polythene bags or foil.

Storage life White fish, six to eight months; oily fish, three to four months; shellfish, two to three months.

Thawing times Large fish in the refrigerator for six hours; fillets and steaks for three hours. Cook thawed fish immediately. Small fish can be cooked from frozen.

VEGETABLES
Most vegetables must be blanched in boiling water before freezing, to destroy enzymes and preserve colour. Vegetables should be young and tender: freeze as quickly as possible after picking.

Most vegetables will keep for 10-12 months and can be cooked from frozen.

FRUIT
Soft fruits, such as raspberries and strawberries, black and red currants, plums, damsons and gooseberries may be open frozen. Clean, place on a baking sheet and leave to freeze until quite solid. Then pack into a freezer bag.

To pack fruit in dry sugar, roll fruit in 225 g–350 g (8 oz–12 oz) sugar for each 1 kg (2 lb) fruit. Either open freeze, rolled in sugar, or layer. In either case, place in a polythene bag.

To freeze fruit in a sugar syrup, use 225–350 g (8–12 oz) sugar to each 600 ml (1 pint) water. Make syrup, cool, then place fruit and syrup in a container leaving about 2.5 cm (1 in) headroom. Cover, label, freeze.

DAIRY PRODUCTS
Freeze in cartons and plastic bottles, then wrap in thick polythene bags.

Storage life Milk tends to separate after freezing unless

it is homogenised. This will freeze in plastic containers for one month. Fresh cream must have a minimum fat content of 35 per cent to prevent separation on thawing. For best results, whip until just softly stiff and freeze in plastic containers. Whipped cream is ideal to freeze in rosettes and can be used from frozen. Hard cheeses freeze well for up to three months in 225 g (8 oz) quantities. Wrap in foil or cling film. Grated cheese is ideal for freezing and can be used from frozen.

Thawing time Thaw all dairy products slowly in the refrigerator for 24 hours.

PREPARED FOODS
Cakes, bread, pastry and dough freeze well. Wrap in heavy polythene or freeze in rigid containers. Cakes and baked pastry will keep for up to six months; bread, bread dough and uncooked pastry

Pies can be ready in minutes if you have all the ingredients in the freezer. Wrap rolled-out pastry in foil and fillings in cling film.

for two to three months. Thaw at room temperature.

Stews, soups and stocks can be frozen in rigid containers. Allow a headspace to allow for expansion. Thaw at room temperature and heat through thoroughly. Once thawed, do not refreeze.

FOOD AND COOKERY

COOKING AIDS

MICROWAVE OVENS

Microwave ovens cook, thaw and re-heat food quickly. Microwaves are high frequency electronic waves, similar to radio waves. They penetrate the food, causing the molecules to vibrate, and generating heat to a depth of 4 cm (1½ in) all round. Thereafter, heat is carried through the food by conduction, as in conventional cookers.

Microwave ovens are widely used commercially and are becoming popular for domestic use. They may be best used to complement your freezer, to thaw and re-heat home-produced, deep frozen food. Because they operate on a totally different basis from conventional cookers, make sure you follow the manufacturer's instructions faithfully.

Place the food in an earthenware, china or throw-away cardboard container. Don't use a metallic dish: the microwaves won't penetrate it. The food will heat very quickly, but it won't brown. When hot, put it under a conventional grill unless you have an oven supplied with a purpose-built ceramic browning dish.

FOOD PROCESSERS

Several models are available with different attachments and blades, such as a double-bladed chopping knife, mixing blade, slicing, shredding disc and grating disc. Basically all can chop, slice, mince, grate, purée or knead food in just a few seconds.

However, they cannot replace an electric mixer for aerating cake mixtures and meringues. It is important to follow the manufacturer's instructions for each different model.

Ensure the correct attachment is fitted, avoid overloading, and use the feed tube attachment for adding liquids.

PRESSURE COOKERS

This is an economical method of cooking at high pressure and temperature, saving time, fuel and nutritional value. When using a pressure cooker, follow the manufacturer's instructions for quantities of food, liquid and timing. The amount of liquid used depends on the length of the cooking time.

The cooker is first brought to pressure by boiling the liquid, with the vent pipe open. When there is a steady flow of steam, the correct pressure weight is added. A loud hissing indicates that the pressure has been reached and that timing for cooking can start.

Reduce pressure first by running under cold water, or gradually, at room temperature for 5-10 minutes before opening. Every pressure cooker must be fitted with a safety device which automatically acts if the pressure control becomes blocked.

SLOW COOKERS

Slow cookers are casseroles, usually earthenware, which heat and cook food very gently, over six–seven hours, by means of an enclosed electrical element. They have two settings, low, which heats to about 82°C (175°F); and high, which reaches 98°C (200°F) after some six hours. Even the highest setting does not reach the lowest heat in an oven.

ENTERTAINING

DINNER PARTIES

Skilful hosts will choose a menu which has been tried out before, successfully. For preference, choose a main course which can be prepared in advance.

Balance flavours, colours and textures, using fresh fruit and vegetables in season. Where possible, offer a choice of dishes. A simple, cold starter is best served before an elaborate casserole; a warming soup before a grill. Follow a rich main dish with a cheeseboard or fruit.

BUFFET PARTIES

Choose dishes which can be eaten comfortably with a fork. Slices of quiche, curries or a goulash are excellent. Serve with a variety of salads and a bowl of savoury rice or garlic bread, hot from the oven.

For the dessert, choose a fresh fruit salad, trifle, cheese cake or caramelized oranges. Prepare a cheeseboard, bunches of watercress, sticks of celery and chicory leaves.

CHILDREN'S PARTIES

Savoury foods are popular with children. Try sandwiches cut in fancy shapes, homemade cheese straws and biscuits, crisps, sausages on sticks and individual quiches. Jellies, blancmanges and ice cream are still a must; so is cake or gateau specially decorated, or shaped like a train, car, drum, animal, clown face or reading book.

Older children are more sophisticated: they may enjoy a lunchtime buffet served with apple juice or a non-alcoholic fruit cup.

TEENAGE PARTIES

Sometimes planning a party based on a theme which includes food, décor and dress is fun. You may try a Greek party, with kebabs and pitta bread; an Indian party with curries and rice; or a South American party, with chilli con carne. Prepare the food in advance, and serve as a buffet.

Fruit punches, based on ginger beer, cider or lemonade are good drinks, served hot or cold.

A setting for a 4-course meal.

BARBECUES

If you use meat, choose lean cuts of beef, lamb or pork (see pp. 10-13). Marinate cubed meat overnight in wine or lemon juice, oil, herbs and seasoning. Thread on to skewers with slices of onion, sweet pepper and tomatoes for kebabs. Use chops, parcelled in aluminium foil, for grilling.

Poultry is often sold in portions. Drumsticks, thighs and wings of chicken or turkey may be devilled.

Vegetables, such as tomatoes, mushrooms, sliced onions, peppers, sweetcorn and aubergines can be threaded onto kebab skewers, or wrapped in foil with a knob of butter and seasoning. You may put potatoes straight onto the embers. Choose medium, floury ones, scrubbed, which will cook in their jackets more quickly. Serve the potatoes with butter flavoured with herbs or garlic and top with grated cheddar cheese.

French bread, sliced lengthwise, spread with herb or garlic butter and warmed in the oven, is a good accompaniment, as are savoury sauces.

PICNICS

The food must be as attractive to eat as it was when prepared. Pies, flans, pasties and scotch eggs have a coating which helps protect the filling: they can be eaten with the fingers or with a knife and fork. Grilled chicken joints, chops or sausages travel well if wrapped in foil.

Prepare sandwiches to include sliced tomato, cucumber or pickle to keep the main ingredient moist, whether it be cheese, egg or meat.

Carry boiling water in a vacuum flask and milk in a separate container so that either coffee or tea bags may be used to make a fresh beverage.

FOOD AND COOKERY

WINE WITH FOOD

This section gives various suggestions for pairing wine and food. These suggestions, based on the general opinions of experienced wine drinkers, are included to help those with less experience and should enable anyone to satisfy the palates of most guests at the dinner table. But the most important opinion about any wine is that of the person drinking it. Personal opinions differ widely. If a person wants white wine with ice to accompany his beef steak, then that is what he should have. In fact, trying the 'wrong' wines with various dishes is essential if the drinker is to acquire any real understanding of why specific wines and dishes tend to make excellent partners.

However, when serving wine to guests, the conventional approach is generally best. Probably the most helpful advice is not to spoil a good meal by serving inferior wine, and not to mask the subtlety of fine wine by serving it with highly spiced or vinegary dishes.

APERITIFS
Aperitifs serve to stimulate the appetite and encourage relaxation. A wide range of wines and spirits are drunk as aperitifs. Many of these are strongly flavoured and tend to numb the palate, rendering it incapable of detecting the subtleties of good food and wine. Still or sparkling dry wine, white or rosé, makes a good aperitif, as does a dry or medium-dry sherry. Dry or medium-dry champagne is an excellent appetizer.

WINES WITH HORS D'OEUVRES
The most difficult part of a meal to match with a wine is usually the hors d'oeuvre. Many hors d'oeuvres are flavoured with vinegar, which tends to make any accompanying wine taste vinegary too. Lemon juice sprinkled on fish also affects the taste of wine, as does the bitter taste of the grapefruit. If table wine is served, a cheap variety will be quite adequate to go with strongly flavoured dishes. Plainer hors d'oeuvres can be accompanied by a better quality table wine or champagne. Some foods, such as eggs, go well with most wines. But, in many cases, care is needed in choosing wine.

WINES WITH SOUPS
Dry, fortified wines are satisfactory with most meat soups. Sherry is generally suitable although, if the soup contains wine, then the same type of wine may prove to be a more suitable drink. If the wine used in the soup is of poor quality, a better version of the same basic type of wine can be served instead. Dry madeira is suitable for many of the heavier, more strongly flavoured meat soups. In most cases, the wine to be served with the main course can be confidently served with the soup too.

WINES WITH MAIN COURSES
Red meat usually demands a dry red wine. A good beef or lamb dish, provided that it is not highly seasoned, justifies a bottle or two of the best red wine available. If the meat itself is of the more

highly flavoured kind —liver, kidneys, or gammon, for example — a full-bodied, medium-quality red wine is usually most suitable. The finesse of a great wine would be difficult to appreciate with dishes of this kind.

Many different types of wine can be enjoyed with white meats, such as veal, pork, and chicken. If white wine is served, it should be dry or medium-dry, and full-flavoured. Rosé, or a light red wine are alternatives, being particularly suited to the more strongly flavoured white meat dishes.

Fish, including shellfish, almost always tastes best with dry white wine. White wine with a slightly sharp, acid flavour can be used to offset the oiliness that is characteristic of some fish dishes. Fish with an extremely delicate flavour needs to be accompanied by a very light white wine. A fuller bodied white wine can be served with the more flavourful fish dishes. If lemon or a strong sauce is provided with the fish, a cheaper variety of wine can be served.

WINE WITH CHEESE
The relatively strong flavour of most cheeses demands a full-bodied red table wine, or port. White wine goes well with most of the milder cheeses.

WINES WITH DESSERTS
Sweet dishes are best accompanied by sweet, rich wine, the contrast of such food with dry wine being rather unpleasant. Heavy, sweet fortified wines are suitable companions for the sweetest dishes.

GLOSSARY OF COOKERY TERMS

Angelica A sweet-flavoured plant, its green stems are candied and used for decorating cakes and sweets.

Arrowroot Starch obtained from the ground root of an American plant, used for thickening sauces.

Aspic Clear savoury jelly made from stock.

Au gratin Food covered with a thick sauce, breadcrumbs, butter or grated cheese and grilled.

Baba Light yeast mixture with currants, baked in a dariole mould and soaked in a rum syrup after baking.

Bain-marie Large pan of hot water in which another smaller pan is placed to cook food or keep foods warm.

Bake 'blind' Pastry case, lined with aluminium foil or greaseproof paper and dried beans and partially baked for 15 minutes without a filling (see p. 66).

Baking powder Raising agent consisting of one part cream of tartar to two parts bicarbonate of soda, with added starch.

Barding Covering dry meat or poultry with pork fat or bacon as it cooks.

Basting Spooning over juices from the roasting tin to keep meat or poultry moist.

Beating Introducing air to food using a wooden spoon, whisk or electric mixer, to make it light.

Béchamel White sauce, thickened with a roux, from which other sauces can be made.

Binding Holding together a dry mixture such as stuffing or croquettes, with eggs, cream, melted butter or thick sauce.

Blanching Immersing vegetables or fruit in boiling water briefly, to retain colour, kill enzymes before freezing, and to loosen skins before peeling.

Blanquette A dish made from the liquor in which meat or poultry has been cooked, with added milk, cream or egg yolks.

Boiling Cooking in a liquid at boiling point 100°C (212°F).

Bouquet garni A bunch of herbs, most often bayleaf, thyme and parsley, used to flavour casseroles and savoury dishes.

Bourguignonne Meat cooked with red wine, mushrooms and onions.

Braising Long, slow cooking with liquid and vegetables after the meat has been first browned in fat.

Bran Valuable source of roughage in the diet. Inner husk of wheat and other grains, which is normally removed in milling.

Brawn Dish made from a stewed pig's head.

Brine Salt and water solution used for preserving.

Brioche Light yeast dough, shaped like a small cottage loaf and baked in a fluted mould.

Brochette Skewer used for grilling assorted pieces of meat, fish and vegetables.

Browning Sealing in juices of meat by quickly cooking outer surface of meat.

Canapé Hors d'oeuvre consisting of small pieces of fried or toasted bread or biscuits topped with a savoury mixture, such as cream cheese with stuffed olives, anchovy fillets, shrimps or crab.

Candied peel The peel of citrus fruits, soaked in a sugar solution to preserve, used with dried fruit for cakes and puddings.

Cannelloni Italian pasta shaped into large tubes, filled with a savoury stuffing and baked, coated with a cheese or tomato sauce.

Caper The flower bud from a bush grown around the Mediterranean, pickled, and used for garnishing and flavouring.

Caramel Sugar dissolved in water and heated gently until brown, used as a flavouring for sweets and puddings.

Carbonnade Meat in beer.

Cardinal Dishes and sauces naturally bright red.

Casserole Long, slow cooking of meat, poultry or fish and vegetables.

Cassoulet French stew of haricot beans, pork, sausages and goose.

Caviar Sturgeon roes served as an hors-d'oeuvre.

Cayenne Red pepper from chillies.

Chantilly Sweetened whipped cream.

Charlotte A moulded pudding served hot, with slices of bread lined around an ovenproof dish and filled with sweetened fruit; cold, with sponge fingers, the centre filled with fruit and cream.

Chasseur A sauce made with white wine, mushrooms, onions and tomatoes, served with chicken or rabbit.

Chaud-froid Creamy sauce dish, glazed with aspic.

Chiffonade Shredded green salad, served as a garnish.

Chining Separating the backbone from the ribs of meat, to make carving easier.

Chowder Fish stew.

Clarifying Clearing fats by slow heating and sieving. Use whisked egg white to clear soups and jellies.

Cochineal Bluish-red colouring, obtained from the cochineal insect.

Cocotte Small, ovenproof egg dish.

Coddling Cooking eggs slowly in simmering water.

Compôte Fruit poached in syrup.

FOOD AND COOKERY

Concassé Roughly chopped vegetables, most often applied to tomatoes.

Condiment Spice or sauce which adds flavour to a dish, such as salt, pepper and mustard.

Conserve Fruit preserved, whole, in a sugar syrup.

Consommé Thin clear soup.

Cornflour A maize-based starch used for thickening sauces and puddings.

Court bouillon Stock made with water, vegetables, herbs, wine or vinegar, used mainly for poaching fish.

Crackling Skin of pork when roasted.

Crêpe Thin pancake.

Croissant Rich, flaky, crescent-shaped roll.

Croquette Shaped savoury mixture, coated with egg, breadcrumbs and deep fried.

Croûton Small toasted or fried piece of bread.

Curd Milk solids, obtained from soured milk.

Curdling Milk separated into solids and liquids through overheating or added acid.

Curing Preserving meat or fish by salting, pickling or cold smoking.

Dariole Mould used for making jellies, creams and puddings.

Deep-frying Frying foods completely covered in hot fat or oil.

Dicing Chopping food into small cubes.

Dough Flour and liquid mixture which is kneaded and shaped to make bread or scones.

Dredging Dusting food with flour or sugar.

Dressing Plucking, drawing and trussing poultry or game, or preparing shellfish.

Dripping Fat obtained from roasting meat.

En croûte Food encased in pastry.

Entrée The main dish in a formal dinner, which is served after the fish course.

Escalope Thin piece of meat, usually veal, which is shallow-fried.

Faggots Savoury rounds of seasoned minced meats, herbs and breadcrumbs.

Fines herbes Mixed herbs — parsley, chervil, tarragon and chives.

Flaking Separating the flesh of cooked fish.

Flambé Food flamed with brandy or wine.

Florentine Usually used to describe fish or eggs on a bed of spinach and coated with cheese sauce. It is also the name for wafer-thin biscuits containing nuts and fruits and coated with melted milk or plain chocolate.

Folding-in Using a metal spoon to introduce one mixture into another.

Fondant Syrup of sugar and water, boiled and used for sweets and cake icing.

Fondue Originating from Switzerland, a melted cheese and white wine dish into which pieces of bread are dipped. In a meat fondue, tender, raw meat is dipped on a fork into hot oil.

Fool Purée of fruit and cream.

Freezing Storing at below freezing point to preserve food.

Fritter Piece of food dipped into batter and deep-fried.

Frosting Coating a cake with icing, or dipping fruit into egg white and caster sugar.

Frying Cooking quickly in hot fat.

Galantine A cold dish of boned and stuffed poultry, game or meat, glazed with aspic.

Garnish A decoration to improve the appearance of a dish.

Gelatine Used to set liquids and available in powder or sheets.

Genoise Rich sponge cake made from whisked eggs and sugar to which melted butter is added with flour.

Gherkin Small cucumber, pickled, used for garnishing and as cocktail savouries.

Giblets Edible insides of poultry.

Glacé Icing or iced dessert; also sugared fruit.

Glaze Shiny finish to food, obtained by brushing with milk, beaten egg or sugar and water before baking.

Gluten Protein in the grain of wheat, important in bread making.

Goulash Beef or lamb stew with onions, tomato and seasoning. Strongly flavoured with paprika.

Griddle (girdle) Thick round metal plate used to bake scones and oatcakes on the top of the cooker.

Haggis Scottish savoury pudding made from offal, suet, onions and oatmeal.

Hanging Suspending meat, poultry or game to tenderize.

Haricot Dried, white bean.

Hash Fried dish made from leftover meat with added potatoes and other vegetables.

Hors d'oeuvre An appetizer served as the first course.

Hot-pot Stew, topped with potatoes; the most famous is Lancashire hot-pot.

Hulling Removing the green calyx from soft fruit.

Icing Sugar coating used to decorate cakes.

Infusing Extracting the flavour of herbs, tea leaves or coffee soaked in water.

Jelly Liquid set with gelatine.
Joint Cut of meat used for roasting or term used to divide meat or poultry into single portions.
Junket Milk set to a curd with rennet.

Kebab Small chunks of meat grilled or roasted on long skewers.
Kedgeree Rice dish containing fish and eggs.
Kirsch Liqueur distilled from the fermented juices of wild cherries, used in sweets, soufflés and Black Forest gâteau.

Lard Rendered-down pork fat used for frying.
Larding Threading small pieces of fat into lean meat, to keep moist during cooking.
Lasagne Wide ribbons of pasta, cooked and layered with meat, tomato and cheese sauce.
Légumes Vegetables with pods, such as peas and beans.
Liqueur Alcohol distilled from spirits, flavoured with fruit, herbs or spices and with variable alcoholic content.

Macaroni Pasta tubes of varying length.
Macaroon Rich almond biscuit, made solely from ground almonds, sugar and egg whites.
Maître-d'hôtel Butter, creamed with chopped, fresh parsley, served as a garnish to steak.
Marinading Tenderizing meat or fish in a mixture of oil, wine or vinegar, herbs and spices for some hours before cooking.
Marzipan Almond paste used in confectionery and as a coating for rich fruit cakes.

Mille feuille 'A thousand leaves' — puff pastry layered with cream and jam.
Mocha A fine-textured variety of coffee, and a term often used to describe a coffee and chocolate flavouring.
Mornay Savoury dish coated with a cheese sauce and browned under the grill.
Moussaka A casserole of minced meat (lamb or beef) with aubergines, onions, tomatoes and herbs, topped with a cheese sauce.
Mousse Light and fluffy, whether sweet or savoury, a mousse contains eggs and cream and is usually set with gelatine.
Muesli A Swiss-originated dish containing rolled oats, diced apple, nuts and dried fruit; served for breakfast with cream or yogurt.

Navarin Brown stew of lamb or mutton and vegetables.
Niçoise Dishes from the district around Nice, containing tomatoes, garlic, black olives, anchovies and onions.
Noodles Pasta shaped into long ribbons and made from hard (durum) flour, water and often added egg.

Oatmeal Ground from oats and available in different grades, used for porridge, black puddings, and oatcakes and scones.
Offal Edible insides of meat, poultry and game.

Paella Spanish rice dish containing shellfish, chicken, vegetables, herbs and spices.
Panada Thick sauce used to bind dry ingredients.
Parboil Partially cook, as with potatoes before they are roasted.
Parfait Sweet made from cream and fruit purée, and frozen.
Parkin spiced gingerbread, made with oatmeal.

Parmentier A dish cooked with potatoes.
Pasty Individual pastry with savoury stuffing.
Pâté A mixture of meats, often including liver, seasoned with herbs and spices, cooked slowly in the oven and served cold.
Patty Individual pie or round of food (potato or fish cake).
Paupiettes Thin slices of meat enveloping a savoury stuffing.
Pectin Starch extract in fruit, which helps set jams and jellies. Commercially prepared pectin can be bought to set jams and jellies made from low-pectin fruit.
Petits fours Small fancy cakes and biscuits, usually eaten with coffee at the end of a meal.
Pickling Preserving food in a salt and vinegar solution.
Pilaff (Pilau) Rice dish cooked in stock, containing meat, poultry or fish, herbs and spices.
Pimento Green or red sweet pepper.
Pith Bitter white skin between the rind and flesh of citrus fruit.
Pizza Flat round of yeast dough, topped with tomatoes, cheese, anchovies, olives or other savoury ingredients.
Poaching Gentle simmering.
Pot roasting Browning meat, before finishing cooking in a covered casserole in the oven.
Praline Mixture of nuts and caramelized sugar.
Preserving Heat, refrigeration, chemical, salt or sugar treatment of foods to keep in optimum edible condition.
Profiterole Small ball of choux pastry filled with cream and covered with chocolate.
Provençale A dish cooked with garlic and tomatoes.
Pulp Softened mass of fruit or vegetables.

FOOD AND COOKERY

Purée Sieved or liquidized fruit or vegetables.

Quiche Savoury tart, using eggs and cream with bacon, onion, cheese or other fillings.

Ragoût Meat and vegetable stew.

Ramekin Small, individual soufflé dish.

Rare Term used for underdone steaks.

Ratafia Small macaroon flavoured with almonds, used in cream sweets. Also a liqueur flavoured with almonds.

Ratatouille Vegetable dish consisting of courgettes, aubergines, peppers, onions and tomatoes fried in olive oil and stewed.

Ravioli Small, savoury, filled squares of pasta, covered in tomato sauce.

Rechauffé Re-heated dish.

Reducing Extended boiling of sauce or gravy to concentrate flavour and thicken consistency.

Relish Sauce made from fruit and/or vegetables.

Rendering Heating and melting fat in a roasting tin to produce dripping.

Rennet Extract from lining of calf's stomach; used to coagulate milk to make junket and cheese.

Rice paper Edible white paper, produced from the pith of a Chinese plant.

Risotto Italian rice dish, cooked in stock, with added mushrooms, tomatoes and topped with cheese.

Rissole Minced meat patty.

Roasting Cooking by radiant heat in the oven.

Roe Eggs from fish reproductive gland. Soft roe are from the male fish and hard roe from the female.

Roux Fat and flour cooked together to form the basis of some sauces.

Sautéing Shallow frying food in hot fat until brown and golden in appearance.

Savarin Rich yeast cake, soaked in a rum syrup after baking, then filled with fruit and fresh cream.

Scalding Plunging food into boiling water to remove skin or to heat milk just below boiling point.

Scoring Making incision, for example, on pork skin or surface of bread dough.

Shortening Fat used in pastry and biscuit making to produce a 'short' texture.

Sifting Removing lumps in flour or sugar by rubbing through a sieve.

Simmering Cooking in liquid, maintained just below boiling point.

Skimming Removing fat from soups, stews and casseroles; scum from jam; cream from milk.

Souse Cook in a vinegar or wine marinade.

Spatula Kitchen implement, flat on both sides, used for scraping bowls and mixing food mixtures.

Steaming Cooking by moist heat, on a plate over a pan of boiling water or in a special steamer.

Steeping Soaking in liquid to produce desired flavour or to remove a strong taste, such as salt from ham or fish.

Stewing Cooking slowly in water or stock in a covered casserole dish.

Straining Using a sieve or muslin to separate liquid from solid.

Strudel Wafer-thin pastry, filled with a sweet or savoury filling.

Stuffing Mixture of breadcrumbs, fruit or vegetables and seasoning as a filling for meat, poultry, fish and vegetables.

Suet Fat surrounding beef and mutton kidneys, used for pastry and puddings.

Syrup Mixture of sugar and water.

Tabasco Sauce from hot peppers.

Tea-cake Yeast bread baked in rounds.

Tenderize Make food tender by marinating or beating.

Terrine Ovenproof dish with lid.

Truss Using string or skewers to secure poultry and joints during cooking.

Turnover Pastry patty containing sweet or savoury filling.

Vanilla Dried pod, used to flavour caster sugar, cream and custard.

Velouté Sauce or soup made with white stock.

Vermicelli Fine pasta strands, used mainly as a garnish.

Vinaigrette Salad dressing containing oil, vinegar and seasoning.

Vinegar Acetic acid, made by fermenting malt, wine or cider.

Wafer Thin biscuit.

Waffle Flat crisp batter cakes made in a special waffle iron.

Whipping Beating cream until thick.

Whisking Beating, to enclose air, until thick and creamy.

Yeast Fresh or dried, used as a raising agent for bread dough or for fermenting in beer and wine making.

Zest Outer rind of citrus fruit, used to flavour cakes and puddings.

HOME MAINTENANCE

HOME MAINTENANCE

BASIC CLEANING TASKS

INTRODUCTION

For most people their home is a refuge from the pressures of everyday life, a place to relax in, entertain in and generally feel secure. So it makes sense to keep it looking as clean and as appealing as possible. This not only means it is more hygienic, but also a more pleasant place to spend your time.

However, there has to be a balance between maintaining a standard of cleanliness which drives you and the family into a frenzy, and being so daunted by the task of cleaning that you never actually begin. Some kind of routine is important, but keep it flexible.

Decide which jobs have to be done daily, such as washing up, bed-making and some general tidying. It can be surprising how much improved a room looks if the ashtrays are emptied, old newspapers removed, and the cushions plumped.

It is up to you to decide when more tiring tasks, such as vacuuming, cleaning, dusting, washing and ironing, have to be tackled. But remember, they will not disappear — merely accumulate — so reasonably regular attention to them is only sensible. There are also the periodic tasks, such as window cleaning, turning out drawers and defrosting the fridge.

Every individual household will cope with these in its own way, but it is important that some kind of system is evolved, preferably with every member of the household taking a turn so

that the home really is the place where everyone can relax and feel secure.

ADOPTING A SYSTEM

A system is important simply because it will avoid such unpleasant events as being faced with three days' washing up, or a bed still unmade when you wish to climb into it at night.

If necessary make a list of jobs to be tackled. It is very satisfying to tick off each item. But remember that the list should be flexible enough to alter and reorganize for the sudden arrival of a visitor, or the event of a sunny weekend when all would benefit from a day in the open air. Divide the list into three sections: daily tasks; regular tasks; and occasional or periodic tasks.

To help you meet these objectives you need to invest in some labour-saving equipment. A comprehensive list of these is discussed on p.89 but the amount and variety of equipment depends on the resources available.

Among the points to consider is *time*. The less time you have, the more helpful is the labour-saving equipment. Do you have a job or not? Are there children, and if so how many and what age group? Older children will be able to help in household tasks; younger ones need more attention, and, therefore, more of your time. *Money* determines what you can spend on labour-saving devices, outside help and home improvements. *People,* too, can be looked on as a resource. If both partners work, or if the children are old enough, everyone should make a contribution to the running of the home — however small. *Equipment:* how much you need will depend on the size of the family and house, storage space and money to buy and keep equipment in good working order. Some tasks really need labour-saving devices — e.g., for many families a washing machine will repay the initial cost many times over.

DRAWING UP A PLAN

The following chart gives a broad outline of the daily, regular and periodic tasks to be done. It is by no means exhaustive, but should act as a helpful guide. If you find the system works, you might improve on it by including reminders for paying the electricity and gas bills, rent, rates, television licence, etc., and even dental appointments or other essential dates which may be overlooked.

When possible, try to do some of the household jobs sitting down or, if the weather is lovely, take portable tasks outside. An extension cable could mean doing

HOUSEHOLD CLEANING TASKS

Area	Essential (Daily)	Regular (weekly/fortnightly)	Periodic
Kitchen	Wash dishes. Clean sink. Wipe cooker and surfaces. (Pay special attention to corners where germs are trapped.)	Clean cooker; refrigerator; larder. Clean sink and drain (take special care of pipes). Clean floor and any open shelves. Clean windows and ledges. Prepare laundry and do washing. Buy cleaning materials when shopping.	De-frost and turn out freezer (choose a day before shopping so that stocks are low). Clean out cupboards; check provisions for date stamps and signs of deterioration. Wipe spice jars and storage containers on display. Wash walls, tiles and paintwork.
Bathroom	Tidy towels. Wipe over wash basin; remove tide marks. Wipe lavatory seat and handle (clean if necessary). Train the family to do this too!	Change towels; flannels; bath mats. Clean and disinfect lavatory; bath; basin; shower tiles; floor; open shelves and mirrors (keep liquid cleanser and cloth handy). Empty waste bin.	Wash walls. Clean windows. Thoroughly clean the floor and remove scuff marks on paintwork. Deal with bad stains in lavatory, bath, and round taps. Clean shower curtains and loose rugs.
Living Rooms	Tidy up and air room. Clean out fire. Dust if necessary. Check flowers and remove dead ones; check plants. Empty waste bin and tidy away newspapers.	Dust and vacuum. Clean (include upholstered furniture and blinds). Feed and water plants. Clean table tops to remove marks. Change flowers.	Wash paintwork. Clean windows. Clean out drawers, cupboards, desks, etc. Polish furniture. Clean pictures and ornaments. Clean or wash curtains. Shampoo carpets and upholstery.
Bedrooms	Air rooms. Make beds. Tidy away clothing. Dust if necessary. Collect dirty laundry for washing.	Change bed linen. Dust and vacuum. Wipe surfaces with damp cloth to remove cup rings, make-up smears, etc. Empty waste bin. Tidy wardrobes – shoes and clothes.	As for living rooms. Air mattresses, pillows and duvets outside in sunshine; vacuum. Turn mattress. Launder blankets and bedcovers or have them dry cleaned.

HOME MAINTENANCE

the ironing out of doors. In fact any way of making the task more enjoyable should be considered — listening to the radio or record player, for instance.

TACKLING THE CHORES

Washing up You could refuse to do it, and make all members of the family responsible for their own plate, knife, fork, etc. However, this will depend upon your relationship with your family and could mean more work for you in the long run!

Do have a bowl large enough to take a load of dishes. *Do* have lots of hot water and a good-quality washing-up liquid — thin, cheap varieties are a false economy. *Do* soak burnt-on pans and dishes beforehand. *Do* scrape and stack plates, and wash and rinse glasses first. *Do* wash dishes from cleanest to dirtiest. *Do* change the water when necessary, that is, when the foam has disappeared or the water has grown cold. *Do not* wipe everything dry. Invest in a good drainer and leave *rinsed* dishes to dry in the air. Glassware and cutlery are usually wiped dry, with a *clean* cloth to avoid smears.

Dusting Use a damp sponge cloth for sticky marks and a soft duster for loose dirt. Work from the top down — *after* sweeping and *before* vacuuming. If you have attachments for your vacuum cleaner, use them to remove dust and cobwebs from corners, curtains and upholstery.

It is a good idea to have ready all the equipment you might need.

Washing walls and paintwork Usually start from the top and work down. If cleaning windows, a well wrung out 'chamois' leather (real or synthetic) will deal with most dirt. Follow with a soft duster to prevent smears. Very dirty marks can be removed with 15 ml (1 tablespoon) of methylated spirits in a little warm water.

Polishing Apply polish with a cloth — do not put it straight on to the surface. Rub hard and buff off with a clean, soft duster. If using a damp cloth to remove sticky marks from wood, do not polish on the damp surface or white patches may appear.

CLEANING EQUIPMENT

DUSTERS AND CLOTHS

Invest in the best you can afford. Non-woven dusters are not as effective as fluffy cotton yellow dusters. Old flannelette sheets make a good substitute. There is a wide range of useful cloths and sponges for washing up, bathroom and window cleaning. These should be washed regularly. Keep synthetic 'chamois' leather cloths moist by storing them in polythene bags.

BRUSHES

Most household brushes have synthetic rather than animal bristles and wear very well. A long-handled soft bristle broom is useful for tiles, lino or wood floors. A carpet brush is useful for the edges where a vacuum or hand cleaner cannot reach, particularly for stairs and corners.

Scrubbing brushes are often replaced by squeezy or cotton mops but occasionally a hard bristle hand brush is useful for dirty marks. Pot brushes are useful for vegetable preparation as well as for cleaning pots and pans. Nylon or metal pot scourers are an alternative. W.C. brushes are shaped for cleaning under rims and into the W.C. bend. They should be regularly disinfected.

MOPS

Squeezy sponge mops are invaluable for lino or tiled floors. The heads can be replaced when worn. They

should be stored hung up, after rinsing. Cotton mops, too, are useful and durable.

BUCKETS AND BOWLS
A washing-up bowl, one for laundry and a couple of buckets should answer most people's requirements. Rinse them out and remove 'tide marks' after use.

Wash mops, brushes and cloths regularly and dry before storing. Brushes, cotton mop-heads, etc. can be put in an old pillow case to wash in the machine.

LABOUR-SAVING EQUIPMENT
As mentioned above, time is important to the housewife and labour-saving equipment can mean much less and much easier cleaning. Here are some suggestions for really useful equipment for the home:

Vacuum and carpet cleaners
There are three basic types of vacuum cleaner:
1 A light-weight or junior upright model, which is reasonably priced and is useful if you want to carry it upstairs. There are attachments for upholstery cleaning and stairs.
2 A heavier, more sophisticated upright model, useful if the whole house or flat is carpeted. It is less manoeuvrable, but efficient. It too has attachments.
3 A cylinder model has the best suction (but no brushing action), is easily stored and useful for small areas and stairs. It can be a nuisance to cart about from room to room.

You can hire very efficient carpet cleaner/shampooers for a reasonable hire fee — usually for 24 hours. You can also buy the cleaning solution on a use-or-re-

turn basis, and 24 hours is usually enough time to clean all the carpets in the house, if you really get down to it. This is particularly useful for an annual spring clean.

Dishwashers These are a luxury. Few people really need one, except perhaps those with a very large family of small children and those who have to entertain frequently. Indeed, many British kitchens are not large enough to take one; most must be plumbed in and take up a lot of space.

However, let us dispel some myths about them, if you really are considering one.

They are quicker than doing the dishes by hand. You could only *stack* them in the time it takes to load and unload your machine. They do cope with pans and baking trays, and they certainly get most if not all the food off.

When loading a dishwasher, be sure to stack dishes rim downwards.

They are more hygienic than doing the operation by hand because the water used is so much hotter than your hands could bear. They dispense with the need for tea-cloths, too.

They will wash almost anything, but care should be taken with cutlery that has handles attached with animal glue, some types of glassware and some plastics — if in doubt, do these by hand.

Dishwashers, however, can be expensive to buy. Add to that plumbing and running costs and they can be an expensive luxury. If your circumstances are such that you feel that having more time is more essential than wasting endless hours washing up, you might consider one. But take a careful look at the whole range before deciding. Size and noise are two priorities; some machines only take four place-settings, others are noisy.

HOME MAINTENANCE

CLEANING MATERIALS

There are a great variety of these on sale in every supermarket, and the choice is bewildering. It is helpful to have some idea of the different categories of cleaners available in order to make a sensible choice to suit your requirements. By doing this you treat all things in your home in the way that is best.

The following table gives a quick guide to the different cleaning problems around the house, the various products available and their suggested uses.

CLEANING TASKS	PRODUCT	SUGGESTED USES
Hard surfaces	Household cleaning liquids are thick liquids usually stored in plastic containers.	Can be used undiluted to remove scuff marks or burnt-on fats on kitchen surfaces. Rinse with clean water. For floors or large surfaces, use diluted on a mop or sponge. Rinsing and drying are unnecessary.
	Scouring powders are cleaners with disinfectant properties. They are stored in canisters and often contain bleach.	Unsuitable for plastic or stainless steel as they will scratch. Very useful for enamel and porcelain articles such as cookers, lavatories and sinks. Apply with a moist cloth; rinse off with water.
	Scouring creams are liquids stored in plastic bottles. They are less abrasive than powder scourers.	Will clean surfaces without scratching. Good for stainless steel and porcelain sinks, cookers, baths and basins.
	Cleaner/disinfectants are dual-purpose household cleaners in plastic packs.	Use diluted on walls, tiles, painted woodwork, floors, baths, basins and all kitchen surfaces. Use undiluted for stubborn marks such as those on skirting boards.
	Disinfectants/ antiseptics. Germicides.	Recommended for sinks, drains, dustbins and lavatories.
Ovens CAUTION All these products are *caustic*; read instructions before using. Do not inhale fumes. Wear rubber gloves and avoid contact with skin or eyes.	Oven cleaners in aerosol, stick or jelly form are caustic and should be used with care.	Use on all oven surfaces except aluminium or stainless steel. They are relatively mild but be sure to follow the instructions.

PRECAUTIONARY ADVICE ABOUT ALL CLEANING PRODUCTS

Although most of the products mentioned here are generally harmless, some care is needed.
If any product is splashed into an eye or on to the skin, wash it off at once with lots of water.
If accidentally swallowed, drink milk or water or undiluted evaporated milk. See a doctor at once.
When using products such as bleaches and lavatory and oven cleaners, wear rubber gloves and follow the manufacturer's instructions.
All household cleaners should be kept away from children. They should *not* be transferred into other containers.

CLEANING TASKS	PRODUCT	SUGGESTED USES
	Oven pads contain a caustic solution which is packed inside an applicator attached to a sponge pad.	Use on stubborn stains in a cold or warm oven. Leave on overnight for burnt-on stains and wash off with clean water.
Lavatories	Cleaning powders are disinfectant and contain bleach. They often come in 'puffer' plastic packs.	Use in the lavatory only, to disinfect and remove iron scale which forms under the rim.
CAUTION Never mix powder and liquid bleaches as together these give off a chlorine gas. Avoid puffing powder into the face or tipping liquid bleach on to skin or clothes. Wash off with lots of cold water *at once*. Always read the manufacturer's instructions given on the pack.	Liquid bleaches have other uses besides cleaning lavatories. They are stored in plastic bottles with a screw cap.	Use undiluted in lavatories; sinks; bath and basin waste pipes; kitchen sink waste pipes; and outside drains.
	Toilet blocks and flush cleaners are sometimes coloured and perfumed and contain detergent.	Blocks are suspended under the lavatory rim to deodorize the area. Flush cleansers are hung in the cistern and immersed in water during flushing. Their blue colour is released into the water in the bowl.
Glass	Emulsion cleaners are opaque liquids containing a mild abrasive.	Used mainly for windows and mirrors. Apply with a soft cloth and buff off with a clean cloth.
	Aerosols for glass cleaning are more expensive but less wasteful.	Spray on as foam and wipe off quickly.
Furniture	Pastes are polishes designed to resist finger marking and to repel water.	Use on wood and open grain surfaces to seal out dirt and create a shiny finish.
	Creams may be hard or softer products, containing either wax or oil.	Use on all types of furniture surfaces. They are particularly good for antique furniture.

HOME MAINTENANCE

LAUNDRY

INTRODUCTION

Laundry is not usually the most popular of household tasks. It can be made much more bearable by using any of a whole range of appliances and sophisticated detergents that are available and which make the task easier, and by investing in clothes, etc. made from the wide choice of 'easy care' fabrics.

However, in spite of all these aids, people often achieve poor results, which can be discouraging and expensive. There are several reasons for this.

People are often confused by the wide range of detergents — why isn't there just one for everything? In addition, every time you look, there seems to be a new fabric on the market, often needing special treatment, which can mean that it shouldn't be washed in your normal load of laundry. And, with so many washing machines, tumble driers and irons on sale, it is often difficult to decide which is the best for your purposes.

Frequently, the reason for poor results lies in not bothering to read instructions on detergent packs, care labels and the manuals that come with washing machines or driers.

The task then is to achieve satisfactory results with the weekly wash, and to attempt to reduce to a minimum disasters such as baggy, faded acrylic sweaters and greying nylon underwear.

The following sections may help to clarify some points related to fabrics, care labels and washing products.

NATURAL FIBRES	
Fibre, Brand name	**Properties and uses**
Cotton/Linen	**Properties:** Absorbent, strong, withstands frequent laundering.
Wash Code: White $\frac{1}{95}$ Coloured $\frac{2}{60}$	**Uses:** Shirts, denim jeans, bed linen, dresses, handkerchiefs. Blended with polyester for dresses, bed linen, etc.
Wool	**Properties:** Warm, soft, sheds creases. Can be machine washed with special finish.
Wash Code: $\frac{7}{40}$	**Uses:** All knitwear. Blended with acrylic, polyester, nylon, for men's suits, trousers, etc.
Silk	**Properties:** Soft lustre, warm, sheds creases, drapes well.
Wash Code: $\frac{8}{30}$ or dry clean only	**Uses:** Scarves, blouses, dresses, lingerie. Sometimes blended with wool for suits.

MAN-MADE FIBRES	
Fibre, Brand name	**Properties and uses**
Acetate Dicel	**Properties:** Silk-like appearance and feel.
Wash Code: $\frac{6}{40}$ or $\frac{8}{30}$	**Uses:** Knitted and woven dresswear, furnishing fabrics, curtainings, linings, velvets.
Acrylic Acrilan, Courtelle, Dràlon, Orlon	**Properties:** Wool-like appearance and feel, durable, soft and warm, easy care.
Wash Code: $\frac{6}{40}$	**Uses:** Sweaters, pullovers, cardigans, carpets, furnishing fabrics, hand-knitted yarns, long-pile fabrics.
Elastane Lycra, Spanzelle	**Properties:** High stretch recovery with good shape retention, resistant to chemicals and perspiration.
Wash Code: $\frac{4}{60}$ or $\frac{6}{40}$	**Uses:** Corsetry, sportswear.

Fibre, Brand name	Properties and uses
Modacrylic Acrilan, SEF, Teklan **Wash Code:** $\frac{6}{40}$	**Properties:** Wool-like appearance flame resistant. **Uses:** Where flame resistance is important, e.g. in furnishings.
Modal Vincel **Wash Code:** $\frac{1}{95}$ $\frac{2}{60}$ or $\frac{5}{40}$	**Properties:** Cotton-like appearance and feel, sheds creases, washes well. **Uses:** Workwear, household textiles, furnishings.
Nylon **Wash Code:** $\frac{3}{60}$ or $\frac{4}{50}$	**Properties:** Durable, good stretch recovery, resistant to wear and tear, easy care. **Uses:** Knitwear, hosiery, underwear, sleepwear.
Polyester **Wash Code:** $\frac{3}{60}$ $\frac{4}{50}$ or $\frac{6}{40}$	**Properties:** Durable, easy care, good for permanent pleating and shape retention. **Uses:** All types of clothing, household textiles.
Triacetate Tricel **Wash Code:** $\frac{6}{40}$	**Properties:** Silk-like appearance and feel, easy care. **Uses:** Knitted and woven dresswear, furnishing fabrics, linings.
Viscose Evlan **Wash Code:** $\frac{5}{40}$	**Properties:** Versatile, absorbent. **Uses:** All types of clothing, linings, carpets. Also industrial uses.

What the Code looks like

  MACHINE   **HAND WASH**
Hand-hot   Hand-hot
medium wash
Cold rinse. Short spin or drip-dry.

 DO NOT USE CHLORINE BLEACH

 WARM

 DRY CLEANABLE

CARE LABELLING IN THE U.K.

You probably have seen some of the wash code symbols (below) which are recommended for the care of various fabrics. However, these represent only part of the 'International Care Labelling Code' which has been adopted for use on clothing and soft furnishings.

This code, adopted in 1974, consists of five basic symbols:

 1. For washing (by hand or machine)

 2. For bleaching

 3. For ironing

 4. For dry cleaning

 5. For drying

The symbols are always presented in the same sequence.

What are the variations?

 The wash tub symbol indicates a particular washing process most appropriate to a group of fabrics.

 The hand in the tub means hand wash only.

 Tub crossed out means articles must not be washed.

 Triangle means household (chlorine) bleach may be used.

 Household bleach may not be used.

 cool

 warm

 hot

 do not iron

 Articles normal for dry cleaning in all solvents.

Ⓟ Dry clean in white spirit, solvent 113 & 11.

HOME MAINTENANCE

DETERGENTS AND OTHER LAUNDRY AIDS

Again, the choice on any supermarket shelf is bewildering, but it helps to have a little knowledge about what all the various products do, to enable you to make the best choice for your particular needs. Remember, although many of the products appear to be similar, not only do they differ but *people* also differ greatly in their requirements.

The chart below will help you to make a quick selection to suit your particular life-style.

HOW MUCH POWDER TO USE

Don't ignore the quantity recommendations on packs. They are there as a guide and not to encourage you to use more powder than is necessary.

Everyone's circumstances differ, and you need to adjust amounts accordingly. One cup holds 85–100 g (3–3½ oz). Recommendations vary for hard and soft water.

For soaking and hand washing use ½ cup of powder for 4.5 litres (1 gallon) water, 1½ cups per sink (23 litres, 5 gallons), ½–¾ cup per bucket (9 litres, 2 gallons).

Machine	Water Type	Quantity (cups)
Twin tubs	Hard	3
	Soft	2
Top loading automatics 8 gallons capacity	Hard	3
	Soft	2
10 gallons capacity	Hard	4
	Soft	3
15 gallons capacity	Hard	5
	Soft	4
Front and top loading drum automatics	Hard	3
	Soft	2
With pre-wash	Hard	2
Without pre-wash	Soft	1/2

PRODUCT	FORM AND APPEARANCE	RECOMMENDED USES
Soap	Powder	Hand/machine (top loaders) washing.
	Flakes	Hand washing of wool/delicate fabrics.
Synthetic	Powder	Hand/machine (top loaders).
	Light duty powders	Hand washing of wool/delicate fabrics.
	Washing up liquids	Dish washing; stain removal.
Low lather	Powder	In suds-sensitive, drum-type machines; soaking/washing badly soiled clothes.
Solvent	Powder (high lather) (heavy duty)	Soaking/hand/machine washing clothes, particularly synthetics, e.g. polyester. Use with care in drum-type automatics.
Enzyme	Powder	Soaking/washing clothes with protein stains, e.g. blood, egg, gravy. Top loading machines only.
Starches and stiffeners	Powders a) cold water b) boiling water	To stiffen and add gloss. Stiffens less, useful for table linen.
Water softeners	Powders Soda Borax	Add to water before soap. White and coloured cottons only. Delicate fabrics.

EQUIPMENT

When choosing equipment for washing clothes from the very wide range available, there are a number of points to consider:

Space What is available? Will the machine fit under a working surface? Will one appliance stack on top of another?

Cost How much can you afford to pay? Do you want to pay outright or by a hire-purchase arrangement?

Size How many members in your family? Do you have a large wash every week or several times a week?

Time How much can you give to the job? Here, the choice between single, twin-tub and automatic would be important.

Before buying Inspect various models in each type and compare prices, finishes, etc. Many shops offer good discounts on electrical goods. Enquire about after-sales servicing and owners-club schemes — they *will* save you money.

WASHING MACHINES

There are three main types:
Single tubs (semi-automatic) Are the cheapest. These compact machines remove the bulk of the water, but do not get clothes dry.
Twin tubs (semi-automatic) Combine wash tub and spin drier. They can be quite expensive and do not take large loads or very bulky items.
Automatic machines Come in two types: top loading with central paddle; and the horizontal drum automatic which can be front or top loading. Both types carry out all the washing processes.

The six essentials of machine washing
1 Read the machine manual carefully.
2 Sort clothes carefully according to the care label.
3 Use the correct water temperature.
4 Use the correct washing product and quantity.
5 Load machine carefully.
6 Rinse thoroughly.

DRYING EQUIPMENT

Wringers Hand operated or electrical. Do not get clothes dry enough for ironing.
Spin driers Can extract 80 per cent of water from clothes. Their loads must be distributed evenly.
Tumble driers Before use consider: the time and the heat (usually three settings) required for drying; and the movement of clothes — do not overload. Wipe them out and remove fluff from filter after use.

OUTDOOR DRYING

Wipe plastic-coated clothes lines before use if out all the time. Remember to dry woollens and synthetics in shade.

IRONS

Recommended iron settings:
'Hot' (210°C): cotton, linen viscose or modified viscose.
'Warm' (160°C): polyester mixtures, wool.
'Cool' (120°C): acrylic, nylon acetate, triacetate, polyester.

There are many types of washing and drying machines from which to choose. Semi-automatic twin tub machines *(left)* combine a wash tub and spin drier. They are useful for people who want to wash only small amounts of clothes. Automatic washing machines, such as this front loader *(centre)*, are usually large enough to take a family wash, offer a minimum of seven washing programmes, and some of them incorporate a tumble drier. Tumble driers as a separate unit *(right)* can often be fitted under work surfaces. They are not very expensive and make ironing easier by reducing the wrinkling of clothes. Some fit on top of automatic washers.

HOME MAINTENANCE

GENERAL HOME CLEANING

THE KITCHEN

Since the well-being of the family may be said to revolve round the kitchen, some basic ground rules are essential for maintaining it in as hygienic a manner as possible.

LARGE APPLIANCES

Depending on the size and space available, the age of the kitchen and the money to spare, large appliances will usually consist of cooker, sink unit, refrigerator/freezer, a washing machine or some appliance for assisting in the laundry process. There may also be items in the luxury bracket such as a dishwasher, tumble drier or freezer. All these are potential germ traps even, surprisingly, washing machines, and a regular routine is required to keep them clean. (See also chart of household tasks to be done on page 87.)

Cookers Turn off electricity or gas.

Half-fill the sink with very hot water and enzyme detergent — marvellous for dissolving burnt-on food.

Remove all shelves, trays, grill pan burners and soak in sink. Rinse, dry and replace.

Wipe all enamel parts with damp cloth and cream cleanser. Rinse well.

For inside oven, use one of the products recommended on pp. 90–91. If oven is very dirty leave cleaner on all night. Rinse off thoroughly and dry.

Toughened glass in oven doors can be cleaned with a nylon scourer and cream cleanser.

A clean and tidy kitchen is both hygienic and well organized.

Solid fuel cookers Wipe spills at once. Use cream cleanser on all enamel parts. Rinse off carefully.

If enamel is really dirty, try soap-filled pads, but avoid using on plastic or aluminium.

Brush out oven regularly.

Kitchen sinks Hot water and washing-up liquid is enough for general cleaning. Stainless steel and enamel sinks should be cleaned with a cream cleanser or special stainless steel cleaner to avoid scratching surface.

A handful of soda and a capful of liquid bleach washed down the drain at regular intervals will help dissolve grease, kill germs and reduce smells.

Refrigerators Do not overload the fridge with food as this prevents circulation of air.

Cover all food to prevent food smells from circulating and penetrating other foods.

Never leave the door open as this will cause the motor to

work overtime thus building up more frost.

Defrost regularly — speed up the process with a bowl of hot water.

Never leave the door closed when the refrigerator is switched off — it will smell dreadful and mould may grow.

Don't use disinfectant. A solution of soda and water will deodorize the interior. Apply on a soft cloth, and rinse with clear water. Never use harsh abrasives on a refrigerator interior.

Inspect the refrigerator regularly for forgotten dishes of food.

Larders Do not put away bottles or jars with drips on them — these will make jars and shelves sticky.

Clean shelves, cans and any containers regularly with warm water and detergent.

Clean floor with liquid floor cleaner.

Regularly wash out cake, biscuit and other storage tins or boxes.

Try to keep a check on date-stamping and move

older cans, packets, etc. to the front of the shelves, for using first.

Kitchen floors (See also section on kitchen floor coverings.)

Kitchen floors collect dirt very quickly. Gaps between units and appliances can harbour germs from scraps of dropped food. Pastry, vegetable peelings, coffee beans, breadcrumbs can all find their way on to the floor, so regular sweeping is necessary followed by a wash with a squeezy mop and a suitable cleaner.

Kitchen units These need regular wiping as working tops and doors get stained and finger marked. Do not use harsh abrasives on plastic or paintwork as these will scratch the surface and attract more dirt. Use scouring creams or disinfectant/cleaners.

A half-yearly turn-out of cupboards can be very rewarding. You will be surprised to find things you thought you had used. Cupboards containing small equipment also benefit from a regular turn-out to check that things have not rusted through being stored while damp. Make sure that shelves are dried before replacing their contents.

Washing machines (See page 95.)

SMALL APPLIANCES AND UTENSILS

Saucepans and frying pans An overnight soak with a warm solution of enzyme detergent will remove burnt-on food. Wash new pans, casseroles, etc. with warm sudsy water before using for the first time.

Cast-iron ware needs careful drying to avoid rust. Nonstick pans also need special care. Avoid harsh abrasives and scourers as these will destroy the surface. Do not put a cold pan directly on to a hot surface or burner.

Do not use metal spoons on iron or non-stick surfaces as these will also damage the surface.

Aluminium pans Use wooden spoons and avoid soda and harsh scourers. Don't put hot pans straight into water, as they could buckle.

Discoloured pans benefit from lemon rinds, or vinegar, and water boiled up for a few minutes in them.

Copper pans These are lined with silver, nickel or tin. Use wooden spoons and avoid harsh abrasives as these might wear away the surface. Unlined copper develops verdigris which is poisonous.

Ovenproof dishes/casseroles Check that they are not only ovenproof but also 'flameproof' before you put them on a gas ring. If they don't actually say 'flame-proof', chances are they are not.

Always put on to a wooden board when hot — the sudden change from a hot to a cold surface could crack the dish. Soak in a biological solution before washing.

Cutlery Any food containing acid — e.g., vinegar, lemon juice — and egg and salt can mark cutlery, other than stainless steel, so wash as quickly as possible. Don't leave silver spoons in pickle jars, or they will tarnish permanently. Do not soak bone-handled knives in water. Cooking knives may not be stainless steel and will need to be cleaned with steel-wool pads.

China and glass Vases and decanters that are stained respond well to being left overnight in household bleach or a warm enzyme detergent solution.

Tea stains on cups can sometimes be removed with a hot solution of soda and water.

Wood Scrub chopping boards in the direction of the grain. Do not soak or dry near heat or they may warp. Wipe teak salad bowls with kitchen paper and cooking oil to preserve the wood.

There are many cleaning products and cleaning aids from which to choose.

HOME MAINTENANCE

THE BATHROOM

This may also double as a mini-laundry room, where underwear and the occasional shirt may be hand washed, or where nappies may be put to soak.

Although the room may appear to be clean, regular attention is necessary to destroy germs.

Standard equipment varies, but normally there will be a bath, wash basin, W.C. and some kind of cupboard. More luxurious additions may be a hand-shower attachment or separate shower, with cubicle, a bidet, a wash basin installed in a 'vanitory' unit, and a heated towel rail.

W.C.s may have a high- or low-level water storage tank, and may be installed in a separate room together with a small hand basin.

All bathrooms should have a waste bin — preferably of plastic or some wipeable surface, with a plastic bin liner. This deals safely with the problem of what to do with soap wrappers, old razor blades, ends of soap, empty shampoo bottles and lavatory rolls and the like.

It is also quite useful to keep the linen bin in the bathroom (this could double as a bathroom stool). Encourage the family to throw their discarded clothes into this before bathing instead of on the floor of the bathroom.

BATHROOM ROUTINE

Clean mirrors, glass shelves and windows regularly to remove soap splashes, hair spray and toothpaste. Hair spray can be removed with surgical spirit.

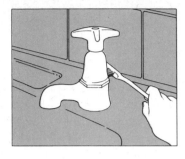

The bath This may be vitreous enamelled cast-iron, fibre-glass or acrylic. If you are considering buying a new bath, remember that acrylic baths are cheaper than cast-iron but damage more easily.

Avoid harsh cleaners on baths as these will scratch. Cream cleansers are more effective and cause less damage than abrasive powder, and can be used on chrome taps, 'grab rails' and other fittings as well as the bath.

If a bath has been badly neglected, fill it with hand-hot water, add a biological detergent, and leave this to soak for several hours; when this solution is rinsed away it will remove all the 'tide marks' and other surface grime very satisfactorily.

For bad coppery-grey stains you can buy a proprietary cleaner designed to remove these, or try smearing lemon juice or vinegar on the stained areas and leave for several hours.

Chrome taps respond well to a polish with a soft cloth after cleaning.

If you do have a hand-held shower, this is very useful for rinsing the bath.

The wash basin This may be vitreous enamel or china. It may be installed in a 'vanitory' unit or boxed in with a

Clean round taps with an old toothbrush dipped in bleach, and pour bleach down the drain to get rid of smells and any germs that might be breeding there.

painted cupboard which may also act as a store cupboard as well as eliminating awkward cleaning behind the pedestal.

The wash basin quickly becomes dirty with soap scum, toothpaste, hair, etc. Swab down regularly with a cream scourer and warm water, and scrub round taps with an old toothbrush dipped in liquid bleach. Bleach or disinfectant poured down the drain at regular intervals eliminates germs and smells.

The lavatory This is made of vitreous china and, if the surface is in good condition, is not difficult to clean. However, if the surface is cracked or 'crazed' this will provide a breeding ground for germs and smells. It may be worth investing in a new loo, rather than hanging on to a potential health hazard.

Lavatory seats are usually plastic and fitted to the pan with bolts. If they fit badly they make another trap for dirt and germs. Wooden seats are less hygienic than plastic and can crack if they are old.

Regular cleaning and disinfecting of the lavatory and surrounding area is essential. A good brush is necessary for this and can be stored in a little water, containing disinfectant; others hang to dry in holders.

Clean the lavatory by pouring bleach or disinfectant into the pan, brush well, paying particular attention to the area under the rim.

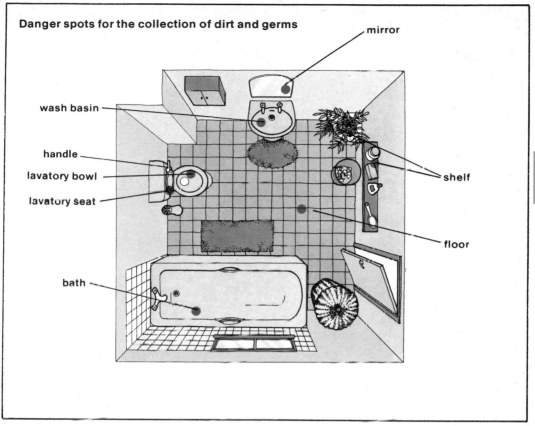

Danger spots for the collection of dirt and germs

mirror

wash basin

handle

lavatory bowl

lavatory seat

shelf

floor

bath

If there are brown stains under the rim, a powder cleaner may be more effective in removing these than disinfectant. However, never mix powder loo cleaners with liquid bleaches as they can give off a dangerous chlorine gas.

For bad stains, puff the lavatory powder on to the stained area and leave for two hours before rinsing off with clean water. There is a proprietary cleaner available for very badly stained lavatories, but wear rubber gloves when using this.

The toilet blocks and flush cleaners discussed on page 91 will dispel unwelcome odours, but will not remove bad stains. You might find it just as effective to open the window!

Remember that lavatories will become blocked if you throw items such as newspaper, tea leaves, sanitary towels or disposable nappies down them. If you do have a blocked lavatory, get a plumber as soon as possible.

Bidets These are sometimes fitted in modern homes. They too are made of vitreous china and can be used for washing and soaking nappies and washing feet as well as for intimate personal hygiene (the purpose for which they are designed). Bidets should be cleaned as you would clean the bath or basin.

General Remember that bathrooms are dusty places, owing to talcum powder and fluff from towels. Try to keep bottles and jars to a minimum or stored in cupboards, as these are time-consuming to wipe clean.

Plants may thrive in the warm, steamy atmosphere of a bathroom, but will also gather dust, so they are best kept to a minimum.

The bathroom floor may be carpeted or covered in any of the coverings discussed on pp. 105–106. Bathroom floors get dirty quickly and should be regularly swept if covered in cork or vinyl tiles. Pay particular attention to the floor surrounding the loo.

In theory, the bathroom should be one of the most relaxing rooms in the house where you can retire to a soothing bath with the radio and a book. However it will only achieve this ideal with regular and careful cleaning and attention.

HOME MAINTENANCE

STAIN REMOVAL

A stain is a discoloration of a fabric caused by the presence of foreign matter.

Always test the removal method on a hidden part first, to make sure that it doesn't harm the fabric.

USEFUL FIRST AID
In all stain removal, prompt attention is most important.

Rinse non-greasy stains away with water.

Sprinkle talc on grease marks to absorb them.

Dab salt on wine or beetroot stains. Soak in cold water as soon as possible.

White wine will remove red wine stains.

Many stains can be removed by soaking and then washing, as long as the fabric is washable.

Professional cleaning is better when expensive garments or furnishings are stained, particularly if the mark cannot be identified or if there is a special finish to the fabric. In this case, avoid home treatment, mark the stain and, if possible, tell the cleaners exactly what was spilt.

THE FOUR CATEGORIES OF STAINS
1 Those removed by normal washing action.
2 Those removed by oxygen bleach (e.g., perborate, present in most washing powders).
3 Those for which soaking before washing helps.
4 Those requiring special treatments.

WARNING
The methods recommended are those most likely to be ef-fective and can be carried out under ordinary domestic conditions. However, there can be no hard-and-fast rules for stain removal. The age and concentration of the stain and the weave and finish of the fabric affect the chances of success. If chemical treatment is carried out on a fabric weakened by age or exposure of any kind it may be further weakened. Extra care must be taken when using chemicals marked 'poisonous' or 'highly inflammable'.

SPECIAL TREATMENTS
For stains which require special treatment a number of products are available.
Laundry borax Safe on most fabrics. Use it in solution 15 ml (1 tablespoon) to 500 ml (1 pint) of warm water for sponging or soaking washables. For white cottons, sprinkle borax on the dampened stain, stretch the item over a basin and pour hot water through.
Glycerine Lubricates and softens stains. Use diluted, 1 part to 2 parts water.
Methylated spirit Use neat as a solvent. It is inflammable and poisonous, so care is needed when using it.
White vinegar (or acetic acid) Useful on certain stains. Keep acetic acid away from acetates, and avoid contact with skin.
Household ammonia Useful for neutralizing acid stains. Use diluted, 1 part to 3 parts water, and use on wool and silk.
Household bleach (chlorine) Use on white cotton or linen only, dilute 14 ml (½ fl oz) to 1 litre (2 pints) of cold water.
Grease solvents These come in several forms. Liquids should be used only in a well-ventilated room. Aerosols contain powder to absorb the stain as it is lifted out by the solvent. Paste/jelly solvents can also be used on wallpaper and stone. Turpentine substitutes, such as white spirit and lighter fuel, are useful as solvents. Petrol can be used as a solvent but it is dangerously inflammable.

STAIN TREATMENT
Treat all stains as soon as possible. The longer they are left on the fabric, the more difficult they will be to remove.

If treated quickly, washing powder and water is often all that is necessary. If this does not remove the stain and alternative treatments are available, try the mildest one first.

Apart from those stains which should be soaked in cold water first, it is best to use warm suds immediately.

Tests must be made to see whether a chemical or solvent is suitable for all colours. Try to do this on an inconspicuous part of the garment or article.

Always place the area to be treated over an absorbent cloth or wad of kitchen paper. An old piece of towelling is ideal for this purpose.

In order to avoid a ring, first treat an area around the stain, and then work in towards the centre.

When a stained part of a fabric has to be dipped or soaked in a solution, hold the cloth by this area and then twist the unstained parts to prevent the solution spreading when the stained area is immersed.

If the stain is to be treated

with solvent first and washed afterwards, the best results will be obtained by washing immediately.

Many solvents are highly inflammable. Never use near a naked flame. Always work in a well-ventilated room, and do not smoke.

Do not use methylated spirits on acetates or triacetates. White spirit may be used.

STAINS AND MARKS ON ALL FURNITURE

Heat and water marks Rub with metal polish in the direction of the grain. For cigarette burns, try rubbing with fine steel wool followed by linseed oil. Alcohol is also effective.
Wine/spirit marks Remove at once. Light marks may be removed with cigarette ash and linseed oil, then polished.
Sticky marks Using a well-wrung cloth, rub with a solution of vinegar and warm water.
Scratches and dents If small, these can be disguised with iodine, shoe polish or commercial 'Scratch Cover' polish. Be sure to polish regularly. Dents may come out if you carefully use a warm iron over a damp cloth on them.
Faded wood Sunlight causes this. Regular treatment with 'Scratch Cover' polish improves this.

CAUTION

Preparations marked poisonous should be kept out of children's reach. The cup or basin used must be very thoroughly washed afterwards.

Never soak wool, silk, leather, non-colourfast articles or articles which have flame-resistant finishes. Some articles which have metal fasteners may also be unsuitable for soaking.

STAINS AND TREATMENTS
Adhesives
Clear or contact adhesives on fabrics and upholstery. Treat with amyl acetate. Hold absorbent pad on stained side and dab from wrong side. Acetate should not be treated with acetone.
Latex adhesive on fabrics and upholstery. If wet, it can be removed with a damp cloth. If dry, loosen with liquid grease solvent, rub off as much as possible, sponge or launder.
Alcohol
Beer Rinse or soak fresh stains in lukewarm water, then launder in heavy-duty detergent.
Spirit Rinse with clear, warm water then launder in heavy-duty detergent at the highest temperature for the fibre type.
Wine Rinse in warm water or soak and sponge in a warm detergent solution.
Blood
(and other proteinaceous stains such as egg, gravy, meat juice, chocolate, ice cream). Soak in cold water and salt, or warm detergent solution. Launder for fibre type. Soak stubborn stains in hydrogen peroxide solution, plus a few drops of ammonia.
Candle wax
Lift off surface deposit with finger-nail. Sandwich stained area between clean blotting paper and melt out remainder with warm iron. Keep moving paper so that clear sections absorb wax. Use grease solvent to remove final traces.
Chewing gum
Harden the gum by placing the garment in a refrigerator, or holding it against a plastic bag containing ice cubes. The gum can then be cracked and picked off.
Coffee and Tea
These stains can normally be washed out in rich suds. Put into soak, or wash as soon as possible.
Creosote and Tar
Scrape off surplus. Treat stains with a grease solvent or petrol over an absorbent pad (caution: this is inflammable). Wash thoroughly to remove final traces of stain.
Dyes
There are no simple rules. For many coloured fabrics and for those which are not washable, professional treatment is needed. Soak white and fast-coloured fabrics (NB. NOT wool, silk or fabrics with flame-resistant finishes) in a solution of heavy-duty detergent. Treat any remaining dye on white articles with dye-stripper. Follow the maker's instructions.
Flowers and Grass
Sponge with methylated spirit. For bad stains, warm spirit carefully first by placing the open container in a bowl of hot water (away from naked flame). Wash in rich suds. To remove green colouring, moisten with glycerine, then wash.
Fruit juice,
see wine stains.
Grease, Fats and Oils
(including boot polish, lipstick, wax polish). Heavy stains should be treated with a grease solvent before washing. Alternatively, soak in a washing solution, preferably of solvent

detergent, then wash at the maximum temperature recommended for the fabric. This will remove most grease-bound stains.

Professional advice may be needed for fabric unsuitable for washing.

Ink

Washable ink Sponge or rub under cold water. Launder in heavy-duty detergent.

Permanent ink Dab with methylated spirit using pad. Wash in detergent solution.

Ballpoint Dab lightly with cotton wool moistened in methylated spirit, or use grease-solvent. Sponge with warm water or launder.

Felt-tip ink Dab small marks with methylated spirit and treat as for ballpoint ink. Felt-tip on wall coverings may be sponged with neat dishwashing liquid or methylated spirits.

Iodine Wash immediately. Old stains can be treated by soaking in a solution of 'Hypo' (sodium thiosulphate) and warm water.

Jam Fresh stains usually wash out. Soak old stains in borax solution of heavy-duty detergent solution. If some remain, try hydrogen peroxide. Launder. For fabrics which cannot be washed, scrape off as much as possible and try sponging with a cloth moistened in a solution of dishwashing liquid. Follow with a clean cloth.

Make-up Wipe fresh stains. Soak for 5 mins in a weak ammonia solution — 5ml–500ml water (1

standard medicine spoon to 1 pint). Rinse well. Launder in a solvent detergent solution at highest temperature for the fibre type.

Dried stains may be softened with glycerine before washing in a solvent detergent.

Mascara Treat with aerosol spray, followed by diluted ammonia. Alternatively, soak if necessary overnight in a strong solution of solvent detergent. Then wash.

Metal polish Blot residue and dab area with white spirit. When dry, brush off powdery deposit. Then launder in heavy-duty detergent (if washable) according to fibre type.

Nail varnish and Hair lacquer Wipe immediately with tissues or cotton wool, holding an absorbent pad under the stain. For all fabrics, use amyl acetate — test a small area first. Be particularly careful with acetates. Dab remaining colour with methylated spirit, followed by careful laundering in heavy-duty detergent.

Paints Prompt treatment is most important. Some of the newer 'silk' paints can be washed out in mild detergent, or sponged carefully when stain is fresh.

Emulsion paint Sponge fresh stains with cold water, then launder.

Oil-based paint Dab fresh stains with white spirit and sponge with cold water. Launder where possible. Dried stains on fabrics

require dry-cleaning.

Perfume Rinse immediately. Lubricate a dried stain with glycerine solution before laundering.

Perspiration Sponge fresh stains with a weak solution of ammonia, then rinse. If colour is affected, sponge with vinegar and then rinse. Bleach white cotton in a solution of hydrogen peroxide or soak in detergent solution. For fabrics unsuitable for washing, dab with white vinegar solution — 5ml of vinegar to 250ml (1 standard medicine spoon to half pint) of warm water — to clear stain and deodorize area.

Scorch marks Rub light marks immediately under cold running water, then soak in warm borax solution. Rinse well and launder if possible. On whites, careful bleaching with hydrogen peroxide (1 part to 4 parts of water) is a last remedy. If fibres are damaged, there is no remedy.

Shoe polish, see Grease, Fats and Oils.

Urine Cold rinse, then launder in heavy-duty detergent. Soak dried marks in detergent solution according to fibre type.

Vomit, Soiled underwear and Nappies Remove surface deposit, rinse well under running cold water. Soak and launder in heavy-duty detergent solution according to fibre type. For fabrics which cannot be washed, remove deposit and sponge in warm water with a few drops of ammonia added. Blot.

WINDOWS, MIRRORS, PICTURES AND BLINDS

Windows If windows are very dirty, use a solution of methylated spirits and a little warm water, applied with a chamois leather and rinsed off.

There are many proprietary glass cleaners — see cleaning table on page 91. After using one of these, polish the glass with a soft cloth to remove smears.

Mirrors/glass-framed pictures Use the same solution of warm water and methylated spirits or a window-cleaning preparation. Never rub dirty glass with a dry cloth or it may mark.

Blinds Venetian blinds should be cleaned with warm water with detergent and a sponge. Wear rubber gloves to protect hands. You can use a special pronged brush for the slats.

Treated fabric blinds: should be wiped with warm water and detergent; do not soak.

Delicate lacey blinds should be washed, with care, with warm water.

WALLS AND CEILINGS

Before you begin cleaning, remove all objects hanging on the walls — mirrors, pictures, etc. — and take down curtains or tie them up so that they are away from the walls. Also move the furniture to the middle of the room and cover it. Using a wall brush (the best is an attachment on a vacuum cleaner) or a cloth-covered broom, begin to dust the walls from the bottom up,

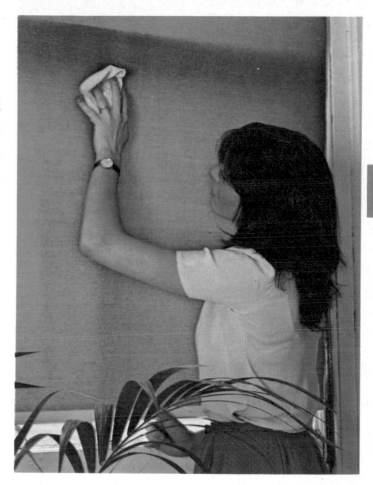

clearing away all cobwebs and threads of dust as you go; then dust the ceiling.

PAINTED SURFACES/ WALL COVERINGS

To wash, use a mild soap or a commercial cleaner designed for this task, and two pails of water, one for washing and one for rinsing. Wash the walls from the bottom up — this is to avoid any water running down on the dry surface: this creates streaks which are very difficult to remove. With a well-wrung cloth or sponge, clean a small area no more than 1 metre (3 ft) square, using a circular motion and overlapping the edges of each

Roller blinds made of treated fabric are simple to install and can be bought or made from a kit. They are easy to wipe clean with sudsy water, but do not soak them.

section you have cleaned. Rinse the area with clean water, dry and continue to the next section until the wall is finished. Remember to change the water in both buckets often.

Do not use scouring powder on walls or ceilings as it can damage the paint; the exception to this is if they are extremely dirty and must be repainted. A little cream cleanser will usually remove scuff marks, and some marks can be removed with a rub-

HOME MAINTENANCE

SURFACE	TREATMENT	CLEANING & POLISHING
Waxed polished furniture	Has been treated with beeswax and turps.	Dust regularly. Polish with good quality wax. Avoid silicones – they give too high a gloss.
High gloss furniture	Is lacquered, varnished or french polished.	Dust. Treat with silicone or good liquid wax polish.
Oiled wood	Linseed oil, turps have been rubbed into wood.	Dust. Rub with oily rag or teak oil applied *sparingly*.
Painted wood	May have matt or gloss finish.	Wash with warm water and liquid cleaner occasionally. Rinse well. Gloss may be restored with furniture cream.
French polished furniture	Treated with layers of shellac dissolved in spirit which has been built up and rubbed down to give gloss.	Dust. Occasionally apply a little furniture cream.
Sealed wood	A permanent seal has been applied.	Dust. Occasionally wipe with vinegar and water to remove marks.
Wickerwork and cane		Wash in hot water and detergent. *Rinse* thoroughly

ber. Whitewashed and distempered walls cannot be washed but must be redone.

To clean glossy enamel paint (on walls or woodwork including doors and windows), use a cloth wrung out in hot water or hot water to which you have added 5 ml (1 teaspoon) washing soda for every 4.5 litres (1 gallon) water; rub gently. Using anything else may dull the finish or leave a film.

WALLPAPER
You should always test to see if your wallpaper is washable by applying your washing solution to a small inconspicuous place before doing the whole wall. If the test is successful, continue to wash using the same method as for painted walls, remembering not to over-wet the paper to avoid soaking the paper off the wall, and to pat, not rub, the surface dry. For thin papers use only clear warm water with no soap or cleaning agent.

Few papers are really washable so you may have to resort to a type of dry cleaner. You can use commercial cleaning dough: wipe the wallpaper with this, turning it so that a clean surface is always in use. Overlap your strokes and be careful that the wall doesn't streak.

For grease marks, make a paste of fuller's earth and a cleaning fluid. After testing an inconspicuous spot, smooth the mixture on the grease spot, leave to dry and then brush off. Alternatively you can try an aerosol cleaner.

FABRIC-COVERED WALLS
Dust these with a vacuum cleaner using the hand attachment. For further cleaning, this should only be done according to the manufacturer's instructions. Do not use drycleaning fluids or upholstery cleaners as these may cause discoloration or

shrinking. Where there is a bad stain, a new piece of fabric could be carefully applied to the area but it will almost certainly be a different colour.

WOOD-PANELLING
See chart for care and cleaning of wood surfaces. These should be brushed or vacuumed and rubbed with soft dusters.

CARPETS AND FLOOR COVERINGS
These can provide the most comfortable and warm of coverings, but need not be really expensive. You may avoid cleaning problems later by choosing carpet with care. Consider, first of all, how much you intend to spend, and how much traffic there is in the room — high heels, children and pets can all be damaging to carpets!

TYPES OF FIBRES
Wool The traditional carpet fibre, now frequently blended with nylon (80% wool/20% nylon) to improve wear, and reduce cost. Wool resists dirt and stains very well.

Acrylic ('Courtelle') An easy-care fibre, tough and durable. Unlike many man-made fibres, it does not cause problems with static.

Modacrylic ('Teklan') A flame-retardant fibre. It is usually used in a blend with other fibres — e.g., wool, which is naturally flame-retardant.

Nylon Very hard wearing but does not retain a good appearance. There are often problems with build-up of static which attracts dirt. There are carpets with anti-static finishes — e.g.,

'Celon'. Nylon can be easily cleaned.

Viscose (Cellulosic) ('Evlan') Resists damage from rubbing by chairs, shoes, etc. and has a good pile. It is anti-static and easy to clean but not suitable for heavy wear.

Polypropylene A relatively new development, used for cheaper carpets such as cords. The pile tends to flatten and there are few colours. It cleans easily, and is a good choice for the bathroom as it is waterproof.

Polyester Often used in carpets, is hard wearing and soft to touch.

Cotton More usually used for bathroom and bedroom rugs. It is absorbent and machine washable.

CARPET CLASSIFICATION
Light domestic Bedrooms, bathrooms, guest rooms.

Medium domestic or light contract Living rooms and dining rooms, hotel bedrooms.

General domestic, medium contract Halls, stairs, public areas in hotels.

Heavy domestic, general contract All general public areas such as hotels, shops, offices and restaurants.

Luxury domestic/heavy con-

tract The most expensive quality suitable for really hard wear in cinemas, hotels, restaurants and the home.

Luxury use Usually a long pile carpet of superior quality.

UNDERLAY
All carpet, unless foam-backed, should have a good underlay, either felt or foam (rubber or synthetic).

Never use old felt or old carpet as this will cause the carpet on top to wear in the same places as the old one. Good quality underfelt will increase the life of your carpet.

CARPET CARE
New carpets will shed fluff at first, so should not be cleaned vigorously. Remove fluff regularly, using a carpet sweeper or a vacuum cleaner.

Regular maintenance: for daily care a carpet sweeper is useful. Regular use of the vacuum cleaner is essential, paying special attention to areas of heavy use. Vacuum cleaning not only cleans the surface but also removes grit in the pile which

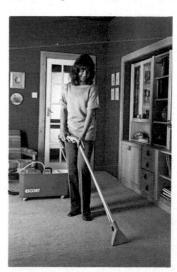

You can clean your carpets with a hired carpet shampooer, using a dry foam shampoo which is mixed with water. This absorbs dust and dries as crystals which can then be removed with a vacuum cleaner, after the carpet has dried completely. Protect the wet carpet, by placing foil under the legs of furniture sitting on it.

HOME MAINTENANCE

FLOOR COVERINGS AND MAINTENANCE	
DESCRIPTION	**CARE AND CLEANING**
Wood (Hard) Oak, beech, walnut (Soft) Pine, cedar, deal	Usually sealed or waxed. Sealing keeps out surface dirt and improves appearance. Sweep and clean with solvent-based wax. Avoid using water- detergent if waxed, remove build-up from time to time.
Wood block Parquet or Mosaic All laid in patterns of alternating squares, or herringbone, with one or more types of wood.	Treat as above. If newly- laid, blocks should be professionally sanded before sealing.
Cork Often tiles, made from bark of cork oak tree, ground, compressed, heated. May be laid on concrete.	Sweep. Vacuum or damp mop. Use liquid floor cleaner occa- sionally. If sealed do not polish, otherwise use a non-slip wax polish and a lot of buffing.
Ceramic tiles Terrazzo marble Made from natural clay, available in various colours, durable and water-resistant, but cold to stand on.	Sweep. Wash by hand or with squeezy mop, using liquid floor cleaner. Do not polish; this is dangerous in kitchens and bathrooms.
Linoleum 'Resilient' floor surface in sheet or tile form and a variety of patterns. Warm, quiet and comfortable.	Clean regularly with squeezy mop and liquid floor cleaner. Do not soak or tiles may lift. Can be sealed with water- based acrylic sealant. Polish with water-based floor wax.
Thermoplastic tiles 'Resilient' surface, which can contain PVC. Tiles are cheap, hard-wearing and water-resistant.	Sweep. Treat with water- emulsion wax. Do not use solvent products. Wash with water and liquid floor cleaner. Use undiluted cleaner on scuff marks.

can wear it away; it also lifts the pile.

Deal with spills *at once*. Solids or semi-solids should be removed gently with a knife, working from the outside to the centre. Absorb moisture with a tissue. Any stain left can be removed with a solution of carpet shampoo. It is useful to keep a tin of aerosol foam specially formulated for spot-removal on carpets and upholstery. A solvent cleaner may be applied to a greasy stain, before shampooing.

Carpet manufacturers often supply a leaflet on carpet cleaning when you buy a new carpet.

UPHOLSTERY

It is surprising how many people forget to pay attention to their upholstered chairs and sofas. Dust settles on and is ground into all fabrics, dulling the colours and wearing the fibres. Upholstered furniture is expensive and will last much longer if cared for.

MATERIALS COMMONLY USED IN UPHOLSTERY

Leather Probably the most expensive material.

Wool Moquette is a looped-pile fabric usually with the loops uncut; flame resistant wool is treated to resist flaring, burning.

Cotton and *linen* Used primarily for upholstery and loose covers.

Velvet May be pure cotton, but is more likely to be a blend of acrylic, polyester and cotton. Acrylic may also be woven.

Brocade Usually a blend of viscose and acetate. Old brocade may be silk.

Tapestry A firm woven fabric containing wool and probably polyester.

Tweed Usually wool with a smaller quantity of synthetic such as polyester.

Plastic Usually vinyl, often made to imitate leather.

CARE AND MAINTENANCE
Regular cleaning Remove all cushions and vacuum, using attachments, or use a good stiff brush. Pay particular

Clean upholstery surfaces and corners regularly with a vacuum cleaner upholstery brush and an upholstery nozzle (*below*). If dust collects on upholstery it can stain the fabric and break the fibres.

attention to inner sides and corners where dust may collect; this can be an attraction to mice. After vacuuming or brushing, fluff up the cushions and replace them, making a point of reversing them if possible as this distributes wear. It is also beneficial to occasionally give cushions an airing out-of-doors.

Stains These should be removed as soon as possible. Follow directions for stain removal on pp. 100–101. Some furniture with loose covers can be totally cleaned; this can be either by washing or dry cleaning — follow the manufacturer's instructions. For small spots and stains, you can sometimes use a solvent. Dry-foam upholstery shampoo is also effective. Always test an inconspicu-

ous place first, for colour fastness if using water, or for any possible reactions to chemicals.

Professional cleaning If the covers are removable and the fabric is suitable, you can have the covers dry cleaned by professionals, or you can do it yourself in a coin-operated dry-cleaning machine. Some fabrics must be cleaned by reliable cleaning services, especially pile fabrics such as plush or velvet. These firms will also be able to advise you if you are unsure about the proper cleaning procedure for a particular piece of upholstered furniture.

Leather This can be cleaned, after dusting, by using saddle soap, following the maker's instructions, or with thick suds made from mild, pure soap and as little water as possible. Wipe the suds off with a damp cloth and polish with a soft, dry cloth. You should keep leather supple by using a good quality furniture cream or hide food on it once or twice a year.

Vinyl Wipe with a damp cloth wrung out in warm, sudsy water; then rinse with a clean damp sponge. Stubborn soil can be removed by further rubbing or scrubbing lightly with a soft-bristled brush.

General maintenance Sharp objects — such as rings, buckles, cats' claws — can 'pluck' or 'snag' fabric. If there is a loose end, don't pull it; cut it off. Prolonged sunlight causes fading and rotting of fabric. Close curtains or blinds during sunny periods. Cover furniture with dust sheets when you are on holiday to prevent dust settling.

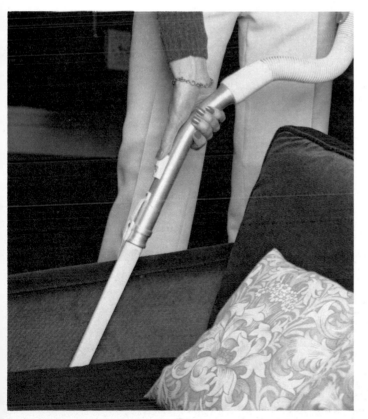

HOME MAINTENANCE

GENERAL HOME CARE

FABRIC REPAIRS
If upholstery cloth has been torn, the easiest repair for a section that is not under strain is to sew a patch to the inside of the upholstery. Cut a piece of cloth that will overlap about 25mm (1in) all round. Pass it through the tear and position it with the end of a table knife. Use the knife or a tapered piece of wood to push through latex adhesive. Spread it around and press the edges tightly, so that it penetrates woven fabric. If the material is a plastic imitation leather, use an adhesive intended for PVC. Fray the edges of a cloth patch before sticking it down, and round the corners of an imitation leather patch. If the plastic patch is thick, thin the edges by sanding underneath.

If the tear or cut tends to pull open there will have to be some stitches as well as a patch. Use stout thread and zig-zag stitches if the pattern will not show them up too much. Do this over a patch if possible, but in some places it may be easier to stick the patch on to the outside of the upholstery, although it will then be more obvious. It may be possible to cut a piece for a patch from a turned-in edge of the old fabric or the bottom of the back.

BUTTONING
If a button comes away from the surface of upholstery, you should replace the piece of thread or twine which runs through to the back. The buttoning keeps the filling in place, as well as looking attractive.

Put the button on a length of twine and pass this through the eye of a needle long enough to go through the upholstery. At the front, push it through at the point where it was sewn previously, but it will probably be stronger if you bring the needle through at a slightly different place at the back. Thread on a flat button at the back and tie the twine under it with a slip knot. Adjust the tension with the slip knot until the front appearance is correct, then lock the knot and push it into the thickness of the cushion.

RE-COVERING
Traditional upholstery was stuffed with a variety of things, most of which tended to settle under pressure and become uneven. Modern up-

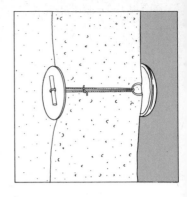

By buttoning through, cover and filling can be held. Use a slip knot for adjustments.

holstery uses plastic or rubber foam and any replacement or repair is better done with this. There are moulded rubber pads shaped to suit standard parts, but plastic foam is bought in large pieces which can be cut with a wet carving knife. Thicknesses vary from a few millimetres to 150 mm (6 in) or more.

A dining chair with a lift-out seat may have a plywood base or be a frame with webbing strained across. Webbing is either formed in parallel strips one way only, or is interwoven at right angles. Tacks which hold the covering material can be lifted off with a screwdriver. Strip off the material as well as any inner lining, then the padding. If the chair has a frame and the webbing is sagging, remove this, but note how it is tacked. Buy new webbing and tack one end of each piece to the frame. At the other end, use a strip of

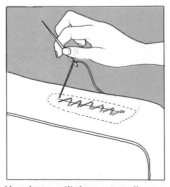

Use a knife to apply adhesive underneath the ripped fabric.

Use large stitches as well as a patch if the tear pulls open.

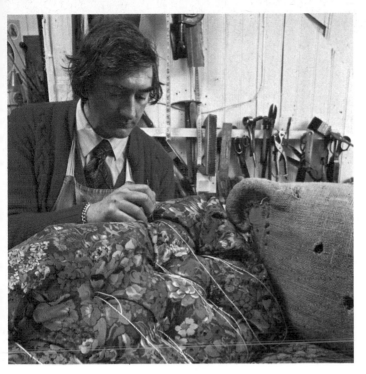

In this typical upholsterer's workroom, the antique sofa is being completely re-covered. This piece of furniture has deep buttoning, which was used in early upholstery to keep stuffing in place.

wood about 100 mm (4 in) long as a lever to tension the webbing while putting in the first tacks there, then cut off and fold over the end for more tacks.

If you are using a new piece of plastic foam as stuffing, cut it slightly oversize so that it is compressed by the covering. Bevel the underside all round so that the cover is stretched, making the edge of the foam curve downwards. Try with a scrap piece of cloth to get this right.

Start tacking the covering to the frame from the underneath. Do the back and front first, working outwards from the centre. When this is satisfactory do the same at the tapered sides. Pull the covering tight over sharp corners, even out any creases and tack underneath. If the corners of the chair are notched to fit legs, cut into the cloth, but do this no more than is necessary to get the top strained into the hollows.

Imitation leather can go directly over the foam filling. A better effect is obtained for woven cloth covering by using an inner covering of unbleached calico or something similar first. The underside of a webbing seat can be finished with a piece of cloth. Turn its edges in and tack it to the frame. Usually, tacking for this and the top cloth is kept far enough in to clear the recesses into which the seat has to fit. If the new covering material is a very different thickness from the old, check the fit before fixing any material, in case the seat has to be planed down or packed out with cardboard.

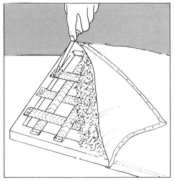

Remove the tacks by levering them off with a screwdriver.

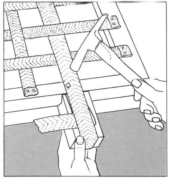

Keep the webbing under tension by using a lever.

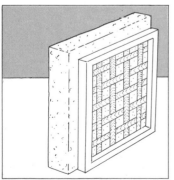

Use slightly oversize foam as it will compress when covered.

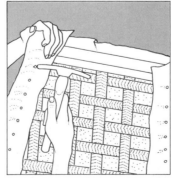

Stretch the covering over the filling and tack it underneath.

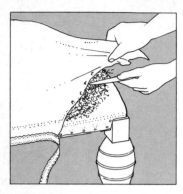

Use a stick to re-arrange the old filling of hair or fibre.

Loose chair cushions have their coverings sewn inside-out. However, part of a seam in the most inconspicuous place has to be sewn from the right side, after the pad has been inserted. In some cases there is a zip fastener. If padding has to be replaced and there is no zip, look around the edges of the back of the cushion for a different stitch pattern. There may be hand stitches or the turned-in edges may be drawn together and machine-stitched from the outside. These are the stitches to unpick so that you can take out the old filling and replace it.

Upholstery that is fixed to a wooden framework often has the tacked edges covered with gimp, which is a sort of tape obtainable in a very large number of patterns, possibly with fringes and tassels. It is held with gimp pins, which are fine black nails. Lever these out carefully. If the old filling of hair or fibre has settled, try lifting an edge so a pointed stick can be inserted. Use this to tease out the compressed material and re-arrange it so that it fills up the hollows to give a better shape. In a bad case, more similar material can be

pushed in or plastic foam can be put under the old material to lift it.

FURNITURE REPAIRS

Cracks or splits in wood can be glued, providing the glue can be spread fully on the meeting surfaces. The glue should be the strongest obtainable if the trouble is not to recur. Avoid general-purpose glues. Buy one intended for boats and follow the directions, as these glues are strong as well as water-proof. If good penetration of the glue into the split is doubtful, screw across the joint, so the screw head comes inconspicuously on an inner surface. Always drill a clearance hole for the neck of the screw, then a smaller hole for the threaded part. Use a countersink bit to let the screw head in level.

If a glued joint has come apart, do not put new glue on top of the old as it will not bond. Scrape through the old glue to expose wood fibres. It helps to draw a fine saw sideways across the wood to roughen it before regluing. Modern glues do not require tight cramping, but the surfaces have to be brought closely together. With framed furniture, such as a

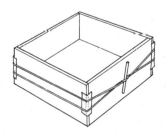

Although, nowadays cramping is often unnecessary, it may prove useful with some framed furniture.

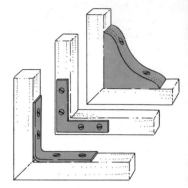

Joints can be strengthened by screwing on brackets.

chair, rope tied across and twisted with a piece of wood to tighten it, can act as a cramp.

If a joint has loosened, but cannot be opened enough to clean and reglue, a strengthening bracket can be screwed on, inside the framing where it cannot be seen. A triangle of wood could be used at the corner of framing under a lift-out seat. Slope the screw holes towards the corner so they draw the bracket in. Metal repair plates can be bought, or an angle bracket, like a small shelf support, can be used in a corner instead of a wood bracket. For a flat repair there are straight and L-shaped plates, already drilled.

A dent in a wooden surface can be brought back level by forcing moisture into the fibres. Hold the surface level and put a little water in the dent. Put a damp cloth over the damaged area and press a hot iron over its centre, so that the water steams and the pressure forces some of this into the wood. Furniture restorers do the same thing with a very hot spoon, which is put into the water. In both cases the process may have to be repeated. Let all moisture dry out, then polish over the wood.

PAINTING

Paint is used both for decoration and protection. Paints intended for outside work are designed to stand up to bad weather. They can be used inside, but there are some inside paints that are unsuitable outdoors. Modern paints have synthetic ingredients and some require different techniques from traditional paints. Read and follow the directions on the can. Varnish may be regarded as colourless paint and treated in the same way.

Tools Good paint brushes produce better work. The widest brush that can be used on a surface would be preferable, but to economize use narrower brushes – 75 mm (3 in) for general use and down to 20 mm (¾ in) for narrow parts.

For broad surfaces and many paints a roller and its tray is quicker to use and produces an even finish. When your brush or roller are out of use overnight, immerse them in solvent for an oil paint or water for emulsion paint. White spirit will clean out oil paint, or you can use a paint cleaner fluid, then wash with detergent and clean water.

Paint can be stripped with a chemical stripper or burned off with a blowlamp (gas or paraffin) and a scraper. A filling or putty knife is needed for pressing stopping into holes or cracks. Glasspaper wrapped around a block of wood can be used for sanding. A wire brush will remove rust from iron. Masking tape is useful for defining areas and divisions between areas of different colours.

STRIPPING

If an old paint surface is sound, there is no need to remove it before repainting. However, it should be cleaned. Wash with warm water and detergent, then wipe over with clean water and allow to dry. If any gloss remains, rub with glasspaper wrapped around a block of wood or scour with water and cleaning powder, followed by clean water. If there are bare patches, paint them and sand the whole surface level before adding an all-over coat.

Tools for stripping and painting: (*top row from left*) stripper, wire brush, sponge, shave hook, blowlamp, putty knife, sanding block; (*bottom row from left*) roller and tray, 75 mm (3 in) brush, 50 mm (2 in) brush, 20 mm (¾ in) brush, white spirit, masking tape.

HOME MAINTENANCE

Use a blowlamp at the correct distance to blister the paint so it can be scraped off.

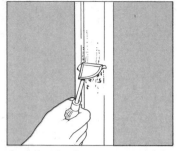

A shave hook removes paint in mouldings and shaped parts; pull it along the surfaces.

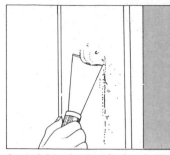

A straight-edged stripping knife will lift paint on broad surfaces; use a pushing action.

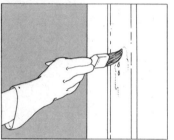

Always wear rubber gloves if using a chemical stripper.

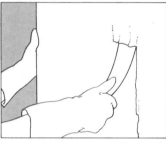

Strip the paint as it lifts and blisters.

Neutralize chemical stripper as directed.

If paint is flaking or is in bad condition, it should be removed. If a chemical stripper is used, *read the directions* — the chemical can damage clothing and skin. The stripper will cause the paint to bubble and it can then be scraped away. For a broad surface use a straight-edged stripping knife with a pushing action. For mouldings and shaped parts it is easier to pull a shave hook. Neutralize the surface as directed by the manufacturers, then leave to dry.

To strip with a blowlamp, experiment first to get the correct distance for the flame. Swing the lamp so as to blister the paint without charring the wood. As the blisters form on the paint, scrape them off. Do not use a blow lamp on plaster, asbestos or around glass.

SURFACE PREPARATION

The quality of the final painted surface depends as much on adequate preparation as on the application of the paint.

Nails should be punched below the surface. Knots, which tend to stand up because of their hardness, should be sanded level. Nail holes and cracks should be stopped. Buy stopping in a tube or a powder which is mixed and pressed in with a filling or putty knife, although an old table knife will do. Leave it slightly raised to allow for sanding. Plastic wood makes a harder stopping and it could be used if wood has broken away and has to be built up to trim to shape. Sand the surface all over after stopping.

Some porous wood also needs filling, using a paste which is rubbed into the wood and sanded to prevent absorption. Some hard-board is also very absorbent.

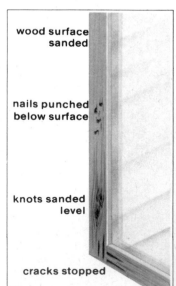

wood surface sanded

nails punched below surface

knots sanded level

cracks stopped

PAINT CHOICE

The traditional paint for most purposes was oil-based, with pigments and natural resins. The modern equivalent is synthetic and has improved drying qualities and durability. A good gloss oil paint is best for outside work on wood or metal. Normally it is applied with a brush. A non-drip version is like a thick jelly, which can also be brushed.

Polyurethane paint in a one-can form has similar qualities to oil paint, with increased waterproofness. A two-can version, mixing the parts before use, is one of the toughest paints made.

Acrylic paint can be thinned with water and is suitable for inside surfaces. Finishes are semi-gloss and matt. It will make steel rust if a primer is not used first.

Emulsion paints can be used on interior walls and ceilings. They are not satisfactory on woodwork. Washable distempers are similar in effect to emulsion paints and are now mostly used for walls and ceilings. Both can be used with a brush or roller. Emulsion comes in matt, silk and gloss finishes; distemper is matt.

Varnishes are made in several qualities. The best for exterior work is boat varnish and this is also toughest for interior use. Normally, varnish has a slightly orange colour. Varnish stain has a colour added, but a better result is obtained by staining the wood and then using clear varnish.

PAINTING TECHNIQUE

Most paints require stirring before use, but read the instructions, particularly if the colour appears even when you open the can.

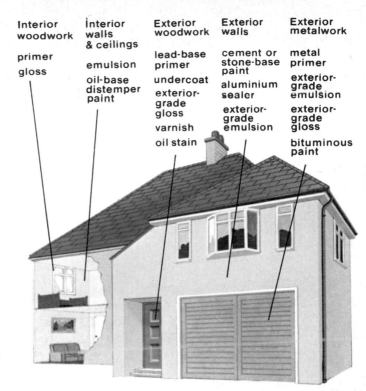

Interior woodwork	Interior walls & ceilings	Exterior woodwork	Exterior walls	Exterior metalwork
primer	emulsion	lead-base primer	cement or stone-base paint	metal primer
gloss	oil-base distemper paint	undercoat	aluminium sealer	exterior-grade emulsion
		exterior-grade gloss	exterior-grade emulsion	exterior-grade gloss
		varnish		bituminous paint
		oil stain		

Some oil paints need a very thorough mixing, using a *clean* wooden stick. Varnishes are better not stirred violently as this causes air bubbles which will mark the surface. Do all stirring before use, otherwise the colour may be affected.

Starting from a bare surface, the first paint is a priming coat. There are special primers, which penetrate wood and grip the grain. For metal, a primer has constituents that bond to the surface. The next coat is undercoat. Both this and the primer finish with a matt surface. In some painting systems the primer is made by thinning undercoat. The colour of the undercoat is complementary to the colour of the top coat, although not necessarily the same. A slightly different shade allows progress of the top coat to be seen more easily. If

there has to be any build-up to get a sufficient covering, this is better done with several undercoats than by repeating the top coat, which may run if glossy paint is used. Normally, each coat has to dry and should be rubbed down before the next coat, but there are some synthetics where following coats have to be applied within a specified time.

It is helpful to hang a wire across the centre of a paint can, so the brush can be wiped against that instead of the edge of the can, where drips will soon run down the outside. So far as possible, only dip about 50 per cent of the depth of the bristles into the paint, because as work progresses, particularly overhead, paint will soon drip back into the brush.

How much brushing to give depends on the paint. Some paints have to be applied with minimum

113

brushing. If no limitations are mentioned in the instructions, dip the brush, wipe off some of the paint, then apply it to the surface, first crossing in at least two directions to spread the coat. Finish with strokes in the direction of the grain or the long way of the piece. As subsequent parts of that surface are painted, make the finishing strokes back towards the previously painted part, lifting the brush as it goes over the edge of that part. In that way, brush marks in the finished surface will be avoided.

If you are painting a vertical surface, you may have to brush across if it is wide and shallow, but if possible finish with up and down strokes. Start at the top, so later painting comes below and the final strokes are upwards. There is then less risk of 'runs', where excess paint forms into lumps as it slides down slightly. However, if brushing is in several directions before the final strokes there is little risk of this happening. If a run or sag occurs, let it dry, then sand it level and paint over. On the top coat, try and brush it out while the paint is still wet.

When dealing with panels

A wire hung across a can of paint helps to keep the drips inside.

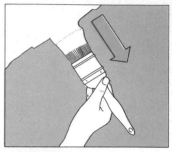

Make sure to spread the paint by brushing from a wet edge.

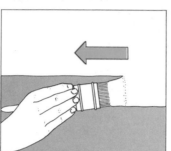

Make sure there are no gaps in the paintwork when resuming.

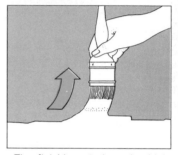

The finishing strokes should be back towards the completed work.

in a door or elsewhere, paint the panels first. Get well into the surrounding angles, but be careful not to have too much paint on the brush, or it will build up in the angles or corners and may run. When dealing with windows, paint the bars and the mouldings before the wider parts of the frame. In other structures, it is normally best to deal with narrow parts before broad.

If there are two colours to be used on one piece, it is usually better to apply the lighter colour first. If it runs over to where the darker colour will come, the darker shade will hide the lighter one. Masking tape can be used to define the edge of the second colour. With some paints that set very hard, leave the tape until the paint is almost dry, then peel it off. If you wait until the paint is very hard, you may finish with a cracked line.

When using a roller for walls and ceilings, have enough paint in the tray and work the roller up and down the slope of the tray. A little experience will show how much paint to take up or

When painting a panelled door, first paint the mouldings and then the panels before the surrounding surfaces.

work out to allow satisfactory use. A roller covers large areas quickly, but is unsatisfactory where edges have to be defined. Use a brush around edges. When dealing with a wall or ceiling, use the brush at the edges, doing small areas at a time ahead of the roller so that both coats are liquid when they meet. If all the edges are done first with a brush, the paint may be dry before the roller reaches it and the meet may be obvious.

For the same reason try to use the roller in such a way that it always meets a previously wetted surface and not one that has dried, although on a large area this is not always possible. Distemper and emulsion paint can be rolled in all directions and they should dry without marks.

For outside work the techniques are very similar, but the main problems are those of access and weather conditions. You have to use ladders and may only be able to reach a limited area at a time. Scaffolding makes working easier, but is a complication. Wood and metal are painted as already described. If stone, brick or cement are to be painted for the first time, use a special sealer (the builders' merchant can advise). This prevents efflorescence, which is the working through of salts in the wall, to show as white deposits on the new surface. It is essential, however, to prepare the surface in accordance with the manufacturer's instructions. Follow this with cement paint, usually two coats. One coat may be all that is needed over an old painted surface.

It is possible to use exterior-grade gloss oil paint on stone or brick. Seal a new surface and apply an undercoat. If the lower colour shows through, apply another coat before the top coat. There are exterior grades of emulsion paint which can be used in a similar way.

WALLPAPERING
Wallpaper is made in so many attractive designs and finishes that it can be used to complement any colouring or furnishing scheme, but for early attempts at hanging avoid the heavier and deeply patterned papers. Lining paper is plain and may be used before wallpaper on painted or poor surfaces. Papering a ceiling is more difficult than a wall, but may be the only way to cover cracks.

Cellulose paste is now the choice for light papers, as it does not stain. The older starch/flour pastes are better for heavier papers.

There are some self-adhesive papers that are moistened in a special trough before hanging. For most papers you will need a pasting table, preferably about 2 m (6½ft) by 80 cm (2½ft), but a kitchen table could be used.

A broad pasting brush is used to apply the paste, which is kept in a bucket. Large paperhanger's scissors are useful, although domestic scissors can be used and a trimming knife with replaceable blades is also handy. A hanging brush is like a narrow clothes brush and is used for smoothing paper. If old paper has to be stripped, a similar scraper to that used for paint stripping can be used.

Preparing the walls Soak any old wallpaper with warm water several times or use a stripping solution. Be careful not to dig the scraper into the plaster. If the old paper has a glazed surface, break through this with a wire brush, so that the water can penetrate. Plasterboard that has not been

Tools for wallpapering: (*from left to right*) paperhanger's scissors, paper stripper, spirit level (to check, when applying patterned paper, if floors and ceilings are level), pasting brush, trimming knife, hanging brush, tape measure (to measure the correct length of each piece of wallpaper, adding a bit extra for insurance).

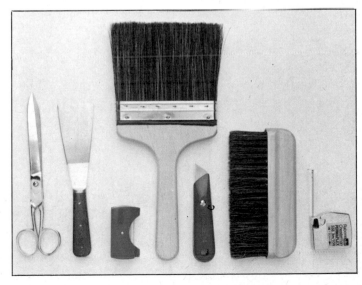

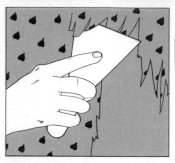

Soak and strip the paper with a broad scraper, being careful not to dig into the plaster.

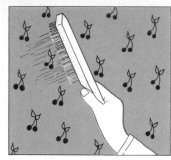

Scour glazed wallpaper with a wire brush so that the water will penetrate and soak the paper.

sealed will soften and become damaged with water. Always try a corner first. If the plasterboard under the paper softens, leave the paper on and put the new paper over it.

In a new house, plaster should be left at least six months before covering with paper. Glue size should be applied to an absorbent wall to prevent loss of adhesion by absorption of water from the paste. This is a thin wood glue to be painted on in the proportions stated on the packet — *this is important*. A painted wall should be sanded and sized before papering.

Fix lining paper horizontally with its edges butting (edge to edge, not overlapping). It may not be necessary to go all over a wall if it is generally smooth. Paper can be pasted over damaged and uneven surfaces only, but hard edges have to be avoided as they may show through the wallpaper. Paste lining paper over the affected area, allowing a small amount to be loose all round. When the paste has dried, tear this surplus away so as to leave a tapered, ragged edge. If there is still any hardness, sand so it blends into the wall.

HANGING WALLPAPER

Check the available length and width of rolls of paper. The shop will charge for trimming, which removes the manufacturer's edge by machine, much more accurately than can be done by hand. Some papers are now pre-trimmed. Measure the walls to be covered and estimate how much paper will be needed. If the paper is plain there will be little waste. If there is a prominent pattern, adjoining pieces will have to be matched and this can mean quite long ends going to waste. Buy enough paper and ensure that all rolls come from the same batch. There may be a slight colour variation in another batch. Obviously, running out of paper could be disastrous.

It is unwise to assume that room corners are square or upright and even doors and window frames may be further from true than is expected. Use a plumb line to get a line for the first edge and not a corner, door or window which may not be truly upright. A plumb line is just a weighted string. Hold or hang it and pencil on the wall at intervals down the string.

It is usually most convenient to start papering the wall with a window in it, so you are working in the light. Always start from the middle of the wall and work outwards.

Cut pieces of paper the length required, but at the same time match patterns and trim to length accordingly as you go. Have the pile of pieces face down on the pasting table. The alternative is to do one piece at a time and match patterns as you go, but this is slower.

The paper will be longer than your table. Paste along the centre as far as you conveniently can, then paste outwards to the edges from this. Pull the paper along and fold over what you have pasted so the pasted surface is inside, while you paste the other section of the sheet in the same way. As you paste towards the edges, it helps to move the sheet so the side you are doing overlaps the table edge slightly. With most papers it is worthwhile to paste a further sheet immediately, so one sheet is soaking up paste while the previous one is being hung.

Take the looped paper to the wall. Use a small step ladder so you can reach the ceiling. Open out the looped top part and position the end against the ceiling, but with a little over for trimming. Hang one edge against the plumb line marks. Stroke the hanging brush down the centre of the paper to force out air then brush to the edges. With the top in place, open the bottom fold and do the same to the bottom edge. The paper should lie as it comes, not be stretched in any direction, or there will be creases.

At top and bottom rub the

Start by using a plumb line to mark a straight line on the wall.

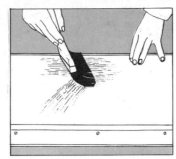

Spread the paste from the centre and smooth it towards the edges.

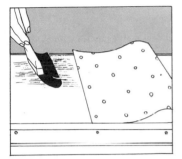

Pull the paper along and fold it as the paste is spread.

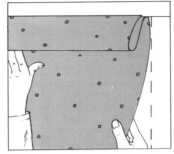

Position the first sheet against the wall on the marked line.

Smooth the hanging brush down the centre first.

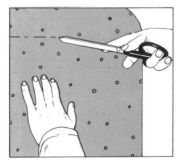

Mark the top cut by pressing scissors into the angle of the ceiling.

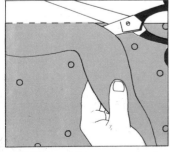

Peel the paper back and cut to this line, then press into place.

Diagonal cuts around a light switch make a tight fit possible.

back of the scissors into the angle of the ceiling or skirting board to mark where the paper has to be trimmed. Peel the paper back and cut to these lines, then press it back. If there is excess paste, use a sponge to remove it before pressing the paper back. Make sure the whole piece is tight against the wall by looking across it towards the light to see whether air bubbles are trapped.

Slide the next piece of paper into position so the patterns match and the edge makes a neat butt joint with the previous piece, then smooth it and trim top and bottom.

CORNERS AND ANGLES

At a corner the angle is unlikely to be accurate enough to allow taking one piece of paper around. Instead, cut the paper so it will reach the corner and wrap around a very small amount. Fix it, then bring the remainder up to it, checking that its further edge is upright. The slight break in the pattern in the corner should not be noticeable.

Where the paper has to be cut around doors and window frames, use a similar technique to that used at top and bottom, rubbing to mark the shape and peeling back for trimming. At a window recess, paper inside from the window and wrap over the edges, then bring pieces from the flat wall over them. When papering around a light switch, first unscrew and loosen plastic covering. Place the paper over the top. Feel for the switch by pressing on the knob, making cuts from this diagonally. Wait until the paper is hung before cutting fully to shape. Screw the switch cover back in position, hiding cut edges.

HOME MAINTENANCE

ELECTRICITY

MAIN SWITCH AND METER

Electricity comes into the home via a main switch and a meter, with sealed fuses, all provided by the supplier of electricity. The main switch is off when it is down and the electricity supply for the whole house is then cut off. *Switching off here is the safety action in an emergency.*

The amount of electricity used is recorded by a meter in kWh (kilowatt-hours). The simplest type to read has a row of figures. Ignore fractions at the right and read the five figures from the left. An older type has six dials with hands and each reading 0 to 9. Ignore the one giving tenths. Read the others in turn from left to right. If a hand is between figures, read the lower. Put your readings together as a five-figure number. A disc turning below the dials indicates that electricity is being used.

FUSES AND CUTOUTS

All electrical equipment is protected from overloading and damage by fuses or cutouts. The whole system is protected by the suppliers' fuse and they must be notified if that fails. Other fuses are in the circuits and are usually located near the main switch. More fuses may be in plugs.

A fuse is a piece of wire that will get hot so that it melts and breaks the circuit if it becomes overloaded. Occasionally a fuse may 'blow' for no apparent reason. *Turn off the main switch if you examine fuses.* A fuse may be

SAFETY PRECAUTIONS

1 *Electricity can kill.* Treat it with respect.
2 If unsure about the safety of any equipment, consult an electrician.
3 Remove plugs before examining equipment and switch off at the mains before working on fixed equipment.
4 Do not overload circuits by using too many adaptors.
5 Do not use wall switches in bathrooms. Have pull-cords.
6 Faulty electrical work is the most common cause of home fires. Do not risk short circuits by using flex with faulty insulation, fixing cables with staples, leaving bare wire at a plug or failing to use earth wires with metal-cased equipment.
7 Use fuses of the correct size.
8 Connect wires to their correct terminals or there could be danger, even when switched off.
9 For an extension, make sure the socket part is on the mains side.

Colour coding: old — neutral / earth / live; new — neutral / earth / live

Electricity meters may have dials or give a digital reading.

Tools for simple electrical repairs: (*top to bottom*) pliers and electrician's wire strippers (both with insulated handles), screwdriver with neon tester (to check if terminal is live), stanley knife. A torch is also very useful, but be sure that it is a rubber one.

replaced, but if the new fuse blows, the cause of the trouble must be discovered. If it is not obvious, get an electrician.

The basic fuse is a piece of wire between terminals on or in a ceramic block that can be pulled away from the fuse box. Fuse wire can be bought wound on a card, usually in 5 amp., 15 amp. and 30 amp. sizes. Do not strain new wire between terminals. There should be some slackness. The ceramic part of the fuse may be marked with a figure to indicate the size wire to use, or it could be colour-coded: white for 5, blue for 15 and red for 30 amp. A cartridge fuse is less troublesome to fit. It is a tube containing the wire, with metal ends to fit into spring clips.

Each cartridge fuse is colour-coded: the most common are 3 amp. (red), used for appliances up to 720 watts, and 13 amp. (brown) for those

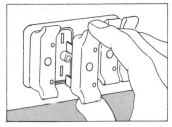

When changing a fuse, be sure to pull it out by using the grips provided at each end.

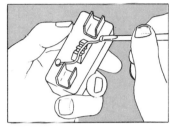

Do not strain new fuse wire when fitting it between terminals.

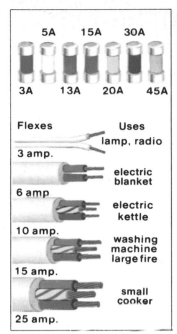

5A	15A	30A
3A	13A	20A	45A

Flexes	Uses
3 amp.	lamp, radio
6 amp	electric blanket
10 amp.	electric kettle
15 amp.	washing machine large fire
25 amp.	small cooker

with a range of 720 – 3000 watts.

A 13 amp. plug can be fitted with a 3 amp. or a 13 amp. fuse. Lightly-loaded equipment, such as radios and clocks, may have 3 amp. fuses, but fires and other heavily-loaded equipment require 13 amp. fuses. Some appliances, although they use below 720 watts, still need a 13 amp. fuse because of the higher starting current required, especially if they incorporate an electric motor.

A circuit breaker may look like a switch or have a projecting knob or button. If it becomes overloaded, the switch jumps to the off position or the button pops out. Both can be reset by moving them back.

WIRING TO PLUGS AND EQUIPMENT

Older wiring had red insulation for the live line, black for the neutral line and green for the earth wire. Newer wires conform to a European standard and have brown for the live line, blue for the neutral line and green and yellow bands for the earth line. Twin cables, with only live and neutral lines are used for lighting and some equipment, including that which is double-insulated and marked with a square within a square. For most other equipment it is important for safety that the earth wire is connected at a plug

Cut away the outer insulation by splitting it lengthwise with a sharp knife and cutting the surplus off with wire cutters. Leave only enough wire for stripping and attaching to terminals.

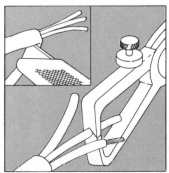

and to a metal part of the equipment.

Modern wiring uses three-pin 13 amp. plugs with flat pins. Older circuits may have plugs with round pins, using 15 amp. plugs for fires and other equipment with heavy loads, and 5 amp. plugs of a smaller size for lightly-loaded equipment.

If new wire is to be fitted to an appliance, make sure the new cable is of the same size and type as the old. Compare the number and size of copper wires. Do not use twin wires where the appliance has an earth connection. For any sort of portable appliance, use flex of the correct size, not cable intended for rigid wiring. If you have any doubt and do not have old cable to compare, tell your supplier what you need the cable for.

Open a plug and check how much of the end of the cable has to be prepared. Cut back the outer insulation. It can usually be split lengthwise and the surplus cut off. Bare the wire ends far enough for them to wrap around screw terminals or fit into those with holes. In most plugs the earth wire has to be

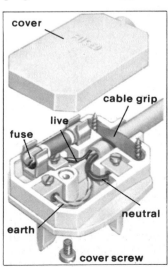

cover
cable grip
live
fuse
neutral
earth
cover screw

HOME MAINTENANCE

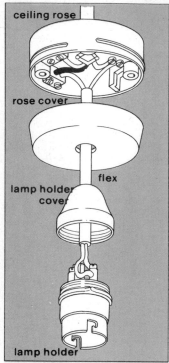

ceiling rose

rose cover

flex

lamp holder cover

lamp holder

A light socket.

longer than the other two.

Wire ends can be bared by careful work with a knife, but there is less risk of cutting the wire as well as the insulation if a stripper, looking like pincers, is used.

If you have a 13 amp. plug with a fuse, the live wire may connect under or alongside the fuse. The neutral terminal (marked N) is at the other side. There will be a flex-retaining clip at the entrance to the plug. This takes any strain, instead of it being transferred to the terminals. Make sure the outer casing will go under that clip when the wires have been cut to length.

If the wires go around screws, wrap them in the direction of tightening. Make sure there are no loose strands. Tighten the re-

taining clip and re-assemble.

At the other end of the cable, connections to an appliance are generally similar, but the outer insulation may have to be cut back more to allow a spread of the wires. Connect brown or red to the terminal marked L and black or blue to that marked N. The earth connection will probably be to an unmarked screw in the casing or a metal part. See that any strain on the cable will be taken by a flex retaining clip and not by the electrical connections.

For a lamp socket connected with twin flex, pull out the plug or switch off the mains, then check how the electrical connections are relieved of load. Usually they loop under a central plastic part and the cover screwing down may further tighten them. Do not bare any more of the ends than are needed to fit into the screwed ends of the contact plungers.

To wire a table lamp with a switch built in, make sure it is the live (brown or red) wire that goes to the switch. The other wire goes to the lamp holder. If a torpedo-shaped switch is to be put in the flex, cut the live wire and bare its ends. The other wire will go straight through the switch casing. Adjust the amount of the live wire ends used to make connections to the switch, so there is equal tension on both parts of the

cable when the switch is assembled.

ELECTRIC FIRES
Electric fires take a heavy load and should be fused accordingly, with a 13 amp. fuse in a fused plug. The element in a fire is a coiled piece of wire with a high resistance. When a current flows through it, it glows.

In the simplest one or two bar fire, each element is made by wrapping wire around a bar insulator, either bare or with silica glass casing. These fires have guards across the front. If a bar fails, pull out the plug and remove the guard. The ends of the element may have sleeve covers over the connections. Slide these clear. The connection is usually a screwed projection held to a bracket by a knurled nut. Release the nuts and spring one bracket to release the element so a new one can be fitted. Make sure the nuts are tight and the guard secure before putting the fire back into use. While the element is out, take the opportunity to polish the reflector.

Another type of fire has the wire element in a fireclay unit, with the coiled wire sprung around grooves. If it fails, it is unsafe to try to link the broken ends. For many fires it is best to get another complete fireclay unit already wired. This has

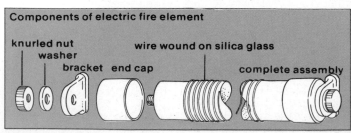

Components of electric fire element

knurled nut
washer
bracket   end cap

wire wound on silica glass

complete assembly

to be screwed into place and the terminals must be connected. Alternatively, it is possible to get a new coiled element to fit into the old fireclay backing. Note how the old fireclay element was fixed. Besides attaching to terminals at its ends there may be clips at intervals through the fireclay. Straighten their ends and pull them out of the front.

The new coil has to be evenly tensioned. Mark it into the same number of divisions as the grooves in the fireclay so each part is pulled the same amount as it is fitted. Join its ends to the terminals and replace the clips. Make sure the fireclay block is fitted securely and any guard is replaced. Fires tend to attract dust and it is worthwhile brushing the fireclay and vacuum cleaning the case when the parts are dismantled.

A bowl reflector fire works in the same way as a flat fireclay unit. If it fails, take off the rear cover, disconnect the element ends from the terminals and fit a new element. It will do the bowl good to give it a polish while the element is out. Make sure the earth wire is connected to the reflector and the guard is replaced securely.

IMMERSION HEATERS
If a domestic water system is heated by an immersion heater, electricity can be saved if its thermostat is adjusted to cut out at the lowest temperature that is acceptable.

The thermostat in the top of the heater usually has three settings, but this is not obvious as it is covered by a plate. If the screw holding the plate is undone this may

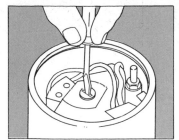

Turn screw to adjust heater thermostat temperature.

expose another cover over a regulator that can be turned with a screwdriver to one of three settings, which may be: 140°, 160° or 180°F (60°, 72° or 82°C). The lowest of these should be adequate for washing up and other domestic uses.

GAS

There is a main gas tap near the meter. In emergency turn this off to isolate all gas appliances. If you smell gas, turn off this tap and notify the suppliers. If you suspect a slight leak, dab any doubtful joint with soapy water. Any bubbles will indicate a leak.

COOKERS
Besides general cleaning of a gas stove, examine the burners. If there are round holes, taper a piece of wood to poke them clear. If there are slots, use a stiff brush to clean them. When clean, all flames should burn blue with

Applying soapy water to a slight leak causes it to bubble.

a clearly defined lighter blue cone inside. If there is any yellowing of the flame, heat is reduced and there is a greater tendency to produce soot. This can be removed by increasing the air to the burner. There may be an adjusting screw under the supply part of the burner. If not, ask the gas board to adjust the burner. If the burner can be lifted out, occasionally wash it through with hot water after clearing the holes.

If a pilot jet fails, it is probably blocked. Use a fine wire pricker to clear it, but not a pin or needle, which might damage the jet.

FIRES
Heat is radiated by flames playing on fireclay bars, called radiants, and these may break and need replacing. There are two modern types: separate bars and box radiants. Older fires have upright honeycomb radiants standing over each jet. A protective grill in front of the fire may be sprung or screwed in place and should be removed before replacing radiants.

Box radiants stand in slots and can be lifted and pulled forward. Put in a new section by engaging the top and lowering it into the slot. Horizontal bars can be lifted one at a time and slid out of its slot, until the damaged one is reached. The upright honeycomb radiants have a bar across their tops to retain them. Release this and lift away the ones to be replaced.

If there is electric ignition from a battery, this can be reached after removing a panel. If there is a fire effect and it needs a new bulb, unplug the fire and lift off the effect panel, then remove any spinners to get at the bulb.

HOME MAINTENANCE

PLUMBING

LEAKING TAPS

If a tap continues to drip after it is turned off, it needs a new washer. If it leaks around the handle when it is turned on, the fault is in the gland around the spindle (the parts of a tap are shown, *right*). If you have to open a tap to replace the washer, turn off the supply of water. This can often be done at the nearest stop tap, but it depends on where the water is coming from (mains or storage tanks). If in doubt, consult your plumber. The gland can usually be repaired without turning the water off. There are only two sizes of tap washer in general use: 13 mm (½ in) for wash basins and sinks, or 20 mm (¾ in) for baths. Older washers were made of leather for cold water taps and fibre for hot water taps, but newer washers are plastic and these are to be used for both systems.

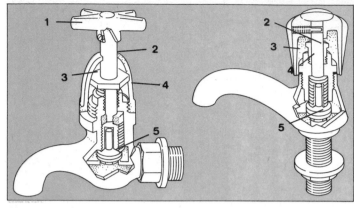

Most taps are basically similar inside and incorporate:
1 Cross handle
2 Spindle
3 Gland nut
4 Dome or cover
5 Jumper and washer

Bib taps (*left*) have horizontal inlets for fixing to the wall, and pillar taps (*right*) have vertical ones which fix into the appliance. Another type is the Supatap whose washer can be changed without turning off the water.

To get at the inside of a tap, remove the handle. If you have a cross type, undo a small screw in its side and lift it off. If it is a deep knob, poke out the little plug at its centre and undo the screw under it so the knob can be lifted off. If there is a shield below the knob, you will find it is screwed on and is often only hand tight. Grip it through a piece of cloth and take it off. Some shields have

If a tap leaks around the spindle, there is slackness at the gland.

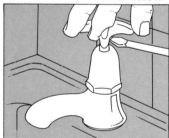

To remove the handle, slacken the screw and lift it off.

The gland nut may be hexagonal or knurled.

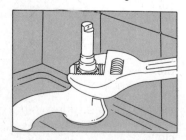

Tighten the gland nut with pliers or spanner.

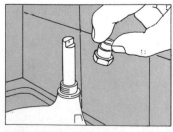

If leak persists, remove gland nut above packing.

Press in more packing string and replace nut.

flats on them to unscrew with a spanner.

The gland nut is the upper part with six flats designed to take a spanner. Use an adjustable spanner rather than pliers, which might damage the brass nut. Tighten the gland nut (turn clockwise when viewed from above). Put the handle temporarily back on the spindle and try running the tap to see if there is still a leak. If the nut will not tighten more, yet there is still a leak, more packing is needed around the gland. Unscrew the gland nut and remove it. String will be found under it and around the spindle. Use a few turns of ordinary soft string, but saturate it with grease first — petroleum jelly will do. Replace and adjust the gland nut.

If the tap drips and a new washer has to be fitted, unscrew at the lower hexagonal part so the top of the tap comes away. The washer is on a metal jumper and is usually held with a small nut.

Remove the jumper, hold the metal part with pliers and undo the small nut with a spanner. Make sure any particles of the old washer are cleaned away before fitting a new one. Re-assemble and try the tap.

CLEARING AN AIR LOCK

Air in a water system will cause a jerky flow of water from a tap and make knocking noises. Usually, the air can be driven out by letting the tap run for a time. Very often the problem is in the hot tap in the kitchen. If this is so, it may be possible to get rid of the airlock by fitting a hose between the hot and cold taps, opening the hot tap in the bathroom, and then opening both taps in the kitchen. The cold tap in the kitchen is usually on mains pressure, and this water under pressure will force the air to escape through the tap in the bathroom. If the kitchen tap is of the mixer type, then the connection to a hot tap will have to be elsewhere.

Fitting a hose between taps can be the first step to remove an airlock.

If there are several taps attached to one pipe, turn them all on, then turn them off in turn, starting from the one nearest the source. Air in a water system will rise. If the same pipe serves taps on different floors, run the lower tap until water flows without signs of air, then close it and do the same with the upper tap. If air becomes trapped in a high part of the system due to pipes being looped higher than the taps and none of these treatments will clear it, the fault will have to be attended to by a plumber.

SINKS AND BASINS

To replace a plug, force open the round or triangular ring on the chain with a screwdriver. Put on the new plug and squeeze the ring ends into the hole with pliers. At the other end of the chain the last link may be held in a similar way to an eyebolt at the back of the basin.

To prevent a blockage of the outlet in a sink there should be a grid to hold back solids. If hot fat is poured down a sink, follow with enough hot water to wash it away. Periodically run water for several minutes through the outlet to keep it clear.

Use a bell-shaped rubber plunger to clear a blocked basin. Plug the overflow hole near the top of the sink with a cloth. Run a small amount of water into the sink. Put the

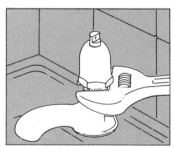
If tap drips, raise shield and unscrew top of tap.

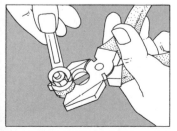
Unscrew small nut holding the washer. Clean jumper.

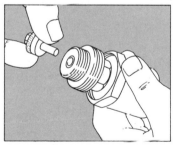
Examine the washer and remove jumper.

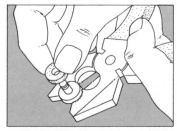
Fit new washer. Tighten nut. Re-assemble tap.

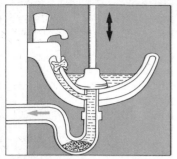

A rubber plunger can clear a blockage under a sink by suction.

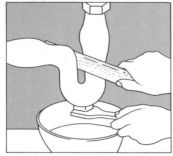

A piece of wood holds the pipe when the drain plug is removed.

Poke out any obstructions at both sides of the bend.

plunger over the outlet, press it down, then work the handle rapidly up and down. Now lift the plunger away. If the water runs away, the blockage is probably now cleared. Remove the cloth from the overflow hole and allow the water to run for a few minutes. If you do not have a proper plunger, a thick pad of cloth tied to the end of a stick will work just as well.

If the sink is still blocked after using the plunger, look underneath. There may be a U-bend with a drain plug at its bottom. Put a bucket underneath the sink. Steady the U-bend while undoing the plug with a spanner. Make sure you do not lose the washer along with the waste in the bucket. Using a piece of wire, poke and loosen any solid matter. Run water in small amounts to wash through anything loosened. If some of the stoppage seems to be further around the bend, poke a piece of flexible curtain wire into it.

There are two other types of traps used under sinks. If the U-bend does not have a drain plug, it will have two nuts so it can be removed completely for cleaning. A bottle trap has a large cylin-

A flexible rod can be used to clear a choked downpipe.

der instead of a U-bend. The bottom can be taken off like an upside-down screwed lid, but you may need a wrench to loosen it. Most waste will come away when this is unscrewed, but poke along the pipes with a wire as well.

Clean outside drains regularly.

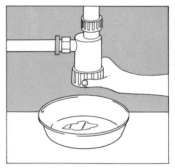

Remove waste by unscrewing the bottle trap under the sink.

Waste water is usually taken to a drain outside. If the waste flow is still unsatisfactory after clearing below the sink, partial stoppage further along may be the trouble. Flexible curtain wire can be poked into the end of the waste pipe. A better tool is a drain cleaner, which looks like curtain rail but is stouter and has a corkscrew end. Directing water up the pipe with a hose may also help. If this drives solid matter back into the sink or bath, remove it so it does not get washed down again. Run hot water through to wash out trapped fat or grease.

Occasionally lift out the iron or plastic grill from the outside drain. Turn it over and poke or wash out trapped hairs and other matter.

BALL VALVES

If a cistern overfills and water runs from the overflow pipe, the inlet valve is not closing early enough and the water is rising higher than the intended level. A metal or plastic ball floating on the water is connected to a lever that works and controls the valve. If the rubber washer, which fits on to the valve, is worn, it will allow too much water to enter the cistern.

Remove the cover of the cistern. Flush the cistern, holding up the ball arm. If this completely stops water coming in, the washer is not worn enough to need replacing. Instead, adjust the valve by bending the ball arm. Be careful neither to strain the valve mechanism nor to damage the ball itself. It is possible to hold the bar in two hands and bend between them very gently. Allow the cistern to fill. Check that the water is reaching the marked level before the valve shuts off. If there is no marked level, water should come to within about 25 mm (1 in) of the bottom of the overflow pipe.

If holding up the ball arm does not completely shut off the water — even allowing just a very slight drip — bending the arm will not stop overflowing and the washer will have to be replaced. Turn off the water supply if

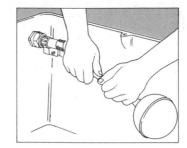

The water level in a cistern can be easily adjusted by bending the arm of the ball valve, up or down

possible, although it is possible to do the repair while water continues to flow, but you have to flush every time the cistern fills.

The ball arm pivots on a cotter pin (split pin). If its ends are spread, pinch them together, then pull the pin out with pliers from the other side. It may be possible to use the pin again, but if it is buckled and worn, use a new brass or stainless steel one. Pulling out the pin allows the arm to be removed, but before doing this, use its extending top to push out the piston that carries the washer, so its end can be gripped.

At the end of the brass piston the washer can be seen as a little pad enclosed by the metal. The metal joint may not be obvious, but the end with its hole is screwed to the main part. Unscrew this cap with pliers, but put cloth in the jaws so they will not

mark the brass. Fit a new washer and re-assemble the parts. See that there are no waste parts of the old washer left in place. Use a cloth on a rod to wipe where the washer is attached to the nozzle. If the valve parts are dull and corroded, clean them with fine emery paper and metal polish, and apply a little petroleum jelly to the piston casing.

Put the parts back together and allow the cistern to fill. Check the water level when the valve closes. With a new washer it will probably not be high enough. Flush the cistern and bend the ball arm up slightly, then try again until the correct level is reached.

If you have a high cistern above a lavatory pan, do not stand on the lavatory seat nor on a board across the earthenware pan. The weight of an adult could break or crack the lavatory frame.

Ball valves are also used for controlling the inlets to water tanks. If water runs from the overflow pipe of a roof tank, it can be repaired in the way described for a cistern. Some 'silent' cisterns have the water controlled in a different way. If removing the top of a cistern shows a system very different from that described, its repair is better left to a plumber.

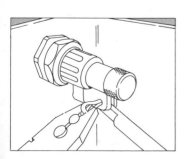

The cistern valve can be opened by withdrawing the split pin.

Carefully coax the plunger out from the valve.

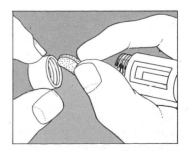

Unscrew the plunger cap and replace the washer.

BATH SEALING

It is important that water does not seep between the edges of a bath, shower or basin and the wall, where it could cause rotting. In the past, sealing was done with plaster and other materials that eventually became brittle and fell out. If this edge sealing has to be replaced, pick out all the old material and clean off the surfaces. Make sure they are dry and free from soap and grease.

The best sealant now is a silicone rubber preparation, available in colours to match basins and tiles, and supplied in a tube with an applicator nozzle, which can be cut to the width needed. Hold the tube at an angle and squeeze while pushing (not pulling), always following the manufacturer's instructions. Smooth within five minutes and leave for 24 hours. Excess sealant can be wiped off with a tissue or cut away when it is dry.

LAVATORY SEATS

If a lavatory seat and its cover are loose, examine the fixing screws and nuts at the back. The nuts underneath may be a wing type for hand tightening. There should be soft washers above and below with screws fitting through loosely into their holes. This is deliberate so as not to risk damaging the glazed earthenware pan. If washers have disintegrated, they should be replaced. Tap washers can be used.

In some installations the lower washers are conical to go into the holes and prevent excessive movement of the seat. Turn the wing nuts only hand tight. If there is a tendency to work loose after a short time, put spring locking washers under the nuts.

When sealing a sink or bath, use a rubber-based sealant which will remain elastic.

Although most seat units are similar sizes, if you do decide to fit a new one, measure the sizes of the holes in the pan and their distance apart, when you go to buy a new unit.

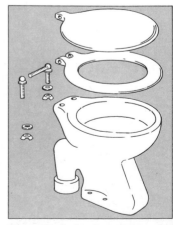

The parts of a lavatory seat.

CENTRAL HEATING

Heating by water circulating through radiators may use gas, oil or solid fuel for the boiler. From the boiler onwards the circuits are basically the same.

Radiators are usually bracketed to a wall. If one becomes loose, the retaining screw may have a head for a spanner, but if it is slotted a screwdriver with a right-angled end may be needed. There are steadying brackets to hold the radiator in position, and these can loosen, but their screws may be tightened with a straight screwdriver.

The usual pipe connections are compression fittings. If one leaks, tighten it with an adjustable spanner. If leaking persists, call a plumber.

If a radiator feels hot at the bottom and much cooler at the top, there is air in it. This is more likely with radiators on the highest floor, as air rises in the system. It is advisable to check for air periodically, particularly after the system is put back into use for the winter. In most radiators there is a recessed square-ended projection at one end of the top. This takes a special key (obtainable from a

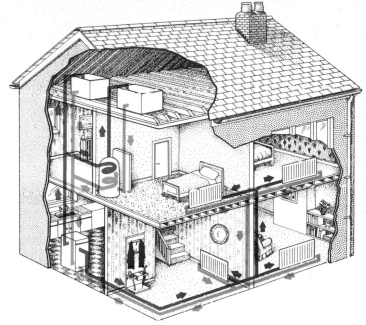

builders' supplier). Use a cloth over the end and hold a jar or other container under the vent. Unscrew the vent until the air is heard hissing out. Leave this open until the air ceases and water comes out, then tighten the vent again. To make sure all the air has gone, let the system operate and try the vent again later.

OIL SYSTEMS

There is a drain cock under the storage tank. Open this briefly once a year and catch what comes out in a bucket.

Typical flow of indirect system of central heating: red = primary circuit; green = secondary circuit. In this type of central-heating system, the circuits are closed and no water can be taken from them. This greatly reduces scaling. In some systems, the hot water rises naturally from the boiler and the cool water returns to it by force of gravity. In other systems, a pump near the boiler is needed. The boiler itself can be heated with gas, oil or solid fuel but, with any of these, the circulation is the same.

There may be sludge, so let it drain until the oil appears clear. Make sure the filler has a cover so that dirt cannot enter. If there is a vent pipe, wire mesh over its end will keep out dirt. If the tank becomes rusty, wire brush the affected parts, rub with abrasive, coat with a rust inhibitor fluid, then repaint the whole tank. Bitumastic paint is a good protection.

Where the supply pipe leaves the tank there should be a filter beside a stop cock. Clean the filter once a year or as necessary. Turn off the stop cock, unscrew the bowl

Loosen the vent screw in the radiator and then release the air until water appears.

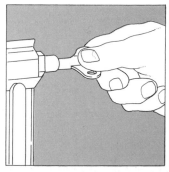

Tighten the vent screw making sure that the radiator heats completely to the top.

HOME MAINTENANCE

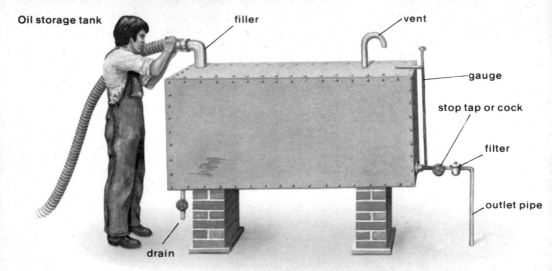

Oil storage tank — filler — vent — gauge — stop tap or cock — filter — outlet pipe — drain

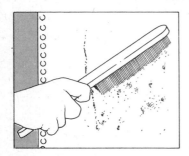

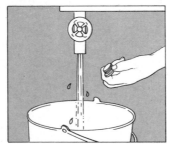

Open the oil tank for a few moments, allowing the sludge to drain into a container.

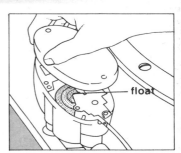

float

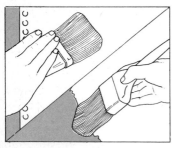

Use a wire brush to remove any rust from within the tank, then coat it with bitumastic paint.

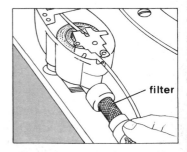

filter

(*Top*) Remove top of filter; check that float moves freely; (*bottom*) clean filter with petrol.

and remove the filter element. Wash out the bowl and the element with petrol. Allow to dry, then re-assemble.

This filter should stop nearly all the dirt passing into the oil. If that element is fairly clean there is no need

to do anything else, but there is another filter on the base of the boiler casing and it is reached by removing the front panel. If the boiler is functioning satisfactorily and the tank filter has been cleaned, leave this other filter for attention at the six-monthly servicing. If you suspect it is blocked, turn off the stop cock and remove any screws holding the lid of the filter. See that the float inside moves freely. The filter unscrews from the side. Place a shallow container under it before loosening. Remove the filter and take it outside to wash in petrol. Dry

and replace it together with the lid.

SOLID FUEL SYSTEMS
Always use the fuel specified and in the correct size. Keep the hopper filled. In modern boilers the fire-bed is automatically refilled from

the hopper, which should be kept full. Ash is easily removed by the ejection system, a simple, dust-free method. The tray needs emptying less frequently than in the old-fashioned boilers.

A solid-fuel boiler should be cleaned every six months. Remove the casing panels and the top. Put a clean cloth over the burner and use a wire brush to remove soot and other products of combustion from the furnace wall. Lift out as much as possible and finish with a vacuum cleaner hose.

Fire bars can be damaged and may need to be replaced. If your fireclay becomes damaged, patch it with fireclay cement which is available from a builders' merchant. Clean the flueway in the boiler when the system is out of use. Open the elbow at its bottom and remove anything deposited there. Have the chimney cleaned annually.

GAS SYSTEMS

A gas-fired boiler does not require attention by the owner comparable with the other two systems and maintenance should be left to the regular servicing by an expert.

In some older systems water circulates naturally, making use of the tendency for hot water to rise, but most modern systems have a circulating pump in the outlet pipe from the boiler. If water does not circulate when the pump is running, this may be due to air in the pump. If there is a vent in the top of the pump, it may need a key similar to that for radiators or a screwdriver may work it. Open the valve and close it when water flows. The vent may be in the flow pipe above the pump and can be

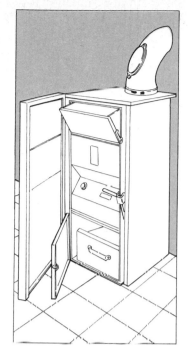

Open the door to gain access to the boiler.

turned with a spanner or key.

There is a flow adjustment on the pump, but this usually requires a special key and its adjustment is better left to an expert.

If the pump fails to run, it may have broken and have to be replaced, or the fault may be electrical. Check that the wiring is intact and look for a

valve
coupling
terminal box
air vent
coupling
valve

A circulating pump: this should be wired into the electrical control system through a 13-amp plug.

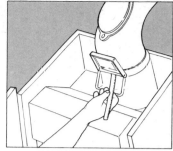

Open the cover at the flue elbow and brush inside.

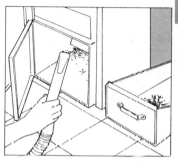

Remove soot and dust with a vacuum cleaner.

blown fuse.

The system is usually controlled by two thermostats: one at the boiler controlling the hot water system and another in a room controlling the heating system. A timing device at the boiler controls whether one or both systems are used and when they go on and off.

Experience will show which are the best settings, but there is no need to set the hot water thermostat higher than the water can be used. If cold water has to be run as well as hot at the sink, heat is being wasted. Water at 140°F (60°C) should be about right. For room temperature 70°F (21°C) is usual, but for economy a few degrees less may be acceptable. Halls and lesser-used rooms may be down to 60°F (15°C) and bedrooms even less. Where the system does not control the heat exactly as wanted in the various places, it is possible

HOME MAINTENANCE

Ideally, the living rooms should be warmer than the rest of the house.

to get radiator thermostats. One of these can be fitted in place of the normal control knob and set to the intended room temperature, independent of heat elsewhere. Obviously, the greatest economy comes with turning off radiators where they are not needed, but there is little to be gained by turning them off for short periods as fuel will have to be used later to restore heat and saving may be nil.

WATER SOFTENING
In a soft water area there is no problem with a hot water system, but if the water is hard it deposits scale or fur and this is a particular problem in pipes, where the deposit has the effect of reducing the bore. Advice should be obtained about any need to soften water, when a new central heating system is installed.

If there is any doubt about the effect of hard water, it might be advisable to try a portable descaler capsule suspended in the supply tank. Chemical descaling kits also exist and it is possible to have a descaling unit fitted in the supply pipe.

A boiler can be installed in a kitchen, as here, and can be unobtrusive but still functional.

OUTDOOR REPAIRS

CONCRETE

Many outside repairs need concrete, mortar or cement. The important constituent is Portland cement, which is bought as a fine powder. It is cheapest when bought in large bags, but as it will deteriorate and harden if kept for long after opening, it may be more economical to buy only sufficient for a job. A mixture of sand and stones, called aggregate, is added to the Portland cement. You can mix sand and stones, or buy them already mixed. When sand and cement are mixed with water a chemical reaction causes hardening. For small repairs, it might be more sensible to buy ready-mixed sand and cement.

The proportions in the mixture have to be varied according to the job. The aggregate in foundations is very coarse, whereas only sand would be used in a mortar mix for pointing or filling a crack.

The maximum size of stone can be specified when ordering aggregate – 20 mm (¾

in) may suit heavy work, 10 mm (2/5 in) would suit paths, while sand only would suit repairs. If you ask for all-in aggregate, sand and stones are already mixed.

For cracks and similar repairs use a proportion of one part cement to three parts coarse sand. For paths use one part cement to three or four parts all-in aggregate. For foundations use one part cement to four or five parts all-in aggregate. If sand

and stones are separate, the second mixture is conveniently remembered as 1:2:3 (cement:sand:stones).

Use clean water to mix concrete. The amount of water should be kept to a minimum, as too much gives a weaker result. Put the aggregate on a flat hard surface in a broad pile, and lay the cement on top. Using a spade or shovel, mix the aggregate from the bottom with the cement until the

Cement and aggregate: amounts for different tasks

Cracks: 1 part cement/3 parts sand

Paths: 1 part cement/1 part sand/2 parts stones

Foundations: 1 part cement/2 parts sand/3 parts stones

Mixing concrete
Mix sand, cement and aggregate together. Pour in a little water. Thoroughly mix until wet, then tamp until the consistency is even, moist, and stiff.

HOME MAINTENANCE

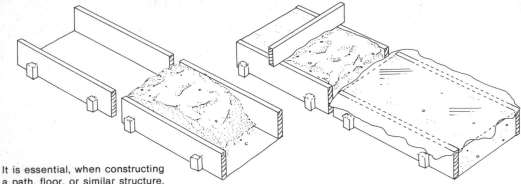

It is essential, when constructing a path, floor, or similar structure, to mark out the width using securely fixed boards.

Put in the concrete above the top and scrape it level.

Cover the concrete to prevent too rapid drying or freezing.

whole pile is an even colour. Make a hollow in the top and pour in a little water, mixing from the edge to the centre. Add more water and continue to mix, turning in dry material until the whole mixture is wet. Try flattening the heap and cut into it with the spade. The ridges formed should stay there. If they flow back into a smoother surface, the mixture is too wet.

There is no need to rush laying concrete. Allow time to do the job properly, but go straight into the work after mixing. If concrete dries too quickly it may eventually cause cracks. Polythene sheeting should be laid over concrete to allow for slow drying. Full drying and hardening will take from four to ten days, according to atmospheric conditions.

Concrete does not wear well in thin sections. In the long run it may be better to increase the area in need of repair, so as to allow for a thicker layer of concrete.

A mason uses several trowels, but most repairs can be done with a small diamond-shaped pointing trowel. For a crack, poke out all loose material with the trowel or a spike and use a stiff bristle brush. Prepare a mixture using one part cement and three parts coarse sand. Brush water into the crack just before you start to work. Using the point of the trowel, force the concrete as far into the crack as possible. Press down and work in more until full, then level with the trowel.

Repairs to cracks may be improved with a PVA adhesive. Put the adhesive directly in the crack and leave to dry. Mix a small amount of the adhesive with the cement and sand mixture.

In a simple crack with fairly sharp edges, filling alone should be sufficient, but if the edge is worn away,

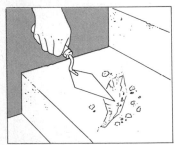

Open, then roughen a crack to key the new concrete.

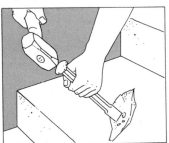

Clean any stones or particles of dirt from the cracks.

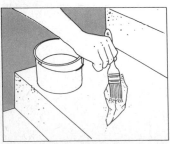

Putting PVA adhesive into cracks helps to strengthen the repair.

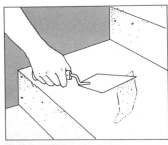

Completely fill the crack and level it off with a trowel.

the feather edge of the new concrete will almost certainly crumble after a short time. To avoid this, use a cold chisel to chop into the old concrete, making a recess with clean angles. The new concrete will have thicker edges.

If concrete is to be laid to extend a path, use pieces of wood to mark the boundary and restrict the new concrete. The surface can be levelled with a straight-edged board moved up and down over it and the border. To achieve a smoother surface, use a float, which is a flat piece of wood or metal with a handle. This can be moved backwards and forwards over the concrete, but do not work it excessively. Leave the wooden boundaries in place until the concrete has set.

POINTING

The mortar between bricks may break away and become uneven. The visible edge is called pointing and keeps a wall both weather-resistant and attractive. If pointing is necessary, use a narrow cold chisel to chop out the old pointing to a depth of about 10 mm (2/5 in). Be careful not to damage the bricks and brush away any dust.

The mortar mixture can be made from a straight cement and fine sand mixture in the proportions of about one to six. If dry hydrate is added there is less tendency to shrink during setting and the mixture will be easy to work. The proportions are then one cement, one dry hydrate and six fine sand.

Have the mixture ready, then wet the joints so that the bricks do not absorb too much moisture from the mortar. Use the edge of the trowel to press the mortar in, and leave it projecting a little from the bricks.

Examine any adjoining undamaged pointing. It may be level as in flush pointing, which is made by wiping

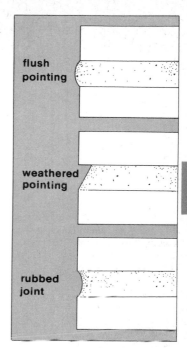

flush pointing

weathered pointing

rubbed joint

over the finished pointing with the trowel. Often weathered pointing is used, which slopes outwards from the upper brick to the one below. Fill the vertical joints, then use the edge of the

Clean out any loose mortar with a cold chisel.

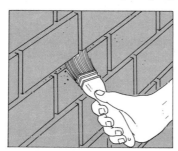

Vigorously brush out the joints to remove any dust.

Trowel in the mortar, making sure it stands above the brick surface.

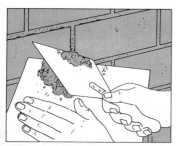

When pointing, the joints can be either weathered or flush.

Brushing gives an even surface and removes waste.

When rubbing a joint, it is best to use a round-ended rod.

trowel to press in the upper edges. Use the trowel along the edge of a board to cut the lower edge straight. When the mortar is almost dry, lightly brush it. If hollow pointing is wanted, fill the joint flush with the surface, then hollow out the joint. This can be done with the rounded end of a rod or tube drawn along the wet mortar.

GUTTERS

Gutters are intended to collect water from a roof and take it to downpipes. These may meet at funnel-shaped containers, called hoppers, and from here the water flows down to a drain. A surprising amount of other debris is washed down with the water and hoppers may become choked with nests and growing plants.

When cleaning gutters, place a bowl under the downpipe to catch debris that might block the drain.

Before cleaning is started, place a bowl under the downpipe to prevent rubbish blocking the drains. Scrape inside the gutters with a piece of wood cut to a slightly smaller curve, then brush loose dirt into a bucket. A rod can be pushed through a straight downpipe. At a hopper head lift out rubbish, rather than pushing it further on. In a bad case it may be necessary to dismantle a downpipe to clear separate sections.

Check the joints and remake them if necessary, by refilling with mastic. Plastic guttering does not need any special treatment, but rust can be removed from iron guttering with a wire brush and the insides should be treated with bitumastic paint. Treat the outside of the guttering to match other painting. Look at the roof and remove moss or anything else likely to wash down and block the gutters

Plastic cage over vent pipe.

later. Cages can be bought to fit over vent pipes and hopper heads to prevent blocking. Pour water into the gutter at its highest point to check the flow and wash through any remaining dirt.

BLOCKED DRAINS

Most waste water runs into a gulley with a trap which can be lifted out. If this is cleared frequently it is unlikely that the drain can become blocked from that source. Lavatory pans connect direct to the drains. If a lavatory does not empty, first try freeing it with a plunger in the same way as described for a sink (see page 124). All drainage systems have manholes over collecting channels, with the one nearest the house being at the highest point. This is the first one to examine if there is a blockage.

If there is liquid in the first manhole, the blockage is further on. If it is clear, the blockage is between it and the house. Start clearing from the manhole without liquid. Superficial clearing can be done with a rod, such as a length of cane, but for more than this a set of drain-clearing rods should be hired. They are flexible and have screwed joints, so that a considerable length can be built up. A cork-screw head or a plunger can be fitted at the end. Block the outlet at a

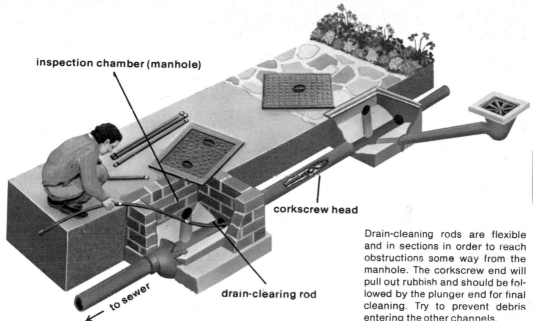

inspection chamber (manhole)

corkscrew head

to sewer

drain-clearing rod

Drain-cleaning rods are flexible and in sections in order to reach obstructions some way from the manhole. The corkscrew end will pull out rubbish and should be followed by the plunger end for final cleaning. Try to prevent debris entering the other channels.

manhole, so that whatever is removed from one pipe cannot go on through another.

Use the corkscrew end to get into the obstruction and pull it out, scooping out the rubbish as it comes through. Follow with the plunger end and run water through to check clearance. While you have the rods, clear any other drains running into the manhole. Poke away dirt and grease from around the manhole rim and clean the cover. Put a small amount of grease around the rim to trap smells.

REGLAZING A WINDOW

Always wear thick gloves and goggles when reglazing. Break out a broken window pane, using a hammer and pliers, and carefully catch and dispose of the glass, wrapping it in several layers of newspaper. Levering out pieces around the edge will also break out putty, but remaining putty should be removed with a woodworking

chisel or a chopping knife, which is a straight-bladed knife with a thick back for hammering. There will be sprigs (headless nails) which held the glass in a wooden frame. Pull them out with pincers. In a metal frame there will be spring clips to remove. Make sure all old putty is cut out and the rebates are level and clean.

Have the glass cut so that it is an easy fit. It should not have to be forced in. Buy the glass of the same thickness as that removed, but if this is not known, most house windows can be 3 mm or

4 mm. Putty will soon become denatured and fall out if put on to bare wood. Paint the rebate, using an oil paint for wood or an aluminium-based paint on metal.

If you need putty for metal frames, ask for metal-casement putty, as ordinary putty does not bond to metal. Mould the putty in your hands until it becomes pliable and you cannot feel any lumps. It should be possible to roll it smoothly into long cylinders. Press the putty into the rebates all round, judging a sufficient thickness to bed the glass in,

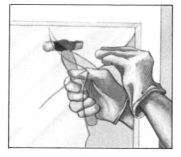

Always wear gloves when breaking out old glass.

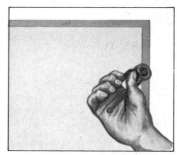

Pull out the sprigs or nails and remove any old putty.

HOME MAINTENANCE

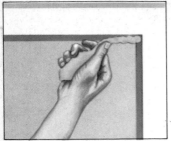

Knead the putty into strips then press it into the rebates.

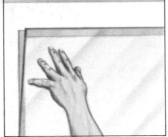

Progressively press in the glass around all the edges.

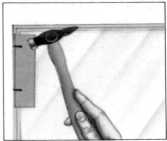

Tap in the sprigs by sliding a hammer across a piece of card.

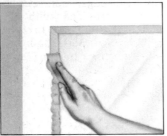

Apply the putty over the sprigs to make a neat angle.

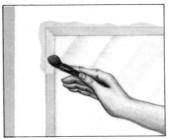

Wiping with a damp brush will smooth down the surface.

Before painting the putty, it must be allowed to harden.

and spread to the edges of the rebate.

Press in the glass, by working with the fingers around the edges. *Do not press at the centre of the glass.* Remember that the point where it is bedded down on the putty will be visible, so try to get an even thickness behind it. Tap in sprigs in the case of a wooden frame or fit wire clips if the frame is metal. The sprigs do not have to go in very far and may be tapped in by sliding the edge of a chisel or a light hammer across some card over the glass.

More putty can be added from the outside with the fingers, but it will have to be pressed in and smoothed with a putty knife. One with a diagonal cut across its end is suitable. Press the putty down so it bonds with that already in the rebate and draw the knife along so the surface

is bevelled to come just below the rebate seen through the other side. Use the straight edge of the knife to make neat mitres at the corners. Surplus putty can be cut away with the knife from both sides of the glass.

Wipe around the putty lightly with a damp brush and leave the putty to harden for about a week. Clean the glass and paint the putty and the frame. Carrying the paint line a very short distance on to the glass may prevent water getting behind the putty and loosening it.

WINDOW FRAMES
Wood expands and contracts according to its moisture content and this depends on the weather for outside woodwork. Wooden window frames set in brick may develop gaps where water has entered and this causes rot. Do not fill these cracks

with concrete, mortar or putty, as these set hard and do not allow for movement.

Buy a mastic sealer from a builders' merchant. This may come in a tube, so that you squeeze the sealer through its nozzle, or it may be in a gun with a lever action. Squeeze this into the gaps. If necessary, press in further with a putty knife, which should be kept wet to prevent sticking. The mastic will set sufficiently hard to take paint, but it remains elastic so that gaps will not form.

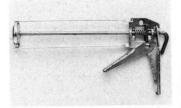

Mastic in gaps gives a permanent flexible seal. It can be applied using a gun (*above*).

GENERAL MAINTENANCE

LOOSE SCREWS

If a woodscrew becomes loose the best treatment is to move it to a new position, when possible. If a door hinge is pulling away it might be moved far enough for the screws to be driven again into solid wood. When this is done, the old holes should be plugged to avoid wood fibres opening towards the new holes and again loosening the screws. In a simple case of a screw loosening it may be sufficient to push a matchstick into the hole and to tighten it again.

If a screw has to be driven into the same place again, the hole should be drilled to take a hardwood dowel, which can be glued in, then drilled for the screw. It may be better to enlarge the hole enough to press in a plastic or fibre wall plug. Push it in below the surface, so that as it expands it does not lift the fitting from the surface.

It may be possible to drive the screw into its old hole, if this is filled with a mixture of glue and sawdust. Do not put any strain on the screw until the glue has set. Driving a longer screw into the same hole only gets the benefit of the grip of the end, but if a stouter gauge screw can be used there should be a good grip along it. If the problem is that the screw is being driven into end grain, it would be a help to drill and fit a dowel across the screw hole, so that part of the screw thread goes into the cross grain of the dowel.

If a door has sagged at the hinges and needs to be rehung, make sure the knuckles of the hinges are in line with each other and that they project from the surface

screw into hardwood dowel

plastic and fibre wall plugs

screw in glue and sawdust

screw in dowel across hole

enough for the door to swing clear. Use a wedge under the door to hold it at the correct height while one screw is driven into each hinge. If the door swings properly then, drive in the other screws. If not, take the screw out and try again using a new hole.

CERAMIC TILES

Glazed tiles make a good finish in bathrooms or kitchens. They will resist most liquids and the range of patterns and colours is considerable. The most common tiles are about 110 mm square and 4 mm thick. Normal tiles have square edges, but others have one rounded edge for a ledge front or the top of a tiled panel, and there are other tiles rounded on two edges for corners.

Tiles can be cut by scoring the glazed surface with a special tool or a glass cutter, then snapping off the surplus. The general-purpose adhesive suits most home jobs, but there are waterproof adhesives for use in very wet areas. Grout is the cement-based material used to seal gaps between tiles, but some adhesives can also be used as grout.

Tiles can be attached to almost any material, providing it is flat. A metal spreader is needed, with a saw-like edge, and this is usually provided with the adhesive. Take care to work squarely. A horizontal line taken from a spirit level or a vertical one from a plumb line will be better than relying on the floor or wall corner.

Spread enough adhesive for more than a tile, then position it and move it a little to bed it down. After a little practice with a few tiles, spread adhesive over a larger area and press in as many tiles as possible. Use the spreader to get an even thickness. The ridges it leaves will help to bed down the tiles.

If an old tile has loosened, lift it off carefully. Most of the old adhesive below it will have to be scraped out so that the tile can be placed level on the new adhesive. Scrape away grout from the surrounding edges, using something like a wood chisel, and remove all dust with a damp rag. Adhesive can be spread directly on to a tile if that is more convenient. Otherwise the adhesive should be spread evenly on the wall and the tile pressed hard on to it. Be ready to prise it out again with a knife or chisel if the level is wrong. When the tile is in position, grout around it and wipe off the surplus.

If a tile is broken and

HOME MAINTENANCE

Tools for tiling: (*top to bottom*) tile scorer, nippers, sponge, adhesive spreader, grouter.

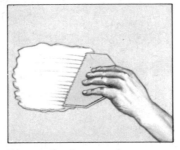

Use an adhesive spreader.

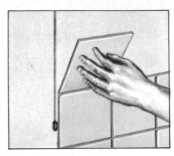

Tiles should be vertical.

Grout all joints.

Wipe clean with a cloth.

loose, but the break is clean and a matching new tile cannot be obtained, use an adhesive intended for crockery along the edges, then refit as described above. The glued joint may not be very strong, so treat it carefully until the tile is in place, when it should hold.

If tiles have to be drilled to allow something to be screwed through them, use a masonry drill. If something has to be hung from a tiled wall, the screws must go through to plugs in the wall. It would be better if the plugs were driven below the level of the tile, so there is no risk of an expanding plug cracking the glaze.

FIREPLACE REPAIRS
A fire should be contained safely, with air entering at the bottom and smoke drawn out at the top. This applies whether it is an open fire or a continuous-burning enclosed one. The lining of the grate is firebrick in sections. If part of this becomes so damaged that it needs replacing, the makers have standard parts available.

However, much can be done with fireclay. This is supplied in a puttylike consistency in a can for easy application. It can be moulded into shape and sets hard enough to have a long life alongside firebrick. Remove dust, moisten the surface, then press in the fireclay. If possible, leave it to set before applying heat, but it can withstand early firing.

DRAUGHTPROOFING
Self-adhesive plastic-backed foam strips can be bought to put around door frames, sealing wide gaps. Peel off the protective strip and press the foam into place. Similar strips can be used in window joints. A more permanent way of achieving the same result is to use metal or plastic hinged strips which have to be pinned into the recesses.

The undersides of room doors need a different treat-

A good way of keeping out draughts is to place a strip of foam or metal into the rebate of a window, or under a door.

ment to prevent draughts. There is a type of fitting that goes across the bottom of a door. It has a bar which drops to seal the gap when the door is closed, but it lifts clear of the floor when the door is moved. Another type of sealer fits across the floor and has a flexible plastic piece at the centre which springs up against the door.

In some houses floor boards do not quite meet the walls and there is a gap under the skirting boards. On a ground floor, cold draughts may come up from the foundations. Carpet may cover the gaps, but, if not, thin splines of wood may be fitted under the skirting board or flexible mastic (as suggested for window frames) pressed in.

INSULATION

Draught prevention contributes to fuel economy. Of the various ways of treating the house to keep in heat, roof insulation is the most efficient, because hot air rises and may otherwise escape through the roof. If the loft is used as a room any insulation would have to be done in the slope of the roof, but otherwise it is better to put an insulation barrier between the ceiling joists, so heat does not go into the roof space.

To keep heat in at the ceiling level, there has to be a thick layer of insulating material. A thin layer will not be worthwhile. Such things as polystyrene tiles on a ceiling offer a small amount of insulation, but it is 100 mm (4 in) or more of insulating material that gives good heat retention.

Glass fibre makes good insulation and it is available in rolls, mostly about 400 mm (16 in) wide to suit the usual spacing between ceiling joists. If there are few pipes or other

insulated cold-water storage tank

lagged pipes

Avoid loss of heat by insulating your loft, either by laying glass fibre (*top*) or spreading loose granules (*left*).

obstructions, this is the simplest effective loft insulation. Work it close into the eaves. Overlap where there have to be any joins.

Another material is mineral wood granules. This comes in bags and is emptied to a sufficient thickness between joists. Include a pad of insulation above the trap door. Do not insulate below a water tank as some heat rising there will help to protect it against frost. With heat held at the bedroom ceiling level, the loft will get colder and insulation of the water tank and pipes becomes especially important.

There are kits of glass fibre and other blanket material for tying around and over tanks. This needs to be at least 75 mm (3 in) thick to be

effective and there must not be any gaps. Similar insulation must be carried around pipes. Bandage-like insulation material can be wrapped spirally around them and it may be advisable to apply more than one layer.

It is difficult to prevent freezing of outside water systems. Lagging pipes may have some effect and the use of polythene pipes may make bursts less likely than using metal pipes, but it is better to have a stop tap and a drain tap if possible, so that the outdoor system can be drained and isolated when frost is expected. If an outside standpipe is in use, the above-ground part, including the tap, should be boxed in so there is 100 mm (4 in) or more space for insulating materials.

HOME MAINTENANCE

FLOOR AND STAIR REPAIRS

An uneven wooden floor is best levelled with a floor-sanding machine, which can be hired. Ask your hire-shop for clear instructions as to how to use this. Walking about and observing the noise of bare boards will show if there are any gaps between boards and joists. Warped boards may be pulled down by driving nails at angles alternately in dovetail fashion or by pulling down with screws.

The boards are laid across joists and their positions can be seen from the nail locations. If a board is in such bad condition that a section should be replaced, saw across it a short distance from the nails to get the cut to one side of the joist. Lever up at the cut and put a strip of wood underneath to support it. If the wood needs to be re-

A floor-sanding machine.

placed past the next joist, try to lever out the nails there. If they will not come, punch them through or split or cut the wood from them. Cut across where the other end is to come. Put battens across the joists to support the ends of the new piece. Trim the ends of the adjoining old board with a chisel if necessary, then cut and fit the new board.

Stairs that creak do so because wood rubs on wood somewhere. Underneath the

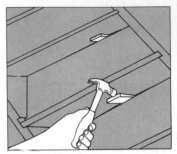

For creaking stairs, tap the wedges tight with a hammer.

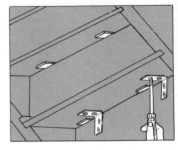

Metal shelf brackets can be used to prevent creaking on stairs.

stairs the ends of the treads may be supported by wedged pieces. Check that these are tight by tapping their ends with a hammer. The treads and risers (upright parts) should have tongued and grooved joints, but there may also be glued triangular blocks in the angles. Failure in these joints may cause creaking. Ask someone to walk on the stairs so that you can observe where the creaking is. Metal repair plates or shelf brackets can be put between offending parts.

ROT AND WOODWORM

There are several kinds of rot, generally divided into two categories: dry rot and wet rot. There is no cure for either type, only prevention.

Dry rot occurs in situations where there is a lack of ventilation and a limited amount of warmth and mois-

Saw across a damaged board away from the nails.

Lever up the damaged part and then support it.

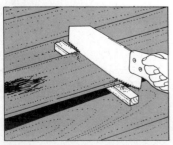

Cut away the damaged section between the joists.

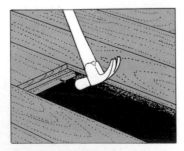

Nail the supports for the new board on to the joists.

ture. A suspended ground floor space is ideal; spores spread very quickly and infect masonry and plaster as well as timber. Treatment is by the total removal and burning of infected timber, and the rot-proofing of surrounding surfaces with a special solution. This has to extend at least one metre (3 ft) beyond the visibly affected area. Dealing with dry rot should be left to experts; they will ensure that all the affected timber — with its almost invisible spores — will be discovered, and they will guarantee.

Wet rot is less serious and, while causing timber to decay, does not develop in the same way as dry rot. First, the source of the additional moisture — leaking pipes, defective gutters, etc. — should be repaired. Then the defective wood should be cut out, and the adjacent timbers treated with preservatives.

Woodworm is annoying, but not as serious as rot. Eggs laid by a beetle in the wood, turn into pupae and emerge as larvae, or woodworm. The holes you see are mainly where the pupae have burrowed. Under the surface the insect digs deeper and makes a network of passages. Fortunately it is only in neglected cases that the effect is serious.

Softwoods are commonly attacked and the first attack in hardwoods is in their sapwood, which is usually a lighter colour. There are special insecticides which can be painted or sprayed on to wood, or even injected into individual holes. Rotproofing solutions may also be effective against attack.

Application before an attack is better than waiting until the trouble has started.

SECURITY

If a thief is determined to get into your home, he probably will, if he is not disturbed and has ample time. Any precautions you take are directed at making his task difficult so that he does not persist.

LOCKS

A mortise lock is fitted into the thickness of the door and is difficult to force. The notches on the key engage with levers. The more there are of these, the more difficult it is to pick the lock. Single or double levered locks are only intended for inside doors. If the lock assembly is withdrawn after removing the retaining screw, screws removed from the faceplate of the lock allow it to be removed and opened. It can then be cleaned and lubricated, preferably with graphite powder, but a light oil can be used sparingly. Too much will attract dust and dirt.

If the lock is difficult to work, a spring in a lever may have broken. A locksmith can provide a new one. If you want to change keys, different levers can be fitted to the lock.

A rim lock fits on the inside of the door and externally there is a cylinder to take the key. Although this type of lock is difficult to pick and the variety of keys is considerable, there are

other ways of forcing it. A piece of flexible plastic, like a credit card, can be pushed through a slight gap to force the bolt back. A snugly fitting door with a good rebate on the frame will reduce this risk.

A catch on the inside of the door will prevent forcing in this way, but if there is a glass panel that could be broken and the lock reached, it is better to have a night latch, where the key can be used inside and removed in a similar way to a mortise lock. Open the lock and lubricate it occasionally. The cylinder can be lubricated by smearing the key with graphite or oil and working it in the lock.

For double security there can be a rim lock and a mortise lock on the same door. Let the mortise lock take the main load near the middle of the door and position the rim lock higher. Fitting it involves the drilling of one hole for the cylinder (usually 32 mm). This is better than having bolts as they cannot be used when you leave the house unattended.

DOOR CHAIN

A chain that allows a door to be opened a little to see who has called before opening fully, provides protection against unwanted callers who may try to enter. The chain hangs from a fitting on the door frame and can be

Both these secure locks fit into the edge of a door.

hooked into a slotted piece on the door, when the door is closed. It cannot be released when the door is partly open. You have to shut the door again to release it.

Fit the piece from which the chain hangs to the door post with screws at a convenient height. The chain hook can usually be left hanging in this when not wanted. Opposite this hold the slotted piece into place on the door edge and mark its position. It has a part that turns over the door edge. If there is much clearance to the door this may not have to be let in, but otherwise cut a shallow notch for the plate, like that for the edge of a rim lock. Screw the slotted plate to the door and test the action.

WINDOWS

Sash windows, where two parts slide vertically and have a catch between them when closed, are particularly vulnerable to potential burglars. The small catch between the two parts can be pushed open easily. There are catches where a screw or spring prevents the swinging arm being moved until it is released inside.

This catch holds the window closed, but if they are to be left slightly open for ventilation there are bolts which can limit the movement of the windows. A plate with a threaded hole is screwed to the side of the upper sash at the point where the lower sash is to come when either is opened. This could be about 100 mm (4 in) without a would-be intruder being able to get his hand in to release anything. A screwed plug is turned with a key

A door chain in place.

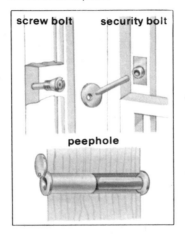

screw bolt   security bolt

peephole

(which can be removed) into the plate and its projection prevents the overlapping sashes being moved further.

Sash windows are counter-weighted by lead weights on cords in boxes at the sides or with helical springs in modern factory produced windows. There are removable strips down the sides called beads, which enable the weights and cords to be reached for repair. The beads act as guides for the windows and are often very lightly attached, so that if one is removed the window can swing sideways.

Casement windows, swinging on vertical hinges, are not such a problem. Make sure the catch on the opposite side to the hinges can go fully home. If it will enter only part way, it may be shaken free. Similarly, if the stay at

the bottom drops fully on to its pegs, it is unlikely to be moved. One of the pegs could be threaded and a nut could be put on it.

See that casement and other swinging windows close tightly, not only against their stops, but into the recesses. A gap does not need to be very wide for a wire to be pushed through and manipulated to move a catch. If a house is to be left unoccupied for some time, screws can be driven to prevent catches being moved until the screws are withdrawn.

Double glazing also provides security. Even if the outer windows can be forced, the intruder is unlikely to try to move the inner glazing panels as well. Lock manufacturers offer window locks which operate with a key.

If you wish to check anyone at the street door there are door answering telephones and even one that gives you a picture of the caller. A simpler (and cheaper) device can be fitted at head level through a hole in the door. By the use of lenses you can have a broad view of the outside of the door, but the visitor cannot look in. Only one hole has to be drilled to fit this.

If you want more sophisticated protection there are systems which sense when windows or doors are opened, carpets are trodden on and things moved. They set off alarms which should scare off an intruder. The better versions of these have to be installed professionally. Partial protection with a simpler installation may give a false sense of security.

HOME IMPROVEMENT

HOME IMPROVEMENT

INTRODUCTION

Your home is for living in, a place in which you can feel as relaxed as possible, so it should be happy, comfortable, attractive to the eye but not overpowering, while providing for your individual needs. It should create the atmosphere you want so that you are able to say: 'There's no place like home'.

Articles on home improvements can be very irritating when your budget is even more limited than the designers' favourite 'shoestring' budget. You don't often read much about ordinary houses worked on by the people who live in them, such as people in rented flats and terraced houses. You may not want, or be able to create, a gallery from your attic, but sometimes such ideas can start you thinking along lines you'd left unexplored. If you can bring a fresh eye to bear on your home, look at its problems and its good points in a clear, unbiased, and even unconventional way; then

you will find that new, exciting and not necessarily expensive ideas will emerge.

Although you can achieve a great deal by redecorating, making some new curtains and so on, you might have to undo your work if your basics are wrong. That might mean rethinking and starting again from scratch to achieve the effect you want. Perhaps you should consider major changes before you start to think of redecorating. You have four elements to combine: the character of your home (its age, fabric, architectural style and location), plus the needs, priorities and personalities of the people who live there.

Every house has an intrinsic character: if you try to impose another style on it, it may look quite ridiculous. This applies particularly to alterations and additions, not just to decoration. What you might think is a modernization, the next owner will probably find outdated, perhaps shabby, and their first task will be to rip it out. If

you always keep in mind the original design of your home, you should be able to choose alterations, such as colour schemes, that won't look out of place, won't date too much and will appeal to those with different tastes.

This is especially true of the exterior. Very few homes are detached, so most houses should blend well with their neighbours. Each house should have an identity —but if it is too individual it will spoil the unity of the group as a whole. In addition, if your house looks odd, it will lessen not only its own retail value on the market but also the value of the area.

In the same way as you have to consider the character of your home, with its good and bad features, you must not forget your own needs. Your home must suit your own tastes, your interests and your way of life. Be honest and emphasize the things that you know you are good at, such as house plants or built-in furniture, and keep away from the areas for which you have no talent.

Don't be influenced too much by magazines or by other people — you must develop your own taste in decoration to feel truly comfortable in your own home. Learn from your mistakes and successes: it will be a slow and sometimes rather painful process, but in the end you'll have something that's unique and suits you absolutely. As a general rule,

The enormous range of colours on the market today makes paint a popular choice when the time for redecorating comes along. It is also relatively inexpensive.

When altering the exterior of your house consider its character and that of the houses on either side.

it's better to be rather cautious — keep things simple and restrained (it will make your rooms look more spacious anyway) until you're absolutely confident. Draw several different plans for each room, and make models. For example, if you're thinking of putting in a new window, hang a piece of paper of the same size on the wall where the window would be.

Each room should relate to the others — a feeling of continuity throughout the house will make it seem like one large living unit, not a lot of little boxes. You can achieve this either by having compatible colour schemes, or by running a consistent feature right through — the carpet, for example.

Try not to have any preconceptions about colour — if you think that you hate blue, remember summer skies and forget-me-nots. A good colour can boost you enormously, and cheaply. If you are at all timid, choose a fairly neutral basic colour and keep the brighter ones for the details. Gather examples (snips, scraps, bits of paper coloured with felt-tipped pens) of everything

you're going to include, then pin them side by side on a piece of card. You will find it most effective if you keep your scheme either mainly monochromatic (shades of one colour), related (similar colours), or contrasting.

Most of us flounder a bit with pattern: we either go overboard and live in a dizzy mixture or fight shy and have everything plain. One way out of this is to reserve your patterns for smaller items — they're easier to live with, and easier to change if you find that you can't. Changes of texture are also extremely important — if everything is too much the same it will make the best of schemes bland and uninteresting.

Often you can achieve a lot by discarding your conventional thinking about which rooms should be where and instead, decide what will suit you best. It's the same with furniture: it's quite likely that you could manage much better with less, even though finding storage space is always difficult. Even re-organizing your furniture in a more rational way will probably give your rooms quite a lift. Altering the actual fabric of your home — moving doors, dividing rooms, putting in a different staircase or pulling down a wall – may achieve something really

worthwhile in terms of the extra space and enjoyment it will provide. *Remember, however, that such activities are governed by various regulations and you must consult your local authorities, and, in the case of removing walls, a builder. Your home is like a house of cards: remove the wrong part and – crash.*

So far as furniture is concerned, don't despise the second-hand. Obviously, the home improvement magazines, the shops and the advertisers all want us to buy, buy, buy. But you must remember that new is not necessarily best, or even necessary. You can get a great deal of satisfaction in finding something old (not necessarily antique) and perhaps renovating it so that you have something which suits your purposes. Alternatively, a collection of small decorative items can become a hobby which will provide an inexpensive and perhaps unique point of interest.

Such details are of surprising importance: they give the feeling that a home is an interesting place, changing, growing, cared for in a way beyond the normal housework chores. It's that sort of environment that will give its occupants something of the security and serenity we all need.

HOME IMPROVEMENT

KITCHENS

Possibly the most complex, expensive and problematical area in the house, many kitchens were planned and built before there was much more than a deep sink and a bulky cooker to think about. Even in modern houses the kitchen is usually one of the smallest rooms, yet it often has to accommodate more work and equipment than anywhere else.

JUST A FACE LIFT

If you're not starting from scratch, and can't afford or don't want major upheavals, try removing all that's unnecessary or ugly — such as old wires, clocks that don't work, threadbare tea-towels, greasy memo pads. Replacing them with fresh pretty things (a jug of flowers, a spice shelf, some nice jars) will give renewed life.

A small whitewood chest of drawers, a painted wardrobe or free-standing bookshelves may easily provide an answer to storage problems, especially in rented accommodation. Industrial shelving or a piece of pegboard could cheaply display a useful and good-looking collection of kitchen equipment. A space where the fire or range used to be might become an alcove for equipment or shelving, perhaps with a wider shelf at waist level as a work surface. A slot at the back of a shelf could keep chopping knives close at hand but out of the way of the children.

A motley group of units all at different levels can be evened up by one single top over the lot. Old pipes might be removable; if not, paint them a decorative colour or box them in. You could unify a hotchpotch of cupboards and equipment by painting everything (including the fridge and cooker) with a bright heatproof paint.

BASIC PRIORITIES

If you are doing more than just a cosmetic job, decide what equipment you really need in your kitchen; if you know that you can't afford it all now, leave space. One of the main things about having a pleasing place to live in is keeping it flexible so that it can grow to meet your changing needs. Question yourself. Will you be eating in there? Will the children want to play there? What sort of meals do you cook and for how many? How much storage do you need and should it be open or in cupboards? Is the water supply, gas, electricity, ventilation adequate? Are you average height, or would it be better to have things custom made? Working surfaces at the wrong height can cause irritation, back ache and slipped discs! Then decide if you could alter the size of it by knocking out walls, a downstairs loo or an unused chimney. But make sure you won't be losing more than you'll gain — a pantry, for instance, can be far better for storing some food than a fridge. It may be best to leave well alone.

It is essential that storage and work surfaces are not only in the right place in your kitchen but at the right height. Stand upright about 450 mm (18 inches) from a wall and raise your arms until your fingers touch the wall: that point is the ideal height for work surfaces.

STORAGE

If you use standard kitchen units you'll have a good idea of what you're getting; some manufacturers also do a planning service to help you organize their selection of products. Many useful extra fittings — wire racks or plastic drawers, for instance — can be bought later, or you can add your own ideas — chopping boards, tiles, etc. — to make it more personal and useful.

If you're confident of your own designing, or have an

odd-shaped kitchen, try custom-built storage. Keep shelving as narrow as possible; that way nothing gets pushed to the back and forgotten. For deeper cupboards, doors with racks on the inside, swinging out to view, are far easier to keep orderly. Ideal doors for high wall cabinets are those sliding up on a sash mechanism — who hasn't cracked their head on a door hanging open at this awkward level?

If things are constantly in use, and the area you live in isn't too dirty, open shelving can have a decorative and unifying effect on the whole kitchen (or you could link it visually with the windows by hanging blinds in front).

REFRIGERATORS
Fridges are bulky, so they usually stand on the floor, though this makes them rather difficult to see into. If you can manage with a small one, try either a wall-hung model or putting it up on a work surface. Two small ones with the doors opening different ways can be very satisfactory.

Large fridges, of course, will give you extras such as freezer sections and ice-makers. Chest freezers are less convenient but cheaper than vertical ones where you can see everything at a glance. Consider the direction of the swing of your fridge door before you buy any particular model.

COOKERS
You probably have your own very definite opinion about whether gas or electricity is better. If you like the cleanliness of electricity, and the flexibility of gas, why not

Even if you can't afford to buy all the equipment shown here when you first design your kitchen, leave room for the items that you know you will want in the long run. Think carefully about the needs of the household when choosing such major, and expensive, items.

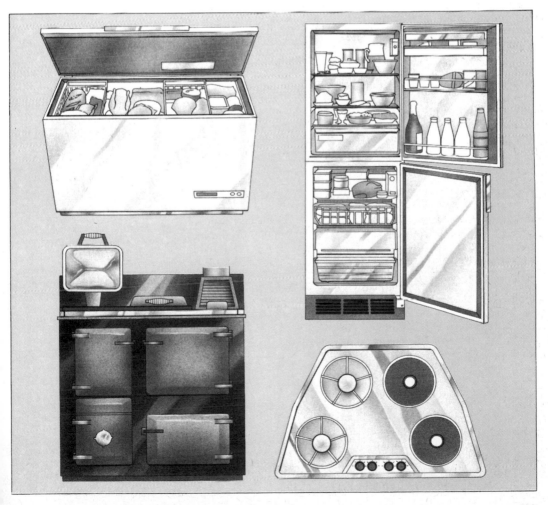

have an electric oven and a gas hob? Conventional cookers always have a gap round the back which gets filthy and is a real nuisance to clean. A split-level scheme does avoid this problem and also cuts out bending to peer at what's cooking.

Some small ovens can be built in or hung on a wall, which saves on space. You could consider micro-wave ovens, especially if you often eat frozen food. At the other end of the spectrum, a cooker incorporating a boiler will give your kitchen a friendly feeling, encourage you to cook slow stews and bake your own bread, and will supply hot water and perhaps heat the radiators as well.

SINKS

Don't necessarily think that you've got to introduce a stainless steel sink to make your kitchen look good. Old ceramic or cast iron ones may be far more in character, and you could always build units around them. Also you don't need to observe the convention of having the sink under the window — unless you have toddlers to watch in the garden. Another time- and space-saver is a wall-mounted plate rack over the sink, and simple wall-mounted taps are the easiest to clean. The sink should be near the hot water supply, with a convenient store for detergents, tea-towels, etc., and it should also be near the cooker, for draining food.

WASTE DISPOSAL

A pedal-bin is essential in the kitchen. Bulky items will need a large plastic container — perhaps attached to the back of a cupboard door. Dustbins should be kept away from doors and windows and the dustbin area should be kept clean, as any scraps of food will attract flies and vermin.

DISHWASHER

If you want one, it's worth buying a good one. You may have to use it several times a day so, if it's too small, unreliable or noisy, it will be very irritating.

HEATING AND VENTILATION

Kitchens usually produce their own heat, what with the cooking, washing and central heating boiler, so if yours is small you'll probably find a temporary quick warmth is all you need — such as that from a fan heater. Under-floor heating would be good for stone or quarry floors.

Condensation and smells seeping out to the rest of the house can be particularly depressing. Some ovens have their own ventilation systems, otherwise an overhead hood is the most acceptable form of ventilation.

LIGHTING

Make sure you won't be in your own light. One answer is to install tungsten tubes under wall-hung cupboards, shining down on work tops. Spotlights will give an efficient and more friendly light than the frequently used strip lights: your kitchen doesn't have to be as dazzling as a supermarket. Make sure the sink is properly lit — it is often the worst lit part of the kitchen at night. Natural light can often be improved — perhaps by altering an old back door to make a sliding window (louvred windows would provide ventilation without draughts). Blinds are probably better than curtains as they are easier to keep clean.

FLOORS, WALLS AND WORK TOPS

Choose something warm, washable, tough, non-slip and

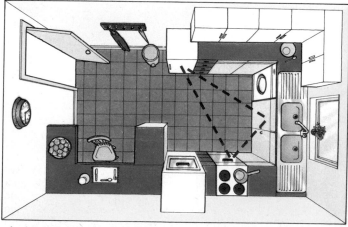

A well-designed kitchen can save a lot of needless walking to and fro. This particular kitchen is a very convenient shape and it has been possible to locate the sink, cooker and fridge at one end of the room and a small, but useful, sitting area at the other. The main work area forms a classic triangular shape. People coming into the kitchen need not disturb the activities of the cook.

not too noisy for your floor covering. Linoleum, cork and vinyl are good. However, don't rush to take out tiles or stone and brick floors if you do have them; you could keep their quality and make them practical by covering them with a matt plastic coating.

Walls in the kitchen have to withstand heat, condensation, splashing and grease, so you must be practical, perhaps even having different types of surfaces in different areas to cope with any of these problems. Ceramic or stainless steel tiles will take splashing and heat; timber, vinyl and cork are fairly resilient and look good. Semigloss paint is better than full gloss — it doesn't show the condensation as much.

There's no ideal work sur-

face, so use a variety for different tasks. Formica is fairly tough, and easy to wipe clean. Stainless steel will withstand heat, wood chopping boards can be movable — large ones can be fixed in the work surface (rub in oil to keep them looking good) – and slate or marble is excellent for pastry making.

LAYOUT
Planning the layout of your kitchen is extremely complex for there are always doors and windows in just the wrong places. The basic idea is to have food storage near where you come in with the shopping, next to a food preparation surface. Cooking facilities should be near the sink, and near a serving area. A dishwasher should be

An air of efficiency is achieved in a busy room by a combination of streamlined units, easy to clean surfaces and a coordinated colour scheme. Yellow is not only a clean and bright colour but is also warm and welcoming.

near the dish storage.

You will need at least 75 cm (2 ft 6 in) of corridor space between units, but avoid having it as a *real* corridor with a flow of people going to and fro — a dangerous situation all too likely to result in burns and scalds. Keep your layout as simple as possible, and try to place all your tall items together so you can have as big an area of uninterrupted work top as possible. Storage is best positioned just above your work surface.

HOME IMPROVEMENT

BATHROOMS

The mood of the bathroom has changed dramatically over the last 25 years, more so than any other area in the whole house. It's far less clinical now, perhaps reflecting our less puritanical attitudes to our bodies.

FITTINGS

The basic British standard bath is 1.65 m x 75 cm x approx. 50 cm high (5ft 6in x 2ft 4 in x 1ft 8in). If you're tall, ask for one of the longer sizes. On the other hand, if you have very little space you might have to use a shorter one, or a hip bath (a split-level affair where you sit on one half, with your feet lower), or a bath to fit in a corner. A bath with a flat bottom is best if you want to have a shower over it. A low-sided bath is best in a small room.

Nowadays baths are either vitreous enamelled steel or acrylic, reinforced with a steel frame. The acrylic ones are lighter and therefore easier to handle; they are also warmer to the touch and come in a greater variety of shapes and colours. However, they scratch easily, a cigarette will melt holes, and they're not absolutely rigid. Some baths have their own panels, or you can buy a hardboard panel with chrome corners. You could even make your own, or cover one to match the walls. If you have elderly people in the house, handgrips may be advisable.

If you want to have a separate shower as well, you must ensure that the area is well waterproofed — you will need about 1m (3ft) square for your shower, and not much less for getting dry. The head

of the shower must be 1 m (3ft) below the level of the cold water tank or you will need a pump.

Basins come in a vast variety — from tiny corner ones for handwashing to a 'vanitory' unit complete with its own storage space. Whatever you choose, it should be about 70 cm (32 in) high.

A new slim-line lavatory cistern can replace a high, large, old one, without having to change the pan. Some have fixed top handles so they can be boxed in. Cisterns concealed behind false walls must have access to them. Avoid cheap flexible

lavatory seats – they snap very easily and are not comfortable to sit on for long. If you want a bidet remember that it takes up more space than a lavatory.

FLOORS AND WALLS

Obviously, the main consideration here is that things should stand up to splashing and condensation — without rotting, peeling, discolouring, etc. Tiles are a traditional answer, but expensive, not suitable for wooden floors, fairly difficult to cope with oneself, and they can give a rather harsh unwelcoming feeling. Strongly patterned tiles will overwhelm a

Light, ventilation and warmth are three important factors in the planning of a bathroom. The hot water tank can be concealed in a

cupboard and provide an invaluable airing cupboard. A matching suite, shower attachment and walls tiled high add a touch of luxury.

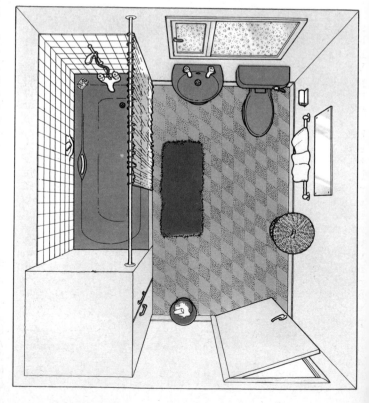

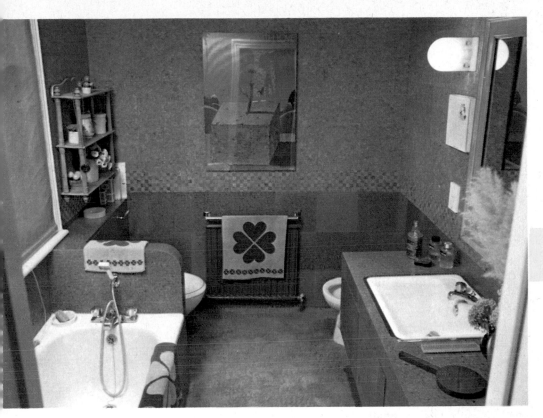

small room. A carpet should be rubber-backed, possibly a non-rotting synthetic fibre. Vinyl or linoleum is very practical, as are cork and non-slip rubber, though these are more expensive.

For walls that are going to be exposed to a lot of water, such as around the shower, try a sheet of Perspex, plastic laminate or tiles, glass, mirror or cork. In other areas you can be a lot more relaxed. Plastic-emulsion or silk-vinyl paint is cheap, easy to apply and available in a wide range of colours. Ordinary wallpaper should be protected with sealer if your bathroom is not very well ventilated; vinyl or waterproof papers are fine. Panelling and tongue-and-groove boarding (again sealed in some way) are good, too, although cheap wood may warp slightly.

LIGHTING AND VENTILATION

Many bathrooms in this country are clammy and dark — windowless ones are often especially depressing. You don't want to go to the other extreme, but varied and pleasant lighting should provide a general glow with stronger light for closer work such as shaving. A white ceiling, lots of mirrors and small concealed strip lights can bounce the light around in an interesting way. Electricity in the bathroom is governed by stringent laws, and rightly so. Check that the fitting you want is suitable for a bathroom and that your wiring and switches are safe.

Remember, good ventilation is much better than deodorizing, and poor heating can ruin the effect of the entire room, no matter what else you've done to it.

An original design and the use of cork in this bathroom make it into a showpiece. The lavatory is well positioned behind a screen wall, while the basin is surrounded by plenty of useful surface space.

MAKING IT YOUR OWN

Bathrooms, more than anywhere in the house, tend to suffer from a lack of personality. It's worth taking extra trouble with the details so you can really feel that it's a good place to wallow in. Shower curtains, for example, can be made of any material at all, as long as it's backed with plastic. Many plants thrive in a warm, damp atmosphere and will love the bathroom. Strongly coloured, matching sets of towels will give a great boost to a dreary bathroom that you can't alter. Additional mirrors, a collection of jars, pretty bottles, tiles etc. will all make it more inviting.

HOME IMPROVEMENT

BEDROOMS

Are your bedrooms unused for much of the day? If so, perhaps you could consider transferring some hobbies or activities there and relieving some of the pressure on the living room. It is certainly a very good idea for children and teenagers. But even if you're going to keep it just for sleeping and dressing, you'll need to consider a few things first: practical problems like whether there is a socket near the bed, if you have enough storage, how important it is to soundproof and whether you're sometimes going to have to put up other people. If it isn't only your room, you must consult the other occupant — his or her taste in decoration may not be the same as yours.

The style of your own bedroom is intimately personal, and you'll relax best in surroundings that you feel are really you. But do a bit of homework first to find out the possibilities; then be wholehearted about what you think is right, whether it's sensual, crisp, dramatic, bright or subdued.

The bedroom is the one place where you can probably take out an old fireplace with no regrets. If your bedroom is small, keep your furniture as low as possible. Also furniture on legs, rather than coming right down to the floor, will add a feeling of spaciousness.

THE DECOR

There are two rules: that it should look relaxing and be flattering to your skin. Strident patterns and harsh colours are probably best avoided. But even if you stick to something plain and muted, you don't have to be terribly practical since, unless it's a teenager's room, it's unlikely to take anything like the wear and tear of the rest of the house. Your carpet, for example, can be of an inexpensive quality or something long-haired and pale and, since you don't have to worry about smoke, water and grease, you can choose less fiercely practical wall coverings or possibly even indulge in wall hangings.

You should give a little extra attention to the ceiling as it's one ceiling in your home you're likely to lie and stare at. You could wallpaper or paint it to match or contrast with the walls, or have a decorative frieze where wall and ceiling meet. For the adventurous, there's stencilling, freehand murals, stars to stick on, even a four poster bed. Sound insulation is often a major consideration in the bedroom — a fitted carpet, cork-lined walls and double glazing are ideal.

FURNITURE

Most concern must be given to the choosing of your bed — we do spend more than a third of our lives there, even if we are asleep for much of that time. What we're lying on affects our bodies, the quality of our rest and, ultimately, how we feel and think. A saggy old bed will eventually damage your

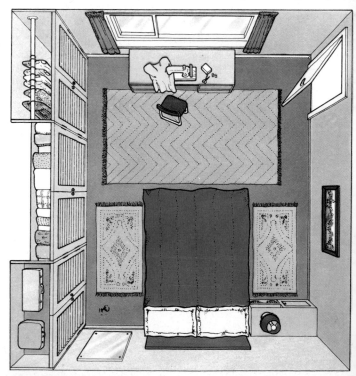

Allow plenty of storage space in your bedroom for bedding and other items as well as clothes. In a large room it may be possible to utilize the space during the day for a hobby, such as sewing. Position your bed so that it will be out of any draughts.

spine. You should have a new bed every ten years, and then as good as you can afford.

Mattresses are either foam (easy to handle and light), old-fashioned stuffed, or interior sprung (the best beds have one thousand springs). A good bed base will prolong the life of your mattress; some sort of base is a necessity because of the amount of moisture you lose during the night.

Beds that fold away are both more comfortable and less expensive than they used to be — avoid ones that crease up the mattress.

The position of the bed is all-important — out of draughts, and so it's easy to make. If you want to include seating in your bedroom but there's little room, you could raise the bed on a plinth and have a step round it to use as a bench, covered with carpet or floor cushions. Or raise the bed right up, add a ladder and have your seating underneath. (You could use this idea for a desk, too.) In either case you can build your own unit or, for seating, buy widely-spaced bunk beds and use the one down below as a sofa with loads of cushions.

Although not strictly necessary, most of us like a chair in the bedroom – even just a low stool to sit on in front of the mirror, or something to throw a shirt on. A light near the bed (even if you don't do much reading) is a good idea, and adequate lighting for making-up your face.

STORAGE

Try to overestimate what you need and then fit it in with the shape of your room. Built-in storage will hold far more than the conventional chest of drawers, etc. — but

The use of green and white, the cane furniture and the brick wall link this elegant bedroom with its attractive garden background. The room is light and airy yet well furnished and comfortable.

make sure it's not going to look like an afterthought. Remember you'll probably have to store spare blankets here too, as well as clothes and hobbies. You could consider covering your cupboard doors with material, perhaps to match your curtains, bedspread or wallpaper. If you are short of space try a bed base with drawers in it — recessed handles are, of course, essential. A lot of bedside junk is rather unsightly so you may want something other than open shelving by your bed. Shelves directly above the bed must be at least 1 m (3 ft) higher or you'll be forever hitting your head on them.

HOME IMPROVEMENT

LIVING ROOMS

A living room has to be the most adaptable of all rooms, yet it's important to create a relaxed atmosphere where your family can recharge, pursue their interests and be themselves. It is best to start with a list of your activities and the equipment needed.

Next draw plans of your living room and its furniture, trying out various ways of incorporating areas for the activities that have emerged.

FURNITURE

Seating is the most important factor in a living room, so give it pride of place in your designing. You won't want a stream of people walking through your sitting area, and it will look rather unfriendly placed all round the walls. On the other hand, if the seats are too close together no one will be able to stretch out their legs. Incidentally, people find conversation easiest if they're seated at right angles to each other. A study area should be tucked away to one side — so you can turn your back on whatever is going on — and preferably lit from the left. If eating is only occasionally done in the living room, avoid large tables taking up too much space and use trolleys and folding chairs instead. You may feel you could fit everything in much better if you moved a doorway, a non-loadbearing wall or a fireplace. The best plan is probably one that gives you the most floor space.

Remember that in this room, more than anywhere, you will need a 'focal point' — that is, something your eyes are drawn to, some-thing you can sit and gaze at. Traditionally this was the fireplace, and it still takes a lot of beating. But an obsolete fireplace does little for anyone's feelings of comfort, so you may have to provide an alternative focal point. A television only fills this need when it is switched on. A really good piece of furniture is better, or a large picture or print, but whatever it is, it should emphasize the room's good points.

Extra room can be created by building a separate unit to house items such as the television set, stereo equipment, drinks and glasses and books. Grouping together these aids to modern living in one unit covering, perhaps, one wall from top to bottom, can create a focal point.

You should also develop secondary points of interest — groups of objects, plants, dried flowers — to balance both the main focal point and each other. You must keep changing these to give a feeling of life to the room.

A three-piece suite is the least flexible of seating arrangements, and three-seater sofas rarely get used by three people — do you really need one? A cheap and simple way of providing seating is to build a low-level platform in a corner and put large floor cushions on it. It isn't necessary to have all your uphol-

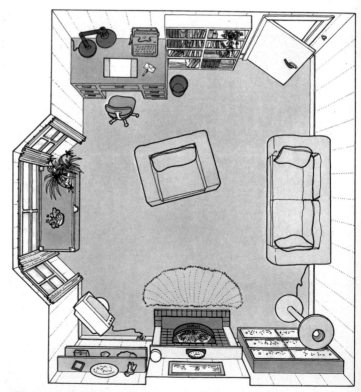

The arrangement of a living room should be flexible, with furniture that can be switched around and pictures that can be changed.

Seating placed round the fire, varied lighting and a quiet corner for a study area make a relaxing but useful family room.

stery matching, as long as each relates to the other. Any low tables should be high enough to eat from.

If you are able to start from scratch, and your ceilings are high enough, you could consider constructing a 'conversation pit'. Build a 1 m (3 ft) high stage around your walls (remembering to include some steps along one side), with a secondary stage half as tall around the other three sides. Cover the main stage and the steps with carpeting and upholster the secondary stage and its backing to form a giant settee.

The equipment you collect in your living room can be quite terrifying, so aim for a lot of storage, either to display or to conceal it. Remember, if you incorporate your television into the storage you will need ventilation. When choosing

any item of furniture, bear in mind all the rest and the eventual atmosphere you want to create. If you are a hi-fi addict, you will want it to be very easily accessible, but remember that dust is the enemy of such equipment and it may be best to keep it behind cupboard doors.

DECORATION
In a much-used room a relatively plain scheme will be easier to live with. Is your living room going to be more of a day-time or night-time room? – for that too will affect your choice of colours. Your windows will have to make it private and interesting. Lighting is, to a degree, a matter of common sense (bright lights for reading etc.), but you should be able to get a bit of extra drama from your lighting arrangements. A display of things

you've collected can be a great focal point — it needn't cost much, it just needs imagination and a little patience. Prints are cheap too — the best quality ones come from museums. If you're going to make a feature of one big print, make sure that that one is well framed. Lots of cushions will add a feeling of relaxation. If your room is very small, a light colour over both walls and woodwork will help. Tidiness, fresh flowers, a plant or a bowl of fruit will give it a lift far beyond its size and cost. Above all you must let your living room evolve continually so that its atmosphere keeps alive.

HOME IMPROVEMENT

EATING AREAS

Wherever you eat (and let's face it, dining rooms are dying out), although it should be near the cooking area, you will want it to be relaxed and comfortable. The table should be your focal point, and the lighting not too harsh.

CHOOSING THE FURNITURE

When buying tables and chairs there are two things to consider: what you will do with them when they're not in use, and if they will be practical and comfortable with enough knee/leg room.

People need a surprising amount of space, and if your space is very limited, a built-in counter with stools or wall benches may be the answer. The counter can double as a work top, but must be at least 20 cm (8 in) wide. Stools should be 25-30 cm (10 in - 12 in) lower. A bench will seat more people, but in that case the table must not be supported from the edges or your eaters will find it difficult to get in and out. Wall seating usually has to be tailor made, but it is quite simple to construct. Stacking or folding chairs look quite good nowadays, though you should have a cupboard or other space to put them in when they're not needed. Chairs with arms or struts may not fit if you want to push them under the table.

A table that folds right away, or an expanding table (with wings or leaves) can be a godsend in a small space. A table should be at least 75 cm (2 ft 6 in) wide if you are using both sides. Each person will need about 60 x 37.5 cm (24 in x 15 in) for their plates, cutlery, glass, etc. So, to seat six people, a round table should be 1.35 m (4 ft 6 in) in diameter, and a square table should be 1.35 m (4 ft 6 in) square. To allow people to push back chairs, and to have space for serving, you'll need at least 90 cm (3 ft) between the table and the wall.

DIVIDERS

If you are eating in the same area as your kitchen, and want to divide it off, there are various possibilities. A curtain to hide kitchen clutter is the cheapest solution. Units built out into the room will provide a partial wall, and louvred doors right across the room will provide a complete one. If the kitchen and eating area are adjacent, a wall 'hatch' (a 'window' between the rooms) is a useful idea, especially if you have two people preparing the meal. In an existing door frame you could fit swing doors (but only if you have plenty of space on both sides) or a 'stable' door, made of two sections, the bottom one remaining closed. If there's often something else happening in the dining area — the kids' homework or grandfather's stamp collecting — there must be adequate storage for that too, to reduce the grumbles when they're forced to clear for tea.

White paint on the walls and low white furniture help to create a feeling of space in this L-shaped room. The folding chairs and table can quickly be removed when they are not needed for dining.

HALLS AND STAIRS

Obviously halls and stairs exist to get us from one room to another, but they can often be a neglected waste of space. First impressions are very important, be it of people or places, and it's your front hall that gives visitors a first glance at the way you live. So it should be friendly and positive and, since you won't spend too much time there, it can probably afford to be more unusual than other areas.

Often the hall is one of the best places to show off a large collection of things hanging on the wall, or for a really large painting that won't fit anywhere else, or for bookshelves. Of course you shouldn't have anything that gets in the way; you don't want to have to edge past bulky items: after all, your hall and stairs must be safe thoroughfares.

Most halls will need a fairly tough and washable wall surface. Though you could opt for a more dramatic colour scheme than you could live with elsewhere, your hall should blend well decoratively with all the rooms leading off it, or it will jar with the others when you leave doors open. A strong focal point at the end of a long hall will appear to shorten it. A wallpaper with a light background and a very widely spaced pattern will add spaciousness.

You will need something hard-wearing and easy to clean on the floor; even in the quietest household in town, it will get relatively dirty. You may also feel you need good sound insulation against the thunder of feet. One type of good economic carpet is a synthetic needleloom, one that is non-woven and has quality hair cords. If you are carpeting stairs, avoid vegetable fibres as they are rather slippery, and make sure that whatever you use is very well tacked down. Also avoid slippery rugs on polished floors.

Light, too, is important for safety's sake as well as for appearance. Consider putting in a glass panel in your door, or a new glass door, although, before you do, consider whether it's going to spoil the appearance or character of your house from the outside. You must certainly guard against dark corners. Putting in spotlights can be a good safety device, as well as adding interest, but make sure no-one will be dazzled coming downstairs.

Heating your hall efficiently it's an airlock anyway; it will help to keep the rooms comfortable and provide a warm greeting. Make sure your front and back doors are as draught-free as possible. A heavy curtain on the type of rod that lifts as you open the door will give an added feeling of comfort and extra sound insulation and will keep out the cold.

NARROW HALLS

Many halls in Britain are long, narrow and rather dark. Often they have to cope with bikes, prams, coats and telephones. If yours is one of these, you will have to plan extra carefully. There's no avoiding these things, but you can try to arrange that most of them can be folded away or hung on a wall: a wall-mounted telephone, a lattice board for letters rather than a shelf, even a seat that folds down if you want to sit for telephone calls (though with rising prices, perhaps that's not something to be encouraged these days).

If you have any sort of recess at all, that's obviously the place to store things. You may be lucky enough to have a space under the stairs where you can put the push chair, or coats and wellies (perhaps with a small hand-basin and long mirror), or even the telephone with a small table and chair for doing the bills. Maybe the recess is big enough to install a downstairs lavatory.

In a narrow hall you will probably need a very unified, simple and fairly light-coloured scheme (if it is too light it will suffer quickly from the dirt brought in through the front door). You will also need a particularly tough wall surface, for it will inevitably get bumped a great deal. If there are lots of doors, you can keep a feeling of continuity by painting them a similar colour to the walls so it doesn't look so broken up. Mirrors will also add a sense of space.

SPACIOUS AND SQUARE HALLS

If you have anything other than a corridor you can more easily consider the possibility of using your hall in some extra capacity. Keep this activity as far away as possible from the bottom of any stairs. You might be able to incorporate a neat dining area, making sure that chairs will push away under the table, or fold up if you're at all tight for space; a round table will be less likely to bruise you if you're edging past. Remember that you will need quite a bit of storage if you're not to be driven mad carrying things in and out, perhaps incorporating it in a cupboard that is there for the inevitable cleaning necessities.

Another possibility for the

HOME IMPROVEMENT

hall is a study area, though you will need it to be out of the main flow of traffic. Alternatively, if you give a lot of parties, often have visitors or have a large family, it is worth considering using the hall as an addition to the main reception area, particularly in conjunction with the lounge and/or dining room. To achieve this, view the house as a series of modules, then work out how you can connect them up with the hall. For instance, if you have a lounge on one side of the house, next to the hall and dining room, between each room you could have double glass doors that could be opened progressively to create a larger gathering area. If you decide to do this, make sure that the decor is consistent in all the rooms and the floor coverings similar so that there are no visual barriers to people circulating.

Other creative ideas depend on the position of the outside walls, ventilation and plumbing. You may be able to put your washing machine, laundry area or even the kitchen in the hall. If you're worried about cupboard doors not having enough space to open, try the type that concertina out — they'll take up half the room.

MAJOR ALTERATIONS
You may be able to improve your hall by moving a doorway, or perhaps blocking one up and using the alcove that is left for storage. In a 'front to back' corridor you might shorten your hall and use the extra space for widening some of the rooms on either side — but you must consult a builder before you take

down any walls. If you partially remove a wall, a low divider will still separate the areas but give added light and a feeling of spaciousness. It won't stop the draughts so effectively, so think hard first. Perhaps you would also benefit from building an entrance lobby.

You may be tempted to take out a staircase that uses a lot of space. This is certainly worth considering, although it can be very expensive. Also there are very many rules and regulations when replacing stairs and you may in any case be removing something rather fine that is a major feature in your house. For example, a spiral staircase may seem like a good space-saver, but you'll still need quite a large square area.

1 It has been possible, in this well-proportioned hall, to create a dining area. The decor is kept very neutral to play down the fact of it being a hallway, and this also increases the feeling of spaciousness. The stairs tone in with the main area to create a completely unified scheme.

2 These stairs are meant to be seen. They are a feature of the house and the bright colour shows them off very successfully. The bold print on the curtains further draws your attention to this interesting corner.

3 The classic combination of black and white tiles adds elegance to this hall where neutral and positive colours have been used most effectively.

4 The bold colour in this hallway provides an excellent background for the framed prints. The spotlights are carefully positioned so as to highlight both the prints and the attractive potted palm, while providing adequate overall lighting. The ceiling reflects the light and provides a relief from all the colour, while the white skirting board forms a precise border between the walls and the dark carpet.

HOME IMPROVEMENT

FLOORS

Flooring is one of the most expensive decorative items, so you can't afford to make mistakes. Be practical first, then make decisions about colour, pattern and texture. Being practical involves thinking about various different aspects of your floor covering. What is it going to cover? – (it's not usually a good idea to put ceramic tiles on a wood floor, or a delicate carpet on the stairs). Then ask yourself if it will be easy to put down, or will the cost be increased by the services of an expert? Once down, will it be easy to keep clean? Pale floors look tempting, but if you've a young family, they're probably not wise. It is also essential that you take into consideration the warmth of the floor, its safety, and whether it will be noisy, or tiring to stand on for long periods.

HARD FLOORS

If you have good floor boards, a cheap way to make them look good is to sand them down (you can hire a machine), then seal or stain them. Floor stain is not only available in the usual woody colours but also in red, blue and green. Plain sealer will bring out the colour of the wood, looks excellent and will show off rugs well, but it doesn't provide insulation. Alternatively you could install a new wooden floor, replacing your old one. Plywood or chipboard can also be used as a surface covering over old floor boards or can be attached directly on to timber joists; both can also be treated by staining or sealing. Hardboard, too, can pro-vide an inexpensive floor covering, and can be sealed, waxed or painted. It isn't very hard-wearing but could perhaps be a first step when carpets are to be laid later.

Tiles are at the other extreme — tremendously hard-wearing and available in a wide range, from glazed or unglazed, ceramic or vitrified, in all sorts of colours, shapes and designs through to the well-known plain quarry tile. All types share the disadvantages of being cold and noisy, and their lack of resilience makes them tiring to stand on for long periods. Many of the more traditional types of flooring share these characteristics — old brick floors, flag stones, slate. Since they have an unusual quality that is irreplaceable, it's probably worth preserving them by cleaning and sealing them.

If you want softer, warmer floors, cork is hard-wearing, a good insulator, resilient and quiet. The only disadvantages with cork are the possibilities of it fading, or crumbling at the edges. Linoleum is better than it used to be, but there is a great variety in quality: the cheapest will give poor service, the thicker and more expensive ones are hard-wearing, resilient and warm underfoot. Rubber flooring is very similar — synthetic rubber is less inclined to mark and plain-coloured embossed industrial rubber flooring is now used in homes, too. Thermoplastic tiles are inexpensive and tough but rather unyielding and chilly. Vinyl asbestos tiles are more resistant to grease but are easily marked by rubber heels, and can soften if they are too near a heat source. Though they need accurate laying, you can create your own individual combination of colours. Vinyl sheeting is durable, resistant to dirt, quiet and warm. The better quality has a cushion backing; it is in the same price range as carpeting.

CARPETING

Carpeting can be made of a bewildering range of fibres, though these fall into two categories — man-made and

A sealed wooden floor complements the kitchen units and the long, attractive wooden table.

Tiles can be highly decorative and very sophisticated. They are also easily wiped clean.

natural. Totally synthetic carpeting, though very hard-wearing, can give rise to static electricity, which gives shocks. One hundred per cent nylon is the worst offender for this, though the problems are being researched. It is extremely tough, but a dropped match will leave a mark. Acrylic fibre is more like wool; it is warm and wears well, but is not fire resistant. Polyester is soft and tough, and also waterproof. Polypropylene is usually used as a backing or blended with something else.

Of the natural fibres, wool has the most luxurious feel and, if blended with nylon, it can be extremely hard-wearing. Other animal hair is not so soft and warm. The vegetable fibres feel harder still, though they can be tough, attractive and relatively inexpensive compared to wool.

As with types of fibre, there are numerous methods of carpet construction. Axminster has a cut pile inserted into a woven backing, often highly patterned and with numerous colours. There is a great variety in price as the quality depends on how much fibre is used in each square centimetre (or square inch). The best blend is 80 per cent wool and 20 per cent nylon. Wilton carpets are made with a continuous yarn, which limits the number of colours usually to five, but many Wiltons are plain. The cost is comparable to Axminster. Tufted carpets are set into a backing and then secured by latex.

Cord carpets are similar to Wiltons but are cheaper and have a ridged appearance; they are often extremely hard-wearing. Needleloom is also inexpensive and tough, utilizing synthetic and vegetable fibres enmeshed in an acrylic backing. Bonded carpets, that is, pile glued to a backing, are being developed rapidly and are now available in many varieties and prices. Carpet tiles are also available in a bewildering assortment of materials and colours; to get the best out of them, you must change them around regularly. Sisal, coir and rush matting is cheap, attractive and very good on cold floors.

Carpet widths range from 67.5 cm (27") to 90 cm (36"), up to 4.5 m (15') and even 5.4 m (18'). It is really best to rely on an expert to lay your carpet, but check on the amounts they estimate you will need. An underlay will soften the unevenness of your floor, greatly prolong the life of your carpet and will give it a far livelier feel, too. An ill-fitting wood floor should be covered with hardboard first. An uneven floor must be levelled up with hardboard (not with newspaper or old carpet) and damp must be eliminated or your carpet will be ruined very quickly. Raw edges can be bound with carpet tape to prevent fraying, or turned under in the case of cord.

Stone mosaic is the ideal floor covering for an area in the house which leads to the garden.

Traditional and tough, quarry tiles always look good, especially in a farmhouse kitchen.

A white carpet in a quiet bedroom adds a touch of luxury and feels good to the feet.

Rush matting is a reasonably cheap floor covering and is practical and hard-wearing.

HOME IMPROVEMENT

WALLS

The decoration of your walls can have a very profound effect on the mood of your rooms — busy, calm, sophisticated, etc. What's more, changing that decoration is the quickest way to alter the whole effect.

PAINT

Paint has become very easy to use, and is the most popular form of decorating. Take a sample of the colour you want with you when buying; manufacturers' colour names vary a great deal. Check the condition of your walls before you start and make sure the cause of any stains has been dealt with. An unplastered good (well-pointed) brick wall can be painted directly, or sealed. A plain painted wall makes an excellent background for a display or collection. But if you want to add individuality to the wall itself, you could be more adventurous — a mural, or stencilled designs cost only imagination. Or try painting the bottom half of your room one colour, the top another. Or combine a painted wall with a paper frieze — there are many to choose from.

WALLPAPER

A patterned paper can help to unify a bitty room, but otherwise there's no need to go floor to ceiling. Try panels, edged with narrow border paper, or dividing your wall

Bold colours in a bedroom may seem unusual but they can be restful as well as impressive. Everything has been carefully chosen to maintain a theme of orange, white and brown.

with friezes as the Victorians did. Then you can have the tough paper at the bottom, where all the wear and tear is, and something more delicate above.

Although most papers come in standard rolls, prices are extremely varied, so you should be able to find something to suit your pocket. The cheapest papers are thin, and both cheap and very expensive papers are harder to hang. Non-washable papers can be protected with a special sealer, but test first to see if the pattern smudges. Hand-printed paper looks sharper than machine printed, but it is much more expensive. Washable paper is water-repellent but not as tough as vinyl. Lincrusta, anaglyptas and embossed paper can be a good solution to bumpy surfaces, especially ceilings where you need

a non-directional design. Like woodchip paper, they can be painted.

Various fabrics are available backed with paper and are hung in the same way as wallpaper. These include hessian (which can be painted, but in its natural state has a very comforting air), felt (which tends to pick up dust but can be vacuumed), linen, wool and jute (some of which can be sponged). Any fabric which doesn't stretch too much can be attached to a framework of battens (bedspreads, for example, make a good panelled effect), but you will have to take it down to clean it. Cork can be bought either attached to paper or as tiles or panels. Polystyrene absorbs noise and condensation and insulates, but it does dent easily and, if there's a fire, it will give off poisonous

fumes. Ceramic tiles are very hard-wearing and easy to clean. Vinyl floor tiles can also be used on the walls for continuity. Mirrors are good used on walls either as tiles or in slabs — they add light and space.

Tongue-and-groove or lapped boarding is good insulation, an excellent inner skin for bad walls and a very sympathetic wall finish. Use it horizontally, vertically or diagonally, depending on what you wish to emphasize. It can be stained or sealed. The same is true of panelling, though it has rather grand connotations and may look out of place. Softboard can be covered with material and attached directly to the wall. Sealed chipboard is good insulation, too, and peg-board is excellent for hanging tools and utensils. Incidentally if you want to construct a deco rative dividing wall, garden screen blocks can look very effective and are unusual.

CREATING ILLUSIONS

If you decorate your walls cleverly, you can overcome many visual problems. Like people, very few houses look perfect, but the right colours and styles can create illusions and emphasize good points, just as the right clothes and make-up do for people. So decide what your rooms' worst features are, and see if you can give them a helping hand. For example, a light-coloured ceiling will appear higher, a medium-coloured ceiling will appear lower (too dark and it will disappear completely if you've low lighting!). Bringing the ceiling colour down to a picture rail, or using horizontal bands of colour

Coordinated wall coverings and curtains are always attractive. The painted window draws out the colour from its cream background and the flower arrangement further complements the scheme.

around the top of a wall will also lower the ceiling. You will need plenty of masking tape to keep the lines straight. You could use a similar method to break up your wall area into panels. A long, narrow space can be opened up by a focal point at the far end. In a complex area, like a hall, have a very carefully coordinated scheme throughout, with perhaps just one or two colours or tones for everything. Add a stripe around an uninteresting room, either at skirting level, at the join with the ceiling or in the middle. This could be batten, a frieze or just a stripe of paint. It will bring it alive.

HOME IMPROVEMENT

WINDOWS

How are you going to dress your windows? For most of us, privacy is one of the major considerations — but if this doesn't apply to you, try leaving a handsome window uncurtained, at least during the day. You don't have to be conventional. For example, you don't have to use curtains — blinds will give an uncluttered look and their patterns won't be broken up with folds. Do consider your windows from the outside too, and how all the windows will look together. Be practical about relating length and weight to headings and rails, etc. — have you considered all the possibilities? Limited funds shouldn't stop you, for there are inexpensive roller-blind kits, cheap louvre panels and many different and efficient heading tapes.

CHOOSING CURTAINS

Curtaining can be expensive, so think carefully how much you can afford and what you want to achieve (noise insulation, complete darkness). Some practical considerations are: will they be fire hazards, how much fullness (better to have masses of something cheap than skimp — you can give quality by lining them) and, of course, colour, texture and pattern. Avoid enormous patterns unless you can afford to change your curtains frequently. If you're already stuck with them, try adding a neutral border to the edges. If you stick to something plain you can always pep the room up with, say, patterned cushions which will be cheaper to change. Also avoid short but heavy curtains — the material just won't hang correctly.

As a general rule it's best to have curtains either 1 cm (1/2in) off the floor or 0.5 cm (1/4in) above the sill; any shorter and it may look as if you ran out of material. The tops should be either ceiling height or at the top of the window. The exception is if you're going to have café curtains which will come half-way down your window. It's best, when you're measuring up for curtains, to put the track up first. Remember to allow for matching pattern repeats, and to check that the material won't shrink! If you've any doubts about your material, your retailer should be able to advise. Always look at your curtain material against the light before you buy it. Incidentally, sheeting and towelling come in out-size widths, good colours and are comparatively cheap, so they are ideal as curtain material. What's more, you can always use them as sheets or towels when you get bored with them as curtains.

Curtains will hang much better if they are lined. Not only does the lining protect the curtain material but it provides an extra insulating layer between the cold glass of the windows and the warm room. Linings can either be sewn to the back of the curtains or can be simply attached to the heading tape with curtain hooks. They can then be taken down and washed separately.

You can also buy ready made curtains. The cheaper ones are unlined and only come in standard lengths but are quick and easy to put up.

HANGING CURTAINS

Basically there are two sorts of heading tape; one with a

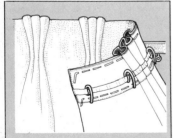

Pinch pleats draw the material together into small pinches rather than in a regular row like pencil pleats. Special heading tape shows you where to insert the hooks when gathering curtains.

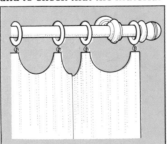

A decorative pole and rings with curtaining with a scalloped top can look effective in a modern room where pelmeting would seem old-fashioned. Poles can be obtained in many finishes.

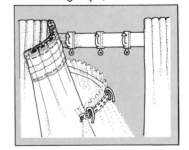

Pencil pleats give a particularly neat and even hang to curtains and are most effective on a long run of full-length curtaining. Use where your curtains are most likely to be admired.

drawstring for pulling your material into folds, and one without. Both are very easy to use. As for curtain hooks, they can be either plastic or metal, can fit into a sliding unit on your track or directly on to the track itself. A track should be hidden discreetly behind your curtains. If attached securely, a track will take even heavy curtains very efficiently. A brass or wooden pole should be grandly displayed in a more traditional way. A tension rod or wire will take light-weight curtaining and is very cheap. Some materials may stretch with hanging, so tack your hem, then finish it when your curtains have been up a couple of days.

BLINDS
The simplest of these are roller blinds. They are neat and inexpensive. There are simple kits available for you to make them yourself with your own choice of material, which should be something quite tough and tightly woven; you can also buy sprays for stiffening roller-blind material. Roman blinds are similar but pull up into concertina pleats. You can make these yourself, too, although they're not quite as straightforward as rollers. Pinoleum blinds are made of fine strips of wood woven together with cotton; there is now a white plastic quill version, too. Balastore and Plea-tex blinds are both made of tough paper, treated like a roman blind. Venetian blinds, with slats of metal or plastic, that you can angle at will to control the light entering or pull right up, are pricey, but consider them as an investment. They are a good answer to sloping windows and are excellent for insulation.

DAY-TIME PRIVACY
Translucent curtains are a well-established method of giving day-time privacy. If they're at all heavy, you'll have to use a second track or a pole but it will be worth the effort to have something rather good. Net curtains can look very wishy-washy. You could be more unconventional and use them as a fixed panel or roller blind. Alternatively you could fit frosted glass or buy glass paint and stencil on a design. If you're not short of light, mirror glass could replace the ordinary sort. A well-tended window box, or shelves of plants across the whole window on the inside are exciting ways to deal with the everyday problem of privacy.

STORAGE

Well-planned storage can give the most hectic house-hold a serene and smoothly-run air. To have a place for everything, most people need twice as much storage as they think, even if they're strong-minded enough to get rid of things that are never used. So, avoiding preconceptions (like jumpers having to go in a chest of drawers), decide if you need something fixed permanently or movable, what you need to store, in what rooms, how various storage schemes might affect those rooms, and how much you can afford.

Here are a few guidelines: allow children at least as much storage as adults; razors and medicines should

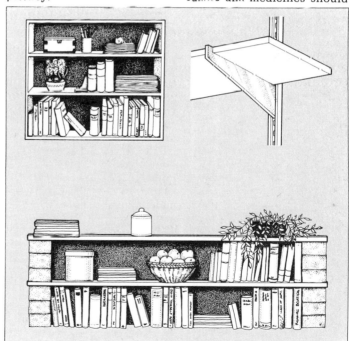

Shelving is a cheap and flexible form of storage. it is easily erected by a handiman, and can be purchased in many forms. The simplest must be using bricks and planks. Paint the bricks to match your decor and paint or varnish the planks. Adjustable shelving has the benefit of being easily moved up or down as the contents change, while a small shelving unit will look more in place with the decoration in a well-furnished living room.

HOME IMPROVEMENT

be stored out of reach of children; you'll need summer storage for eiderdowns and blankets; cups should be stored resting on their sides; brooms and the vacuum cleaner needn't be stored in the kitchen — after all, you use them everywhere.

SHELVING
This is the cheapest, simplest and most versatile storage. Check that the wall you want to put shelves on is sound and solid, and doesn't have any pipes or cables hidden in it. Measure the weight and size of what you want to put on them. If the contents on your shelves are going to remain the same you won't need adjustable shelving — just brackets attached directly to the wall. Otherwise you'll need wall-mounted uprights, with tracks or lots of sockets for movable brackets. The heavier the load, the more supports you'll need. Shelves come in a variety of materials and in standard widths to fit brackets. DIY shops will often cut them to any length you want. Light plastic drawers with their own runners can be fixed to the underside of a shelf. You can make your own shelving with planks supported on bricks arranged in double rows, 90 cm (3ft) apart. Whitewood bookshelves or stacking bins are other alternatives.

FREESTANDING STORAGE
Freestanding storage, like wardrobes and chests, tends to be less efficient than the built-in type. If you're in rented accommodation, you'll probably have to rely on it. Old tin and wicker trunks can

be a godsend too. A basket by the kitchen door for slippers, a bag hanging on the back of a child's door for dirty clothes, metal rails on castors (such as those in the clothes shops) — a simple and inexpensive idea can often help. In an old cupboard with deep shelves that are wide apart, you could fix a narrow shelf between two old ones.

BUILDING IN
When you're short of space — in the bedroom or spare room perhaps — it may be best to devote an entire wall to storage and have very little furniture. You will have to give careful consideration to the space needed. Decide what you've got to store and which type of doors would be best. Sliding doors save space but there will always be a section inside the cupboard that you can't reach. Wide, hinged doors need a lot of clearance. Narrow, hinged doors will make it more expensive because you will need more of them. Hinged, concertina doors will need a slightly deeper cupboard to fold into. Louvred doors are available in a wide range of sizes and are inexpensive.

MODULAR SYSTEMS
These enable you to build up your storage, using units of standard height, depth, and perhaps several different widths. They're often chipboard veneered, but there are various different finishes. Metal storage is usually intended for the office, but could provide a cheap alternative. Not all systems turn a corner well, and prices vary enormously. It may be worth using the same units throughout to give continuity.

LIGHTING

All too often lighting is limited to a single dangling bulb and lampshade; yet it has an enormously important and all-pervading effect on your house. No matter how good your decorating is, if the light is bad a room will look uninteresting. Good lighting can transform a very ordinary setting. What is good lighting then? Again, there's no straight answer; it will depend on your personal needs. Clever use of light and shadows can appear to alter the shape of your rooms; a ceiling that is too high can be 'brought down' by remaining shadowy, while wall lights will appear to increase your space. Leave your room's deficiencies in the shade and high-light its good points. An even all-over light can be depressing; areas of light and shadow will give interest.

LIGHTING NEEDS
Plan where you'll need light, what sort and how much. Apart from the usual bedside light, this will mean considering where you do the mending, pay the bills, listen to records, and so on. Then make sure the switches and sockets are where you need them. If they're not and you can't afford or aren't allowed to do any electrical work, look for standard lamps with adjustable spotlights, use the central ceiling outlet for a track with a number of spots, or use extension leads from skirting sockets. You could have a long flex from that outlet with a lamp attached to the end, and loop the flex over a hook, perhaps above the coffee table. You may

think that lights inside cupboards are too much of a luxury — but a spotlight could be angled to shine into them. In a child's room, make sure that the fittings are out of reach, and use safety plugs and childproof sockets. You will need stronger light for an elderly person. Lights should not shine on to mirrors but on to you when you look in them. Also, you don't want them directly above the mirror or they'll shadow the bags under your eyes.

Reading lights should shine down over your shoulder, and ideally should be used in conjunction with a background light to avoid glare. If you're right-handed, you will need it to come over your left shoulder. For dining, watching television and for stairways, make sure no one's dazzled by low lights; for other activities, low-level lighting can be effective and look very glamorous.

HOW TO CHOOSE

What is there to choose from? You probably won't want to do away with your general light — but could it be more gentle? There are diffuser shades for strip lights, and paper globes and glass and plastic bowl-type shades which make sure you can't see the glaring bulb from below. Frosted glass light bulbs can help. Table or standard lamps with opaque shades, and spotlights and desk lamps will give direct light (a beam on a specific area), but if you point a spotlight at a wall or ceiling it will give a much more gentle and widespread illumination. Or you could train it on a collection or item that you want to highlight. If it's a picture, you may find non-reflecting glass is necessary.

This brings us to the question of direction — do you want your light in one direction permanently, or should it be flexible? If so, make sure your lamps, etc. are tough enough to stand up to being altered regularly. Another aspect of flexibility is that it's easy to replace your on/off switch with a dimmer, so you can turn your lights from bright to a soft glow. Unless your lamp specifically requires low wattage, always have bright bulbs. Fluorescent tubes should not produce a green or bluish light — they will make you look ill! They are also bad for your eyes if used alone. There are varieties of diffuser shades you can buy for them to soften the glare, or try setting them under and behind ledges. A 'rise and fall' pendant lamp fitting, where you can adjust the height of your light, can be useful and effective over a table, although for a really romantic light you can't beat candles.

Warm shades of red and the highly polished finish of natural wood create a relaxing mood in this dining room. A single light over the table provides a general light that is central and not too bright.

167

HOME IMPROVEMENT

HEATING

Better to be warm but undecorated and unfurnished, than look fantastic and feel cold. Central heating is expensive, disruptive and complex to install, but it is a good investment and an excellent solution to heating problems. There are many different heating systems to choose from. Basically, the categories are: a fire with or without back boiler/radiators; under-floor heating; warm-air heating; a hot water boiler with radiators (sometimes incorporated in a cooker); and unit heating (convectors or radiant). There isn't space to go into detail here, but solid fuel, gas, electricity and oil companies will be able to give you all the information you need. If you can't afford central heating or are in rented accommodation, you could build up a system of storage radiators or other heaters — a combination of radiant and convected heat is best. Whatever your system make sure it's quiet and doesn't dry the air too much. Most important of all, make sure you minimize your heat loss by installing thorough and efficient insulation throughout your home.

HEAT LOSS

Damp is the worst heat eater — do your best to eradicate it. Windows let in draughts and lose heat through the glass. Self-adhesive rubber or foam draught-stripping will keep out cold air and dust, as will shredded newspaper, which is cheaper. Double glazing will keep heat in and possibly noise out, but condensation can cause problems. Factory-sealed units (two sheets of glass with space between, to fit directly into your window frame) are comparatively cheap, although the gap in between the sheets of glass isn't really big enough to cut out much sound. You can add an independent secondary frame, which can be opened, to your window your-

A room full of interest. A fire blazing in the hearth provides a welcome focal point while the shelves packed with books and the comfortable furniture draw you further into this homely, 'lived-in' room.

self, or ask a specialist firm. An easier do-it-yourself method is to attach a second frame directly on to your existing window.

Heavy curtains will, of course, help keep in the heat more than light-weight ones. Remember that, if you stop all ventilation, you'll have dreadful condensation, but you can help by producing less steam yourself (turn down the thermostat on the water heater; buy a kettle with an automatic switch) and so avoid the necessity of throwing open a window. Outside doors allow great gusts of warm air to escape — do you have a porch you could glaze to provide an air lock, or could you build an internal lobby? If not, treat your door as a window.

More heat is lost through the floor than most people realize. Damp floors are, of course, especially bad; you should take them up and put down a damp-proof membrane. A handsome stone floor that you don't want to disturb should be sealed with polyurethane to stop rising damp. On a sound floor, an insulating floor covering — foam-backed carpet, vinyl sheeting, cork, for instance — will work wonders.

Have you insulated your loft? If you can't get up there, how about treating your ceilings with an attractive material which will cut out heat loss, too — cork, tongue and groove boarding, etc. Heat rises, especially up the chimney: a throat restrictor and tray will ensure air for combustion comes from outside, not from your warm room. Unused fireplaces should be blocked off — though it's probably best to do it in a way that's temporary: a fireplace can be a valuable and welcoming

focal point. If you are sure that you will not want to utilize the chimney again, it can be blocked off (an air brick must be inserted) and the recess plastered round. Tiled or simply painted and then filled with plants, your fireplace can still provide a very attractive focal point for your room.

FIREPLACES AND RADIATORS

Out-of-character fireplaces can be replaced simply by putting an electric or gas fire in the recess. Or it may be possible to alter fireplaces sufficiently by painting them another colour which blends better with the room. Alternatively, your fireplace may already have been painted and, by stripping it down, you may reveal something well worth preserving. One young couple removed pink gloss paint from their large living room fireplace to find what appeared to be black marble. This was only a fake finish though, over a fine, dull black slate which is now a showpiece and the central feature of their home. You may find you can rearrange the draught on an existing fire by running a tube or pipe from the outside direct to the foot of the grate. Stoves, either solid fuel or wood burning can be extremely attractive and can be kept going all night.

Your flue may be much bigger than you need, especially if you're installing a slow burner of some sort. To adjust this you could fit an asbestos pipe and fill in around it with insulating cement. Your radiators needn't stick out like sore thumbs either; bulky ones can be put in a recess, or they can be painted to match the colour of the walls.

EXTENSIONS AND CONVERSIONS

If you're settled and comfortable living where you are but need more space, it's obviously important to consider making your property grow by using space that's wasted now — converting your attic or cellar, or adding extra space in the form of an extension. There are many regulations covering this and you must take professional advice from builders and local planning authorities on both what is practical and what is legal. You must think very hard, too, about what will look right; you can easily ruin the outside appearance of a house by incongruous additions. You will also have to check that there's nothing against changing or extending your home contained in the deeds of the house.

ATTICS

Any work involving your roof may bring to light all sorts of defects and weaknesses, so be prepared to spend more than you think. Depending on the authorities in the part of the country in which you live, you may have to build a permanent staircase to your attic if it's going to be 'habitable' — that is, a living room or bedroom. If it's just for storage, you may get away with a ladder. But in either case there must be headroom of at least 2 m (6ft 6½in.) as you go into the attic space. In a 'habitable' attic the ceiling height must be at least 2.25 m (7ft 6in.) over half of the unobstructed floor area, but you can reduce the total floor area with built-in cupboards.

A dormer window is another very acceptable way of getting a larger area, plus sufficient light. Although roof lights are the easiest windows to install, they may not be allowed by the by-laws governing ventilation, and they can make a low attic extremely hot. A dormer will open up new vistas and, if inverted, can give space for a tiny roof garden or balcony. When choosing your window, remember that maintenance may be difficult; if so, pick something with a tough and long lasting finish.

If your attic is too small to use as an extra floor, you could still use it as a gallery by opening it up to the floor below (this won't have so many legal restrictions). Then part of your top floor will have an impressive, high ceiling, with some sort of staircase to an informal, unusual, cosy balcony. This is liked particularly well by youngsters, although the elderly may find it rather too open and more like an adventure playground.

Of course, either in a full conversion or a balcony, weatherproofing and insulation are imperative; you stand to lose a high percentage of your heating if it's neglected. You can weatherproof the underside of your roof by spraying on a sealer to stop leaks. It will last 25 years. Boarding nailed on to the joists over a layer of glass fibre will give added insulation and will look very pleasant. Make sure your attic floor joists are strong enough to take continued walking. Plywood or blockboard will be cheaper than floor boards. Carpeting will give added insulation and soundproofing. One good way of using the lowest corners of your sloping ceiling is to build beds under them.

CELLARS

Modern houses rarely have cellars, but up to the last war they were fairly common. Damp, dark and depressing, they're the obvious places now for central-heating oil tanks. There are about as many rules for converting your cellar to be habitable as there are for the attic, but adequate light, ventilation and height are the most important. If it is to be habitable it must have an area of window equal to one-tenth of the floor area, and half of that window must let in fresh air. You will also need 2.25 m (7ft 6in) headroom; you may be tempted to lower your cellar floor to achieve this, but it is virtually impossible and can be extremely dangerous — even if you keep well away from the supporting walls. It is probably better to open up part of your ground floor down to the basement level.

However, if you've enough space, a cellar can provide an excellent soundproof room for your hi-fi. It may even be a good place for your kitchen, though you would certainly have to discuss that with your local authorities. In extreme cases, you could turn it into a completely self-contained flat, though there will be fire regulations to consider, and probably an increase in the rates. If you're just seeking to use your existing cellar more efficiently, you could clean it up and use it as a workshop or as a wine store.

One of the brightest and most popular ideas is to turn your cellar into a bar area. Space can be maximized by using a spiral staircase, or by using the space under conventional steps for storing soft drinks (which are usually very bulky), stereo equipment or heating units. Much of the original brick or stone work can be retained to give a pub-like atmosphere. Carrying this decor a step further, you should aim to make your cellar bar as conducive to conversation and fairly active enjoyment as your 'local' — where many a gathering in your bar will doubtless begin.

One of the easiest ways to construct the bar is to build it from plain bricks and cover the top with wood or formica — far cheaper than buying a separate unit from a furniture shop. Wine racks can be built into such a unit to use the restricted space behind the bar more efficiently than shelving. You can also get away with using very inexpensive decorating material — such as indestructible office carpeting — in a cellar, making its construction less costly than many people might imagine. All sorts of novel ideas can be used to advantage. Should there be a wall beside the stairs leading down to the cellar, why not put a fish tank into the wall so that the aquarium can be seen from both sides, at the same time saving space?

A cellar bar can be an enjoyable and well-used addition, introducing a completely new dimension to your home, while providing what amounts to an extra room. For example, teenagers can have a party while their parents find a bit of peace and quiet in the comfort of the lounge upstairs.

Just as insulation is the major consideration in your attic, so damp-proofing must

be in your cellar, though you are more likely to need the services of an expert here. Air bricks, vertical damp-proof membranes, asphalt floors — there are many possibilities and you will need to explore your own problems thoroughly and discuss the possible solutions with a builder. Even when you feel confident, it is best not to decorate with anything likely to be damaged or to peel should damp recur. Similarly, think of your cellar floor rather like a bathroom floor

in terms of dampness and you can't go wrong. Enlarge any windows and give a lot of attention to your artifical lighting as it's likely to be more often on than off. You might find mirrors a very useful way of increasing what light you have. Good heating can really make or break a cellar conversion: it should retain heat well, so one of the cheap storage systems should prove to be particularly suitable.

One of the main problems associated with installing

An inspiring idea for what to do with your attic space. The new room is light and airy yet cosy, with low seating and shelving, and the attractive surround of steeply sloping walls-cum-ceiling.

kitchens, lavatories or bathrooms in cellars is what to do with waste water. Most cellars are below ground level, so complicated plumbing and waste-disposal facilities relying on electric pumps are likely to be needed. This tends to negate the attractions of turning the cellar into

171

HOME IMPROVEMENT

an additional toilet, bath-room or kitchen, no matter how desperate the need for space might be for people with large families.

EXTENSIONS
An extension can be any-thing from a study to a con-servatory and is often a great joy. Decide just what your extra space is to be used for — it might be adequate (and certainly cheaper) to buy a shed for the garden. If you feel that it is an extension you want, then make sure it's going to look suitable, in keeping with the outside of of your house, and not too cold or inconvenient to use. An off-the-peg extension may need your own lining to make it usable all year round and will not be as sturdy as something custom built. However, the manufacturers usually provide plans for the local authorities and, often, an assembly service.

You may have a single-storey garage on which you could build. You will be most successful if, when finished, the extension looks like part of the original house, so match the slope of the roof, tiles and windows as closely as possible. Even if you're buying a package extension, try to match it closely to the style of your house. If it does look odd, you can soften the effect with quick-growing plants such as virginia creeper. If your extension has a flat roof it might be usable as a balcony — a very attractive finishing touch.

An extension should look as though it is part of the original building. The careful choice of building materials and shrubs and creepers will ensure this.

It is important to heat the new extension thoroughly by extending your existing central heating system or perhaps by installing new under-floor heating. If you have a lot of glass it may be worthwhile to double-glaze. Timber walls should be insulated with glass fibre. A solid roof will obviously give better insulation, but you may find that you are obliged to have glass in it so that the room to which you are attaching the extension doesn't become too dark. If you want to use your exten-sion all year round you must

give your floor a good con-crete foundation and an in-sulating and damp-proofing layer. Cork, linoleum or vinyl are excellent floor coverings for this type of room.

Light, plain and simple furniture will probably look best, with plenty of plants. If you've lots of windows, blinds will almost certainly be cheaper than curtains. If your new extension is less of a room in itself and more of an addition to an existing room, it is probably best to make the decor and furnish-ings link as closely as poss-ible with the original room.

GARDENING

GARDENING

PLANNING A GARDEN

If you have just moved house and are faced with a rubble-strewn, barren plot of ground, or a mature garden totally unsuitable for your needs or taste, then garden planning on a large scale is necessary. On a smaller scale, you may have a garden you are quite pleased with but feel it needs improvement in the form of a new border, a change of planting scheme or a bit of additional paving.

Whatever the scale of the operation, the same factors need consideration. It is inadvisable to rush immediately to a nursery or garden centre and buy whatever catches your fancy at the time. Plants, paving and walling materials, garden tools and furniture are expensive. A few hours spent with graph paper, pencil and nursery catalogue will save you time, money and effort in the long run.

Take note of and record all aspects of the site as it exists. These include the actual size of the garden, contours and levels, views from it and to it from the house (both good

Buy a few, well-made garden tools to start with. Leave the more specialized equipment until necessary. You may then find you can borrow the particular tool, or rent it at an economical rate.

When buying tools, make sure they are strong but not too heavy for comfort. Equipment such as large watering cans and wheelbarrows can get unwieldy when full.

Stainless-steel tools are initially expensive, but easy to clean and use and are very long lasting. All tools should be cleaned after use and stored in a dry shed or garage. If hung up, they are less likely to be stepped on or tripped over. Electrical and sharp tools must be kept out of children's reach.

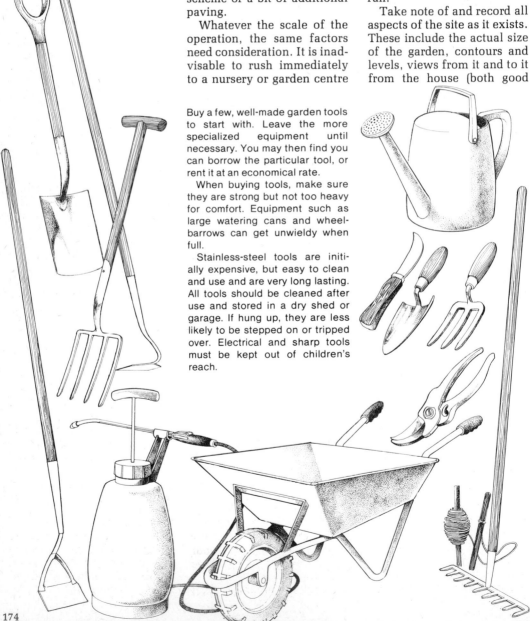

and bad), vegetation, the sunny and shaded spots and the sheltered and exposed positions. Some will be immediately obvious as good points. Others, such as a badly drained, stagnant patch of soil, can be turned to advantage: for example, the creation of a bog garden.

After this site appraisal, list what you want from your garden. The garden needs of a family with young children — safety, indestructibility, total enclosure and amusement in the form of play equipment — would be diametrically opposed to those of a gardener who is a keen exhibition grower, and envisages his plot as a source of perfect fruit, vegetables and flowers.

It is important to have a good idea of how much time you are prepared to give to your garden. The idea of an immaculate lawn may appeal to you, but an enormous amount of maintenance and upkeep is involved. However a badly kept lawn is better than no lawn at all.

Similarly, raising your own fruit and vegetables needs quite a commitment of time, on a regular basis rather than in sporadic bursts of activity.

Not everything in the garden can be beautiful. Space is usually required for clothes drying, refuse storage, car and bicycle maintenance. Hard-wearing surfacing will be necessary in these areas, to stand up to constant use, and adequate provision should be made for it. Screening is useful for such situations, either in the form of hedging or walls or opaque fencing.

Screening is additionally useful for boundary demarcation, particularly if you want a bit of privacy. The minimum height for a feeling

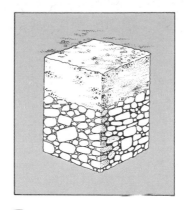

To make a soakaway, dig a 1 m x 1 m (3 ft x 3 ft) hole, in dry weather. Keep the topsoil and cart away the subsoil. Fill the hole to within 30 cm (1 ft) of the top with hardcore, firming as you go. Place a 2.5 cm (1 in.) layer of pea gravel over the hardcore and cover with the topsoil. Some settling is likely and the surface may need topping up with some extra topsoil.

To level, hammer a peg into the ground to the soil level required. Hammer in a second peg 2.5 m (8 ft 3 inches) away and join them with a piece of string. Place a plank on top of the two pegs, with a spirit level on top, as shown. Hammer the second peg into position until the spirit level shows the plank is level. Tighten the string around both pegs until taut; use it to indicate the level to which the soil has to be raked.

of privacy is 1.5 m (5 ft); anything less will leave you quite visible from neighbouring gardens.

Walls and screening offer additional advantages; they provide shelter and act as wind breaks, and also provide growing space. Not only can conventional climbers, such as clematis and honeysuckle, be trained up walls, pots and other containers can be bracketed to walls to allow for vertical gardening.

One note of advice: before beginning any boundary demarcation, particularly of a permanent or expensive nature, make legally sure that you have the right to do so. Planning permission from your local authority is necessary for the construction of a garage, the building of a new driveway off an existing road and the removal, or even the pruning, of trees in your garden which have tree preservation orders.

Do not lay out new paths if you have just moved house. It is far better to wait for a couple of months to see where paths naturally occur; worn-out grass between the kitchen door and the shed or vegetable garden will indicate the shortest and most convenient route. Unnecessarily curving or less direct concrete paths will be totally ignored.

In considering costs, the time-scale must be kept in mind. In general, quick results and instant effects cost more than having your garden develop over several years. This is particularly true if you envisage employing contractors for hard landscaping. Herbaceous perennials, shrubs and even trees can be grown from seed at a fraction of the cost of buying a mature specimen. However, this exercise demands enormous patience and it may be many years before they make any worthwhile contribution.

GARDENING

When making decisions on colour schemes, it is important to decide whether short, but spectacular, displays in spring and summer are the effects you want, or a more moderate display over the whole year. Except in the smallest gardens, it is a mistake to include too many colours, randomly mixed together. It is far better to have groups of plants, all of a single colour, although the garden as a whole might include many such groups.

Neighbouring gardens, nearby public parks and even woods give a clear indication of the types of plants most successfully grown in surroundings similar to your garden. It is sensible to take note of these plants.

The rise and fall of undulating ground can add interest and charm to any site, depending upon the scale involved. In small modern gardens, however, limited opportunities are available for changes of level, which are largely determined by existing features, such as buildings, roads, drives and neighbouring boundaries. Where changes in level are contemplated, these should be carried out in conjunction with drainage. Earth moving, which is usually costly and time consuming, is best kept to a minimum. The rise and fall of the land has a number of practical implications. Where slopes are steeper than one in three — the ground rises or falls more than 1 m for each 3 m travelled — walking as well as grass mowing becomes difficult. Where gradients are too steep for slopes or banks, steps, terraces and retaining walls become desirable and necessary.

When planning the layout of the garden, it simplifies the task if you have a predetermined idea of the character you want. Three broad styles are recognised — formal, informal and natural. Formal gardens are those with a regular, symmetrical arrangement of beds, borders and bedding plants. Informal gardens are less rigid in their layout and can combine lawns with herbaceous borders and/or shrubs, and perhaps make use of specimen trees. Wild or natural gardens are intended to resemble nature, and here the attention of the gardener is minimal.

When starting a garden for

Although the traditional English country garden is very beautiful, it may prove difficult to recreate in urban areas.

the first time, resist the temptation to obtain all the tools imaginable, some of which will almost certainly prove unnecessary. Buy a few well made basic items, and build up gradually as the need for different tools becomes apparent. Be sure that any tools bought are reasonably strong, but are not too heavy for the user.

Throughout the planning process, safety should always be to the forefront of one's mind. Water, walls, machinery, chemicals and poisonous plants are all potential hazards. With young children and pets extra care is needed. Drives, paths and any other building work, should be carried out in a competent manner. Smooth, well laid surfaces are usually easy to keep clean, but potholed paths, or collapsing walls resulting from poor workmanship, can be dangerous as well as irritating.

When planning a garden always bear in mind the nature of the site and what you want from it. Isolate any problems and then carefully work out an overall garden plan.

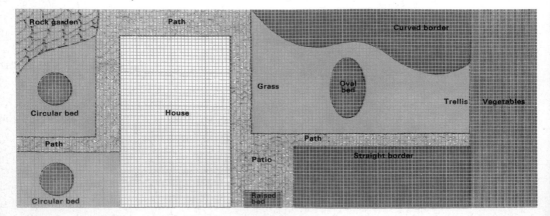

GARDENING

UNDERSTANDING THE SOIL

The soil type greatly influences the range of plants which can be grown. Most rhododendrons, for example, cannot tolerate chalky soil, while clematis absolutely thrive on it. The basic soil types are listed below, and all can be made to produce good crops or ornamental displays, given suitable soil management and improvement.

LOAM

The ideal soil is loam and it is the one most gardeners would opt for if they had the choice. It is very fertile and easy to cultivate. Although there are plants which prefer sandy or chalky soil conditions, there are very few plants which fail to thrive in loam. All other factors being equal, it offers the widest range of growing potential, for both ornamental and edible plants.

Loam is made up of particles of sand, clay and decayed organic matter (humus), as well as air, moisture, plant nutrients and micro-organisms. It is free-draining enough not to become waterlogged, unlike clay, although it is moisture-retentive enough not to dry out in summer, unlike sand.

CLAY

Although clay soils are usually fertile, they are notoriously difficult to cultivate. They have a tendency to become iron hard when dry in summer and, in winter or after a heavy rainfall, lack of natural drainage leads to sticky, waterlogged conditions.

Clay soils are very slow to dry out and late to warm up in spring.

Never walk on clay soil when it is wet or, worse still, attempt to dig it or push a wheelbarrow over it. The individual particles of clay are minute, and when compressed, the tiny pockets of air which normally keep the soil 'sweet' disappear. Technically, the beneficial, aerobic bacteria are replaced by harmful, anaerobic bacteria and the soil turns 'sour'.

Providing drainage, in the form of land drains and soakaways, improves clay soils, as does digging in well-rotted organic matter and sand. Peat will also help to improve the condition.

BUILDING A COMPOST HEAP

Compost is the converting of pest- and disease-free vegetable remains, including kitchen waste, and lawn clippings, into a useful substitute for farmyard manure. Perennial weeds should not be used in composting, as the seeds may survive intact. Evergreen leaves should also be avoided as they are slow to break down, and any animal remains, such as bones and fat, will attract rodents.

To make a heap, stack up 15 cm layers of moist vegetable remains. Alternate layers should be covered first with an activator, such as sulphate of ammonia, at 20 g/m² and then with ground limestone at 160 g/m². Proprietary activators are available and should be used according to the manufacturer's instructions.

Wood ash (but never coal ash) can be added to the heap in thin layers, and provides a valuable source of potash. In dry spells, water the heap to speed decay. Do not over-water, though, as waterlogged compost will putrify rather than rot down.

Oxygen is also necessary for decomposition and compost heaps should be allowed to settle of their own accord, not forcibly compressed.

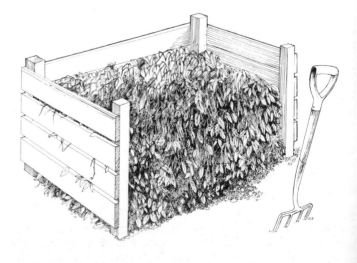

LIGHT/SANDY

Usually free draining and early to warm up in spring, sandy soil is rather more demanding than loam. It needs regular applications of bulky organic matter together with quick-acting chemical fertilizers to get the best results. This is because, whenever it rains, the nutrient content gets washed down, or leached, to the lower layers of subsoil and is inaccessible to plants' roots.

A related problem with sandy soils is that of drying out in summer. This can be partially remedied by digging in bulky organic matter which helps to retain moisture. Artificial irrigation is usually necessary, and mulching is also beneficial, provided the soil is thoroughly soaked before the mulch is applied.

CHALK AND LIMESTONE

Chalk and limestone soils are usually pale; the humus-containing topsoil level is often shallow, with the pure chalk or limestone very close to the surface. They are free draining and tend to dry out in summer, although stickiness is a problem after heavy rain.

Because of its alkaline nature, certain elements, such as magnesium, iron and potassium, become 'locked' in the soil and unavailable to the plants. Liberal quantities of manures and fertilizers are necessary, year after year, as nutrients are quickly leached out of chalk soils.

It is best to stick to plants which thrive in chalk soils, such as many alpines, rather than suffer defeat with known lime-haters.

PEAT

Peat soils are dark, spongy and contain large amounts of

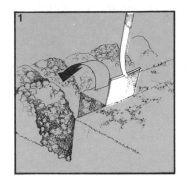

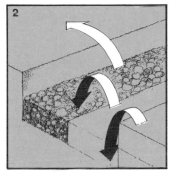

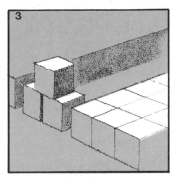

1 *Digging.* Push the spade vertically into the ground and lift.

2 *Double digging.* Fork up the base of the first trench and cover with soil from the second.

3 *Ridging.* Useful on wet land.

partially-decomposed vegetable matter. They usually occur in areas of high rainfall and humidity, so drying out is not a problem. However, they tend to have high water-tables, and special provision for drainage is usually necessary.

Acidity and lack of nutrients are additional problems with peat soils, but when regularly limed and dressed with fertilizers, excellent results can be had.

Peat, as purchased in bags at garden centres, has no nutrient value at all but is excellent for improving the soil conditions of sandy, chalky and clay soils. Always wet peat thoroughly before using.

MULCHING

Mulching, or top dressing, is the practice of covering the surface of the soil, usually to prevent evaporation. Additionally, mulching helps keep down weeds and, in hot weather, can keep the soil cool. Bulky organic matter, such as well-rotted compost, spent hops and grass cuttings are often used as mulches, as they provide humus and nutrients.

DIGGING

Soils act as reservoirs for nutrients and moisture, and the deeper a plant's roots can travel, the better the plant's growth will be. During autumn or winter, when the soil is neither frozen nor waterlogged, prepare new beds by digging to at least a spade's depth.

For plain, or single, digging, excavate a trench a spade deep and a similar width, heaping the soil to one side. Fill this trench with soil from a second, repeating the process until the last trench dug is filled with the soil from the first.

To break up compacted subsoil and improve aeration and drainage still further, dig a trench one spade deep and 60 cm (2 ft) wide. Fork over the bottom of the trench and work in well-rotted compost or manure. Fill with the soil dug from a second trench, and so on.

GARDENING

The Gardening Year

Outdoor vegetables – see pp. 185–88 for details

Crop	J	F	M	A	M	J	J	A	S	O	N	D
Beans, broad	*	*S	*S	*S		H	H	H		*	*S	*
Beans, dwarf	*	*	*	*S	*S	*SP		H	H	H	*	*
Beans, runner	*	*	*	*	*S	*P			H	H	*H	*
Beetroot	*	*	*	*S	*S	*S		H	H	*H	*	*
Broccoli, sprouting	*	*	*H	*H	*S	*S	*P	*P			*	*
Brussels sprouts	*H	*H	*HS	*S	*P	*P			H	*H	*H	*H
Cabbage, summer	*	*	*S	*SP	*P	H	H	H	H	*	*	*
Cabbage, winter	*H	*	*	*S	*SP	*SP	*P			*H	*H	*H
Cabbage, spring	*	*	*H	*H	*H	*	*S	*S	*P	*	*	*
Cabbage, Savoy	*H	*H	*H	*S	*SP	*P			H	*H	*H	*H
Carrot	*	*	*S	*S	*S	*S	H	H	H	*H	*	*
Cauliflower	*	*	*	*SP	*SP	*P		H		*H	*H	*H
Cauliflower, winter	*H	*H	*H	*H	*SH	*P	*P			*	*	*
Leek	*H	*H	*H	*P	*P	*P			H	*H	*H	*H
Lettuce	*	*	*S	*SPT	*SP TH	*SP TH	*SP TH	H	H	*H	*	*
Marrow/courgette	*	*	*	*	*P	*P		H	H		*	*
Onion, bulb	*	*	*P	*P			H	HS	H	*	*	*
Onion, salad	*	*	*HS	*HS	*S	*S	*HS	H	H	*H	*H	*
Pea, round	*S	*S	*S			H	H	H	*	*	*S	*S
Pea, wrinkled	*	*	*S	*S	*S	*S	*SH	H	H	H	*	*
Potatoes	*	*	*	*P			H	H	H	*H	*	*
Radish	*	*	*S	*SH	*SH	*SH	*SH	*SH	*SH	*H	*	*
Shallot	*	*P	*P	*P			H	H	*	*	*	*
Spinach	*	*S	*S	*ST	*SHT	*HT	*H	*H	*H	*H	*H	*H
Swede	*H	*H	*H	*	*S	T	T			*H	*H	*H
Tomato	*	*	*	*	*	*P		H	H	*	*	*

Key:

S = Sowing

P = Planting

H = Harvesting

T = Thinning

* = Digging,
preparatory
cultivations

GARDENING

The Gardening Year

Covered Crops – see pp. 195–207 for details

Crop	J	F	M	A	M	J	J	A	S	O	N	D
Food												
Cucumber				S	S	P	H	H	H			
Lettuce	S	S	P	PH	H			S	TP	H	H	
Marrow/courgette				S	S	P	H	H	H			
Radish		S	S	H					S	H		
Sweet corn				S	SP	P		(H)	(H)			
Sweet pepper			S	S	P	P		H	H			
Tomato			S	S	P	P	H	H	H			
Brussels sprouts, cabbage and cauliflower	S	S		P				H	H	H	H	H
Leeks and onions from seed	S	S		P				H	H	H	H	H
Dwarf and runner beans				S	SP	P		(H)	(H)			
Flower and Foliage Plants												
Summer bedding plants F/Lv	S	S	S		P	P	P	H	H	H		
Begonia, tuberous F	O	St	St			P	P	H	HL	O	O	O
Fuchsia mainly F	O	St	St	C		P	H	H	HL	O	O	O
Pelargoniums F, Lv	O	O	O	O	O	P	P	HC	HCL	O	O	O
Spring-flowering bulbs F, (daffodils, hyacinths, tulips)	H	H	H	H				St	St	St	O	H
Aluminium plant Lv	H	H	HC	HC	HC	H	H	H	H	H	H	H
Christmas cactus F and Lv	H	H	HC	HC	H	H	H	H	H	H	H	H
Easter cactus F and Lv	H	H	H	H	HC	HC	HC	H	H	H	H	H
Ivies Lv	H	H	H	H	H	H	H	H	HC	HC	H	H
Kangaroo vine Lv	H	H	HC	HC	HC	H	H	H	H	H	H	H
Maranta Lv	H	HD	HD	H	H	H	H	H	H	H	H	H
Peperomia Lv and F	H	H	HC	HC	H	H	H	H	H	H	H	H
Rubber plant Lv	H	H	H	HC	HC	HC	H	H	H	H	H	H
Saintpaulia F and Lv	H	H	H	H	H	HLc	HLc	HLc	HLc	H	H	H
Sansevieria Lv	H	H	HD	HD	H	H	H	H	H	H	H	H
Shrimp plant F and Lv	H	H	C	HC	H	H	H	H	H	H	H	H
Spider plant Lv	H	H	HD	HLa	H	H	H	H	H	H	H	H
Sweetheart plant Lv	H	H	HC	HC	HC	HC	H	H	H	H	H	H
Wandering Jew Lv	H	H	HC	HC	HC	HC	HC	HC	HC	H	H	H

House plants (Winter): from October to March give maximum sunlight, reduce watering and maintain minimum temperature.

House plants (Summer): from April to October increase watering, feeding, humidity and ventilation. Shade from strong sun.

Key:

S = Sow	H = Harvesting	D = Divide
P = Plant	St = Start into growth	La = Layer
T = Thin	L = Lift	Lc = Leaf cutting
(H) = Outdoor crop, started under cover	O = Overwinter/store	F = Flowering plant
	C = Take cuttings	Lv = Foliage plant

GARDENING

see pp. 190–95 for details

The Gardening Year

The Care of Outdoor Decorative Plants – see pp. 190–95 for details

Crops and Cultivations — Time of Operations

Operation	J	F	M	A	M	J	J	A	S	O	N	D
General all subjects												
Preparations for planting	•	•	•	•	•	•	•	•	•	•	•	•
Water		•	•	•	•	•	•	•	•			
Hoe and weed			•	•	•	•	•	•	•	•		
Spray				•	•	•	•	•	•	•		
Deadhead				•	•	•	•	•	•	•	•	•
End of season cultivation	•	•	•						•	•	•	•
Trees, shrubs and climbers												
Plant deciduous subjects	•	•								•	•	•
Plant evergreens				•	•				•	•	•	•
Plant container-grown subjects	•	•	•	•	•	•	•	•	•	•	•	•
Provide/fix stakes and supports	•	•	•	•	•	•	•	•			•	•
Firm new-planted subjects	•	•	•	•	•	•					•	•
Mulch			•	•	•	•	•	•				
Train, tie	•	•	•	•	•	•	•	•	•	•	•	•
Prune	•	•	•	•	•	•	•	•	•	•	•	•
Lop branches				•	•			•	•	•	•	•
Layer shrubs			•	•								
Herbaceous plants												
Plant, natural season	•	•	•	•						•	•	•
Plant, container-grown subjects	•	•	•	•	•				•	•	•	•
Stake and tie				•	•	•	•	•				
Lift and divide plants			•	•	•			•	•	•	•	
Feed			•	•								
Bedding plants												
Prepare/water beds					•	•			•	•		
Plant summer bedding					•	•						
Clear summer bedding									•	•		
Plant spring bedding									•	•		
Clear spring bedding					•	•						

Key: • Can be carried out now

GARDENING

The Gardening Year

Hardy Fruits – see pp. 185–88 for details

Operations

Operation	J	F	M	A	M	J	J	A	S	O	N	D
Preparations for planting	●	●	●	●	●●	●●	●●	●●	●●	●●	●	●
Provide and fix supports	●	●	●	●	●	●	●	●	●	●●	●●	●●
Plant trees	●	●								●●	●●	●●
Plant bush/cane fruit	●									●●	●●	●●
Plant strawberries								●	●●	●●		
Plant container-grown top bush/cane fruits	●	●	●●	●●	●			●	●●	●●		
Firm newly-planted stock	●●	●●	●●	●●	●	●	●	●	●	●	●●	●●
Hoe	●	●	●●	●●	●●	●	●●	●●	●●	●●	●	●
Mulch		●	●●	●●	●●	●●	●●	●				
Water				●	●●	●●	●●	●●	●	●		
Weed	●	●●	●●	●●	●●	●●	●●	●●	●●	●●	●	●
Top dressing feed		●●	●●	●								
Net crops against birds	●	●			●●	●●	●●	●	●	●	●	●
Spray top and bush fruits	●●		●	●●	●●	●●	●					●●
Spray strawberries		●	●	●●	●	●		●				
Summer prune top and bush fruits							●●	●●	●			
Harvest top fruit							●	●●	●●	●	●	
Harvest bush, cane and strawberry crops						●	●●	●●	●●	●		
Winter prune top and bush fruit	●	●	●						●	●●	●●	●●
End-of-season clean up	●	●						●	●	●●	●●	●●
Take cuttings of bush fruits									●	●●	●●	●

Key:

●● Main time

● Can be carried out now

GARDENING FOR FOOD

The cultivation of vegetable and fruit crops provides healthy exercise, helps the housekeeping budget and produces good, wholesome food. For ease of cultivation and crop-rotation planning, vegetable crops are divided into three types; pod, bulb and stem crops (beans, peas, onions, leeks and celery); root crops (potatoes, turnips, carrots, beetroot); and green crops (cabbage, Brussels sprouts, broccoli, kale).

For pod, bulb and stem crops, deeply dig and generously manure the ground, ideally in autumn. Digging and the addition of fertilizer is usually adequate for root crops, although potatoes benefit from manuring. Carrots, parsnips and beetroot tend to be misshapen and split when grown on freshly manured ground. Green crops need well-limed, firm land and fertilizer rather than manure, but there must be at least a one- to two-month interval between the application of ground limestone, at 200 g/m², and compound fertilizer, at 100 g/m².

SEED SOWING

Seeds are offered for sale uncoated, much as they are in nature, or pelleted. Pelleted seeds are covered with a chemical preparation to feed and protect them from pests and diseases. Though expensive, pelleted seeds are easier to sow individually and they eliminate the need for thinning later on.

Drills that are V-shaped are used for small, fine seed. Peas are sown in broad, flat drills, 5 cm (2 in.) deep and 10—15 cm (4—6 in.) wide.

After the seeds are covered and firmed, place netting or cotton over the drills to discourage birds. Sow beans in narrow, 5-7.5cm (2-3in.) deep drills, taken out with a draw hoe and filled with fine soil after sowing. Always mark the end of each row with a label noting the crop and date on which it was sown.

If you are sowing a tender crop, then you must wait until all threat of frost has passed. You can get a quicker start if you warm up the seedbed soil beforehand by placing cloches over where you intend to sow. Do this about a fortnight before the sowing date, and leave them there once the seeds have been put in.

1 Before sowing prepare the ground thoroughly. Rake the earth down to a fine tilth.

2 Seeds are sown in a small furrow known as a 'drill', which can be prepared by using a draw hoe. The shape and depth of the drill differs for different types of seed. Make a shallow V-shaped drill for small seeds and a wide flat-bottomed drill for larger seeds such as garden peas.

3 Sow small seeds thinly and evenly by hand. The correct spacing is important: sow 5 small seeds to every 2.5cm (1 in.) run of drill. Scatter peas 5–7.5 cm (2–3 in.) apart in a flat drill.

4 Cover the seeds with a fine soil and lightly firm with the back of a rake. When this is done, always mark the end of each row sown with a label noting the crop.

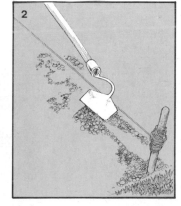

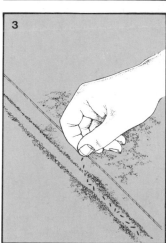

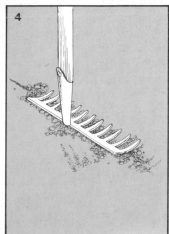

GARDENING

PLANTING

Planting out is a critical stage in the growth of any plant. Do it with care.

Always water seedlings and small plants thoroughly, both before and after planting. A calm, dull, showery day is best for planting out, and always plant at the same depth as before their move. Most planting is done with a trowel, but small cabbages and leeks are better planted with a dibber. Their roots are not widespreading when young and planting with a dibber saves time. Place leek seedlings 5–10 cm (2–4 in.) deep in dibber holes, water them in, but do not firm.

Plant onion and shallot sets with a trowel, with their tops, or shoulders, level with the soil surface.

THINNING AND CARE

Vegetables sown in situ often need thinning, in two or more stages. Start as soon as the seedlings are large enough to handle. The space between each remaining plant at this stage should be one third to one half the final distance required. Thin again as soon as the leaves of adjoining seedlings touch, disturbing the remaining plants as little as possible. Remove all traces of thinnings, particularly of carrots and onions, to avoid attracting carrot fly and onion fly.

Subsequent care consists mainly of hoeing and weeding the ground regularly, and watering young plants and those bearing heavy crops, particularly during periods of dry weather.

Runner beans, courgettes and tomatoes can give increased yields when fed with diluted liquid fertilizer; begin watering in fertilizer at pod-forming and fruit-swelling stages respectively. Hoe in 70 g/m^2 of balanced compound fertilizer around spring cabbage and purple sprouting broccoli during late February or early March.

Peas, runner beans and tomatoes usually require supports. Push in twiggy pea sticks among pea seedlings, or provide stakes and netting. Poles for runner beans should be in position at sowing or planting time. Stake and tie tomatoes when setting them out in their final positions. Remove the side shoots of tall tomato varieties when they appear and cut out

Growing Food
Outdoor vegetables

Crop	Variety	Treatment	Sow	Plant	Spacing cm Plant	Row	Harvest
Beans, broad	Windsor	Pod/stem	Feb-Apr		20	20	Jul-Aug
Beans, runner	Scarlet Emperor	Pod/stem	May	Jun*	30	40	Aug-Oct
Beetroot	The Globe	Root	Apr-Jun		10	30	Aug-Oct
Brussels sprouts	Early & late types	Greens	Mar-Apr	May-Jun	75	75	Sep-Mar
Cabbage, summer	Hispi F1 Hybrid	Greens	Mar-Apr	Apr*-May	45	50	Jun-Sep
Cabbage, spring	Durham Early	Greens	Jul-Aug	Mar-May	30	45	Mar-May
Carrot	Quick maturing types	Root	Mar-Jun		8	30	Jul-Oct
Cauliflower	Summer/ autumn type	Greens	Apr-May	Apr*-Jul	60	60	Aug-Dec
Leek	Musselburgh	Pod/stem		Apr-Jun*	15	35	Sep-Mar
Lettuce	Butterhead Cos, crispy types	Pod/stem	Mar-Jun	Apr*-Jul	23	30	May-Oct
Marrow/courgette	Bush	Pod/stem		May-Jun*	60	75	Aug-Sep
Onion, bulb (sets)	Sturon	Pod/stem		Mar-Apr	10	30	Jul-Sep
Pea	Wrinkled seeded	Pod/stem	Mar-Jul		5 dwarf tall	60 120	Jul-Oct
Potato	Early type	Root		Apr	30	60	Jul-Aug
Radish	Summer type	Pod/stem	Mar-Sep		13	25	Apr-Oct
Shallot	Hative de Niort	Pod/stem		Feb-Apr	10	30	Jul-Aug
Spinach	Long-standing round	Pod/stem	Feb-May		23	30	May-Nov
Tomato	Bush & outdoor	Pod/stem		Jun*	45	60	Aug-Sep

*Plants are raised under glass

the growing point at the second leaf beyond the fourth truss. Bush types of tomatoes do not usually need side-shooting, staking, tying or stopping, but place straw under the fruit to protect it and keep it clean.

POTATOES

In late winter, prepare, or chit, seed potatoes. Put them in shallow trays in a light, frost-free place to sprout. Those the size of hens' eggs are best, although larger tubers can be split before planting; be sure each piece contains two healthy sprouts. Plant when the sprouts are 2.5–5 cm (1–2 in.) long, sprout end up.

Plant from March onwards in 10–15 cm (4–6 in.) deep drills. Potatoes are frost tender, so in cold seasons or districts, delay may be necessary. Ideally the soil should have been manured the previous autumn. If this was not done, top-dress the soil with 5 cm (2 in.) of well-rotted manure, after backfilling the trench. Begin earthing up immediately, to protect the shoots and tubers from damage by heavy frosts.

FRUIT GROWING

Fruits can be successfully grown in confined spaces, and produce crops within one to three years after planting. While they generally crop best in sunny positions, gooseberries, blackcurrants, raspberries and strawberries grow satisfactorily in light shade. Shelter from cold north and east winds, particularly at flowering time, is necessary to ensure pollination and fruit set.

Most cultivated land is suitable, as long as it is free-draining, with 25 cm (10 in.) of topsoil. Soil preparation, including weed eradication, should be thorough, as fruit trees occupy the land for a number of years.

Selection and purchase Points to consider when selecting fruits to grow and deciding where to plant them include personal preferences, available space, ultimate plant size, length of time from planting to picking, suitability of climate and site, and cultural requirements.

The ultimate plant size depends on the variety and plant form. Bush apples require more space than cordon, but both are best when budded or grafted on to dwarfing root stock. Cordon and wall-trained fruits require more attention.

Purchase healthy, well-shaped plants, with good roots. Blackcurrants, raspberries and strawberries should be Ministry-certified as disease free. Many tree fruits cannot set heavy crops without pollen from another, closely related variety.

Family trees, having branches of two or more different varieties on the same plant, overcome the pollination problem and avoid the

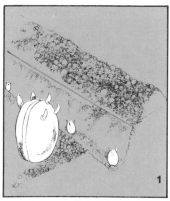

1 Cut large potato tubers in half, leaving two or three buds. Plant when the sprouts are 2.5–5 cm (1–2 in.) long. Plant in March, sprout end up.
2 Place fork clear of potatoes when lifting to avoid damage.

1 Support standards with a stake.
2 Bushes are easy to pick, spray and prune.
3 Cordons produce excellent apples where space is limited.
4 Fan-trained forms are suitable for blackberries and loganberries.

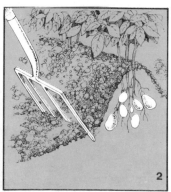

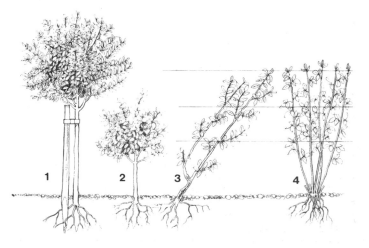

GARDENING

need to plant two trees.

Planting is best done in autumn, although pot-grown fruits can be planted whenever the soil is not frozen, waterlogged or baked solid. Stakes and supports should be in position before planting. The planting hole should be large enough to hold the roots comfortably. Make sure the plants are the same depth after planting as before their move, and water them in unless the soil is very moist.

Care and cultivation Hoe bare ground around all fruits to kill weeds and loosen the soil surface. Apply 70–100 g/m² of balanced compound fertilizer, and mulch fruits each spring. Water new plants in dry weather until well established.

Pruning It is easiest to buy trees and bushes with a ready-formed framework of branches. Subsequent treatment consists of cutting out dead and inward-growing shoots of bushes and trees. Cordon and wall-trained fruit should have new growth shortened by half to two thirds in summer. The stumps are then cut back, when dormant, to within two or three buds of the main branches or stems.

Black currants should have their fruiting branches cut out completely every year after harvesting, and the same is true for fruited raspberry and blackberry canes. Remove surplus strawberry runners from between the rows when picking ceases and the beds are cleaned up. Cut off all the old foliage to minimize the risk of disease and infestation setting in the following year.

Harvesting and storing Plums, cherries and berried fruits are picked as they ripen; some form of protection from birds is usually necessary. Gather apples and pears when they part readily from the tree, but some varieties need to be stored before being eaten. Avoid storing damaged or bruised fruits as they quickly rot and infect others. Cool, frost-free storage conditions are best.

Exercise care when picking fruit from tall trees. Make sure that the ladder is secure. Well cared for older trees can give substantial yields of fruit. In order to get the best from your trees, harvest at the correct time.

Gardening for Food

Fruit			Space		Years, planting to	
Crop	Form	Plants m.	Rows m.	picking	Harvest
Apple	Bush	3-4	3-4	3-4	Aug-Oct
Apple	Cordon	1	2	2-5	Aug-Oct
Apple	Standard	6	6	5-8	Aug-Oct
Blackberry	Fan or Rod	3	2	2-3	Aug-Sep
Blackcurrant	Bush	1.8	1.8	2-3	Jul
Cherry	Fan	5	2	4-5	Jun-Sep
Cherry	Standard	7.5	7.5	5-7	Jun-Sep
Gooseberry	Bush	1.8		3-4	Jun-Jul
Gooseberry	Cordon	75 cm	1.8	2-3	Jun-Jul
Loganberry	Fan or Rod	3	2	2	Aug-Sep
Pear	Cordon	1	2	3-4	Aug-Oct
Pear	Espalier	4.5	1.8	4-5	Aug-Oct
Pear	Dwarf pyramid	1	2	4-5	Aug-Oct
Plum	Bush	5	5	3-5	Aug-Oct
Plum	Fan	5	2	3-6	Aug-Oct
Raspberry	Upright Cane	75 cm	2	2	Jul-Sep
Redcurrant	Bush	1.8	1.8	2-3	Jul
Redcurrant	Cordon	75 cm	1.8	2-3	Jul
Strawberry	Single plant	45 cm	75 cm	1	May-Oct

GARDENING

FLOWERS

INTRODUCTION

Garden flowers are divided according to their life-cycles, into three types. Annuals complete their life-cycle, from sowing to flowering and seed production, within 12 months. Many summer bedding and cut-flower plants belong to this group.

Biennials require two growing seasons to complete their life process from sowing to seed production. Pansies, foxgloves and evening primroses are examples. Perennials, which live and grow for more than two years, include trees, shrubs, bulbs, climbers and herbaceous plants.

SEED SOWING

To sow seeds outdoors, whether for annual, biennial or perennial plants, work well-cultivated soil down to a fine, crumb-like consistency; leave the surface level and firm. Mark the rows using pegs and a garden line. Use a draw hoe to make shallow, V-shaped drills; water the drills if the soil is dry. Annuals sown *in situ* should be scattered in drifts, rather than rows, to give a more natural arrangement.

After sowing, cover the seeds with fine soil and gently firm with the back of a rake. Keep the seed bed well watered and weed free. Seedlings sown *in situ* should be thinned in two stages, as with vegetables. Stake and tie tall varieties, or support them with twiggy sticks.

The division of bulbs and tubers is an easy method of increase. This should be done when the plants are dormant.

Transplant wallflowers when they are 7.5-10cm (3-4 in.) high into nursery beds for growing on to final size. Space them 15 cm (6 in.) apart with 30 cm (1 ft) between the rows. Set them out with a trowel, making the holes large enough to take the roots comfortably.

PLANTING

Dig, manure and cultivate the ground for bedding and border plants and rake in 70 g/m² of balanced fertilizer. Open-grown plants are best set out while dormant, between autumn and spring. Container-grown plants may be planted any time of the year, as long as the soil is reasonably workable.

When planting, make sure the roots are well spread out, and fine topsoil worked back into the roots, so there are no air pockets. Make sure the plant is set out at the same depth as before its move, and watered in if the soil is dry.

DIVISION

Many plants form clumps, crowns or stools which can be divided or split up to provide a ready means of increase. This is usually done while the plants are dormant, in autumn or early spring. The older, central portion of the clump is the least valu-

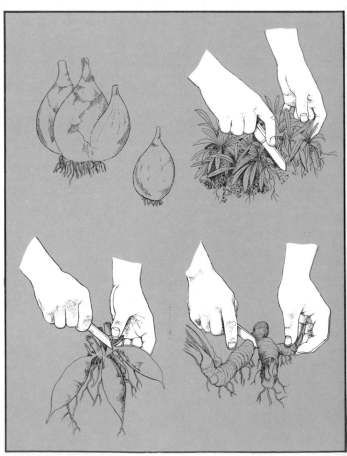

able in terms of growth or flowering capability. It can be discarded, and the younger, outer growths replanted in prepared beds or borders. Doronicums, Michaelmas daisies and most herbaceous subjects are examples of plants easily propagated by division.

If the clumps have very tough roots, two garden forks, inserted back to back in the centre of the clump and then levered apart, will break up the roots. Make sure there is a growth bud on each bit of the plant that you replant.

CUTTINGS

Some flowers, such as lupins, delphiniums and chrysanthemums, are best propagated from cuttings of new shoots. In early March, lift and bring under glass, or cloche outdoors, the dormant stools or clumps. This hastens the growth of tender, succulent shoots, which make ideal cutting material You can use unforced growth, but these shoots, unless taken when young, are tough and hollow and do not make pleasing cutting material.

When the shoots are 5–7.5 cm (2–3 in.) long, cut them as close to the base as possible. Using a sharp knife or razor blade, remove the small leaves closest to the cut and dip the base of the stem into hormone rooting powder. Insert the prepared cuttings individually into 7.5 cm (3 in.) pots, or put several around the edge of a larger pot filled with a mixture of peat and sharp sand or grit.

Water and place in a greenhouse or cold frame, or on a sunny window sill. Rooting will be quicker if you enclose the pot in a clear polythene bag. Insert canes or wires into the pot to keep

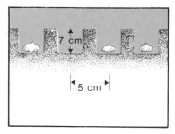

1 Crocuses should be planted in autumn to flower in spring. Plant them 5 cm (2 in.) apart and 7 cm (2½ in.) deep.

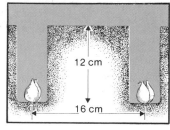

2 Plant narcissi and daffodils between August and October to flower in spring, 16 cm (7 in.) apart and 12 cm (5 in.) deep.

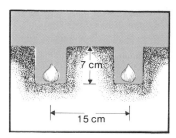

3 Hyacinths, to flower in spring, are planted from September to November. Set them 15 cm (6 in.) apart and 7 cm (2½ in.) deep.

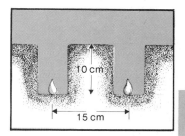

4 Plant iris in September or October to flower in spring. Set them 15 cm (6 in.) apart and 10 cm (4 in.) deep.

the polythene from resting on the cuttings.

Once roots have formed and new growth has appeared, pot on into containers filled with John Innes No. 2 and harden off in a cold frame before planting out.

Sea hollies, dicentra and oriental poppies are propagated by root cuttings taken while the plant is dormant. Clean off any soil clinging to the roots and cut them into 5 cm (2 in.) lengths. The cut closest to the crown should be flat across and the lower one angled. Insert this end vertically into a pot filled with a mixture of peat and sand. Several cuttings can be accommodated in the same pot, as long as they do not touch each other.

Some primulas are propagated by root cuttings, but because the roots are very delicate, they are laid horizont-

ally on the surface of the compost and covered with a layer of sand.

LAYERING

To increase border carnations, remove the lower leaves from a non-flowering side shoot in summer. Make a slanting cut part of the way through the underneath of the stem, 15–20 cm (6–8 in.) from the growing point. Be careful not to sever the stem entirely. Bend the shoot where it has been partially severed and peg it down into sandy soil or specially prepared compost; you can bury a pot in the soil so the shoot roots directly into the pot. Once the roots have formed, cut the new plant free.

BULBS

When buying bulbs, corms and tubers, look for firmness, solid texture and even colour.

1 Standard roses should always be tied to a stake. The top of the stake should be at least 5 cm (2 in.) below the lowest branch.

2 Prune bush roses back to an upward pointing bud placed 12–15 cm (5 6 in.) above soil level, in late March or early April.

Avoid soft, punctured, sprouting or mouldy bulbs, and any which are exceptionally large or small. Large gladioli corms, for example, may be old ones and will give less value for money than more

Wistaria and wallflowers provide abundant colour and scent in spring. Note the support which Wistaria needs when grown as a freestanding specimen.

moderate-sized corms.

To naturalize bulbs in grass, let them fall from your hand in roughly the area where you intend them to grow. Plant them where they land, rather than formally setting them out in rows.

Special bulb planters are available; these remove plugs of turf and soil so the bulb can be planted and the turf

returned with a minimum of effort. If the soil is at all heavy, a light sprinkling of sharp sand or peat in the bottom of the hole improves the drainage and keeps the bulb from rotting. Once the bulb is planted, return the plug of soil and turf and firm with your feet.

Bulbs in turf need little attention other than remov-

GARDENING

ing dead leaves and long grass. Lift, divide and replant when overcrowded, or the quality and size of flower will deteriorate.

Never cut green leaves from bulbs, or future flowering will be sacrificed. If the bulbs have finished flowering and you wish to use the space they occupy for annuals or biennials to follow on, lift the bulbs with the leaves still intact. Once dried out, they can be stored in a cool place until the following autumn, when they can be replanted.

Some bulbs and corms, such as some lilies and gladioli, are not frost hardy and must be lifted before the first of the winter frosts.

ROSES

Roses are the most popular of all cultivated shrubs and there are hundreds of species and named cultivars (varieties) available. Basically, there are four types: shrub roses, grown for their flowers and brightly coloured hips; hybrid teas, which carry one large bloom per stem; floribundas, producing several blooms per stem; and climbing and rambling roses.

Many roses are sold as bare-rooted, dormant plants. When selecting one, make sure the roots are firm and plump, rather than thin, dry and shrivelled.

Choose a sunny site and rich, well-drained soil, away from over-hanging trees.

Dig a hole 15 cm (6 in.) wider and deeper than the root spread. Carefully fork over the bottom of the hole, incorporating a bucketful of well-rotted manure and a handful of bonemeal. Plant the rose firmly, working fine

topsoil between the roots. As most roses are grafted, make sure that the join between the root stock and the named variety is at the same soil-mark level as it was when bought. If suckers appear from the roots, pull these off with your hands.

If you are planting standards or half standards, hammer in a stake before planting, to avoid damaging the roots. The top of the stake should be at least 5 cm (2 in.) below the lowest branch. Tie the trunk to the stake once near the top and again halfway down the stake. Mulch round the plants each spring to conserve moisture and keep down weeds. Check and adjust stakes and ties as necessary during the year.

PRUNING

Initial rose pruning consists of cutting the branches back to about 20 cm (8 in.), to an outward-facing bud. This prevents the bush rocking in strong wind. Roses planted in the autumn should not be pruned back hard because severe frosts could kill all above-ground growth, leaving only the rootstock living.

In autumn, shorten the stems of established hybrid tea roses by about half, removing all old blooms. During March or early April, cut each stem back to a strong bud, 10–15 cm (4–6 in.) from the base.

Established floribunda roses are pruned in much the same manner as hybrid teas. Being naturally more vigorous, however, they are pruned less severely in spring. Cut back to an outward-facing bud 15–20 cm (6–8 in.) from the base.

TREES, SHRUBS AND CLIMBERS

Trees are among the most important features in garden design, and a single tree can make a garden. Because they are long lived, the eventual size, shape and habit of growth should be considered very carefully before you choose a tree. A tree which outgrows the available space can be costly, embarrassing and even dangerous to live with. The importance of specific names and varieties cannot be overemphasized; there are named cultivars of cedars which form dwarf hummocks and others which grow to 30 m (100 ft) or more in height.

The usual distinction between a tree and a shrub is whether a single, main trunk or several, smaller stems form at ground level. However, some trees, such as some birches and magnolias, are naturally multi-stemmed, while shrubs, such as lilac or cotoneaster, can reach tree-like heights and proportions.

Colour, not only of the flowers but also the leaves, bark and berries, should be considered. A tree or shrub that blooms lavishly for one week and is dull for the rest of the year is of less merit than one with more modest flowers, but a longer flowering period followed by perhaps brightly-coloured berries or autumnal foliage. This is particularly true if your garden is small and the space for planting limited.

Trees and shrubs vary enormously in their hardiness and the amount of care and maintenance they need. If you are a weekend gardener, then tough, self-sufficient plants, which give a reasonable display for little effort, are best.

The same factors which determine the selection of trees and shrubs are valid when selecting climbers. The easiest are self-clinging climbers; once established, they need virtually no attention. Best known is ivy. As well as the common garden, dark-green form, there are many named cultivars, often beautifully variegated. Other self-clinging climbers are Virginia creeper and climbing hydrangea.

Typical climbers needing support are wistaria, honeysuckle and clematis. These will need tying in at 15–20 cm (6–8 in.) intervals, to keep them close against a wall and minimize wind damage.

PRUNING

The pruning of trees, shrubs and climbers ensures the continued provision of new growth, particularly important for plants which only flower on new wood. Secondly, it keeps plants from becoming too large for the space allotted them.

Where shrubs and trees have been obtained with a good framework of branches and the soil is fertile, little pruning is needed. Dead and diseased wood should always be cut out, though, and any which is awkwardly shaped or spoils the plant's shape should also be singled out and eliminated.

Generally, the harder the pruning, the more vigorous the growth; light pruning results in weak growth. Prune evergreens (other than conifers) in spring or summer, but only if essential, and deciduous plants while dormant, or immediately after flowering if they flower on the previous year's wood.

The frame can be opened and ventilated on fine days. Ensure that the light is firmly fixed.

Seal the ends of cloches in order to prevent damage by animals, birds and wind.

GROWING UNDER GLASS

Growing under glass offers many advantages: early, extended and out-of-season cropping, improved quality and quantity, and less dependence on the weather. Greenhouses, cold frames and cloches outdoors, and window sills and sun lounges indoors, provide basically similar growing conditions.

All such structures should be drip- and draught-proof. Ease of access, sufficient work space, ventilation and provisions for watering and heating are all essential. Greenhouses need a minimum height of 1.8 m (6 ft); frames and cloches need at least 30 cm (1 ft). A sunny, sheltered site is ideal, with a hard-paved access for wet-weather work.

COMPOSTS AND CONTAINERS

Plants require different composts or rooting media according to their condition and stage of development. Seed, cutting and potting mixtures are all available ready-mixed, and there is little difference between the various proprietary brands. Potting composts are available with different concentrations of fertilizer; those with the

heaviest concentration are used for strong-growing plants.

Containers can be pots, either clay or plastic, purpose-made seed trays, or shallow wooden trays, often available from greengrocers. All containers should be clean, free-draining and of a suitable size and depth for the intended purpose.

SOWING IN CONTAINERS

Cover the bottom of the container with a thin layer of pea gravel for drainage. Top up with damp seed compost to 6 mm (¼ in.) below the rim after levelling and light firming. Sow large seeds, like marrow, individually in small pots, cover with a sprinkling of compost and water in, using a fine rose.

For smaller seeds, water the compost 30 minutes before sowing, using a fine rose on the watering can. Scatter the seeds thinly on the surface, covering those of medium size with finely sifted seed compost to a depth equal to twice their diameter. Cover the containers with a pane of glass or some transparent plastic sheeting and place a sheet of folded paper on top. Keep warm and moist, removing the glass (or plastic) and paper when the seedlings appear. Protect the seedlings from strong sun.

PRICKING OUT AND HARDENING OFF

When the seedlings are large enough to handle, prick them out, either singly into small pots, or 4–5 cm (1½–2 in.) apart into boxes containing potting compost with a low fertilizer content.

To harden plants off for outdoor cultivation, place in unheated frames about three weeks before setting out. Gradually increase the venti-

1 Water gently.

2 Sow the seed thinly.

3 Cover with a sheet of glass.

lation to acclimatize the plants. Tomatoes and cucumbers, for planting in unheated greenhouses and frames, are best stood in their new surroundings for two or three days before planting out.

SOFT-STEM CUTTINGS

Chrysanthemums and dahlias are best raised from cuttings rooted in warmth during spring. Start the stools and tubers into growth in slight heat, about a month before cuttings are required. Cut new growths, 5–10 cm (2–4 in.) long, just below a leaf joint. Remove the bottom two or three leaves. Dip the cut end in hormone rooting powder and insert around the edges of pots or boxes filled with cutting compost. Keep moist, lightly shaded and in a minimum temperature of 10°C (50°F). When new growth is visible, pot up the cuttings.

STORING AND OVER-WINTERING

Many popular flowering plants should be stored under cover during winter. Corms of gladioli and begonia tubers are lifted, dried, cleaned and

4 Pricking out young seedlings.

stored loose in shallow trays, in an airy, frost-free place. Cut the tops of dahlias and chrysanthemums back to 15 cm (6 in.) above ground level and carefully lift the roots, shaking off the old soil. Store the roots and tubers in boxes filled with peat in a cool greenhouse or frame.

ORNAMENTAL PLANTS

Many annuals and bedding plants can be started under glass and then moved outdoors, once all danger of frost is over. Alyssum, antirrhinums and pansies are examples of such plants.

Fibrous-rooted begonias are raised from seed each year. Tuberous-rooted varieties are started off in boxes of moist peat, in a minimum temperature of 10°C (50°F), and then potted on.

Chrysanthemums under glass are grown from cuttings and potted up into their final pots in late spring. Large-flowered chrysanthemums are stopped, by removing the growing tip when six to ten leaves have formed, to encourage a bushier plant. To disbud to develop larger blooms, remove all flower buds below the main bud as soon as they can be rubbed out.

Daffodils, narcissi, hyacinths and tulips can be grown under glass. Place the bulbs in bowls or pots of moist bulb fibre in early autumn. Keep in dark conditions, at about 7°C (45°F), until growth appears. Then move the bulbs into a light, airy room or greenhouse. The warmer the temperature, the quicker the flowering. Avoid temperatures above 16°C

Flowering plants

Name	Height m	Season of interest	Plant	Colour shades
Herbaceous				
Aubretia	8-10cm	Apr-May	Sep-Oct	Maroon and mauve
Delphinium	30cm-1.8	Jun-Jul	Sep-Mar	Blue, pink, purple, white
Dianthus (Pinks)	20-38cm	Jun-Jul	Sep-Nov	Pink and white
Doronicum	60cm	Apr-Jun	Oct-Mar	Yellow
Helenium	1.2-1.8	Aug-Oct	Oct-Apr	Bronze and yellow
Kniphofia, Red-hot Poker	45cm-1.5	Jun-Oct	Sep-Oct	Red and yellow
Lupin	90cm-1.5	May-Jul	Oct-Mar	Various
Phlox	45cm-1.2	Jul-Sep	Sep-Mar	Pink, red, white and wine
Solidago, Golden Rod	15cm-1.8	Jul-Sep	Oct-Mar	Yellow
Shrubs				
Buddleia	3	Jul-Oct	Oct-Nov	Pink, purple, white and wine
Cytisus, Broom	2.5	May-Jun	Sep/Oct Mar/Apr	Cream, mahogany
Erica, Winter flowering	25cm	Nov-May	Oct-May	Pink and white
Forsythia	2.5	Mar-Apr	Oct-Mar	Yellow
Hydrangea	1.2-1.8	Jul-Sep	Oct/Nov Mar/Apr	Blue, pink and white
Magnolia soulangeana	3-4.5	Apr	Mar-Apr	White, tinged purple
Mahonia	90cm-1.5	Mar-Apr	Oct-Mar	Yellow
Potentilla	60cm-1.5	May-Aug	Oct-Mar	Tangerine, white and yellow
Rhododendron	30cm-4.5	Mar-Jun	Sep-Apr	Various
Rosa, Rose	45cm-2.5	Jun-Oct	Oct-Mar	Various
Weigela	1.8	May-Jun	Oct-Mar	Pink
Trees				
Crataegus (Thorn)	4.5-6	May Sep-Nov	Oct-Mar	Pink, red, white
Laburnum	3-6	Apr-Jun	Oct-Mar	Yellow
Malus (Crab)	4.5-7.5 3-6	Mar/Apr Aug/Sep	Oct-Mar	Pink/white Red/yellow
Prunus (Cherry)	6-7.5	Mar-May	Oct-Mar	Pink and white
Climbers/wall plants				
Clematis, hybrids	2.5-6	May-Oct	Oct-May	Various
Jasminum, Jasmine	3	Nov-Apr	Oct-Nov	Yellow
Pyracantha	3-4.5	Sep-Nov	Oct-Mar	Orange and red
Rosa, Rose	3-4.5	Jun-Oct	Oct-Mar	Various
Wistaria	9	May-Jun	Oct-Mar	Mauve and white

GARDENING

(60°F), however, and keep out of direct sunlight once the buds are open.

Raise fuchsias from soft-stem cuttings taken in spring. Pot on and harden off those for outdoor use. Mature plants can be over-wintered successfully at a minimum temperature of 5°C (41°F); keep fairly dry while dormant. In spring, cut the previous year's growth back to the main stem, increase the temperature to 10°C (50°F), syringe daily, and new growth will start.

Pelargoniums are raised from 8–10 cm (3–4 in.) long stem cuttings, taken in summer. Pot up rooted cuttings singly, into small pots, and provide a minimum winter temperature of 10°C (50°F).

CROPS UNDER GLASS

Many outdoor crops will benefit from being sown under glass and then transplanted outdoors. French and runner beans, cabbages, cauliflowers, leeks and onions are examples. Although the earliest lettuces are raised entirely under glass, the outdoor-grown crops will give quicker results if sown under glass.

Marrows, courgettes and ridge cucumbers crop well in frames and under cloches. Male flowers must be retained.

Tomatoes Tomatoes are probably the most popular greenhouse crop. Bush varieties can be grown indoors or out, while standard varieties are grown under glass, train-

ed as single-stem plants. Sow seeds of both sorts thinly and cover with a 3 mm (⅛ in.) layer of sifted seed compost. A minimum temperature of 16°C (60°F) is necessary for germination.

Prick out the seedlings singly, into 9 cm (3½ in.) pots, and grow on at a minimum temperature of 14°C (57°F). Shade from strong sun and ventilate freely in warm weather. Harden off outdoor varieties before planting out in June. Set plants about 40 cm (16 in.) apart, with 60 cm (2 ft) between rows.

Train greenhouse standard varieties up canes or other supports. Remove all side shoots, and stop each plant at two leaves above the fourth or fifth truss. Start feeding plants weekly with dilute

Growing under cover

Flowers started under cover

Crop	Position		Method	Time	Temp °C	Use
Ageratum	I	O	Seed	Mar-Apr	16	B & P
Alyssum	O		Seed	Feb-Mar	12	B & P
Antirrhinum	I	O	Seed	Feb-Mar	17	B & Cf
Aster	O		Seed	Mar	16	B & Cf
Begonia	I	O	Seed, C & Tuber	Apr	18	B & P
Chrysanthemum	I	O	C	Mar-Apr	14	B, P & Cf
Daffodil/narcissi	I		Bulb/Offsets	Aug-Sep	7	P & Cf
Dahlia	O		Seed, C & Tuber	Mar-Apr	14	B & Cf
Fuchsia	I	O	C	Mar-Apr	16	B & P
Hyacinth	I		Bulb	Aug-Sep	7-10	P
Impatiens	I	O	Seed	Feb-Mar	17	B & P
Marigold, French	I	O	Seed	Feb-Apr	16	B & P
Matthiola	I	O	Seed	Feb-Mar	14	B, P, & Cf
Pansy	I	O	Seed	Jan-Mar	16	B & P
Pelargonium	I	O	C	Jul-Sep	10	B & P
Petunia	I	O	Seed	Feb-Mar	16	B & P
Salvia	I	O	Seed	Feb-Mar	18	B & P
Tulip	I		Bulb	Aug-Sep	7-10	P & Cf

I = grown indoors O = raised indoors, matured in open B = bedding P = pot work
Cf = cut flower C = Cuttings
Time = period of sowing, taking cuttings or starting off Temperature = minimum required for sowing/starting off plants; growing temperature usually at least 3°C lower.

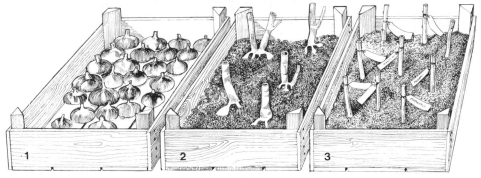

liquid feed as soon as fruits on the bottom truss start to swell.

Cucumbers Sow cucumber seeds on edge, 2 cm (⅘ in.) deep, in pots of moist seed compost. A minimum temperature of 16°C (60°F) is needed for germination. Once the seed leaves have started to grow, pot the seedlings into 12.5 cm (5 in.) pots filled with moist potting compost.

When four or five leaves have developed, set the plants out in their final positions. In the greenhouse, set the plants 60 cm (2 ft) apart on raised beds consisting of equal parts of well-rotted manure and John Innes No. 2 compost. This mixture is also suitable for frames.

Train and tie the main stem of each greenhouse plant up a single cane. Tie in the side shoots at 15 cm (6 in.) intervals to horizontal

1 Lift gladioli after flowering in September. Dry and clean the corms when the foliage is dry. Store in shallow layers in an airy frost-free place. Replant in April.

2 Cut down dahlia stems and lift tubers in September or October. Dry and clean. Dust with flowers of sulphur and store in dry peat in a frost-free place.

3 Cut chrysanthemum stems back to 12 cm (5 in.), lift and clean. Store in clean soil or potting compost over the winter. Keep slightly moist. Start growth in spring.

Growing under cover

Food crops sown under cover

Crop	Position	Sow	Temp °C	Plant	Pick
Beans, dwarf	O	Apr	10	Jun	Aug-Sep
Bean, runner	O	Apr	12	Jun	Aug-Oct
Cabbage	O	Feb	10	Apr	Jun-Sep
Cauliflower, summer	O	Feb	12	Apr	Jul-Sep
Courgette	I O	Apr	12	May/Jun	Aug-Sep
Cress	I	Year round	7-10	Year round	Year round
Cucumber	I	Apr	17	May	Jul-Sep
Egg plant	I	Feb	18	May (pot)	Aug-Sep
Endive	O	Jul	Unheated	Aug (thin)	Sep-Nov
Leek	O	Feb	10	Apr	Sep-Jan
Lettuce	I O	Jan-Apr	10	Mar-May	Apr-Jun
Marrow	I O	Apr	12	May/Jun	Aug-Sep
Mustard	I	Year round	7-10	Year round	Year round
Onion	O	Feb	17	Apr	Aug-Sep
Radish	I O	Feb-Mar	Unheated	Mar-May	Apr-May
Sweet Corn	O	Apr-May	17	May-Jun	Aug-Sep
Sweet Pepper	I	Feb-Mar	17	May (pot)	Aug-Sep
Tomato	I	Feb-Mar	17	Apr-May	Jul-Sep
Tomato	O	Mar-Apr	17	Jun	Aug-Sep

O = plant outdoors   IO = plant/sow under frames/cloches and uncover as crop matures   I = start off and mature under cover

wires running at 20 cm (8 in.) intervals. Remove the growing point as soon as the top wire is reached. Stop side shoots at the second leaf, and sublaterals at the first. Pick off any male flowers, which are those without embryonic fruits attached, to prevent pollination and inferior fruits.

In warm weather, damp down the greenhouse. Once the fruits begin swelling, give weekly feeds of dilute fertilizer.

Greenhouse-type cucumbers grown in frames can be treated as above, except that the training procedure differs slightly. Stop the young plants after the fifth leaf and train out four shoots, one into each corner of the frame. Stop these at the ninth leaf. The laterals and sublaterals are then stopped as for greenhouse culture.

Ridge cucumbers are grown in frames and cloches, and should not have the male flowers removed. Training depends on the variety chosen; follow instructions on the packet.

HOUSE PLANTS

INTRODUCTION

There is a wide range of house plants available today. Some were originally collected from the wild on plant-hunting expeditions, while others were bred or developed for indoor growth by commercial growers.

Whatever their origins, house plants must meet certain requirements. They must be attractive — in flower, foliage or both — and they must be tolerant of the unnatural growing conditions found in a house. Relatively low light levels, dry atmosphere and central heating, rapid fluctuations in temperature, fumes and draughts and erratic water supply are some of the problems.

House plants vary enormously in their ability to tolerate these conditions. When buying a house plant or deciding where to put it, try to match the requirements of the particular plant with the environment you have to offer.

There are three basic categories of house plants, according to their temperature requirements. Those requiring cool conditions are grown between 4°C (39°F) minimum and 16°C (60°F) maximum; normal, or intermediate, temperature, 7°C (45°F) minimum and 19°C (66°F) maximum; and warm conditions 10°C (50°F) minimum and 21°C (70°F) maximum.

Foliage plants generally tolerate shade better than flowering subjects, which also need protection from intense sun when flowering. Most house plants grow well in positions where there is plenty of natural light, but out of direct sunlight, particularly in summer.

MATERIALS

You need a healthy plant to start with, as plants which are sold in poor condition rarely recover. Also necessary are suitable containers, troughs and composts, canes and ties for tall plants, a

The basic materials required for growing house plants can be bought relatively cheaply.

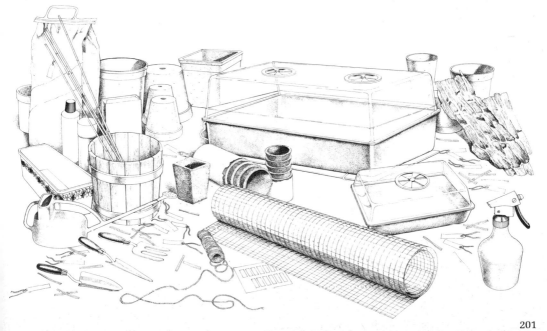

GARDENING

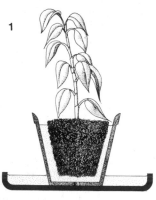

sharp knife, liquid feed, insecticide and fungicide, a small sprayer and a room thermometer.

Optional extras include a watering can with a narrow spout or a fine rose, and a small propagator, but a small jug and a polythene bag make admirable substitutes.

CONTAINERS
Containers for growing plants should look nice, be of a suitable size and depth, be well drained and easy to clean. Clay and plastic pots are most often used, but timber and glazed-ware containers are popular for display purposes. Clay containers are heavier than plastic ones and so provide stability, particularly important if you are using a light, soil-less compost. Plastic pots are easier to clean and dry out more slowly.

Pot size is measured by the diameter across the top. Those in common use are 6.5 cm (2¼ in.), 9 cm (3½ in.), 10 cm (4 in.), 12.5 cm (5 in.), 15 cm (6 in.) and 17.5 cm (7 in.).

COMPOSTS
Soil-based mixtures are easier to manage than soil-less composts if the plant is likely to remain in its pot for a year or more.

Some plants, such as dumb cane (Dieffenbachia), are offered for sale in hydro-culture packs, consisting of a plant, a container and a granular material around the

1 When the compost is very dry, water will run down the inside.

2 Water will collect in a pool if the compost is too compact.

3 Submerging the pot in water will saturate the compost.

When potting, ensure good drainage. Cover base with a shallow layer of crocks, overlay with peat and top up with potting compost.

roots. These specially treated granules are soil or compost substitutes and are moistened with a very weak, balanced fertilizer solution.

WATERING
Once a healthy plant has been positioned to give it the optimum heat and light to suit its needs, then watering, feeding and general maintenance become important.

Watering is the most difficult process to get right. There are moisture meters available which indicate by lights or numbers the moisture content of the soil when a metal probe is inserted into the compost. These are no substitute for experience and judgement. The type of plant, the season, its position, the amount of heat and light available all affect the amount of water needed. Plants resting in winter need little water compared to their spring and summer requirements. Always use tepid water, to avoid shocking the plant's roots.

One watering method is to fill the top of the container until water runs out the bottom. If the compost is very dry and has shrunk away from the pot, water will simply run down the inner sides of the pot. Submerge the entire pot, up to the level of the soil surface, in a large container of water. Leave until all the air bubbles have stopped rising to the surface; this indicates the compost is saturated. Remove and drain.

If, on the other hand, water sits on the top of the compost surface in a pool, it means the compost is so compact that water cannot percolate through. You can try gently pricking over the surface with a fork and standing the pot in a container of water, as above. It is usually better, though, to repot the plant into fresh compost.

Never allow plants to stand permanently in water. Empty out any surplus from the saucers or plant holders 30 minutes after watering. Small seedlings and plants with hairy leaves, like African violets, are best watered by submerging the container, so as to avoid water settling on the leaves and causing rot. Cyclamen corms are also best watered from below, as water settling on the corm can lead to rot.

Always water thoroughly rather than wetting the surface of the compost alone. Although there are exceptions, the compost should be allowed to nearly dry out between waterings.

During winter, many plants suffer from dryness of

the air when radiators are on. Regular sponging of the leaves or misting of all except hairy-leaved plants will help remedy the situation. Small pot plants can be stood on gravel-lined trays filled with water. The water evaporating creates a humid atmosphere immediately around the plants.

FEEDING

Plants which are growing rapidly need feeding; for most plants, this is during spring and summer. Those which are producing flower buds or are very large in size also need feeding. In winter, or when plants are resting,

the amount and frequency of feeding should be reduced or stopped altogether.

Plant fertilizers consist of balanced amounts of nitrogen, phosphates and potash, together with other chemical elements. These materials can be absorbed only when dissolved in water, so liquid feeding is the quickest way of supplying essential nutrients to growing plants.

Never apply liquid fertilizer to plants when their roots or compost are dry, or when the plants are in a wilted condition. If the compost is dry, water thoroughly at least half an hour before applying liquid feed.

Window boxes and hanging baskets can make a colourful display. Make sure they are firmly secured and that any dripping water will not cause a nuisance.

GARDENING

Never give stronger solutions than the makers recommend, or the roots of the plant may be burned.

Proprietary feeds are obtainable in different formulations. Standard feeds are useful for average needs. High-nitrogen feeds are beneficial if growth is poor and an extra boost is needed in late spring or summer. High-potash feeds are usually reserved for winter use, if growth is soft and sappy. They are also used to improve the quality and colour of blooms and foliage.

POTTING

If you propagate house plants yourself, or buy small specimens, potting becomes a necessary routine. It involves a sequence of moves for seedlings, cuttings and small plants into increasingly larger pots.

All pots should be clean, both for appearance's sake and to lessen the risk of pests or diseases spreading. Avoid

A slow-growing pot plant with roots protruding from the base. It needs potting on.

Remove plant from the pot carefully. Ease out old crocks and the matted mass of roots.

putting slow-growing plants from small pots into excessively large containers in a single operation, or the compost becomes sour before the roots can fill the space.

Drain pots by crocking; place a few clean, small

stones or pot shards over the bottom for drainage. Follow this with a thin layer of peat and then fill with the chosen compost. Always water plants thoroughly before moving them.

Gently spread out any

Types of indoor plants
1 *Hedera canariensis*
2 *Hedera helix*
3 *Philodendron scandens*
4, 6 *Rhoicissus rhomboidea*
5 *Neoregelia*
7 *Sansevieria trifasciata*
8 *Cordyline terminalis*
9 *Anthurium andreanum*
10 *Hibiscus rosa-siensis*
11 *Ficus elastica*
12 *Pelargonium domesticum*
13 *Thunbergia alata*
14 *Monstera deliciosa*
15 *Aglaonema crispum*
16 *Dracaena marginata*
17, 25 *Begonia tuberhybrida*
18 *Coleus blumei*
19 *Dieffenbachia picta*
20 *Adiantum tenerum*
21, 29 *Selaginella*
22 *Chlorophytum comosum*
23 *Saintpaulia ionantha*
24 *Sinningia speciosa*
26 *Platycerium bifurcatum*

27 *Fuchsia*
28 *Rebutia violaciflora*
30 *Echeveria*

31 *Echeveria multicaulis*
32 *Opuntia microdasys*
33 *Notocactus tabularis*

With old plants, trim dead roots before repotting. Remove the original compost at the same time.

curled roots when setting plants in their new containers. Work compost into the space between the rootball and the edges of the container, leaving room at the top for watering.

Repotting is necessary when mature plants reach their final size, their growth slows down and potting into larger containers becomes undesirable or unnecessary. It is best carried out while the plant is resting. Remove it from its container, carefully scrape away the old compost, trim off dead roots and leaves, and repot it into the same sized container. Work fresh compost in and around the roots to replace the compost removed while repotting.

When potting, do not firm soil-less mixtures more than is sufficient to keep plants in position. With soil-based composts, the firmness of potting follows the degree of hardness of the plant's stems. Woody stems require firm potting but soft stems require only light potting.

PROPAGATION

Many houseplants can be grown from seed, the techniques of which are outlined on page 195. If you are using polythene bags over pots or seed pans, remove them as soon as the seeds have germinated or the cuttings rooted.

The aluminium plant, *Pilea cadierei*, and the shrimp plant, *Beloperone guttata*, can be propagated from soft-stem cuttings. The iron-cross begonia, *Begonia rex*, is easily increased by leaf cuttings. Remove a healthy leaf and nick the main leaf veins

GARDENING

1 The iron-cross begonia, *Begonia rex*, can be easily increased by leaf propagation.
2 Both *Saintpaulia* and ivy can increase by leaf propagation.

in several places on the undersurface with a sharp knife. Pin the prepared leaf to the surface of a pot or seed pan filled with cutting compost; use bent wire or hair pins to hold the leaf in place. Alternatively, cut the leaf into 3 cm (1¼ in.) squares, including a section of main vein on each square, and insert them edgeways, 1.5 cm (⅗ in.) deep. Keep the leaf cuttings in warm, moist conditions and tiny plantlets will soon appear from the vein cuts.

Clump-forming plants,

House plants providing year-round interest

Name	Watering	Nature of Interest		Condition of room	Temp °C and siting	Method of Increase
African violet	A	F	L	Warm	13-16 Light	Leaf
Aluminium plant	A		L	Average	8-13 Shade	C
Begonia	A	F	L	Warm	10-16 Shade	C Leaf
Christmas cactus	A	F	L	Warm	13 Light	Leaf
Cordyline	A		L	Warm	10-13 Light	Suckers
Dumb cane/Leopard lily	M		L	Warm	13-16 Light	C
Easter cactus	A	F	L	Warm	13 Light	Leaf
Ferns various	M		L	Average	7-13 Shade	Division
Grape Ivy	A		L	Average	7-10 Shade	C
Hedera various	A		L	Cool	5-10 Shade	C Ivy
Mother-in-law's tongue	D		L	Warm	10-13 Shade	Suckers
Parlour palm	M		L	Warm	13-16 Shade	Seed
Peperomia	A	F	L	Warm	10-13 Light	C Leaf
Rubber plant	D	A	L	Warm	13-18 Shade	C Leaf bud
Shrimp plant	A	F	L	Average	7-10 Light	C
Spider plant	A		L	Average	7-10 Shade	Layer
Star blossom	A	F	L	Cool	5-10 Light	Leaf
Sweetheart plant	A		L	Warm	13-16 Shade	C
Swiss cheese plant	A		L	Warm	10-12 Shade	C
Wandering Jew	A		L	Average	7-10 Shade	C

KEY   A = Average watering   D = Keep dryish   M = Keep moist
      F = Flower interest   L = Foliage interest   C = Cuttings

Temperatures are minimum for overwintering. Shade indicates plant's tolerance or liking for medium shade. Light indicates need for good winter illumination. All kinds listed will grow well under good natural lighting but not in full sun.

such as *Clivia miniata* and aspidistras, can be split up into several smaller clumps to increase numbers. Many cacti and succulents form suckers which can be removed and potted up separately. To propagate the Christmas cacti, *Schlumbergera* x *buckleyi*, place 3–5 cm (1–2 inch) long leaf segments upright in shallow pots or seed pans filled with potting compost. Given warm, moist conditions, new roots will grow from each segment.

PLANTS FOR FREE
Many plants can be grown for free, from vegetables or even vegetable parings. While these are not long lived or particularly beautiful, children enjoy experimenting in this way, especially so because the results are very rapid.

The tops of carrots, if placed in a shallow dish of gravel or sand topped up with water, produce masses of ferny new leaves. Other roots, such as beetroot, parsnip and swede, can be similarly treated. Cut all the old leaves and stalks back to within 3–5 cm (1–2 in.) of the top when starting.

Grapefruit, orange and lemon plants can be grown from pips if you can provide a constant temperature of 16°C (60°F). Although the plants are unlikely to produce fruit in temperate climates, the foliage is very attractive and pleasantly scented. The date palm can also be raised from pips, but it requires a minimum temperature of 23°C (73°F) in order to germinate.

Pineapple tops can sometimes be persuaded to root if you cut off the foliage with about 2.5 cm (1 in.) of fruit still attached. Pare around the edges of the attached pulp so the sides are vertical and form a plug. Leave this to dry out for a day or two, to lessen the risk of rotting, and plant in a cutting compost.

PALE, TALL, LEGGY PLANTS
These symptoms are often caused by excessive shade, particularly when accompanied by high temperatures. Avoid overcrowding and excessive heat. Provide plenty of indirect sunlight and fertilizer.

WILTING
When plants lose water more quickly than it can be replaced, leaves become limp and droop. Avoid dry atmospheric and root conditions, draughts and strong sunlight. Keep plants in the shade, especially those with diseased and damaged roots, and immediately after repotting. Although some plants flower better when pot-bound, others resent this condition; the latter should be potted on whenever necessary. Excessive water can also cause wilting, as it fills the tiny air pockets in the growing medium and literally suffocates the plant's roots.

BROWN OR SCORCHED LEAF MARGINS
This often follows severe wilting (see above). Try to prevent wilting and, in particular, keep plants warm and out of cold, drying draughts and wind, and hot dry atmosphere.

WATER MARKING
Plants with hairy leaves, such as African violets, develop pale or scorched patches on the leaves if water lodges on the leaf surface. The problem is made worse if foliar feeding is done in direct sunlight. Avoid feeding or watering plants in direct sunlight, and take care not to splash water on hairy-leaved plants.

SLOW-GROWING, PALE PLANTS
These symptoms, particularly when combined with hard stems, indicate starvation. Use the correct compost and start feeding plants within a month of potting. Pot on plants into increasingly large containers. Repot long-lived plants into fresh compost when the final-sized container is reached. Avoid draughts, chills and periods of neglect.

NON-FLOWERING OR BUD DROPPING
Give flowering plants well-lit conditions, avoiding heavy shade, low temperatures, dry atmospheres, and violent fluctuations in temperature, light, feeding and watering.

CHLOROSIS
Yellow leaves which seem fairly healthy and do not wilt indicate growing conditions which are excessively alkaline. Other symptoms are small leaves and delayed or poor flowering and a whitish encrustation or covering on the leaves. Where possible, use rainwater instead of water from a tap. Applications of iron and magnesium chelate often correct the situation by supplying the plant nutrients required.

LOSS OF VARIEGATION
Some variegated plants, such as tradescantia, develop shoots with all-green leaves. Remove such shoots as soon as they appear and avoid overfeeding. Move the pot into more light, which encourages variegation.

GARDENING

ANIMALS IN THE GARDEN

Frog This amphibian eats slugs, worms, flies and grubs. It is a cold-blooded animal and hibernates in the winter. Although its habits are similar to the toad's, its skin is smoother and moister.

Toad This is an amphibian related to the frog, but its skin is dry and rough or warty. Its diet is much the same as that of the frog, and both can live on land or in water.

Hedgehog This is a small animal whose back is covered in spines like the porcupine. It eats all kinds of insects and also eats worms and bird's eggs. It rolls itself into a ball when threatened.

Common lizard This is a reptile closely related to the snake. It generally eats insects, which makes it a beneficial addition to the garden. Unlike most lizards, it gives birth to live young.

Mole This is a small mammal that lives almost entirely underground, and is almost entirely blind. Although it does eat grubs, it can cause much damage to lawns.

Squirrel This is a small rodent that eats nuts, insects, eggs and small birds. The grey squirrel, which is very destructive to trees, has ousted the red squirrel from many places.

Woodpigeon This bird of woodland is often seen in gardens, where it eats seeds and can be damaging to cabbage crops. It lives in flocks outside the breeding season.

Collared dove This bird, originally from the Middle East, first bred in Britain in 1955 and is now widespread. It is considered to be a pest.

GARDEN PESTS AND DISEASES

WARNING

Pesticides and fungicides should be handled with extra care. Always keep them away from children and household pets. Before using any chemical preparation in the garden, first read the label and follow the manufacturer's instructions.

Aphids (greenfly and black-fly) The growing points and leaves of many kinds of plants, both ornamental and edible, can be affected. Spray with derris or malathion.

Apple scab Infected fruits and leaves of apples and pears develop black spots. Spray with benomyl or captan from green flower-bud to fruitlet stages.

Big-bud (gall mite) The buds of blackcurrants become swollen and fail to open. Spray bushes with lime sulphur at the flowering stage and again three weeks later. Pick off and burn infested buds in mild attacks, or destroy severely infested bushes completely.

Birds Bullfinches often strip buds off trees and shrubs in winter. If only a few plants are involved, black cotton thread or fine mesh woven among branches acts as a deterrent. Blackbirds and thrushes feed on ripening berries, which need similar protection. Fruit cages, although initially expensive, are the only real solution.

Sparrows create havoc in seed beds by making dust bath hollows and by eating seedlings. Pigeons are particularly fond of brassica seedling leaves. In all these cases, cloches, fine netting or black cotton thread will help minimize damage and are more effective than bird scarers.

Black spot The upper surfaces of rose leaves develop black spots. Spray infected plants with captan and spray again at fortnightly intervals. Rake up and burn infected leaves.

Carrot fly Yellow or white maggots bore holes into carrot and parsnip roots. Treat seed beds before sowing with an application of diazinon or trichlorphon.

Caterpillars The larvae of many moths and butterflies damage leaves, buds, shoots and roots of ornamental and edible plants. Hand pick and destroy caterpillars in mild infestations and spray affected plants with fenitrothion or derris.

Club root Members of the cabbage family become stunted, with swollen and foul-smelling roots. Practise crop rotation and avoid growing brassicas on infected soil. Dress seed bed or planting holes with calomel dust before sowing or planting. Remove and burn diseased plants.

Codling moth Whitish grubs tunnel through apple and pear fruits. Spray trees with fenitrothion in mid-June and twice more at three-week intervals. Place bands of sacking round the trunks in late June to trap the larvae; remove and burn the bands during the winter.

Cutworm Root vegetables and flowering plants are attacked by soil-dwelling caterpillars. The pests are active at night and the plants are chewed or severed completely at ground level. Treat soil with an application of diazinon or chlorpyriphos.

Earwig The buds, petals and leaves of chrysanthemums, dahlias and other plants are eaten by these shiny brown pests with pincer-like tail ends. Apply gamma HCH (formerly BHC) dusts or sprays to affected plants, treating the surrounding area of soil as well.

Flea beetles Seedlings of turnips and other members of the brassica family, including wallflowers, are attacked; holes, looking like gunshot, appear on the leaves. Use seeds treated with insecticide and dust or spray infested seedlings with derris or gamma HCH (BHC).

Grey mould (botrytis) This fungal infection is one of the most troublesome garden problems. Fruit, vegetables, bulbs and herbaceous plants are all vulnerable. A grey, fluffy growth is the main symptom. Remove infected parts if the infection is mild, otherwise destroy badly infected plants. Treat plants with captan, benomyl, thiram or thispanate-methyl systemic fungicide.

Mealy bug Patches of white, woolly covering on the stems of greenhouse plants are symptoms of mealy bug infestation. The insects are concealed underneath the covering. Spray with malathion or dimethoate.

Mildew White powdery patches, on both indoor and hardy plants, are symptoms of mildew. Spray apples with benomyl, thisphanate-methyl systemic fungicide or dinocap at the pink-bud stage, and other crops as soon as the disease is seen. Repeat once or twice weekly.

Onion fly White grubs eat the bulbs of spring-sown onions; onions grown from sets often escape attack. Treat soil near infested onions with calomel dust or chlorpyriphos. Attacks carrots and cabbages too.

GARDENING

Potato blight Brown spots or blotches appear on the leaves and stems of potato and tomato plants. Unless the disease is checked quickly, the crops will be ruined. Apply copper fungicide spray in late June and repeat at least twice.

Red spider mite Both indoor and outdoor plants are vulnerable; the tiny red or yellow mites live on the leaf undersides. Leaves become mottled and bronzed and sometimes fine webs are visible. Spray with derris or malathion.

Scale insects These small, limpet-like pests mainly attack plants grown under glass, although occasionally hardy trees and shrubs are infested. Treat with malathion or petroleum oil sprays. Dabbing the individual scales with cotton wool dipped in methylated spirits is effective in the case of mild infestations.

Slugs and snails Slime trails and irregular-shaped holes in leaves indicate the presence of slugs and snails. Place metaldehyde or methiocarb slug baits near affected plants, particularly freshly transplanted crops.

Thrips These small dark insects are extremely numerous in the summer. Attacks can result in silvering or streaking on leaves and flowers. Spray affected plants with malathion.

Whitefly These tiny, winged, moth-like pests attack indoor and outdoor plants. They feed on the undersides of the leaves and produce a sticky honeydew, which in turn encourages the growth of sooty mould. Spray infested plants with gamma HCH (BHC) or malathion.

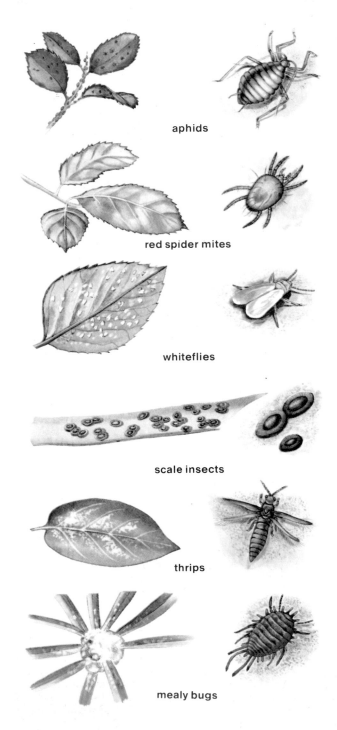

aphids

red spider mites

whiteflies

scale insects

thrips

mealy bugs

GLOSSARY

Acid soil Soil with a pH of less than 7.0, containing little or no lime.

Aerate To relieve soil compaction and improve underground ventilation by hoeing, forking, or digging.

Alkaline soil Soil with a pH of more than 7.0, containing more than an average amount of lime.

Ameliorant Any material added to the soil which improves its fertility.

Annual A plant which germinates, grows, sets seed and dies within a year.

Bedding Plants set out in beds or borders, mainly for spring or summer effect, which are disposed of at the end of their flowering season.

Bi-colour Flowers or foliage with two main colours.

Biennial A plant which germinates, grows, sets seed and dies within two years.

Blanch To exclude light from leaves and stems to improve colour, texture and flavour.

Brassica A member of the cabbage tribe, such as the cauliflower.

Bulb A swollen food storage organ consisting of overlapping scales, such as an onion.

Bush A shrub or tree with branches which do not grow to more than 75 cm (30 in.) above soil level.

Catch crop A quick growing crop taken between two main crops.

Compost Partly decomposed vegetable matter for use as a manure substitute. Seed, cutting and potting composts contain mixtures of peat, sand or similar materials, with or without loam, and usually with fertilizer, for use as a growing medium.

Conifers Usually evergreen trees and bearing cones.

Container-plant A plant which has been grown, or is growing, in a container.

Cordons Tree forms, usually fruit, which are restricted to a single main stem.

Corm A swollen stem, resembling a bulb, which acts as a food storage organ.

Crock A piece of broken clay pot or small stone placed in the bottom of pots to maintain free drainage.

Crown The framework of branches in trees and shrubs, or the clump of roots of herbaceous plants.

Curd The edible white flowery head of a cauliflower.

Cutting A piece of stem, root, shoot or leaf which can be used for propagation.

Deadhead The removal of faded or dead blooms.

Deciduous Term applied to plants which shed their leaves, usually in autumn, and follow this by a period of dormancy.

Dibber A piece of wood used to make holes for planting, available in a variety of thicknesses.

Disbud The removal of secondary buds, leaving the main or terminal bud to develop upwards.

Division The splitting up of crowns or root clumps for the purpose of propagation.

Dormant Term applied to plants when active growth has visibly ceased, as with leafless but living bulbs or trees in winter.

Double digging Digging to double the depth of a spade.

Earthing up Drawing soil around the stems of crops, such as celery or leeks, and covering developing potato tubers, for protection.

Evergreen Plants having leaves all year round, such as the conifers.

Fertilizer A substance containing concentrated plant foods essential for growth.

F1 hybrid The result obtained by crossing two related, but dissimilar, plants.

Fruitlet stage Applied to fruit trees and bushes, when the young fruits are swelling.

Fungicide Material used to prevent or destroy fungi.

Germination The first stages of seed growth, when shoots or leaves appear.

Green-bud stage Term applied to fruit trees when the flower buds are green, but unopened.

Grow on The care of plants from pricking out, potting or planting, until they reach maturity.

Hardening off Acclimatizing plants raised under cover to cool or outdoor conditions.

Hardy Term applied to plants which can be grown outdoors all year round.

Herbaceous Term applied to plants having non-woody stems, particularly perennial flowering plants.

Herbicide A substance used for killing weeds.

Insecticide A substance used for killing insects.

Intercrop When two crops are grown together — e.g. spring onions with lettuce.

Lateral A side shoot or growth developing from a main stem.

Lime A material containing calcium, usually in the form of ground limestone.

Loam Fertile soil composed of a balanced mixture of sand and clay and decayed organic matter.

Manure Usually a mixture of vegetable and animal waste.

Marginal plants Those which grow happily round the edges

211

GARDENING

of ponds or water.

Mulch A surface dressing of rotted manure, peat or compost, placed around plants.

Naturalize The informal planting of bulbs or other plants, usually in grass, where they can grow and increase naturally.

Neutral Term applied to soils and composts which are neither acid nor alkaline.

Node The swollen junction of a leaf and stem.

Offset A bulb or shoot arising at or below soil level from the parent bulb or stem.

Open Condition of soil through which water drains freely and which roots penetrate easily. Also, winter weather without hard frost or heavy rain, suitable for planting.

Organic gardening Methods in which no inorganic fertilizers are used, only organic manures and compost, and the use of herbicides and pesticides is restricted.

Perennial A plant, usually non-woody, which develops over three or more years.

Pink bud The stage when pink petals are just visible on the buds of apple trees.

Plunge The practice of sinking plant pots up to the rim in soil or peat, to prevent them drying out or being blown over.

Pollination The transfer of pollen, from one flower to another or from one part of the plant to another part, to effect fertilization of fruit blossom and setting of seeds.

Pot-bound The condition when the roots of a containerized plant have outgrown the pot.

Pricking out Transferring seedlings from a seed pan into boxes, pots or beds.

Propagation The reproduction of plants.

Pruning The systematic cutting out of unwanted shoots.

Resting periods Phases when active growth ceases — e.g. during winter.

Ring culture Method of greenhouse tomato growing. So called because the containers are bottomless cylinders of compost standing on a layer of some water-holding but sterile medium. Useful where plants cannot be watered frequently.

Rootball A collective mass of roots with soil or compost surrounding them.

Rootstock The root part of a budded or grafted plant.

Runner An above-ground stem connecting a plantlet to the parent plant.

Scarify To aerate turf with a wire rake.

Scions The upper parts of grafted plants when they are of a different variety to the lower part, or rootstock.

Seed bed An area of ground prepared for seed sowing.

Seed leaves The first pair of leaves that seedlings produce after germination.

Selective weedkiller A herbicide which kills certain types of plants (weeds) but leaves others unharmed.

Set A partly developed bulb, such as an onion or shallot, which has been specially treated and used instead of seed for crop production. Set, applied to fruit trees, means that seeds or fruit have formed successfully.

Shrub A plant with woody main branches which start at or near ground level.

Specimen plant Describes a plant grown for its individual beauty.

Spit A spade's depth, usually 25–30 cm (10–12 in.) deep.

Standard Trees and roses with a minimum clear stem of 1 m (3 ft) between soil level and the lowest branches.

Stopping The removal of the growing point of a main stem or branch.

Sucker A shoot or growth arising from below or near soil level.

Tender Term applied to plant needing frost protection during the winter months.

Terminal shoots These are leading growths of plants.

Tilth Condition of soil surface. Fine tilth consists of granular, finely divided soil, without large lumps.

Top-dressing A surface application of plant food: fertilizer or compost.

Topsoil Fertile, top layer of soil, varying in depth to 30 cm (12 in.).

Transplanting Lifting plants and replanting them in a new position.

Tuber A swollen or thickened underground stem or root which acts as a food store.

Variegated A term applied to leaves, or sometimes petals, with distinctive markings of two or more colours.

Waterlogged A term applied to soils which are saturated with water so that air, essential for growth, is absent from between soil particles.

Weed A plant, usually of little value, which is growing where it is unwanted.

White bud A stage in pear development when the buds first reveal the white, unopened flowers.

HOME CRAFTS

HOME CRAFTS

KNITTING

Despite the innovations of home knitting machines and the availability of inexpensive ready-made knitwear, hand knitting is a popular pastime as well as being a money-saver. Unusual and beautiful yarns are made especially for hand knitting and new designs and instructions are continually produced to meet increasing popular demand.

The most popular items to knit are sweaters, cardigans and accessories such as hats, scarves and gloves. You will find available a great variety of designs with printed instructions, either in yarn shops or in magazines. The designs are usually linked to a specific yarn, so that the sizing and quantity of yarn required can be calculated accurately. With basic yarns it may be possible to use a

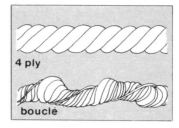

4 ply

bouclé

A selection of yarns.

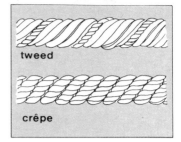

tweed

crêpe

substitute quite successfully providing it is of similar thickness, but this is not usually so with speciality yarns because the tension may not work correctly.

ABOUT YARNS

Knitting yarn may be in wool, cotton or synthetic fibres, or a blend of one with another. Yarn is sold by ball, hank or spool, usually in weight rather than length.

The amount required for an item is specified on the pattern you intend to follow. It is wise to buy all your yarn at once because the colour of balls dyed at different times may vary slightly, and this may show up in a finished garment. Check the dye lot number which is printed on the yarn label, and buy only from one dye lot. If you cannot afford to buy a large quantity at one time, you may find that the shop will reserve some for a while.

Yarns are made by twisting together single spun threads and the term 'ply' describes how many threads have been used. It may be two, three or four. Ply does

---

CASTING ON

1 Make a slip loop with your fingers about 10 cm (4 inches) from the end of the yarn. Insert a knitting needle through the loop and hold the needle in your left hand. This loop has now formed the first stitch.

2 Insert the right-hand needle into the loop from front to back and wind the yarn clockwise round the point. Pull the needle back through the first stitch towards you, drawing the yarn through the slip loop to form a new stitch.

3 Insert the left-hand needle into the new stitch and withdraw the right-hand needle. Continue in this way, until you have made the required number of stitches, inserting the needle into the stitch just formed to create the next stitch.

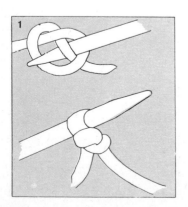

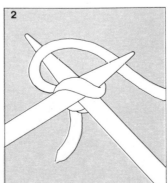

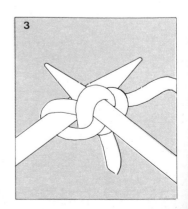

not describe thickness and it is quite possible that a two-ply could be thicker than a four-ply. All plies may have a crêpe texture.

Baby yarns These are available in three- or four-ply weights. They are soft to wear and may be washed repeatedly without harm.

Double knitting This knits up quickly and is double the thickness of a normal four-ply yarn. Use for classic sweaters and cardigans.

Chunky or double-double knitting. As its name implies, this is a heavy yarn, ideal for thick sweaters.

Speciality yarns These have an unusual feature such as the addition of a lurex thread or a special texture as in bouclé yarns.

Quicker knit is a baby yarn thicker than four-ply but less thick than double knitting.

ABOUT NEEDLES

As well as yarn, you also need needles, usually a pair, in the appropriate size for the yarn. The size of a needle is the metric measurement taken round its shaft. Needles of the same size can vary in length. Choose the needles according to the width of garment being made so that the stitches are held easily.

The needle size is specified in the pattern you wish to follow, but you may well find you need one size smaller or larger to knit to the correct tension.

Special needles are made with points at each end, in sets of four, for making a circular fabric without seams, or in short lengths for cabling.

You may also require a stitch holder for reserving certain stitches while you work on others.

For sewing up finished garments, use a blunt-ended yarn needle.

HOLDING THE NEEDLES

Hold the needle with the stitches to be worked in your left hand and the one which forms the new stitches in your right hand, wind the yarn over the fingers as shown to control the tension. When forming the stitch, carry the yarn round the needle point with the right hand index finger while still holding the needle.

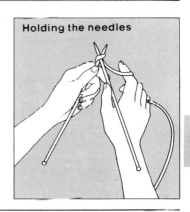

Holding the needles

KNIT STITCH

1 With needle holding stitches in left hand, insert right-hand needle from front to back into first stitch on LH needle, so that RH needle and yarn are behind it. Take yarn under RH needle and wind it round clockwise.

2 Pull yarn through the stitch on the LH needle, thus forming a new stitch on the RH needle.

3 Keeping the new stitch on the RH needle, drop the stitch worked from the LH needle. Work into each stitch in this way on the LH needle,

keeping the new stitches on the RH needle, to the end. Turn the work round to hold the needle with the stitches on the left hand for the next row.

This is the most basic knitting stitch, producing a neat, firm fabric.

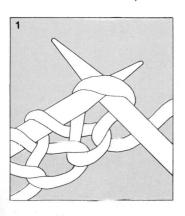

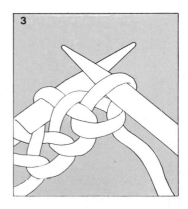

HOME CRAFTS

PURL STITCH

This is the other basic stitch used in knitting and, combined with knit stitch, can form innumerable patterns and textures, the most common being stocking stitch.

1 With needle holding stitches in your left hand, insert right-hand needle from right to left into the first stitch on LH needle so that RH needle and yarn are at the front of it.

2 Take yarn over needle and wind around clockwise. Pull yarn through stitch on LH needle to form a new stitch on the RH needle.

3 Keeping the new stitch on the RH needle, drop the one worked from the LH needle. Repeat to make successive purl stitches.

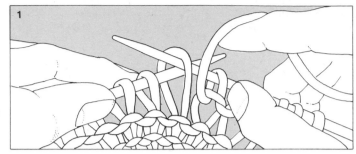

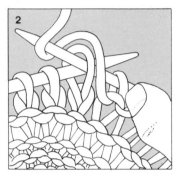

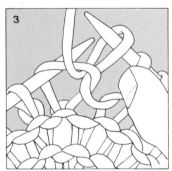

CASTING OFF

This secures the stitches at the end of a piece of knitting and forms a firm edge. To ensure the edge does not become too tight, use a larger needle in the right hand.

1 Knit the first two stitches on the LH needle as if beginning a new row.

2 Insert the point of the LH needle into the first stitch knitted and lift it over the second one and then off the RH needle.

3 Withdraw the LH needle, leaving the second stitch on the RH needle. Knit the next stitch from the LH needle in the usual way and repeat the process.

4 When all the stitches are off the LH needle and only one stitch remains on the RH needle, break the yarn leaving a 10 cm (4 inch) end. Thread the end through the last stitch, withdraw the needle and pull the end tight.

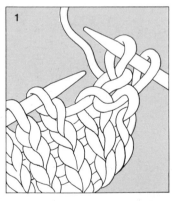

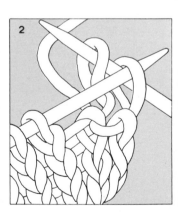

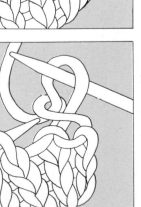

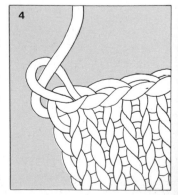

TENSION

Knitting patterns always give instructions for checking 'tension', which describes how many stitches and rows there should be to a specific measurement, in order to knit the design to the required size.

Although it may be tempting to ignore the check and to start knitting the design immediately, you then risk the finished item being too large or too small. This is because some individuals knit more tightly or loosely than others; by working a small sample first you can compare your own tension with that of the designer of the pattern.

Even if you find your knitting usually corresponds to the pattern tension, it is always worth checking because tensions can vary with different yarns or in different stitch patterns. It is even more important to check if you are not using the recommended yarn.

If the tension check gives 20 stitches and 35 rows to measure 10 x 10 cm (4 x 4 inches), cast on the required stitches plus a few extra. Knit at least 10 cm (4 inches) in the stitch pattern of the design.

Count the 20 stitches in the middle of your sample, marking them with pins. Lay a tape measure between the pins. If the stitches measure less than 10 cm (4 inches), the tension is too tight and you should make another sample with one size larger needles. If the stitches measure more than 10 cm (4 inches), you should try needles one size smaller. If these samples are not right, try again with needles of the next size up or down.

With simple-stitch patterns, the width measurement is more important than the length, because you are usually instructed to work to a specific length measurement and it should not matter how many rows this involves. However, with more complicated patterns, length is just as important.

Lay your sample on a flat surface and count out twenty stitches. Mark them with pins. Is the distance between them 10 cm (4 in.)?

HOME CRAFTS

BASIC PATTERNS

Garter stitch This is the pattern made by working knit stitch into every stitch on every row.

Stocking stitch This is one of the most common stitch patterns. Simply work the first and following alternate rows in knit stitch. Work the intervening rows in purl stitch. The right side of the fabric, which faces you when you are working in knit stitch, has interlocking V shapes.

Reverse stocking stitch In this pattern the reverse side of stocking stitch, which resembles garter stitch but is firmer, becomes the right side. Work rows of purl and knit stitches alternately, beginning with a purl row.

Single rib This is a very elastic stitch, ideal for cuffs, welts and neckbands. It can be worked on any number of stitches. Work knit stitch and purl stitch alternately across the row, bring the yarn forward before a purl stitch and take it back again for a knit stitch. On the second and following rows, work a knit stitch into each purl stitch, and purl stitch into each knit stitch of the previous row.

Moss stitch This is also worked by knitting and purling alternately across the row, but by knitting into each knitted stitch and purling each purled stitch of the previous row. The pattern is seeded and not stretchy.

Double rib For this stretchy pattern to work you must have a multiple of four stitches plus two extra in the row. In the first row, knit and purl two stitches alternately

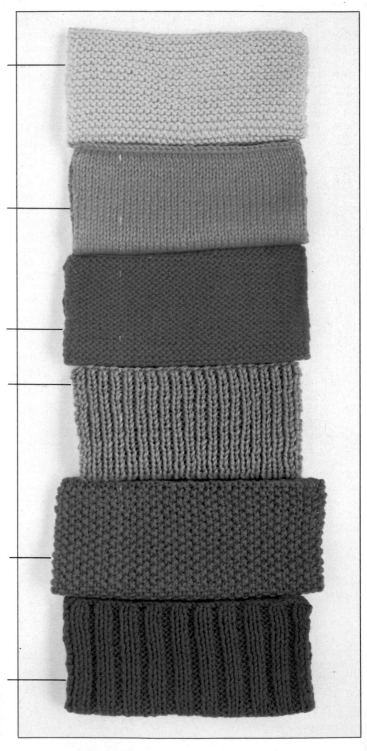

to the end. In the next row, do the same but begin with a purl. Repeat the two rows to make the pattern.

Stripes Working in stripes — horizontally or vertically — is an easy way of creating a pattern without complication. It is also a useful way of using up left-over yarns, providing they are all of similar thickness and so do not affect the tension.

The patterns can consist of regular-sized stripes, each with the same number of rows or stitches, or you could make a more random effect by varying the numbers.

For horizontal stripes, introduce the yarn for the stripe at the beginning of the row as if joining a new ball. You should do this at the beginning of a knit row for a smooth, unbroken line in stocking stitch.

You do not need to break off the old colour if you need it again in a few rows. Simply carry it up the side of the work and twist it round the last colour before using it. You can carry as many colours as wished up the side in this way.

Vertical stripes are best made with up to five stitches in each so that you can swap colours easily and carry the yarn between them across the back. Twist the yarns together before using the new one to avoid making a hole, and carry the colour not in use loosely across the back of the stripe being worked.

Embroidery Simple motifs, worked in embroidery stitches, such as blanket stitch, chain stitch or cross stitch, can be used most effectively to embellish plain knitting. Add them in yarn of similar type after the knitting is complete.

SHAPING

Shaping in knitting is often done by increasing or decreasing the number of stitches in use.

Simple increasing This is most easily worked in a knit stitch row, although it may be applied to purling. To make one extra stitch, knit into a stitch on the left-hand needle as usual but do not drop the loop. Insert the right-hand needle into the back of it and knit it again.

Multiple increasing This may be necessary at the beginning of a row. Simply cast on the required number of extra stitches, work back across them and continue on the old stitches to the end of the row.

Simple decreasing These methods may be worked at any point in a row. Because they form a slanting effect, choose the method to produce a slant in the desired direction to give a balanced effect on the garment.

To make a decrease which slants to the left on the right side in stocking stitch, slip the next stitch to be worked from the left-hand needle onto the right-hand needle without knitting it. Knit the next stitch, then, using the point of the left-hand needle, lift the slipped stitch over it and off the right-hand needle.

To make a decrease which slants to the right, simply insert the needle through the next two stitches and knit or purl them as if they were one.

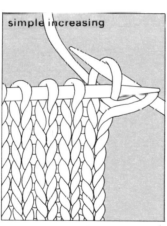

simple increasing

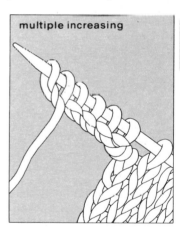

multiple increasing

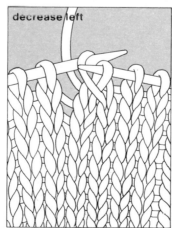

decrease left

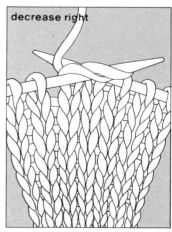

decrease right

HOME CRAFTS

FOLLOWING PATTERNS

Knitting patterns often include instructions for making a design in a choice of three or more sizes. These are body measurements and any necessary allowances for movement have been made by the designer. For an average garment, this is 5 cm (2 inches), although it might be less on a garment intended to be clingy and more on a garment intended for outdoor wear.

The instructions on multi-size patterns are given for the smallest size first, followed by the other sizes, which may be separated by strokes or brackets, so: cast on 22/24/28 stitches or 22 (24, 28) sts. To avoid confusion while working the pattern, read through it first and underline the correct figure for your size.

Always work the pattern pieces in the order instructed, as you may have to complete and then join pieces before continuing.

Patterns usually contain abbreviations to save space, and words preceded by asterisks or enclosed by brackets may be used to indicate a set of instructions which has to be repeated across a row or later on.

STANDARD ABBREVIATIONS	
alt alternate(ly)	p2sso pass 2 slipped stitches over
approx approximate(ly)	P up pick up and purl
beg begin(ning)	P-wise purlwise
cont continu(e/ing)	rem remain(ing)
dec decreas(e/ing)	rep repeat
DK double knitting	rev st st reverse stocking stitch
foll follow(ing)	RH right-hand
g st garter stitch	RS right side
inc increas(e/ing)	sl slip
K knit	sl st slip stitch
K up pick up and knit	st(s) stitch(es)
K-wise knitwise	st st stocking stitch
LH left-hand	tbl through back of loop(s)
M1 make 1	tog together
no. number	WS wrong side
P purl	ybk yarn back
patt pattern	yfwd yarn forward
psso pass slipped stitch over	yon yarn over needle
	yrn yarn round needle

JOINING ON NEW YARN

This should be done at the beginning of a row. If ending a ball of yarn, check that you have enough to complete the row — about four times the width. Leaving an end of 10 cm (4 inches) on the new ball, start the row with it. Cut the old end to the same length and darn both ends in later.

PICKING UP STITCHES

If you drop a stitch, do not leave it because it may become a ladder. Dropped stitches are picked up most easily on a knit-stitch row.

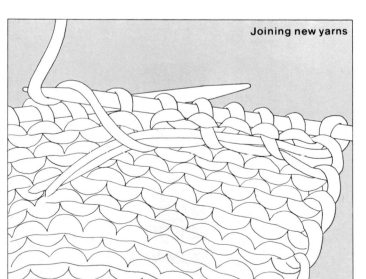

Joining new yarns

220

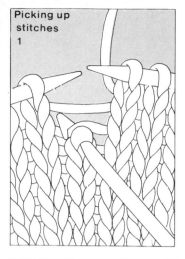

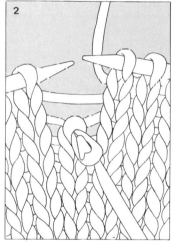

MAKING UP

Use matching yarn and a blunt-ended needle.

Seams along shoulders, sides and sleeves may be joined by backstitching. For seams in ribbing, such as on welts and cuffs, the seam is flatter if joined by oversewing the ridges together.

Try to match row ends and do not pull the yarn tightly.

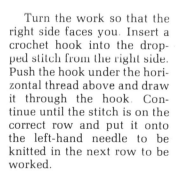

Turn the work so that the right side faces you. Insert a crochet hook into the dropped stitch from the right side. Push the hook under the horizontal thread above and draw it through the hook. Continue until the stitch is on the correct row and put it onto the left-hand needle to be knitted in the next row to be worked.

MEASURING

Use a rigid ruler and lay the knitting flat. Always measure depth in a straight line, parallel to the vertical line of stitches. Measure width by laying ruler along the rows.

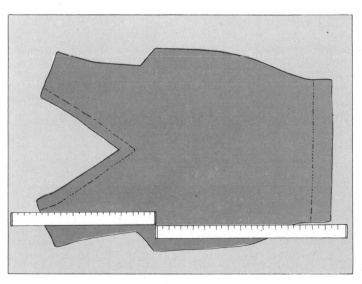

HOME CRAFTS

BASIC SEWING

EQUIPMENT
The type of equipment you need obviously depends on the type and amount of sewing you intend to do. For most basic tasks, including mending, you should have:
Packet of 'sharps' hand sewing needles in mixed sizes, to suit different yarns
Small, sharp scissors, used only for sewing
Thimble
Tape measure
Dressmaker's pins
Bodkin for threading elastic

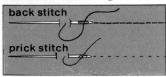

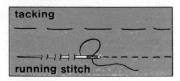

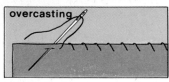

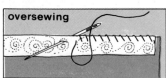

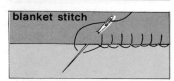

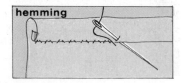

Sewing thread — you can, of course, buy this as you need it, but it is also useful to have some basic colours for emergencies, perhaps to match shirts, uniforms, dominant colours in wardrobes or household furnishings, towels etc.

Although you cannot anticipate what you will need for the next job, it often helps to save re-usable zips and buttons from old garments. You should also keep any fabric cut off altered garments and left-over yarn from knitting.

BASIC STITCHES
Hand sewing has not been superseded by today's elaborate sewing machines because in many cases it can be easier, and even quicker, to make simple repairs or do fiddly jobs by hand. The stitches described here are the most basic ones you will need for all types of sewing at home.

BACK STITCH
This is the hand stitch most like machine stitching and holds very firmly.

Insert the needle into the fabric at the starting point and bring it up 2–3 mm (⅛ inch) further along stitching line.

Re-insert needle at starting point and repeat step 1 twice to prevent thread from pulling through.

Re-insert needle at starting point and bring out 4–6 mm (¼ inch) further along.

Re-insert needle 2–3 mm (⅛ inch) behind, to meet previous stitch, and bring out 4-6 mm (¼ inch) ahead. Continue like this to the end.

Finish with three back stitches, as in the beginning.

PRICK STITCH
Use to insert zips by hand. Working from the right side of the fabric, work in a similar way to back stitch, but re-inserting the needle only two threads behind. The stitches will thus overlap underneath, but show as tiny dots on the right side.

TACKING
This is sometimes known as basting. It is a temporary stitch, used to hold the fabrics in place while machine stitching, pressing or fitting.

Use purpose-made tacking cotton thread, which is easy to remove, or oddments of sewing thread in a contrasting colour to your fabric. Start and finish stitching with a triple back stitch.

Weave needle in and out of fabric, following the required line, making even stitches and spaces about 15 mm (⅝ inch) long.

Remove tacking stitches when no longer required.

RUNNING STITCH
Use instead of back stitch where strength is not required (as in a run and fell seam), or for gathering.

Work like tacking but make stitches and spaces 2–3 mm (⅛ inch) long. Weave needle in and out of fabric, making several stitches, before pulling through the thread.

OVERCASTING
Work along raw edges of fabric to prevent fraying.

Start and finish by making three diagonal stitches in the same place over the edge.

Work along the edge, making evenly-spaced diagonal stitches over it. The stitches should be about 3 mm (⅛ inch) deep.

OVERSEWING

This is sometimes known as whip stitch. Use for joining edges, closing openings, and for applying trimmings. Work as overcasting, but making small, neat stitches over edge of trimming and into fabric below.

BLANKET STITCH

Use to neaten raw edges of woollen fabric.

Work as shown. Taking shallow and deep stitches alternately is another way to prevent the fabric fraying and curling.

HEMMING

Work as shown. To prevent hem showing through on the right side of the garment, lift hem edge so that stitches may be made on underside. Take a tiny stitch on main fabric and longer ones on hem. Do not pull stitches tight. Start and finish with stitches on hem, not on main fabric.

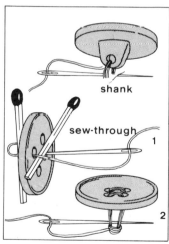

shank

sew-through

1

2

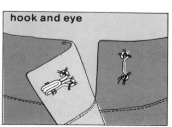

hook and eye

BUTTONS

With all but lightweight fabrics, buttons should have a shank between the button and the fabric to allow for the thickness of the overlap. Some buttons are made with a shank, or you can form one with the thread as you stitch the button on. Attach buttons with buttonhole twist in a colour to match your fabric.

Mark exact position of button and secure thread with three back stitches over the mark.

Shank buttons Pass needle through shank and make another stitch in the fabric in the same position. Repeat several times, taking care not to twist the button. Finish off with more back stitches into fabric.

Sew-through buttons Pass needle through one hole in button, lay a matchstick over button and stitch over the stick to second hole. Pass needle through fabric in position as before. Repeat several times until button is secure. If button has four holes, work stitches through the second set of holes as for the first. Remove matchstick, hold button away from fabric and form a shank by winding the thread around the stitches. Finish off with back stitches through the shank.

HOOKS AND EYES

Where the edges overlap, position the hook on the wrong side of the fabric, away from the edge. Align the eye on the underlap.

On abutting edges, position the eye loop to protrude by 2–3 mm (⅛ inch) and place the hook the same distance from the opposite edge.

Fix hook and eye to fabric with oversewing stitches

radiating around the holes. Work extra stitches over shank.

PRESS STUDS

Separate halves of stud and face ball section flat side down on wrong side of overlap fabric. Attach with three or four oversewing stitches in each hole, passing thread below stud between holes for neatness.

Locate position for socket on underlap fabric by inserting a pin through centres, and oversew as for the ball section.

NAME TABS

Leaving a 1 cm (⅜ inch) margin at the left-hand edge, write the name on the tape. Cut the tape leaving a 1 cm (⅜ inch) margin on the right.

Fold under 5 mm (¼ inch) at each edge of the tape. Place on the inside of the garment in an easily-seen position. Oversew firmly at each end. Woven name tapes can be attached in the same way.

HANGING LOOPS

Make loops with 7.5 cm (3 inch) of 1.5 cm (⅝ inch) width tape. Apply as for name tabs, in a suitable place for hanging the garment, oversewing it as firmly as possible.

press studs

HOME CRAFTS

SEAMS

A plain seam is the most usual way of joining one piece of fabric to another. It may be machine-stitched or back-stitched by hand.

The edges of the fabric should then be neatened to prevent fraying. There are various neatening methods for different fabrics and garments. Decide the finishing method before beginning the seam, as this may affect its construction.

1 Level together the edges of the fabric to be joined with right sides facing unless otherwise directed. Pin at the ends, at the centre, at any notches and then at 5 cm (2

inch) intervals in between. Tack along the stitching line.

2 If machine stitching, place fabric under the presser foot with the edges to the right, and lower the needle onto the stitching line about 15 mm (⅝ inch) from the back edge. Reverse stitch to edge and then stitch forward to opposite edge close to the side of the tacking. Reverse stitch for 15mm (⅝ inch) and cut threads.

If hand stitching, work along the tacking in back stitch, keeping the stitches even in size and tension.

3 Press the seam flat, as stitched. Then bring the fabric under it and open out the turnings; press again. Leave like this or close the turnings and press to one side, according to finishing method.

Joining straight fabric to a curved edge Prepare straight edge by stay stitching (see page 229) outside seam. Clip the edge, up to the stitching, at 2 cm (¾ inch) intervals. Pin the straight strip to the curve,

allowing the clips to open out on outward curves or to overlap on inward curves. Machine stitch.

Joining straight fabric to an angle

Measure the edge of the angled piece along the seamline. Mark the same measurement on the straight strip.

Stay stitch the seamline for 2.5 cm (1 inch) on either side of the mark and then clip to the mark from the edge.

Pin the straight strip to the angled piece, allowing the clip to open as it turns the corner.

Stitch the first edge of the seam as far as the mark, leave the machine needle down and turn the work to stitch the second side.

Joining a concave edge to a convex edge Stay stitch seam lines and clip the concave edge. Stitch the seam and press open.

FINISHING METHODS

For simple finishes, the edges

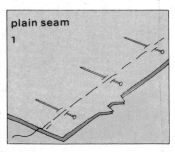

plain seam
1

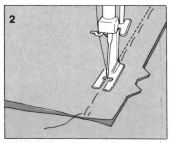

2

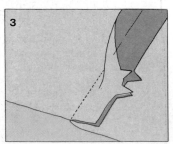

3

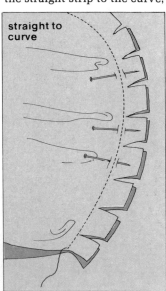

straight to curve

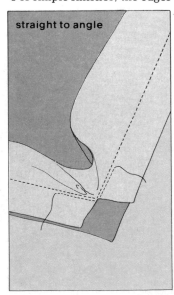

straight to angle

of the seam allowances may be stitched and pinked; zigzagged; turned under for 3 mm (⅛ inch) and then stitched; blanket-stitched or overcast.

French seam This is a good seam finish for fine fabrics and for items frequently washed, such as blouses, nightwear and pillowcases. The edges are completely enclosed.

Make a plain seam, placing the fabric edges with wrong sides together; stitch, taking *half* the total seam allowance. Press as stitched.

Trim the edges to 5 mm (¼ inch) of the stitching and press the seam open.

Turn the fabric right side out and fold along the line of the seam. Baste and stitch along the stitching line. Press as stitched.

Machine fell seam This is a strong flat finish, suitable for shirts and sports clothes.

Make a plain seam and press the turnings flat to one side of the stitching.

Trim the under-seam allowance to half the original width and fold under the edge of the upper allowance for 3 mm (⅛ inch). Pin down to the main fabric, over the trimmed edge, and tack and machine stitch close to the fold through all thicknesses.

Note: to make this seam with two rows of machine stitching on the right side, as for jeans, make the first seam with the wrong sides of fabric together.

Run and fell seam This is a flat seam finish suitable for baby clothes.

Work as for a machine fell seam, using running stitch to form the first seam and oversewing for the second stage.

GATHERING
Gathering may be worked by hand in running stitch or by using a long machine stitch. For a wide area of gathering, divide the edge in quarters and mark in the same way the piece to which the gathering is to be joined.

Work two rows of gathering stitches 3 mm (⅛ inch) each side of the seamline, leaving the ends loose. Repeat on each section.

Pin the edges together, matching right sides and divisions. Start to pull up the gathering threads from one end by holding the threads together and moving the fabric away from them until the gathering is tight enough to fit the opposite edge.

Arrange the gathers so they are evenly spaced across the width and secure the threads by winding a figure eight around a pin.

Baste and machine stitch along the seamline, keeping the gathered side facing up to avoid puckering.

Press carefully with the point of an iron. Pull out the gathering threads.

MAKING A FRILL
A frill is simple to make from a straight strip of fabric or from a purpose-made edging, such as broderie anglaise or lace, which needs no hem. The desired length should be 1½-2 times the length of the edge to which it is to be attached. Add on seam and hem allowances. If the frill is a shallow one in fine fabric, it is easier to make it in double fabric so that you do not need a hem along the outer edge. Fold the fabric double with right side out and treat the layers as one for the gathering process.

Finish by trimming the turning of the gathered edge to within 3 mm (⅛ inch) of stitching. Fold under flat edge and stitch to seamline.

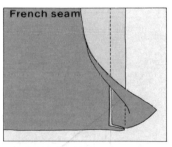
French seam

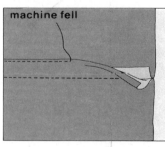
machine fell

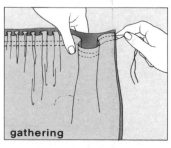
gathering

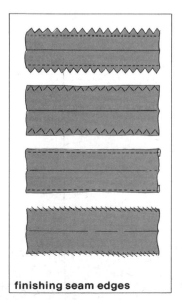
finishing seam edges

225

HOME CRAFTS

BINDING

This is a strong seam finish ideal for woollens, unlined jackets, etc. It can also be used on exposed edges such as armholes and necklines, or as an alternative to a hem. Binding may either match or contrast with the main fabric.

Use straight seam binding or straight edges and pre-folded bias binding — which is more flexible on curves.

Straight binding Cut to required length. Fold binding over edge with slightly more underneath than above. Tack and machine stitch along edge through all layers.

Bias binding Do not cut to length. Unfold one edge, place on fabric with right sides together, stretching it slightly on inward curves and easing it on outward curves.

Tack and machine stitch along binding fold line. Turn binding to wrong side of fabric and place the second fold to line of stitching. Tack and machine stitch or oversew through all layers.

Making your own binding To cut bias strips, fold a piece of fabric diagonally so that the selvedge lies parallel with the weft. Press the fold lightly with your fingers, taking care not to stretch it.
1-2 Unfold the fabric and, using a ruler, chalk along the crease line. Mark successive lines 4 cm (1½ inches) away from this and cut along them to form the strips.
3 To join the strips, cut the ends on the straight grain slanting the same way. With right sides together, place the ends as shown and stitch 5 mm (¼ inch) from edge.
4 Press seam turnings open;

trim off protruding corners.

Apply in a similar way to bought bias binding, stitching 10 mm (⅜ inch) from the edge in the first stage and folding under the same amount before stitching the second stage.

At internal corners, clip fabric at an angle and open out so that binding can be applied in a straight line. At external corners, fold the binding diagonally at the angle so it continues at 90° to the first edge. After stitching turn binding to the reverse side of fabric, mitring the fullness neatly at the corners.

MAKING PIPING

Piping is made by enclosing cord in a bias strip which is then sandwiched into a seam to give a ridged decorative appearance. It also adds strength to seams subject to

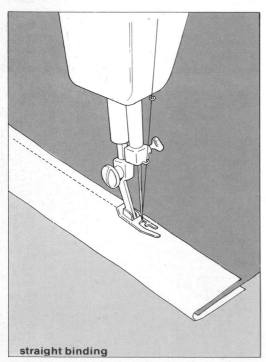
straight binding

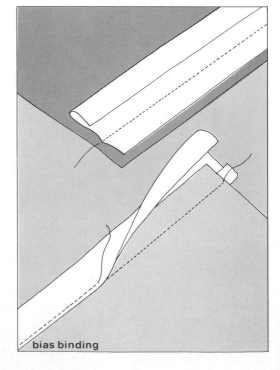
bias binding

continual chafing, as in loose covers.

Purpose-made cord is sold for piping and varies from quite a fine diameter for clothing to very thick for furnishing. It is always wise to pre-wash the cord before making up as it is liable to shrink. Cut the bias strips wide enough to wrap round the cord and give a seam allowance along both edges.

Apply the bias strip to the edge as for the first stage in binding. Lay the cord along the centre and fold over the free edge of the strip to lie level with the first edge. If the piping is to be enclosed in a seam, lay the next layer, right side down, on top. Pin, placing the pins at right-angles to the edge.

Fit the piping foot to your machine so that the needle is to the left. Machine stitch through all thicknesses, keeping the needle as close to the edge of the cord as possible.

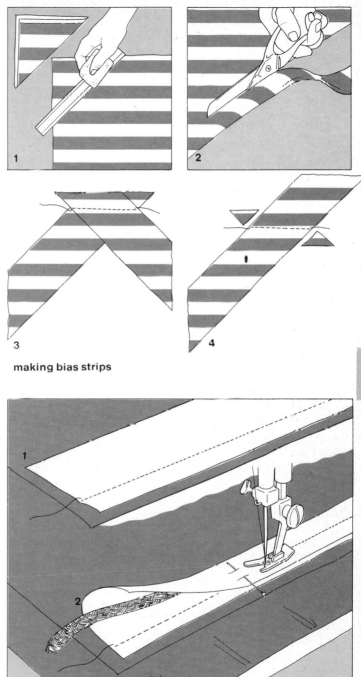

making bias strips

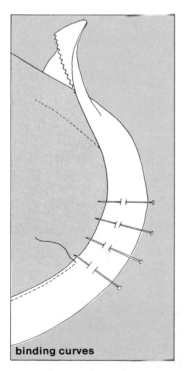

binding curves

piping

HOME CRAFTS

DRESSMAKING

EQUIPMENT

A sewing machine is really a necessity for dressmaking. You can, of course, make entirely hand-stitched clothes, but it takes so much longer. If you are buying a sewing machine, spend time researching the various makes by asking friends and looking in shops. A swing-needle machine is certainly more useful than one with only straight stitch. But consider carefully whether you can justify the high cost of an elaborate machine with several embroidery stitches if basically all you need is plain sewing.

Do ask for a demonstration of buttonholing — the technique varies with the machine and it *should* be easy. You should also try lifting the machine and remember to check on easy availability of spare needles, bobbins, bulbs and other accessories. Make sure the machine has an adequate instruction book and spend time reading it and practising stitches before attempting a garment.

Other equipment As well as the items listed on page 222, you will need good dressmaker's shears for cutting out, tailor's chalk for marking fabric, a seam ripper and a piping foot for your machine.

FABRICS

There is such a wide variety of fabrics available for home dressmaking that it helps to know a few facts before buying.

Fabrics may be made from natural fibres, such as cotton, wool, silk or linen, or from synthetic fibres such as nylon, polyester or acrylic, or from combinations of the two. With any of these yarns, the fabrics fall into two main categories, woven or knitted, according to their construction.

Knits are stretchier than wovens and should be stitched with a synthetic thread which has a similar stretch to prevent seams and hems from popping. Knits should be stitched with ball-pointed needles which do not pierce the yarns. Choose threads for stitching wovens by fibre: silk thread for silks; cotton for cotton, wool and linen; polyester thread for synthetics.

When buying fabric always ask for the fibre content, as this will affect the garment you make, the way you sew it, and washing and pressing.

PATTERNS

Apart from a few very simple items, it is always worth buying a paper pattern for the garment you wish to make. Patterns for children and men as well as for women come in a range of sizes and designs which are updated every season and can be seen in shop catalogues.

Paper patterns are sold by body measurement — assumed to be taken over underclothes — and they are cut with allowances for comfort and movement in the same way as ready-manufactured clothes.

Choose the size that most nearly corresponds to the one you require, basing it on the bust or chest measurement for shirts, blouses or dresses, or on the hip measurement for skirts and trousers. Other measurements can be altered to fit if necessary.

If you are new to dressmaking, choose a pattern marked 'simple' or 'easy'. The instructions will be straightforward with clear diagrams for each step.

Make up the pattern in one of the fabric types suggested for the design on the pattern envelope. Choosing the wrong fabric for a style is one of the most common problems in home dressmaking.

TERMS AND TIPS

The instruction sheet given with patterns is usually very clear, but it may contain unfamiliar terms. Here are some of the most common ones.

Basting Tacking stitches, see page 222.

Bias Any line running diagonally across the woven threads. Fabric cut 'on the bias' is more stretchy than fabric 'cut on the straight grain'.

Bodkin A large-eyed, blunt-ended needle used to thread elastic, etc. through casings.

Clipping curves Method of making curved seams smooth. Using sharp scissors, cut from raw edge to within one thread of stitching. On inward curves the clips may be triangular to reduce bulk.

Crosswise threads The weft threads of woven fabrics which run from selvedge to selvedge.

Dart A triangular tuck taken in fabric to give shaping.

Ease Slight gathering.

Facing Shaped section, found inside a garment, stitched on to finish an edge.

Grading Trimming seam allowances to different widths where several layers have been stitched together to reduce bulk.

Grain The lengthwise or warp threads on woven fabrics.

Interfacing Special fabric used inside collars, cuffs, etc. to give body and stiffness. It is made in a variety of weights to suit different fabrics and should always be bought with the fabric to ensure correct type.

Nap A soft surface on fabric.

Pile The raised surface of fabrics like velvet. Pile must lie in one direction on all sections of a garment or the colour appears different.

Seam allowance The amount of fabric left between the seamline and the raw edge. It is usually 1.5 cm (⅝ inch).

Seam line The line along which the stitching is to be worked. It is marked on paper patterns but need not be transferred to fabric.

Stay stitching Stitching on a single thickness of fabric along the seamline to prevent stretching.

Top stitching 'Show' stitching worked from the right side of fabric, usually through several layers.

Trimming seams This is done after stitching to reduce bulk and make curves smoother: cut seam allowances to within 5 mm (¼ inch) of stitching.

HOME CRAFTS

MARKING
Paper pattern pieces have several construction marks which are usually indicated by dots for darts, gathering, etc. These marks need to be transferred accurately onto the fabric and in a way that marks both layers of fabric simultaneously. This may be done by making tailor's tack stitches or by using a tracing wheel and dressmaker's carbon paper, obtainable from haberdashers.

Tailor's tacks **1** Using thread in a contrasting colour, make a single back stitch through the pattern and all layers of fabric underneath at every dot. Cut thread and loop after each stitch, leaving long ends.
2 Unpin the pattern and lift it off carefully so that the stitches pull out of the paper but stay in the fabric. Slowly separate the layers of fabric, cutting through the threads of

the tacks as you reach them. You are then left with little tufts of thread which are easily removed when the garment is finished.

Tracing wheel and carbon Use a shade of paper either lighter or darker than the fabric and practise on spare fabric first. To mark a dart on two pieces of fabric with right sides together, use a strip of paper slightly wider and twice as long as the dart. Fold the strip in half widthwise with the coated sides together.

Place one end under the bottom layer of fabric and one between the fabric and pattern, removing any obstructing pins.

Mark by rolling the wheel away from you, over the centre and outside lines of the dart, using a ruler as a guide for straightness. Mark the end of the dart and other dots with intersecting lines.

FORMING DARTS
Fold the fabric, with right sides together, along the centre line of the dart so that the dots on opposite sides correspond. Baste along a line joining the dots and check for fit before finally stitching.

Work the final stitching from the wide end to the point, cutting off the threads with 5 cm (2 inch) ends. Tie them firmly in a double knot and trim the excess.

Press the dart to lie in the direction indicated on the pattern.

BUTTONHOLES
On light and medium weight fabrics buttonholes may be stitched by hand or machine. On heavier weight fabrics buttonholes are best made by binding, as this prevents fraying. For any method, practise on a piece of leftover fabric from the garment and check the size of the but-

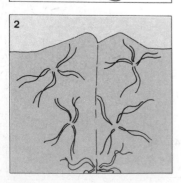
tailor's tacks
1
2

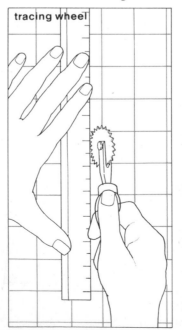
tracing wheel

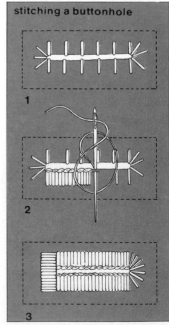
stitching a buttonhole
1
2
3

230

tonhole by inserting the button.

Never make buttonholes before you have bought the buttons. The fabric should always be interfaced to strengthen and maintain the buttonhole's shape.

Stitched buttonholes should be worked through all layers of the garment — top, interfacing and facing — but bound buttonholes should be started on the top and interfacing layers and finished after the facing has been applied.

Machine-stitched buttonholes
Mark buttonhole positions but do not cut. Work the stitching, carefully following your machine instructions. Slit the holes with a seam ripper.

Buttonhole stitch Use to make slit or loop buttonholes or to finish cut edges.
1 Working from left to right, insert needle through back of fabric 2–3 mm (⅛ inch) from edge. Before pulling through, form a loop by bringing thread from needle under point. Pull forward into a small knot on the edge. Do not pull too tightly.
2 Work following stitches closely, but not so tightly that the edge wrinkles.

Hand-stitched buttonholes
Use regular sewing thread for light-weight fabrics and button twist for medium weights.
1 Mark all the buttonholes but do not cut until just before you are ready to work.
2/3 Overcast edges of the slit. Beginning at the lower inside end, work along the slit in buttonhole twist. At the outside end work straight stitches in a fan shape, then continue buttonholing along the opposite edge. Work buttonhole stitches across the inside end in a bar shape.

For vertical buttonholes, work a bar at both ends.

Bound buttonholes For each buttonhole cut a bias rectangle 5 cm (2 inches) wide x 4 cm (1½ inches) longer than the buttonhole.
1 Centre the rectangle over the buttonhole position with right sides together. Machine stitch a rectangle to finished size of buttonhole.
2 Cut along the centre of the rectangle and into each corner, taking care not to cut stitching.
3 Poke fabric through slit to the wrong side so that it forms a binding on the front; roll the edges of the binding to meet and oversew them.
4 On the wrong side, arrange the fabric to form an inverted pleat at each end of the buttonhole; oversew in place.
5 After attaching the facing, baste it to the main fabric around each buttonhole. Slit the facing in line with the buttonhole, turn under the edges and hem down neatly.

Loop buttonholes Mark ends of loop. Secure thread at top, take tiny stitch at bottom, leaving required loop. Repeat, working back. Buttonhole stitch over loops.

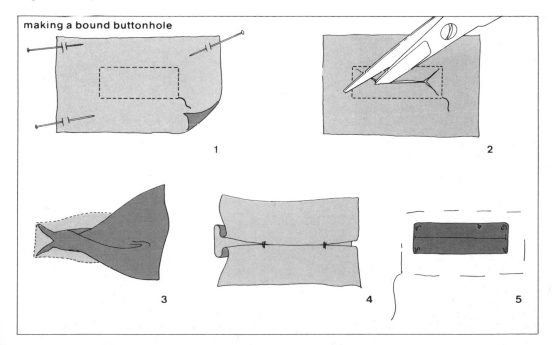

making a bound buttonhole

1

2

3

4

5

HOME CRAFTS

REPAIRS AND ALTERATIONS

Even if you are not a dress-maker, it is useful to be able to repair or alter your clothes. Many jobs can be done either by hand sewing or machine, and you do not need much equipment apart from that described on page 222. For darning, however, you will require a darning mushroom and a darning needle.

UNPICKING

Mending and altering usually involves careful unpicking of existing stitching to avoid damaging the fabric. Use either small, sharp-pointed scissors or a seam ripper. Insert the point of the ripper or scissors under a stitch and cut the thread. You can then insert the point under the next stitch and pull the thread loose. Continue for about 2.5 cm (1 inch) and then try pulling the thread through the remaining stitches as if drawing up gathering. If this does not work, you will have to go along the row cutting stitches at 2.5 cm (1 inch) intervals.

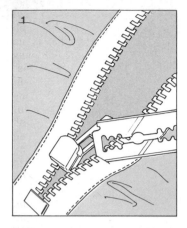

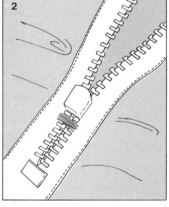

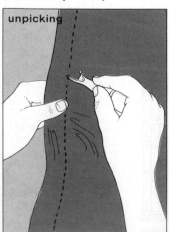

unpicking

Pull out any tufts of remaining thread between cuts.

REPAIRING ZIPS

This can be done if the slider is not catching the teeth on one side of the zip. It reduces the zip length by about 1.5 cm (½ inch).

1 With a sharp razor blade, carefully cut the zip tape 1 cm (⅜ inch) from the bottom of the zip on the appropriate side. Lower the slider on the opposite side until level with the slit and insert the tape above the slit into the slider (as if fixing an open-ended zip).

2 Close the zip in the usual way. Work oversewing stitches across the teeth just above the slit to act as a stop for the slider when opening the zip.

REPLACING ZIPS

This has to be done when a zip cannot be repaired.

To remove the old zip, use small pointed scissors and

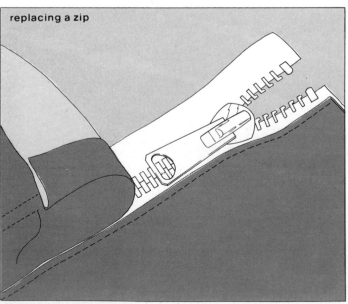

replacing a zip

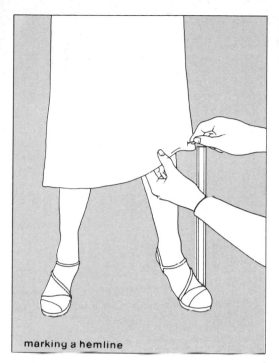

marking a hemline

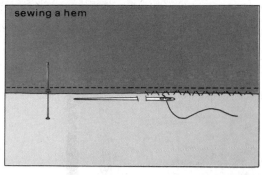

sewing a hem

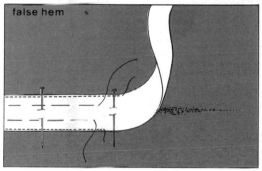

false hem

carefully unpick the stitches. On skirts and trousers you may have to unpick some of the waistband in order to free the tape at the top. Note how any facing layers and flies are attached as you work.

When the zip is out, straighten and measure it along the length of the teeth only to learn its size.

Pin the new zip in position as it was for the old one, tucking the tapes into the waistband and ensuring that it is facing right side out. Tack firmly, then fix the facings and flies. Machine stitch, using a zip foot, or prick stitch by hand, following the original stitching line. Stitch down the waistband neatly.

ALTERING HEMLINES
Whether you are lengthening or shortening the garment, first unpick the stitches holding the original hem. Carefully press the fabric flat. Try on the garment, wearing the appropriate shoes.

The new hemline is most easily marked by someone else holding a rigid ruler. Decide the required level of the hemline and mark with a pin. Measure the distance from the floor and turn slowly so that pins may be inserted all around the garment at the same height.

Take off the garment and turn up the hem along the pinned line. Tack along the fold. Decide how deep you wish the hem turning to be and mark with pins. For a child it is worth having up to 10 cm (4 inches) or even more to allow for growth. For an adult about 4–5 cm (1½–2 inches) is appropriate. Cut off any surplus.

If you have let the hem down and there is less than 2.5 cm (1 inch) for the turning, you can make a false hem with tape as described below. Or if there is no room at all for a turning, you could bind the edge (see page 226).

Alternatively, neaten the raw edge by one of the me-

thods described on page 225, and tack it to the main fabric. If the edge is fuller than the main fabric it will not lie flat unless you make tiny darts at intervals.

Hem edge in position.

FALSE HEM
This can be made with straight or bias tape. If there is almost no hem turning at all, use bias tape 2.5 cm (1 inch) wide.

If using straight tape place one edge over the hem edge for 3mm (⅛ inch). Tack and back stitch or machine stitch. Keeping the hem and tape flat, hem the free edge of tape to the main fabric.

If using bias tape, unfold one edge of the tape and place to hem edge with right sides together. Machine or back stitch along foldline. Turn tape right side out, keeping it flat on the main fabric. Hem along the opposite fold.

To finish off, press hem on wrong side.

HOME CRAFTS

MAKING A PATCH

A patch is the best way of mending a hole in non-knitted fabrics. A rectangular or oval patch can be inserted behind the hole for neatness. A patch in a decorative shape can be applied over the hole.

If you wish the patch to be as inconspicuous as possible, cut the fabric for it from a facing, hem or pocket of the garment, matching the direction of weave and any pattern. Otherwise you could use contrasting fabric of appropriate weight or buy a decorative patch. Leather patches can be used for elbows on jackets and coats, and denim ones are available for jeans, etc.

Inset patches Decide the shape of the patch and mark the area on the item, leaving a good margin round it. Cut out the area, leaving 1 cm (⅜ inch) fabric inside the tacked marking line.

Cut the patch to shape, making it 5 mm (¼ inch) larger all around than the marked area. Turn this 5 mm (¼ inch) to the right side.

Now place the patch, right side facing out, in position on the wrong side of the garment. Tack and back or machine stitch around the edge.

On the right side of the garment, fold under the edges for 5 mm (¼ inch), clipping into curves and angles. Stitch the folded edges to the patch.

Applied patch If making your own patch, cut it to the required size, leaving no margin for turnings. Place the patch, right side facing out, over the hole on the right side of the garment. Tack, then zigzag or blanket stitch around the edges.

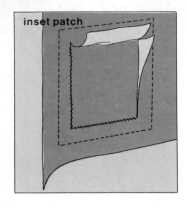

inset patch

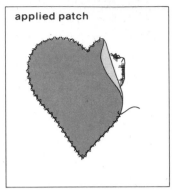

applied patch

MENDING TEARS

One of the simplest ways to do this is with a piece of iron-on fabric made for this purpose. Following the manufacturer's instructions for heat settings, place the iron-on fabric on to the wrong side of the fabric behind the tear and iron it in position.

DARNING

You will need a darning needle and mushroom plus yarn to match the item being mended.

Place the mushroom under the hole and hold the mushroom stem in your non-stitching hand. Starting at the top right hand corner, about 1 cm (⅜ inch) from the hole, work close rows of running stitch up and down the fabric, turning them 1 cm (⅜ inch) below the hole and moving progressively towards it.

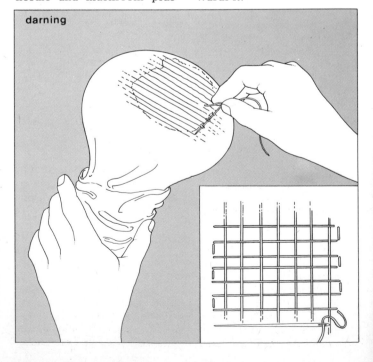

darning

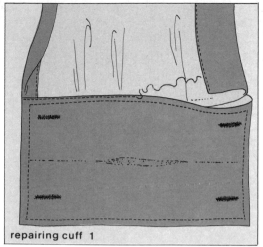

repairing cuff 1

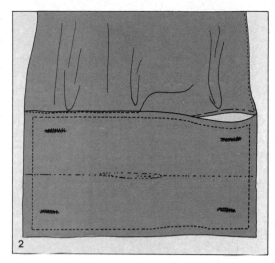

2

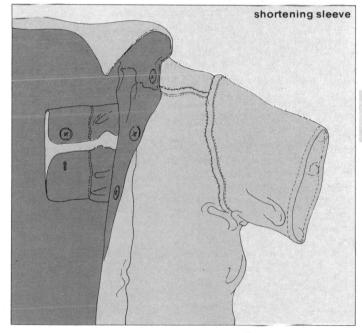

shortening sleeve

When you reach the hole, lay the yarn flat across it and continue in running stitch on the other side. When the hole is filled in, work running stitch on the left-hand side to match the right.

Work in a similar way from right to left, weaving the yarn in and out of the strands covering the hole. Never pull the yarn tight. Finish with a few extra running stitches at right angles to the last row worked.

TURNING FRAYED COLLARS AND CUFFS

This method can't be used for collars with stiffeners or for cuffs fastened by buttons unless you make a new buttonhole on the opposite edge.

1 Carefully unpick the cuff or collar from the garment, noting how it was attached. Turn it over so that the 'good' side will show when worn. Keeping the edges of the collar or cuff turned in, insert the edge of the garment between the layers of the collar or cuff and pin and stitch along the original lines. Refold and press carefully.

2 If the cuff fastens with a button, make the new buttonhole on the appropriate side.

Close the old buttonhole with neat oversewing and sew the button in the correct position over it.

SHORTENING SLEEVES

If the sleeves have a plain hem, follow the general method for shortening garments on page 233. If they have a cuff, the simplest way to shorten them without removing the cuff is to take a tuck halfway up. Two tucks,

about 2.5 cm (1 inch) apart, can be made for growing children, so that one may be unpicked before the other.

With the wrong side of the garment facing out, fold the sleeve back into the armhole until the underarm seam measures about 5 cm (2 inches). Straighten the fold neatly and stitch around the sleeve half the required shortening amount from it.

Turn to right side. Press.

235

HOME CRAFTS

MAKING CLOTHES FIT
The way clothes fit obviously depends on their style and construction, but the principles described here apply in most cases.

DARTS AND SEAMS
You can take in all garments by increasing the amount of fabric taken at the seams or other shaping areas such as darts, tucks, pleats or gathers. To let out garments reduce the amount taken at these places. Unfortunately on many modern manufactured garments, this may present a problem because the amount allowed for seams is so small.

As well as the affected seams or darts, you may have to unpick and remove a waistband or seam joining a skirt to a bodice to give access to the area. You may also have to remove zip fasteners. These can all be re-inserted after the alteration.

BALANCE
The alteration must not affect the balance of the garment. The total amount to be let in or out should be halved between the left and right hand sides so that the centre front or back lines are not moved. If you alter a dart at the left front, you must alter one on the right front to correspond.

If you alter darts or seams on a skirt, you will probably also have to adjust the bodice of a dress or waistband.

Gussets If you cannot let out seams enough, particularly at underarms or at the waist, you could insert a triangular gusset of matching fabric.

Decide how much you wish to let out. Cut a triangle to fit, plus 1 cm (⅜ inch) seam allowance all round.

Unpick the seam to be altered to the required depth and open it out by the re-

quired amount. Place the triangle under the opening and tack and stitch neatly in place.

If altering the underarm seam of a bodice, repeat the process on the sleeve seam and then resew the sleeve to the bodice.

If altering the seams on a skirt or trousers, increase the waistband as described below and resew the waistband in place.

WAISTBANDS
Alterations to seams and darts will also affect the waistband. Turn the waistband inside out at the underlap end, removing any hooks and eyes, to see its construction. To reduce the length you can usually sew the required distance from the end. To increase length you may have to join on a piece at the end. If you are lucky, the new piece may form the underlap of the opening.

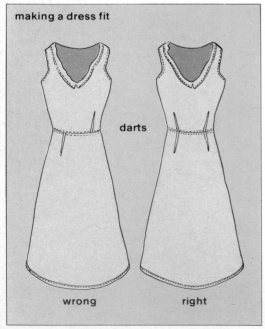

making a dress fit

darts

wrong   right

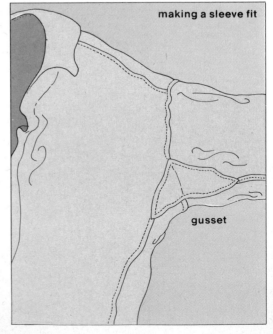

making a sleeve fit

gusset

HOME CRAFTS

HOME FURNISHING

Home furnishings, such as curtains, cushions and bedspreads are often simpler to make than clothes because they are usually made from rectangles cut to measure and then seamed and hemmed. The two most critical factors are the choice of fabric and the accuracy of the measurements for the item being made.

For the best, long-lasting results, always use soft furnishing — not dressmaking — fabric of a type specified for the item (curtains, bedspreads, loose covers, upholstery, etc). A good quality curtain fabric should not fade, rot or shrink and it should give several years' wear as curtains, but if you use it for loose covers the result may not be as good.

British-made furnishing fabrics are mostly 120 cm (48 inches) wide (net curtains are the main exception), but the width of imported fabrics may vary considerably. Patterned fabrics have a specified repeat size for their design, so that a particular motif, for example, is repeated at regular intervals down the length. They are also carefully designed so that the pattern along one edge will match the edge of another piece when seamed together.

Before you can buy your fabric, you must know both its width (preferably less the borders which form the selvedges) and the size of the pattern repeat, in order to be able to calculate how much to buy.

Start by taking the overall measurements — described on the next pages in detail

under the appropriate item — and note them down. In many cases you may have to join the fabric to make it wide enough, which may also involve careful pattern matching at seams. Or you may be making cushion covers and need to know how many you can cut from a width of fabric.

If possible, make two visits to the fabric shop. On the first visit, choose the fabric, learn its measurements, and try to take a sample home to check the colour before you calculate quantities. Buy the fabric on the second visit. If only one visit is possible, allow as much time as you can and take with you all the measurements you need, plus the formulae here for calculating quantities. Choose your fabric and then go away and quietly work things out before buying.

Never rely on the shop to do it for you because if they make a mistake it will be at your expense.

CALCULATING FABRIC QUANTITIES

Wide items Measure the fabric width, less the borders. Divide this figure into the width of the item, rounding up the answer to a whole figure. This gives the number of fabric widths required.

If using patterned fabric, divide the repeat (motif) length into the length of the item, rounding up to a whole figure. Multiply this figure by the pattern repeat to give the total length of fabric you must allow for each width to match the pattern at seams. You will be trimming off the excess length.

Multiply the total length by the number of widths required to give the amount of fabric to buy.

Narrow items Divide the fabric width by the item width. If this gives the number you require, then simply buy a length of fabric equal to the length of the item.

Otherwise, divide the number given into the required number; multiply the answer by the length of the item to give the amount of fabric to buy.

LAYOUTS

If you are dealing with several rectangles of different sizes, the only sure way to calculate the total amount is by making a chart. If it helps you could even do it to scale, using graph paper. Keep your layout for reference when cutting out.

Draw and then cut out a shape to the same scale for each section of the item. Label the shapes and mark their dimensions.

On another piece of paper, draw two parallel lines to represent the fabric width. Arrange the shapes closely on this layout with their length measurements parallel to the lines.

Measure the length of the layout used, and convert back in scale to give the total amount of fabric required.

CUTTING OUT

If you are cutting out rectangles, whether for cushions or curtains, they must be on the straight grain. All lengthwise edges should be cut parallel to the selvedges and widthwise edges at 90° to the selvedges.

Check that the first cut

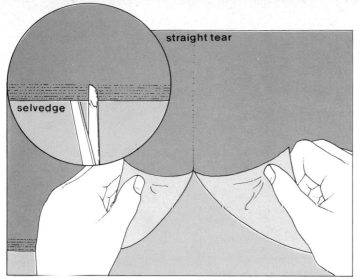

straight tear

selvedge

chalk

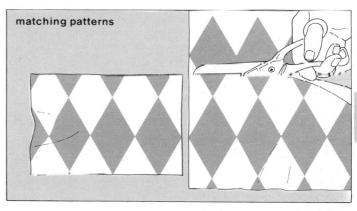

matching patterns

edge is straight, either by snipping the selvedge and tearing the fabric across to the other edge, or by pulling out a weft thread completely to the opposite edge. Or you could align a set square along the selvedge, place a long ruler against it across the width and draw along the line with chalk. Cut along this line.

Measure the length of your first rectangle from this line, using the selvedge as a guide, and cut across the width using the same method as for the top edge.

To match the pattern for the next rectangle, lay the first piece out flat and fold under the selvedge on one side. Place the folded edge over the selvedge of the uncut fabric, adjusting it until the pattern matches from one piece to the next. Cut off any excess fabric at the top edge of the second piece. Then measure your length for the second piece and cut the bottom edge. Cut subsequent pieces in the same way.

JOINING THE PIECES

Have the edges in the same position as for pattern matching when cutting out. Tack them together from the right side by alternately inserting the needle along the fold on one piece and then making an ordinary stitch alongside the fold on the other piece. You can then stitch them on the wrong side in the usual way.

AVOIDING A CENTRE SEAM

On flat items, such as a roller blind, bedspread or table-cloth, a centre seam can be very ugly. To avoid it, when using two fabric widths, cut one piece in half lengthwise. Join the selvedges of the halved piece to the selvedges of the other piece, then trim off any excess width equally from each cut edge.

On patterned fabrics, if

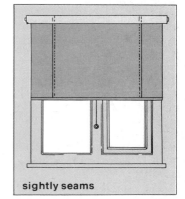

sightly seams

you match the design one hundred per cent accurately, the seamlines will hardly be noticeable. On plain fabrics you can disguise the lines made by the seams by covering them with coloured braid or ric-rac binding.

HOME CRAFTS

CURTAINS

Curtain making is simplified by the use of drawstring tapes to form the curtain head into gathers or pleats and, if you want lined curtains, by detachable linings.

Taking measurements Take all measurements from your curtain track. For the width of the curtains:

Measure the track from end to end. Divide by the number of curtains required. If you wish the curtains to overlap add 5 cm (2 inches) to each for the finished width.

Decide on the type of heading you want and multiply the finished width by 1.5 for simple gathers, by 2 for pinch pleats or by 2.5 for pencil pleats.

To give the total width, add 10 cm (4 inches) for hems along each side edge.
For the length:

If you wish the curtains to cover the track when closed, measure from just above the track down to the required length, i.e. sill, just below sill or to floor. If you wish the track to remain exposed, measure from just below it to the required length.

To give the total length, add 2.5 cm (1 inch) for a turning at the top and 15 cm (6 inches) for a hem at the bottom.

Fabric quantities Calculate how much fabric is required for one curtain following the method above. Multiply this by the number of curtains being made to give the amount of fabric you need to buy.

Tape Subtract 7.5 cm (3 inches) from the total width of each curtain to give the length of heading tape needed per curtain. Multiply by the number of curtains being made to give the amount to buy.

Lining Calculate the amount of lining fabric in a similar way to the amount of cur-

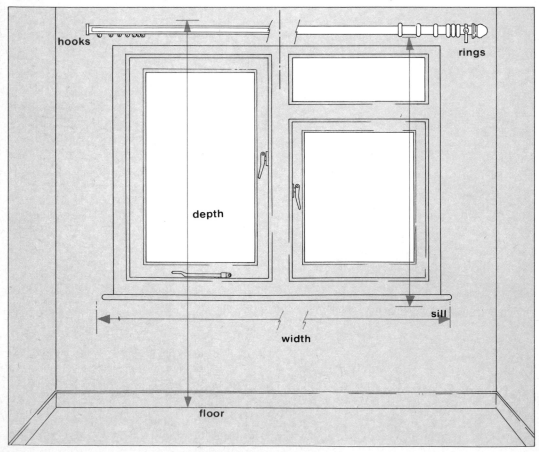

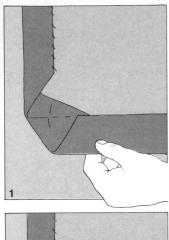

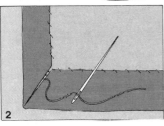

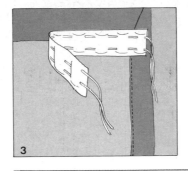

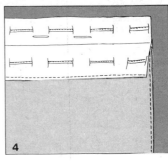

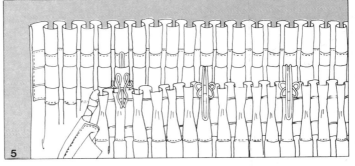

tain fabric, multiplying the finished width by 1.5 and adding 10 cm (4 inches) to give the total width and 10 cm (4 inches) to the measured length to give the total length.

For the lining tape, buy a piece equal to the total width of each lining per curtain.

Making up the curtains Cut out and join the fabric for each curtain as described. Repeat for the linings.

Make double hems along the side edges of each curtain by folding the selvedges to the wrong side for 2.5 cm (1 inch) and then again for the same amount. Press lightly.

Make a double hem along the bottom, folding up 7.5 cm (3 inches) each time. Press lightly.

1 Mitre the bottom corners by unfolding the hems and refolding diagonally as shown so that the new folds intersect the old ones. Refold the remaining portion of the sides and bottom hems as before.

2 Stitch the hems down by hemming or machine stitching.

Fold the turning along the top edge to the wrong side for 2.5 cm (1 inch). Check that the length of the curtains is correct and adjust the amount of the top turning if necessary. Baste the turning in position.

3 Pull out the drawstrings from the heading tape for 2.5 cm (1 inch) at each end. Knot the strings together at one end but leave them free at the other. Fold under the ends of tape for 2 cm (¾ inch).

4 Place the heading tape in position on the wrong side of the curtain about 5 mm (¼ inch) from the top and side edges (this amount may be increased for plain gathered headings). Baste the tape to the curtain along both edges.

Insert a few curtain hooks and hang the curtain from the track to check length and the position of the tape. Make any adjustments and machine stitch the tape to the top edge of the curtain.

Pull up the unknotted drawstrings until the curtain is the correct width. Arrange the gathers or pleats evenly and knot the strings together. Do not cut off the excess length as you may wish to release the heading when the curtains are taken down for cleaning.

Make the linings in a similar way, but before turning the side hems insert the unfolded top edge between the layers of the lining tape and machine stitch. Pull out the drawstrings for 5 cm (2 inches) at one end and fold under the tape ends with the side hems. Pull up the gathers to size.

5 Insert the curtain hooks first through the slots in the lining tape and then into the pockets of the heading tape. Place a hook at each edge of the curtain and then at 10 cm (4 inch) intervals in between on gathers or pencil pleats, or at each group of pinch-pleats. Hang the finished curtains.

HOME CRAFTS

CUSHIONS

Cushions may be square, oblong, round, oval or any shape and size you choose. Cushion covers may be in virtually any fabric, and all are made in a similar way, from two pieces, either stitched together to make a bag or with a strip between them to make a 'wall'. The edges of the cover can be plain or you could include piping or a frill in the seam. Alternatively you could stitch cord around the edge afterwards.

The cushion filling can be firm or soft depending on how you want to use it. Cushion pads of foam rubber are available in a wide variety of sizes and shapes, but for anything unusual you will have to make the pad yourself.

Cutting out Square or oblong cushion covers can be cut to measure. Simply decide the size and add 2.5 cm (1 inch) each way for the seam turnings. For other shapes it is advisable to make a paper pattern. Decide the shape you want, and outline it on your fabric. Draw a second line 1.5 cm (½ inch) outside the first for the seam turn-

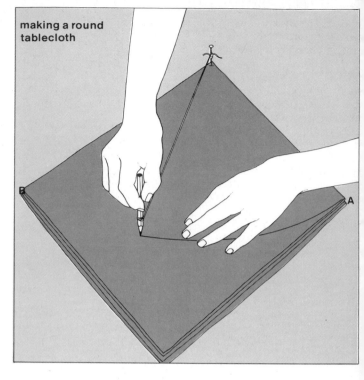

making a round tablecloth

ings. Cut two pieces of fabric to the shape of the pattern.

Making the cover Place the cover pieces with right sides together and stitch 1.5 cm (½ inch) from the edge, leaving an opening on one side to insert the cushion pad.

Neaten the raw edges of the seams, clipping them at angles, corners and curves.

Turn the cover right side out, insert the cushion pad and fold under the seam turnings along the opening. Slip stitch them firmly together. This slip stitching may be pulled out easily if the cover is removed for cleaning.

Cushion pads Use a cheap fabric to make the casing of the pad and foam chippings, polyester wadding or kapok for the stuffing. Make the casing like the cushion cover, but omitting any piping or frill. Stuff well and oversew the edges of the opening firmly together.

TABLECLOTHS

To calculate the size of the cloth, decide the length of the overhang and add twice this

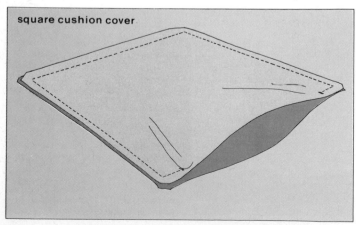

square cushion cover

mount plus 10 cm (4 inches) or hems, to the dimensions of the tabletop.

Calculate the amount of fabric required, cut it out and make any joins, following the general method on page 239.

Square or oblong cloths Make double hems all round the cloth by folding 2.5 cm (1 inch) to the wrong side and then another 2.5 cm (1 inch). Press the folds firmly.

At each corner, unfold the hems and refold in mitres. Stitch the hems by hand or machine.

Round cloths Start by cutting a square of fabric with sides equal to the required total diameter of the table-cloth. Fold the square in half lengthways and then width-ways.

Tie a piece of string to a dressmaker's chalk pencil, and pin it at the intersection of the folds, leaving half the diameter length between pencil and pin.

Draw an arc from corner A to the corner B, keeping the string taut.

Cut around the arc through all thicknesses of fabric and open it out to give the circle. Finish the edges of the tablecloth either by binding or by turning a narrow hem and machine stitching.

SHEETS
Sheeting fabric can be bought in two widths — 178 cm (70 inches) for single beds or 130 cm (51 inches) for double beds.

To calculate the length you require to make flat sheets, add twice the depth of the mattress to its length, plus a further metre (yard) to give good tuck-ins and hems.

Making the sheets For the top hem, turn 1.5 cm (½ inch) to the wrong side and then 4 cm (1½ inches). For the bottom hem, turn 1 cm (⅜ inch) and then 1.5 cm (½ inch). Machine stitch and press both hems. There is no need for side hems because of the selvedges.

Repairing worn sheets Sheets tend to show first signs of wear down the middle, and it is advisable to remedy this before tears occur.

Cut the sheet in half lengthways. Turn the pieces over so that the edges are at the centre, and lap one edge over the other by 1.5 cm (½ inch). Pin and machine stitch twice, once along each edge. Make narrow hems along the new side edges.

DUVET COVERS
Sheeting material can also be used to make duvet covers. The dimensions of duvets vary, so don't take a chance: measure it properly.

Cut two rectangles of sheeting to the dimensions of the duvet, plus 5 cm (2 inches) each way.

Join the rectangles with French seams on three sides, taking a total of 1.5 cm (⅝ inch) in the seam allowance.

Make a hem around the edges of the fourth side, with 1 cm (⅜ inch) in the first turning and 2.5 cm (1 inch) in the second.

To close the opening, either apply press studs or sew on touch-and-close tape.

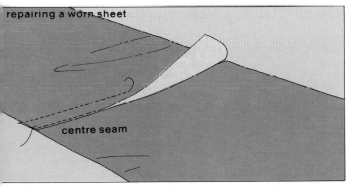

repairing a worn sheet

centre seam

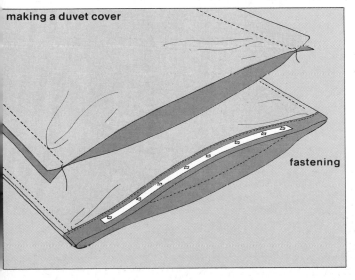

making a duvet cover

fastening

HOME CRAFTS

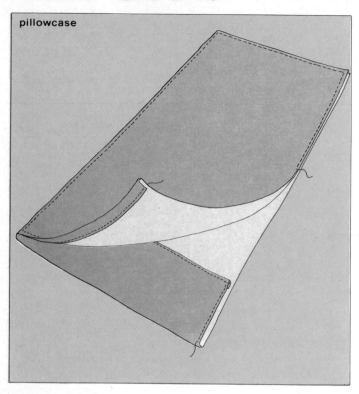

pillowcase

PILLOWCASES

Cut one piece of sheeting to the dimensions of the pillow plus 5 cm (2 inches) each way. Cut another piece of the same length but 15 cm (6 inches) wider.

On both pieces, make a hem along one of the shorter sides, with 1 cm (⅜ inch) in the first turning and 2.5 cm (1 inch) in the second. Machine.

Turn down the hemmed edge of the wider piece for 15 cm (6 inches) on to wrong side. Place both pieces wrong sides together and join on the remaining three edges, taking 5 mm (¼ inch) in the seam turnings. Trim and press the turnings.

Turn the case right side out and fold the pocket over the narrower piece. Stitch again round the three sides, taking 1 cm (⅜ inch) seam turnings. Turn right side out and fold the pocket inside.

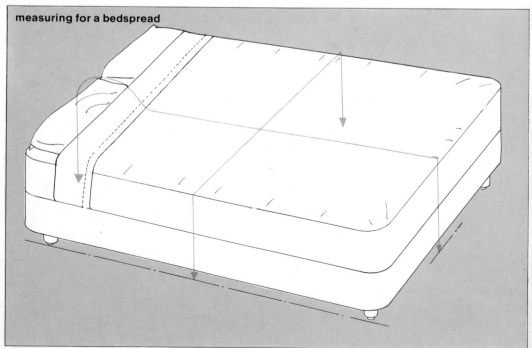

measuring for a bedspread

THROWOVER BEDSPREADS

Measure the bed with bedding and pillows in position. For length, measure from the mattress base at the top, over the pillows to the desired length at the base. For width, measure across the bed to the desired length on each side. Add 5 cm (2 inches) to both measurements. If you are going to round off the corners, note the overhang measurement which is from the edge of the mattress to the desired length plus 2.5 cm (1 inch).

Calculate the amount of fabric required, cut out and make any joins, following the general method on page 239.

For square corners, make double hems all round the edge, mitring the corners. For rounded corners, mark in each corner a square with sides equal to the overhang measurement. Then, using X as the centre, draw an arc from Y to Z. Cut off the corner outside the arc. Turn up a double hem round the edge.

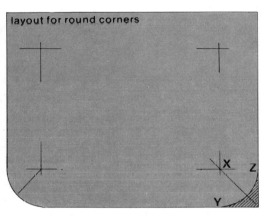

layout for round corners

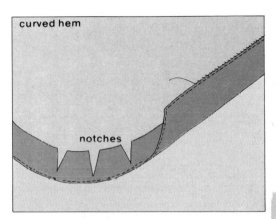

curved hem

notches

making a valance

FLOUNCED BEDSPREAD OR VALANCE

For a flounced bedspread, measure dimensions over bedclothes. For a valance, take measurements over mattress. Measure the width and length of the bed and then the desired length of the flounce — for a bedspread this will be from the upper edge of the mattress, but for a valance it will be from the lower edge.

Allow fabric for the main panel of the bedspread or valance to be the width by the length of the bed, plus 3 cm (1¼ inches) each way. For the flounce, add the width to twice the length of the bed and allow fabric to this length by the height of the flounce plus 4 cm (1½ inches).

Calculate the amount of fabric required, cut out and make any joins (see page 239).

Work gathering threads along the top edge of the flounce. Pull up gathers and join to sides and bottom edges of the main panel.

Turn up a hem along the top edge of the flounce and main panel and round the bottom of the flounce.

HOME CRAFTS

DRIED FLOWERS

There are three basic ways of drying flowers, depending on their types. Some, because of the nature of their petals, dry quite naturally. A second type are dried quickly in places such as airing cupboards. And the third variety are dried using desiccants (drying agents).

Helichrysums and statice or limonium are examples of the first variety. Others, closely related, known collectively as everlastings or immortelles, include acroclinium, rhodanthe, lonas and ammobium, all easily grown from seed. It is not practical to allow them to dry on the plant, because they continue to develop and make seed or become weathered and dull. Instead, they should be gathered little by little as they open. Strip the leaves from the stems, tie tightly in small bunches and hang them upside down, well spaced apart, in a cool, airy and shady place. When they are dry to the touch, they are ready for use. Everlastings remain decorative for years, keeping their colours the best of all.

In some seasons the heads of helichrysums become easily severed from their stems after drying. The flowers are then best mounted on false stems: when fresh they are easy to thread on to florist stem wires or on to grasses (see below). Some people gather only the heads from the plants and dry them by spreading them out on newspaper. Flower heads can also be used in flower pictures and other types of montage.

The second method of drying is for flowers which, although not naturally of a papery or straw-like texture, actually dry quite well. Many of these provide attractive contrasts of shape and texture to the daisy-like everlastings. Some are quite large and can be used in arrangements on a grand scale. They include many ordinary garden flowers: acanthus or bear's breeches; achillea (the garden varieties dry better than the wild species); alchemilla or lady's mantle; amaranthus or love-lies-bleeding; celosia or cockscomb; catananche or cupid's dart; delphinium and its annual form, the larkspur; echinops or globe thistle; eryngium, the blue sea holly — this cultivated kind is not as spiny as the wild; gypsophila; polygonum or bistort; solidago or golden rod. Among the shrubs are hydrangeas, which should be dried after the heads change colour; roses in bud and young ramblers and some spireas. All of these are best dried very quickly; an airing cupboard provides perfect conditions.

The third method, in which desiccants are used, gives you scope to dry almost any kind of flower you fancy, but it has its drawbacks. Flowers dried this way, although exciting at first, do not last like the true everlastings nor do they keep their colour. One of the best ways to keep them is to enclose the arrangement inside a covered glass jar or under a glass dome.

One desiccant is clean, dry sand. Unfortunately this is so

Stemless dried flowers are ideal for flower pictures.

heavy that it often presses the flowers, sometimes spoiling them. It suits flat flowers such as pansies, narcissi, hellebores and some daisies. Two other desiccants are domestic borax and silica gel, both available at chemist shops. It is possible to mix sand and borax, thus lightening both weight and price. Silica gel, the more expensive of the two, can be combined with the dry foamed plastics used for flower arrangement. After drying out, all of these can be used time and time again.

Use airtight boxes, and be sure they are deep if the flowers are to be left on long stems. These last also call for a large (and expensive) quantity of desiccant. To economize, shorten them and mount the flowers on false stems later.

First, make a layer of desiccant or foamed plastic at the bottom of the box. Keep to one kind of flower in each box. According to their shape, either lay them flat or stand them upright or at an angle — this is where the foamed plastic comes in handy. Flowers can be quite close together and at different levels but they should not touch. Gently pour in the desiccant so that it gradually buries each flower, trickling into all spaces without alter-

ing the shape of the blooms. Gently shake the box from time to time. When everything is covered, close the box and keep it in a warm, dry place. Inspect the flowers often. It is not possible to say how long drying will take: according to their type and moisture content, some flowers take only a few hours, others a few days.

Most grasses, including pampas and farm cereals, are delightful mixed with dried flowers, offering as they do good contrasts in shape. It is important to gather all of these soon after they emerge from their sheaths while they are still young. They then keep a good colour and do not disintegrate easily.

Whole grasses and stem ends from those you shorten make splendid natural-looking false stems. All you need to attach them is a touch of adhesive under the base of the bloom or on the end of the flower stem. Allow them to dry before arrangement. Helichrysums can be pierced at the centre and a grass then threaded through.

Bear in mind that, because dried flowers are light in weight, their containers should be heavy or weighted in some way. You can half-fill them with sand or shingle and then rest wire netting or dry foamed plastic on top.

FLOWER ARRANGING

Standing a bunch of fairly uniform flowers in water, and making a flower arrangement from them are two very different things. There are, it is true, some flowers which never seem to call for arrangement: snowdrops, primroses, forget-me-nots, wallflowers, nasturtiums, sweet peas, even roses can stand in a favourite vase or pitcher and look simply lovely. However, if you adopt this method for all flowers, especially the large long-stemmed kinds, results can be very unsatisfying. Arrangement's great advantage is that, like good cooking, it gives you full value for the ingredients you use and you can make a little go a long way with delightful results.

(*Above*) Containers with a built-in rim are designed to hold a standard block of Oasis. Insert the central flower first to establish the height of the arrangement. When the foam stands above the rim, stems can be inserted in its sides to hide the container. Discard Oasis when it becomes full of holes.

(*Left*) Pinholders support stems in an upright or angled position. They are used in low dishes or bowls. Pinholders with wide-set pins are for holding Oasis or Stemfix.

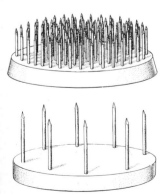
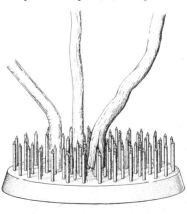

247

HOME CRAFTS

If you are able to visualize how you want a flower arrangement to look when it is completed, and if you have suitable vases or other vessels, you really should have no problem in assembling it. Style, size, colour harmony, content, are all personal matters. The trick, shared by all, is to employ some aid which will securely hold any material the way you want to see it, so begin by spending a little money on a water-retentive foamed-plastic stemholder such as Oasis or Stemfix. This is good practising material. One large block should suffice for several average-size arrangements, so you can use the piece several times. Sappy stems are not easily inserted into this so avoid these, but any firm stem should stay in place immediately it is inserted into the block, even if only a short length goes in. This means that you can use many short-stemmed flowers effectively, and stems can be arranged at any angle, even downwards. Well-soaked plastic nurtures all stems it holds, even those outside a vessel, but it must be kept moist.

You will have most scope if you cut a block deep enough to stand a little way above the rim of a vessel. Once the arrangement is complete, the plastic should be well hidden.

Once you have grasped the essentials and found a style you like, you can switch to wire netting as a stemholder. This is cheaper, adaptable and lasts for ever. It accommodates all thicknesses and textures of stems. These are held in place by the mesh. You can insert them deeply or

just below rim level. At first they may not stay in place instantly as they do in the plastic, but you will soon get used to the netting. Use large, 4 cm (1½ in) or 5 cm (2 in) mesh, which will crumple up easily and tightly, yet give way sufficiently to accommodate thick stems.

To fill a vessel, cut a piece of netting (kitchen scissors or old secateurs are best for this purpose) which measures twice the depth of the container and as wide or even a little wider than its widest part. Fold the piece into a U and squash it down into the container. Hook a few of the cut ends over the rim to keep the netting from moving if you think this necessary.

Sometimes it is helpful to combine a block of plastic and netting, for instance when you are arranging long, firm stems and short, sappy ones, such as, say, blossom branches and little flowers and individual leaves at rim level. Stand a block of plastic, or place a mass of much-used pieces in the bottom of the container and rest wire

In arrangements for a table centre, balance is easily achieved by arranging the tallest, most upright stem at the centre.

Stemholders enable the arranger to make attractive designs and to place flowers in low-lying positions.

netting on top.

When using clear glass containers, restrict stemholders to the top part of the container only. So long as it has had a good drink beforehand and so long as you keep the water level topped up, it is not necessary that a great length of stem goes under water. Stems can be arranged in the top few inches only. Low-lying flowers, leaves and other materials arranged early on in assembly will hide all traces of the stemholder, leaving just clear water visible through the glass.

If you fancy arrangements in low dishes, troughs and bowls, foamed plastic or metal pinholders can be used. Wire netting is not suitable for these except to be hooked on the front of a pinholder to take flowers whose stems are too slender to be impaled on or wedged between the points. The way you hide these holders becomes an important part of the design.

Flowers that are just placed in water usually stand all round the rim, but most arrangements are best made with flowers facing one way. These call for fewer flowers, etc. than all-round designs. It helps first to establish a centre stem and to make the heart of the design at its base. Work from the outer stems to the centre, which should be the focal point. The important thing is to stand the first stem as far back as possible. This way you provide plenty of space for the other stems.

When filling a bowl for a table, the centre stem should stand vertically in the middle, and it should remain the tallest. All the others should radiate from its base. Turn the bowl as you fill it to get all stems evenly balanced.

BEER AND WINE MAKING
BEER

If making beer for the first time, simplicity is the keynote and the instructions and suggestions given here are based on this assumption. Beermaking kits containing ingredients, equipment and instructions also make a good introduction to the hobby and, if you find you enjoy it, there are lots of ways to experiment and add variety to your beers. However you begin, try to buy from a good home-brewing supplier.

TYPES OF BEER

Light and pale ales and bitters Pale gold in colour and have a dry and bitter taste. They are made from light malts and have a relatively high hop content.

Brown ales Made with darker malts, contain fewer hops and are generally sweeter than bitters.

Stout Almost black in colour and is made from very dark malt. It has a high hop content so is bitter but some varieties are sweetened to give a smoother flavour.

Lager Originated in Europe, is pale in colour and has a light, fresh taste. It is produced by a different fermentation process to British beers.

BASIC INGREDIENTS

Malted barley Varies in colour from light to dark depending upon the degree of roasting. Before use it needs to be cracked and then mashed by steeping it in hot water for a time at a controlled temperature to convert the starch to sugar; the resultant liquid is known as the 'wort'. Alternatively, light or dark malt extract in syrup or powder form may be used as the basis for the wort. It may be combined with small quantities of malted barley or crystal malt (crack them with a rolling pin or in an electric blender and boil them with the hops) or other cereals to vary the flavour.

Hops Add aroma and bitterness to beer and also act as a preservative. Different varieties are available like the aromatic yellow Goldings or the more bitter, green Fuggles hops. Imported hops such as Saaz are used for lagers. Hop extract and ready-hopped concentrated worts are also available.

Sugar Adds sweetness and will increase the alcohol content of the finished beer; plain white is ideal. Since beer is a long drink, it should not be overly alcoholic and 3–6 per cent alcohol content is normal. Moist brown sugar or glucose chips may be used instead of sugar to vary the flavour, and glucose adds extra body. Sugar is also used to prime beer after bottling to cause a secondary fermentation and produce a sparkling brew. Add 1–2 ml (¼–½ teaspoon) sugar per bottle (the more sugar the more fizz), using a small funnel and then seal.

Water Hard water is particularly good for making bitters and light and pale ales, while soft water is best for milds and stouts. Tap water may be treated with small amounts of water-treatment chemical to make it soft or hard.

Yeast Brewers' yeast is available in liquid or powder form and should be added when the wort is between 18–21°C (65–70°F). This temperature should be maintained throughout fermentation which lasts for about one week. Beers are generally made with a top fermenting

HOME CRAFTS

yeast which should form a thick head after 24 hours and last for 2–3 days. Scum should be skimmed off and discarded. The beer will then 'simmer' with small bubbles rising to the top. This stage should stop after 5–6 days when fermentation will have ceased; a hydrometer will help determine this point. The beer is then ready for bottling.

Irish moss Boiled with the wort acts as a clearing agent. Beer finings may be added to clear a finished beer but are not generally necessary when the beer is to be bottled.

EQUIPMENT
Make sure that *all* nylon, plastic or polythene items are white or clear in colour and of good quality. Never use strongly-coloured items. All equipment must be sterilized with boiling water before use.

Saucepan Use large aluminium, stainless steel or un-chipped enamel pans to boil the hops. An old Burco boiler is ideal or you can use any electric boiler.

Strainer Used to strain the hopped liquid into the fermentation bin.

Fermentation bin A wide-necked lidded polythene bin roomy enough to allow for vigorous fermentation; a small plastic dustbin will do. Mark any 'topping up' levels on the outside before you begin.

Spoon Long-handled wood or plastic for stirring and skimming.

Thermometer To check the temperature of the wort before and during fermentation.

Hydrometer Measures the specific gravity of a liquid and will indicate how much sugar is in the wort and therefore the potential alcohol content of the brew. It should give a reading of 1006 or lower when beer fermentation has finished. If the reading is higher, leave the beer for another day and test again.

Polythene tubing About 2 m (6 ft) and a glass U-tube for siphoning beer into bottles.

Storage Containers Beer or cider bottles are ideal and can

1 Dustbin
2 Electric boiler
3 Insulated food container
4 Boiling pan
5 Fermentation bin
6 Bottles
7 Siphon tube
8 Spoon
9 Cracked malt
10 Sugar
11 Yeast
12 Dried hops
13 Electric blender

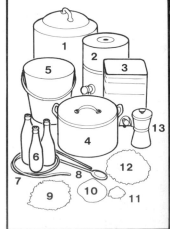

be collected easily. Bottles may be sealed with crown corks or polythene stoppers. The advantage of the latter is that they can be fitted by hand and can be reused. Crown corks need to be fitted with a crown-corking machine. Beer may also be stored in bulk in a pressurized container.

BITTER BEER
(makes 23 litres, 5 gallons)

1.8 kg (4 lb) malt extract (light)
5 ml (1 teaspoon) Irish moss
5 ml (1 teaspoon) water-
    treatment crystals for pale
    ale
85 g (3 oz) hops (Goldings)
0.90 kg (2 lb) sugar (white or
    soft brown)
14 g (½ oz) beer yeast

Dissolve the malt extract in 13.6 litres (3 gallons) of warm water and boil for about 30 minutes with the Irish moss and water-treatment crystals. Add hops and boil for about 30 minutes more. Strain this hopped wort into the fermentation bin and rinse (sparge) the hops with a kettleful of hot water. Add the sugar and stir well. Top up to 22.5 litres (5 gallons) with cold water and add the yeast when wort is 18–21°C (65–70°F). Stir and cover and leave in a warm place. Check that fermentation is progressing and skim as necessary. When fermentation is complete, siphon the beer into bottles, filling them to within about 2.5 cm (1 in) of the top. Prime the beer by adding 1–2 ml (¼–½ teaspoon) sugar per bottle and then seal, and keep in a warm place for 2 days to allow secondary fermentation to begin. Store in a cool dark place for about 2 weeks before tasting — if you can wait! The beer will improve for up to about 3 months.

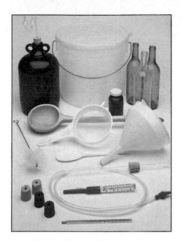

In wine-making, it helps to have proper equipment, such as a demijohn, fermentation bin, hydrometer, thermometer, PVC tubing, sieve, funnel, etc.

WINE

Delightful country wines can be made at home with almost any fruits, vegetables, flowers, grains, etc. (providing they are not poisonous!). A simple recipe for apple wine is given overleaf, along with information about the basic equipment needed to begin winemaking. A reputable supplier will certainly stock the items mentioned and will be pleased to give advice on any problems. Grape concentrates may also be used to make good vins ordinaires quickly and simply.

BASIC INGREDIENTS
Must Prepared fruit, vegetables, grain, etc., which give the wine its flavour, colour and name. Small quantities of grape concentrate, raisins or sultanas are sometimes added to other musts to lend a true wine flavour.
Wine yeast Changes the sugar in the must to alcohol and carbon dioxide. Some yeasts may be added direct to the must, others need to be activated first. Follow the instructions on the packet for best results.
It is very important to remember that the yeast must be kept at a temperature of about 24°C (75°F) throughout fermentation.

White granulated sugar Helps the yeast attain the required alcohol content in the wine — generally 10-15 per cent for table wines — and adds sweetness.

Other additives: Campden tablets (sodium metabisulphite) are used to sterilize the must and to prevent further yeast activity after fermentation; pectozyme destroys pectin in the must which may cause haziness in the wine; and yeast nutrient and energizer help the yeast to multiply and aid fermentation.

EQUIPMENT
All nylon, plastic, polythene or PVC items should be clear or white in colour and of food-grade quality. All items that come in contact with the wine should be washed, then sterilized in a solution of sodium metabisulphite and drained dry before use to prevent contamination.
Fermentation bin Wide-necked plastic or polythene container with a lid, such as a small dustbin, needed for fermentation of the pulp.
Glass jar (demijohn) Ideal for the second stage of fermentation and a second one will be useful when racking the wine. Mark the jar(s) on the outside at the 4.5-litre (1 gallon) level as a guide when topping up.
Airlock Sits in a bored cork in the neck of the demijohn, sealing out oxygen and wild yeasts while allowing carbon dioxide gas to bubble off the wine. Put a little diluted sterilizing solution in the airlock to kill bacteria.

HOME CRAFTS

Hydrometer Measures the specific gravity of a liquid. In winemaking it will indicate the amount of sugar in the must, allowing the potential alcohol in the finished wine to be calculated. It will also give an indication of when fermentation has ceased by giving the same reading consecutively. The specific gravity of a dry wine at the end of fermentation should be close to 996.

PVC tubing Use approximately 1.5 m (5 ft) and a glass U-tube for racking the wine.

Bottles Collect empty wine bottles at home or from a wine bar. A long-handled bottle brush is useful for cleaning them.

Corks New cylindrical corks make a good seal and can be fitted by hand — soak in water overnight, then dip them in diluted sterilizing solution before fitting. Store the bottles on their sides to keep the corks moist. Plastic stoppers are easy to fit by hand and are reusable. Bottles sealed in this way should be stored upright.

Other equipment A long-handled plastic spoon, a sieve, funnel and a thermometer will also be required.

APPLE WINE
(dry white)

5.4 kg (12 lb) mixed apples
225 g (½ lb) sultanas
3.4 litres (6 pints) warm water
1 Campden tablet
5 ml (1 teaspoon) pectic enzyme
1 sachet (10 g) general purpose wine yeast
10 ml (2 teaspoons) yeast nutrient and energizer salts
1 kg (2¼ lb) sugar

Wash apples, removing bruised or bad bits, then chop them with the sultanas and place in a wide-necked

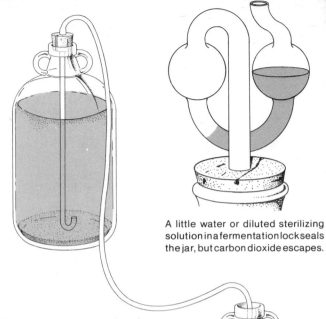

A little water or diluted sterilizing solution in a fermentation lock seals the jar, but carbon dioxide escapes.

Racking — siphoning wine from the sediment deposited in the jar to one at a lower level.

fermentation bin with the warm water, Campden tablet and the pectic enzyme. Cover closely and leave for 24 hours.

Dissolve half the sugar in 500 ml (1 pint) hot water and add to the must. When it cools to about 24°C (75°F), add the yeast nutrient and energizer salts, stir, then add the yeast. Stir again then cover and leave in a warm place for a week stirring daily.

Strain the pulp through a sieve, squeezing it gently. Dissolve the rest of the sugar in the strained juice, funnel it into a demijohn and top up to 4.5 litres (1 gallon) with tepid water. Fit an airlock and leave to ferment for 5–6 weeks.

Rack the wine off the sediment into a clean demijohn, top up with more tepid water, fit an airlock and leave to fer-

ment out. Fermentation is over when there are no bubbles rising in the wine; this will take several weeks.

Rack the wine again, add 1 Campden tablet, top up with cold water and seal the demijohn with a cork bung. Leave to clear before racking again as above.

After three rackings the wine should be clear and bright and ready for bottling. Siphon finished wine into bottles, seal and store in a cool dark place for at least 3 months before drinking.

PET CARE

PET CARE

INTRODUCTION

In many homes the pets are introduced by the children, who understandably cannot resist the thought of an interesting new companion in their lives. Yet, when young children ask for pets and still more pets, they are not taking into account all the responsibilities involved. These concern the parents, and it is they who must decide which animals, if any, are suitable pets for the family.

Is it, for instance, humane to keep a bird in a cage, or a goldfish in a bowl? Is it right to keep any gregarious animal alone? Should we continue to import as pets, such exotic animals as tortoises? Is it fair to shut up a dog all day in a house vaca-ted by the whole family? Is it responsible to keep an uncastrated tom cat who may sire dozens of unwanted kittens in the neighbourhood? It is not only the children who fail to visualize just how much a puppy may grow. When it does, who will exercise it? Most dogs need long walks every day. How would the family manage with a bitch on heat or a cat with fleas? Who will dig the goldfish pond and maintain it afterwards? Who will care for the tropical fish? Will caged birds have sufficient space? What about cleaning out the rabbits and the guinea pigs?

FINANCE

The most obvious costs, initial housing and feeding bills, are only a proportion of the total sum involved. In particular, veterinary fees must be expected, not only for illnesses and accidents, but also for vaccinations, booster inoculations, neutering and worming, and for old and suffering animals.

LEGAL RESPONSIBILITIES

Since an owner is liable in law for third party damages if his animal is responsible for an accident, adequate insurance cover should be bought.

Furthermore, owners are legally responsible for ensuring that their pets never suffer unnecessarily.

Children and animals together make an idyllic picture, which often belies the work and problems involved in keeping pet animals.

CATS

BREEDS
Most pet cats are mongrel but there are many varieties of pedigree cats available from breeders. They fall into three main categories: foreign short-haired breeds, such as the Siamese, Abyssinian and Burmese; British short-haired breeds, including the British Blue, Bicoloureds and Manx; and long-haired breeds, such as the Angora and Persians.

ACQUIRING A KITTEN
Between the ages of nine and twelve weeks, a kitten is old enough to be taken from its mother and introduced to a new home. Those kittens which are welcomed into the family and whose needs are understood and provided for, grow into delightful and affectionate pets. Kittens are intelligent and playful — it is inadvisable to leave them alone for too long.

FEEDING
At nine to twelve weeks a kitten needs four small meals a day of suitable protein food, such as flaked fish, minced raw beef, minced cooked chicken, liver and scrambled egg. Milk can give some kittens diarrhoea, but is acceptable if mixed with baby cereal. Tinned cat food can also be introduced at this stage.

Adult cats need two meals a day of either meat, fish or offal, with some cereal such as wholemeal bread. Meat can be fed raw as can heart, liver and kidney. However, regular feeding of offal alone should be avoided. A varied diet is always best.

Tinned and packet foods if used must be fed exactly according to the manufacturer's instructions. In addi-

A family of Abyssinians. Do not take kittens away from their mother until they are weaned.

tion offer a large marrow bone occasionally, as this helps keep teeth and gums in the best possible condition.

Clean drinking water must always be available although many cats choose to ignore it and drink from dripping taps and puddles. When dehydrated food is fed to cats, plenty of fresh water is particularly vital.

ACCOMMODATION
Every cat needs a warm dry bed in the house, to which it has access both day and night. A cat flap fitted into an external door will provide for this quite adequately.

The bed which may be a basket, box or manufactured cat bed, should be designed to stand off the ground and be deep enough for the sides to cut off all draughts. A washable cushion or blanket, if frequently laundered, makes excellent bedding.

HOUSE-TRAINING
Kittens, town cats and some older cats need to be given a litter tray to use in the house. Any shallow box filled with sand, dry earth, or a manufactured cat litter sprinkled with a handful of earth will serve, provided it is kept clean and positioned in a quiet corner. Cats are far too fastidious to use a soiled tray.

GROOMING
Short-haired cats are able to groom themselves adequately except when they are moulting. At that time they need to be thoroughly combed to remove loose hairs that would otherwise matt with food to form hair-balls in the digestive tract. These balls cause blockages that can be dangerous and often

255

PET CARE

cause ill-health.

Long-haired cats, whether pedigree or mongrel, need to be groomed every day. They are unable to keep knots and tangles out of their coat and are dependent on their owner for considerable attention. Although delightful to look at their long hair may make them unsuitable as pets in busy households.

CLAWS
A cat's claws are weapons used in both defence and attack and they are careful to keep them well sharpened. A scratching post should be provided for a kitten before it selects a piece of furniture instead and damages it irreparably.

INOCULATION
Kittens are very susceptible to infectious diseases and must be taken to a veterinary surgeon for inoculation between the ages of eight and twelve weeks. Annual boosters are usually necessary.

PARASITES
A variety of parasites, including fleas, lice, ticks, mites and worms, may affect a cat. Aerosol sprays are available for use against fleas and lice, but mites in the ears require veterinary treatment.

NEUTERING
Since it is impossible to control the breeding of pet cats both the males and females should be neutered to prevent unwanted litters. A veterinary surgeon will perform the spaying or castration under a general anaesthetic, preferably before the age of six months, although an older cat that has already bred can still be neutered.

256

DOGS

BREEDS
It is most important to choose a dog — regardless of whether it is a pedigree or mongrel — whose size and temperament suits the family. By general consent the middle-sized dogs such as the Border Collie, the Labrador and Golden Retrievers, number among the quietest and most agreeable of companions. They are known for their tolerance of children but need plenty of exercise.

ACQUIRING A PUPPY
Puppies are ready to be taken into a new home at about the age of eight weeks. At this age in particular they need a great deal of human companionship and should not be left alone except for short periods. The transition to a new home is often best made by puppies who come into a household where there is already an adult dog. In fact it is often kinder to keep two dogs rather than one, since they are company for each other.

FEEDING
Like babies, puppies need frequent small meals. At eight weeks they should be fed four times a day at four-hourly intervals. Two of the meals should contain puppy meal and wholemeal bread, or baby cereal with a little milk. The others should be of minced or scraped meat. An occasional hunk of meat, or a safe bone that will not splinter or fragment, is good for the puppy's teeth, gums and jaws, and will happily engross it for hours.

Adult dogs, by the time they are nine months old,

should have one main meat meal a day fed to them in the evening, with a bowl of milk and cereal each morning. It is normal for dogs to swallow their food very quickly, stopping only to tear it into manageable chunks. Large marrow bones are good for adult dogs and puppies, and particularly so for those fed on soft tinned food instead of fresh food.

Clean drinking water must be accessible to dogs and puppies all day whether they are indoors or outside.

ACCOMMODATION
In the house a dog needs a comfortable, warm, dry bed. Large-sized manufactured beds are expensive, but if the bed is too small, the dog will not use it. If the expense is too great, then a large box or an otherwise unused chair will suffice.

Dogs which are expected to sleep outside the house need a substantially built kennel, with deep bedding for severe weather. Even dogs which sleep indoors benefit from having a kennel they can retreat into at times during the day.

TRAINING
As soon as the puppy is introduced into the family house-training can begin. Success depends on anticipating the puppy's needs. Take it outside to urinate and defecate each morning and evening, and every time it finishes a meal or wakes from sleep. Stay with it until it has finished, then congratulate it.

While young the puppy must be handled quietly and discouraged from jumping up at visitors and barking.

age, breed and health. A big, energetic dog such as an Irish Setter, can walk 16 km (10 miles) a day throughout the year.

As well as its daily walks, a dog needs to spend part of every day in the garden. A walled garden is ideal but at least part of any garden must be made dog-proof with good fencing, gates and secure catches.

INOCULATION
Puppies should receive their first inoculations against infectious diseases at the age of nine to twelve weeks. Avoid walking the puppy in public until the first course of injections is complete. The veterinary surgeon will advise how frequently boosters are needed — often annually.

PARASITES
Of the various kinds of parasite that may infest a dog fleas and worms are the most common. Flea powders and sprays are available for use on the dog's fur but also clean the bedding thoroughly, since that is where the fleas breed.

Puppies should be given a routine worming for roundworms at three to six weeks with their first injections. If these worms are suspected again or if segments of tapeworm are found seek veterinary advice.

NEUTERING
It is advisable to have a pet bitch spayed to prevent it coming into season twice a year, for three weeks at a time, and producing litters of 1-12 pups. However, some vets advise waiting until after the first season.

Pet dogs can be neutered by castration.

From the age of six months, puppies can be taught to sit, lie down, walk to heel and to come when called, but further training is not usually appropriate for pet dogs.

GROOMING
The amount of grooming required varies according to the coat. Long-haired dogs, such as the Yorkshire Terrier, should be groomed daily, those with medium-length, short or wiry coats need much less attention. Baths should be given when necessary but it is important to dry the dog immediately afterwards with a towel or hair dryer.

Some dogs do not always wear down their claws naturally and any new growth needs to be trimmed off periodically with animal nail clippers, taking great care not to cut into the nerve and blood supply at the base of the nail.

COLLARS AND LICENCES
Owners have a legal obligation when dogs are six months old to obtain a licence which must be renewed annually together with a collar which states the owner's name. The collar must be worn whenever the dog is in a public place — e.g., a street — and local Councils are empowered to designate certain roads where dogs are not allowed off a leash.

EXERCISE
All dogs need walking every day although the distance will vary considerably, depending on the dog's size,

PET CARE

RABBITS

BREEDS
Pedigree rabbits are classified as normal fur breeds which include Chinchillas, Californians and New Zealands; fancy breeds, including English, Dutch, Angoras, Lops, Netherland Dwarfs and Flemish Giants and the Rex and Satin breeds.

The smaller rabbits, whether mongrel or purebred, are to be preferred as pets to the larger breeds, which may be very difficult for a child to handle. Rabbits such as the English, Dutch and Netherland Dwarfs have proved to be suitable household pets.

ACQUIRING A RABBIT
Young rabbits — known as kits — are born very imma-ture and helpless after a pregnancy of about thirty-one days. If there is any undue disturbance of the nest the doe is liable to kill its own young. During the third week of life they begin to leave the nest of their own accord, but they are not ready to be taken from the mother until fully weaned at about eight weeks.

The bucks and does must be kept apart after they mature sexually, which is at nine months in small breeds and six months in large breeds, to prevent recurring pregnancies and many unwanted litters. The bucks normally need to be housed on their own to prevent fighting although several does may live together peaceably.

FEEDING
By nature grazing animals, in captivity rabbits need a daily mixture of crushed oats, flaked maize, mixed corn and bran, either fed dry, or made into a crumbly mash with hot or cold milk or water. Wholemeal bread also makes a satisfactory base for a mash.

In addition, a rabbit needs to graze during the day or have another meal consisting of green and root vegetables, fruit and suitable wild plants, such as dandelion, clover, sow thistle and groundsel.

It is essential for rabbits to have hay, which should be of the best quality and offered in a hay net or rack to stop it being trodden underfoot.

Rabbits must be provided with clean water in a drip-

Always support a rabbit's weight when lifting it up.

feed bottle. The amount taken may vary according to the amount of fresh green-stuff eaten.

ACCOMMODATION
A good rabbit hutch should measure at least 150 x 60 x 60 cm (60 x 24 x 24 in) and be sturdily constructed with two compartments. It needs to stand off the ground at about table height and be designed to make cleaning easy.

The floor will need some protection from urine and a thick layer of newspaper covered by wood chippings, peatmoss litter or cat litter will keep it dry.

Inside the sleeping area there will need to be lots of straw for bedding but even that will not be sufficient in severe weather. Then the hutch needs to be moved into the shelter of an outhouse or at least covered over at night to make it frost-proof.

Wild rabbits are considered hardy but they are free to burrow deep under an insulating layer of earth. The smaller breeds of tame rabbits in particular may be at risk in harsh winter weather.

EXERCISE
No matter how good the hutch it provides insufficient accommodation for a rabbit. There also needs to be a safe place in which to exercise and if possible to graze. Ideally, part of the garden should be made rabbit-proof and the rabbits allowed free run of a big enclosure.

If a safe enclosure cannot be made, then a portable ark, is recommended, as it will allow a little exercise to be taken and give some scope for limited grazing.

GROOMING
All but the Angoras can groom themselves but some grooming is recommended. Overgrown claws may need trimming and overgrown teeth can sometimes be avoided by providing a gnawing block.

HANDLING
Support a rabbit's weight when lifting it, particularly one of the larger breeds. If a rabbit is returned to its hutch hind first it cannot kick out at its handler.

INOCULATION
Tame rabbits in rural areas may be at risk from an outbreak of *myxomatosis*. Veterinary advice should be sought about possible protection by inoculation.

Rabbits can share a big enclosure with other pet animals such as guinea pigs and tortoises. To stop the rabbits escaping, the fence should be 1 m (39 in.) in height.

PET CARE

GUINEA PIGS

VARIETIES

Guinea pigs, which are also known as cavies, are originally from South America. They have been selectively bred in captivity and they now occur in a variety of colours as well as having three distinct types of coat; the smooth-haired or English, the rough-haired or Abyssinian, and the long-haired Peruvian.

The comfortable size and weight of guinea pigs, together with their gentle, docile nature, means they continue to remain popular as children's pets. It is very rare for a guinea pig to bite and while the smaller, more agile rodents, such as the gerbil, may prove difficult to handle, the guinea pig can be lifted competently even by young children.

ACQUIRING A GUINEA PIG

The young are born, usually in rather small litters, fully furred, able to move around and with their eyes open. In two or three days they begin to eat solid food such as fine oatmeal.

They are mature enough to be adopted into their new home at the age of four to five weeks and since they are gregarious animals, it is best to keep more than one; a boar with several females for breeding, otherwise two sows.

FEEDING

These are entirely herbivorous animals which thrive on a diet of fresh vegetables, grass, hay and a cereal-based mash with some bran. The mash may be whole-meal bread with milk, or crushed oats and bran softened to a crumbly consistency with hot water or milk. Vitamin C and green food is essential. Guinea pigs must be offered fresh drinking water in a drip-feed bottle. Sometimes they will be seen to drink thirstily, whereas at other times they seem to take all the water they need through grazing.

ACCOMMODATION

The most suitable accommodation for guinea pigs is a good rabbit hutch. Two or three guinea pigs will need one measuring a minimum 120 x 60 x 50 cm (48 x 24 x 20 in). It will have to be moved into a warm outhouse for added protection in severe weather and furnished with lots of straw for bedding.

EXERCISE

An indoor box and an outdoor ark should be provided for exercise. Do not keep guinea pigs on wiremesh as this surface may cause sore hocks and mouths.

GENERAL CARE

The fur may be groomed with

Guinea pigs are gentle and docile animals. They are good pets for children to keep.

a brush or a non-scratch comb. Groom the way the fur grows and do not try to make the rosettes of fur on an Abyssinian lie smooth. The long-haired Peruvian guinea pig is clearly the most difficult variety to keep as a pet, but if kept with a companion of the same breed, each will do the other the service of gnawing off very long hair.

It should be noted, however, that excessive stripping of hair is an abnormality among guinea pigs, thought possibly to be caused by insufficient hay in their diet.

A wooden gnawing block will allow guinea pigs to trim their own front teeth which grow continuously.

When lifting a guinea pig, support its weight with both hands, one around the shoulders and one around the pelvis.

Avoid handling the abdomen of sows during their sixty-three day long pregnancy, for fear of harming the developing young.

HAMSTERS

VARIETIES

The Golden hamster, sometimes known as the Syrian from its country of origin, is the species kept as a pet, but not all are golden as they are bred in several colours.

ACQUIRING A HAMSTER

Hamsters are usually born in large litters after a very short pregnancy of sixteen days. As they weigh only 2g (1/14 oz) at birth, they are in danger of being killed by the mother if the nest is disturbed during their first two weeks of life. Weaning is complete by the end of the fourth week and the young can then be safely rehoused.

These are solitary, nocturnal animals, only coming together as adults to mate. They have to be housed individually after the age of five weeks or they may fight to the death.

FEEDING

A selection of grains, seeds, nuts, vegetables and fruit are the basic ingredients of a hamster's diet. Fruit cake makes an acceptable titbit, but chocolate may poison it.

It is a characteristic of hamsters to carry food in cheek pouches which is then hoarded, usually in their sleeping compartment. This is a survival technique in the wild and although not necessary in captivity, the behaviour persists. Only disturb the store to ensure that the food is not decaying.

The cage should be at least 50 x 30 x 25 cm in size and made of metal or hardwood. A galleried upstairs compartment gives extra space and ease of movement around the cage. Use sand on the floor.

Clean drinking water must always be available from a drip-feed bottle. It is a dangerous fallacy to suppose that hamsters, as desert animals, can manage without water.

ACCOMMODATION

Ideally the cage should be made of timber sturdy enough to withstand constant gnawing. This habit can be satisfied by providing the hamster with a wooden gnawing block.

Hamsters must not be allowed to become cold or they will go into hibernation and appear to be dead. If in doubt, warm them up in your hands.

A sleeping compartment is vital, for, as underground animals they must be able to retreat into the dark. Nesting materials should not include straw, which can damage the cheek pouches.

EXERCISE

A solid exercise wheel will allow the hamsters some movement but it is best to let them out of their cage for a run every evening. Keep them under close supervision as they are likely to escape.

Hamsters are solitary animals and must be housed on their own or they will fight to the death.

GENERAL CARE

Avoid using household aerosol sprays in the same room as a hamster for, if their fur becomes contaminated, they can be poisoned during one of their frequent bouts of grooming. Hamsters are shortsighted and should never be left unattended on a tabletop. As they can bite, do not point a finger at one.

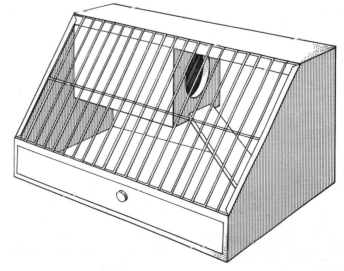

PET CARE

MONGOLIAN GERBILS

Many species of gerbil have been kept as pets, but of all the different kinds it is the Mongolian gerbil, with its distinctive black claws, that has established itself as a very successful pet.

ACQUIRING A GERBIL
Gerbils are born after a pregnancy of twenty-four days. The young are very immature and small with dark red skin. Both parents stay with the young who are suckled for three to four weeks. They can be rehoused between the seventh and tenth weeks, at which time they have to be paired, for if adult gerbils are introduced later than this, serious fighting can break out. A breeding pair, housed before ten weeks of age, will live together for life. If this is undesirable, two females from the same litter will also live together companionably for life.

FEEDING
Mainly herbivorous, these little rodents need a diet of mixed canary seed, sunflower seed, wheat, oats, maize and barley. They may be expected to take a tablespoonful of this cereal mixture each day. In addition some will eat small amounts of animal protein, such as hard-boiled eggs. Fresh fruit and vegetables is another daily necessity, and raisins are a favourite titbit for hand-feeding.

It is quite often said — and erroneously — that desert animals such as the gerbil and hamster do not need to be given water to drink. This is

Gerbils are friendly, curious animals and can become quite tame.

not the case and tests have shown that, given the choice, gerbils will drink about a teaspoonful of water daily, unless they are old, ill or pregnant, in which cases they drink far more. Although this seems to be only a small amount, it is very important to realize that daily drinking water is absolutely essential to gerbils. They will of course, use it economically, practising survival techniques evolved under desert conditions. They do not waste water by sweating and their urine is highly concentrated.

ACCOMMODATION
The most satisfactory type of cage for a pair of gerbils is a roomy box cage with ramps and ladders leading to a galleried upper storey. This greatly increases the floor area and the opportunity for movement within the cage.

In the wild, gerbils spend much of their time underground in burrows, and the opportunity to dig in deep litter and retreat from the light, is essential to their welfare.

A far better way of providing gerbils with an underground retreat that approximates, albeit on a very small scale, to their natural environment, is to convert a tank into a gerbilarium. Use as big a tank as possible and fill it with a mixture of Irish moss peat mixed with chopped straw. This is just right for burrowing. The mixture needs to be compacted down and possibly covered with grass turves. A pair of gerbils will busily dig tunnels that will hold their shape and will soon have built a network of underground burrows.

Clean kitchen paper may

be offered as bedding and, although a nocturnal creature such as the hamster would spend all day underground, gerbils are active during the day and not lost to sight.

Since gerbils urinate so little and the peat mixture is so absorbent, the gerbilarium needs cleaning only two or three times a year. Gerbils do not hoard food in captivity and although some is inevitably buried when they dig, decaying food is not normally a problem. For this reason, fresh foods, that would rot down quickly, must be removed daily.

The gerbilarium will need to be fitted with a ventilated cover to prevent these highly agile creatures escaping. It is usually convenient to fix the water-bottle to an attachment in the cover.

EXERCISE

The gerbilarium enables the gerbils to move around the tank as they would move around their own burrow system in the wild. Those which allow themselves to be handled may be brought out for a period of exercise each day, but it will need to be supervised since they are quick moving and liable to escape.

Caged gerbils can use a wheel for exercise, but as their long tails can become caught up in a spoked wheel, a solid one is to be preferred.

All caged gerbils should be taken out of their cage for a period of exercise each day, since there is scope only for limited movement within it.

GENERAL CARE

A pair of gerbils will groom each other and need no help from their owner. They do not smell unless kept in very inadequate conditions.

Mongolian gerbils have teeth which continually grow, as is common to all rodents, and they must be allowed wood or big nuts, such as Brazil nuts, to gnaw on. They are able to keep their teeth in perfect trim this way.

Mongolian gerbils are known for their curiosity and friendliness to humans, and most will walk onto an outstretched hand with no fear.

Those less reluctant to do so may be picked up by cupping them in the hands, and tamed over a period of time by hand-feeding.

Gerbils can be provided with an underground retreat that approximates to their natural habitat.

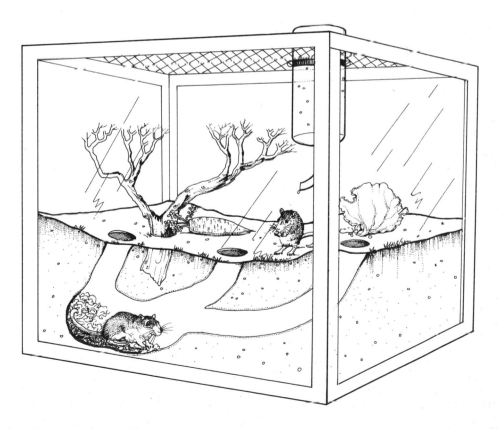

PET CARE

CAGE BIRDS

VARIETIES
The two most popular kinds of cage bird are the budgerigar and the canary. The first is a small Australian parrot and is by nature a roving flock bird from semi-arid grasslands; the other is a flock bird of the finch family and is native to the forests of the Canary Islands.

The care of budgerigars and canaries varies a little according to their different requirements, but it is true of both that although usually known as cage birds, they are far more suitably housed in an aviary. The two must never be housed together, for the frailer canary is at risk from the bolder and more assertive budgerigar.

BUDGERIGARS
These birds are bred in a host of colours and varieties, but four major colours predominate: blue, green, yellow, and white.

ACQUIRING A BUDGERIGAR
The young — with the possible exception of the first two — hatch on alternate days after an eighteen day incubation. At birth budgerigars are blind and without feathers. They are reared in the nest box by both parents, emerging at about four weeks fully feathered and able to de-husk seed. During this period the cock continues to part-feed them and by the age of six weeks they can be re-housed.

It is unfair to keep flock birds singly, but when housed in mixed groups there should be an equal number of each sex. If there is a spare female, one of the cocks will serve two hens, but surplus males will become very frustrated.

Adult budgerigars are easily sexed by the colour of the cere, which is the area just above the beak. Blue denotes a cock bird, brown denotes a hen, but on young fledgelings the cere colouring may be indistinct.

FEEDING
A good seed mixture, supplemented with an occasional segment of fruit or small quantities of greenstuff is a suitable diet. Packeted mixtures usually contain canary seed and millet enriched with artificial grains of vitamins and minerals.

Grit is needed by budgerigars as it aids the digestion of seed in the gizzard. Cuttlefish 'bone' is a source of calcium and a useful tool on which the birds may trim their own beaks.

In the wild budgerigars may have to go a day or two without water and they may choose to do so in captivity, but clean drinking water must always be available to them.

ACCOMMODATION
The type of cage illustrated, which is used by fanciers as a breeding cage, provides good accommodation all year round. It is easy to build and costs less than a traditional wire cage.

It should be made as spacious as possible, with plenty of room for these active little birds to flit from

The great advantage of a breeding cage is its spaciousness: the birds have room to fly and climb the cage-front. Fit a nest box, which should be dark and snug.

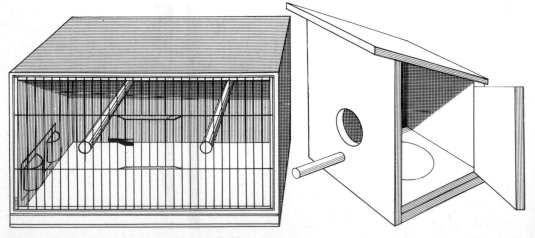

Adult budgerigars can be easily sexed by the colour of the cere, which is just above the beak. On the cock bird the cere is blue, on the hen it is brown in colour.

ACQUIRING A CANARY

The young are reared in a nest constructed in a nest-pan inside the breeding cage. The parents need to be fed special canary rearing food, which in turn they feed to the young. At three weeks the young begin to leave the nest and most are independent at five weeks and can be re-housed.

As flock birds they should not be kept singly, but it is advisable to keep only one sex unless breeding. The males are in most demand for their song, as females do not sing.

FEEDING

Canaries dehusk seed before eating it, feeding just like budgerigars. However, they need a higher fat content in their food and special canary mixtures provide for this by including niger or linseed.

Although a budgerigar may survive a few days without water, canaries very quickly succumb to thirst and need their drinking water changed every day.

Canaries also need to bathe more frequently and regularly than budgerigars, and must have a birdbath in their cage.

HANDLING

Owners accustomed to the hardy budgerigar — which can tolerate handling and readily becomes finger tame — should note that the canary has a much more delicate and retiring nature. Canaries are not easy to train and many are reluctant to leave their cage for exercise. For this reason they are best housed in an aviary.

perch to perch and to climb on the wire cage-front.

A size of 100 cm long; 60 cm wide; and 75 cm high (36 x 24 x 30in) will be needed for two budgerigars.

When the nest box is in place and the birds are busy rearing a family, no cage accessories other than the normal perches and the food and water pots will be necessary. At other times the birds may enjoy the added interest and stimulation of swings, mirrors and ladders. Such toys are particularly valuable to a single budgerigar kept in a cage.

Budgerigars are hardy enough to live in an outside aviary all year round, providing they have access to a weather-proof sleeping area at night.

EXERCISE

Aviary birds enjoy a certain freedom of movement and association with other birds. As a substitute, solitary budgerigars need human companionship, and some — notably cocks not yet six months old — may learn to 'talk'.

All caged budgerigars will need daily exercise out of their cage. If it is left open in a safe room for part of every day and providing food and water are never available elsewhere, then the birds will return to their own perch after a period of freedom.

CANARIES

Not all canaries are yellow, although that colour is associated so closely with their name. They are bred in a range of colours, from white to red and in several types, such as the Roller, Lizard, Border, Yorkshire, and Norwich.

PET CARE

TORTOISES AND TERRAPINS

VARIETIES
Tortoises are land animals, turtles are marine and terrapins live in freshwater, although in America the word 'turtle' is used to describe all three. Those kept as pets are usually Mediterranean tortoises, European pond terrapins and tropical Red-eared terrapins.

None of these animals is well enough suited to our northern climate to successfully breed, and as a result their continued importation depletes wild populations. For this reason they are not recommended as pets.

MEDITERRANEAN TORTOISES
Tortoises must feed well during the summer months to build up their fat reserves for winter hibernation. They feed almost exclusively on green plants such as cabbage, peas, lettuce, green beans and dandelion, together with fruits and root vegetables. Some will also take wholemeal bread and drained tinned beans, e.g., kidney beans, which are valuable for their high protein content. A sprinkling of a vitamin or mineral supplement is very beneficial.

Grate, shred, mince or chop food if it entices small specimens to eat more and provide artificial light and heat to keep them eating when the weather is dull.

Water provided in a large shallow pan will suffice for both bathing and drinking and must be constantly available.

ACCOMMODATION
A safe enclosure is needed for exercise and, although sunlight is essential for their health, tortoises need shelter from excessive sun and rain. A box-like shelter with abundant bedding, or access to a greenhouse or outhouse is invaluable.

During the coldest months, tortoises can hibernate in a large box of earth and dry leaves. This must be ventilated, and be both rat-proof and frost-proof. Do not keep them warm; they must be allowed to hibernate.

EUROPEAN POND TERRAPINS
Terrapins are carnivorous and need a diet of raw meat, whole fish, and such freshwater life as *Daphnia,* *Gammarus* and *Tubifex.* Both crustaceans and molluscs will be taken complete with their shells, which are valuable for their calcium content. Terrapins will also eat pond weeds and lettuce.

ACCOMMODATION
Terrapins should be kept in a garden pond with access to an island or an enclosed shore area where they can rest and bask.

In the wild, terrapins hibernate in the mud at the bottom of ponds.

RED-EARED TERRAPINS
Tropical terrapins have the same diet as the European variety, but they suffer from a lack of natural sunlight and need food rich in vitamins and calcium.

ACCOMMODATION
The Red-eared terrapin will only survive outside in this climate in high summer. Throughout the rest of the year it needs to be accommodated in an aquarium tank heated to a constant 24–29°C (75–85°F), and equipped with a basking area.

A European pond terrapin. Being native to Europe it is hardy and can survive in a garden pond equipped with a small island.

FISH

GOLDFISH
The Common goldfish is the type most often kept in garden pools and cold water aquariums, but there is also a wide range of fancy goldfish available. These have exaggerated fins and body shapes, and there is some colour variation, but all tend to be more delicate and shorter lived than the hardy Common goldfish from which they derive.

ACQUIRING A GOLDFISH
Goldfish are usually sold in a plastic bag, from which it can be dangerous to tip them directly into a pond or tank. If the opened bag is floated on the surface for about 10 minutes until the water temperatures have evened up, then it is safe to empty out the fish. However, it can be more harmful to leave them in the bag if it is too small.

Young goldfish are a dull khaki colour, and do not show the full adult colouration until they are one year old.

As gregarious creatures, goldfish should be housed together in small shoals rather than kept singly.

FEEDING
Most of the time it is convenient to feed goldfish on dried, packeted food, but this should be supplemented when possible, with chopped lettuce and such freshwater invertebrates as *Daphnia, Gammarus,* and *Tubifex* worms, all available in frozen form from pet shops.

As coldblooded animals, fish are only active enough to feed well when they are warm. In summer they may need two meals a day; in winter perhaps only one meal on alternate days. Providing more than they can finish in about a quarter of an hour merely fouls the water with decaying matter.

A feeding ring in a tank keeps food from spreading across the entire surface of the water.

Fish kept in an established pond, with water plants and flourishing freshwater life, need no extra feeding.

ACCOMMODATION
Ideally, Common goldfish and all the hardy fancy varieties, such as Comet, London Shubunkin and *visibly* scaled Fantails should be kept in a garden pool all year. Other successful fish in ponds are Golden Rudd and Golden Orfe.

In autumn, cover the pond with a net to prevent it becoming choked with fallen leaves. Avoid smashing any ice that forms in freezing weather as the fish beneath will usually survive unless disturbed by shock waves. It is possible to float planks and balls on the surface at night and remove them in the day to open up air holes.

If fish are to survive under the ice, the pond must be 1m (3 ft) deep in part. A pond of varying depth will enable a variety of plants to grow, and a shallow margin which warms up quickly in springtime will encourage the fish to spawn.

Small specimens of Common goldfish and the more delicate fancy varieties, such as Veiltail, Black Moor and Bristol Shubunkin, need to be kept in a tank. Big aquariums are costly, but a large surface area is of paramount importance.

Tanks may be furnished with gravel and a few smooth rocks, but most important are the plants that provide both shade and green food for the fish. Suitable plants for coldwater tanks include Canadian pondweed, horn-wort, curly pondweed, and water milfoil.

A ventilated cover will help keep dust off the surface and keep the fish safe. It may house a light that will encourage the plants to thrive if left on 8-10 hours a day.

The Common goldfish is the variety most often kept as a pet.

PET CARE

As fish have no eyelids, avoid subjecting them to the direct rays of the sun in summer. The tank can be shaded by a paper frieze or by painting part of the exterior dark green.

TROPICAL FISH

As tropical fish display such a variety of colour and line, it is not surprising that keeping them has become something of a cult. Since many are incompatible, and some — notably the piranha — are deadly carnivores, beginners should take an aquarist's advice before attempting to stock a community tank. Among the fish most likely to be recommended are Guppies, Mollies, Swordtails, Zebra fish, Beacon fish, small-sized Angel fish and the Tetras.

WARM WATER AQUARIUMS

Tropical fish have to be kept at an even temperature of 24° C (75° F). If the water temperature falls to 18° C (65° F) for a protracted period both fish and plants are likely to suffer. Small fluctuations in temperature are seldom important.

AQUARIUM PLANTS

A tropical tank does not differ from the coldwater type but must contain plants of tropical origin that will flourish in warm water. These include sword plants, cabombas and ludwigias, as well as the more familiar eel grass which is also grown in cold tanks.

When stocking a community tank remember that certain species are incompatible. Some fish are deadly carnivores and should be excluded.

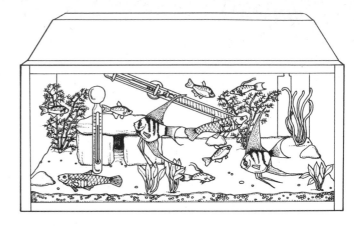

AQUARIUM MAINTENANCE

In order to maintain a tropical fish tank certain equipment is needed: a thermostatically controlled water heater, with thermometer; top lighting for 10-12 hours a day; and a vibrator pump to aerate the water. All this

If the common fault of overcrowding is avoided, tank maintenance will be much easier. Fish require differing amounts of space. If in doubt, consult an aquarist.

equipment is available in a range of prices and qualities and the better pumps may be used both to aerate and filter water.

BEAUTY AND HEALTH

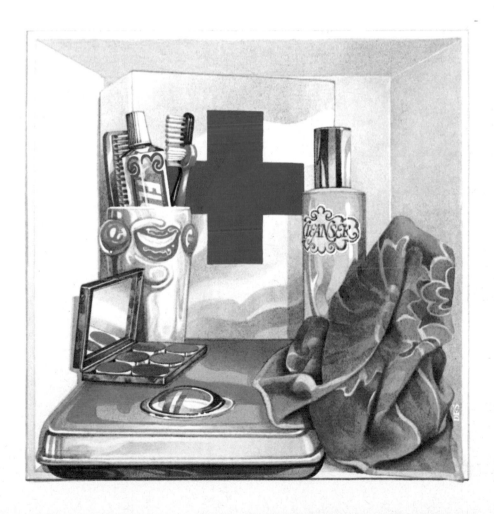

BEAUTY AND HEALTH

FAMILY DIET AND EXERCISE

Wouldn't it be marvellous if we could eat as many cream cakes, chips or chocolates — or whatever your favourite fantasy food is — and still look slim and glowing with health! Alas, even eating food that is considered good for us, such as meat, eggs or cheese, can be unhealthy if we do so to excess.

A 'balanced' diet is an eating pattern that contains a bit of everything. Bodies have different requirements at different stages, but everybody needs to eat balanced, regular meals. This is a habit that is the foundation of good health and good looks and it's something careful parents can help their children establish early, getting them into the habit of eating well — and properly — all their lives.

WHAT IS A BALANCED DIET?

All foods contain at least one of these nutrients, and each nutrient has a specific function in the body-building process. They are:

CARBOHYDRATES and FATS which provide bodily energy. Anything left over is stored in the body as fat.
PROTEINS help body growth and repair.
MINERALS also help with growth and repair and, with VITAMINS, help to regulate body processes.

Carbohydrates are sugars, starches and cellulose (dietary fibre) or roughage. Main sources for these are all sweetened items such as jams, ice cream, etc., as well as items containing natural sugar such as fruits and milk. Starches are found in all flour-based items such as bread and in processed foods with thickened sauces.

Main sources of fats are butter, cream, cooking oils, hard cheeses, fatty meats such as pork. All dairy products contain a certain amount of fats although this is quite low in the case of milk, eggs and cottage cheese.

Proteins are found in all meats, fish, cheese and pulses, with useful amounts in bread and milk.

Most balanced diets contain sufficient of the 15 or so minerals that are essential for good health. The minerals calcium, phosphorus and magnesium are very important for strong bones and teeth. Iron is particularly important as it is involved with the use of oxygen. If there is a deficiency of iron it results in anaemia. Other minerals are also necessary for the body's well being but only in small quantities.

Vitamins are essential in minute amounts for normal body growth and general good health. Vitamins fall into two main types: the fat soluble vitamins which are found in fats and oils, meat, fish and dairy products; and the water soluble vitamins which are found in cereals, fruit, vegetables and, like fat soluble vitamins, in dairy products.

Here are some of the major 'building' foods and what they contain:

MILK contains nearly every constituent of nutritional importance although it is somewhat deficient in iron and vitamins C and D.

EGGS are good sources of iron, protein and vitamins A and D. Colour depends more on the breed than nutritional value.

MEAT is a major source of protein, iron and B vitamins while liver and kidney also contain vitamin A.

FISH The flesh of fish is a very valuable source of protein. The fat soluble vitamins

A and D are both present in fatty fish such as herring and mackerel. They are also found in the livers of cod and halibut.

VEGETABLES contain dietary fibre to help the digestive process, vitamins A, C, iron and other minerals. Pulses, such as beans, peas (fresh), are also rich in protein.

FRUITS contain vitamin C and fructose (fruit sugar) — especially dried fruits — an important source of energy. Nuts are high in protein and fat and a good source of B vitamins.

CEREALS: most breakfast cereals are reinforced with vitamin and mineral ingredients, as is white flour. Wholemeal flour has a natural content of iron, vitamins and dietary fibre.

WHAT EVERY BODY NEEDS

Although we all need a good proportion of these different foods to help us function efficiently, individual needs vary as the body changes. One important thing to remember is that children's eating habits are established very early in life.

Children should be given a wide variety of different foods to try from a fairly early age and a stable meal pattern should be encouraged as well. A well-balanced diet will provide all the energy needed. High-energy, snack-type foods are best avoided as they can help to encourage both obesity and dental decay.

For instance, all the sugar we need can be found in the fruit we eat, all the fats in items such as milk, cheese, toast and butter, and in vegetable oils. Cream cakes, sweets, and jams are really 'treats'. We honestly don't need them to maintain life — although they do make life that much more pleasant!

And here's a further dire warning — sucrose (the sugar found in sugars and sugar-based items like sweets) can wreak havoc on young teeth and cause a lot of trouble all through your child's adult life. (See 'Dental Care' below.)

But don't worry if your *pre-teenage child* displays a big appetite. This is really 'healthy' and should be encouraged — but in the right way.

During their schooldays, children are extremely active and, as they are growing very rapidly at that time in their lives, their dietary requirements are high in relation to the actual size of their body. However, bulky-type foods that fill up but only

have a very low nutritional value such as sweets, soft drinks, cakes and biscuits should not be allowed to spoil the child's appetite so that they do not want to eat when it is time for their proper meals. 'Snacks' should be discouraged.

Milk is a good source for calcium, riboflavin and protein and should form a regular part of your children's diet. Add bread, cheese, meat (particularly liver), fish, eggs, fruit, green vegetables and potatoes and you have the basis of a good balanced diet that will ensure that they have all the nourishment they need and that they will probably never have a weight problem when they grow up. *Adolescents* basically require the same varied, well balanced, easily converted diet, although their own fads and fancies often defeat this aim. Obesity (overweight) among school children is now a very sad but common sight and it is due entirely to bad eating habits.

On the other hand, *anorexia nervosa* is also becoming increasingly common among teenagers, particularly girls. This is compulsive dieting to the point of malnutrition and, in extreme cases, it can be fatal.

As far as the nutritionist is concerned, although Johnny is grossly overweight and his sister looks like a scarecrow, both are suffering from a form of malnutrition because both, in their own separate ways, are not eating the foods they need to maintain their bodies.

There's no easy answer to these difficult problems and, although they represent extremes, most parents have had to cope with 'difficult' teenage eating at some stage or another. Nagging doesn't

BEAUTY AND HEALTH

really help; neither does pointing out that something is 'good for you'. Delicious-smelling meals, attractively presented and which just happen to contain all the right things, may go a long way to helping the teenager adjust his cravings to his real needs.

Like pre-teen children, they do need a lot of energy. A big appetite isn't neces-sarily a bad thing and should be fully indulged. Probably at no other time in their lives will they require so much energy, and energy-giving food will help build up bodies beautifully.

Adults are frequently less active than they were when they were adolescents and, in consequence, their energy re-quirements decline. How-ever, it is often the case that appetites remain the same as they were before.

If your weight was right for you at 20, then ideally it should remain the same at 40 — but has it? Women tend to be more weight-conscious than men, but with more and more people doing sedentary jobs with a minimum of exercise, and probably not eating pro-perly — e.g., filling up at the pub at lunch with beer and crisps — it's no wonder that obesity is becoming more and more of a problem with adults, too.

It is also a health prob-lem. A heavy body puts undue strain on the body's organs, particularly the heart. An unexercised, over-weight body means slack muscles that cannot easily cope with the added weight strain, and bad health is the all-too-common result. It

isn't vanity to want to stay slim all your life — just plain common sense!

The elderly, on the other hand, are often in danger of suffering from another form of anorexia, particularly if they live on their own. Be-cause energy requirements diminish with age, nature adjusts by lessening the appe-tite. But this natural process can be extended unhealthily by the eating habits of the senior citizen.

Very often they lose interest in their food, particu-larly if they have to pre-pare it for themselves and there is no-one else to cook for. They will tend to heat up a tin of something or other, or skip meals altogether. A balanced diet is just as impor-tant for them as for everyone else. Eggs and other dairy products should form a large part of their diet, as well as items containing natural roughage such as greens and wholemeal bread to help with digestion.

STAYING SLIM — SENSIBLY

For most people, weight-gain happens over a period of time. You step on the scales one morning and suddenly see that you're five kilo-grams (11 lb) heavier than you were just the other day, or, at any rate, a few months ago . . . or a year ago.

But there can be a world of difference between what you would like to be, and how nature intended. Perhaps never as sylphlike as the fashion pundits would wish, but if your figure is in propor-tion (waist 25 cm (10") slim-mer than bust; bust 5 cm (2") smaller than hips), if you

look well put together, then there is very little to worry about.

On the other hand, love can be blind, certainly when it comes to the odd 'spare tyre' or two. 'Oh my fam-ily/husband/wife like me this way' is a common excuse. Do they really — or are they just being kind? And, if it comes to that, are you really being loving when you serve your portly (all right, cuddly) hus-band or wife a favourite meal of fish and chips followed by spotted dick and a couple of pints to wash it all down? On the whole, a slim family is a healthy family. And there's just as wide a gap between fat and slim as there is between slim and gaunt!

A two-pronged attack is needed to effect a lasting weight-loss — diet and exer-cise. *Diet* will actually make the pounds melt, however slowly. *Exercise* will help speed up the process, and will help trim slack muscles to give you a slimmer, more streamlined figure. Many people often feel that, be-cause they're a bit lumpy and bumpy, they're overweight, although the scales tell them differently. Quite often this can be corrected by regular exercise — all that is needed is some firming up.

The two most popular types of dieting are calorie counting and carbohydrate counting. Calories are a measurement of energy; for instance, it is estimated that the average adult woman can burn up 2000 calories a day — anything over that will be stored in the body as fat. The average adult man needs about 3000 a day. Or, if you prefer carbohydrate count-ing, then 60 g (2 oz) a day is

Calories values are given in Calories per ounce.

Calories

	Calories
Almonds	165
Apple, fresh eating, (medium about 4 oz)	15
Apricot, tinned	30
Apricots, dried	50
Asparagus, fresh	5
Bacon, lean, fried	125
Bacon, lean, grilled	90
Bananas, fresh, peeled	20
Barley, pearl	105
Beans, broad, fresh	20
Beans, butter, boiled	25
Beans, green, runner	5
Beef, corned	60
Beef, roast, lean & fat	100
Beef, roast, lean	65
Beer, bottled, pale or brown	10
Beer, draught, bitter or mild	10
Beetroot, boiled	10
Beverages	
Chocolate, drinking	115
Cocoa powder	130
Coffee	0
Tea	0
Biscuits, plain	120
chocolate	140
Blackberries	10
Bread	70
Broccoli, boiled	5
Brussels sprouts, boiled	5
Butter	205
Cabbage, boiled	5
Cakes	
plain sponge	130
fruit	100
jam tarts	105
Carrots, fresh, boiled, raw, tinned	5
Cauliflower, boiled	5
Celery, fresh, raw	5
Cereal, breakfast (varies from about 90-115)	
Cheese, Cheddar	115
Cheshire	115
Cottage	30
Cream	120
Danish Blue	100

Calories

	Calories
Cherries, fresh,	15
Chicken, roast	40
Chips, potato, fried	70
Chocolate, milk	160
Chocolate, plain	150
Cooking fat, lard	255
Cooking oil	250
Corn on the cob	35
Cream, fresh, single	60
Cream, fresh, double	130
Cress, fresh, raw	5
Crisps, potato,	150
Cucumber, raw	5
Damsons, fresh, raw or stewed	10
Dates,	60
Doughnuts, jam	100
Egg, boiled or poached	45
Egg, fried	70
Egg, raw	45
Fish, white	20
fried in batter	55
herrings	65
kipper fillets	60
Fish, canned	
pilchards in tomato	40
salmon	40
sardines in oil	60
shrimps, drained	35
tuna in oil	75
Fish fingers, grilled	50
Flour, white or wholemeal	100
Fruit, dried	
sultanas	70
raisins	70
Gherkins	0
Grapes, white	15
Grapefruit, fresh	5
Grapefruit, canned	15
Ham	75
Ice cream	55
Lamb chop, grilled	75
Leek, boiled	5
Lemon, fresh	5
Lemon barley water	30
Lentils, boiled	25
Lettuce, raw	0

Calories

	Calories
Liver sausage, cooked	65
Margarine	205
Marmalade	75
Marrow, boiled	0
Melon, yellow, fresh	5
Milk, fresh, dairy	20
Milk, evaporated	50
Milk, dried, whole	140
Mushrooms, raw	0
Olive oil	255
Olives	30
Onion, fried	100
Onion, raw	5
Orange, sweet, fresh	10
Orange, juice, fresh	10
Orange squash, concentrate	30
Parsley, raw, fresh	5
Parsnip, boiled or raw	15
Pasta	
dry weight	105
Peaches, canned	25
Peanuts, shelled	170
Peanut butter	175
Pear, fresh, raw, eating or fresh, cooking, stewed	10
Peas, frozen	20
Peas, fresh, boiled	15
Peppers, red or green	5
Pineapple, fresh, raw	10
Pineapple, canned	20
Plums, dessert, fresh	10
Potatoes, boiled	25
Potatoes, roast	35
Prawns	10
Prunes, canned	25
Rabbit, stewed	50
Raspberries	5
Rhubarb, stewed	0
Rice, boiled	35
Salad cream	90
Sauce, Worcestershire	5
Sausages, pork, fried	95
grilled	90
Spinach, fresh, boiled	5
Spirits, alcoholic, average	60-70
Sugar, white	115
brown	115
Sweet Pickle	40

BEAUTY AND HEALTH

The ideal weight charts illustrated on this page and opposite are not intended to be clinically accurate. They are, however, a rough guide to those on a diet and the figures given are an approximation of the 'right' weight in relation to height and build.

a usual dieter's allowance.

Most people prefer calorie counting because it gives you a wider choice of foods, even allowing sweets or chocolates as an occasional treat. But the low carbohydrate — or high protein — diet has many devotees and works well. Starches and sweets are virtually taboo in this diet but it does allow a certain amount of alcohol (high in calories), and dieters can eat as much as they want of the 'allowed' foods.

	IDEAL WEIGHT (WOMEN)		
Height Ft In	Small Frame St lb	Medium Frame St lb	Large Frame St lb
4 11	7 10	8 1	8 10
5 0	7 13	8 3	8 13
5 1	8 2	8 7	9 2
5 2	8 5	8 10	9 5
5 3	8 7	8 13	9 8
5 4	8 11	9 2	9 11
5 5	8 13	9 5	10 2
5 6	9 3	9 9	10 6
5 7	9 6	9 13	10 9
5 8	9 9	10 3	10 12
5 9	9 12	10 7	11 3
5 10	10 3	10 12	11 7
5 11	10 6	11 2	11 11

EXERCISES FOR EVERYONE

Many people start off on an exercise programme with high hopes and enthusiasm, but fall by the wayside very shortly afterwards. Sports — running, tennis, badminton, squash, swimming, riding — are very good, complete exercise but not everyone has the time, inclination or facilities to enjoy them. But a regular exercise programme at home will be just as effective in toning muscles and keeping fit.

There's safety — and fun — in numbers. Here's an exercise programme for all the family. Do it first thing in the morning (just by getting up ten minutes earlier).

GENERAL TONER. Run on the spot, bringing knees up high, for 30 seconds.

BUST AND CHEST. Bring hands to chest height. Clasp them together with the heels against each other. Push hard — heel against

heel. Relax. Push hard again. Repeat 20 times.

WAIST. Stand up, legs about 30 cm (12 in) apart. With left hand on left hip, slide your right hand down your right leg as far as you can, bending your trunk sideways. Slowly come back to starting position and repeat with left

side. Repeat 10 times each side.

TUMMY. Lie flat on the floor with heels resting on a pile of books so that they're about 30 cm (12 in) higher than the head. Clasp hands behind head. Raise trunk, keeping legs straight, to sitting position. Very fit people can show off by leaning forward and touching

Whichever diet you choose, please don't try to lose more than 1–2 kg (2–3 lb) a week for every 6 kg (14 lb) you are overweight. Quick weight-loss is harmful and is not long-lasting. The first amount of weight you will lose is body fluid — 'crash' diets simply eliminate this and then, the minute you revert to your usual eating pattern, all of it comes on again. A slow but steady diet will help your body adjust to its weight-loss and will also re-educate your stomach to expect less.

Two final golden rules: remember that every diet should be balanced for health and effectiveness. You want to look good and feel on top of the world when you're slimming, so always include body-building foods (another reason why you should avoid fad diets). And, if you are grossly overweight, always consult your doctor first. He will help monitor your weight-loss and advise you on the best diet to follow.

IDEAL WEIGHT (MEN)			
Height Ft In	Small Frame St lb	Medium Frame St lb	Large Frame St lb
5 2	8 9	9 3	9 9
5 3	8 11	9 6	9 13
5 4	9 1	9 9	10 3
5 5	9 4	9 13	10 7
5 6	9 8	10 2	10 11
5 7	9 12	10 6	11 1
5 8	10 1	10 11	11 5
5 9	10 5	11 0	11 8
5 10	10 9	11 4	11 10
5 11	11 0	11 9	12 4
6 0	11 4	11 12	12 9
6 1	11 8	12 4	13 2
6 2	12 1	12 9	13 7
6 3	12 6	13 0	13 12

knees with their forehead. Try — and if at first you don't succeed. . . . Repeat 5 times.

BOTTOM AND THIGHS. Squats are super for this problem area. Hold on to the back of a chair or anything that is firm and chest high. Keep feet flat on the floor about 30 cm (12 in) apart. Squat down, holding on to the chair or whatever, keeping your back straight and feet flat. Come back to standing position. Do this very quickly and as often as you can manage, starting with 10.

LEGS. Bicycle in the air, preferably from a shoulder stand position, for at least a minute.

FINAL BREATHER. Stand up, arms at side, legs slightly apart. Flop forward from the waist, arms hanging loose, touching the floor. As you flop, breathe out. Stretch up slowly, breathing in. Reach for the ceiling with your hands and stand on tiptoe, still reaching. Then flop forward. Repeat 5 times or more.

BEAUTY AND HEALTH

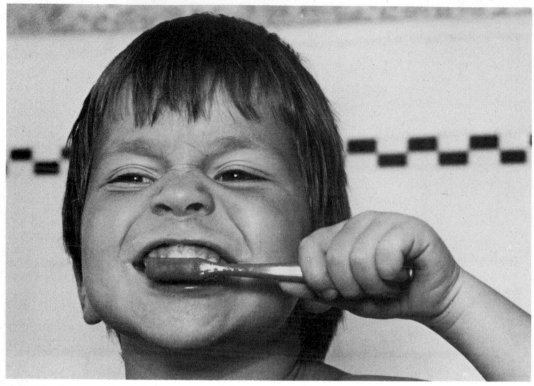

DENTAL CARE

For such a modern nation, Britons don't have much to boast about when it comes to oral hygiene. Thirty-one per cent of the adult population have no teeth, 75 per cent of all children have active dental decay and 99 per cent of young people have gingivitis (gum disease).

The sad thing about these statistics is that they can, and should, be zero per cent in every case. Nobody should ever have a filling again or an extraction; the makers of false teeth should go out of business.

The cause of both caries (tooth decay) and gingivitis is 'plaque' — a sticky film made up of food and saliva deposits and harmful bacteria which adheres to the surface

enamel area of the teeth.

Sugar is particularly active in helping to form plaque and this is the main reason why all oral hygiene experts advise parents to watch the amount of sweets, cakes and biscuits their children eat (also important for skin and weight problems later) and always to encourage them to brush their teeth afterwards.

STARTING FROM SCRATCH

There are three major things that should all be done together to help make teeth less vulnerable to attack. They are:

(1) Correct brushing;
(2) Use of fluoride;
(3) Regular visits to the dentist.

Correct brushing This must start with having the right toothbrush. Always make sure that everyone in the family has his own toothbrush, and that it's changed about four times a year. A toothbrush with broken or bent filaments simply won't do the cleaning job.

A few years ago, the fashion was for hard bristles that would really clean thoroughly. Nowadays, it's recognized that a too-hard bristle can scratch and damage tooth enamel. The ideal brush should have a small head that fits comfortably into the mouth, with multi-tufted nylon filaments trimmed flat. They should also be flexible. Soft/medium bristles are quite adequate in removing food particles, plaque, etc. Using dental floss is an excellent way of cleaning between teeth.

Use of fluoride Fluoride is a naturally-occurring mineral which has been conclusively proved to substantially fortify teeth against plaque. It can be taken in a variety of forms — the most common is in toothpaste. However, you can also take fluoride tablets (of particular benefit for pregnant women to help both their own and their unborn babies' teeth); it can come in the water supply (your area water authority will tell you if your water contains it); and your dentist can make an application of fluoride directly on to the teeth — which brings us on to the next point.

Regular visits to the dentist Everyone should visit their dentist at least twice a year, even if nothing seems to be wrong. Your dentist can detect early warning signs of damage; he can also tell if teeth are being looked after correctly and will advise on correct brushing. He will also show you and your children how to use dental floss properly — and flossing is an important part in the cleaning process as it removes food and other particles from crevices that your toothbrush can't penetrate efficiently. So don't put off the evil day until it becomes one.

WHY TAKE ALL THIS TROUBLE?
If you could cut a tooth in half lengthwise, you'd see that there are five different sections. The outer layer is the one we see — hard white enamel. This encases the whole tooth above the gum line. Under the enamel is soft dentine, which in turn contains the pulp cavity with the nerve and blood supply. Cementum covers the root below the gum surface. The germs in plaque convert its sugar content to acid, which eats away at the enamel. Once that has been penetrated, the dentine is easily attacked and unless a filling is made, the whole tooth can rot away. This is 'caries'.

The same plaque can also attack the gums and, while a rotting tooth is painful, apart from the give-away initial bleeding, this is a painless process. Then the supporting structure of the tooth is attacked, and the tooth will eventually fall out or will have to be extracted. This is 'gingivitis'.

Because plaque takes about 24 hours to develop, this whole process can be controllable. In bad cases, plaque can be detected as a yellowy film and the affected teeth feel rough when you run a tongue over them. But your teeth don't have to reach this stage to be in danger from plaque.

THE FIGHT AGAINST PLAQUE
The first step in the battle against plaque is to establish a regular brushing routine — first thing every morning and

Stages in tooth decay

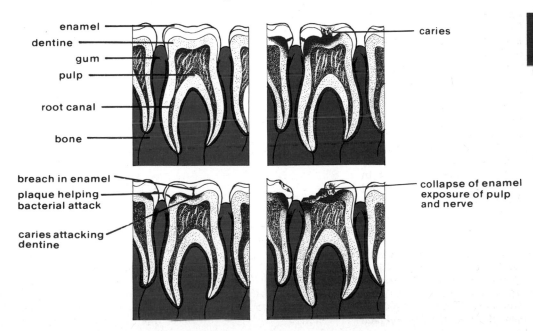

enamel
dentine
gum
pulp
root canal
bone

caries

breach in enamel
plaque helping bacterial attack
caries attacking dentine

collapse of enamel
exposure of pulp and nerve

BEAUTY AND HEALTH

last thing every night. Involve your children from an early age, and make it an amusing occasion. Use an egg-timer — three minutes is the correct length of time — for them to time their brushing, and always make sure that they brush correctly. Here's how:

1 First, brush the top teeth downwards from the gums to the tip.
2 Then brush lower teeth upwards.
3 and **4** Brush backs of all teeth from gums to tips.
5 Finally, brush biting surfaces backwards and forwards.

Remember, the generally accepted method of brushing from side to side (instead of upwards) isn't very effective in removing plaque as the brush tends to skip the crevices where plaque is lurking, and it may also damage the gums. So always make sure that your children are brushing correctly from the very first. It could make a world of difference as to whether or not they wear false teeth by the time they're 30.

SPECIAL CARE FOR SPECIAL PEOPLE

The mother-to-be It's an old myth that the foetus takes calcium from the mother's teeth; however, this does reflect the all-too-sad fact that many pregnant women find their teeth particularly prone to decay during this time.

There are two main reasons for this: the first is that pregnancy does weaken the gum's resistance to disease, and gingivitis will occur more readily if the gums aren't kept free from plaque.

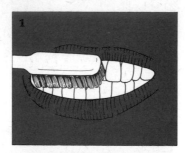

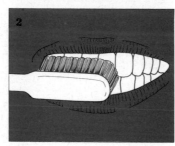

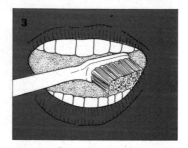

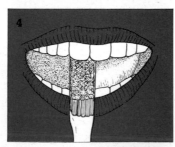

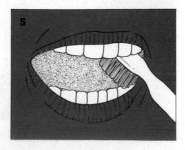

To brush your teeth correctly, follow the instructions given in the text on the left. You should also use dental floss in the crevices.

The second reason is more individual, and rests largely on how well the expectant mother looks after herself. It's quite possible, particularly during the early, morning-sickness months, that she will skip the morning brush (anything she puts in her mouth will make her feel nauseous). If this is the case, she should use a child's-size tooth-brush to help overcome the problem. Often, too, cravings mean that she's eating far more sweets, cakes and so on than usual. In pregnancy, as at every other time, sugar is the main cause of plaque. *Always* brush teeth after eating sweets.

As an added precaution, the expectant mum can take fluoride tablets (as directed on the bottle) during the last three months of pregnancy. They will help fortify her teeth and those of her baby.

Baby's milk teeth Many parents believe that, because milk teeth aren't permanent, it doesn't really matter if they're lost a bit earlier than usual because of dental decay. This isn't true, and every care should be taken to ensure that a baby's milk teeth are as well looked after as his 'grown-up' ones.

Milk teeth give a growing guide to the permanent teeth beneath. If they're lost prematurely, the secondary teeth can grow out crooked and, indeed, may be affected by the decay or abscess started in the milk tooth.

It's also very important that children be taught good eating habits from the begin-

278

ning — for their general health as well as for their teeth.

Parents can start the good work by properly cleaning the baby's teeth right from the outset. As soon as they appear through the gum they are vulnerable to plaque attack, and should be regularly cleaned with a piece of gauze coated with fluoride toothpaste. As the baby gets older, you can progress to a properly-made child's toothbrush. Mothers should also continue to take fluoride tablets and should give them to their babies, too.

Many of the medicines and anti-teething products for children contain some form of pleasant-tasting sweetener. It's not always possible to avoid giving them to babies, but their teeth should always be cleaned afterwards. And when it comes to teething, they should be encouraged to bite on a teething ring or a hard, unsweetened rusk.

Children This is the time when they can be properly taught about oral hygiene — but it's also the time when they're not too bothered about their appearance, and the time when they find all kinds of sweet temptation at school!

Watching their parents brush their teeth regularly gives them a very good example to follow, as are regular visits to the dentist.

Something all children find fun to use are 'disclosing' tablets — harmless red tablets that stain the teeth where plaque is present. They show children exactly where they're missing out when it comes to proper brushing, and makes their mouths look deliciously gruesome!

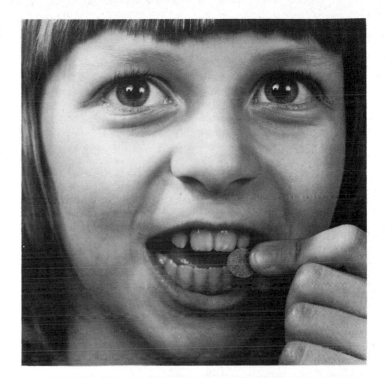

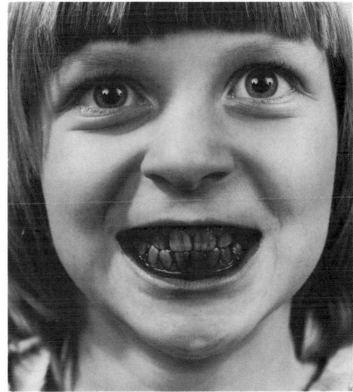

Disclosing tablets stain teeth red where plaque is present.

BEAUTY AND HEALTH

The teenage rebel. Teenagers are notorious for wanting to do things their own way, and for showing a very marked disinclination to follow any suggestions made by fuddy-duddy adults. Fortunately, though, they can be very vain and concerned about their appearance.

The best way to encourage them to brush their teeth regularly is not to tell them that it's 'good for them', but to point out how unattractive bad breath and yellow teeth are — and do they really want to take out their teeth every night like granny does?

And because they are undergoing various hormonal changes, their gums are particularly low on resistance against infection. Unless they are cleaned thoroughly of plaque, gingivitis and the painful ulcerative gingivitis may develop. Bleeding gums are the first sign that this is occurring and very often people stop brushing because of the pain. It's absolutely essential to carry on brushing — good and regular brushing is the very best method of removing the plaque.

Sweets, as ever, are the killers; they will cause overweight as well as rotten teeth — two reasons why the figure-conscious teenager should avoid all unnecessary sugar-containing foods.

YOUR ORAL HYGIENE CHECK-LIST

The toothbrush is the basis of all good oral hygiene. Make sure you use one professionals recommend — your dentist will always advise you about this — and change it regularly.

Make sure that all the family has a good toothbrush in proper working order. Shared brushes shouldn't exist in plaque-free homes.

Cultivate the habit of using dental floss. Remember that each tooth has five sides and a brush can clean only three of them. Flossing (again, properly demonstrated by your dentist) will help remove all bits of food and other particles stuck between each tooth.

Alternatively, you may prefer softwood sticks or a waterpick. Both are designed to remove plaque from between the teeth — often the first place where decay occurs.

Toothpaste — naturally! Whenever possible, always choose a fluoride one. Always make sure that you have enough — it's not a good idea to get into the habit of occasionally skipping a brush, for whatever reason.

Disclosing tablets are the final proof of how well, or otherwise, you brush your teeth. Show the kids how to use them — and use them on yourself, too.

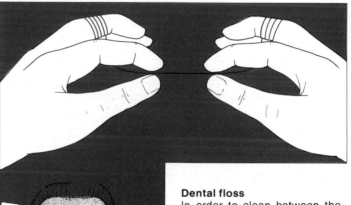

Dental floss
In order to clean between the teeth thoroughly, use dental floss. This is a nylon thread, made of many fine strands that fan out and glide gently under the gum margins to remove plaque in this vital area. Take 25–30 cm (10–12 in) of the floss and wind one end around the middle finger of each hand (*above*). Holding them about 2.5 cm (1 in) apart, work the floss gently up and down between the teeth (*top left*), cleaning the surfaces of each tooth, including the area below the gum line (*bottom left*). Be careful not to cut into the gum. As you work your way right around the mouth, move your fingers to change the angle you need. You can also buy flavoured dental floss which acts in the same way as the usual type but leaves your mouth with a pleasant taste.

HAIR AND SCALP

Technically speaking, the hair you see on your head is 'dead'. Who would have believed it when your hair is really looking its best — soft, shiny, easy to manage. Scientists have recently confirmed that hair is a good barometer of health; anyone who has experienced that less than top-of-the-world feeling (and who hasn't?) can often put it down to the fact that one's hair isn't quite right. And what feels better than walking out of a hairdresser's with a perfect, attractive, eye-catching coiffure?

BASIC STRUCTURE OF THE HAIR

Strangely, your hair and nails are very similar in composition — both are mainly composed of a protein called keratin and both are 'dead' when they are visible. This doesn't mean to say that they can't be looked after, improved.

If you looked at a cross-section of a hair under a microscope, it would look like the sawn-off trunk of a tree since it is composed of three concentric rings — the outer layer or cuticle, the inner layer or cortex, and the heart or medulla.

The cuticle consists of thousands of tiny, overlapping scales. When the hair is in good condition, these scales lie flat on top of each other. They are lubricated by the hair's natural oil and the result is soft, shiny hair. Damaged or broken hair results in torn or uplifted scales that give hair a dull appearance and coarse, wiry texture.

The cortex principally contains the hair's natural pigmentation which is made

up of thousands of tiny cells called 'melanocytes'. Each one is either black, yellow or red and the combination of these cells gives us our overall hair colour — 'mouse', for example, is a more or less equal combination of all three with often an underlying preponderance of red. As we grow older, the cortex loses its ability to manufacture this pigment and the result is the hair becoming grey, then white — i.e., colourless hair.

No-one quite knows what function the medulla has, and in some hairs it is missing entirely.

Each hair has a root

When hair is in good condition (top) the keratin scales of the hairshaft lie flat and smooth overlapping each other, giving a shiny look. Damaged or broken hair results in torn or uplifted scales (bottom).

lodged just underneath the skin's surface. This is the living part of the hair; it feeds from the skin and the hair shaft is lubricated by an oil from a sebaceous gland situated right next to the root.

Each hair has an average life span of about three years. After that, it will simply fall out of the scalp and is usually replaced by another — we've all noticed a certain amount of hair-loss whenever we brush or comb our hair. This is why some people will never have waist-length hair, even if they never cut it — it simply can't grow fast enough.

Curly hair or straight, platinum blonde or black, thick or fine — all these factors are determined by our own heredity. We can't change the basic pattern that dictates what our hair will be like, but we can help it look its very best.

HAIR TYPES AND HOW TO LOOK AFTER THEM

The usual definition of hair types depends mainly on how efficiently it is lubricated by the sebaceous gland. This natural lubrication affects the whole look and feel of the hair. There are dry, normal and oily categories.

DRY hair is often brittle and lifeless in appearance, with a rather wiry texture. The ends split easily and it has little natural sheen. It's most common from the age of 30 upwards although this isn't a hard-and-fast rule.

Washing and grooming Looking after dry hair means two things — keeping it clean while not washing away any natural oil, and supplementing your own oil supply. So, always choose a gentle shampoo specified for this hair

BEAUTY AND HEALTH

type. Often, shampoos for dry hair also contain a conditioning agent; if the shampoo of your choice doesn't then always apply a creme rinse after shampooing. You'll probably find you need only shampoo about once a week.

Twice a month, give your hair a deep conditioning treatment. After shampooing, towel dry your hair and then apply a conditioner all over it, gently working it in. Then wrap your hair with a towel and leave for 20–30 minutes. Rinse out thoroughly.

Gently massaging your scalp regularly between shampoos will also help stimulate the sebaceous glands and get a little more oil moving.

Because dry hair is prone to split ends, you will need to visit your hairdresser regularly for a trim. A style that doesn't need much in the way of electrical appliances (which can be very drying) to maintain it, and has a simple straightforward line, whose uncluttered appearance will make the most of the fine texture of your hair, is the ideal look for this hair type.

NORMAL hair should more properly be called 'ideal hair'! Most people have problems with their hair of some sort or another, although normal-haired people do exist. For these lucky folk, the main object is to ensure that the *status quo* is maintained.

Washing and grooming Usually this couldn't be more straightforward. Simply use whatever shampoo happens to please you at the moment. Occasionally, women will experience some excess greasiness just before their periods — if this happens to you, use a shampoo designed for oily hair and shampoo your hair twice a week instead of your usual once. Illness or pregnancy may cause dryness. Alternate your own shampoo with a conditioning shampoo, or apply a creme rinse after every second shampoo.

Hair doesn't grow at the same rate, so a trim by your hairdresser every two months will smarten your hair as well as strengthen the ends.

GREASY hair is most common during the teens and closely allied to greasy skin. It will tend to settle down during the twenties although it often results in the annoying *combination hair* condition — oily roots but dry ends.

Washing and grooming The amount of oil produced by the sebaceous glands is related to the body's hormonal activity, and there's not much we can do about that. Teenagers who wash their hair every second or third day at least show pride in their appearance, while clean hair is less likely to deposit excess oil along the hairline, often a cause of an embarrassing margin of spots.

Therefore, shampoo as often as seems necessary. As far as combination hair is concerned, dry shampoos play a useful part in curbing the roots' oiliness although most people tend to wash as for oily hair and then apply a conditioner on to the ends only.

Short to medium-length hair is the easiest to manage if you do shampoo often, while a body perm will take away the characteristic 'lankness' and add some fullness and will also help dry up the oil a little.

FAMILY HAIR CARE

Hair grooming for most families tends to be a communal thing. Parents buy a large economical bottle of family shampoo and there are towels, brushes and combs in the bathroom for everyone to use.

There is nothing wrong in that, as long as everything is kept scrupulously clean. Brushes and combs should be washed at least twice a week so that they are purely grooming tools, not passers-on of someone else's oil and dirt. Hairdressings and hairsprays get picked up by brushes and combs which are then vigorously applied to another, newly-shampooed head!

If, however, any member of the family suffers from dandruff then he *must* have his own towel, brush and comb and should see a trichologist as soon as possible. Dandruff is as infectious as it is unsightly and, by using the hair accessories of a dandruff sufferer, you immediately lay yourself open to risk. Scurf looks like dandruff but isn't nearly so persistent and is often only caused by inefficient rinsing out of shampoo or by a temporary dryness of the scalp. If you have dandruff, a good anti-dandruff shampoo will certainly help, but professional advice should be sought. If you suffer from scurf, try using a shampoo for normal or dry hair, and rinse it out well.

Looking after one's hair means taking a pride in one's

Young children must be taught at an early age to care for their hair so that, when they get older, it still looks good.

appearance — it's all part of developing self-esteem. Many younger children have an aversion to anything that smacks of cleanliness, so it's important that shampooing should be made as enjoyable as possible. Parents can set the example by demonstrating that *they* think that nice-looking hair is important, and this can be reinforced by regular visits to a hairdresser.

Shampooing, regular brushing and regular trimming are just as important for young hair as for adult hair so choose your child-

ren's shampoo and hair equipment with care.

THE TOOLS OF THE TRADE

Just as important as the correct shampooing routine is the use of the right hair equipment to maintain your hair properly. Brushes and combs are so commonplace that no-one really gives them much thought nowadays — any type will do, won't it?

The answer to that is an emphatic *no!*

Badly or incorrectly made brushes and combs can actually tear hair, breaking the ends and weakening the structure. Always choose a brush that is either pure natural bristle or a natural bristle and nylon mix. Nylon fila-

ments alone are too rigid; they won't give easily so the hair must — if hair is pulled too hard, it will break. Combs should have rounded teeth that are set sufficiently far apart so that the comb can slide through the hair easily. Fine-tooth combs should be reserved for children and for very fine hair, and metal combs should never be used.

Today most homes have their fair share of electrical hair appliances. The most popular, for women, are undoubtedly heated rollers, while almost everyone uses a hand-held dryer of some sort. In addition, there are curling tongs or wands, hooded dryers, hand-dryers with various brush attachments and so on. The list grows

BEAUTY AND HEALTH

longer each day but it all adds up to ease of styling and quickness of grooming —two very important assets.

But regard these as tools only. And depending on how well, or badly, you use them, so will your hair be affected. Whatever you use, there are some basic rules (illustrated below) to ensure that hair is always groomed beautifully, but never damaged.

WHAT STYLE SUITS ME?
Very few people can look at themselves objectively in the mirror and recognize exactly why they look best with long hair or short, curly or straight. We are so used to the way we look that an unbiased outsider's opinion is often the best. This is why, if you have a trusted hairdresser, he should be allowed to do what he thinks suits you — he is probably right.

But you are asking for trouble if you have someone totally unknown give you a dramatically new look. Let him get used to you, and your hair, before any drastic restyling takes place. And, most important, always ensure that your hairdresser knows you as a person — not just as a head with a body wrapped in overalls sitting in front of a mirror. If he sees you standing up and dressed normally, he can then see your height and width (so he can design a hairstyle in proportion to the rest of your body), and he can also see you as an individual who would look best with a simple, uncluttered style, or who is crying out for something really sophisticated or dramatic.

You too can take an intelligent interest in what your hairdresser is doing by understanding the proportions of your own face. There are two simple rules which everyone knows and everyone forgets — vertical lines make things look longer, horizontal lines make things look broader!

HOME PERMING AND COLOURING
Home perms and colourants are so safe these days and come in such a variety that there's no question that they can be used very effectively at home.

Never brush hair when it is wet. Hair has a very elastic quality and it is at its most stretched when wet. Any harsh pulling will tend to break it, so a gentle comb-through is all that is really needed.

When using a hand-held dryer, hold it about 30 cm (12 in) away from the head, and move it up and down all the time. Heat will 'cook' the hair and overdry it. Make sure your dryer just speeds the drying process.

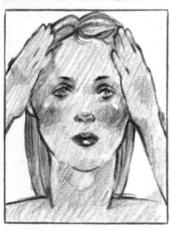

A setting lotion applied on your hair before using any heated appliance will protect your hair from the heat while ensuring a longer-lasting set. A creme rinse/conditioner will also protect your hair and make it shiny.

Imitate your hairdresser and wrap heated rollers in tissues (or toilet paper) before rolling your hair in them. Again, this will protect your hair from the heat as well as from possible tearing by the filaments which are the prongs of the rollers.

If you have a longish, narrow face (1a), broaden it by having a medium-length, curly or wavy style (1b), avoiding having it pulled back, and perhaps also having a perm. A plump face (2a) can look much thinner when surrounded by a classic page-boy cut (2b), which will cover a wide jawline that a pulled-back style would reveal.

A long forehead (3b) can be effectively hidden with a fringe (3a), but be sure to always clean the skin under it carefully as this area can be prone to spots. A low forehead (4b) should have hair swept off it and then brought round on either side of the face (4a). You should always avoid wearing a fringe as this accentuates a low forehead.

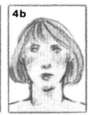

Safety doesn't mean foolproof, however — manufacturers of these products have files of letters that often boil down to one thing: the consumer didn't read the instructions. That's a rule that should never, never be broken, simply because perming and permanent colouring actually alter the basic structure of the hair.

If you apply a permanent colour on your hair which you don't like, then there's no point in trying to cover it with another colourant — you will simply get a strange combination of the two. Permanent colourants remove the pigmentation in the melanocytes and replace it

with their own colour so, if you don't like it, you'll have to try to get a professional to strip out the colour first and then apply another colour which is an approximation of your own. Often professionals will not correct wrong treatment, and you should contact the manufacturers of the colourant who can often suggest a professional willing to do something about it.

The same goes for perming. It alters the structure of the cortex so, again, if you're not happy with it, you'll have to get your hairdresser to do a professional straightening.

If you want to go from

straight to curly, know exactly what you will look like when the process is completed. If you want to go from dark to light, understand that your skin tone and make-up should be adapted accordingly. In both cases, if you're not sure of the results, do it gradually or go to a local department store and try on a wig of the style or colour you had in mind. And take your best friend with you! In addition, you should always check with your hairdresser that your hair is suitable for perming. For example, hair that has been bleached or has had highlights put in should never be permed immediately afterwards.

BEAUTY AND HEALTH

SKIN CARE

We all take our skin for granted. Did you know that it is our body's largest organ that acts as a waterproof barrier and insulator, as well as a protector of all our internal organs?

As far as most people are concerned, the outward appearance of the skin *is* the body — it tells us the approximate age of the person and is a major contributor to his/her good looks. However, what most people think is the skin is merely the surface — a tiny network of interlinking cells that are regularly sloughed off and replaced by new ones.

In fact, the skin consists of two layers — the epidermis (or top) and the dermis, which houses blood vessels, sweat and oil glands and hair follicles. The highly efficient replacement of old cells by new on the skin's surface starts in the dermis, for this is where the skin's natural moisture is stored as well as collagen and elastic tissue which give young skins that smooth, unlined appearance.

As we get older, this process of renewal slows down. At the same time, the epidermis becomes thinner and the dermis changes so that the skin loses its elasticity and tone. This process can be hastened by exposure to the elements — sun, wind, cold weather — as well as atmospheric pollution. You have only to compare the facial skin of adults with that of their bottoms or inside thighs: the first is beginning to line, the second is still soft and smooth — and the difference is simply due to a daily confrontation with the outside world!

Fortunately there's a great deal we can do to minimize these effects and, while the ageing process is still one of science's question marks, people today are in the lucky position of knowing that, if they look after their skin regularly and well (from the inside out), they really will look younger than their years. Of course, needs change with the years, but the basic skin care for everyone from 18 to 80 is summed up in three words: cleanse, tone, moisturize.

THE TROUBLED, OILY ADOLESCENT SKIN

Telling an impatient teenager that his spots are all due to hormonal changes in his body that will right themselves with time isn't going to console him much, even if it is the truth! Spots are closely allied with greasy skin so treatment for the one is often the same as treatment for the other. These hormonal changes affect the whole body and obviously something as complex and as profound as these may often have undesirable side-effects. The most common is that the sebaceous, or oil, glands in the dermis start over-producing. Excess oil with dirt may then combine to plug up the skin's pores and the result — blackheads and, of course, spots.

Very bad cases should be taken to your GP who may refer the sufferer to a skin

STRUCTURE OF THE SKIN

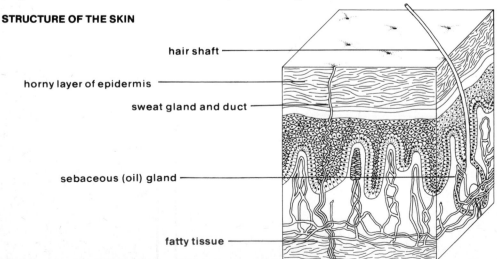

hair shaft

horny layer of epidermis

sweat gland and duct

sebaceous (oil) gland

fatty tissue

specialist, but less severe conditions can be controlled by oneself. The word 'control' is important; at the moment, only certain antibiotics available from the doctor will actually clear up the problem for any great length of time. Such extreme measures aren't always necessary or desirable, and the skin-care routine teenagers learn now will stand them in good stead all their lives.

A good teenage skin-care routine should have three main objectives: it should control the excess oil; it should keep the skin scrupulously clean; and it should be mildly antiseptic to discourage bacterial activity that works with the oil and dirt to cause spots. So the emphasis in the classic 'cleanse, tone, moisturize' routine is on *cleanse* and *tone.*

Many people think that washing their face with soap and water is sufficient. It isn't! Ordinary toilet soap is not formulated to wash away efficiently all the detritus on the face including, often,

make-up. So always ensure that your teenage son or daughter uses a properly-formulated soap or liquid soap to do the job. Granulated skin-care products used once or twice a week will help the circulation and get rid of dead skin cells that may clog the pores. Cleaning should take place every night and morning to ensure maximum effect, and should be followed by toning. Face cloths and towels should be used only by one individual, and they should be washed (by boiling) every day to get rid of all germs. For a teenager, an astringent or toner especially formulated for greasy skin is the one to use. Pour a little on a dampened piece of cotton wool and rub lightly over the face.

The biggest temptation for all spot sufferers is to have a good pick at the offending areas. This is the best way of spreading the infection! Each spot should be covered with an antiseptic cream and then, when it is ready and only then, lightly squeezed with clean hands and a clean tissue and dabbed with a

medicated lotion.

The third part of the skin-care routine — moisturizing — probably won't apply for this skin type, although it's worth remembering that loss of moisture can occur even with greasy skin. If this happens, and the skin takes on a dry, flaky appearance, apply a light, non-greasy moisturizing lotion as and when necessary. There are several on the market that are formulated for this skin type.

SKIN AT ITS BEST
Skin is at its peak when you are in your twenties — the production of oil will have modified and its mechanism for retaining moisture will still be highly efficient. This is the time to establish a good skin-care routine to help keep it looking good as long as possible.

From now on, the most important part of the skin-care routine is moisturizing, for natural moisture is the most valuable single item of a young-looking skin. A very simple analogy is to look at a prune and compare it with a plum. Both are the same

Blackheads

A spot

Acne

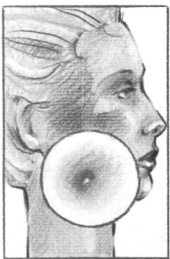

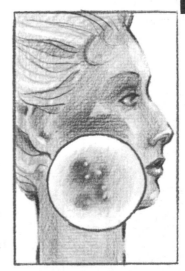

BEAUTY AND HEALTH

fruit, except the prune has been dried of its moisture and it has wrinkled up, just like human skin would in the same circumstances. Natural moisture plumps out the skin cells, making them look smooth and soft.

To help your skin maintain its natural moisture content, you need to protect and replenish it. Because the face is exposed almost constantly to the elements, facial moisture evaporates much more quickly than from any other part of the body. There are also areas on the face that contain little or no natural oil or moisture, and these are therefore the parts that will begin to wrinkle first.

First start with cleansing. This is really the time, if you haven't done so before, to break the habit of using toilet soap when cleansing your face. That tingly, tight feeling that many people associate with cleanliness is

(Left) For young-looking skin, protect and add to its natural moisture.

Cleanse: wipe off cleanser using an upward movement.

Tone: non-alcoholic type, with astringent for greasy patches.

Moisturize: apply moisturizer from neck to top of face.

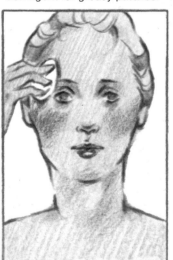

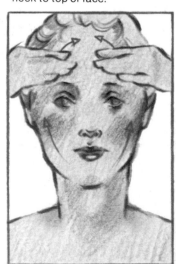

really a drying of the skin — it is contracting to fill in the gaps left by the removal of natural oil and moisture. Another point: most make-up foundations are oil-in-water based which means they need specially-formulated products to remove them from the face. Soap can't do this efficiently, so it probably won't leave your skin very clean anyway.

There are now many well-formulated facial washing products on the market and, if this is the type of cleansing routine you prefer, then do choose one of these. It's worth remembering, though, that excessive contact with water can be drying, and dry skin shouldn't really be washed more than necessary.

People in their twenties often suffer from combination skin — an oily T-shape that covers the forehead, nose and chin, leaving the rest normal or dry. This skin type will probably benefit from a wash once or twice a week, particularly for women just before and during their periods, when they may still find the odd spot appearing — most annoyingly!

For normal and dry skins, a good cleansing milk or lotion should do the trick. Pour a little into the palm of your hand, then lightly massage it over your face, starting from the neck and moving upwards. Don't pull or stretch the skin in any way — simply work in the cleanser using a gentle, circular movement. Afterwards wipe it off thoroughly with a cotton wool pad, again using an upward movement. Then apply your toner. Greasy skin patches may benefit once or twice a week from an astringent — otherwise, use a toner, non-alcoholic for preference.

This should be done at night and in the morning and it is a good idea, too, to put the cleanser on during your bath or shower. The steam will open the pores, giving the cleanser a chance to penetrate and remove all deep-lying dirt.

Finally, the all-important moisturizer, designed for your skin type, should be applied religiously. Apart from replacing lost natural moisture, a good moisturizer will create a barrier on the skin's surface to help prevent further moisture-loss, and it also enables make-up to go on smoothly and evenly. No-one should ever forget to use it!

THE OLDER SKIN

Skin treated with tender loving care will repay this kindness lavishly in the years to come. We have all admired elderly ladies with beautiful skin; we have all admired women of forty plus who look at least ten years younger than they are.

We can't escape the onslaught of age and nothing short of surgery will remove bags and wrinkles once they have appeared. But the older skin does have its compensations. It will now be free from blemishes and will have regulated itself, although the moisture-loss will have speeded up.

From the early thirties onwards, the skin-care routine should be supplemented by other, extra action for 'maintenance'. This is the time to invest in extra items that will help you always to look your best. The most important of these are an eye cream and a richer night cream to reinforce the action of the day-time moisturizer.

Eye cream is so important because the delicate skin around the eye contains very little natural oil and moisture and what little it does contain escapes very readily into the atmosphere. This is why crow's feet (or laughter lines) are among the first wrinkles to put in an appearance.

A night cream is necessary because the efficient manufacture of the skin's collagen content is beginning to slow down and the skin will start to sag and line instead of remaining firm and smooth. A night cream will help replace this loss. Both night cream and eye cream should be used sparingly at first — not every night — and only when your skin needs them. Of course, both these products should be used in conjunction with your 'cleanse, tone, moisturize' routine which should be second nature by now!

BEAUTY EXTRAS

These are the bare bones of a good beauty skin-care routine. Do the following and you won't go far wrong. But, like everything else, the more you put into it, the more you get out and there are very few women who are so busy that they don't have the odd hour — or even afternoon when they can give themselves a really professional beauty treatment.

First, get together everything you'll need — your cleanser, a large towel, a kettle of boiled, steaming water, some dried camomile flowers or sprigs of fresh mint and your face mask. There are many masks on the market specially formulated for all skin types. Choose one that best suits your skin and one which you can reasonably afford.

Cleanse your face thoroughly. Once you've done this, reapply the clean-

BEAUTY AND HEALTH

Older skin needs special attention to replace the loss of natural oil and prevent skin sagging.

wipe off the cleanser. You'll be amazed how much extra dirt appears! Now apply the face mask, following the instructions on the pack. For best results, lie down for about 15–20 minutes, propping up your feet so that they're higher than your head. This gives the blood a chance to flow easily to your head. Remove the mask when it is set, and apply a light covering of moisturizer over your face.

Do this regularly about once a week and you will really notice the difference in both your appearance and feeling of well-being.

These are all things you can do from the outside, and they will all be helped immeasurably if you look after your skin from the inside, too. A correct, balanced diet will not only help you keep your figure trim, give you the vitality and energy you need — it will also 'feed' your skin (as it does the rest of you), helping it to look its very best.

Nourish your skin inwardly as carefully as you do outwardly; make sure, for instance, that your daily diet always includes green vegetables and an amount of fibre and fresh fruit. A model's tip is to drink at least one litre (2 pints) of water a day — it will flush all impurities out of your system, getting rid of that 'stodgy' look!

Facial exercises are important too for, when you exercise the face muscles to prevent them going slack, you are also exercising your skin. Before you put on your make-up in the morning, follow the simple routine on p.291 — watching yourself in the mirror.

ser on to your clean face. Pour the boiled water into your wash basin and throw in the camomile flowers or mint. Then bend over the steam, covering your whole head with the towel.

Steam your face for about five minutes (you can use a kitchen timer), then gently

Lift your jaw and turn your head from side to side, rapidly biting at the air. Then drop your jaw to normal level and slap your chin quickly with the backs of each hand. These two exercises are very good for firming jaw and mouth muscles, and help prevent a double chin.

Roll your eyes around clockwise, pausing at each corner. This is good for eye muscles.

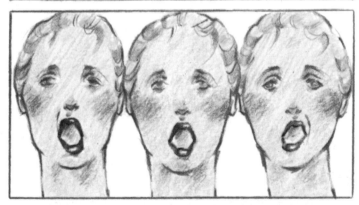

Pretend you're an opera singer of the worst tradition and open your mouth as wide as you can, close it, twisting it from side to side just as if you are singing an aria. If you like, you really can burst into song! This is good for mouth and cheek muscles.

Finally, using the backs of your hands, smooth your forehead, starting from your eyebrows and the bridge of your nose. This is good for reducing frown and forehead lines.

BEAUTY AND HEALTH

THE ART OF MAKE-UP

If you want to take making-up beyond a touch of lipstick and a bit of powder on the nose, the first thing to do is to learn to look at your face as an artist would an untouched piece of canvas.

And, like an artist, you need to start with some basic equipment to make the most of the potential your face represents. You need:

A set of make-up brushes ranging from the very wide to the very thin — about four to six in all. These can be obtained from any good chemist or department store.

Foundation.

Transparent loose powder.

At least two lipsticks, preferably one slightly darker than the other, and a lip glosser.

Blusher. Highlighter. At least two eyeshadows. Eyeliner. Mascara. Shader. Eyebrow pencil.

Most of these items come in a choice of creams or powders, and it's entirely up to you which type you choose.

CHOOSING COLOURS TO SUIT YOU

The next question is, of course, what colours do you choose? Your selection may be largely dictated by the fashion colours of the season if you feel confident enough to follow the latest look, whatever it may be.

Even if you are someone who prefers to keep to a more classic style, always be aware of fashion trends. Nothing is more ageing than a dated make-up; and, in any event, the present fashion looks always take in the latest make-up innovations — always something to look for.

It's quite possible for you to adapt a look to suit yourself if you understand how the colours you choose will look on your face — before you buy them.

Remember that your own colouring is made up of a combination of many pigments and, depending on how you like it, you can modify or emphasize it. Take eyes, for instance. If you put a blue shadow above blue eyes, they will look greener. Put a green shadow above them and you bring out the blue. Brown eyes work this way with brown and green shadow. Darker shades are recessive, lighter colours will make something stand out.

When it comes to choosing foundation, always test it on skin that is the closest shade to your face — on the back of your hand, for example. Even though you have fair skin, perhaps, it will have either an over-all pink or yellow tone and you need to decide whether to emphasize this by choosing a colour close to your own skin tone or to disguise it by choosing a contrasting colour.

Most lipsticks contain either blue or yellow in the colour — if you have yellow to olive-toned skin, choose blue lipsticks to serve as a contrast.

MAKING THE MOST OF THINGS

Even the most beautiful women in the world have their share of bad features — most of us are a pretty mixed bag of good and bad ones. Good make-up will do two things: it will emphasize the good, play down the bad.

First make a list of what you consider your good points. A clear complexion, for instance. Pretty eyes or mouth. Study the shape of your face carefully, pulling your hair right back so you can see your face properly. A nice oval, perhaps? Jaw a bit too square? Forehead too high/low? Write all this down.

There are many kinds of make-up and make-up equipment from which to choose. Here is just a selection of the hundreds of varieties available. Many types come in cream or powder form and in a multitude of colours and shades.

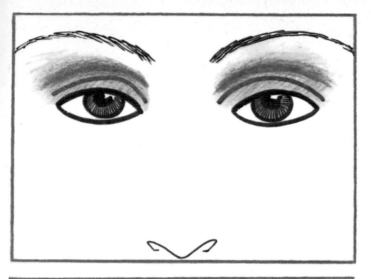

And, finally, study the proportions of your face. Ideally, it should divide into three equal parts lengthwise with forehead/nose/nose-to-chin all the same length, and the same measure breadthwise from the hairline to the bridge of the nose. Ideally, too, this should be the broadest part of your face, with it reducing down to an oval which will be half the width at the chin. Even if you don't have any particularly outstanding features, if your face is in proportion this is a great help in creating an over-all make-up that could make you look stunning.

SOME TRICKS OF THE TRADE

Next to your list of good points, set out the bad ones! Nice coloured eyes, but too small/prominent/close set. Mouth too thin/generous. Chin too long/weak. Skin tone rather murky/lacking colour. And so on.

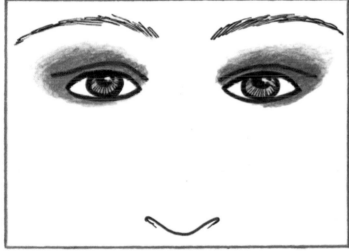

Most people regard the eyes as the most important feature in the face, and certainly a pair of beautiful eyes do give an immediate impression of beauty. Fortunately, nowadays there are very few eyes that can't be called that after a little help!

Remember that light colours pull things out, that dark ones are recessive. If you have deep-set eyes, for

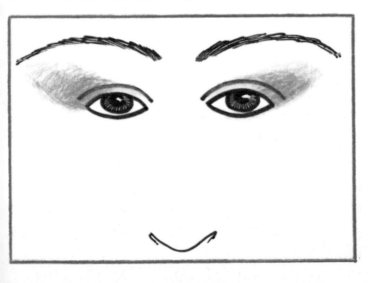

With make-up you can improve the appearance of your eyes. Deep-set eyes (*top*) should have light-coloured shadow over the whole lid with darker shadow running along the top line; the rest of the area under the brow should have highlighter. Prominent eyes (*centre*) should be dealt with in the reverse with dark shadow on the lower lids. Close-set and small eyes (*bottom*) have a light colour on the lids, with a darker one extending out from the side corners.

BEAUTY AND HEALTH

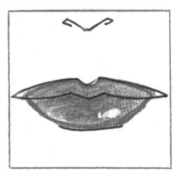

(*Clockwise from top left*) Thin lips: with a paler shade of lipstick, draw a line around the outside of your lips and fill in with a slightly darker shade. Badly proportioned lips: use a paler shade of lipstick around outside of thin lip and a darker just inside fuller lip, blending the colours as they meet. Wide lips: draw around the lips just short of outer corners which you cover with foundation. Full lips: using a darker colour draw a lipline just inside natural outline and fill in with a paler shade.

instance, put a light-coloured eyeshadow over the whole lid, extending it right over the eye socket, beyond the lid line. Run a very subtle darker shadow along this top line, then cover the rest of the area under the brow with your highlighter. Reverse the process with prominent eyes, and also run your dark shadow around the lower lids just under the lower lashes.

Close-set and small eyes can look bigger and wider apart by, again, placing a lighter colour on the lid up to the socket, then taking the darker colour and winging it up from the outer corners, extending it beyond the eyes' natural edge and lifting it towards the brow.

Thick, lustrous lashes are a definite beauty plus. Always make sure you apply two coats of mascara, waiting for the first to dry before applying the second.

Next problem is the mouth. Too thin, too shapeless, too thick. This is where that very fine brush you bought comes in handy. Cover it with your darker lipstick and very carefully draw the outline of your mouth as you would like it. It can't be too exaggerated, but you can extend the outer boundary and shape of your mouth, or not cover it as far as nature dictated. Then fill in with the slightly lighter lipstick.

A heavy jaw can be disguised by using the shader as a shadower. Lightly run it along the jaw line, and blend it into your foundation. The same can be done for a thick nose; a long, pointed one should have the shader running along the bridge and over the point.

Remember — the trick of camouflage is that no one can see it; they just see the results!

LOOKING AFTER NAILS

Nails are an important part of your total look, and should be cared for regularly. Always wear rubber gloves when doing hard chores and washing up, and always use a good hand cream regularly.

Before you think of applying a nail enamel, give your nails a good grooming first. Start by setting aside at least 30 minutes once a week. Then you can be sure that you have enough time in which to do the job properly.

Assemble all the tools you will need: cotton wool; nail varnish remover (non-alcoholic if possible); emery board; cuticle hoof, orange sticks or cotton buds; base coat; nail varnish; top coat.

First, immerse your fingers in a bowl of lukewarm water for a couple of minutes to soften the cuticles. Then remove all old nail varnish thoroughly with a cotton wool pad soaked in the remover. Go over your nails twice if necessary.

Next, push back your cuticles gently, using the hoof, orange sticks or cotton buds. Don't break the skin — if you're gentle enough you won't.

If your nails need shaping,

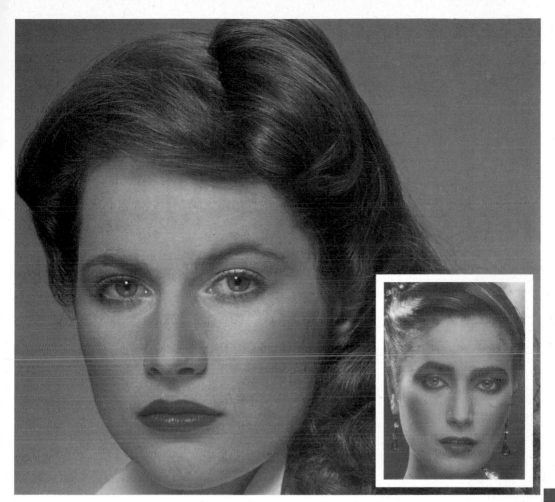

do so with the emery board, rubbing it against each nail in one direction only. Steel nail files are too hard and may splinter the nails, so don't use them.

Finally, the three coats of varnish. First apply the base coat, moving the brush from the cuticle to the tip of the nail in a smooth, even motion. Make sure that there's enough varnish on the brush to cover the nail — but not so much that it drips. The base coat will help set the colour, and both it and the top coat will help prevent chipping.

This regular grooming and polishing will not only make your nails look good — it will strengthen them, too.

DAY-INTO-EVENING MAKE-UP

Once you know what you need and why you need it, the best way to get used to using make-up is to practise. Don't just keep it for high days and holidays but apply it whenever you have a reasonable excuse — like fetching the kids from school!

First make up your eyes, following the camouflage ideas. Don't forget your eyebrows. Never draw a single straight line; always lightly feather it to give the brows a natural emphasis. Don't forget your mascara!

Foundation next. Dot spots of it on your forehead,

Make-up, whether it is for the daytime when you are working or for the evening when you are entertaining or being entertained, is basically the same, with evening make-up being more adventurous. You have to take account of artificial light at night, so use your make-up to emphasize your features.

each cheek, nose and chin, then evenly blend it over your face, making sure there's no 'high-tide' mark around the chin and hairline. Apply your shader where necessary. Apply your blusher now, and remember that both your blusher and shader give colour and shape to your face. Use them to mould, to

295

BEAUTY AND HEALTH

1 Dots of foundation.
2 Smoothing on foundation.
3 Square jaw: take your shader from the jaw line to the cheekbone and blend it.
4 Long chin: apply your shader to the bottom of your chin and work it up the jaw line a little way.
5 Long nose: put some shader on the tip of your nose and blend it in.
6 Broad nose: put shader down the side of each nostril and blend into your foundation.
7 Apply your blusher from the hairline at the sides of your face and along your cheekbones, forming triangles.

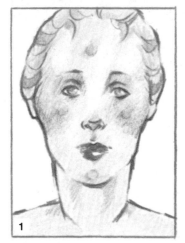

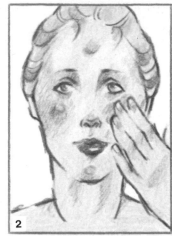

highlight or to hide. This means that you can emphasize your best features. Always start the blusher at the sides of your face against the hairline, then smooth it (if you use a powder, use your widest make-up brush) right across your cheekbones. You should have made a triangle with the widest part against the hairline.

Now, dust loose powder all over your face to set your make-up.

Finally, your lips. Outline first, then fill in with lipstick. Blot them between a tissue, then apply a second coat, and finally use your glosser. That way the lipstick will last longer.

Because your eyes and your mouth are your two most important features, you must balance both of them — giving them more or less importance. People see your face as a whole — too much emphasis on one area gives that whole a strange, uneven look!

Your evening make-up is basically the same, except that it should take into account the artificial light that you'll be in. Emphasize your eyes with a fine eyeliner drawn along the upper lids against the lashes. Use glitter highlighter above the eyeshadow and above your blusher to emphasize the shape of your face. Be bolder with your blusher and lipstick.

Of course, once you feel confident about using and wearing make-up, the sky's the limit.

Always look out for a look or a colour that suits your style — and never be afraid to experiment.

HOME NURSING

Relatively few of the illnesses and emergencies which affect people at home or at work need emergency help. What is important, however, is to be quite clear whether or not the problem is serious before deciding to treat it yourself. Check with this book, or any other reference book to see if the course of treatment is clear; if not, have no hesitation in calling

BEAUTY AND HEALTH

the family doctor for more advice, or going to hospital if that appears necessary. For quick reference, all the following entries are arranged alphabetically.

BACK PAIN
Each year, in Britain alone, 13 million working days are lost, and a million and a half people consult their doctors because of back pain. Very little is known about the causes of this very common and often temporarily crippling condition, although as the spine, with its 24 fragile bones and the associated cartilage and tendons is extremely complex, and supports the whole bodyweight, it is not surprising that it sometimes goes wrong.

The most common cause is strain caused by abuse; lifting too heavy weights or abusing the back some other way. Slipped discs can follow, when the rubbery cushion between the vertebrae becomes damaged. General aches and pains in the back become more frequent as we age, sometimes due to an arthritic condition. In women, several gynaecological problems can cause back pain; even a perfectly normal period.

Because some of these conditions can be severe, it is advisable to see the doctor about a painful back if it persists for more than a few days. If, as sometimes happens, your back pain is one of those conditions which can recur, you will have to try to avoid starting it up again.

If you know that over-exertion has caused the problem, be sensible and take things easy. Make sure you sit erect as far as possible, with a cushion supporting the small of the back. A firm bed, or a special orthopaedic mattress can also help considerably. If your mattress is sagging or very soft, put a rigid board beneath it.

Take aspirin, according to the dose specified on the bottle. This is not only a pain-killer, but will also relieve inflammation which is sometimes associated with back pain. Paracetamol is also a useful anti-inflammatory analgesic.

Your doctor may prescribe stronger drugs, heat treatment, or a course of mild exercise. In other cases, a surgical corset may help.

BED SORES
Lying in one position for a long time causes pressure which cuts off the circulation from the parts of the body touching the bed. This eventually causes damage to the tissues, especially in the elderly bedridden, who already have poor circulation. In these pressure points, such as heels, buttocks, hip bones and elbows, the damage eventually causes large ulcers or bed sores. The solution is simple; prevent them by turning the patient as often as possible, without causing too much discomfort. Encourage them to move about in bed, and periodically shift them from side to side. Look out for red patches on the pressure points, and tell the doctor if you see one developing. Bedsores are much easier to prevent than to heal, so keep patients dry and comfortable, and straighten out creases in the sheet which can irritate the skin.

COLDS
Unfortunately no magic cure exists. Don't bother to try any antibiotics you may have been previously prescribed — they have no effect. Neither does whisky or brandy. Aspirin is about the only remedy which has a worthwhile effect. It will ease the discomfort and reduce the high temperature. Some commercially available decongestants help dry up the runny nose too, but should not be used for more than a few days at a time.

DIARRHOEA
In Britain, diarrhoea in adults and adolescents is usually caused by virus infections, which cannot be treated directly. The symptoms can be eased by the traditional kaolin and morphine mixture or tablets, or by medicines containing codeine.

Holiday diarrhoea, picked up abroad, is quite likely to be caused by bacteria. Take kaolin and morphine and if it does not clear up in few days, consult the doctor.

Diarrhoea in babies needs careful attention. Many babies naturally have loose bowel action up to age six months, due to their liquid diet. But sudden attacks of copious watery diarrhoea mean that the baby probably has an infection. Take it off solids, and give it boiled water with a teaspoon of sugar and half a teaspoon of salt per pint. Consult the doctor if it persists for more than one day, or call him immediately if the baby is vomiting or seems to be weakening.

FEVER
See **Temperature**

GASTROENTERITIS

This is a group of diseases in which there is inflammation of the stomach or part of the intestine. Its symptoms are typically vomiting, diarrhoea, and often, pains in the abdomen. The causes can be food poisoning due to bacteria, food allergies, or most commonly, a virus infection, usually called 'gastric flu'. Diarrhoea and vomiting in infants is also a form of gastroenteritis.

Because the delicate lining of the stomach is likely to be inflamed, most medicines are immediately vomited up (especially aspirin, which irritates the stomach further). A bland medicine like magnesium trisilicate soothes the stomach, and large quantities of water, squashes, or milk should be drunk to replace lost body fluids. Consult the doctor if symptoms persist for more than a day.

Diarrhoea and vomiting in infants under one year is potentially dangerous. Dehydration can develop rapidly. Consult the doctor immediately if diarrhoea and vomiting persist for more than six hours.

STOMACH ACHE

There are seldom any obvious causes for stomach ache, and most attacks are due to either indigestion or wind. A teaspoon of bicarbonate of soda in half a glass of water usually eases indigestion pain, helped by a hot water bottle rested on the stomach. If the pain is caused by wind, it will usually relieve itself quickly. If the pain lasts more than eight hours, seek medical advice. In children it may not be wise to wait this long. Seek medical advice in any case if the pain worsens.

TEMPERATURE

A thermometer is a useful item for the family medical chest, but should be used with discretion. Body temperature varies quite considerably throughout the day, and from person to person. First thing in the morning, the temperature is at its lowest, and rises steadily throughout the day. There is a 'normal' temperature however, which falls somewhere between 98.4°F and 98.6°F (36.9°C to 37.0°C).

Generally, a person with an active infection has a raised temperature or fever, caused by the body's efforts to fight the disease.

Thermometers are not very easy to use, until you have learned the knack of shaking down the mercury before starting to take a temperature.

The scale is marked in divisions of 0.2°F, and has a range of from 94°F to 106°F. Unlike a room thermometer, the silvery thread of mercury will not return to the bulb unless it is shaken down. This is done by holding the stem of the thermometer at the end away from the bulb, and shaking it with a sharp flick of the wrist, until it goes down to the lowest number on the scale.

In adults and adolescents, take the temperature by laying the thermometer under the tongue. In very young children, use the armpit, which can be kept warm by holding the child's arm firmly down against its side. Keep the thermometer in place for at least two minutes. Don't attempt to use the rectum to take the temperature; this is a skilled job, to be carried out only by the doctor or nurse.

Shake the mercury down after use, then wash the thermometer thoroughly in cold

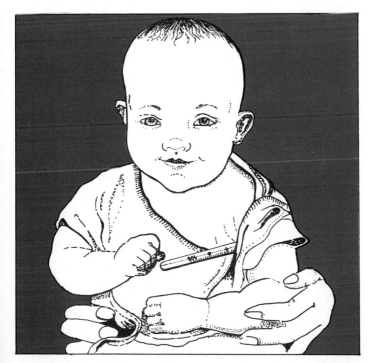

Use the armpit for taking the temperature of young children.

BEAUTY AND HEALTH

soapy water. If you will need it again shortly, stand the thermometer in a jar of diluted disinfectant (but rinse it before using it again).

A temperature 3°F (2°C) above the 'normal' range usually means that something is wrong. However, remember that a baby's temperature can rise sharply when it is crying, or in an older child, during a tantrum. Even in an adult, temperatures can rise markedly during exercise.

Because the temperature varies so much normally, it is not possible to be precise over what is 'serious'. A temperature of 101°F in a child usually means that they are feeling quite ill, and you should contact the doctor. In an adult, this sort of temperature is not unusual during a severe cold, or more commonly, with influenza.

Except with the elderly, it is not usually necessary to contact the doctor for these illnesses, which usually resolve themselves without treatment.

You can help reduce a raised temperature, by giving aspirin in the maximum dose recommended on the bottle (never exceed this dose). Aspirin effectively reduces temperature. Always give aspirin with plenty of water or some other drink, to avoid stomach irritation. If the patient already has stomach pain, feels queasy, or is vomiting, paracetamol may be given. For children under five years give 'junior' or paediatric formulations.

You can also help bring down a high fever by some commonsense measures. This is useful when dealing with young children. Turn down room heating and open windows to cool the air, and avoid bundling up the patient with masses of bedclothes. Bathe the body with tepid water, which will bring a child's temperature down rapidly. Give plenty of cold drinks.

Contrary to popular belief, uncovering and cooling the patient won't make their illness worse, but be prepared to wrap them up again as soon as their temperature has dropped.

In a patient whose temperature has already dropped back *below* normal, it is obviously important to keep them warm, and to give them warm drinks.

A new and convenient method of measuring approximate temperature is a temperature-sensitive strip which changes colour when laid against the forehead.

VOMITING

Vomiting is intended to rid the stomach of anything which is irritating it. While the stomach is still sore, eating anything else will only cause more vomiting. Just drink plenty of water, and wait until the vomiting eases. If it persists for more than a day, contact the doctor for advice. With young children consult the doctor if it persists for six hours. See **Gastroenteritis.**

SAFETY FIRST

Your medicine cabinet contains many powerful poisons; relatively safe if taken properly, but very dangerous if taken by a young child. Painkillers are potentially lethal, and undiluted disinfectants can cause severe internal burning if taken by mouth. Many prescribed drugs are even more dangerous. Commonsense tells you to keep *all* medicines high up, out of reach.

Commonsense also extends to following the instructions with all medicines, whether bought at the chemists, or prescribed by the doctor. Take particular care that you take the right number of doses each day, at the times specified, and never *stop* taking prescribed medicine before the doctor tells you it is safe to do so; this is particularly important with antibiotics. If you have any doubts about this, ask the doctor for a precise set of dose instructions. Never save any prescribed medicines you have left over after completing a course of treatment. Misuse of drugs can be highly dangerous and some of them actually 'go off' within a short time after mixing. The safest way of disposing of left-over medicines and tablets is to take them back to the chemist.

Elderly people often have to take several different medicines each day, and they easily become confused. This can be dangerous, and if you think there could be a problem, draw up a medicine chart, showing when to take each drug, and how much to take (e.g., Breakfast — 1 red tablet, 1 teaspoon of medicine).

The well stocked medicine cabinet should include the following items:
Pain killers Paracetamol, aspirin and junior aspirin.
Dressings A range of bandages, gauze, and adhesive plasters.
Cleansing materials Antiseptic liquid (e.g. TCP), lint and cotton wool.

BEAUTY AND HEALTH

FIRST AID

First aid should never be thought of as a substitute for professional medical advice, and valuable though it is when performed properly, over-zealous first aid treatment can be worse than no treatment at all. If in doubt, don't treat; call a doctor. Remember that such thoughtless acts as helping an injured person to sit up could kill them, and be very cautious if there seems the slightest possibility of serious injury. An unconscious person should be placed in the 'recovery' position (p.307).

The entries that follow are in alphabetical order.

ARTIFICIAL RESPIRATION AND CARDIAC MASSAGE

These two measures need to be learned by everyone, as they can both save lives by keeping a badly injured or sick person breathing, and their heart pumping, until they reach hospital for more thorough treatment. Artificial respiration is essential whenever breathing has stopped, due to any reason. Accidents such as head injury, drowning, electrocution, poisoning, or inhalation of vomit can cause breathing to cease. For anyone other than a trained first-aider, mouth to mouth artificial respiration is best, as other types involving pressure on the ribs can cause injury if done incorrectly.

Roll the casualty on his back, and using the finger, remove any obstructions from the mouth, including false teeth, vomit, or bits of food. Make sure the tongue has not doubled back down

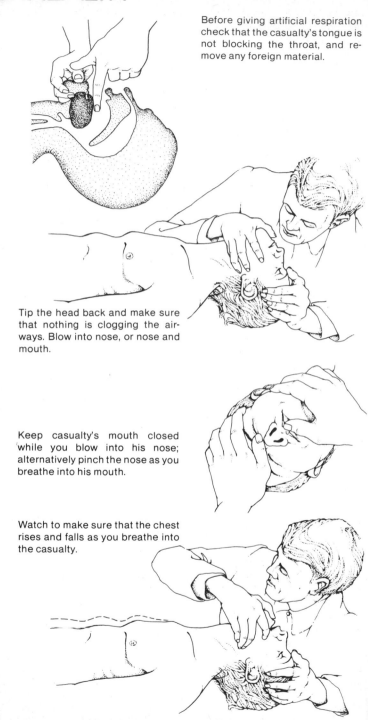

Before giving artificial respiration check that the casualty's tongue is not blocking the throat, and remove any foreign material.

Tip the head back and make sure that nothing is clogging the airways. Blow into nose, or nose and mouth.

Keep casualty's mouth closed while you blow into his nose; alternatively pinch the nose as you breathe into his mouth.

Watch to make sure that the chest rises and falls as you breathe into the casualty.

the throat. If it has, pull the tongue forward.

Tilt the head back, holding the jaws forward to keep the tongue off the back of the throat. Pull open the clothing around the neck.

Pinch the casualty's nostrils shut, then, taking a deep breath, seal your lips around his open mouth and exhale into him. Watch to see if the casualty's chest rises. If not, there is an obstruction in the windpipe, which means checking the mouth again to make sure you have not missed any object blocking the flow of air. Otherwise, press the casualty's chest to try and dislodge the obstruction.

When the chest is seen to rise, remove your mouth while air is expelled once more and repeat the process, at a rate of about 20 times per minute.

In babies and small children, it is usually better to cover both nose and mouth together as you breathe into them. Especially with small children, never blow forcibly into them, but use only the small amount of air which is contained in your puffed-out cheeks.

Check periodically to see if the casualty has started to breathe naturally. Make absolutely certain that they are breathing strongly before ceasing artificial respiration. Never give up if the patient shows no sign of responding; continue until medical assistance can be obtained.

Cardiac arrest sometimes follows asphyxiation, or can occur due to other causes, such as a heart attack or electric shock. When the heart stops, the casualty very quickly becomes bluish or grey in colour, and the pupils of the eye become widely dilated. Breathing stops, consciousness is lost and no pulse can be felt. Keep the patient breathing as the first priority.

If cardiac massage is to be attempted, roll the casualty on his back. Now thump the casualty sharply on the lower part of the breastbone. In babies, a sharp tap is all that is necessary. If the heart does not start immediately, external heart massage is needed.

Place the heel of one hand over the lower part of the breast bone, and heel of the

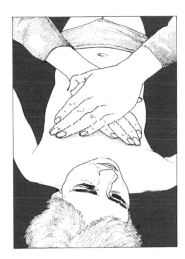

Heart massage.

other hand on top of this. Keep the arms stiff and straight, and rock forward so that the breast bone is pushed in by about 1½ inches (4 cm). Repeat the movement once per second for adults; 80-90 times per minute for children. Use firm, regular pressure, and don't push harder than you need. (Keep up the mouth to mouth respiration.) Continue treatment until the heart re-starts, when the colour will improve, pupils return to normal, and a pulse can be felt. Then get medical aid immediately.

BANDAGES AND DRESSINGS

Dressings are probably more often used than bandages for household first aid.

The purposes of a dressing are to keep out infection and prevent further injury. Because it is in close contact with an open wound, a dressing must be sterile. It must also be porous to absorb blood, and be of material which will not adhere to the wound as it dries.

Adhesive dressings, or plasters, are most useful,

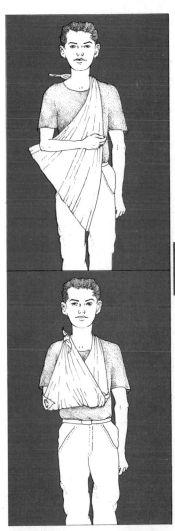

Triangular sling for a broken arm.

303

BEAUTY AND HEALTH

being pre-sterilized, and available in a range of sizes. They will not adhere to damp skin. Use the porous type which allow skin to 'breathe'.

BRUISING

Bruises are caused by bleeding from the tiny blood

Dressings for a broken finger.

Bandaging a leg broken below knee.

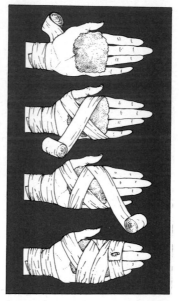

Bandaging an injured hand.

vessels beneath the skin. Once a bruise has formed, there is little that can be done to remove it. The body clears up the leaked blood gradually, and the discoloration fades. If you catch it in time, however, a cold compress may stop the bruise forming, or at least stop it getting too big.

BURNS

Burns require rapid treatment, especially serious burning. Burns caused by contact with fire, boiling water, steam or corrosive chemicals must be treated by plunging the affected part under cold flowing water.

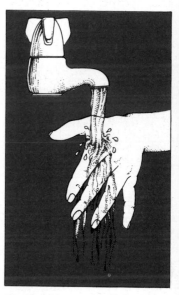

Treating burns with flowing cold water.

Never coat the burned area with creams or ointments. If the burns are extensive, deep, or if severe blistering has occurred, hospital treatment is needed without delay. Shock, infection, and scarring can occur without proper treatment. Burns are especially dangerous in the very young or the very old. For chemical burns, remove affected clothing as soon as possible. For other burns, don't remove clothing or damaged skin — leave it to the doctor.

Mild burns need no treatment. Just clean them, and cover with a dressing or bandage.

Mild sunburn is best

304

treated with calamine, or with antihistamine cream if it is painful. Blisters need medical treatment, and if the sunburned person is shivering or vomiting, treat as a fever and get medical help immediately, as they may have sunstroke.

CARDIAC MASSAGE
See **Artificial respiration**

CHOKING
Blockage of the windpipe causes choking. Treat by

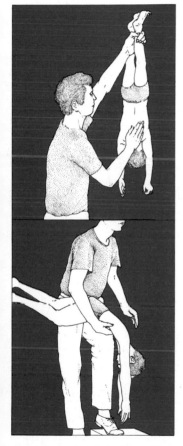

Two methods of dealing with a choking child.

thumping firmly between the shoulder blades, two or three times. A small child can be held up by the feet, and a larger child laid over the knee face down, before thumping

the back. Hook out any obstruction in the mouth with the fingers. If choking continues, and the casualty turns bluish, give mouth to mouth respiration and rush them to hospital immediately. Choking with a bone in the throat is painful, but less of an emergency. If you can't hook it out with a finger, seek medical help.

CONVULSIONS
In infants, convulsions usually occur because of a high temperature during infectious illness. These are called febrile convulsions, where there is usually a brief loss of consciousness as the temperature soars. Get the temperature down quickly, as described under **Temperature** (page 299). Bathing the body with tepid water is probably fastest. Call the doctor meanwhile, and watch the baby carefully until the doctor arrives.

Adult convulsions are usually due to the disease epilepsy, although there are several other possible causes. Some epilepsy sufferers wear a bracelet or medallion warning of their condition. In such a convulsion, the person falls down and jerks all over. Don't try to stop this, as you will cause them more harm. Just loosen clothing to prevent breathing difficulties, and try to stop them injuring themselves. In particular, epileptics may bite their tongues, and it is sometimes possible to force a rolled up handkerchief between their jaws to prevent this.

After the convulsion they will be sleepy and confused, and may not realize what has happened. Reassure them, and then get them to a doctor for a check up.

CUTS AND GRAZES
Clean the wound by washing under cold running water. Obvious dirt can be wiped off carefully, wiping away from the wound. Mild antiseptic can be used, especially in grazes which are particularly likely to be dirty, and become infected. Never use at full strength. Use as in the directions.

Bleeding will normally stop naturally after a few minutes. Don't try to wipe off clotted blood or the wound will bleed again. Cover the wound with an adhesive dressing, or non-adhesive dressing and bandage. Once bleeding has stopped, petroleum jelly can be applied to stop the dressing sticking.

DROWNING
See **Artificial respiration**

ELECTRIC SHOCK
First switch off the electrical supply, or get the person away from the source of shock. If you cannot switch it off, pull out the plug, or pull the cable free. Make sure that you do not come into contact with any

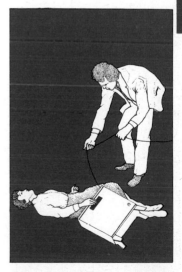

Pull appliance away by its cable.

BEAUTY AND HEALTH

exposed electrical part or conductor of electricity. This means not touching the casualty until you are sure the electricity has been disconnected. If you can't be sure of this, stand on dry wood, cardboard, or a mat to insulate yourself, or try to roll them away with a length of wood. Always seek medical advice after an electric shock, as there may be severe internal damage, which is not always apparent. Use **artificial respiration** if breathing has ceased, and **cardiac massage** if the heart has stopped.

FAINTING

Faints are caused by a partial interruption of the blood supply to the brain. There is usually some warning, such as a feeling of giddiness or 'cold sweats'. If the affected person lies down, or puts their head down between their knees, the distance the heart has to pump blood to the brain is reduced, and the blood supply improves. Get the casualty to breathe deeply, and loosen clothing around the neck.

Faints are not usually serious, and can happen if a person has a developing illness, or has been standing for a long while in crowded or hot conditions.

FOREIGN BODIES

If a child swallows a coin or other small object, place him face-down over the knee to see if he will vomit it up. If not, check with the doctor to see if hospital treatment is necessary. Most objects pass through the system within a few days, without causing any harm. Sharp objects are potentially dangerous, so

advise the doctor immediately.

Small objects pushed up the nose or into ears require special treatment. Never try to get them out, as they may be accidentally pushed further in. Take the casualty to the doctor or hospital for treatment.

Foreign bodies in the eye can cause damage if not properly treated. Usually tears will dislodge them and carry them into the corner of the eye, where they can be gently removed with the edge of a clean cloth. If not, pull the upper eyelid down over the lower, holding it by the lashes. The lashes on the lower lid will then sometimes brush the object out. Pull the lower eyelid down and remove any visible dirt with a clean cloth. Never touch the eye with any hard object. Seek medical attention without hesitation if you cannot remove the foreign body easily.

HEAD INJURIES

Any head injury which causes even a short loss of consciousness could be serious, and the ill-effects can be delayed. Always report such injuries to the doctor, and watch the casualty for such symptoms as sleepiness, dizziness, persistent headaches or vomiting. Report these conditions to the doctor without delay.

HEART ATTACKS

Symptoms of a heart attack are varied, and may not even be felt in the area of the heart. Common warning signs are heaviness and pain in the upper chest, spreading to the shoulders and arms, and even to the jaw.

Feelings of weakness are common, together with sweating and breathlessness. The symptoms may fade and then return. Immediate medical attention is essential, and if the doctor is not available, call an ambulance. If breathing stops, give mouth to mouth respiration. If the heart stops, give cardiac massage.

HEART FAILURE See **Artificial respiration and cardiac massage.**

INSECT BITES AND STINGS

Bites and stings are seldom serious, although they can be painful. Most can be treated with calamine lotion, or with an antihistamine cream which eases the itching. Bee stings break off in the skin, and must be removed with

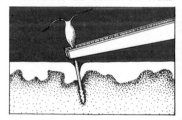

Removing a bee sting.

tweezers. Try not to squeeze the sting, as this will only pump more venom into the wound. Avoid scratching bites, as this leads to infection. Sometimes there is a severe allergic reaction to a bite, which can cause breathing difficulties. This needs immediate medical attention. This condition is fortunately extremely rare. Similarly, although a single bee sting is no cause for alarm, multiple stings can be dangerous, and if a stung casualty collapses, artificial respiration may be necessary while awaiting medical aid.

NOSE BLEEDS
A nose bleed is seldom more than a nuisance. It often follows a cold, where the nasal tissues have been damaged by sneezing violently, or by congestion. Get the casualty to sit, with the head forward, and breathing through the mouth. Hold the soft part of the nose pinched closed for 10 minutes, after which the bleeding will usually have stopped. Stop the casualty from sniffing or blowing the nose as this will disturb the clot and start the bleeding again. If bleeding persists for an hour or more, seek medical aid.

POISONING
Corrosive poisons: disinfectants, petrol, paraffin, cleaning fluids, caustic soda, some insecticides. Try to dilute the poison by getting the casualty to drink water or milk. Don't try to make them vomit, as this will lead to more burning. Rinse the mouth out and wipe away any deposits of the corrosive material around the lips.

Non-corrosive poisons: medicines, weedkiller, poisonous plants. If you are certain that the poison is not corrosive, try to make the casualty vomit, by placing a finger far back in the throat. Don't give the casualty a drink, as this could worsen his condition.

In all cases of poisoning, seek medical aid immediately. If the casualty is conscious, try to obtain details of what he has taken, and tell the doctor. Some drugs have a delayed action and if the casualty deteriorates, give artificial respiration and cardiac massage as necessary. Try to save a specimen of the original poison, its container, or any vomited material to send to hospital with the casualty.

ROAD ACCIDENTS AND MAJOR INJURIES
Don't do anything to make matters worse. Never try to move the casualty or straighten obviously damaged limbs. If the casualty is unconscious put him in the recovery position, but if conscious don't move him at all. Give **artificial respiration** and/or **cardiac massage** if necessary. Never give drinks, as internal damage may have occurred. Call an ambulance immediately.

Severe bleeding needs emergency treatment on the spot, by pressing a pad of cloth over the wound. Add more thicknesses of cloth if this is insufficient. For small wounds, press the sides of the wound together with the fingers to check bleeding. Do not attempt to cut off the blood supply with a tourniquet unless you know exactly what you are doing, as this can worsen the damage. Cover the casualty with a warm blanket or a coat, while waiting for help to arrive.

See **Shock**

SHOCK
Shock is a condition in which the circulation begins to fail. It can sometimes be fatal. It can follow severe injury, burns, bleeding, ruptured appendix, fright, or even bad news. The symptoms are rapid, shallow breathing, fainting or dizziness, sweating, and sometimes, blurred vision.

Lay the casualty down, cover him and keep him warm. Do *not* give hot drinks or anything else by mouth, in case internal injury has oc-curred. Get medical help quickly.

SWALLOWED OBJECTS
See **Foreign bodies**

UNCONSCIOUSNESS
Check that an unconscious person is breathing. If not, give artificial respiration. Check first that the airway is not blocked by the tongue, and make sure that any vomit is removed from the mouth.

If the casualty is breathing satisfactorily, turn him over into the 'recovery position' (see below). Loosen clothing around the neck, and keep him warm until medical help can be obtained. Watch him carefully while waiting for assistance, to make sure that breathing is maintained. Use artificial respiration if breathing seems to stop or to be very weak.

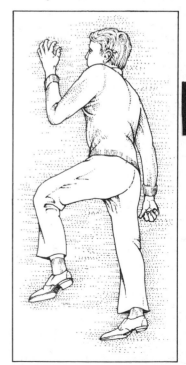

The recovery position.

BEAUTY AND HEALTH

PREGNANCY

Having a baby is probably the most important experience in a woman's life, and is one which most women approach with joy and anticipation.

The changes in the body which take place during pregnancy are quite drastic, and in some women, can lead to discomfort, or to emotional disturbances, which could mar the otherwise happy experience of producing a child. But pregnancy is not an illness. Many women feel fitter during their pregnancy than at any other time, and indeed, some chronic illnesses like arthritis may clear up temporarily in pregnancy. Most problems of pregnancy can be overcome with a combination of commonsense and good antenatal care. As soon as a woman thinks she is pregnant, she should seek her GP's advice on antenatal procedure.

FOOD

One of the best ways to cope with nausea and vomiting in early pregnancy is to have frequent small snacks. Milk and sweet biscuits are usually the best for between meals. Meals should be small and simple. Eat a small supper before retiring and leave a glass of milk and biscuits alongside the bed to have on waking during the night or in the morning. Get up slowly and do not rush your breakfast if you are going out to work.

If you get heartburn in late pregnancy, only have a small evening meal and not much after that, except small drinks of milk and antacid powders prescribed by your doctor.

Overeating and getting fat can be a problem for some women. It may be caused by frequent nibbling to overcome nausea or heartburn or to satisfy a craving. Sometimes it is because of boredom, loneliness, anxiety or just simply being at home more than usual. If you desperately want something to eat, between meals, try raw carrot, celery or an apple.

When you are having a meal try to relax. Eat slowly and chew the food thoroughly. If you sit down to meals at regular times, it is easier to eat less than if you snatch a meal here and there. Cutting out meals does not help — it normally means you eat more later.

CONSTIPATION

Constipation, the infrequent passing of rather hard bowel motions, is an unpleasant ailment which is quite common. The straining sometimes involved can aggravate piles and the hard motion can cause a split in the anus, resulting in bleeding and sharp pain. Although some women blame iron tablets for causing constipation, this is most unlikely. Even if they were responsible they are so important in the prevention of anaemia that any consti-

The illustration below shows the development of the foetus at 6, 16, 20, 25, 30 weeks and finally at full term — 40 weeks. By this time the foetus has moved into position for a normal 'head first' delivery.

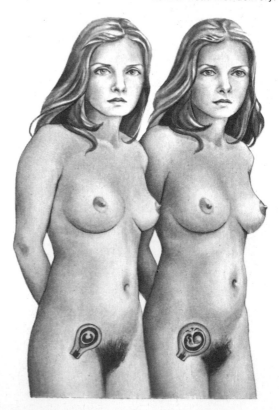

pation should be offset by modifying the diet rather than by stopping the iron. Suitable changes to the diet can be made once nausea ceases to be a problem.

Relying too much on laxatives tends to reduce normal bowel activity. It is easy to become dependent on them. Try to develop regular bowel action.

A cup of tea on waking will often stir the bowel into action. Eating vegetables, fresh and dried fruits, wholemeal bread, stewed prunes and rhubarb all help to keep the bowels active and the motions soft and easy to pass. Sprinkle natural bran on food or mix it with custard or yogurt.

NO SMOKING

Giving up smoking can be fairly easy for some women who only have a few cigarettes a day, or for those who develop an aversion to smoking when they become pregnant. Other women are unlucky enough to be dependent on the nicotine in cigarette smoke. The nervous system has adapted to the presence of this drug in such a way that nervousness, anxiety and headaches develop when smoking is stopped. It requires a great effort of will to break the habit.

Smoking mothers risk having babies of lower birth weight and associated problems: respiratory disorders and mental retardation. In a very small proportion of women, giving up smoking early in pregnancy can mean improvement in the blood supply to a failing placenta. The baby who might have died in the uterus is therefore born healthy. The fact that no one knows just whose baby will be saved in this way is sufficient reason for all women to give up smoking. Even being in a room with smokers increases the risk. Consequently husbands and friends should offer encouragement and give up smoking themselves if necessary.

DRINKING

Small amounts of alcohol do not have any harmful effects on pregnancy, although they do exaggerate flushing, sweating and faintness which bother some pregnant women. However, it is often after having a drink that a woman gives in to temptation when cigarettes are handed round. Do not forget about the combination of drink and drugs. Anti-sickness tablets taken in early pregnancy can also exaggerate the effects of alcohol.

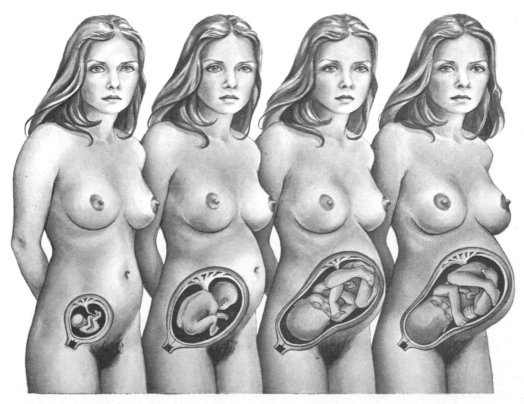

BEAUTY AND HEALTH

DRUGS

Pills and medicines must be avoided unless they have been prescribed by your doctor. If you have difficulty in sleeping, try simple measures like taking a warm drink or practising complete relaxation and concentrating on controlled breathing. This helps to divert your mind from other things.

TRAVEL

Providing the journey is not too far or strenuous, travelling is all right. But pregnant women tend to tire more easily and particularly in late pregnancy are often reluctant to go far from home. Perhaps this has something to do with the nesting instinct, or merely that they want to stay close to a hospital.

Women should not drive if they are taking anti-sickness tablets because they create drowsiness and reduce reaction time. Even without these, women in late pregnancy tend to be more dreamy, so they must exercise more care and be extra cautious about speed and anticipating the unexpected from other drivers. At all times seat belts should be worn.

Air travel is safe in modern pressurized cabins but, as with cars and trains, it involves sitting sometimes in a cramped position. This tends to slow the flow of blood back from the legs, which could cause dangerous clotting in the veins. It is essential for women to get up and walk about a little at least hourly and not to have any restricting garments around the legs. On a long car journey it means stopping hourly.

WHEN TO STOP WORK

When to stop work is an individual decision. It depends on how well you feel, how busy and demanding your job is, how much you need the money and how much you have to do at home. If you can, it is a good idea to stop early rather than late — late pregnancy is a time to take things easy and to have extra rest. Lie down for an hour in the afternoons and avoid late nights. Always put your feet up when you are sitting and never move heavy furniture by yourself.

Women can feel isolated, bored and cut-off at this time. It is a good idea to call in at your work a couple of times a week to keep involved and in contact with your friends. It is also a good time to take an interest in your friends' babies and young children.

ANTE-NATAL CLASSES

Try to learn as much as you can at the ante-natal childbirth preparation classes. And talk to the other women and possibly make friends with those who live nearby. You will find you have a lot in common and can benefit from exchanging ideas, anxieties and experiences. Do not make the mistake of attending two or more different sets of classes. You may think you will be able to pick and choose from the methods each teaches, but often the result is confusion when you find yourself in labour. You need simple, clear concepts to cling to. Practise your relaxation and breathing exercises and get your husband to do this with you.

Make sure you attend the ante-natal clinic regularly. It might seem unnecessary when you are feeling fit and well, but remember that it is only frequent examination which will detect problems at an early stage. If you are advised to have extra rest because blood pressure is slightly up, take the advice seriously. Quite a few women are unexpectedly admitted to the ante-natal ward at short notice because a clinic visit detects high blood pressure. Often the rise proves to be a false alarm and you are allowed home again in a day or two. At other times women stay in hospital until delivery.

If your husband seems disinterested and bored, try and get him involved as much as possible. He may just be feeling a bit left out. However attending the fathers' class usually works wonders. Once your husband feels involved you may find as a result that you both start communicating freely on the subject for the first time. Some men at first think that it is not quite manly to be too involved in pregnancies and babies, and in all probability will have had some ragging at work. Leave your books around so that he can have quiet glances which might stimulate his interest.

SEX DURING PREGNANCY

Some couples are anxious that pressure on the abdomen might squash the foetus or harm him in some way. Others worry that the penetrating penis might bump the developing baby or damage him. But there is no basis for either anxiety because the foetus is cushioned in the fluid, protecting it from all but the most severe bumps.

The effects of pregnancy on a woman's desire for intercourse or on her response to sexual stimulation varies widely. Partly they are influenced by the hormonal changes in her body. Some women have an increased desire and reach orgasm more easily, perhaps because of the freedom from contraception. Others can go off sex for varying periods, even the whole of pregnancy. Men too are sometimes affected in this way.

Couples should make every attempt to discuss their anxieties and fears with each other and should seek the help of a doctor or marriage counsellor if necessary.

These meals are economical and easy to prepare and contain all the elements for a balanced diet. They are based on the fact that most women having their first babies will be working up to 11 weeks before childbirth.

WEEKLY DIET DURING PREGNANCY

	Breakfast	Lunch	Dinner
Sunday	fruit juice grilled bacon & tomato, bread/ toast & butter tea/coffee/milk	roast chicken roast potatoes & vegetables lemon meringue pie	sardines/cheese on toast yogurt pear
Monday	boiled egg bread/toast & butter tea/coffee/milk	chicken sandwich yogurt orange	egg & bacon flan fresh vegetables fresh fruit/ cheese & biscuits
Tuesday	cereal (bran if constipated) & milk, toast tea/coffee/milk	egg & bacon flan apple	stewed beef, carrots & onions jacket potato fruit crumble
Wednesday	poached egg on toast tea/coffee/milk	cheese sandwich with onion/tomato /salad, pear	cottage pie & fresh vegetables fruit fool
Thursday	scrambled egg on toast tea/coffee/milk	liver sausage sandwich yogurt fruit	soup, grilled cheese on fresh vegetables rice/potatoes
Friday	boiled egg, bread/ toast & butter tea/coffee/milk	braised liver & onions, green vegetables, jacket potato fruit salad	grilled fish, fresh vegetables & parsley potatoes fresh fruit salad
Saturday	wheat cereal/ porridge & milk, toast tea/coffee/milk	cottage or cream cheese & crispbreads, tomato/salad apple	herb & tomato omelette bread orange

BABY AND CHILD CARE

The prospect of bringing up a first child is a daunting one, but for most women, proves much easier than might be expected. We possess powerful instincts which are seldom wrong when it comes to very young babies. Mothers don't need to be told when to pick up and comfort a crying child. Cuddling has a definite purpose in the young baby. It encourages his attachment to his mother, and comforts him by making him feel secure. It also has very definite psychological benefits for the mother.

Parents know their own child better than any other person can. Sometimes a doctor or nurse will be unable to detect the subtle changes of mood or behaviour which worry the parents of a baby, who have become very familiar with his normal state.

BREAST FEEDING

Breast feeding is undoubtedly better for the baby and can be very satisfying for the mother. There are difficulties sometimes in getting started, but persistence is frequently rewarded so do not worry if feeding is a problem to begin with. Even when you have been one of the unfortunate ones for whom breast feeding did not work out with your first baby, you will be pleasantly surprised how much easier it is the second time.

The baby's bowel movements can tell you quite a lot about how the feeding is going. At first you get a

Cuddling and talking to your baby will give you a pleasurably relaxed feeling. Eye-to-eye contact is of great importance.

BEAUTY AND HEALTH

Breast feeding can benefit child and mother.

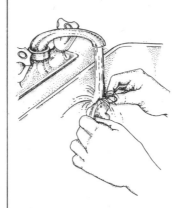

sticky greenish-brown stool. After a few days this gradually changes to stools which are soft and orangey-red with whitish curds. They have a faint inoffensive smell. Bowel motions may become infrequent as breast milk is almost completely digested and absorbed. The baby is never constipated but can go for as long as a week and then pass a rather large soft motion. A baby's bowels often open during or just after feeds, so changing afterwards is most practical. If he is temporarily getting insufficient milk, he may pass a few green stools with slime or mucus in them, but as you feed him more often and the milk supply improves the green colour disappears.

BOTTLE FEEDING
For successful bottle feeding you need to be more careful and pay attention to detail.

The milk, the bottle and the teat must all be germ-free to prevent the risk of gastro-enteritis. After 9 months, the baby will have built up his own resistance and thereafter sterilization of his food containers will be unnecessary.

Set aside a special work surface for preparing feeds, close to running water and facilities for boiling. Plastic laminate surfaces are ideal, being easily cleaned and free of germ-harbouring cracks. Bottles and teats can be sterilized either by boiling or by soaking in a special chemical solution for 3-4 hours.

Boiling, which takes only 15 minutes, is far quicker. Clean the bottle and teat carefully first. To clean the bottle, use washing-up liquid and a special wire-handled brush. Rinse the bottle inside and out with tap water before boiling. Clean the teat as shown, under a running tap. It is easier to do this preliminary cleaning immediately after the bottle has been used. Then immerse both bottle and

teat in a saucepan of water.

For ideal sterility only one bottle should be sterilized at a time. It is not desirable to boil several bottles in a large saucepan because after an hour or so the water in which the bottles are immersed will no longer be sterile.

The chemical method allows a large number of bottles to be sterilized at one time. The most commonly used solution is sodium hypochlorite (trade name Milton). It is sold in a concentrated form and requires dilution. A special container for the solution and bottles can be purchased. However, a plastic bucket is just as good, providing it is used only for bottle sterilization and is cleaned out regularly. It is helpful to number the bottles with a marking pen to ensure each one remains in the solution for at least 3 hours. The bottles do not require rinsing after removal from the container, though some parents like to rinse out the insides with boiling water.

Bottle milks are being manufactured to closely simulate mother's milk and are safe and wholesome. *But you must be careful to follow instructions about measuring milk powder.* The chief

danger is in making the milk too strong. It means that the baby will take in too much salt which makes all the body solutions too concentrated. It is a good idea to offer drinks of water after or occasion-

Weight gain Normally the infant will lose some weight over the first 3 days and then return to his birth weight by 8-10 days. Then he should gain steadily. This formula can be used to calculate weight gain: age in days minus 10 = number of ounces more than birth weight, e.g. a 30-day-old baby should have gained 20 ounces (30-10). The formula is valid up to 3 months of age. The birth weight will double by age 5 months and treble by age 1 year. The graph shows the gain in weight from birth to 90 days.

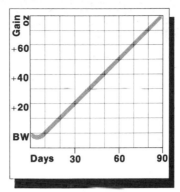

ally between feeds if the baby is thirsty. The extra water enables him to make the urine necessary to get rid of the extra salts in the milk. If he vomits, has diarrhoea or is in a warm centrally heated atmosphere, he can easily get short of water without you realizing it.

Do not change milks without asking the advice of your doctor or health visitor. If your baby seems unhappy, cries a lot or brings up feeds, changing to a different brand of milk will not be helpful.

WINDING
Whether breast- or bottle-fed, all babies swallow air when feeding and will need encouragement to expel it — 'winding'. There are two basic methods. One is to sit the young infant on the knee with one hand supporting the chest and the other gently tapping the back. The other is to hold the infant over your shoulder and gently tap his back. The essential principle is to hold the child upright, in order to allow the air bubble in the stomach to rise to the right position for expulsion.

Wind is blamed, usually mistakenly, for a variety of discomforts. Unnecessary air swallowing should be avoided by attention to the teat hole.

WEANING
'Weaning' means gradually replacing a total milk diet with solids. Weaning should begin when milk alone does not satisfy the child, a stage usually arrived at when he is about 4 months of age, or slightly earlier with some infants. It should not be left later than nine months because after that age it will become progressively more difficult. Unless introduced to solids and spoon-feeding in good time the infant may react by spitting out his food; he will also need vitamins to supplement his milk diet. Start with one semi-solid feed a day, gradually increasing to three a day over the next two months. At about eight

months the food can become coarser. By one year most children should be eating a finely chopped-up version of an adult diet.

IMMUNIZATION
Immunization, or vaccination, is the process of protecting small children against diseases by giving them injections, skin scratches or drops by mouth.

For some conditions one disease is given because it gives protection against another. Smallpox vaccine is in fact an inoculation with the disease cowpox.

In certain instances, a virus that causes a disease is treated in the laboratory so that it becomes relatively harmless. This virus is then used in the vaccine. Poliomyelitis vaccine is prepared in this way and is administered by oral drops.

Whooping cough vaccine has recently been the subject of much debate. There have

Babies should be winded after a feed, since they usually swallow a certain amount of air with their milk. They need help to expel it otherwise they may get stomach pains. Below two possible positions for holding the baby are shown.

BEAUTY AND HEALTH

been a few very rare cases of brain damage resulting from abnormal reactions to the vaccine, but at the same time whooping cough is a dreadful disease, killing some infants and leaving others with permanent damage to their lungs. It may be that whooping cough, like scarlet fever, is gradually dying out. But on the other hand, if we do not protect our children with the vaccine then we may run the risk of getting another epidemic of whooping cough. Children who should not receive whooping cough vaccine are those who are ill at the time, those who have had previous abnormal reactions to vaccinations, and those who themselves or whose families have any history of epileptic fits.

Diphtheria and tetanus vaccines have few significant side effects, and provide good protection. BCG vaccination (against tuberculosis) and measles vaccine also seem to be worthwhile. So is German measles vaccine for girls who did not get it in childhood but who hope later to have children. German measles during pregnancy is dangerous to the unborn child.

ILLNESS IN BABIES AND YOUNG CHILDREN

Babies always seem (to their parents at least) to be suffering from illnesses of varying types. As they get older, and especially when they begin to go to school, they pick up even more infections from their friends.

In many ways, this is desirable, though a nuisance to the parents, and thoroughly uncomfortable for the child.

Most of the common illnesses picked up by children cause few problems at an early age, and because immunity develops to most illnesses after one attack, it should not recur. But if a 'childhood' disease like mumps or chickenpox strikes an adult, it can be very severe indeed. Far better to take care of them early in life.

When to call the doctor is usually a problem. Don't panic. Remember that you know your own child better than anyone else, and be sure that it really is ill before calling the doctor.

Most signs of serious illness are obvious, but some can be confusing. The following are all cause for concern in a young child and should be reported to the doctor:

Persistent vomiting and diarrhoea.
Blood in urine, faeces, or vomit.
Epileptic fit lasting more than 10 minutes, or recurring.
Bluish lips or tongue.
Persistent headache, and obvious discomfort in light.
Sudden abdominal pains, with vomiting.
Raging thirst, together with very frequent urination.
Coughing and fever, with very rapid breathing.
Obvious difficulty in breathing.
Failure to pass urine for long periods.
Head injuries from which the child does not recover in a few minutes.
Refusal to take feeds in a baby.

In addition to these warning signs, none of which can be safely ignored, common-sense tells you to call the

doctor if a sick child is obviously deteriorating. Respiratory disease and a number of other conditions can develop very rapidly in a young baby. Lesser emergencies can still be very worrying. Earache and toothache are both common causes of emergency calls to the doctor at night. Both are better treated initially with the specified dose of painkiller like aspirin or junior aspirin. There is little your doctor can do for toothache in the middle of the night, and for earache, he will probably prescribe an antibiotic, which you will not be able to obtain until the morning.

COMMON CHILDHOOD ILLNESSES

Chickenpox comes 12 to 20 days after contact with a child with chickenpox or an adult with shingles. The child is infectious and may have a fever for two days before the rash appears.

The rash comes on the body, face and limbs, and can be particularly sore if spots appear on the eyelids or in the mouth.

The spots do not all develop at the same time. Some spots will just be forming at the same time as others have already blistered and crusted.

The best treatment is to give a simple antihistamine syrup to stop itching, and to apply calamine ointment to the spots. Junior aspirin in the correct dosage should be given to reduce the fever. The child is no longer infectious when all the crusts have gone.

Diphtheria is deadly. This is what the advertisement for

immunization used to say — and it is true. Immunization has dramatically reduced the number of deaths from diphtheria to almost nil. If worries about the effectiveness of other vaccines and the risks from them (such as the risks from whooping cough vaccines) lead to mothers failing to immunize their children against diphtheria, then we could see terrible outbreaks of this disease again.

Diphtheria causes a sore throat, cough and very high fever, and a grey membrane develops on the back of the throat. It has a high mortality rate. Vaccination against the disease is highly successful and there are minimal side effects.

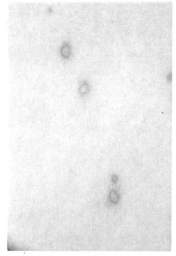

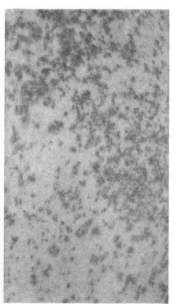

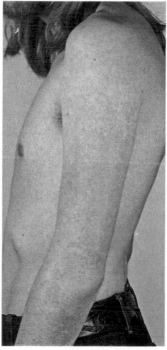

It is often quite difficult to know whether a child's rash is an allergic reaction to something or an infectious illness. The three illustrations show different types of rashes associated with different diseases. Above left is a close-up of chicken pox spots. The rash is much less densely distributed than the German measles rash, shown above. Left is the rash of a fairly unusual condition called Purpura. It is a purplish blotchy rash caused by a fault in the blood clotting mechanism. It can sometimes occur as the result of a reaction to certain drugs.

German Measles (Rubella) comes on two to three weeks after contact and causes a fine pin-point rash on the face and body. In typical cases the glands at the base of the neck can be felt, and this helps to diagnose this condition from other skin rashes. Young infants often get a skin rash that looks like German Measles but is not. This may give rise to the belief that one can get German Measles twice. Like other infectious fevers this is probably not true. Either way, it is not a very significant disease except for the effects it can have on an unborn child when it is caught by a pregnant mother within the first three months of pregnancy. Girls should therefore be vaccinated against it. Once the rash has gone, the child is no longer infectious.

Measles The rash comes up between one and three weeks after contact. The first sign of infection may be small white spots inside the cheeks, and they appear several days before the rash appears. The child is already infectious even before the rash comes out and remains infectious until the rash has gone. The rash usually starts on the face and spreads all over the body. The eyes may be sore and the child may find it more convenient to be in a dark room if they hurt.

One of the main problems of measles is that it commonly gives rise to complications such as ear infections or pneumonia. It is well worth being vaccinated against measles.

Whooping cough Unlike many other diseases, immunity to whooping cough is not transmitted before birth by the mother. It may there-

BEAUTY AND HEALTH

fore affect young infants and can be very serious. The child gets paroxysms of coughing, and a typical 'whoop' is heard as the child draws in breath again. Permanent lung damage can occur. The child may be infectious for many weeks.

TEETH

Most children are unable to manipulate a toothbrush properly until they are seven years old or more. Encourage them to try by all means, but make absolutely sure they clean their teeth properly. Clean their teeth yourself, then let them try afterwards.

Make sure children have a brush with a small head, which will easily reach to the back of the mouth. Show them how to remove food particles from between the teeth, with an up and down movement, rather than a simple polishing action.

Impress on your children the need for at least one thorough cleaning each day; this is far better than several cursory attempts at cleaning throughout the day.

Try to educate your children to see the dentist as a friend, who can help them avoid the unsightly teeth they see in many adults. It is not too early to take the child to the dentist when it has only a few teeth; even as early as six months.

FEET

The younger the child, the more important it is to ensure that their shoes are correctly fitted. If you cannot find a shop which specializes in fitting children's shoes, ask at your local Citizen's Advice Bureau to

see the Children's Foot Health Register, which lists shops which stock shoes in various fittings, and which have specially trained staff to measure your child's feet.

Sizes of shoes can vary between different manufacturers, so just specifying the shoe size you want is not enough. The feet must be measured in each shop, on each occasion you buy shoes. Make sure both feet are measured, as some children have feet which differ by as much as two sizes.

A correctly fitted shoe allows about 1.5 cm (½ in) between the longest toe (which may not be the big toe) and the end of the shoe. The toes should be able to spread under the child's weight as it stands, without being restricted by the side of the shoe. At the same time, the shoe should not slip about as the child walks.

This is particularly painful and damaging if poor fit allows the heel of the shoe to rub up and down at the back of the foot, where it will cause a painful callus.

Resign yourself to having

to buy new shoes at frequent intervals; for children of three to four years, they should last for about three months, and for five to ten years, for up to six months. They may well need changing at lesser intervals, however.

It goes without saying that fancy fashion shoes do no good to the feet, appealing though they are to a fashion-conscious child.

It is also important to remember that too-tight socks can also constrict a child's feet and be as uncomfortable as shoes which are too small. When buying a new pair of shoes it might also be useful to check your child's supply of socks. The same can apply to 'baby-grows'. While your baby might still fit into the arms and body, the feet could be getting tight and painful. Sometimes children may suffer from dropped arches or flat feet. This can be helped by foot exercises and by wearing the right shoes.

It is important that children have *both* their feet measured for shoes.

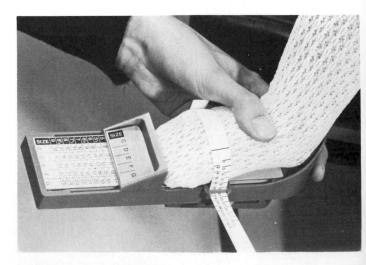

THE ELDERLY

The proportion of elderly people in our population has risen steadily. In the UK at the moment, about 14 per cent of the population are 65 or over. This is due to a number of factors. Many diseases have been overcome; we are better fed and housed than previously; we have better welfare services than were available to earlier generations.

This does not mean that we can all expect to live on to a great age without any illnesses. Unfortunately, some illnesses become more apparent as we age. Old age itself is not a disease, and very few people die simply of 'old age'; rather, from the complications which appear when the ageing body cannot cope with disease.

Old age need not be a catalogue of diseases. Many elderly people enjoy life as never before, though at a rather quieter pace. Understanding of the causes of some of the problems of the elderly can make their life a lot easier.

SIGHT
Many visual problems of old age can be overcome with the use of the correct glasses. When these are worn, other problems like headaches often clear up. Eyes should be checked annually by an optician. If vision is badly deteriorated, go to a specialist hospital's outpatient unit where advice on aids for the partially sighted can also be obtained.

HEARING
Deterioration of hearing causes many elderly people needless distress. Certainly, acuteness of hearing may be less with advancing years, but actual deafness can usually be eased by use of a hearing aid, which can restore almost normal hearing and eliminate the embarrassment which the hard of hearing often feel. In addition, wax often causes partial deafness, and when removed after softening with drops which can be bought at a chemist's, hearing is often markedly improved.

TEETH
When dentures are worn, changes in the shape of the jaw take place in old age, which can affect their fit. Loose dentures make eating uncomfortable and sometimes embarrassing, so see the dentist if they give any trouble. Don't neglect remaining natural teeth either; regular dental checks are essential.

SLEEP
Many elderly people complain of difficulty in sleeping. We actually sleep progressively less as we age, and the elderly don't need much sleep. Many also add to their total sleeping time by taking odd naps during the day. Elderly people may not take sufficient exercise to tire them thoroughly. Rather than asking the doctor for sleeping tablets, which are best avoided unless absolutely necessary, try some commonsense measures which may improve sleeping habits, or allow prolonged sleep.

Don't take tea or coffee before going to bed. They are mild stimulants, which will keep you awake. Instead, take a warm milky drink, or even a small amount of alcoholic drink, to help you relax. Don't drink too much of anything late at night, or you will have to get up to use the toilet.

Make sure your mattress is comfortable, and that you have sufficient warm clothes on the bed. If you can't sleep once you are in bed, don't lie there tossing and turning; put the light on and read until you are really tired.

FEET
Many elderly people are now suffering as a result of the ill-fitting shoes they wore in childhood. Bunions, corns, and ingrowing toenails can be excruciatingly painful, and need proper treatment by a chiropodist if they are really bad. Always try to wear soft comfortable shoes, and consult the doctor about foot problems which cause much pain.

Duncan Maclean, photographed here when in his late 80s was still running every day at Crystal Palace, London. Of course very few people are capable of keeping up this very strenuous sort of exercise in old age, but it does show that small amounts of sensible exercise can stop ageing muscles and joints from stiffening.

BEAUTY AND HEALTH

EXERCISE

It is only too easy to tell an elderly person to take plenty of exercise, but the elderly do not have the stamina and reserves of strength possessed by a younger person. Indeed, too much exercise of the wrong sort could be harmful.

Violent exercise should also be avoided as far as possible. For example, if you propose to take up jogging, you would need a thorough check up by your doctor first, to make sure your heart could take the unaccustomed strain. And even then, you would have to work up to it very gradually.

Most people are content with more leisurely forms of exercise, which don't carry such risks. Walking is probably the best form of exercise. Don't push yourself to walk too far. Several short strolls are better than a long hike, preferably with a rest between strolls.

Swimming is another excellent form of exercise which works on most of the muscles of the body. There is no need to be self-conscious about wearing a swimming costume; if you can't swim, it's never too late to learn, at classes run by many local Colleges of Further Education.

Exercise need not mean getting the whole body into action. Writing and knitting are good for stiff fingers, and the more you exercise, the looser your joints will become.

All joints tend to become stiff with lack of use, especially the many joints in the spine. Regular exercise keeps the ligaments which join the bones together quite

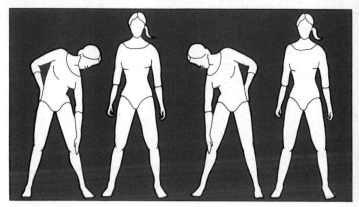

Trunk

Starting position: Stand with feet shoulder width apart and arms at sides.
Bend body sideways to left as far as comfortable.
Return to starting position.
Bend body to right as far as comfortable.
Return to starting position.
Perform at moderate speed.
Week 1: 3 times
Week 2: 4 times
Week 3: 5 times
Week 4: 6 times

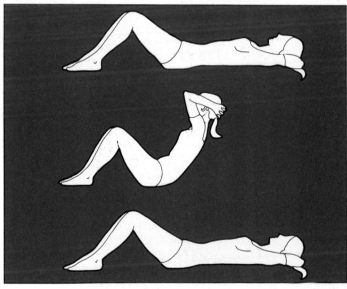

Starting position: Lie on back with heels on floor, knees bent at a right-angle and hands behind head.
With chin tucked into chest, slowly curl forward raising shoulders off the floor as far as possible.
Hold this position for two seconds.
Slowly return to starting position.
Perform at slow speed.
Week 1: 3 times
Week 2: 4 times
Week 3: 5 times
Week 4: 6 times

If you are not able to do the above exercise and need to gradually build up to it then start in a sitting position and *lower* your body to the curl position. Hold for two seconds then sit up again.

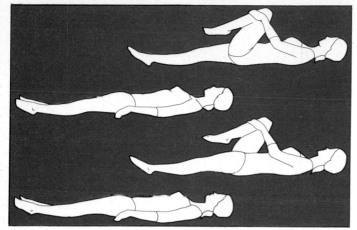

Hips, thighs, buttocks

Starting position: Lie on back with feet together, legs extended and arms along sides.

Clasp left knee with both hands and pull slowly towards your chest.

Return left leg to starting position.

Repeat exercise with right leg and return to starting position.

Perform at slow speed.

Week 1: 3 times
Week 2: 4 times
Week 3. 5 times
Week 4: 6 times

Balance

Starting position: Stand erect. Hold out your arms to balance.

Walk in a straight line, placing the right foot in front of the left foot with the right heel touching the left toe. In this way walk the number of steps indicated below. Return to the starting position by walking backward, toe to heel.

Perform at slow speed.

Week 1: 5 steps
Week 2: 6 steps
Week 3: 7 steps
Week 4: 8 steps

Have someone at your side if you are uncertain of your balance.

Neck, arms, shoulders

Starting position: Stand with feet shoulder width apart, head up with buttocks and stomach in. Extend your arms out from shoulders parallel to floor.

Rotate arms backwards the prescribed number of times, palms up.

Put arms to sides and relax.

Rotate arms forwards with palms down.

Slow increasing to moderate speed.

Week 1: 5 each direction
Week 2: 6 each direction
Week 3: 7 each direction
Week 4: 8 each direction

flexible, and makes movement easier. Constant exercise will also keep muscles healthy. Muscles easily waste away with disuse, as sometimes happens under the cast on a broken limb.

When you start exercise, your movement will probably be restricted to some extent. Don't force movement in any joint. Just try to move each joint naturally, and stop if it becomes too uncomfortable. Each day you will get a little more movement in the joint, until you can move it quite freely once more. Then keep up the exercise to maintain your new-found freedom of movement.

THE HEART

The heart is mainly muscle, so like any other muscle, it needs exercise to keep it in good condition. Inactivity means that the heart seldom has to work hard, so it becomes soft and flabby, and the heart muscle which pumps blood around the entire body shrinks in size. Then the heart cannot cope with overloads, leading to faintness and shortness of breath when you take any heavy exercise.

The heart and blood vessels have to work hard throughout life, so it is not surprising that they are not so efficient in old age.

Regular exercise keeps the heart working at its peak, and also improves blood flow around the entire body.

Restrictions or alterations in the blood flow lead to a good many of the problems of old age, such as angina, which causes severe chest pains on exercise. This is a warning sign, not to be ignored. Get medical advice as soon as possible.

Don't put too much of a strain on your circulation,

BEAUTY AND HEALTH

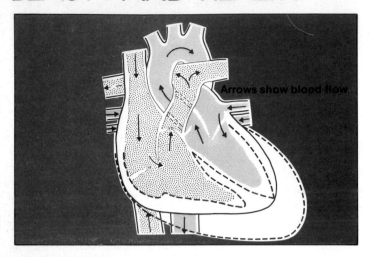

Arrows show blood flow

The powerful muscle making up the bulk of the heart forces blood around the body and lungs. During exercise, the body's demand for oxygen carried in the blood increases, so to meet this extra demand, the heart must pump harder. With frequent exercise, the extra work means that the heart muscle can increase in size significantly (shown dotted above), making it better able to cope.

Sitting down for a long time, or in an awkward position, can interfere with the blood flow. If your circulation is not in good shape, you may feel dizzy when you stand up, as blood drains away from the brain. It is always best to get up slowly, especially if you have been sitting for a long while.

There are several warning signs that things are not well with the heart, and they should not be ignored. The doctor can usually treat heart problems provided they are identified early enough.

Tell your doctor if you experience dizziness, palpitations, shortness of breath, chest pains, or swollen ankles. None of these necessarily means heart trouble, but it pays to have a check up to avoid trouble later on.

If you do have a heart problem, take your doctor's advice seriously. Stick rigidly to the dosage he prescribes for any medicine, and take the medicines at the proper time of day. Don't take two doses just because you might have forgotten the earlier one; make a chart to help you remember when to take them. And give up smoking completely. It will make your condition worse.

EATING WELL
Like sleep, elderly people need less food than the young. They take less exercise, and thus burn up less of the energy provided by food. If they do eat heartily, they usually become overweight, which is in itself a hazard, and puts an undue strain on the heart and other organs. Far better to keep slim, though not too slim, as the body needs some fat reserves.

The sense of taste is not so acute in the elderly, so food may not taste so appetising. Eating small savoury meals often appeals more than larger, bland-tasting meals. This lack of interest in food means that elderly people sometimes have an unbalanced diet. If they have dentures, they may find fruit difficult to eat, so they do not have an adequate vitamin intake. They may feel it is too much trouble, or too expensive, to eat adequate meals, or may eat convenience foods which may not contain the right balance of nutrients.

Constipation often bothers the elderly, and can usually be avoided by eating plenty of vegetables, which are cheap, or by eating cereals containing added bran to provide roughage.

PAINFUL JOINTS
Being overweight puts an additional strain on the joints. In old age, joints begin to show some wear and tear, as the body's repair mechanism becomes less effective, and this usually shows first in knees, hips, and the spine, which take all the weight of the body.

Worn or damaged joints usually become swollen and painful. Don't accept this as a normal part of growing old, as the doctor can almost always prescribe something to make the joints less painful, and to reduce swelling.

The usual causes are common disorders like osteoarthritis, rheumatoid arthritis, or gout. Of these, osteoarthritis tends to cause chronic nagging pain and stiffness, while rheumatoid arthritis and gout flare up into painful episodes, which can be controlled with the proper medical treatment.

If you get joint pains, always check with your doctor before starting a course of exercises, as these could further damage your joints.

SEX AND THE ELDERLY
Sexual activity can continue well into old age. In fact, it can continue as long as both partners wish, the exercise alone being beneficial, quite apart from the pleasure it brings. Elderly women sometimes find intercourse painful, due to the drying up of vaginal secretions after the menopause. This minor problem can be overcome with the use of suitable lubricants. Your doctor can provide advice on these.

MOVING AROUND
In spite of exercises, mobility is a problem to many old and infirm people, some of whom are very unsteady on their feet. The home can be organized to make life a lot easier and more safe. Polished floors are an obvious hazard, as are loose or torn carpets, which can cause a fall. Severe handicaps need special means to overcome them. A walking frame can help even the unsteadiest person, providing a secure handhold to rest on. Handrails can be fitted to the walls near the toilet and on the stairs, making life much safer. For the elderly person with arthritic hands, special gadgets can be obtained for fitting to taps, opening bottles, and coping with all the other everyday problems which are so difficult if the hand cannot grip strongly. Obtain details by writing to the Disabled Living Foundation, 346 Kensington High St, London W14, or from a community nurse or social worker.

GLOSSARY

Allergy: Abnormal reaction to otherwise harmless substances which can cause rashes, sneezing, watery eyes, asthma or swelling of lips and eyes. Commonly caused by inhaled grass pollen, but sometimes related to home dust, foods, or almost anything else.

Angina: Very severe 'crushing' pain in the chest, caused by poor blood supply to the heart muscle. Usually comes on with exercise, and is a warning to take things more easily.

Antenatal: Literally 'before birth'. Usually implies check-ups and relaxation courses for a pregnant woman.

Antibiotic: Substance which attacks bacteria. It has no effect against disease caused by viruses.

Antibody: Substance produced by the body in response to an infection, or to the presence of a foreign substance in the blood. Antibodies help the body inactivate bacteria, viruses, or substances capable of causing damage.

Antihistamine: Drug which reduces the effects of an allergy. It frequently causes tiredness as a side-effect and for this reason is sometimes also used as a sedative.

Bacteria: Micro-organisms which are frequently capable of causing infectious diseases. Bacteria are attacked by antibiotics.

Breech Delivery: Birth in which the baby emerges bottom-first, instead of head-first as is normal.

Bronchi: Thick-walled tubes which carry air to and from the lungs during breathing.

Bronchitis: Inflammation of the lining of the bronchi, causing breathlessness and coughing. Very common in Britain, and made much worse by smoking. Can lead to more serious disease if unchecked.

Caries: Tooth decay.

Cataract: Cloudiness in the normally clear lens of the eye, obscuring vision. Generally affecting the elderly, but sometimes appearing after eye injury such as chemical burns. Can be removed surgically, spectacles or contact lenses being worn to replace the lens.

Cystic Fibrosis: Hereditary disease affecting various glands. Can lead to clogging of the lungs and breathing difficulties. Digestive disorders are also common. Often requires continuous antibiotic treatment to prevent lung infection.

Cystitis: Painful inflammation of the bladder, most common in women. Frequently follows sexual intercourse. Needs medical treatment, and can recur.

Dehydration: Shortage of water in the body, often following persistent vomiting or diarrhoea. Quickly replaced by drinking large amounts. Especially dangerous in infants.

Diabetes: Disease caused by failure of the body to produce sufficient insulin. This in turn allows levels of sugar in the blood to rise to dangerous levels. Can be treated with drugs, or by injection of insulin.

DPT: Abbreviation for triple vaccine, against diphtheria, pertussis (whooping cough), and tetanus.

Enuresis: Bed-wetting; inability to control the flow of urine during sleep, in persons over five years of age.

BEAUTY AND HEALTH

Febrile Convulsions: A fit caused by the effect on the brain of a high fever.

Gall Bladder: Small sac in which bile produced by the liver is stored temporarily. Bile is released into the intestine, stimulated by the passage of food, where it helps to digest fats. The gall bladder sometimes becomes blocked or inflamed.

Haemoglobin: Red pigment in the blood, which transports oxygen around the body. Low levels of haemoglobin can cause anaemia.

Heart Murmur: An unusual sound in the heart, which can be heard with a stethoscope. It does not necessarily mean that there is any heart problem.

Hyperactivity: State of constant physical activity in young children.

Hypertension: Abnormally high blood pressure. Can cause damage to the heart and in later life if allowed to remain untreated.

Immunization: Protection against a disease by giving harmless, weakened or dead germs or viruses by mouth, skin scratch or injection. Their presence stimulates the body to produce antibodies.

Jaundice: Yellow discolouration caused by the inability of the liver to break down old red blood cells. Usually follows a liver infection or disorder.

Meningitis: Inflammation of the layer of tissue covering the brain and spinal cord. Can cause very serious illness, especially in young children.

Mongolism: Physical and mental retardation present when a child is born. Affected babies have an 'oriental' appearance. Mongol babies are born more frequently to mothers who have babies in late middle age.

Neonate: New-born baby, up to one month old.

Obesity: Gross overweight. Obese people put themselves at risk due to heart and circulatory problems, and may damage joints.

Pertussis: Whooping cough.

Placenta: Organ through which the unborn child obtains its nourishment. The placenta is attached to the womb, and is expelled shortly after the birth of the child. It is sometimes referred to as the afterbirth.

Prophylactic: Measure to prevent disease — e.g. hygiene, immunization.

Prostate Gland: Gland close to the bladder, in males. With increasing age it may swell and impede the flow of urine.

Retina: The layer of tissue at the back of the eye containing light-sensitive cells.

Rickets: Bone disease caused by a deficiency of vitamin D or calcium in the diet. Can cause marked bending of the shin bones, as well as other deformities in children.

Roughage (or dietary fibre): Material in the diet which will be incompletely digested, and therefore produces soft, bulky stools. Many modern foods are over-refined to remove roughage, and constipation and disorders can result. Vegetables are a good source of roughage, as is bran.

Rubella: German measles.

Scabies: Skin disease caused by invasion of microscopic burrowing mites. Very infectious, and needs medical attention. Usually treated with special creams.

Scarlet Fever: Now fortunately rare, scarlet fever results from reaction to poisons produced by a particular throat infection, causing a rash appearing first on the face, neck, and upper chest. Well controlled by antibiotics.

Stroke: Damage caused by interruption of the blood supply to the brain, due to a blockage or ruptured blood vessel. Severe strokes cause paralysis, complete or partial, and often affect speech. There is usually some degree of recovery.

Thrombosis: Blockage of a blood vessel by a blood clot (thrombus). Can be dangerous if the clot forms in the brain (stroke) or heart (heart attack).

Trachea: The wind pipe, a tough armoured tube leading to the bronchi and the lungs.

Ulcerative Colitis. Painful and severe illness in which the lower part of the bowel becomes ulcerated, causing continuous diarrhoea.

Umbilical Cord: The cord connecting the unborn baby to the placenta, supplying nourishment to the baby and removing waste material.

Ventilator: Machine used to help the breathing of a severely ill person.

Weaning: Gradual transfer of babies from milk to a solid diet.

LAW AND FINANCE

LAW AND FINANCE

If money makes the world go round, then it is the law which regulates its speed. There are numerous limits placed by the law on how we acquire money, how much of it is taken away by the State, and what we can do with the rest. There are controls, too, on those who seek to take our money from us. The ways in which goods are described, their suitability for the purpose for which they are sold, and means of redress if they turn out to be no good, are all governed by various laws. Insurance, credit facilities, social security, banking are all examples of how the law and the financial side of our lives are inextricably bound together. If the rules are understood and observed, problems will be few and far between. But if they are not, the outcome can be truly chaotic.

HOUSEHOLD BUDGETS

Unless money is no object, it is essential to give some thought to planning the household budget. If the amount of money coming in each week or month is fixed, then care must be taken to ensure that the outgoings do not exceed it. Certain items must rank as necessities, though, and the amount involved will be fixed. Others will also be necessary, but the sums which can be devoted to them will vary. And others still will be optional luxuries, to be bought only if there is enough money left over.

Each household must determine its own priorities, but housing must head the list, along with food, of course. Unless there is a sudden rise in the mortgage rates, the cost of housing usually does not fluctuate from week to week, but the amount spent on food can and probably will. Since it is an essential item in the budget, food should have the first claim on the money that is left after other bills have been paid.

Nonetheless, it is sensible to try to work out an average weekly expenditure on food, and then proceed to divide up the rest. Other important items are gas and electricity. The difficulty in budgeting to meet fuel bills, though, is that they come in only four times a year and are not necessarily for the same amounts. If the money available is limited, this can cause problems. One way round it is to enter into arrangements with the gas or electricity boards to pay an average pre-determined monthly sum towards the annual bill. Any balance will then be refunded or demanded at the end of the year.

Telephone bills too are payable every quarter. The rental element is fixed, but the charge for the number of calls made cannot really be worked out in advance. It is possible to buy devices which record the cost of calls, but they are not cheap and they do not save you money unless you use them to ensure that you do not spend too long on the phone. But you can buy special stamps from the Post Office in advance to put towards the bill when it comes in and, if you are doubtful whether you can afford to dole out a large lump-sum in one go, they are clearly worth buying.

Unless you live in furnished or council accommodation (where the rates are included in the rent) you will have to pay domestic rates on your home. The level of these is fixed early each year, and must then be paid in two instalments — half in

April and the other half in October. But if you apply in writing to the local council, you can pay by ten instalments over the year.

The amount of your other outgoings will depend on how you choose to spend your money. Clothes will obviously have to be bought. There may be fares to work or to the shops. You may take holidays. Most televisions these days are rented, and the rentals are payable monthly. Anyone using a television must have a licence. This is bought outright, but you can buy stamps from the Post Office in advance to put towards the cost.

If you own a car, it will be another drain on your resources. If it has been acquired on HP, there will be the monthly payments. Then there is the cost of maintenance, insurance, the road fund licence, and petrol.

CASH OR CREDIT?

Some people prefer to pay all their bills as soon as they arrive, and prefer to pay immediately they make a purchase. Others are happy to take advantage of whatever credit facilities may be available. There is nothing intrinsically wrong with buying on credit, so long as you do not overload yourself and finally find it impossible to meet the repayments.

A sensible course to follow is to buy only 'capital' items on credit, such as furniture, expensive clothes, a car and so on. If you make routine and regular purchases in this way, you could be heading for trouble, because these ought to come out of a normal weekly or monthly budget. However, if you prefer to use credit cards, and always pay the bill from the credit card company immediately it comes in, then that is good budgeting, as you are using the card as an alternative to carrying cash, and not to provide you with money that does not really exist.

How the bank can help Most banks operate what are called 'budget accounts' for those of their customers who want them. These are accounts into which you pay a fixed sum each month over a year. From it, the bank will let you draw whatever cheques are needed to pay large irregular bills as they come in, even if that leaves the account temporarily overdrawn. As you work out in advance what these bills are likely to come to, the account should eventually balance. There is a small service charge for using the account and normal overdraft rates are charged, but if you would otherwise have difficulty in meeting these bills, this kind of account may be the answer.

INSURANCE

The essence of insurance is that you pay now to cover yourself against future risks. If there is anything that is capable of happening then, in theory at least, you can insure against it. In practice, of course, the kinds of things for which people do take out insurance are against death, or other likely hazards such as road traffic accidents (if you drive a car, you must, by law, be insured), and theft of or damage to the contents of your house.

Apart from the compulsory car insurance cover, any other insurance is optional. Nonetheless, it is obviously a sensible way of providing for both yourself and your family, especially if you are not in a position to cope with the financial consequences without the benefit of insurance.

15% Housing, rates and rent

6% Fuel light and heat

24% Food

5% Alcoholic drink

3% Tobacco

8% Clothing and footwear

7% Household goods

7% Leisure goods

14% Transport — fares, petrol and cars

10% Services, telephone, TV Licences and holidays

1% Miscellaneous

If income is fixed, it is very important to plan expenditure. In this way you can be sure that there will be enough to meet the various outgoings, and you will also know how much to spend.

LAW AND FINANCE

If you are injured, or cause injury to others, the financial consequences could be serious. It is possible to obtain insurance that will compensate you in the event of being injured, and there are also schemes which provide cover if you are the cause of someone else being injured.

LIFE INSURANCE

There are a number of ways in which you can take out insurance on your life. Strictly speaking, it is *assurance* that you take on your life, because you will, of course, die at some point in the future. You might want a policy which provides a lump sum for your dependants; or a policy which will provide income, or a mixture of capital and income. You can go for a whole-life policy or, if you can afford it, what is called an endowment policy. The differences between these various policies are considerable, and it is worth looking at each.

Whole life policies: with and without profits A whole-life policy is one that pays out only when you die. You pay premiums during your lifetime, although some policies allow you to stop paying when you reach a given age — usually retirement age. If you die early, then your dependants will collect what might be quite a large lump sum, depending on the amount for which you were covered. This is a fairly inexpensive type of insurance, but then if you are in good health it is not really very good value.

If the policy allows you to cash it in at a certain point, you will get back a lump sum. It will obviously be a lot less than would have been paid out on death, but it might be more than the total premiums paid. Allowing for the effects of inflation you are most unlikely to end up ahead if you do surrender the policy, but it is worth bearing the possibility in mind when making your initial choice.

Whether or not the policy is with or without profits will make a lot of difference at the end of the day. If it is without profits, then the eventual payout will be the sum quoted at the outset, and no more. A with-profits policy, on the other hand, is more expensive, in that a given premium will buy you a lot less basic life cover than will the same premium on a without-profits policy. But you will have added to the benefits which will ultimately be paid out, annual bonuses based on the level of profits secured by the company on the life insurance investments. These will be added to the minimum sum assured. If you can afford it (on the basis of the level of life cover that you must have) then a with-profits policy is better value.

Endowment policies These are more a form of saving than providing adequate life insurance cover. You agree to pay premiums for a set number of years. At the end of that period, the insurance company will pay out a sum which has been determined at the outset. It is possible (and sensible) to take out an endowment policy with profits, given that it is a method of saving, and this will mean an additional and possibly substantial payment to take account of any bonuses.

This amount of cover provided is the annual premium which you pay, multiplied by the number of years the policy is to run, though this varies from company to company. So it would be very expensive to carry the same level of cover as you will get on an ordinary whole-life policy, where the sum assured is calculated on the basis that it will probably be a very long time before you (or your family) become entitled to it.

Endowment policies are usually very effective savings devices, because the sum eventually paid is tax-free, and you qualify for tax relief on the premiums. (This is discussed further below.) Because they acquire an increasing surrender value, and will provide a guaranteed lump sum at a known point in the future, endowment policies are often used as security for loans, particularly mortgages.

Other forms of life insurance The range of other kinds of policies is considerable. There are schemes which offer an annual income for dependants for an agreed number of years. Another possibility is a policy which offers a fixed level of cover for an agreed number of years. After that point has been reached, you get nothing. Alternatively, the level of cover might diminish over the years, as your need for security reduces — as children grow up and leave home, perhaps. These policies, cheaper than whole-life and endowment policies, are on the whole perfectly adequate and therefore worth looking into.

Tax relief Within limits laid down by law, you are eligible for tax relief on insurance premiums. Very roughly, you halve the basic rate of tax and apply that percentage to the premium. So, if basic rate is 30 per cent, and the annual premiums total £200, your tax saving comes to £30. This sum is deducted by the insurance company, so that you pay only the net amount — £170 in the above example.

MOTOR INSURANCE

By law, everyone must be insured if they drive motor vehicles. It is a serious criminal offence to drive if you do not have the benefit of at least third-party insurance. This covers you for any harm or damage inflicted on passengers, pedestrians or other drivers, but not for damage to your own car. For that you will need a different type of insurance, known as comprehensive cover, which is obviously more expensive.

Unless someone is hurt in an accident, the police are not usually involved. The procedure is for the parties concerned to exchange names and addresses and insurance details and the respective insurance companies will deal with the case from then on.

LAW AND FINANCE

Few people could afford to replace all of their possessions if they were stolen, damaged by fire or flood, or were lost. House contents insurance enables you to pass the risk involved in ownership to an insurance company. In return for your premium, the company will undertake to compensate you for any loss.

HOUSE INSURANCE

If you are burgled, or your house is damaged by, say, fire, a contents policy will help with all or part of the cost of replacing what has been lost. Some policies provide you with enough to meet current replacement costs (known as 'new for old' policies), while others, which are cheaper, will only pay out what the goods were worth when they were lost. Premiums vary according to several factors, including the level of cover required and where you live.

Fire and structural insurance is normally one of the conditions of a mortgage and the building society often pays the premium and collects it back from the house owner. Otherwise, obtain quotes based on clearing the site and rebuilding. Choose the most competitive policy available from a broker or an insurance company.

TAKING OUT INSURANCE

When you apply for insurance cover, you will have to fill in an application form. It is essential that you answer all the questions asked accurately, and also that you mention anything else which you feel might be relevant. If you fail, for instance, to mention that your son has a conviction for burglary, you might find the insurance company turning round at some point in the future and refusing to meet a claim on the ground that that was something which they were entitled to know when deciding whether to take your business.

WHERE TO GET ADVICE

If you are new to the world of insurance, your best bet is to get in touch with an insurance broker. He will be able to advise you on what kind of policy will best suit your needs, and which company might be able to help. But remember that he has a vested interest in getting you to take a policy — he gets paid commission by the insurance companies. So insist on seeing details of as many options as possible, and take them away to look at them at your leisure.

TAXATION

There are very few ways of acquiring money in this country which escape the demands of the Inland Revenue. If it is earned, then it is taxable. If it is unearned, in the sense of coming from interest payments on savings, then again it is taxable, and sometimes at a higher rate. If you sell something (other than your home) at a profit, a tax bill will eventually follow. Presents of cash or property can be taxable, if they are large enough, although the tax is normally payable by the donor. Similarly, bequests attract tax.

Income tax is the main source of revenue for the Government. Anyone who earns enough money to come within the tax net will have to pay a proportion of that income by way of income tax, and the greater the level of earnings, the greater the proportion of tax.

INCOME TAX

As indicated, and as is obvious from its name, this is a tax levied on income. It is a progressive tax, in that the percentage payable rises according to the level of income. At present, the lowest rate is 30 per cent, the highest 60 per cent.

Anyone who is employed will be taxed under the PAYE scheme, and the employer will simply deduct enough money each week or month to settle the tax bill up to that point. But although that undoubtedly simplifies matters, it does not mean that the employee can afford to ignore what is being done.

For a start, mistakes can be made. The tables produced by the Inland Revenue which set out the tax deductions to be made are fairly complicated, and the wrong figures could be read off. By adding together your reliefs and allowances, it is possible to work out roughly what your regular tax bill should be. So, if the amount actually taken, and your own calculations, are wildly out, you should query it.

Secondly, it is up to you to make sure that you claim the reliefs and allowances to which you are entitled. This means filling in your tax return as soon as it is sent to you by the Inland Revenue each year, and also notifying your local tax office if there is any change in your circumstances.

These include getting married, taking on a mortgage (or having to pay extra mortgage interest), losing or acquiring certain fringe benefits, incurring expenses related to work (especially if you are not reimbursed by your employer) and reaching retirement age. Other things are likely to increase your tax liability, and these too must be notified to the tax authorities. Apart from ceasing to be eligible for any of the above reliefs and allowances, any interest which you receive from investments on which tax has not been deducted at source, will mean that you have to pay income tax on it.

The Inland Revenue looks at all of these factors, and works out the total that you are allowed tax-free. This is then converted into a code number, and using that code, your employer can calculate your ongoing tax liability.

Income tax is a progressive tax, in that the more you earn the greater the percentage of your income that will have to be paid over to the Inland Revenue. Thus the person on £20,000 a year pays over 31 per cent of his total earnings in income tax, while the person on £6,000 pays only 19 per cent. The chart relates to income tax without allowances and shows approximate percentages.

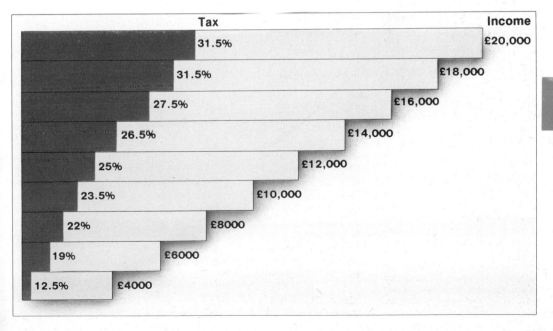

Tax	Income
31.5%	£20,000
31.5%	£18,000
27.5%	£16,000
26.5%	£14,000
25%	£12,000
23.5%	£10,000
22%	£8000
19%	£6000
12.5%	£4000

LAW AND FINANCE

Changing jobs, or becoming unemployed, can affect your tax position, for obvious reasons. If you do lose your job, then, under PAYE, you may be entitled to a tax refund. Either your ex-employer or the local unemployment office or tax office will advise you.

Because PAYE is self-correcting, any refunds due to you are normally implemented in the course of the tax year. However, delays can occur, particularly if there is some dispute over whether you are entitled to particular allowances, for instance.

Husbands and wives There are a number of ways in which the incomes of husbands and wives who both work can be taxed. For those with relatively high incomes the decision as to which method to opt for can have important consequences, and advice should be sought from an accountant.

The self-employed Only those who are employed can be taxed under PAYE. Those who are self-employed are responsible for making their own arrangements to pay tax. The procedures are quite complicated, and will often require the services of an accountant, because it is necessary to draw up profit and loss accounts for the business.

However, the tax due on the profits (if any) is paid in arrears, which is obviously advantageous. And the self-employed enjoy much more favourable rules regarding business expenses than do employees. As long as it can be shown that a particular expense was incurred in connection with the business activity, then it is tax deductible.

IF YOU DISAGREE WITH THE AMOUNT OF TAX DEDUCTED

It is fairly unusual for employees to have any serious disputes over their tax position. Far more disagreements crop up between the tax authorities and the self-employed. Profit levels may be queried, expenses may not be allowed as deductions and so on. Often agreement can eventually be reached by negotiation, but if that is not possible the matter is likely to end up before the Income Tax Commissioners, referred either by the tax inspector or by the taxpayer.

The Commissioners will hear the arguments and then decide whether a particular assessment to tax should be upheld or not. The dispute can revolve round either the interpretation of facts, or points of law, or both. In any event, such proceedings, while relatively informal, are nonetheless rather involved, and it would be unwise to pursue an appeal to the Commissioners unless the sums involved are reasonably large, because help from an accountant may well be needed (and will have to be paid for).

TAX-SAVING HINTS

Unless you earn large amounts of money, it is really not worth worrying about devices for minimizing your tax bill. By and large, it is better to have a mortgage on a property than to use capital to finance a purchase, because of the generous tax relief on the interest. If you want to save, a pension scheme is a good way of doing it, if you do not already belong to an occupational pension scheme, because again the tax treatment of the premiums is favourable. If you have children going through university or college, and are paying their grant, the use of a covenant will reduce the overall cost. Many firms offer staff a range of fringe benefits such as company cars, cheap loans and free insurance. From the tax viewpoint, these benefits are usually worth having, because you will be taxed less on the benefit than on a comparable amount of extra salary.

IF YOU DO NOT PAY YOUR TAX BILL
Those taxed under PAYE have no choice but to pay, because the money is taken from their pay before they get it. The self-employed, though, pay their own tax, in two annual instalments. Any delay in paying on the date specified in the tax assessments will mean that interest, currently 12 per cent a year, must be paid. And if the delay persists, the Inland Revenue can take action to obtain the money.

They can either remove your goods and sell them to meet the debt, or take action through the courts. If suing does not bring forth payment, then the usual procedure is to commence bankruptcy proceedings. If the Inland Revenue does obtain judgement against you, it is essential to pay up immediately because proceedings can start at once.

In Victorian Britain there were special prisons for debtors, which were stark and dismal places. Today it is still possible to be sent to prison for bankruptcy.

BENEFITS AND ALLOWANCES

The social security system in the UK is designed to ensure that anyone needing financial help in order to subsist will receive it. The amounts paid may not be generous, and will as a rule cover only bare essentials, but everyone is entitled, if the circumstances are right, to have help from the State if they are without any means of support.

Unfortunately, the system has become extremely complicated, with a number of different kinds of benefit being administered by different agencies, and with different levels of payment, and different methods of calculating entitlement.

SUPPLEMENTARY BENEFIT
This is the safety net of the social security system. The criterion is need, and factors such as length of employment, previous earnings and so on, do not enter into it. Anyone who is not in paid full-time employment can apply, and if they are found to have needs which cannot be met from other sources they will be eligible for supplementary benefit.

There is a basic level of payment, which is periodically increased to take account of inflation, with additional payments to cover dependants and certain outgoings such as rent, children's clothes and the like. It is permissible to earn a small amount of money without entitlement being affected, but the social security office should be consulted to ascertain the current position. Many people who claim supplementary benefit do so because they are not eligible for unemployment benefit or sickness benefit on technical grounds, although a claimant may still be entitled to supplementary benefit if he is receiving certain other benefits.

LAW AND FINANCE

There are a number of benefits available to handicapped or disabled people who are unable to work, such as home help, meals on wheels, industrial disablement benefit and mobility allowances.

CHILD BENEFIT
This is a payment made to mothers for each of their children, meaning those under 16, or under 19 if they are in full-time education. It is paid via the Post Office, and was brought in to replace the old tax allowances for children.

FAMILY INCOME SUPPLEMENT
Whereas supplementary benefit is not payable to those in work, FIS is a benefit which is available to families on very low earned incomes.

SICKNESS BENEFIT
If you are unable to work because of illness, you may be entitled to sickness benefit from the DHSS. This is paid for 27.5 weeks, after which invalidity benefit will be normally payable. Eligibility for sickness benefit is based on the length of time you have been in employment, because the DHSS looks at how long national insurance contributions have been paid. The calculations are rather involved, but for the first year or two in work you are unlikely to be entitled to sickness benefit, although thereafter there should be no problem unless there is a significant break. Women who take time off to have children are therefore somewhat vulnerable. The amount paid is based to some extent on how much you have been earning. To claim, you need a certificate from your GP, which must be sent to the DHSS. No benefit is paid for the first three days. And most firms which operate their own sick pay scheme will deduct from what they pay you an amount equal to what you should be getting from the DHSS.

UNEMPLOYMENT BENEFIT
Those who lose their jobs can claim unemployment benefit if they do not immediately start a new job. (Those who resign may be eligible in certain circumstances.) The rules governing eligibility are rather detailed — for instance, you can be denied benefit for several weeks if the Department of Employment official thinks that it was your own fault that you lost your job. And, as with sickness benefit, length of total employment is relevant. However, those who fail to qualify because they do not have enough national insurance contributions to their name, may still be entitled to supplementary benefit. Unemployment benefit will normally be paid for a maximum of 12 months, after which the claimant will have to rely on supplementary benefit.

PENSIONS
Most people are entitled to a pension from the State when they retire. The retirement ages at the moment are 60 for women and 65 for men. It is possible, though, to continue working beyond those ages, in which event the pension will not be paid until work is finally stopped (or the age of 70 — 65 for women — is reached), although it will then be paid at a higher rate. And the rules currently allow people to earn quite a lot after attaining retirement age without their pension being withheld.

The amount of the pension is based primarily on National

Insurance contributions, on how many years have been worked and how much was earned. In view of the importance of knowing what your pension will be, and what rules govern any work you might want to do after retiring, it is clearly sensible to ask the Department of Health and Social Security for advice.

HOUSE PURCHASE

Buying a house or flat is not an easy business. There are seemingly innumerable stages to go through, and the whole process can often take three months or more to complete. A good deal of expense is also involved.

Looking for a suitable property can itself take some considerable time. Once something likely has been located, it is necessary to make an offer. Deciding how much to offer is not easy. Factors such as the asking price, the condition of the property, how much you want it and the availability of finance must all be taken into account.

When the offer has been accepted things become even more complex and hectic. For a start, until contracts have been exchanged, there is no binding contract, and either party can therefore withdraw. Apart from the distress and inconvenience that this can cause, it can also be expensive, because money may have been spent in preparing contracts, surveys, etc., and this cannot be recovered.

A great deal of work needs to be done, usually by solicitors, before contracts are exchanged. The deeds to the property need to be checked; searches at the Land Registry must be conducted; local plans at the Town Hall should be studied to see if any major development is envisaged for the area.

CONVEYANCING

Although it is possible to do all this yourself, or entrust it to a conveyancing organization, most people use solicitors to handle the legal work involved in house purchase. When all the preliminaries have been completed, and each party is satisfied, contracts can be exchanged. The property is then at the buyer's risk and he should immediately take out insurance. The exchange of contracts is an important step, because the deal then becomes binding, and failure to go through with it on the appointed day will prove very costly. To comply with legal requirements, a conveyance must be drawn up. This is the formal document transferring ownership of the property to the purchaser. It is possible to do yourself, but without any knowledge of law, it can be most time-consuming, and could cause untold problems later if any mistakes are made.

SEARCHES AND SURVEYS

As indicated, it is crucial that Town Hall records be checked. If any development is proposed — such as a new housing estate or road — it could have a powerful effect on house prices, and might make you think twice about buying the property in question. At the same time it is usually the case that a check is carried out to see that any building work carried out on the house was, where appropriate, covered by planning permission or building regulation consent.

Details of most properties are now stored at the Land Registry, and a check will reveal whether, for instance, there

LAW AND FINANCE

are any limitations on the disposal or use of the property that you are intending to buy.

Unless you are extremely confident, it is wise to commission a private survey of the property. This should reveal any structural defects and will cover the general condition of the place. It might affect your decision to buy, or at least warn you of any work that might need to be done. Surveyor's reports vary enormously, as do their prices. Ask your solicitor or friends to recommend one.

All new properties are covered by the NHBC (National House Building Council) guarantee, which will meet the cost of defects arising in the first ten years, though if a house is sold while the guarantee is still in effect, the NHBC must be notified.

STAMP DUTY

This is a form of tax on the purchase price of private homes. The stamp duty varies from, at present, nil for a house sold for under £20,000, to 2 per cent of the purchase price for a house over £35,000. The important thing to bear in mind is that stamp duty is payable only on the price of the house. But the price that is sometimes agreed upon contains a sum for carpets, curtains, etc. Work out what this sum is and deduct this from the total price for the purposes of stamp duty, because it could make quite a difference to the amount of duty payable. For instance, if you offer £30,500, but £750 of that is for fixtures and fittings, only £29,750 is for the house. Stamp duty is thus 1 per cent of £29,750 rather than 1.5 per cent of £30,500 — a saving of £160. In addition to stamp duty, the buyer will normally have to pay Land Registry fees.

FINANCE

Most house purchases are financed with the aid of a mortgage. This is a loan under which, in return for advancing the money, the lender takes the deeds, and can prevent any sale of the property until the loan is repaid, as well as taking legal proceedings to acquire possession of the property if the repayments are not kept up.

The great majority of loans for house purchase come from building societies, although banks, insurance companies and local authorities will also lend money for that purpose in certain circumstances.

There are strict rules laid down by each society as to how much they will lend. The usual formula is based on earnings and the age and value of the property. Thus a society might lend up to three times the husband's income, with a ceiling of 85 per cent of the valuation or price (whichever is the lower) of the property, subject to a maximum advance of, say, £20,000, repayable over 20 or 25 years.

Some lend more than others; some give more weight to the wife's earnings; some will not lend on old properties or conversions; and most insist that you have saved with them in the past. So shopping around is often a good idea, as is regular saving with a building society.

There are two basic types of mortgage — combined interest/capital and endowment.

Under the combined interest/capital type, you pay a monthly sum which meets the interest and makes a small contribution towards the capital sum. You can then claim tax relief on the interest element. These schemes are so arranged that after a few years you have repaid almost all the interest that will fall due over the term of the loan, so that the bulk of the repayments then go to reducing the debt itself. Thus the proportion eligible for tax relief gradually diminishes.

Under an endowment mortgage, you only pay interest to the building society over the length of the loan. But you also finance an endowment insurance policy. At the end of the 20 or 25 years or whatever, the insurance company pays off the mortgage and hands over the balance, if there is any. These mortgages are more expensive, but give added security and are a form of savings, and, because of the higher tax relief and the possibility of a tax-free lump sum at the end of the day, may be the best way of buying a home for those with higher incomes.

If you have a small income you could consider an 'option mortgage' where you get a subsidy from the Government to pay part of your interest, instead of income tax relief. Also possible for the first-time buyer is the Government's 'Homeloan Scheme' for a grant and an interest-free loan.

RENT AND RATES

RENT

The alternative to buying a home is to rent one. The rented sector can, broadly speaking, be divided into two — private renting and local authority renting. The whole of the country is covered by councils with housing responsibilities, and they must make available accommodation not just to the homeless but also to those who might have difficulty in obtaining any other form of housing.

The rules regarding eligibility for council housing are not uniform, and the councils have different procedures for dealing with applications. Anyone wishing to obtain a house or flat from the local authority should, therefore, contact the Housing Department of the council and make appropriate enquiries, or write to their MP. Rents charged tend to be lower than those prevailing in the private sector, and normally a charge inclusive of rent, rates and heating will be levied, weekly or fortnightly. There is as yet no security of tenure for council tenants, who can be transferred to other accommodation within the borough or district at the behest of the council, and can be evicted with comparatively little redress if, say, the rent is unpaid. Some councils are operating a policy of selling property to their tenants, and all councils may eventually be obliged to do so if the tenant wishes to buy.

The privately rented accommodation market is shrinking, largely, it is thought, because of the effect of the Rent Acts, which make it very difficult for landlords to evict tenants, and also because of the low rents sometimes fixed by rent tribunals. Privately rented property can be furnished or unfurnished. The distinction mainly concerns the rent which can be charged, as furnished accommodation will obviously be more expensive, although unfurnished property usually requires quite a large

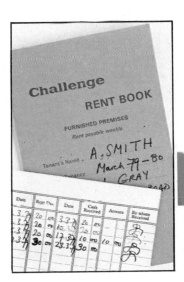

A rent book is a useful reminder to both landlord and tenant as to when rent has been paid or is due. For most types of tenancy the landlord must supply one, and certain benefits will be denied you if you cannot produce your rent book.

LAW AND FINANCE

initial payment in respect of fixtures and fittings. The law on security of tenure is extremely complicated. The type of tenancy determines the degree and nature of any protection.

If you occupy a separate dwelling as your home (as opposed to a room in a house) you will normally be classed as a 'protected tenant', and you cannot be evicted unless you are in breach of the tenancy agreement. It is irrelevant that the landlord may have said that you could only occupy the premises for a given period. You can only be evicted if you do not pay the rent or, in some cases, if the landlord needs the property for himself or a member of his family, or is able to provide alternative accommodation. Also if you have sub-let without permission, or damaged the premises or if you have been causing a nuisance to other tenants. There are other grounds on which eviction can be sought, but they are less usual.

You cannot, in any event, simply be thrown out into the streets. The landlord must take out possession proceedings in the local County Court. And the court does not have to grant immediate possession. If you have remedied the grievance — such as having cleared the rent arrears, or most of them — the court can suspend the possession order on condition that you continue to keep up with the payments. If you receive an eviction notice, or a possession summons, you should take legal advice, either from a solicitor, or from a local Citizens Advice Bureau, Rent Office or law centre, so that you know what will

Although under the current Rent Act it is harder for tenants to be evicted, if it is proven that the tenant has no intention of paying the rent, eviction can still take place.

happen next and can take whatever action seems appropriate.

The landlord is limited in raising the rent, if you are a protected tenant. If the tenant disagrees with the proposed rent, the landlord must apply to the local Rent Office for a fair rent to be fixed, and the figure laid down will take account of factors such as the condition of the property and the outgoings incurred by the landlord. Tenants too can apply to the Rent Office for a fair rent to be fixed. It is also possible to get a rent rebate or allowance for council or privately rented accommodation.

RATES

Rates on domestic property are assessed by, and payable to, the local council. They are the charges levied for all local services provided by the council. Sometimes they are included in the total rent payable to the landlord, in the case of council or furnished rented property. Otherwise, they are the responsibility of the tenant or owner-occupier.

The rates are payable in two instalments — half in April and the other half in October. But you can apply in writing for permission to pay ten instalments in the course of the year. A failure to pay will lead to court proceedings. If payment is still not forthcoming, the council will usually ask bailiffs to collect the money, and they are empowered to remove sufficient of your goods to sell and meet the debt. As a final resort, you can be brought before a court and committed to prison for non-payment. You may be entitled to a rates rebate if you are an owner-occupier, council or private tenant.

BANKS AND SAVINGS

The number of people with bank accounts is growing all the time. Although many are still paid in cash, and prefer to conduct all their purchases with cash, the use of cheque books is becoming increasingly common. They are convenient, because you do not have to decide in advance what you are going to buy and take that amount of money with you, and they are safer than cash because they are not as easily lost or stolen.

CURRENT ACCOUNTS

A current account is an account with a bank into which you pay money (or have it paid for you) and from which you withdraw money by writing cheques. The bank will then pay out to the person who presents the cheque or pays it into his/her account. As a rule, no interest is credited to the account in respect of the money in it, and in fact you will have to pay charges based on the use you make of the account, although these are usually only levied if there is little or no money there. People with more than £100 in their account are not normally charged.

There are a number of ways that money can be taken from this type of account. You can go into your own branch of the bank, write out a cheque, and you will then be given the sum required. Or you can go into another bank or branch. But then they may have to check with your own branch that you have enough money to meet the cheque (they will charge you a small sum for the telephone call). That can be avoided if you possess a bank cheque card (see p.340), or if you have made a written arrangement to draw money from another branch. This is sometimes done by people who have an account in one place but

For small savers there are various deposit accounts which give good interest rates, such as the Post Office and building societies.

LAW AND FINANCE

The details that need to be filled in on a cheque are: the date, your signature and the amount written twice (once in numerals and once in full). If you are cashing a cheque you should write 'cash' at the top or if you are paying someone, their name. A cheque card is usually required in shops and restaurants and guarantees that the bank will pay out up to £50.

cannot normally reach it during banking hours — if you have an account near your home, but work some distance away, for instance.

You can buy goods and pay for them with a cheque (though normally a cheque card is required for identification and guarantee of payment), or send a cheque in payment of a bill. The recipient of the cheque then pays it into his own account, and the banks then have their own arrangements for transferring the money.

What happens if you do not have enough money to meet a cheque? You can only take out what you put into your account, unless the bank has agreed to lend you some money, either as a loan with fixed repayments, or by way of an overdraft. But if you do not bother to make one or other arrangement, and you try to cash a cheque, you might find the bank refuses to cash it. And if you have given someone else a cheque in payment of a bill, the bank could 'bounce' it if there is not enough money. That means that it will be sent back unpaid, and the person to whom it was given will then look to you to come up with the amount you owe. Although this can happen by accident — many people simply forget how much (or little) money they have — it should be remembered that to give someone a cheque, knowing full well that there is not enough money to meet it, is a criminal offence, and you could be prosecuted.

Cheque cards If you have run an account satisfactorily for several months, the bank manager will probably be prepared to issue you with a cheque card. This will enable you to cash cheques to the value of £50 at any bank in the UK, and even some abroad, simply by tendering the cheque and the card to the cashier. It is, in other words, a guarantee that the cheque will be paid.

Similarly, you can use the card in shops to guarantee a cheque. If you have a valid card (i.e., one where the time-limit has not expired), and the number of the card is written on the back of the cheque by the shop assistant, the bank must pay the amount of the cheque, so long as it does not exceed £50. However, if you use a card in this way, you cannot later stop the cheque. If you could, shops would not be prepared to accept them, because they still could not be sure of getting their money. But if you use a cheque card when you are overdrawn, the bank might insist that you return it, as you will be forcing them to pay out in circumstances which would normally have resulted in the cheque being sent back.

Your cheque card should also be kept separate from your cheque book so that if you lose or have your cheque card or book stolen, they will be of little value to anyone.

Stopping cheques If you lose your cheque book, you should inform the bank immediately, so that a warning can be sent out to all other banks not to pay any cheques on that account. You can also instruct the bank to withhold payment on any other cheques (so long as you have not used a cheque card to guarantee them). You might want to do this if you have sent someone a cheque by mistake. You can also do it if there is a dispute over what you have bought, but legally you could then be sued for the face value of the cheque, and it would be up to you to counterclaim (see p.349) for the disputed amount. Nonetheless, it is a lever which is available to you in such cases.

Bank statements The bank will send you, at periodic intervals, a statement showing what transactions have been going through your account. You should check these off against the counterfoils in your cheque book and paying-in book, and tell the bank if there are any mistakes.

OTHER TYPES OF BANK ACCOUNT
If you want to save money, there is no point in using a current account for the purpose as there is no interest. It is better to open deposit and savings accounts. Interest is paid on money invested in these accounts, but you are sometimes required to give several days notice if you want to withdraw money. Often the higher the interest paid, the longer the notice of withdrawal you must give. You cannot write cheques on a deposit account.

STANDING ORDERS
Regular fixed payments that you make can be handled by asking the bank to execute a standing order in favour of the person to be paid. This is an instruction to the bank to pay a given sum on a given day or date. It will be done automatically, and the amount simply deducted from your account.

CREDIT CARDS

The use of credit cards is growing. All the major banks are involved in running credit card schemes, as are a number of other commercial concerns. They can be used to withdraw money from a bank, to pay for goods, even in some instances to guarantee cheques.

HOW TO OBTAIN A CREDIT CARD
When they were first being launched, many people were sent credit cards through the post, quite unsolicited. This practice has been frowned upon, largely because it led some people to incur debts that they could not meet and would not, in the normal course of events, have run up anyway. Nowadays you must apply for a card, although you may well receive literature through the post inviting you to do so, or see advertisements in the press or leaflets at the bank which proclaim the advantages of possessing these cards.

If you decide to apply, you will have to provide a considerable amount of information about yourself. This is so that the credit card company can carry out checks into your credit status, in order to establish whether you are a good risk or not. It benefits no one in the long run if cards are handed out at random to people who cannot or will not keep up the necessary repayments.

The principal credit cards in the UK are 'Access', 'Visa' (Barclaycard) and 'Diners Club'. Strictly speaking 'Diners Club' and also 'American Express' are not credit cards, as you must pay immediately the bill comes in.

People are finding increasingly that it is more convenient to pay by credit card than to carry large amounts of cash around with them.

LAW AND FINANCE

USING CREDIT CARDS

Credit cards fall into two categories. There are those which can be used as cash substitutes, where the money used must be repaid as soon as the bill comes in from the credit card company. And there are those where you have an option either to repay it all at once or to spread the repayments over a comparatively long period, with interest added to the outstanding balance each month. It is a matter for personal choice which type of card you use, and whether or not you choose to repay all the money at once. The danger lies in using a card to make regular purchases and then spreading the repayments over several months, because the debt is likely to mount at an alarming rate, as it will always be added to. In addition, the interest continues to be added to the balance so long as the debt is outstanding, and this interest can be *very* expensive.

IF YOU LOSE YOUR CARD

A credit card can be used by anyone who finds it, so long as he or she can produce a reasonable forgery of the signature it carries. Thus it is very important to notify the credit card company immediately you lose — or even think you might have lost — your card. If you do, they can then inform all the numerous outlets which accept them that a particular card has been lost and to phone them or the police if anyone tries to use it. You will not normally be held responsible for any such illegal use once you have notified the company. It is, though, possible to take out insurance to cover yourself against any liability arising from such misuse. This costs very little and given that credit card fraud is growing, it is a wise precaution.

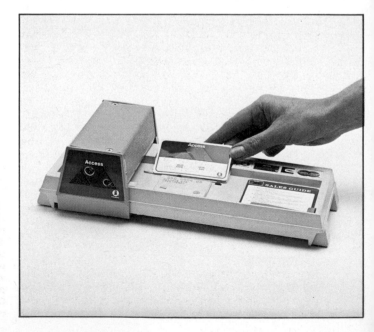

When purchasing with a credit card, simply present the card and the retailer will write out a sales voucher. You check the details and sign it. He then puts the voucher through an imprinter to record the details of your name and card number, returns the card and copy of the voucher to you, together with the goods.

CREDIT SALE

This is the name given to a form of credit whereby you pay over five or more monthly instalments. The goods belong to you from the outset — hence the name — but, if you want to dispose of them before you have paid off the debt, you will probably, under the agreement, have to pay off any balance left. Sometimes there is no interest charged on credit sales.

LOANS

Several organizations make loans to people wishing to buy goods on credit. Banks and finance companies are the principal sources of loans. The interest rates can be high, partly because, since you will own the goods, there will be no real security. However, if you wish to make several purchases in different places, or you want a very large loan, or you want to be free to decide how and when you will make your purchases, or if you are buying not goods but services, these loans are worth investigating.

The interest will be worked out at the beginning, and added to the advance, which will then be divided by the number of monthly repayments to work out the size of each repayment. If you default, the bank or finance company will have to take you to court, but will not be able to repossess the goods because they will be your property.

HIRE-PURCHASE

The alternative to paying cash for your purchases is to buy them on credit. There are several ways in which this can be done, and the method chosen will depend partly on what options are open to you and which you feel would be the most appropriate for the purchase in question.

A distinction can be drawn between hire-purchase (and various other forms of loan) and credit cards. It is an important distinction, because the two kinds of credit are quite different in their effect and legal implications.

The important point to note about hire-purchase (HP) is that you do not own the goods that you have acquired until the final payment under the agreement has been made. Only then does ownership pass from the finance company which put up the money to the person who has, until then, been merely hiring them.

With most HP transactions, an initial deposit is required. The percentage needed varies according to the type of goods and, sometimes, the period over which repayments are to be made. The balance will then be repayable over a given number of months — for example 12, 24 or 36. For certain purchases the maximum period is, in fact, laid down by law, so cars must be paid for over 24 months, if they are for private use. Interest will be added to the balance, at the rate prevailing when the transaction is entered into. In addition, there will be a nominal charge of £2 or so which represents the actual purchase price needed to transfer ownership. This will be added to the final payment.

When something is bought on HP, the vendor sells it to the finance company, and the finance company then enters into a hiring agreement with the person wishing to acquire the goods. Legally, therefore, they belong to the finance company until

Hire purchase is often used as the means for acquiring expensive items like cars. The seller, often a garage or car dealer, will sell the vehicle to a finance company, which will in turn 'hire' it to the person who wishes to acquire it. Only when the final payment has been made will he actually own it.

LAW AND FINANCE

Investment is a way of using money to make more money. You can apply it in a number of ways, depending on the kind of return you want or need. Some investments produce only interest, which will provide an income; others yield mainly capital growth; and some offer both.

that final payment has been made. They cannot be disposed of until then, without the consent of the finance company, and to do so could amount to a criminal offence, because the hirer will, to all intents and purposes, have stolen the goods.

When seeking an HP loan, it is vital to provide correct information about yourself. The finance company will want to carry out a check to see if you are credit-worthy, and false information could obviously mean that they come up with the wrong answers. To deliberately give false information is also a criminal offence. If you fail to keep up with the repayments, the finance company may be able to repossess the goods. They can do so if you have paid less than 33 per cent of the total credit price (the initial price plus the interest you have to pay). If more than that has been paid, the finance company must go to court to try and regain the goods. Provided you have a good reason to explain the non-payment, and so long as it seems that you can and will keep up with future payments and also pay off the arrears, the most likely outcome is a suspended possession order. Under this you have to keep up with the future instalments and make a regular payment towards clearing the arrears. So long as you keep to that, you will be allowed to retain the goods.

INVESTMENT

If you are fortunate enough to have a lot of money to invest, you should without delay seek competent professional advice. Your bank manager, solicitor or accountant should be able to point you in the right direction. Alternatively, if you have already used the services of a stockbroker, and had no cause for complaint, you could go back to him. Those with smaller amounts at their disposal — perhaps only a few hundred pounds, or maybe a thousand or two — have a number of options open to them.

Advice rarely comes free, and so it may not be worth your while consulting, say, an accountant when his charges will make appreciable inroads into your capital. A bank manager will be able to advise, and he will not charge anything. He will be in a position to outline the various possibilities for the 'small' investor, and you can then make your own decision. Obviously he will press the advantages of investing in a bank deposit account, but if he does his job properly he will also tell you what else is available.

Of course, it is also possible to make your own inquiries, and evaluate the information thus collected. There are several organizations seeking funds from investors, each with their own terms and conditions. The banks have already been mentioned. Their rates of interest fluctuates in line with what is called the Minimum Lending Rate (MLR) and can change from week to week.

Then there are the building societies. They now offer a range of different investment options, depending on how much you want to invest and for how long. They pay good interest, and also pay the tax due on your interest for you, which, for those who are working and so paying tax, makes them an attractive bet. But it can take some time to extract your money, and they are not so advantageous if you do not pay income tax.

The Post Office and the Trustee Savings Bank (TSB) also need money from investors, and might be worth looking at. The Post Office also, of course, sells premium bonds and savings certificates.

If you do not see yourself becoming a large-scale operator on the Stock Exchange, you can still buy shares of a kind by purchasing what are known as unit trusts. See your bank manager for details.

One possibility if you want to save regularly over a period of time (as opposed to investing a single lump sum) is to join a Save-As-You-Earn scheme, under which you agree to pay a fixed monthly sum for a fixed number of years. The tax treatment of the interest is favourable, and after a given period you qualify for an extra tax-free bonus. Details of this scheme are available from the Post Office and most building societies.

It is also possible to combine saving with life insurance, with the bulk of the money being invested in unit trusts and the rest being used to pay the insurance premiums.

CONSUMER RIGHTS

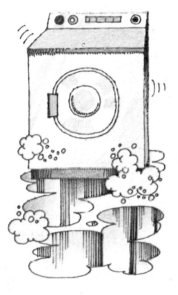

The past ten years have seen a phenomenal increase in consumer protection of all kinds. There are laws which prevent most kinds of misleading advertising and attempts by traders to pull the wool over your eyes. Faulty goods can be returned far more easily than was previously the case, and in some instances it is easier to enforce your legal rights than was hitherto possible. And many of the unfair practices which were rife in certain spheres have been restricted by codes of practice negotiated between the Office of Fair Trading and the professional and trading bodies concerned.

ADVERTISING
It is illegal to give false information in advertisements or description of goods and the prices charged for them. The Trade Descriptions Act bans any false description (which includes prices), and any offender faces prosecution. In one case a car dealer was fined because he had turned the mileage clock back on one of the cars he was selling.

Consumers enjoy a wide range of rights in respect of goods and services that turn out to be defective or inadequate. For example, if you buy a washing machine that leaks or a pair of shoes that fall apart shortly after purchase, you can usually demand a refund if you no longer wish to retain the goods.

A descriptive sign in a shop must be correct too. To state that the price has been reduced, when in fact the article has always been sold at that price, is illegal, because again it conveys a false impression, leading people to think that they are getting a bargain. There are, though, some exceptions to this rule. If prices are brought down for a sale, they must normally have been sold at the higher price for at least 28 days before the trader can announce that he has made the reduction. But if that is not the case, and they were not on sale at that higher price for that period, he can still state that the price has been reduced, so long as he also states that the previous price was not in force for 28 days. In other words, he can charge any amount he wishes so long as he does not mislead people into thinking that they are getting a better bargain than they in fact are. If you think you have been misled by false descriptions or pricing, you should take your complaint to the local Trading Standards Officer.

LAW AND FINANCE

Traders who make unwarranted claims about their wares, or who apply false descriptions to them, can face legal action.

FALSE REPRESENTATIONS

If you are given misleading factual information about goods bought, you might be able to return them. What is important is whether you were duped into making the purchase by what you were told about it. So if a shop assistant makes incorrect claims, even in all innocence, you might be able to bring them back and insist on a refund. Good examples are if you are told, erroneously, that, say, a raincoat is waterproof, when that is not correct, or if you are told that a piece of kitchen equipment — a food mixer, for instance — can be used for certain jobs when it cannot in fact be so used. Because the misrepresentation led you into making a purchase that you would not otherwise have made, you can, on discovering the true state of affairs, terminate the contract and ask for your money back.

DEFECTIVE GOODS

You also have the right to a refund if you buy goods which turn out to be defective. The goods should comply with the description applied to them, be of 'merchantable quality' and be reasonably fit for their ordinary purpose.

If you buy something that is intended to be washed, such as an item of clothing, and it shrinks after having been washed correctly, then again it is not, in law, fit for the purpose for which it was sold. Nor are shoes which fall to bits within a few days of being worn. And so on.

If you rely on the seller's skill in making a purchase, then if he misleads you or makes mistakes, you might be entitled to return the goods and demand a refund. So if you ask for advice and are given a wrong answer, and if the seller admits that he gave you this advice, then you have the right to complain.

Problems of this kind often arise in relation to clothing, particularly for children. Parents often have to rely on the shop assistant to fit children's shoes, for instance, and if this is not done correctly considerable harm could result. And, because the seller was supposed to be providing the necessary skills, the contract can be terminated if he in fact failed to do so.

When goods are not defective. A trader must take back faulty goods and give a refund. But he does not have to take back goods which are not faulty or were not wrongly described. Some shops will in fact do so, in order to foster goodwill. So if someone buys a sweater in the wrong size, for instance, the shop may be prepared to take it back, even though the customer tried it on before buying it. There can, however, be problems with clothing, because if there are no facilities to try things on, the customer can only rely on the label or the opinion of the assistant, in which case there might be a right to return the goods anyway. But if that does not apply, it is purely at the discretion of the management as to whether or not they accept returned goods. If they do operate such a policy, they can give refunds, or issue credit notes, or accept returns only if something else is bought there and then. As they are doing you a favour by taking the goods back, you cannot insist on having your money refunded.

REMEDIES

When goods are returned because they are faulty or because they were wrongly described, the customer is entitled to a refund. If the shop assistant tries to fob you off by saying that it is not the policy to give refunds, and that you must accept a credit note, you can and should refuse. They have no legal right to operate such a policy, even if there is a large notice proclaiming it in the shop, although many will make refunds for public relations purposes. If you have a legal right to return the goods you have a legal right to your money back.

HOW TO ENFORCE YOUR RIGHTS

In most cases where you have a grievance, matters can be settled perfectly amicably between the trader and yourself. Sometimes, though, you encounter difficulties. To be fair, it might not be a case of the shop refusing to accept its obligations. People who complain are not always in the right.

To help resolve some of the more common complaints about difficulties in sorting out grievances, the Office of Fair Trading (OFT) has drawn up codes of practice with certain bodies. So, for example, complaints about laundries and dry cleaners are now governed by rules set out in such a code. They lay down what the firm ought to do when a customer complains, and the extent of their responsibility. Likewise complaints about cars are regulated by a code. The idea is to ensure that complaints will be dealt with properly and fairly, and not just rejected without proper consideration. The customer will at least get a hearing, and if the trader proves unreasonable, a complaint can then be made to the trade association concerned, which might discipline its member.

In business sales, exclusion clauses are normally valid but a Court may declare such a clause void if it is 'unfair' or 'unreasonable'. 'Reasonableness' depends upon all the circumstances, including the relative bargaining strength of the parties. In consumer contracts for services, exclusion clauses are valid if they are reasonable. In business contracts for services on 'own standard written terms', they must also be

The Office of Fair Trading does not normally get involved in individual cases, but has negotiated a number of codes of practice designed to make life easier for the consumer. As a final resort, though, it is sometimes necessary to bring legal proceedings in the County Court.

reasonable to be valid. But in other business contracts, exclusion clauses will normally be upheld, regardless of reasonableness.

If you cannot reach agreement on a complaint, you will have to decide on your next move. The local Trading Standards Officer may be able to intervene on your behalf, as might the Citizens Advice Bureau. But at the end of the day, the only answer might be to bring legal proceedings against the trader. This, it must be emphasized, can be expensive, although much less so if the amounts involved are small. But then you have to decide if it is worth all the bother of going to court. It is not enough just to allege that the goods are no good. You must be able to specify in what respect they are defective, and that is not always as easy as it might sound. Sometimes, if there is a code of practice in existence, it will provide for arbitration, and that might be an answer. Nonetheless, if you cannot obtain satisfaction yourself, you have to decide how much time, effort and money you are prepared to devote to pursuing the matter. Only if a fair amount is involved should legal proceedings be contemplated, as you might otherwise win the case but still end up out of pocket because of solicitor's fees and possible court costs.

LITIGATION

Certain unresolved grievances can be pursued through the courts. For instance, a failure to pay your bills could well result in the creditor suing you. Equally, of course, if someone owes you money, you could take them to court to recover it, if all else fails. Legal action can also be initiated following road accidents (or any other kind of accident); if you are saddled with defective goods and the trader will not take them back; if you are libelled; and many other kinds of grievance.

Going to court is expensive for all concerned, and it should be avoided wherever possible. If you are dithering over paying a bill, you should bear in mind that the legal and court fees you will incur if you are sued will be quite large. Likewise if you decide to take someone to court, you might, if the sums involved are on the low side, end up by paying out in expenses a sizeable chunk of the sum you recover.

If any legal proceedings are going to be conducted in the County Court (which is the usual venue if less than £2,000 is involved) then it is worth considering handling the matter yourself, and not using the services of a solicitor. But if you do decide to do this, then get hold of the booklet produced by the Lord Chancellor's Department on handling County Court claims, or else the book published by the Consumer's Association on the subject, so that you are aware of the various steps to be followed.

However, do not be misled into thinking that it is all very simple, and if you have any doubts whatever about the merits of your claim, or the procedures to be followed, then a solicitor would indeed be a good 'investment'. If you are being sued, and you cannot understand what is involved, then again it is important to seek legal advice. There are fairly strict time limits

This book produced by the Consumer's Association is a step-by-step guide to suing in the County Court, from legal rights through to enforcing a judgment.

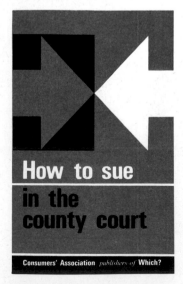

How to sue in the county court

Consumers' Association *publishers of* **Which?**

to be observed, and delay could mean that you lose by default.

A County Court claim is started by the issue of a summons. This is a formal document setting out the names of the parties, the court involved (usually the one nearest to where you live), and certain other details. If a fixed sum of money is sought (as when a bill has not been paid) then the summons will specify a date on which the case will be heard. The summons will be accompanied by a statement setting out what the claim is about. There will also, in a fixed-sum claim (known as a default summons) be a form on which you can admit the claim in full, or in part, or deny it, or accept that it is valid but counterclaim in respect of your own grievance. For instance, if you bought an item of electrical equipment, and, when it went wrong, refused to pay, you might be sued for the price. One option open to you would be to accept that you owed the sum in question, but then claim against the trader for the cost of having repairs carried out.

The accompanying documents will specify the time limits, and you must keep to them. If you admit that you owe the money claimed, but want time to pay, it is imperative that you return the relevant form as soon as possible, setting out your offer.

A claim of this kind does not usually end in a court hearing. But if liability is not an open-and-shut issue, or if the amount involved is not clear, then there will have to be a hearing. For instance, if someone alleges that you injured them in a road accident, you will almost certainly need to go to court to sort things out.

That type of claim is obviously complicated, and you should see a solicitor with a view to his advising you. An insurance company will probably be involved, and they might help with legal representation. As a rule, though, go to a solicitor if you are in any doubt whatever over whether you are liable. And if you are suing someone, and handling the case yourself, bring in a solicitor if you feel that you are no longer in control of what is happening.

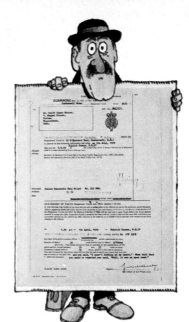

A summons to attend a magistrates court (e.g. for a driving offence) will normally be posted or can be delivered by the police. A County Court summons can be served either by post or by being personally delivered by a bailiff who is a court official.

It is always preferable to take good legal advice before deciding to take action in the courts.

LAW AND FINANCE

A court is an imposing place if you are not familiar with the proceedings.

IN COURT

Giving evidence in court can, for some people, be very frightening. There are strict rules governing court procedure, and for the layman they can be most intimidating. Small claims are sometimes dealt with by an official called a registrar. He is less senior than a judge, but is legally qualified, and tends to handle the simpler cases. For some small claims, there is a procedure known as arbitration. This is less formal than a full-blown trial, and if you feel that it would be appropriate you can ask that the case be disposed of in this way.

Big claims The County Courts are used for the smaller claims — those where the amount of money involved is not that large, and also for possession claims in respect of property and goods (see pp.338, 343 and 344). In cases where large sums are involved, the scene shifts to the High Court. The rules and procedures involved there are far too complex for anyone to handle on their own, and it would be foolish to try. So, if you are being sued in the High Court, or decide to bring proceedings against anyone which will have to be heard in the High Court, you should seek legal advice without delay.

OBTAINING LEGAL ADVICE

The obvious source of legal advice is a solicitor. There are plenty of them about. Either go to someone you know, or who has been recommended by a friend or, if that does not yield anyone, ask the local Citizens' Advice Bureau for names of firms in the area who handle the kind of work in question. Failing that, there are always the Yellow Pages.

Solicitors charge for their time, and can therefore prove very expensive. Try to find out at the beginning what sums could be involved. Ask the solicitor to advise you on the likelihood of winning, how much it will cost you if you do not and what you might still have to pay even if you do. Normally, the loser pays the legal costs of both sides, but not always all of them, so you could still have a bill to pay.

You might qualify for legal aid or advice, whereby the State would foot all or part of the bill. The solicitor will be able to advise you further on that.

WILLS

If you have any property to leave when you die, it would be extremely foolish not to make a will. It will prevent considerable inconvenience for your dependants if there is a will, and it will avoid any bad feeling which not knowing could cause. A will is a formal legal document which sets out the wishes of the person making it. To be valid it must fulfil certain conditions, of which the most important are: that it is unambiguous; that it is signed at the bottom by the testator (the person whose will it is); and that it be witnessed by two people. If one of the witnesses is a beneficiary, the will can stand but the particular gift to the witness will not be allowed.

That said, the wording of the will can be extremely simple, running perhaps to only a couple of lines. It can be on elegant parchment with lots of heavy Gothic lettering, but it does not have to be. A sheet from a notebook will do just as well, although it might not look terribly authentic.

You can consult a solicitor and ask him to draft the will for you, but it is not necessary. However, there are obvious risks with a 'do-it-yourself' job, because it may not meet the requirements about witnesses and signatures, or actually express your true wishes. A botched effort is often worse than no will at all — in the absence of a will, everything goes to the next-of-kin, but if the instructions are unclear, the wrong people may end up by benefiting.

While solicitors certainly are not infallible, they are more likely to know the dangers, and to ask questions designed to elicit all the relevant information. From there they can fashion the will into a form of words that will ensure that when you die your property reaches the people you wanted it to. A lot of people make wills when in hospital, and there will usually be someone on the hospital staff available who can help with the drafting, and there should be no shortage of witnesses on hand.

Certain events cancel out any previous wills. Making a new one can have that effect, but to be on the safe side it is best to start the new one off by saying that it revokes all earlier wills. Getting married also cancels any will made before the marriage, so that if you want the disposal of your property to be governed by a will you will need to make a new one. When someone dies intestate — that is without leaving a valid will — the division of the estate depends upon its value and what family survives. But even if your present intentions coincide with the intestacy rules, it is almost always better to make a will.

A will is usually set out in a formal and specially printed document, but this is not necessary. So long as the will is properly signed and witnessed, it will be valid, regardless of what it is written on.

LAW AND FINANCE

GLOSSARY

Cheque A cheque is an instruction to a bank to pay a stated amount to a stated person. Although it is standard practice for specially printed cheques provided by the banks to be used for the purpose, they could in fact be written on anything.

Conveyancing This is the legal process whereby freehold property is transferred from one person to another. It is usually undertaken by a solicitor, and involves a considerable amount of fairly complicated paperwork.

Credit If a purchase is made on credit, it means that part or all of the cost is paid after the goods have been acquired. There are many forms of credit, ranging from simply paying a bill rendered after delivery of the goods, to paying off a loan over several years.

Hire-purchase This is perhaps the most common form of credit. Once the goods have been selected, they are then sold to a finance company which in turn enters into an agreement with the consumer. Under that agreement the consumer literally hires them from the company, paying an agreed monthly sum over a given number of months. Only when the final payment has been made do the goods belong to him. Until then, they are the property of the finance company, and cannot therefore be sold or otherwise disposed of.

Insurance This is a means of passing a particular risk over to someone else. Insurance can be obtained for a very wide range of possibilities, but the most common are motor insurance, house contents insurance, and life insurance. In return for a premium, an insurance company will undertake to pay either a fixed sum or a sum based on the actual loss if the event which has been insured against actually happens.

Investment This is a means of using money to earn interest or bring capital gains. It can be put into some form of savings account, or used to buy shares or property, depending on the kind of return that is sought.

Legal Aid Those who are unable to afford to instruct lawyers to represent them in legal proceedings can apply for legal aid, which is assistance provided by the state to help with legal expenses. There are different procedures for applying for legal aid in civil and criminal cases. One of the principal factors that go to determine whether legal aid will be granted, and how much will be made available, is the disposable income and capital of the applicant.

Merchantable quality — Goods can be returned to the seller if they are not of merchantable quality. This concept is defined as meaning fit for the purpose for which they are sold. So if, for example, an item of electrical equipment will not work at all, it is hardly fit for its intended purpose, and thus it is not, in law, of merchantable quality.

Mortgage A mortgage is a form of loan used to finance house purchase. The purchaser mortgages the property to the organization putting up the money — usually a building society. Under such a transaction, the society advances the money and acquires certain rights over the property. Although it will not own it, it can prevent it being sold, and can impose conditions on how it is used.

PAYE This is the system under which income tax is deducted from the earnings of employees. The employer takes off each week or month an amount to meet the income tax liability that has arisen. It differs from the arrangements applying to the self-employed, who are responsible for paying their own tax.

Rates Local authorities raise a significant part of their money through rates. They are a kind of tax, payable on property, according to a rather complicated formula. A value, called the rateable value, is fixed for each property, every few years. The council then decides each year what percentage rate to levy. So, if a house is given a rateable value of £300, and the rate for the year is fixed at 80p. in the £, the rates payable for that year will be £240. Half will then be payable on 1 April, and the rest on 1 October, unless a written application has been made to the council to pay in ten instalments over the year.

FAMILY OCCASIONS

FAMILY OCCASIONS

INTRODUCTION

Some occasions stand out as landmarks in a lifetime: getting married, having a baby christened or moving house. Arranging events like these may seem overwhelmingly complex, and this chapter is designed to guide you smoothly through the pitfalls. Thoughtful planning is the key to successfully organising anything from that first formal dinner party to a happy and fulfilling retirement. Finally, we deal with the formalities surrounding a bereavement, a subject that people prefer to ignore, until they have to cope with it, and at a time when sorrow makes them least able to do so.

WEDDINGS

A wedding is a particularly special time which everyone would like to look back on with joy and happiness. The event can be as simple or as elaborate as the couple and their families want it to be, from a quiet Register Office marriage to the grandeur of a church service with choir and pealing bells.

There are legal requirements to be met before any marriage can take place. The couple must be over 16, sane, free to marry, and not related

For most church weddings the groom usually wears a dark suit or morning suit and the bride a long dress. Since most men nowadays do not own a morning suit and top hat, the usual procedure is to hire one. The bride's dress can range from an original Edwardian antique (which can also be hired) to a modern dress which can usefully be worn as an evening dress at a later date.

within the forbidden degrees by blood or marriage. They must fulfil certain residential requirements, and others, depending on where and by what religious rites they wish to be married. In case of doubt about the procedures to follow in particular circumstances, advice can be obtained from the local Superintendent Registrar (look under Registration in the telephone directory), or the clergyman for the parish.

IN THE CHURCH OF ENGLAND

There are three ways of marrying in the Church of England: Marriage by Spe-

cial Licence, Marriage by Banns and Marriage by Common Licence.

A Special Licence enables a wedding to take place at any time and any place in England and Wales. It is granted by the Archbishop of Canterbury and is given in outstanding circumstances — such as a deathbed or prison cell marriage.

The first step in arranging a Marriage by Banns is to approach the clergyman of the local church. If he is satisfied that both parties are free to marry, and is willing to conduct the ceremony, he will then arrange to read aloud the banns on three

It is permissible to wear anything from jeans to traditional wedding dress in a Register Office, but the majority of people choose smart everyday clothes.

separate Sundays. If the couple do not live in the same parish, then the banns must be called in both. Sometimes a couple choose to marry in a Church of England church which is not in either of their local parishes. In this case the banns are still called in each of their parish churches, in addition to the church in which they are marrying.

There is, incidentally, no obligation on a clergyman to marry people who are not his own parishioners but at least one of the couple in question will have to be put on the 'Electoral roll' of his church. After the banns have been published, and providing no objection has been raised, the wedding must take place within three months.

To be married by Common Licence the bride or groom must have lived in the parish of the church in which the wedding will take place for 15 days prior to applying for the licence. Again, the first step is to approach the clergyman of the church. Once issued, the licence is valid for three months.

IN THE ROMAN CATHOLIC CHURCH
If bride and groom are both Catholic, banns will be read

in the parish of each on three Sundays. The couple must also give notice of marriage and obtain a certificate from a Superintendent Registrar,

as for a Register Office (see overleaf). The procedure is the same for all Christian weddings other than Church of England.

The marriage certificate is concrete evidence of a wedding having taken place between the couple concerned, should the need to prove this ever arise. It is sometimes necessary to produce the certificate for purposes such as tax or insurance. These days, however, being married is no longer a necessary criterion for getting a mortgage on a property and this can now be either a joint or a single mortgage.

FAMILY OCCASIONS

A CIVIL WEDDING

A civil marriage, or Register Office wedding, may take place by authority of a certificate(s) — with or without a licence. — issued by a Superintendent Registrar. The first step is to give notice to a Superintendent Registrar whose address can be found in the telephone book.

This notice of marriage involves giving full details of names, addresses, ages, occupation, marital status. The applicant also has to sign a declaration that there is no impediment to the marriage.

For a certificate of marriage without licence, notice must be given to the Superintendent Registrar in the district where at least one of the couple have lived for a minimum of seven days before the application. If the other half of the couple lives in a different district, then he/she must also give notice in his/her respective district, and obtain a certificate. 21 days after notice is given, the certificate authorizing marriage will be granted. It is valid for three months.

For a certificate of marriage with licence, either bride or groom must have lived in the district for at least 15 days before notice is given. The same particulars must be supplied as for a certificate of marriage without licence. This licence can be issued a few days after notice has been entered.

The difference in price between a large wedding at a smart church and a small parish affair can be quite staggering. Bear in mind that in a larger church you may be required to pay for heating, lighting, a choir and the verger, instead of the standard fee plus a fee for an organist in a small church.

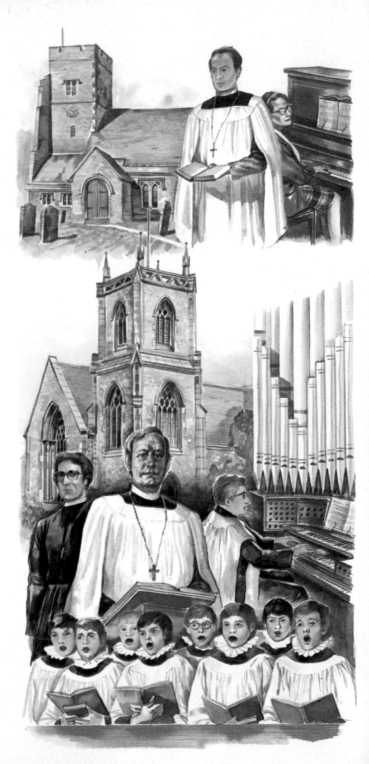

SCOTTISH WEDDINGS

No qualifying period of residence is necessary in Scotland before giving notice of intention to marry. This notice is issued to the Registrar in the district in which the marriage is to take place.

The names of the parties and the dates of the proposed marriage will then be displayed outside the Registrar's office for a minimum of 14 clear days; after which — providing no successful objection has been raised — the Registrar will prepare a Marriage Schedule (a form).

If a religious marriage is intended, the Schedule is issued to the couple and must be delivered to the appropriate minister at the time of the service: to be signed, witnessed and returned to the Registrar's office again within three days.

For a civil wedding, the Registrar will retain the Schedule himself until the ceremony.

In exceptional circumstances the Registrar General may agree to reduce the 14 days waiting period.

Time and place of marriage
There is no official restriction on the time or place at which a religious marriage may be solemnized in Scotland, but civil marriages always occur in a Registration Office. Exceptions are made for humanitarian reasons, however, when for example, a hospital wedding, may be conducted.

Marrying outside Scotland
Scots wishing to marry elsewhere in the UK should consult their Registrar for the correct procedure to follow. Scots who married outside the UK and have doubts about the validity of their wedding may undergo a second ceremony inside Scotland — again the local Registrar is the person to approach.

PLANNING THE WEDDING DAY

Traditionally, it is the bride's privilege to be married in her own parish church. In practice, the couple decide between them the kind of wedding they want, bearing in mind their circumstances and family circumstances — a particularly important point if the expenses of the wedding and reception are being paid for in the traditional way by the bride's family.

The best man is traditionally responsible for the smooth-running of the wedding day from keeping the ring to looking after the reception guests.

If they decide on a church service, the couple should make an appointment to see the clergyman concerned to book a date and time. The earlier they start making arrangements, the more likely they are to find their first choice of date available. This also applies if they have a particular photographer or car-hire firm in mind.

When discussing wedding plans with the clergyman, the couple can also take the opportunity to mention the hymns and music they would like during the service, so that he can approve their choice. He will most probably want to talk to the couple, either then or at a later date, about the solemnity and meaning of the vows they will take, and go through the marriage service with them.

The other participants in the wedding party, best man

and bridesmaid, must be chosen. If there is to be only one bridesmaid, normally the bride will ask someone in her family or a close friend to take on this role. If the wedding is a large one, and she is having more than one bridesmaid, then it is a friendly gesture to invite someone from the groom's family, perhaps a sister, to be bridesmaid also.

The best man, who is normally a near-relative or friend of the bridegroom's, should be calm and well-organized, ready to cope with any situation, as well as to soothe the bridegroom's nerves.

The ushers can be chosen from both families. When deciding whether or not to have very young bridesmaids and pages in the bridal procession, it is as well to bear in mind the demands the occasion will put on them. They can look absolutely delightful, but they should, in fairness, be of an age to cope without becoming bored or unhappy.

PHOTOGRAPHIC ARRANGEMENTS
If the couple would like to have photographs taken inside the church and during the service, then they must ask the clergyman if this is agreeable to him. The same courtesy applies regarding tape-recording or filming.

FLOWERS
When the bride and bridesmaids have chosen their dresses, they can discuss suitable bouquets with the florist. Also to be arranged — sprays of flowers for the bride's mother and the groom's mother; buttonholes for the groom, best man, bride's father and other male relatives. Also to be considered: floral arrangements in the church and at the reception.

TRANSPORT
Usually, three cars will be needed for the bride, her immediate family and attendants. There will be one for the bride's mother, a second for the bridesmaids, and a third for the bride and her father. The bride's father should book these three cars and arrange transport for any relatives, such as grandparents, staying with them for the wedding. The bridegroom should arrange for cars to take him and his best man to church, and for himself and his new wife to leave the reception.

OTHER ESSENTIALS

The bridegroom must buy the wedding ring. If the couple plan to exchange rings during the service — a point, incidentally, to discuss with the clergyman — then the bride, too, will need to purchase a ring. The bridegroom should also buy presents for the best man and bridesmaids to give them a token of thanks and memento of the occasion. Bride and bridesmaids will want to make hairdressing appointments, mentioning at the time of booking if they wish to take along their headdresses so a suitable style can be devised. If the men are wearing morning dress, this may have to be hired. Organist, choir and bellringers will have to be booked, and the reception and wedding-cake organized.

WHO PAYS FOR WHAT?

The bride's family, strictly speaking, should pay for the invitations, service sheets, press announcements, wedding reception, the bride's dress, the flowers in the church and the cars to take the bride to church and from church to reception.

The bridegroom pays for the licence, the church fees, the bride's wedding ring, the bride's and bridesmaid's bouquets, a floral spray for the bride's mother, gifts to bridesmaids and best man, the car to take him and the best man to church and the car to take him and his wife from the reception.

INVITATIONS

When time, date and place have been settled, the invitations can be ordered. For a formal wedding, printed invitations should be sent by the bride's family about six weeks before the wedding.

When it comes to deciding the guest list, both families are involved, though if the bride's family are following tradition and paying for the reception, they should be deferred to on numbers.

Stationers will have a range of styles available for consideration, and examples of wording. Most couples like to have Order of Service sheets in a style which matches the invitations and these can be selected at this stage.

Replies to the invitation are sent to the bride's mother, and it is courteous to send them as quickly as possible so she can gauge the number of guests to be catered for at the reception.

The bridegroom's family, best man and bridesmaids are assumed to be attending, and so they do not receive invit-

Mr & Mrs John Brown
request the pleasure of your company
at the marriage of their daughter
Susanna

to

Mr Hugh Williams
at Saint John's Church,
Walton
on Saturday, 24th November, 1979
at 2 p.m.
and afterwards at
10 Holly Lane

Malm Cottage,
South Harting,
Petersfield,
Hampshire.

R.S.V.P.

Jane and George Smith have much pleasure in accepting the kind invitation of Mr. and Mrs. Brown to their daughter Suzie's wedding at 2 o'clock on Saturday, 24th November, at St. John's Church, Walton, and to the reception afterwards at 10, Holly Lane.

FAMILY OCCASIONS

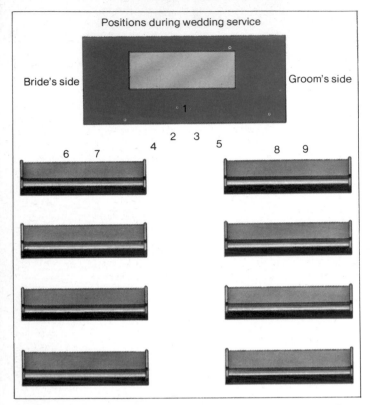

Positions during wedding service

Bride's side   Groom's side

1 vicar **2** bride **3** bridegroom
4 chief bridesmaid **5** best man
6 bride's mother **7** bride's father
8 groom's father **9** groom's mother

ations as other guests do, but if the bride's mother sends them an invitation with a note to say she thought they would like to have it as a keepsake, the gesture will be appreciated.

THE WEDDING DAY

The bridegroom and best man arrive at the church and sit in the front pew to the right of the aisle. The best man, of course, has the wedding ring or rings in his safe keeping.

As the guests arrive, the ushers greet them and enquire 'Bride or groom?' Relatives and friends of the bride are shown to pews on the left of the aisle, with groom's relatives and friends on the right of the aisle. The ushers should ensure that close relatives are shown to front pews.

The bride's mother arrives at the church and is escorted to the front left-hand pew by a son or other male relative. She leaves the aisle seat free for her husband (or the person who will give the bride away).

As the bride arrives, the bridegroom stands on the right of the chancel steps, with the best man slightly behind him on his right. The bride takes her father's right arm and walks down the aisle, the bridal attendants behind her, the chief bridesmaid keeping a watchful eye on the bride's train, if she is wearing one, in case it catches

on the edge of a pew.

The bride stands at the chancel steps on her bridegroom's left. The chief bridesmaid takes the bride's bouquet, and all is ready for the marriage service to begin.

Although the couple will probably have rehearsed the form the service will take with the clergyman, he will be wise in the ways of nervous brides and grooms and will guide them through this great event in their lives.

After the bride's father has passed his daughter's hand to the clergyman, he steps back to the aisle seat on the left beside his wife.

If the bride and groom wish to exchange rings, they should let the clergyman know beforehand. In any case, the bride's engagement ring should have been transferred earlier to her right hand.

When the service is completed, the bridal party follow the clergyman to the vestry, the bride on her husband's left arm. Beside them come the chief bridesmaid with the best man, and the parents of the happy couple. After the register is signed, the bride using her maiden name, the party re-forms for the procession down the aisle: the bride on her husband's left arm, and with the rest of the party in pairs behind. The bride's mother is escorted by the groom's father, and the bridegroom's mother by the bride's father.

After photographs have been taken, the couple leave for the reception. Confetti is usually thrown at this point, and it is tactful to have enquired beforehand if this is allowed.

It is part of the best man's

duties to organize the cars to take the bride and groom, followed in a second car by their parents, to the reception. Bridesmaids and guests follow on. The best man should check that all guests are safely on their way before he leaves the church for the reception. He will have paid all fees at the church on behalf of the bridegroom, who will then reimburse him.

THE RECEPTION

The celebration that follows the marriage service can be anything from a meal in a restaurant for the couple and a few close friends, to a buffet or sit-down meal for as many people as they care to invite, bearing in mind the expense of the occasion if the bride's father is footing the bill.

Whether the reception is a party at home, or a formal occasion, the guests should be greeted by the bride's parents, as host and hostess, the bride's mother first, then her husband, bridegroom's mother and father, then bride and groom.

If there is to be a sit-down meal, the seating plan has the bride and groom at the centre of the top table, the bride on her husband's left. The bride's father sits on her left, then the groom's mother. The bride's mother sits on the groom's right, groom's father next to her. The best man sits next to the groom's mother, and the chief bridesmaid beside the groom's father. Grandparents should also be

invited to sit at the top table, as should the clergyman if his duties allow him to accept the invitation.

If he is present, he will then say Grace. When the cake has been cut by bride and groom, the speeches and toasts follow. There are usually three speeches.

The first speech is to toast the health of bride and groom. The bride's father, an uncle or close friend of the family speaks — briefly — expressing delight that so many people are there to take

If the bride's family have a reasonably sized garden and the couple are having a spring or summer wedding, a marquee in the garden provides the ideal setting for the wedding reception.

part in this joyous occasion and share their happiness, and to raise their glasses in the toast to the future of the couple.

The bridegroom replies, and by tradition begins 'My wife and I . . .' His speech includes a toast to the bridesmaids, thanking them for taking part in such a memorable day, and complimenting them on adding their most delightful presence to the occasion.

The best man replies on behalf of the bridesmaids, and after that, he may read out the telegrams and cards of congratulation.

It is part of the best man's duties to make sure that bride and groom leave the reception on time to catch the train or plane taking them on their honeymoon journey. When the couple have changed into their 'going-away' outfits, they say their farewells and thank-yous, then depart to begin their honeymoon, and new life together.

REGISTER OFFICE WEDDING
Essentially, in a Register Office wedding, the bride and groom make their solemn declarations before the Superintendent Registrar and two witnesses. It can either be as simple as that, or the couple can decide to be married without religious significance but with much of the ceremonial surrounding the traditional church wedding.

For example, when it comes to deciding how many guests to invite, the main factor is how many people the Register Office will hold. Some are more spacious than others, and when the form-filling formalities are being completed, the couple can enquire how many guests this particular Register Office can accommodate.

If the couple feel that they wish to marry with only their very closest relations or friends present, then they may decide the ideal arrangement is to invite very few to the Register Office, but have a reception for many more, on the same lines as any other wedding reception.

When the decision is to confine guests to those few who are dearest and closest, then hand-written notes of invitation can be sent rather than the formal printed kind. If a reception is being held for a large number of guests, then printed invitations stating 'wedding reception' rather than 'at the marriage of' can be sent instead.

Couples who would like to have a Service of Blessing after a Register Office wedding should talk to the clergyman.

SPECIAL CIRCUMSTANCES
A bride, traditionally, is escorted to the altar by her father. If he has died, and her mother has remarried, the bride may wish to ask her step-father to take on this role. If her parents are divorced, and depending on family feeling, her father may still be asked to 'give her away'; otherwise a brother, grandfather, uncle or close friend could escort her.

THE DIVORCED
If either or both of the partners has been divorced, the Registrar will require evidence that the divorce has been granted.

MARRIAGE OF MINORS
The Superintendent Registrar for the area will advise on the necessary formalities.

In England, Wales and Northern Ireland, those aged between 16 and 18 must have written consent from their parents or guardians before they are allowed to marry.

BIRTHS

The birth of a baby is a momentous event in any family. The first people the father usually contacts to tell the news of the happy event are the grandparents. Then others in the family circle, and friends, can be informed.

After the birth, the baby has to be registered, and this must be done within certain time limits, depending on where the birth takes place.

In England, Wales and Northern Ireland, the baby must be registered within six weeks. In many hospitals and nursing homes, a member of the Registrar's staff makes regular visits, and the birth can be registered then.

Otherwise, the father or mother must go to the local Registrar of Births, Deaths and Marriages (look under Registration in the telephone book).

In Scotland, the birth must be registered within three weeks. This can be done only at a Registration Office. The office can be the one for the district in which the birth took place, or the one for the district in which the mother usually lives.

THE BIRTH CERTIFICATE

A birth certificate is an important document, issued at the time a birth is registered. It should be kept in a safe place, because it will be required fairly frequently in the future.

There are two types of birth certificate. The short version, which does not give details of the parents and is issued automatically, and the standard version, which does give details of the parents and is available on payment of a fee. However, for most purposes, the short version is accepted.

Should the birth certificate get lost or mislaid, or another copy be needed, then it can be obtained as follows. For England and Wales, from your local Register Office or the General Register Office, St Catherine's House, 10 Kingsway, London WC2B 6JP. The certificates are not normally available from the General Register Office until a year after the registration.

Charges vary depending on whether you apply in person and collect the certificate a few days later, or apply by post, for which

there is an additional charge.

For Scotland application should be made to the General Register Office, New Register House, Edinburgh EH1 3YT and for Northern Ireland, the address is the General Register Office, Oxford House, 49-55 Chichester Street, Belfast BT1 4HL.

If you require another copy of a birth certificate, it does help to supply as much information as you can: the full name on the original birth certificate, the full names of the parents, the date and place of birth.

BIRTHS IN FOREIGN COUNTRIES

The procedure varies according to the country, and also in instances when the baby is born to the family of a member of the armed forces, serving outside the United Kingdom.

In this case, the birth may be registered by the Service Department. For civilians, a birth in a foreign country may be registered with the British Consul or British High Commission.

A birth certificate is a form of identification and should be kept.

CF 888455   CERTIFIED COPY of an   ENTRY OF BIRTH   [Printed by authority of the Registrar General.] B. Cert. S.R.

The statutory fee for this certificate is 3s. 9d. Where a search is necessary to find the entry, a search fee is payable in addition.   Pursuant to the Births and   Deaths Registration Act 1953

Registration District *Redbridge*

1967 Birth in the Sub-district of *Ilford South* in the *London Borough of Redbridge*

No.	When and where born	Name, if any	Sex	Name and surname of father	Name, surname, and maiden surname of mother	Occupation of father	Signature, description, and residence of informant	When registered	Signature of registrar	Name entered after registration
494	Twenty fourth May, 1967 106 Castleview Gardens Cranbrook	James Patrick Robert	Boy	Patrick Joseph Hayde	Mary Rita Hayde formerly Thomas	Clerk Paint manufactory	Mr L. Hayde Mother 106 Castleview Gardens Cranbrook	Nineteenth June 1967	J. Peters Registrar.	/

I, P. P. SHORTER. Superintendent Registrar for the District of *Redbridge*, in the *London Borough of Redbridge* do hereby certify that this is a true copy of the entry No. *494* in the Register of Births No. *2B* for the above-named Sub-district, and that such Register is now legally in my custody. WITNESS MY HAND this *18th* day of *June*, 19*69*

CAUTION—Any person who (1) falsifies any of the particulars on this certificate, or (2) uses a falsified certificate as true, knowing it to be false, is liable to prosecution.

Superintendent Registrar

FAMILY OCCASIONS

ANNOUNCING THE BIRTH

A formal announcement of the birth in a newspaper does not normally include the name of the child: 'SMITH — On September 4, 1980, at Some Town Hospital, to Caroline, wife of Charles Smith, a daughter.'

But frequently, nowadays, the name of the child is given in brackets, and the wording is less formal: 'SMITH — On September 4, 1980, at Some Town Hospital, to Caroline and Charles, a daughter (Belinda Susan), a sister for Matthew and Robert.'

The other way of informing friends of the birth, and telling them of the child's name, is to send out informal printed notes, available from stationers. But, no matter how distant family relationships may be, it is a courtesy to inform the grandparents before the news is announced either formally in a newspaper or to family and friends.

HOW TO SEND BEST WISHES

On hearing the news, relatives and friends will send flowers and cards to the mother. She should reply to these good wishes when she can. And the senders should appreciate that the mother may not be feeling her energetic self so soon after the momentous event.

However, it is a much-appreciated gesture if the mother does acknowledge these expressions of kindness as soon as she is able to do so.

To respond to a newspaper announcement of the birth, instead of sending a card, friends may prefer to write a letter. There is no need for it to be lengthy.

ADOPTION

Many couples who adopt a child wish to make this known in a formal newspaper announcement of the adoption.

The usual form this takes is 'JONES — On September

A photograph of a new-born baby and mother is a memento that will be treasured by friends and relatives and can be the start of a beautiful family album.

1, 1980, by Clare and Robert Jones, a son, now aged three months.' The child's names can be included, too, according to the wishes of the adoptive parents.

CHRISTENINGS

There is no legal need to have a baby baptized or christened. Indeed, some parents nowadays feel that baptism should be deferred until the child is old enough to understand the meaning and purpose of baptism. Accordingly, baptism may be deferred until the child is confirmed, or seeks full membership of the church.

However, if parents do decide to have their baby baptized in infancy, then the first step is to choose the godparents. In the Church of England, there should be two godmothers and one godfather for a girl, and two godfathers and one godmother for a boy.

Being a godparent has far more than social significance. After all, godparents make solemn promises on behalf of the child and vow to look after the child's spiritual welfare. Anyone who is invited to be a godparent should feel honoured, but at the same time ask themselves if they can truly fulfil the bond they will be entering into. By Church of England law, the godparents must have been baptized and confirmed, but some clergy may be willing to waive the confirmation condition.

ARRANGING THE CEREMONY
The vicar who will conduct the service should be approached in order to arrange a suitable date and time. Baptisms are normally held on a Sunday, after the children's service in the morning.

When details of time and place have been agreed, the invitations can be sent out. As this ceremony is normally one for family and close friends, these will be letters from the mother, rather than formal printed invitations. If a prospective godparent is unable to attend the service, it is in order for someone else to act as proxy.

CHOOSING THE NAMES
The prospective parents may well have decided on a first name for the child before its arrival, and depending on its sex. As to the other names, they could plan to include names which run in their respective families, and this compliment will undoubtedly give great pleasure to relatives.

The most important consideration, however, is to avoid inflicting on the child a name which will be an embarrassment in later life. Or a combination of initials with the same effect. Names, like everything else, go through fashions. If in doubt, consider how prospective names may sound in thirty or forty years time!

FAMILY OCCASIONS

THE CEREMONY

Parents, godparents and the guests sit in pews at the front of the church. The baby is usually dressed in a white christening robe. As the service begins, the participants go to the font, the baby in the mother's arms. As the service reaches the point of the actual giving of names, the baby is transferred to the chief godmother who hands it to the vicar, so that the baby's head rests in the crook of his left arm.

Printed service sheets will be given out in church to guide the participants through the proceedings. The godparents make their responses together, and after the baby has been christened, the vicar will hand the child back to the godmother.

When the ceremony is over a Certificate of Baptism is issued. This should be kept safely, because it will be needed when the child is confirmed later. It is usual to make a donation to church funds.

ROMAN CATHOLIC BAPTISM

In this case, there should be one godfather and one godmother, aged at least 14, and both godparents are normally practising Catholics, although it may be acceptable for one to be a non-Catholic. Baptism usually takes place within six weeks of the birth.

AFTER THE SERVICE

It is usual to hold a small celebration for the guests present at the service. If this takes place in the morning, then the guests are invited to lunch; if in the afternoon, to tea. The clergyman is normally invited to attend.

The centrepiece of the celebration will be the christening cake. This is cut by the mother, then everyone drinks a toast to the child.

Whether guests are invited to a lunch or a tea, the mother should try to prepare as much as possible beforehand: tables ready-laid, glasses assembled for the toast and so on. If she can obtain the assistance of a few close friends, guests who will start to bring food from refrigerator to table, so much the better. This will leave the mother and godparents free to entertain the other guests and admire the central figure of the event — the baby.

If the clergyman is present, though other duties may prevent his attendance, he will say Grace before the meal commences.

CHRISTENING GIFTS

By tradition, godparents mark the event with gifts which can be suitably inscribed: napkin ring, silver tankard or mug, spoon, bangle. But the choice is vast. Many godparents and close relatives prefer to give the child the start of a collection to which they will add on each succeeding birthday: a standard design in crystal, glass or china, or some cutlery.

Then there are beautifully bound Bibles or prayer-books and, increasingly popular nowadays, financial gifts like Premium Bonds.

As a general guide, perhaps the best presents to choose are those which can be kept safely by the parents until the child is old enough to appreciate them and to realize their significance as reminders of an important event in his or her life.

HOLIDAYS

APPLYING FOR A PASSPORT

There are two types of passport. A British Visitor's Passport is valid for one year, and is non-renewable. It can be used for short holiday visits only to certain countries, basically the Western European countries and Canada. The alternative is a full United Kingdom passport, valid for ten years.

To obtain a British Visitor's Passport, application forms are available at any main post office in England, Scotland and Wales, and in Northern Ireland from the Foreign and Commonwealth Office Passport Agency in Belfast.

The completed and signed form should be taken to the main post office with suitable identification — birth certificate, NHS medical card, retirement pension book, expired but uncancelled UK passport or previous British Visitor's Passport (if issued after March 1, 1966) — plus two recent passport photographs.

If a wife is to be included in the same passport, she must accompany her husband to the post office, and provide identification as above. Children must be at least eight to hold their own Visitor's Passport, but any child under 16 may be included on that of an older brother or sister, or on the parents' Visitor's Passport. Once over 16, they must have their own Visitor's Passport.

To obtain a United Kingdom passport, application forms are again available from any main post office in England, Scotland and Wales, and from the Foreign and Commonwealth Office Passport Agency in Belfast for Northern Ireland. Also there are passport-issuing offices in Glasgow, Liverpool, London, Peterborough and Newport (Gwent).

The completed form must be counter-signed by someone of the standing of doctor, lawyer or clergyman, who has known you personally for at least two years, and who is a British subject. This person must also sign the two passport photographs required. The completed application form, with the photographs and identification documents necessary (listed on the notes for guidance supplied with the form), plus fee may be posted or taken to the passport-issuing office for the area.

Allow at least a month for your application to be dealt with, and preferably longer if you apply in spring or summer. In an emergency, telephone the local passport-issuing office for advice on the procedure to follow.

FAMILY OCCASIONS

A PASSPORT FOR THE HONEYMOON

If you plan to go abroad immediately after your wedding, you can apply for a post-dated passport in your married name, or you can have your married name shown on your current United Kingdom passport. Obtain the special form for the purpose from the passport-issuing office for the area. This procedure applies only to full United Kingdom passports.

WHAT TO DO IF YOU LOSE YOUR PASSPORT

If in this country, inform the office which issued the passport, and the police. If abroad, inform the nearest British Consul. It is helpful if you can inform the authorities of the number of your passport.

VISAS AND VACCINATIONS

Some countries outside Western Europe require visas which should be obtained from the country's embassy. Check when you make your travel arrangements.

The Department of Health issues a booklet, *Notice to travellers — Health Protection,* which gives valuable guidance on international vaccination requirements and general advice on health care when abroad. For information about current vaccination requirements, contact the embassy of the country you plan to visit.

MEDICAL TREATMENT

Should you become ill while on holiday in this country, you may register temporarily with a doctor locally for treatment. Some coun-

tries abroad have reciprocal arrangements whereby British subjects may receive emergency treatment free or at reduced cost. Local offices of the Department of Health and Social Security have leaflets (SA 28/SA 30) available describing these arrangements in EEC countries and others. Medical treatment abroad can be extremely expensive, and your travel agent or insurance broker should be able to advise you about taking out a private insurance policy to make sure you are adequately covered.

A DISAPPOINTING HOLIDAY

If you have complaints about your holiday, do not wait until you return home to raise them. Take up the matter on the spot with the courier or travel firm representative or the hotel. If this does not resolve the problem, then on your return home, ask your travel agent to take up your case with the tour operator. Make sure you keep any documentation, and a note of the people with whom you

raised your complaints at the resort.

If the tour operator says there is no case to answer, there are other courses open to you if you wish to take the matter further. The next step depends on whether or not the travel operator is a member of the Association of British Travel Agents. If he is not a member of ABTA, then you have recourse to the local Trading Standards Officer.

If the travel operator is a member of ABTA, then there is a free conciliation service. If that fails to resolve the matter, you can take the case to arbitration, under a fully-independent service subsidized by ABTA.

ENTERTAINING

The secret of success lies in the planning, whether you are giving a party for the children or a formal dinner. Although food suggestions are given below, more detailed advice for party food and dinner parties can be found on page 79.

CHILDREN'S PARTIES

In general, the younger the age group, the fewer children you should invite: a dozen four-year-olds need more adult attention than a similar number twice their age. Team games are easier to organize with an even number of guests.

The games which will amuse four-year-olds would seem downright childish to a twelve-year-old, so the party is easier to run if the children are roughly in the same age group. Plan the games you will have, and work out what equipment will be needed. Buy it in good time and put on one side before your own children get their hands on it.

PLANNING THE FOOD

Children like to sample everything available, so have small-size sandwiches and sausage rolls, dainty cakes and biscuits to save waste. Older children like to feel they are having 'grown-up' food, so a cheese dip accompanied by crisps and biscuits will be popular. Things on cocktail sticks are best avoided in case of accidents.

Jellies, ice cream, fruit salad, and of course, a birthday or Christmas cake, depending on the occasion, will complete the food. Choose a sponge-type cake with an attractive icing rather than the heavy fruit kind. For drinks, serve squashes.

ORGANIZING THE PARTY ROOM

Clear the room of anything fragile or valuable. Remove, or push furniture against the walls to make a clear games-playing area. Make sure the fire is well guarded, and check for any hazards like trailing lamp flexes. Fairy lights get hot, so arrange them out of reach. Cake candles must be set firmly in their holders.

Paper plates, cups and tablecloth are best for children, but no tablecloth should have dangerously trailing edges. Decorate the room with colourful streamers and lots of balloons. Decide where coats will be left; organize an emergency kit: first aid equipment, plus plenty of tissues and kitchen towels for mopping up spills, a damp face flannel and towel to deal with sticky faces and fingers.

Children start going to parties as early as one year old. As well as being a chance to have fun, eat and drink and play with other people's toys, a party is also part of their introduction to 'social life'.

THE PATTERN OF THE PARTY

Try to intersperse quiet games with energetic ones. After tea, concentrate on the sit-down variety to allow time for food to settle. Or you could organize an entertainer — a magician or puppeteer. Your local paper may carry advertisements, or other parents may recommend someone.

Make sure parents know what time to collect their children, and to send all the guests happily on their way home, organize a lucky dip for the last event. Fill a box with crumpled tissue paper and hide in it a variety of wrapped presents — crayons, colouring books, games and toys, depending on the age of the children. It saves complications if the gifts are unisex!

BUFFET PARTIES

Arrange to hire glasses from a local off-licence, allowing twice as many as the number of guests. Order wine on a sale-or-return basis. Have a selection of soft drinks, too.

When planning food, choose dishes which can be eaten with fork or fingers. Try to arrange the buffet table against the longest wall of the room, or failing a table large enough, provide two separate locations for food. Leave plates, cutlery and napkins on the table. Candles look pretty on the table, but they can be dangerous if knocked over, or placed where someone may stretch across them. Arrange dishes of crisps, peanuts at strategic points. Provide ashtrays, too.

DINNER PARTIES

When planning the menu, choose dishes for some courses that can be prepared in advance, or the hostess will spend too much time in the kitchen.

Lay the table earlier in the day: pretty flowers and soft candlelight are wonderful scene-setters, but guests should not have to peer at each other awkwardly through the table decor, so avoid tall arrangements.

Cutlery should be placed so that it is used from the outside working inwards through the different courses. Pudding spoon and fork may take their order in this sequence, or be positioned above the place setting.

Decide the seating plan beforehand, rather than keep guests hovering uncertainly round the table while the hostess makes up her mind who should go where. The general rule to follow is that the most important, or oldest, lady sits on the host's right.

The most successful social events are the ones which have been planned carefully beforehand, and the most successful dinner parties depend a great deal on how smoothly the hostess copes in the kitchen. It is far better to serve something simple that is cooked to perfection than to attempt something too ambitious and panic when the soufflé refuses to rise!

WEDDING ANNIVERSARIES

Everyone knows about silver, gold and diamond anniversaries but there are traditional gifts for some of the others, too.

First: cotton. Second: paper. Third: leather. Fourth: silk. Fifth: wooden. Sixth: iron. Seventh: woollen. Eighth: bronze. Ninth: pottery. Tenth: tin. Twelfth: linen. Thirteenth: lace. Fourteenth: ivory. Fifteenth: crystal. Twentieth: china. Twenty-fifth: silver. Thirtieth: pearl. Thirty-fifth: coral. Fortieth: ruby. Forty-fifth: sapphire. Fiftieth: golden. Fifty-fifth: emerald. Sixtieth: diamond.

The 'look' of a buffet table is almost as important as the taste of the food itself. Serving colourful dishes, attractively presented, is more enticing than colourless food simply 'plonked' on a plate.

MOVING HOUSE

At some point in the middle of the upheaval of moving house, most people wonder why they ever decided to embark on the project! But there is a lot that can be done to simplify the event. Everyone accumulates junk, for example: don't wait till moving day is upon you before you sort it out. In the panic, you may throw out what later you'll wish you had kept, and keep what you don't want.

Depending on the bulk and quantity of your possessions, you can opt for a do-it-yourself removal, or engage the services of a professional firm.

If you decide on the do-it-yourself variety and hire a van, then you can drive one of up to three tons capacity on an ordinary driving licence. The secret of success in this kind of removal is to pack small items from books to china well in advance. Then moving day means loading and unloading a series of boxes, instead of an endless procession of loose items. Label each box with a list of contents so you can distinguish between essentials and non-essentials. Do not unpack non-essentials until carpets and furniture are in position.

If you are going to use professional removers, ask for quotes from at least three different firms. Start enquiries well in advance of your moving day. Make sure you know exactly what is included in the estimate. Will the removal firm provide packing cases and do the packing and unpacking? Will your goods be insured against loss and damage at all stages of the removal? How long do they estimate the removal will take?

AUTHORITIES TO CONTACT

You must notify gas, electricity and telephone authorities in good time to turn off services at your old address, and in the case of gas and electricity, have the meters read on your day of departure. Give a week's notice. They may be able to cope with less, but as moving day approaches you will have more than enough on your mind. Ask for services to be connected at the new address, and arrange for appliances like cookers to be disconnected and re-connected.

Arrange with your local post office to forward your mail. Write down in a notebook the telephone numbers of the people you have contacted — this is especially useful if you are moving to a new area and may not have instant access to the telephone directories for the old area.

FORWARD PLANNING

Start to eat up the contents of the freezer, and have this and the refrigerator defrosted by moving day. Make arrangements for the safekeeping of vital documents like birth

FAMILY OCCASIONS

certificates, bank books and jewellery. Check that the electrical fitments in your new home match the existing ones, and if not, buy new ones.

PLANNING YOUR NEW HOME

You must provide the removal men with all the information they need so they can place each item of furniture in its new location. Removal day is no time to wonder if the oak bookcase would look better in the sitting-room than the pine one. You sort out the finer points of positioning at a later date.

For removal day, make out a plan of each room, showing where each piece of furniture will go. Label the furniture with tie-on or sticky labels and mark each with the corresponding letter on

This picture shows the unfortunate result of bad forward planning.

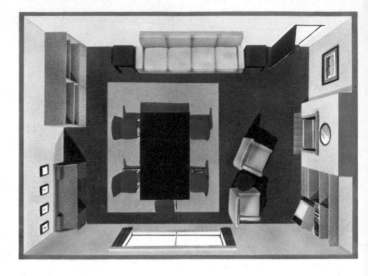

the plan. Tie furniture keys firmly to the items they belong to.

COPING WITH CHILDREN AND PETS

Children, if it is possible to arrange it, are probably best left in the care of obliging relatives or neighbours, at least until the packing and loading stages are completed. Be careful not to pack favourite books, games and toys and have to hand a few specially bought new distractions.

Pets rarely take kindly to an upheaval in their familiar surroundings. If your dog or cat is likely to react badly, and there is a long journey ahead of them to the new house, ask your vet about the possibilities of tranquillizers for them. Alternatively, it may be worth putting them into boarding kennels or cattery until the worst of the upheaval is over. Book in advance, and make sure that they have valid vaccination certificates or they may not be accepted by the kennels or cattery.

By drawing up a room plan to the proper scale, you can quickly see how your furniture will fit into your new home.

When they arrive at the new house, be on your guard that they do not escape and wander off to lose themselves in a strange neighbourhood. Cat experts recommend confining a cat indoors for a week or so until it makes itself at home. If you plan to do this, invest in a cat litter tray, and supply of litter.

EMERGENCY SUPPLIES

Plan in advance how to feed the family on moving day — sandwiches or take-away food are easy solutions — and make sure that it's not early-closing day.

Pets may be off their food, but keep a can of pet food and opener on hand, plus dishes, especially a water-dish. For human comforts, do not let the electric kettle vanish and have the appropriate plug for the new home available, together with milk, sugar, tea-bags, instant coffee, mugs and tea-spoons.

STARTING SCHOOL

Starting school is a momentous event in a child's life, and parents can do a tremendous amount at home to help ensure that their child will find going to school an enjoyable experience. These first impressions could colour a child's attitudes for the rest of his school life, so it is vital to help him start off on the right foot. Preparation for the transition from home life to the hurly-burly of school should begin long before the first day of term.

Children who are accustomed to the almost constant presence of their mother may find her sudden absence in the early days in the classroom upsetting. If you can leave your child to play at a friend's house sometimes, it will help him get used to being without you.

Learning to play happily in a group, and to share toys and books with other children, will also give a child a head start in the classroom. As well as learning to share

possessions, children need to realize that they have to share adult attention, too. A teacher in a classroom has to divide her attention among far more children than a mother at home with the family, so the child who is accustomed to being one of a group will settle into school life more quickly.

These children at playgroup are learning that there comes a time when they must accept sharing adult attention.

Likewise, the child who has mastered practical matters, like fastening buttons and zips, and knowing his left shoe from his right, will not feel helpless when he has to dress after physical education lessons, so guide him into being as independent as possible. Write his name in simple letters on his clothes, from coat to wellington boots, and help him to recognize it.

Do not wait until the first day of term before showing him where the school is. It is a good idea to walk there with him, talk to him about all the things he will do there, let him watch the children in the playground. If you have done your homework properly, then your child should be eager and enthusiastic to start school, and find it an enjoyable experience.

This little girl has mastered the art of putting on her socks by herself.

FAMILY OCCASIONS

PRE-SCHOOL PLAYGROUPS AND NURSERY SCHOOLS

These can give your child opportunities to learn to play with other children and develop the skills which will help him when he starts school proper.

The Pre-School Playgroups Association has about 370 branches around the country. Playgroups are for children from three to five years, and there are also Mother and Toddler groups for children up to five years. For the address of your local branch, write to the Pre-School Playgroups Association, Alford House, Aveline Street, London SE11 5DH.

To find out if there are nursery school places available in your area, contact your local primary school or education office. Nursery classes normally cater for three- and four-year-olds.

ENROLLING YOUR CHILD FOR PRIMARY SCHOOL

The school term following a child's fifth birthday is the compulsory deadline for starting school. In practice, many children can attend school from the beginning of the term in which they have their fifth birthday, depending on the pressure for places in different parts of the country.

Make an appointment with the head of the school you would like your child to attend to discover the position there. An added advantage in contacting the school well before your child is due to start is that you will have the opportunity to find out about any arrangements that particular school makes to help

ease new pupils into school life. For example, some encourage children to visit their future classroom to familiarize themselves with the surroundings.

KEEPING IN TOUCH

When your child has started school, do give him every chance to chat to you about the happenings of his day. As well as providing him with opportunities to develop his conversational abilities, it could also give you an early warning of anything that is

Reassure your children as much as possible before they start their first term at school. Everything including their new uniform will probably seem strange and awe-inspiring at first.

worrying him about school. Young children can so easily become anxious about trivialities. Resolving worries sooner rather than later prevents a child from letting them grow out of proportion.

And finally, starting school can be an upheaval to the child. It can be just as dramatic to a mother!

RETIREMENT

The people who enjoy a happy and fulfilling retirement are those who see it as yet another phase of life, to be lived as fully as possible. That presentation gold watch, to them, marks not an end, but a beginning. They think back to their days at work, and remember the times they said 'If only the office didn't keep me so busy, I'd . . .' and it could be anything from lowering their golf handicap to classifying the stamp collection.

Certainly, after a lifetime governed by the disciplines imposed by the routine of work, the freedom of retirement can seem overwhelming, unless it has been planned for. The people who have planned and considered how to shape their lives and develop them in this new situation are the ones who will stand the best chance of a fulfilling, happy time. The past is past, and an exciting future beckons.

WHERE TO LIVE

Retirement, of course, can impose restraints, not the least of which may be financial. It is almost inevitable that income will drop. People whose retirement seems so far in the future as to be barely worth a thought should refer to page 334 for advice on how to protect their financial interests in retirement. The earlier you make provision for it, the better off you will be.

The more freedom you have from financial worries, the greater the choice you will have when it comes to considering, for example, where you will live. Many people have a vision of spending retired life in some cottage with roses round the door, often in a place where they have spent happy summer holidays.

Before taking the plunge, consider. Have you actually spent time during the winter in this same place? Will that large garden that you are longing to put into shape become a burden in 10 or 15 years rather than a pleasure?

The peace and quiet of an isolated spot may be appealing now. But could neighbours near at hand be an immense asset in later years? Will you always be able to drive and run a car — and if you think perhaps not, then how is your home situated

for access by public transport to essentials like shops, doctor, library, cinema?

Even if you have no thoughts of moving out of the neighbourhood, is the place that has been home for all the years the children were growing up going to seem a vast and expensive burden to heat and maintain on a pension? Instead of abandoning the area you know, would the wiser plan be to find a smaller house in the same district? Would it be expensive, and exhausting, to visit sons and daughters, if you moved far afield? And what would life be like for the partner left behind when the other dies? As with any other major decision in the course of a life, there are no easy answers to the questions retirement poses. But at least give time to considering the issues that could arise.

Should you decide that you do wish to move house, then providing the distance between your new home and work does not make it totally unmanageable, it can be a good idea to make the move before retirement. It means you do not have to cope with finding your feet in a new neighbourhood, and adjusting to the idea of retirement.

USING TIME WISELY

The person who retires from a mentally-taxing, demanding job one day, does not turn into an apathetic cabbage the next — unless they let their abilities slide through lack of use. A fascinating hobby, an Open University course, an evening or afternoon class which you can discover through your local library or town hall, all provide opportunities to do something you

have always wanted to do but have never had the opportunity. Husbands should not be unmindful, either, of the effect of their sudden, and constant, presence on a wife who has got into her own routine over the years when he was at work! There are also opportunities for voluntary service: for example, a local hospital may be desperate for volunteers to man library trolleys and coffee bars.

TAKING ADVANTAGE OF WHAT IS AVAILABLE

A pension book is a passport to a great many financial concessions. Some people make the sad mistake of regarding this as 'charity', and prefer to go their own way, even if it means a financial struggle. In working life, everyone contributes handsomely so that such concessions can be available to others. When it is your turn, take advantage of them. You are reclaiming a part of what you have given over many years. Bus passes, rail cards, rent and rates rebates, help with fuel bills; the Social

Services department at the local town hall will provide details. Never be afraid to ask what you might be entitled to. You have made your contribution during your working life and it is only fair that you should benefit now.

FINDING OUT MORE

Local public libraries are a good starting point on almost any enquiry. For information about rent and rates rebates, contact your local authority. Citizens Advice Bureaux (see telephone directory for your local branch) will advise on how to obtain specific information, if they cannot help you directly.

Age Concern (Bernard Sunley House, 60 Pitcairn Road, Mitcham, Surrey) is a very helpful source of information on all aspects of retirement, while the Pre-Retirement Association (19 Undine Street, London SW17) will advise on planning retirement.

There are passes for pensioners which allow them reduced rates on, for example, buses and trains.

BEREAVEMENT

The death of a loved member of the family circle is a most shattering blow. While coping with the enormity of the personal loss, someone in the family or close to the bereaved must take in hand the practical arrangements a death entails, as well as comforting and sustaining those most deeply stricken by the tragedy of their loss.

REGISTERING THE DEATH

If a death should occur at home, then the doctor to the deceased should be telephoned at once. In the instance of a death in hospital, the authorities there will call a doctor and inform the next of kin.

In England and Wales, a death must normally be registered within five days with the office of the Registrar of Births, Deaths and Marriages for the district. The address can be found under Registration in the local telephone directory. Neither a burial nor a cremation can take place until the Registrar has been informed and the appropriate documents are obtained.

The medical certificate setting out the cause of death must be shown to the Registrar. This certificate is issued by the doctor who attended during the last illness or who was called in after the death.

If there are complicating circumstances, for example if the doctor had not attended the deceased in this last illness, then the Registrar will report to the coroner. If the death took place in hospital, then the certificate will usually be issued there.

In normal circumstances, a relative will go to the Regis-

trar and give the relevant details: name, age, address, occupation, date of birth and the place the death occurred. The Registrar will need various documents — medical card, pension book — if relevant.

When these formalities have been completed, the Registrar will provide a certificate of disposal. This is the authority for the burial to take place.

CREMATION

The formalities to be fulfilled are different, and more complex in the case of cremation. In their lifetime, some people will indicate their feelings on the matter. This is not something to be put in a will, because this document may not be referred to until the funeral has taken place. Those who have strong feelings may save their next-of-kin, already in a state of deep distress, from agonizing over fulfilling the wishes of the deceased if someone close to them knows if burial or cremation is their choice.

If, however, the deceased desired to be cremated rather than buried, or if this is the wish of the next-of-kin in the case of no prior indication otherwise on the part of the deceased, then there are further formalities to be fulfilled.

After the application for cremation has been completed, then a certificate must be obtained from the doctor who attended the deceased. In addition, a further certificate must be obtained from a doctor of five years' standing. This second doctor must be independent, unconnected by family or medical partnership to the first doctor, and not related to the deceased. The certificates they issue are then put be-

FAMILY OCCASIONS

fore the crematorium authorities who issue the certificate to cremate.

THE FUNERAL DIRECTOR

He will take on various duties, or assist with advice, whoever is completing the formalities associated with these tragic circumstances. Depending on the wishes of the family, the funeral director will take in hand the arranging of newspaper announcements of the death and even escort whoever is designated to register the death and obtain the necessary certificates. The doctor may be able to suggest a local firm, or look in the classified telephone directory for the area.

THE FUNERAL

After the various certificates have been obtained, then the final arrangements for the funeral can be made. The immediate family and those closest to the deceased will, of course, have been told of the sad event immediately. A newspaper announcement of the death will normally be made to reach more distant connections.

These notices usually give the facts and when and where the death occurred, and mention surviving members of the family. Details of funeral arrangements follow in the notice: the time and place, then any specific wishes.

Perhaps donations to a particular medical research foundation will be preferred to flowers and wreaths. Or the service for all mourners who wish to attend will be followed by a private interment or cremation attended only by the close members of the family.

The funeral director can attend to the newspaper announcements. If they are telephoned directly to the newspaper, then, in order that the facts may later be confirmed, a telephone number will be requested.

According to the wishes of the family, relatives and friends should be allowed, as they most likely will desire, an opportunity to pay their last respects to the deceased. This can be done at home, or at the chapel of rest, depending on where the relatives wish the deceased to lie. In either case, a suitable time should be arranged and the mourners should be notified.

If the deceased was a practising member of a church, then the relatives will have been in touch with priest or clergyman. Otherwise, the funeral director will contact church or crematorium authorities to arrange the service.

The next-of-kin will be asked to give their choice of music and hymns for the service. If desired, they may have special service sheets printed. The funeral director can arrange this.

SENDING WREATHS

Flowers and wreaths should arrive at the funeral director's or the family home, on the morning of the day the funeral is to take place. The reverse side of the card should show who sent the flowers. On the other side, the message from the sender of the wreath appears. This is phrased according to the closeness of the relationship: the formal 'With deepest sympathy' from acquaintances, to more personal messages from those closest to the deceased.

AFTER THE FUNERAL
The relatives will probably wish to have an opportunity to talk to the people — friends or relatives — who have made a long journey to attend, and whom they may not have seen for some time. It is a courtesy to invite them back for some refreshment after the funeral.

IN SCOTLAND
A death must be registered within eight days. The formalities are completed at a Registration Office for the district in which the deceased usually lived, or the one in which the death occurred. At the Registration Office, the same basic questions will be asked as in England.

WRITING A LETTER OF CONDOLENCE
Every relationship, and every circumstance of death, may differ. If there were but one form of letter of condolence it would automatically cease to have anything but totally formal significance and would mean little, in terms of consolation, to the bereaved person.

This kind of letter is one of the most personal anyone will ever write, and therefore only the most general of guidelines can be given. The substance of the letter must, in large part, be left to the sensibilities of the person who writes, bearing in mind their relationship, and the circumstances of the bereavement. On the whole, it is better to write a simple and sincere letter of consolation than pages of well-meaning sentiment.

Dear Mrs Smith,
Charles and I are so grieved to hear of your tragic loss. We know that Michael will be most sadly missed by so many people for his unfailing kindness, and his total thoughtfulness and consideration for others. Please do not hesitate to get in touch with us if there is anything we can do to help in this most tragic time. Our thoughts are with you and your family.
Yours sincerely,

My dear Margaret,
I cannot tell you how terribly saddened I am to hear news of your father's death. I offer my very deepest sympathy to you and your family. I do most sincerely hope that if there is anything I may do to help, then you will let me know at once. I know that my sense of loss is little consolation in your time of grief. I can only assure you that my thoughts and prayers are with you in this most sad time.
With my love,

It is always especially comforting to the bereaved if you can include a personal memory of something the deceased did for you, or some example that their life set you. It is only basic courtesy to acknowledge all condolence letters, but if the next of kin is too distressed to cope with writing a letter, then it is permissible to send cards instead.

Replies to letters of condolence can be phrased only according to the sentiments expressed, and the relationship of the writer to the bereaved family. Any outline of a reply can be but an indication of what to say.

Dear Mrs Brown,
Thank you so much for your kind letter, which has

FAMILY OCCASIONS

Dear Margaret,

I cannot tell you how terribly saddened I am to hear the news of your father's death. I offer my very deepest sympathy to you and your family and hope that if there is anything I may do to help, you will let me know at once. I know that my sense of loss is little consolation in your time of grief but I can only assure you that my thoughts and prayers are with you in this most sad time.

With my love,

Dear Mrs. Brown,

Thank you so much for your kind letter, which has brought me such comfort. To know that you are thinking of me gives me strength to face the future. David will be so grievously missed in our family circle, but to realize that so many others will also feel our terrible loss is a great consolation at this time.

Thank you again for your most comforting words.

Yours Sincerely,

Two possible models for a letter of condolence.

time. Yet they do not want to appear as objects of pity. They therefore will tend not to approach the people who would like to offer all the help and will need different kinds of support in the time of adjusting to their loss, and the terribly changed circumstances of their life.

When it comes to choosing between doing nothing, or doing something, then surely it must be better to extend the hand of friendship and then be guided for the future by reaction to that invitation, than to discover long afterwards that the tragedy would have been more easily borne with the sympathetic support of caring friends instead of in lonely isolation.

AFTER THE FUNERAL

The local office of the Department of Health and Social Security will be able to provide leaflets to give guidance on the entitlements due according to circumstance. These may range from widows' benefits to supplementary pensions.

A standard Death Grant may be payable if application is made within six months of occurrence of the death. Again, the local office of the Department of Health and Social Security can provide details, but normally a certificate to take to the DHSS will be supplied by the Registrar.

Normally, all charges made with reference to the funeral will be met by the funeral director, and then he will submit his account.

brought me such comfort. To know that you are thinking of me gives me strength to face the future. Charles will, as you say, be so grievously missed in our family circle.

Thank you again for your most comforting words.

Yours sincerely,

When a family has suffered a tragic loss, friends and neighbours may be most willing and anxious to do whatever they can to help — but the best and most helpful form of action to take remains a mystery. They may feel, sometimes rightly, that the bereaved will find most consolation in quiet and solitude, and be reluctant to intrude on this mourning and grieving time.

On the other hand, the bereaved may find great comfort in the company of those who feel for them at this

INDEX

CREDITS

Editors
Susan Condor
Brenda Clarke
Bridget Daly
Nancy Duin
Jim Miles
Vic Rigby
Linda Sonntag
Jane Taylor
Claire Walsh

Consultants
James Allcock B.V. Sc.,
   M.R.C.V.S.
Janet Browne
Dr C. F. Donovan N.B.B.S. B.R.O.G.
Christopher Gilchrist
Elizabeth Gundrey
G. N. Henderson M.R.C.V.S.
Celia Hunter
Margaret Leeming
Patricia Pett
Garry Porter D. Arch., R.I.B.A.,
   F.F.A.S.
Paul Secher L.L.B.
Rosemary Wadey
Maureen Walker

Designers
Peter Benoist
Rosemary Bullen
Camron
Nicola Diepering
Anne Isseyegh
David Shapley
David Worth
Hank Young

Art Direction
Camron

Artists
Anne-Julia Dawson
Leslie Forbes
Ron Hayward Art Group
Sally Launder
David Mostyn
Oxford Illustrators
David Parr
QED
Ilric Shetland
Jeff Riddle/Great Art Fraud
D. Farwell Smith/Great Art Fraud
Tony Streek
David Worth

Production
Philip Hughes
Penny Kitchenham

Picture research
Jenny de Gex
Frances Miller
Lynda Poley

Typesetting
Technical Editing Services

Picture Credits
Access 342
Heather Angel 49, 262, 266, 267
Ardea 265
Ardea/J. P. Ferrero 255, 257
Elizabeth Arden 283 (Inset)
Art Directors Photo Library 288, 290
Banbury Home Extensions 172
British Gas 130
Camera Press/Dimitri Kasterine 357
Chubb 142
Clairol 281T, B
Clark's Shoes 318
Mary Evans Picture Library 333
Fleximent Ltd/Dow Corning UK
   Distributors 126
John Garrett 313
Richard & Sally Greenhill 371
Susan Griggs Agency 283
Susan Griggs Agency/Michael
   Boys 96, 153, 156
Guide Dogs for the Blind
   Association 334
Hackney Gazette 338
Health Education Council 279T, B
John Hillelson Agency/Michael
   Hardy 369
Hire Technicians Group Ltd 140
The Home Office 349B, 350
Hoover 107
Hotpoint 89, 95
Camilla Jessel 254, 258
Leslie Johns 246, 248T, B
Macdonald Educational/Barry
   Bullough 54, 55, 77
Macdonald Educational/David
   Cripps 109
Macdonald Educational/Chris
   Drake 9, 10, 11, 12, 13, 14, 23,
   27, 31, 39, 189.
Macdonald Educational/Paul
   Forrester 47, 69, 250
Macdonald Educational/John Lee
   57, 63, 71, 79
Macdonald Educational/Fran
   Miller 124, 134
Macdonald Educational/Margaret
   Murray 314
Macdonald Educational/Peter
   Myers 19, 50, 52, 53, 79, 88, 97,
   103, 105, 111, 115, 118, 136,
   138, 144, 215, 217, 218, 221,
   251, 292, 297, 301, 337, 339,
   340, 341, 348, 349T, 356, 363,
   376
Macdonald Educational/Mike
   Newton 58
Macdonald Educational/John
   Sims 205
Milk Marketing Board 44
Pat Morris 260
MW Publicity/John Adrian 295
Peter Myers 86, 184
St. Bartholomew's Hospital 317
St. Mary's Hospital Medical School
   317
Liz Scott 354
Mark Shearman 319
John Sims 192
Spectrum 329
Sterling Health 105
Syndication International 370
Syndication International/John
   Miller 149
Tessa Traeger 177, 203, 375
Vision International/John
   Govren 355
Vision International/Anthea
   Sieveking 361, 364, 373T, B,
   374
John Walmsley 365
Westminster Hospital Medical
   School 317
Elizabeth Whiting Associates 151,
   161BL, 171, 237.
Elizabeth Whiting Associates/
   David Cripps 163
Elizabeth Whiting Associates/
   Clive Helm 159T, 161BR.
Elizabeth Whiting Associates/
   Graham Henderson 151
Elizabeth Whiting Associates/
   Mike Nicholson 158B, 161TL,
   162, 168, 200.
Elizabeth Whiting Associates/Tim
   Street-Porter 158T, 161TR
Elizabeth Whiting Associates/
   Jerry Tubby 155, 159B, 160T,B
   167
Zefa 261, 268, 312

Grateful thanks to the following for
supplying items for photography.
Addis Ltd. for domestic cleaning
   ware pp. 88, 97
Boots for winemaking equipment
   p. 251
Butcher & Edmunds for poultry and
   game p. 19
Crown Paints Ltd. for paint from
   their *Plus 2* range p. 144
Nicholls & Clarke Ltd. for tools and
   equipment pp. 111, 115, 118,
   136, 138, 301.

The publishers wish to thank the
following organizations for their
assistance.
British Meat
British Safety Council
Consumers Association
Danish Agricultural Producers
The Electricity Council
The Fresh Fruit and Vegetable
   Information Bureau
Royal Society for the Prevention
   of Cruelty to Animals
White Fish Authority